P9-DNU-978

GRE
词汇精选

俞敏洪◎著

群言出版社
Qunyan Press

图书在版编目(CIP)数据

GRE 词汇精选 / 俞敏洪编著. —北京：群言出版社，
2011 (2012.10 重印)

ISBN 978-7-80256-233-2

Ⅰ．①G… Ⅱ．①俞… Ⅲ．①英语—词汇—研究生—
入学考试—美国—自学参考资料 Ⅳ．①H313

中国版本图书馆 CIP 数据核字(2011)第 032810 号

FLIP

GRE 词汇精选

出 版 人	范 芳
责任编辑	孙春红
封面设计	大愚设计
出版发行	群言出版社（Qunyan Press）
地 址	北京东城区东厂胡同北巷1号
邮政编码	100006
网 站	www. qypublish. com
读者信箱	bj62605588@163. com
总 编 办	010—65265404 65138815
编 辑 部	010—65276609 65262436
发 行 部	010—62605588 62605019
经 销	新华书店
读者服务	010—65220236 65265404 65263345
法律顾问	中济律师事务所
印 刷	北京朝阳新艺印刷有限公司
版 次	2012 年 10 月第 1 版第 5 次印刷
开 本	720mm×990mm 1/16
印 张	30.5
字 数	700 千
书 号	ISBN 978-7-80256-233-2
定 价	58.00 元

新东方图书策划委员会

主任　俞敏洪

委员　（按姓氏笔画为序）

王　强　　包凡一

仲晓红　　沙云龙

陈向东　　张洪伟

邱政政　　汪海涛

周成刚　　徐小平

谢　琴　　窦中川

美丽的鞭策 (代序)

我做任何事情都不太容易抢占先机，因为天性有点与世无争，反映到学习和追求上就是不够上进，或者说没有进取心。1985年大学毕业后被留在北大当了老师，不是因为成绩优秀，而是因为当时北大公共英语迅速发展，严重缺老师，结果把我这个中英文水平都残缺不全的人留了下来。尽管当时我的教学水平不怎么样，但是却很喜欢北大宁静的生活，准备把一辈子托付给北大，在北大分给我的一间八平米的地下室里自得其乐，天天在见不到一丝阳光的房间里读着马尔克斯的《百年孤独》。整个楼房的下水管刚好从我房间旁边通过，二十四小时的哗哗水声传进耳朵，我把它听成美丽的瀑布而不去想像里面的内容。后来北大可怜我，把我从地下室拯救出来，搬到了北大十六楼同样八平米的宿舍里。每天早上打开窗户就能见到阳光，我感激得涕泗横流，决定把一辈子献给北大。

我是一个对周围事情的发展很不敏感的人。到今天为止，我对国内国际的政治形势和变化依然反应迟钝，认为这是大人物的事情，和我这样的草民没有太多关系。我对周围的人在做些什么反应也很迟钝，认为这是人家的私事，我没有知道的权利。在这种迟钝中，我周围的世界和人物都在悄悄地发生变化。中国已经向世界开放，出国的热潮在中国悄然兴起。我周围的朋友们都是奔走在风口浪尖上的人物，迅速嗅到了从遥远的国度飘过来的鱼腥味，偷偷地顺着味道飘来的方向前进（当时大家联系出国都不会让单位知道，甚至不愿意让朋友知道）。过了一段时间，我发现周围的朋友们都失踪了，最后收到他们从海外发来的明信片，才知道他们已经登上了北美大陆。

我依然没有生出太多的羡慕。我能从农村到北大就已经登天了，出国留学对于我来说是一件奢侈得不敢想的事情，还是顺手拿本《三国演义》读一读更加轻松。但不幸的是，我这时候已经结了婚，我不和别人比，我老婆会把我和别人比。她能嫁给我就够为难她的了，几乎是一朵鲜花插在了牛粪上，如果我太落后，这脸面往哪里搁呀？突然有一天我听到一声大吼：如果你不走出国门，就永远别进家门！我一哆嗦后立刻明白我的命运将从此改变。后来我发现，一个女人结婚以后最大的能力是自己不再进步，却能把一个男人弄得很进步或很失败。

老婆的一声吼远远超过了马克思主义的力量。从1988年开始我被迫为了出国而努力。每次我挑灯夜战TOEFL和GRE的时候，她就高兴地为我煮汤倒水；每次看到我夜读三国，她就杏眼圆睁，把我一脚从床上踹下。我化压力为动力，终于考过了TOEFL，又战胜了GRE，尽管分数不算很高，但毕竟可以联系美国大学了。于是开始选专业。但我的学习虽然是涉猎甚广，却对任何专业都没有真正的爱好和研究。病急乱投医，我几乎把美国所有的大学都联系了个遍。美国教授一个个鹰眼犀利，一下就看出来我是个滥竽充数的草包，连在太平洋一个小小岛屿上的夏威夷大学都对我不屑一顾。挣扎了三年，倾家荡产以后，我出国读书的梦想终于彻底破灭。

出国不成，活下去变成了我的第一选择，于是每天晚上出去授课赚取生活费用。三年多联系出国的经历，使我对出国考试有了很深的了解。而此时的中国已经进入了九十年代，大家已经开始明目张胆地为出国而拼命。北京的TOEFL、GRE班遍地开花。北大里面有TOEFL、GRE班，北大外面有很多培训机构也有TOEFL、GRE班。北大里面的班轮不到我去教，老资格的人把职位全占了，于是我就只能到外面去教，结果就影响了北大的生源，就得罪了北大，就被不明不白地给了一个行政记过处分。偷鸡不成反蚀一把米，出国没弄成，教书没挣到钱，反而连北大都待不下去了。我尽管不好胜，但也要脸，不像今天已经练就了死皮赖脸的本领，被处分了还怎么在学生面前露面啊？只能一狠心从北大辞了职。

于是就一心一意地搞英语培训。先是为别人教书，后来就发现自己干能挣更多的钱，就承包了一个民办学校的外语培训中心，先是搞TOEFL培训，后来又发现开GRE班比开TOEFL班更受欢迎，于是就开始搞GRE班。招来了几十个学生才发现没有任何老师能够教GRE的词汇，只能自己日夜备课，拼命翻各种英语大辞典，每天备课达十个小时，但上课时依然捉襟见肘，常常被学生的问题难倒，弄得张口结舌。为维护自己的尊严，我只能收起懒散的性情，开始拼命背英语词汇，家里的每一个角落都贴满了英语单词，最后居然弄破两本《朗文现代英汉双解词典》。男子汉不发奋则已，一发奋则几万单词尽入麾下。结果我老婆从此对我敬畏恩爱，如滔滔江水，绵绵不绝。

后来呢？后来就有了新东方学校，就有了《GRE词汇精选》这本书。最早写这本书时，中国还没有普及电脑，我就用一张卡片写一个单词和解释，在写完几千张卡片以后，再按照字母顺序整理出来送到出版社，结果出版社不收卡片，我只能又把几千张卡片抱回家，我老婆就在家里把一张张卡片上的内容抄在稿子上，每天都到深夜不辍。书终于出版了，由于用了红色封面被学生戏称为"红宝书"。后来为了不断跟上时代，又几经改版。由于有了电脑，修改起来也变得容易，不再需要任何人伏案抄写。但对我来说，这本书唯一的意义，就是直到永远都留在我感动中的——我老婆在灯光下帮我抄写手稿时的美丽背影。

新东方教育科技集团董事长兼总裁

1993 年初版序言

GRE 考生最头疼的事情就是背单词。要在两三个月内熟记大量的 GRE 词汇，并且还要了解这些单词的精确含义，真让人恨不得生出三头六臂来。本书的目的就是为了减轻考生背单词的负担，加快背单词的速度，让考生将更多的时间用在考题本身的学习上。下面我先谈一下本书的特色：

一、本书收词量是目前 GRE 词汇书中最多的一本，所选单词几乎全部来自 GRE 真题，并且对一些将来可能会考到的新单词进行了预测。所以只要背完本书，考试中的词汇量问题就能基本解决。

二、本书对大部分单词的记忆方法进行了说明，使考生记单词的速度至少提高一倍，有些单词甚至可以做到过目不忘。同时，部分单词配有例句或词组，使考生对单词的使用方法一目了然。

下面我再谈一下本书所提到的记忆方法。

一、**词根词缀记忆法**　大部分英语单词都可以分成几个部分来记，它们通常的形式是：前缀 + 词根 + 后缀，如 auto(自己) + bio(生命) + graph(写) + y(后缀)，autobiography(写自己的生命→自传)，这样就可以避免一个字母一个字母地死记硬背。英语中的基本词根、词缀不超过 500 个，只要了解了它们，就可以通过它们轻而易举地记上几千个单词。本书对反复出现的词根进行了详细解释和说明，并列举同根词进行参考，使记单词达到举一反三的效果。

二、**分割联想记忆法**　对于没有词根的单词或词根难以记住的单词，本书采用了分割联想记忆法。所谓分割联想记忆法就是把一个单词分割成几个单词或几个部分，并用联想的方法记住。如：charisma(领导人的超凡魅力)可以这样记：cha 看作 China，ris 看作 rise，ma 看作 Mao，连起来为 China rises Mao (中国升起了毛泽东)→超凡魅力。再如：adamant(坚定的)可以看作两个单词的组合：adam (亚当) + ant (蚂蚁)，亚当和蚂蚁是坚定的人和动物。这样，"坚定的"一词就记住了。有一点需要说明的是，这种方法是极不科学的，甚至是荒谬的，但为了记住单词，可以用尽一切手段。

三、**寻根探源记忆法**　有些英文单词是外来词或因为某个人、物或社会事件所产生的单词，对于这一类的单词，只要了解其来源，一下子就能记住。如 chauvinism(极度爱国主义)，即来自一剧中主角 Chauvin，他是拿破仑的士兵，狂热崇拜拿破仑及鼓吹以武力征服其他民族。再如，tantalize(惹弄，逗引)即来自希腊神话人物 Tantalus，他因泄露天机，被罚立在齐下巴深的水中，头上有果树。口渴欲饮时，水即流失，腹饥欲食时，果子就被风吹去。本书对这一类单词的来源都作了说明，使大家一看到该单词即过目不忘。

四、**比较记忆法**　有些英文单词拼写极为相似，这类单词如果并列在一起，就可以进行比较，并加强记忆。如：minnow(鲦鱼)和 winnow(吹去杂质)；taunt(嘲弄)和 daunt(恐吓)。如果将这些单词以比较的方式呈现，考生就能够一次记几个单词。本书把词形相同的单词都放在一起，使大家可以达到一箭数雕的目的。

五、单词举例记忆法　对有些很短的单词和用法很特殊的单词，本书把它们放入具体的例句或词组中，使大家对于这些单词的用法十分清楚，以增强记忆，如 shoal（浅滩；一群），例：strike on a shoal（搁浅）/ a shoal of tourists（大批游客），两组短语便把 shoal 的两个含义清楚地表达了出来。又如 table 一词，GRE 中考的意义为"搁置，不加考虑"（table a suggestion），是所谓熟悉的单词不熟悉的意义，本书对这一类单词都进行了强调，并附例句说明。通过阅读本书，GRE 中的常考多义词便能全部掌握。

　　本书的记忆方法讲完了，我还想再谈一下记 GRE 单词要注意的几个问题。

　　一、记 GRE 单词讲究的是迅速，只要你眼睛看到英文单词，能想起其中文意思，这个单词就算记住了，所以是"认"单词而不是"背单词"。如看到 dilettante 知道是"外行，业余爱好者"，看到 emancipation 知道是"解放"，这就够了，至于这些单词怎么拼写可以先不管，以后再说。本书把英文单词和释义部分分开，目的就是为了让你能够单独思考单词的含义。你在背完一页单词后，可以盖住右边的解释，再看一遍单词，边看边想这些单词的含义，能想起来就算过了关。

　　二、记单词讲究反复性。不管运用了什么样的记忆方法，说到底反复记忆是最好的方法，比如你今天背了 100 个单词用了 30 分钟，明天复习一下只要 5 分钟，再过几天复习一下仍只要 5 分钟，再过一星期复习一下还是 5 分钟，复习的间隔时间不断延长，记得就会越来越牢固。如果你记了 100 个单词 10 天都不看，一定会全部忘光，还得从头来，这就不合算了。请记住：学而时习之，不亦乐乎？

　　三、每天要给自己规定一定的任务量，或 100 个单词，或 200 个单词，不背完绝不罢休。可以采取自我奖惩的方式，如果完成了任务，就奖励一下自己，或美餐一顿，或看一场电影，或交朋会友。如果完不成则惩罚自己一下，惩罚方式当然由自己选择。另外，也可以采取互相监督的方式，找一个 GRE 的考伴，一起背单词，看谁能把规定的任务先完成，事实证明这种方法能激发起很高的积极性。

　　总之，记 GRE 单词不是件轻松的事情。本书只不过希望起到抛砖引玉的作用。如果你有更好的记忆方法，请主动运用到记单词中去，也希望你能告诉我，以进一步提高本书的质量。由于本书写作时间很短，所以中间一定会有大量的错误和不到之处，甚至会有很可笑的地方，希望得到大家的谅解和批评指正。对于在本书写作过程中给予我极大鼓励和帮助的各位朋友，以及给予我督促和动力的广大 GRE 学员，我在此表示衷心的感谢。

俞敏洪谨识
1993 年 12 月 15 日深夜两点，于北京

本书特点

特点〈1〉《GRE词汇精选》被广大G族亲切地称为"红宝书"，自1993年首版以来一直深受广大考生青睐，迄今为止已改版九次，是一本久经考验的GRE词汇精品书。本书影响了几十万的GRE考生，凡是认真背过本书的考生，都在GRE考试中取得了优异的成绩。

特点〈2〉最新《GRE词汇精选》与以往版本相比有了重大的调整：单词数量有所减少。凡是在考试中出现的重要单词都一一收录，删去了在历年考试中从未出现过的单词。顺应GRE考试改革的需要，这次改版对选词又进行了一次大幅度的筛选和调整。大致步骤如下：（1）对真题词汇进行计算机词频及题型建模统计，以此为改版依据。（2）筛选出核心词汇（填空词和阅读词）、拓展词汇和数学词汇。分为计算机和人工两次加工完成，确保单词筛选的权威性和完整性。（3）考虑到核心词汇的重要性，根据韦氏词典给出英文释义并进行人工筛选，同时根据真题给出单词短语和例句。（4）针对GRE改革后考试填空同义词题型特点，根据韦氏词典对核心词汇给出同义词，并对其进行加工筛选。

特点〈3〉改版后本书分为两个部分：第一部分的"核心词汇"收录了所有重点单词，第二部分的"拓展词汇"则根据对历年试题及GRE考试形势的分析给出。改版后的分类编排使本书成为迄今为止唯一一本涵盖此前GRE考试中出现的所有重点词汇并具有前瞻性的词汇宝典。

特点〈4〉《GRE词汇精选》为每一个重要单词配出了贴切、精练的记忆方法，正文中以"记"标出。其中包括：词根词缀记忆法、分割联想记忆法和发音记忆法等。本书所倡导的记忆方法已经成为中国考生记忆单词的主流方法，其中联想记忆和发音记忆均是本书的独创。这些方法使英语单词记忆由枯燥的劳役变成了生动的游戏，极大地克服了考生对背单词的恐惧心理，增强了记忆单词的趣味性，提高了学习效率。此次改版对书中的记忆方法做出了一定程度的调整，修改后的记忆方法更加贴切、接近生活。此外，本书还在每页的底部设置了"返记菜单"，考生在结束每页的学习后可以及时进行复习和自测，有助于巩固对单词的掌握。

特点〈5〉《GRE词汇精选》给大量的重要单词配上了同义词"同"等，扩大横向词汇量，起到了记单词举一反三的效果，使记单词的自然重复率达到三倍以上。

特点〈6〉《GRE词汇精选》给单词配上了简单明了的英文注解。英文注解所使用的参考词典为ETS出题常用的Webster's Merriam-Webster、New World Thesaurus等词典，以助于考生更准确地理解单词释义。

特点〈7〉 为了增加学习的趣味性，加深对单词的记忆，本书为一些单词配上了生动有趣的漫画插图。这使得记单词由枯燥的劳役变成了生动的游戏，极大地克服了考生对背单词的恐惧心理，提高了学习效率。

特点〈8〉 本书配有600分钟MP3光盘一张，对书中所有英文单词（美式发音）及其中文释义进行了朗读。考生在听单词发音的同时可以更有效地提高对单词的理解和记忆。

祝每位在备考中的考生都能痛并快乐着，在考试中超越自我，取得理想的成绩，做到"无愧我心"！

如何使用本书

联想记忆通过单词的分拆、谐音和词与词之间的联系将难词化简，轻松高效地记忆单词。

本书对反复出现的词根进行了解释和说明，使记单词达到举一反三的效果。

幽默有趣的插图在解释单词含义、帮助考生记忆的同时，增加了学习的趣味性。

ambitious [æm'bɪʃəs]	*adj.* 有抱负的，雄心勃勃的（having a desire to achieve a particular goal） 同 emulous
ambivalent [æm'bɪvələnt]	*adj.* （对人或物）有矛盾看法的（having simultaneous and contradictory attitudes or feelings toward sb. or sth.）
amble ['æmbl]	*v.* 缓行，漫步（to saunter） 记 词根记忆：amble 本身就是一个词根=ambul（走路）
ameliorate [ə'mi:liəreɪt]	*v.* 改善，改良（to improve） 记 词根记忆：a + melior(=better 更好) + ate → 改善，改良
amenable [ə'mi:nəbl]	*adj.* 顺从的；愿接受的（willing; submissive） 记 联想记忆：a + men(人) + able(能…的) → 一个能共事的人 → 顺从的 搭 be amenable to 服从
amend [ə'mend]	*v.* 改正，修正（to put right）；改善（to change or modify for the better） 记 词根记忆：a(加强) + mend(修理) → 修正
amendment [ə'mendmənt]	*n.* 改正，修正（a correction of errors, faults）；修正案（a revision made in a bill, law, constitution, etc.）
amiability [ˌeɪmɪə'bɪləti]	*n.* 亲切，友善（the state of being friendly） 同 agreeableness, cordiality, geniality, pleasance, pleasantness
amicable ['æmɪkəbl]	*adj.* 友好的（friendly in feeling；showing good will） 记 联想记忆：am(是) + i(我) + cable(电缆) → 我是电缆，友好的通向别人 → 友好的
amicably ['æmɪkəbli]	*adv.* 友善地（in an amicable manner）
amorphous [ə'mɔ:rfəs]	*adj.* 无固定形状的（without definite form；shapeless） 记 词根记忆：a + morph(形状) + ous → 无固定形状的
anachronistic [əˌnækrə'nɪstɪk]	*adj.* 时代错误的（an error in chronology） 记 词根记忆：ana(错) + chron(时间) + istic → 时代错误的
anaerobic [ˌæne'roʊbɪk]	*adj.* 厌氧的（of, relating to, or being activity in which the body incurs an oxygen debt）*n.* 厌氧微生物 记 词根记忆：an(不，无) + aero(空气) + bic → 不要空气的 → 厌氧的
analogous [ə'næləgəs]	*adj.* 相似的，可比拟的 搭 be analogous to... 与…相似 同 akin, comparable, corresponding, parallel, undifferentiated
anarchy ['ænərki]	*n.* 无政府（absence of government）；政治混乱（political disorder） 记 词根记忆：an(不，无) + archy(统治) → 无统治 → 无政府
anathema [ə'næθəmə]	*n.* 被诅咒的人（one that is cursed）；（天主教的）革出教门，诅咒（a formal ecclesiastical ban；curse） 记 联想记忆：ana(错误) + them(他们) + a → 他们做错了所以被诅咒 → 被诅咒的人

□ ambitious	□ ambivalent	□ amble	□ ameliorate	□ amenable	□ amend
□ amendment	□ amiability	□ amicable	□ amicably	□ amorphous	□ anachronistic
□ anaerobic	□ analogous	□ anarchy	□ anathema		

本书为重要单词提供了同义词等，扩大了横向词汇量。

每页底部设有返记菜单，考生结束每页的学习后可以及时进行复习和自测，有助于巩固对单词的掌握。

epic ['epɪk]	*n.* 叙事诗，史诗(a long narrative poem) *adj.* 史诗的，叙事诗的；英雄的；大规模的(of great size) 例 Telling gripping tales about a central character engaged in a mighty struggle with events, modern biographies satisfy the American appetite for *epic* narratives.
epidemic [ˌepɪ'demɪk]	*adj.* 传染性的，流行性的 (prevalent and spreading rapidly in a community) 记 词根记忆: epi(在…中) + dem(人民) + ic → 在一群人之中 → 流行性的
episodic [ˌepɪ'sɑːdɪk]	*adj.* 偶然发生的(occurring irregularly)；分散性的 记 来自episode(*n.* 片断)
epitome [ɪ'pɪtəmi]	*n.* 典型(sb./sth. showing all the typical qualities of sth.)；梗概(abstract; summary; abridgment) 记 词根记忆: epi(在…上) + tom(切) + e → 切下来放在最上面 → 梗概；单词tome 意为"卷，册"
epoch ['epək]	*n.* 新纪元(the beginning of a new and important period in the history)；重大的事件(a noteworthy and characteristic event)
equate [i'kweɪt]	*v.* 认为…相等或相仿(to consider sth. as equal to sth. else) 记 词根记忆: equ(相等的) + ate(表动作) → 使相等 → 认为…相等或相仿
equation [ɪ'kweɪʒn]	*n.* 等式(two expressions connected by the sign"=")；等同，相等(action of making equal)

If you would go up high, then use your own legs! Do not let yourselves carried aloft; do not seat yourselves on other people's backs and heads.

如果你想要走到高处，就要使用自己的两条腿！不要让别人把你抬到高处；不要坐在别人的背上和头上。

——德国哲学家 尼采(F. W. Nietzsche, German philosopher)

MP3

□ epic　　□ epidemic　　□ episodic　　□ epitome　　□ epoch　　□ equate
□ equation

目　录

美丽的鞭策（代序）
1993 年初版序言
本书特点
如何使用本书

核心词汇

拓展词汇

核心词汇

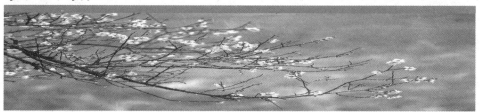

abatement [əˈbeɪtmənt]	*n.* 减少，减轻（the act or process of abating） 记 来自 abate（*v.* 减轻，减弱）
abbreviate [əˈbriːvieɪt]	*v.* 缩短（to make shorter）；缩写（to shorten a word or phrase） 记 词根记忆：ab（加强）+ brev（短）+ iate → 缩短
aberrant [æˈberənt]	*adj.* 越轨的（turning away from what is right）；异常的（deviating from what is normal） 记 词根记忆：ab + err（错误）+ ant → 走向错误 → 越轨的
aberration [ˌæbəˈreɪʃn]	*n.* 越轨（being aberrant） 记 词根记忆：ab + err（错误）+ ation → 错误的行为 → 越轨
abet [əˈbet]	*v.* 教唆，鼓励，帮助（to incite, encourage, urge and help on） 记 联想记忆：a + bet（赌博）→ 教唆赌博 → 教唆
abeyance [əˈbeɪəns]	*n.* 中止，搁置（temporary suspension of an activity） 记 发音记忆："又被压死" →（事情）因搁置而死 → 搁置 搭 in abeyance 搁置；暂停使用
abhor [əbˈhɔːr]	*v.* 憎恨，厌恶（to detest；hate） 记 词根记忆：ab + hor（恨，怕）→ 憎恨，厌恶 同 abominate, execrate, loathe
ablaze [əˈbleɪz]	*adj.* 着火的，燃烧的（being on fire）；闪耀的（radiant with light or emotion） 搭 ablaze with sth. 闪耀、发光
abolition [ˌæbəˈlɪʃn]	*n.* 废除，废止（the state of being abolished；prohibition） 记 来自 abolish（*v.* 废除、废止）
abrasive [əˈbreɪsɪv]	*adj.* 研磨的（tending to abrade） 记 来自 abrade（*v.* 磨损）
abreast [əˈbrest]	*adv.* 并列，并排（side by side） 记 联想记忆：a + breast（胸）→ 胸和胸并排 → 并排 搭 abreast of 与…并排
abridge [əˈbrɪdʒ]	*v.* 删减（to reduce in scope or extent）；缩短（to condense） 记 联想记忆：a + bridge（桥）→ 一座桥把路缩短了 → 缩短

□ abatement　　☑ abbreviate　　□ aberrant　　□ aberration　　□ abet　　□ abeyance
□ abhor　　□ ablaze　　□ abolition　　□ abrasive　　□ abreast　　□ abridge

1

absent	*v.* 缺席，不参加(to keep (oneself) away) *adj.* 缺席的
[æbˈsent]	记 联想记忆：ab + sent(送走) → 把某人送走 → 缺席
	例 Although Irish literature continued to flourish after the sixteenth century, a comparable tradition is *absent* in the visual arts: we think about Irish culture in terms of the word, not in terms of pictorial images.
abstain	*v.* 禁绝，放弃 (to refrain deliberately and often with an effort of self-denial from an action or practice)
[əbˈsteɪn]	记 词根记忆：abs(不) + tain(拿住) → 不拿住 → 放弃
abstract	*n.* 摘要(summary) *adj.* 抽象的(disassociated from any specific instance)
[ˈæbstrækt]	记 词根记忆：abs + tract(拉) → 从文章中拉出 → 摘要
	搭 an abstract sense of the concept 对于概念抽象的理解
abstruse	*adj.* 难懂的，深奥的(hard to understand; recondite)
[əbˈstruːs]	记 词根记忆：abs + trus(走，推) + e → 走不进去 → 难懂的
absurd	*adj.* 荒谬的，可笑的 (ridiculously unreasonable; ludicrous)
[əbˈsɜːrd]	记 词根记忆：ab + surd (不合理的) → 不合理的 → 荒谬的
	搭 absurd assumptions 荒谬的推断
abut	*v.* 邻接，毗邻(to border upon)
[əˈbʌt]	记 联想记忆：about 去掉 o；注意不要和 abet (*v.* 教唆)相混
abysmal	*adj.* 极深的(bottomless; unfathomable)；糟透的(wretched; immeasurably bad)
[əˈbɪzməl]	记 来自 abyss(*n.* 深渊，深坑)
academic	*adj.* 学院的，学术的 (associated with an academy or school)；理论的 (theoretical)
[ˌækəˈdemɪk]	记 来自 academy(*n.* 学院，学术团体)
	搭 academic field 学术领域
accede	*v.* 同意(to give assent; consent)
[əkˈsiːd]	记 词根记忆：ac + cede(走) → 走到一起 → 同意
	搭 accede to 答应
accelerate	*v.* 加速(to increase the speed)；促进(to develop more quickly)
[əkˈseləreɪt]	记 词根记忆：ac(加强) + celer(速度) + ate → 加速
accentuate	*v.* 强调(to emphasize)；重读(to pronounce with an accent or stress)
[əkˈsentʃueɪt]	记 词根记忆：ac(加强) + cent(=cant 唱，说) + uate → 不断说 → 强调
accessible	*adj.* 易接近的(easy to approach)；易受影响的(open to the influence of)
[əkˈsesəbl]	搭 accessible to 达到
	同 employable, operative, practicable, unrestricted, usable
accidental	*adj.* 偶然发生的(occurring unexpectedly or by chance)
[ˌæksɪˈdentl]	记 来自 accident (*n.* 事故，意外)

absurd

□ absent	□ abstain	□ abstract	□ abstruse	□ absurd	□ abut
□ abysmal	□ academic	□ accede	□ accelerate	□ accentuate	□ accessible
□ accidental					

accommodate [əˈkɑːmədeɪt]	*v.* 与…一致(to make fit, suitable, or congruous); 提供住宿(to make room for); 顺应, 使适应
	记 联想记忆: ac + commo(看作 common, 普通的) + date(日子) → 人们适应了过普通的日子 → 使适应
	同 attune, harmonize, reconcile
accompany [əˈkʌmpəni]	*v.* 伴随, 陪伴(to walk with sb. as a companion)
	记 词根记忆: ac + company(陪伴) → 伴随, 陪伴
accomplice [əˈkɑːmplɪs]	*n.* 共犯, 同谋(associate; partner in a crime)
	记 词根记忆: ac + com(共同) + plic(重叠) + e → 重叠一起干 → 同谋
accomplish [əˈkɑːmplɪʃ]	*v.* 完成, 做成功(to succeed in doing sth.)
	记 词根记忆: ac + compl(满) + ish → 圆满 → 完成
	同 achieve, attain, gain, realize
accredit [əˈkredɪt]	*v.* 授权(to give official authorization to or approval of)
	搭 accredit sb. to 委任、委派
accuracy [ˈækjərəsi]	*n.* 精确, 准确(precision; exactness)
	记 词根记忆: ac + cur(关心) + acy → 不断关心才能保证精确 → 精确
accuse [əˈkjuːz]	*v.* 谴责, 指责(to blame)
	记 词根记忆: ac + cuse(理由) → 有理由说别人 → 指责
	同 arraign, charge, criminate, incriminate, inculpate
accustom [əˈkʌstəm]	*v.* 使习惯(to make familiar with something through use or experience)
	记 词根记忆: ac(一再) + custom(习惯) → 使习惯
acerbic [əˈsɜːrbɪk]	*adj.* 尖酸的; 刻薄的(bitter; sharp; harsh)
	记 词根记忆: acerb(尖, 酸) + ic → 尖酸的, 刻薄的
acidic [əˈsɪdɪk]	*adj.* 酸的, 酸性的(acid)
	记 词根记忆: acid(*n.* 酸) + ic → 酸的
acknowledge [əkˈnɑːlɪdʒ]	*v.* 承认(to recognize as genuine or valid); 致谢(to express gratitude)
	记 联想记忆: ac + knowledge(知识, 知道) → 大家都知道了, 所以不得不承认 → 承认
	同 admit, avow, concede, confess
acolyte [ˈækəlaɪt]	*n.* (教士的)助手, 侍僧(one who assists the celebrant in the performance of liturgical rites)
	记 发音记忆: "爱过来的" → 爱过来帮忙的人 → 助手
acoustic [əˈkuːstɪk]	*adj.* 听觉的, 声音的(having to do with hearing or sound)
acquiescence [ˌækwiˈesns]	*n.* 默许(the act of acquiescing)
	记 来自 acquiesce(*v.* 默认, 默许)
acquiescent [ˌækwiˈesnt]	*adj.* 默认的(inclined to acquiesce)
acrimonious [ˌækrɪˈmoʊniəs]	*adj.* 尖酸刻薄的, 激烈的(caustic, biting, or rancorous)
	同 indignant, irate, ireful, wrathful, wroth

☑ accommodate	☑ accompany	☐ accomplice	☑ accomplish	☐ accredit	☑ accuracy
☑ accuse	☑ accustom	☐ acerbic	☐ acidic	☑ acknowledge	☐ acolyte
☐ acoustic	☐ acquiescence	☐ acquiescent	☐ acrimonious		

acrimony [ˈækrɪmoʊni]	*n.* 尖刻，刻薄(asperity) 记 词根记忆：acri(尖，酸) + mony(表示名词) → 尖刻
activate [ˈæktɪveɪt]	*v.* 刺激，使活动(to make active or more active) 例 The burglar alarm is *activated* by movement.
actuate [ˈæktʃueɪt]	*v.* 开动，促使(to motivate; activate) 记 词根记忆：act(行动) + uate(动词后缀) → 使行动起来 → 促使
acute [əˈkjuːt]	*adj.* 灵敏的，敏锐的(keen; shrewd; sensitive)；剧烈的(characterized by sharpness or severity)；急性的 记 联想记忆：a + cut(切) + e → 一刀切 → 剧烈的
adamant [ˈædəmənt]	*adj.* 坚决的，固执的 (unyielding; inflexible)；强硬的 (too hard to be broken) 记 联想记忆：adam(亚当) + ant(蚂蚁) → 亚当和蚂蚁都很固执 → 固执的 搭 remain adamant in 对…很固执 同 obdurate, rigid, unbending
adaptability [əˌdæptəbɪləti]	*n.* 适应性(capable of being or becoming adapted) 记 来自adapt(*v.* 适应)
adaptable [əˈdæptəbl]	*adj.* 有适应能力的 (able to adjust oneself to new circumstances)；可改编的(capable of being adapted) 记 词根记忆：adapt(适应) + able(能…的) → 有适应能力的
adaptive [əˈdæptɪv]	*adj.* 适应的 (showing or having a capacity for or tendency toward adaptation)
addict [ˈædɪkt]	*v.* 沉溺；上瘾(to be an addict; devote oneself to sth. habitually) 记 词根记忆：ad(一再) + dict(说，要求) → 一再要求 → 上瘾
address [əˈdres]	*v.* 处理，对付，设法解决(to tackle sth.)；致辞(to deliver a formal speech to)
adept [əˈdept]	*adj.* 熟练的，擅长的(highly skilled; expert) 记 词根记忆：ad + ept(能力) → 有能力 → 熟练的，擅长的 搭 be adept at 擅长
adequate [ˈædɪkwət]	*adj.* 足够的(sufficient) 记 词根记忆：ad(加强) + equ(平等) + ate(…的) → 比平等多的 → 足够的 同 competent, satisfactory
adhere [ədˈhɪr]	*v.* 粘着，坚持(to stick fast; stay attached) 记 词根记忆：ad + here(粘连) → 粘着 搭 adhere to 坚持
adhesive [ədˈhiːsɪv]	*adj.* 粘着的，带粘性的 (tending to adhere or cause adherence) *n.* 黏合剂 (an adhesive substance) 记 联想记忆：ad + hes(=stick 粘住) + ive → 带粘性的；粘合剂
admonish [ədˈmɑːnɪʃ]	*v.* 训诫(to reprove mildly)；警告(to warn; advise) 记 词根记忆：ad(一再) + mon(警告) + ish → 训诫；警告

□ acrimony □ activate □ actuate □ acute □ adamant □ adaptability
□ adaptable □ adaptive □ addict □ address □ adept □ adequate
□ adhere □ adhesive □ admonish

adopt [əˈdɑːpt]	v. 采纳，采用（to take up and practice or use）；正式接受，通过（to accept formally and put into effect） 记 词根记忆：ad + opt(选择) → 通过选择 → 采纳，采用

好！就用你的方案吧！

adopt

adoration [ˌædəˈreɪʃn]	n. 崇拜，爱慕(the act of adoring) 记 来自 adore(v. 崇拜)
adore [əˈdɔːr]	v. 崇拜（to worship as divine）；爱慕（to love greatly; revere） 记 词根记忆：ad + ore(讲话) → 不断想对某人讲话 → 爱慕(某人)
adorn [əˈdɔːrn]	v. 装饰(to decorate; beautify) 记 词根记忆：ad + orn(装饰) → 装饰
adulation [ˌædʒəˈleɪʃn]	n. 奉承，谄媚(excessive or slavish admiration or flattery)
adulatory [ˈædʒələtɔːri]	adj. 奉承的(having excessive or slavish admiration or flattery)
adumbrate [ˈædəmbreɪt]	v. 预示(to foreshadow in a vague way) 记 词根记忆：ad + umbr(影子) + ate → 影子提前来到 → 预示
advantage [ədˈvæntɪdʒ]	n. 利益，益处(benefit) v. 有利于，有益于 搭 have the advantage of... 有…优势 同 allowance, avail, interest
adventurous [ədˈventʃərəs]	adj. 爱冒险的，大胆的(disposed to seek adventure)，充满危险的(characterized by unknown dangers and risks) 同 adventuresome, audacious
adversary [ˈædvərseri]	n. 对手，敌手（one that contends with, opposes, or resists）adj. 对手的，敌对的(having or involving antagonistic parties or opposing interests)
adverse [ˈædvɜːrs]	adj. 有害的，不利的(not favorable)；敌对的(hostile)，相反的(contrary) 记 词根记忆：ad(坏) + verse(转) → 不利的；敌对的
adversity [ədˈvɜːrsəti]	n. 逆境，不幸（a state, condition, or instance of serious or continued difficulty or adverse fortune）
advertise [ˈædvərtaɪz]	v. 做广告(to call public attention to arouse a desire to buy or patronize)；通知(to make publicly and generally known)
advocacy [ˈædvəkəsi]	n. 拥护，支持(the act or process of advocating) 记 来自 advocate(v. 拥护，支持)
aesthetic [esˈθetɪk]	adj. 美学的，审美的(relating to aesthetics or the beautiful) 记 词根记忆：a + esthe(感觉) + tic(…的) → 美学的；审美的
aesthetically [esˈθetɪkli]	adv. 审美地（according to aesthetics or its principles）；美学观点上地（in an aesthetic manner）

□ adopt	□ adoration	□ adore	□ adorn	□ adulation	□ adulatory
□ adumbrate	□ advantage	□ adventurous	□ adversary	□ adverse	□ adversity
□ advertise	□ advocacy	□ aesthetic	□ aesthetically		

affable [ˈæfəbl]	*adj.* 和蔼的(gentle; amiable); 友善的(pleasant and easy to approach or talk to)
	记 词根记忆: af + fable(说, 讲) → 可以说话的 → 易于交谈的 → 友善的
affection [əˈfekʃn]	*n.* 喜爱(fond or tender feeling)
	记 词根记忆: affect(*v.* 影响, 感染) + ion → 喜爱
affectionate [əˈfekʃənət]	*adj.* 亲爱的, 挚爱的(having affection or warm regard)
	例 He is very *affectionate* towards his children.
affective [əˈfektɪv]	*adj.* 感情的(relating to, arising from, or influencing feelings or emotions), 表达感情的(expressing emotion)
affinity [əˈfɪnəti]	*n.* 相互吸引(a mutual attraction between a man and a woman); 密切关系(close relationship)
	记 词根记忆: af + fin(范围) + ity → 在范围内 → 密切关系
affirmation [ˌæfərˈmeɪʃn]	*n.* 肯定; 断言(the act of affirming or the state of being affirmed; assertion)
afflict [əˈflɪkt]	*v.* 折磨; 使痛苦(to cause persistent pain or suffering)
	记 词根记忆: af + flict(打击) → 一再打击 → 折磨; 使痛苦
affluent [ˈæfluənt]	*adj.* 富有的, 丰富的(rich)
	搭 affluent western countries 富裕的西方国家
affordable [əˈfɔːrdəbl]	*adj.* 负担得起的(being able to buy sth.)
	记 词根记忆: afford(*v.* 买得起) + able(*adj.* 能) → 负担得起的
affront [əˈfrʌnt]	*v.* 侮辱, 冒犯(to offend)
	记 词根记忆: af + front(前面, 脸面) → 冲着别人的脸 → 冒犯
	同 confront, encounter
aggrandize [əˈɡrænˌdaiz]	*v.* 增大, 扩张(to make greater or more powerful); 吹捧(to praise highly)
	记 词根记忆: ag + grand(大) + ize → 增大
	搭 aggrandize oneself 妄自尊大
	同 augment, extend, heighten, magnify, multiply
aggravate [ˈæɡrəveɪt]	*v.* 加重, 恶化(to make worse; intensify); 激怒, 使恼火
	记 词根记忆: ag + grav(重) + ate → 加重
	同 exasperate, irritate, peeve, pique, provoke
aggressive [əˈɡresɪv]	*adj.* 好斗的(militant; assertive); 有进取心的(full of enterprise and initiative)
	记 词根记忆: ag(加强) + gress(行走) + ive → 到处乱走的 → 好斗的
	搭 aggressive entrepreneur 有进取心的企业家
	同 assertory, pushful, self-assertive
aghast [əˈɡæst]	*adj.* 惊骇的, 吓呆的(feeling great horror or dismay; terrified)
	记 联想记忆: a(⋯的) + ghast(=ghost 鬼) → 像看到鬼的 → 吓呆的
	同 frightened, scared, scary
agility [əˈdʒɪləti]	*n.* 敏捷(the quality or state of being agile)
	记 来自 agile(*adj.* 灵活的, 敏捷的)

agitate [ˈædʒɪteɪt]	*v.* 鼓动，煽动 (to argue publicly or campaign for/against sth.)；使不安，使焦虑 (to cause anxiety) 记 词根记忆：ag（做）+ itate（表示不断的动作）→ 使不断地做 → 鼓动，煽动
agitation [ˌædʒɪˈteɪʃn]	*n.* 焦虑，不安（anxiety）；公开辩论，鼓动宣传 (public argument or action for social or political change)
agony [ˈægəni]	*n.* 极大的痛苦 (very great mental or physical pain) 记 词根记忆：agon（挣扎）+ y → 拼命挣扎 → 极大的痛苦；谐音："爱过你"
agoraphobic [ˌægərəˈfoʊbɪk]	*n./adj.* 患旷野恐惧症的(人)
agrarian [əˈgreriən]	*adj.* 土地的 (of land) 记 词根记忆：agr（田地，农业）+ arian（表形容词）→ 土地的
airborne [ˈerbɔːrn]	*adj.* 空运地 (transported or carried by the air)，空降的 (trained for deployment by air and especially by parachute)；空气传播的
akin [əˈkɪn]	*adj.* 同族的 (related by blood)；类似的 (essentially similar, related, or compatible)
alienate [ˈeɪliəneɪt]	*v.* 使疏远，离间 (to estrange; cause to become unfriendly or indifferent) 记 词根记忆：alien(外国的) + ate → 把别人当外国人 → 使疏远 同 alien, disaffect
alienation [ˌeɪliəˈneɪʃn]	*n.* 疏远，离间 (a withdrawing or separation of a person) 搭 alienation from 与…疏远
allegiance [əˈliːdʒəns]	*n.* 忠诚，拥护 (loyalty or devotion to a cause or a person) 记 词根记忆：al(加强) + leg(法律) + iance → 拥护法律 → 拥护
allegory [ˈæləgɔːri]	*n.* 寓言 (fable) 记 联想记忆：all + ego(自己) + ry → 全部关于自己的寓言 → 寓言
allot [əˈlɑːt]	*v.* 分配 (to assign as a share or portion)；拨出 (to distribute by or as if by lot)
alloy [ˈælɔɪ]	*n.* 合金 (a substance composed of two or more metals) 记 联想记忆：all(所有的) + oy → 把所有金属混在一起 → 合金 同 admixture, amalgam, composite, fusion, interfusion
allude [əˈluːd]	*v.* 暗指，影射，间接提到 (to refer in an indirect way) 记 词根记忆：al + lud(嬉笑) + e → 在嬉笑中说 → 暗指，影射
allure [əˈlʊr]	*v.* 引诱，诱惑 (to entice by charm or attraction)
allusion [əˈluːʒn]	*n.* 暗指，间接提到 (an implied or indirect reference esp. in literature) 记 来自 allude(*v.* 暗指，间接提到)
allusive [əˈluːsɪv]	*adj.* 暗指的，间接提到的 (containing allusions) 记 词根记忆：allu (=allude 暗指) + sive → 暗指的

□ agitate	□ agitation	□ agony	□ agoraphobic	□ agrarian	□ airborne
□ akin	□ alienate	□ alienation	□ allegiance	□ allegory	□ allot
□ alloy	□ allude	□ allure	□ allusion	□ allusive	

ally	[əˈlaɪ] v. (使)结盟，(使)联合(to associate)
	[ˈælaɪ] n. 同盟者，伙伴(one that is associated with another)
	记 联想记忆：all(全部) + y → 把全部人都聚集在一起 → (使)结盟
aloof [əˈluːf]	adj. 远离的(removed or distant either physically or emotionally)；冷淡的，冷漠的 (cool and distant in manner)
also-ran [ˈɔːlsou ræn]	n. 落选者(a contestant that does not win)；不重要的参与者(one that is of little importance)
alternate 	[ˈɔːltərnət] adj. 轮流的，交替的 (occurring or succeeding by turns)
	[ˈɔːltərneɪt] v. 轮流，交替(to perform by turns or in succession)
	[ˈɔːltərnət] n. 候选人，代替者(one that substitutes for or alternates with another)
	记 词根记忆：alter(改变) + nate → 来回改变 → 轮流的，交替的
	同 alternative, backup, surrogate
alternative [ɔːlˈtɜːrnətɪv]	adj. 轮流的，交替的 (alternate)；两者择一的 (offering or expressing a choice)
	记 词根记忆：alter (改变状态，其他的) + native (…的) → 改变状态的 → 轮流的，交替的
	同 backup, substitute, surrogate
altruism [ˈæltruɪzəm]	n. 利他主义；无私(selflessness)
	记 词根记忆：altru(其他) + ism(主义) → 利他主义
amalgam [əˈmælgəm]	n. 混合物(a combination or mixture)
	记 联想记忆：am + alg + am → 前后两个 am 结合 → 混合物
	同 admixture, composite, compound, interfusion
amateur [ˈæmətər]	n. 业余爱好者 (one who engages in sth. as a pastime rather than as a profession)
	记 词根记忆：amat(=amor 爱) + eur(人) → 爱好的人 → 业余爱好者
amaze [əˈmeɪz]	v. 使大为吃惊，使惊奇(to fill with wonder)
	记 发音记忆："啊美死" → 使惊奇
	同 astound, dumbfound, flabbergast
ambidextrous [ˌæmbiˈdekstrəs]	adj. 十分灵巧的(very skillful or versatile)
	记 词根记忆：ambi(两个) + dextr(右的) + ous → 两只手都像右手一样灵巧 → 十分灵巧的
	同 bimanal
ambiguity [ˌæmbiˈgjuːəti]	n. 模棱两可的话(an ambiguous word or expression)；不明确(uncertainty)
	同 amphibology, equivocality, equivocation, equivoque, tergiversation
ambiguous [æmˈbɪgjuəs]	adj. 含糊的(not clear; uncertain; vague)
	记 词根记忆：ambi(二) + guous(做…的) → 两件事都想做的 → 含糊的

☑ ally　　☑ aloof　　☐ also-ran　　☐ alternate　　☑ alternative　　☑ altruism
☐ amalgam　　☑ amateur　　☑ amaze　　☐ ambidextrous　　☑ ambiguity　　☑ ambiguous

ambitious [æmˈbɪʃəs]	*adj.* 有抱负的，雄心勃勃的（having a desire to achieve a particular goal） 同 emulous
ambivalent [æmˈbɪvələnt]	*adj.* （对人或物）有矛盾看法的（having simultaneous and contradictory attitudes or feelings toward sb. or sth.）
amble [ˈæmbl]	*v.* 缓行，漫步（to saunter） 记 词根记忆：amble 本身就是一个词根=ambul（走路）
ameliorate [əˈmiːliəreɪt]	*v.* 改善，改良（to improve） 记 词根记忆：a + melior（=better 更好）+ ate → 改善，改良
amenable [əˈmiːnəbl]	*adj.* 顺从的；愿接受的（willing；submissive） 记 联想记忆：a + men（人）+ able（能…的）→ 一个能共事的人 → 顺从的 搭 be amenable to 服从
amend [əˈmend]	*v.* 改正，修正（to put right）；改善（to change or modify for the better） 记 词根记忆：a（加强）+ mend（修理）→ 修正
amendment [əˈmendmənt]	*n.* 改正，修正（a correction of errors, faults）；修正案（a revision made in a bill, law, constitution, etc.）
amiability [ˌeɪmiəˈbɪləti]	*n.* 亲切，友善（the state of being friendly） 同 agreeableness, cordiality, geniality, pleasance, pleasantness
amicable [ˈæmɪkəbl]	*adj.* 友好的（friendly in feeling；showing good will） 记 联想记忆：am（是）+ i（我）+ cable（电缆）→ 我是电缆，友好的通向别人 → 友好的
amicably [ˈæmɪkəbli]	*adv.* 友善地（in an amicable manner）
amorphous [əˈmɔːrfəs]	*adj.* 无固定形状的（without definite form；shapeless） 记 词根记忆：a + morph（形状）+ ous → 无固定形状的
anachronistic [əˌnækrəˈnɪstɪk]	*adj.* 时代错误的（an error in chronology） 记 词根记忆：ana（错）+ chron（时间）+ istic → 时代错误的
anaerobic [ˌæneˈroʊbɪk]	*adj.* 厌氧（of, relating to, or being activity in which the body incurs an oxygen debt）*n.* 厌氧微生物 记 词根记忆：an（不，无）+ aero（空气）+ bic → 不要空气的 → 厌氧的
analogous [əˈnæləgəs]	*adj.* 相似的，可比拟的 搭 be analogous to... 与…相似 同 akin, comparable, corresponding, parallel, undifferentiated
anarchy [ˈænərki]	*n.* 无政府（absence of government）；政治混乱（political disorder） 记 词根记忆：an（不，无）+ archy（统治）→ 无统治 → 无政府
anathema [əˈnæθəmə]	*n.* 被诅咒的人（one that is cursed）；（天主教的）革出教门，诅咒（a formal ecclesiastical ban；curse） 记 联想记忆：ana（错误）+ them（他们）+ a → 他们做错了所以被诅咒 → 被诅咒的人

☑ ambitious	☑ ambivalent	☐ amble	☐ ameliorate	☐ amenable	☑ amend
☑ amendment	☑ amiability	☐ amicable	☐ amicably	☐ amorphous	☐ anachronistic
☐ anaerobic	☑ analogous	☑ anarchy	☐ anathema		

9

anatomical [ˌænəˈtɑːmɪkl]	*adj.* 解剖学的(of, or relating to anatomy) 记 来自 anatomy(*n.* 解剖学，解剖)；ana(分开) + tomy(切) → 切开 → 解剖
ancestor [ˈænsestər]	*n.* 祖先，祖宗（one from whom a person is descended） 记 词根记忆：ance（看作 ante，先）+ stor → 祖先，祖宗
ancestral [ænˈsestrəl]	*adj.* 祖先的，祖传的（of, relating to, or inherited from an ancestor） 记 词根记忆：ances(原始的) + tral → 祖先的
anecdotal [ˌænɪkˈdoʊtl]	*adj.* 轶事的，趣闻的（of, relating to, or consisting of anecdotes） 记 来自 anecdot(*n.* 逸事，趣闻)
angular [ˈæŋɡjələr]	*adj.* 生硬的，笨拙的（lacking grace or smoothness; awkward）；有角的（having angles）；（指人）瘦削的(thin and bony)
animated [ˈænɪmeɪtɪd]	*adj.* 活生生的，生动的(full of vigor and spirit) 记 来自 animate(*adj.* 有生气的)
animosity [ˌænɪˈmɑːsəti]	*n.* 憎恶，仇恨（a feeling of strong dislike or hatred） 记 词根记忆：anim(生命) + osity → 用整个生命去恨 → 仇恨 同 animus, antagonism, enmity, hostility, rancor
annex [əˈneks]	*v.* 兼并（to obtain or take for oneself），附加（to attach as a quality, consequence, or condition）
annotate [ˈænəteɪt]	*v.* 注解（to provide critical or explanatory notes） 记 词根记忆：an + not(标示) + ate → 注解
anomalous [əˈnɑːmələs]	*adj.* 反常的（inconsistent with what is usual, normal, or expected）；不协调的（marked by incongruity or contradiction） 同 aberrant, abnormal, deviant, divergent, irregular
anomaly [əˈnɑːməli]	*n.* 异常，反常（deviation from common rule）；异常事物（sth. anomalous） 记 词根记忆：a + nomal(看作 normal, 正常的) + y → 异常
antagonism [ænˈtæɡənɪzəm]	*n.* 对抗，敌对 同 animosity, animus, antipathy, opposition, rancor
antagonistic [ænˌtæɡəˈnɪstɪk]	*adj.* 敌对的，对抗性的（marked by or resulting from antagonism） 同 adverse, antipathetic, opposed, opposing
antagonize [ænˈtæɡənaɪz]	*v.* 使…敌对，与…对抗（to arouse hostility; show opposition） 记 词根记忆：ant(反) + agon(打斗，比赛) + ize → 对着打 → 与…对抗
antecedent [ˌæntɪˈsiːdnt]	*n.* 前事（a preceding event, condition or cause）；祖先（a person's ancestors or family and social background）*adj.* 先行的（preceding in time and order）

ancestor

☐ anatomical ☑ ancestor ☐ ancestral ☐ anecdotal ☐ angular ☐ animated
☐ animosity ☐ annex ☐ annotate ☐ anomalous ☐ anomaly ☐ antagonism
☐ antagonistic ☐ antagonize ☐ antecedent

antedate [ˌænti'deit]	*v.* (在信、支票等上)填写比实际日期早的日期；早于(to assign to a date prior to that of actual occurrence) 记 词根记忆：ante(前面) + date(日期) → 在现在的日期前面 → 早于 同 antecede, forerun, pace, precede, predate
anterior [æn'tiriər]	*adj.* 较早的，以前的(previous; earlier)
antibiotic [ˌæntibai'ɑːtik]	*adj.* 抗菌的(of, or relating to antibiotics) *n.* 抗生素(substance that can destroy or prevent the growth of bacteria) 记 词根记忆：anti(反) + bio(生命) + tic → 抗生素

1

Today is the first day of the rest of my life, I wake as a child to see the world begin. On monarch wings and birthday wonderings, want to put on faces, walk in the wet and cold. And look forward to my growing old, to grow is to change, to change is to be new, to be new is to be young again, I barely remember when.

——美国乡村歌手约翰·丹佛(John Denver)

Word List 2  MP3 - 02

anticipatory [æn'tɪsəpətɔːri]	*adj.* 预想的，预期的(characterized by anticipation) 记 来自 anticipate(*v.* 预测，预料)
anticlimactic [ˌæntiklaɪ'mæktɪk]	*adj.* 突减的(of, relating to, or marked by anticlimax) 记 词根记忆: anti (相反) + climac (=climax 顶点) + tic → 与顶点相反 → 突减的
antidote ['æntidoʊt]	*n.* 解药(a remedy to counteract a poison) 记 词根记忆: anti(反) + dote(药剂) → 反毒的药 → 解药
antipathy [æn'tɪpəθi]	*n.* 反感，厌恶(strong dislike) 记 词根记忆: anti + pathy(感情) → 反感 同 animosity, animus, antagonism, enmity, hostility
antiquarianism [ˌænti'kweəriənizəm]	*n.* 古物研究，好古癖(study, collection or sale of valuable old objects) 记 词根记忆: antiqu(古老的) + arian + ism → 古物研究
antiquated ['æntɪkweɪtɪd]	*adj.* 陈旧的，过时的(outmoded or discredited by reason of age)；年老的 (advanced in age) 搭 antiquated idea 过时的想法 同 antique, archaic, dated
antique [æn'tiːk]	*adj.* 古时的，古老的(existing since or belonging to ealier times) *n.* 古物，古董(a relic or object of ancient times) 记 词根记忆：anti(前) + que → 以前的 → 古 时的
antiquity [æn'tɪkwəti]	*n.* 古老 (the quality of being ancient)；古人(the people of ancient times)；古迹 (objects, buildings or work of art from the ancient past)
antiseptic [ˌænti'septɪk]	*n.* 杀菌剂(any substance that inhibit the action of microorganisms) *adj.* 防腐的(preventing infection or decay) 记 词根记忆: anti(反) + sept(菌) + ic → 杀菌剂
antithesis [æn'tɪθəsɪs]	*n.* 对立；相对(a contrast or opposition) 记 词根记忆: anti(反) + thesis(放) → 反着放 → 对立
antithetical [ˌænti'θetɪkl]	*adj.* 相反的(constituting or marked by antithesis)；对立的(opposite) 同 contradictory, contrary, converse, counter, reverse

apathetic [ˌæpə'θetɪk]	*adj.* 无感情的(having or showing little or no feeling or emotion); 无兴趣的 (having little or no interest or concern) 搭 be apathetic about 对…冷淡
apex ['eɪpeks]	*n.* 顶点, 最高点(peak; vertex) 搭 reach the apex 达到顶点 同 acme, climax, crest, crown, fastigium
aphorism ['æfərɪzəm]	*n.* 格言(maxim; adage) 记 词根记忆: a + phor(带来) + ism → 带来智慧的话 → 格言
appall [ə'pɔːl]	*v.* 使惊骇, 使胆寒(to fill with horror or dismay; shock) 记 词根记忆: ap + pal(=pale 苍白) + l → 脸色变白 → 使惊骇
apparition [ˌæpə'rɪʃn]	*n.* 幽灵(a strange figure appearing suddenly and thought to be a ghost); 特异景象(an unusual or unexpected sight) 记 词根记忆: appar(出现) + ition → 出现的幽灵 → 幽灵; 和 appearance (*n.* 出现; 外貌)来自同一词源 同 phantasm, phantom, revenant, specter
appease [ə'piːz]	*v.* 使平静, 安抚(to pacify or quiet) 记 词根记忆: ap + pease(和平) → 使平静 同 assuage, conciliate, mollify, pacify, propitiate
appetizing ['æpɪtaɪzɪŋ]	*adj.* 美味可口的, 促进食欲的(stimulating the appetite) 同 delicious, tasty
applaud [ə'plɔːd]	*v.* 鼓掌; 称赞(to show approval by clapping the hands) 记 词根记忆: ap(加强) + plaud(鼓掌) → 鼓掌 同 acclaim, commend, compliment
applicability [ˌæplɪkə'bɪləti]	*n.* 适用性, 适应性 记 来自 apply(*v.* 应用, 适用)
apply [ə'plaɪ]	*v.* 应用(to put to use); 适用(to have relevance or a valid connection) 记 和 supply(*v.* 提供)一起记 搭 apply to 适用于 同 bestow, employ, exploit, handle, utilize
apportion [ə'pɔːrʃn]	*v.* (按比例或计划)分配(to divide and share out according to a plan) 搭 apportion sth. among/between/to sb. 分配, 分发
apposite ['æpəzɪt]	*adj.* 适当的, 贴切的(appropriate; apt; relevant) 记 词根记忆: ap + pos(放) + ite → 放在一起 → 适当的; 注意不要和 opposite(*adj.* 相反的)相混淆
appreciate [ə'priːʃieɪt]	*v.* 欣赏(to understand and enjoy); 感激(to recognize with gratitude) 记 词根记忆: ap + preci(价值) + ate → 给以价值 → 欣赏
appreciative [ə'priːʃətɪv]	*adj.* 赞赏的; 感激的(having or showing appreciation) 记 来自 appreciate(*v.* 欣赏, 感激)

applaud

☑ apathetic	☐ apex	☐ aphorism	☐ appall	☐ apparition	☐ appease
☐ appetizing	☐ applaud	☐ applicability	☑ apply	☐ apportion	☐ apposite
☑ appreciate	☐ appreciative				

13

apprehensive [ˌæprɪˈhensɪv]	*adj.* 害怕的(anxious or fearful that sth. bad or unpleasant will happen); 敏悟的(capable of apprehending or quick to do so) 记 联想记忆:ap + prehen(看作 prehend, 抓住) + sive → 抓住不放 → (因为)害怕的
apprise [əˈpraɪz]	*v.* 通知, 告知(to inform or notify) 记 联想记忆:app(看作 appear) + rise → 出现 + 升起 → 通知 同 acquaint, advise, warn
approach [əˈprəʊtʃ]	*v.* 接近, 靠近 (to come nearer); 着手处理(to begin to handle) *n.* 方法(method) 记 词根记忆: ap + proach(接近) → 靠近 搭 approach to …的方法
approaching [əˈprəʊtʃɪŋ]	*adj.* 接近的, 逼近的
approbation [ˌæprəˈbeɪʃn]	*n.* 赞许(commendation); 认可(official approval) 记 词根记忆: ap + prob (=prove 证实) + ation → 证实是好的 → 赞许
appropriate [əˈprəʊpriət]	*v.* 拨款(to set money aside for a specific use); 盗用(to take improperly) *adj.* 恰当的(fitting) 记 词根记忆: ap + propr(拥有) + iate → 自己拥有 → 盗用
approximate [əˈprɑːksɪmət]	*adj.* 近似的, 大约的(much like; nearly correct or exact) 记 词根记忆: ap + proxim(接近) + ate → 近似的, 大约的
apropos [ˌæprəˈpəʊ]	*adj./adv.* 适当的(地)(seasonabl(y)); 有关(with reference to; regarding) 记 联想记忆:a+prop(看作 proper, 适当的) + os → 适当的/地
aptitude [ˈæptɪtuːd]	*n.* 适宜(a natural tendency); 才能, 资质(a natural ability to do sth.) 记 词根记忆:apt(能力) + itude(状态) → 才能, 资质 搭 aptitude for 有…方面的才能
aquatic [əˈkwætɪk]	*adj.* 水生的, 水中的(growing or living in or upon water) 记 词根记忆: aqua(水) + tic → 水中的
arable [ˈærəbl]	*adj.* 适于耕种的(suitable for plowing and planting) 记 联想记忆: ar(看作 are) + able → 是能够耕种的 → 适于耕种的 搭 arable field 可耕地
arbiter [ˈɑːrbɪtər]	*n.* 权威人士, 泰斗(arbitrator; a person fully qualified to judge or decide) 记 词根记忆:arbit(判断, 裁决) + er → 判断之人 → 权威人士, 泰斗
arbitrary [ˈɑːrbətreri]	*adj.* 专横的, 武断的(discretionary; despotic; dictatorial) 记 词根记忆: arbitr(判断) + ary(…的) → 自己作判断 → 武断的 同 autarchic, autocratic, monocratic
arboreal [ɑːrˈbɔːriəl]	*adj.* 树木的(of or like a tree) 记 词根记忆: arbor(树) + eal → 树木的
arcane [ɑːrˈkeɪn]	*adj.* 神秘的, 秘密的(mysterious; hidden or secret) 记 词根记忆: arcan(秘密) + e → 神秘的 同 cabalistic, impenetrable, inscrutable, mystic

approach

□ apprehensive	□ apprise	□ approach	□ approaching	□ approbation	□ appropriate
□ approximate	□ apropos	□ aptitude	□ aquatic	□ arable	□ arbiter
□ arbitrary	□ arboreal	□ arcane			

archaeological [ˌɑːrkiə'lɑːdʒɪkl]	*adj.* 考古学的
archaic [ɑːr'keɪɪk]	*adj.* 古老的（of, relating to, or characteristic of an earlier or more primitive time）
archetypally ['ɑːrki'taɪpəli]	*adv.* 典型地 记 来自 archetype(*n.* 典型)
architect ['ɑːrkɪtekt]	*n.* 建筑师（person who designs buildings and supervises their construction） 记 联想记忆：archi(统治者，主要的) + tect(做) → 统治造房的人 → 建筑师
architectural [ˌɑːrkɪ'tektʃərəl]	*adj.* 建筑上的；建筑学的(of or relating to architecture) 搭 architectural design 建筑设计
archive ['ɑːrkaɪv]	*n.* 档案室（a place where public record or document are kept）
arduous ['ɑːrdʒuəs]	*adj.* 费力的，艰难的（marked by great labor or effort） 搭 arduous march 艰难行军
argumentative [ˌɑːrgju'mentətɪv]	*adj.* 好争辩的，好争吵的（characterized by argument） 记 来自 argument(*n.* 争论，争辩)
arid ['ærɪd]	*adj.* 干旱的(dry)；枯燥的(dull；uninteresting) 搭 an arid discussion 枯燥的讨论
aristocratic [əˌrɪstə'krætɪk]	*adj.* 贵族（化）的（belonging to, having the qualities of, or favoring aristocracy）
armored ['ɑːrmərd]	*adj.* 披甲的，装甲的(equipped or protected with armor) 搭 an armored car 装甲车
aromatic [ˌærə'mætɪk]	*adj.* 芬芳的，芳香的(having a strong pleasant smell) 记 词根记忆：aroma(芳香，香味) + tic → 芳香的
arresting [ə'restɪŋ]	*adj.* 醒目的，引人注意的(catching the attention) 记 来自 arrest(*v.* 吸引，注意)
arrogant ['ærəgənt]	*adj.* 傲慢的，自大的(overbearing；haughty；proud)
articulate [ɑːr'tɪkjuleɪt]	*v.* 清楚地说话（to express clearly）；（用关节）连接（to put together by joints） 记 词根记忆：articul(接合) + ate → 连接 同 enunciate
artisan ['ɑːrtəzn]	*n.* 技工(skilled workman or craftsman) 记 词根记忆：arti(技术) + san(人) → 技工
artistry ['ɑːrtɪstri]	*n.* 艺术技巧(skill of an artist) 记 词根记忆：artist(艺术家) + ry → 艺术技巧

archive

☐ archaeological	☐ archaic	☐ archetypally	☐ architect	☐ architectural	☐ archive
☐ arduous	☐ argumentative	☐ arid	☐ aristocratic	☐ armored	☐ aromatic
☐ arresting	☐ arrogant	☐ articulate	☐ artisan	☐ artistry	

15

artless [ˈɑːrtləs]	*adj.* 朴实的，自然的（without artificiality；natural）；粗俗的（uncultured；ignorant）
ascent [əˈsent]	*n.* 上升，攀登（the act of rising or mounting upward）；上坡路（an upward slope or rising grade）；提高，提升（an advance in social status or reputation）
ascetic [əˈsetɪk]	*adj.* 禁欲的（self-denying）*n.* 苦行者（anyone who lives with strict self-discipline） 记 来自希腊文，原意是"刻苦锻炼并隐居的人" 同 astringent, austere, mortified, severe, stern
asceticism [əˈsetɪsɪzəm]	*n.* 禁欲主义
ascribe [əˈskraɪb]	*v.* 归因于，归咎于（to consider sth. to be caused by） 记 词根记忆：a + scribe（写）→ 把…写上去 → 归因于，归咎于
aseptic [ˌeɪˈseptɪk]	*adj.* 净化的（not contaminated）；无菌的（not septic） 记 词根记忆：a(无) + sept(菌) + ic → 无菌的
aspect [ˈæspekt]	*n.* （问题等的）方面（a particular status or phase in which sth. appears or may be regarded）；面貌，外表（appearence） 记 词根记忆：a+spect(看) → 看向的地方 →（问题等的）方面
aspen [ˈæspən]	*n.* 白杨 记 联想记忆：as + pen(笔) → 像笔一样直的树木 → 白杨
aspiration [ˌæspəˈreɪʃn]	*n.* 抱负，渴望（strong desire or ambition） 记 词根记忆：a + spir(呼吸) + ation → 屏住呼吸下决心 → 抱负
aspiring [əˈspaɪərɪŋ]	*adj.* 有抱负的，有理想的 记 来自aspire（*v.* 渴望成就…，有志成于…）
assail [əˈseɪl]	*v.* 质问（to attack with arguments）；攻击（to assault） 记 词根记忆：as + sail(跳上去) → 跳上去打 → 攻击 同 aggress, beset, storm, strike
assertion [əˈsɜːrʃn]	*n.* 断言，声明；主张（declaration；affirmation） 记 来自assert（*v.* 明确肯定，断言）
assertive [əˈsɜːrtɪv]	*adj.* 断言的，肯定的（expressing or tending to express strong opinions or claims）
assessment [əˈsesmənt]	*n.* 估价，评价（the action or an instance of assessing） 记 来自assess（*v.* 评价，评定）
assiduous [əˈsɪdʒuəs]	*adj.* 勤勉的（diligent；persevering）；专心的（attentive） 记 词根记忆：as + sid（坐）+ uous → 坐得多的 → 勤勉的 搭 be assiduous in... 专心于… assimilate
assimilate [əˈsɪməleɪt]	*v.* 同化；吸收（to absorb and incorporate） 记 词根记忆：as + simil（相同）+ ate → 使相同 → 同化

16

□ artless　　□ ascent　　□ ascetic　　□ asceticism　　□ ascribe　　□ aseptic
□ aspect　　□ aspen　　□ aspiration　　□ aspiring　　□ assail　　□ assertion
□ assertive　　□ assessment　　□ assiduous　　□ assimilate

assorted [əˈsɔːrtəd]	*adj.* 各式各样的(consisting of various kinds); 混杂的(mixed) 记 词根记忆: as + sort(种类) + ed → 把各种东西放到一起 → 混杂的
assume [əˈsuːm]	*v.* 假定(to accept sth. as true before there is proof); 承担, 担任(to take on duties or responsibilities) 记 联想记忆: as(加强) + sume(拿, 取) → 拿住 → 承担
assuming [əˈsuːmɪŋ]	*adj.* 傲慢的, 自负的(pretentious; presumptuous)
assure [əˈʃʊr]	*v.* 保证(to tell sb. positively); 使确信(to convince) 记 词根记忆: as(一再) + sure(肯定) → 一再肯定 → 使确信
assuredness [əˈʃʊrdnəs]	*n.* 确定; 自信 记 来自 assure(*v.* 使确信)
astigmatic [ˌæstɪɡˈmætɪk]	*adj.* 散光的, 乱视的(affected with, relating to astigmatism) 记 词根记忆: a + stigma(污点) + tic → 看不见污点 → 散光的
astound [əˈstaʊnd]	*v.* 使震惊(to overcome sb. with surprise) 记 联想记忆: as + tound(看作 sound) → 像被大声吓倒 → 使震惊
astounding [əˈstaʊndɪŋ]	*adj.* 令人震惊的(causing astonishment or amazement)
astray [əˈstreɪ]	*adj.* 迷路的, 误入歧途的(off the right path or way) 记 联想记忆: a + stray(走离) → 走离正道 → 误入歧途的
astronomical [ˌæstrəˈnɑːmɪkl]	*adj.* 极大的 (enormously or inconceivably large or great); 天文学的(of astronomy) 记 词根记忆: astro(星星) + nomical → 星星的, 星体的 → 极大的 搭 systematic astronomical and weather observations 系统的天文气象观察
astute [əˈstuːt]	*adj.* 机敏的, 精明的(showing clever or shrewd mind; cunning; crafty) 记 来自拉丁文 astus(灵活)
asunder [əˈsʌndər]	*adj./adv.* 分离的(地)(apart or separate); 化为碎片的(地)(into pieces) 记 分拆记忆: as + under → 好像在下面 → 分离的
asymmetric [ˌeɪsɪˈmetrɪk]	*adj.* 不对称的(having sides that are not alike) 记 词根记忆: a(不) + sym(相同) + metr(测量) + ic → 测量不同 → 不对称的
atheist [ˈeɪθiɪst]	*n.* 无神论者(one who believes that there is no deity)
atomic [əˈtɑːmɪk]	*adj.* 原子的(of, relating to, or concerned with atoms); 微小的(minute) 记 来自 atom(*v.* 原子)
atonement [əˈtoʊnmənt]	*n.* 弥补(reparation for an offense or injury) 记 来自 atone(*v.* 弥补, 赎罪)
atrocity [əˈtrɑːsəti]	*n.* 邪恶(state of being atrocious); 暴行(an atrocious act)

□ assorted	☑ assume	□ assuming	☑ assure	□ assuredness	□ astigmatic
□ astound	☑ astounding	□ astray	□ astronomical	□ astute	□ asunder
□ asymmetric	□ atheist	□ atomic	□ atonement	□ atrocity	

atrophy	*n.* 萎缩, 衰退(decrease in size or wasting away of a body part or tissue)
[ˈætrəfi]	记 词根记忆：a(无) + troph(营养) + y → 无营养会萎缩 → 萎缩
	同 decadence, declination, degeneracy, degeneration, deterioration
attenuation	*n.* 变瘦；减少；减弱 (the act of attenuating or the state of being
[əˌtenjʊˈeɪʃn]	attenuated)
attest	*v.* 证明, 证实(to declare to be true or genuine)
[əˈtest]	记 词根记忆：at + test(证明) → 证明
	搭 attest to 证实, 证明
	同 certify, testify, witness
attribute	[əˈtrɪbjuːt] *v.* 把…归于(to assign or ascribe to)
	[ˈætrɪbjuːt] *n.* 属性, 特质(a characteristic or quality)
	记 词根记忆：at + tribute(给与) → 把…归于
	搭 attribute... to... 把…归于…
	同 trait, virtue
attrition	*n.* 摩擦, 磨损(the act of wearing or grinding down by friction)
[əˈtrɪʃn]	记 词根记忆：at + trit(摩擦) + ion → 摩擦, 磨损
attune	*v.* 使调和(to put into correct and harmonious tune)
[əˈtuːn]	记 联想记忆：at + tune(调子) → 使调子一致 → 使调和
audacious	*adj.* 大胆的 (daring; fearless; brave)
[ɔːˈdeɪʃəs]	记 词根记忆：aud(大胆) + acious(多…的) → 大胆的
audible	*adj.* 听得见的(capable of being heard clearly)
[ˈɔːdəbl]	记 词根记忆：audi(听) + ble → 能听的 → 听得见的
audience	*n.* 听众, 观众(a group of listeners or spectators)；读者(a reading public)
[ˈɔːdiəns]	记 词根记忆：audi(听) + ence → 听众
audit	*v.* 旁听 (to attend (a course) without working for or expecting to receive
[ˈɔːdɪt]	formal credit)；审计, 查账(to examine and check account)
augment	*v.* 提高, 增加(to become greater; increase)
[ɔːɡˈment]	记 词根记忆：aug(提高) + ment → 提高
	同 enlarge, expand, heighten, mount, wax
auspices	*n.* 支持, 赞助(approval and support)
[ˈɔːspɪsɪz]	记 词根记忆：au + spic(看) + es → 看到(好事) → 赞助
auspicious	*adj.* 幸运的(favored by future; successful)；吉兆的(propitious)
[ɔːˈspɪʃəs]	记 联想记忆：au + spic(看) + ious → 看到(好事)的 → 吉兆的
austere	*adj.* 朴素的(very plain; lacking ornament)
[ɔːˈstɪr]	记 词根记忆：au + stere(冷) → 冷面孔 → 朴素的
authentic	*adj.* 真正的, 真实的(genuine; real)；可信的(legally attested)
[ɔːˈθentɪk]	记 词根记忆：authent(=author 作家) + ic → 自己就是作家 → 真正的
authenticate	*v.* 证明…是真实的(to prove or serve to prove the authenticity of)
[ɔːˈθentɪkeɪt]	

□ atrophy	□ attenuation	□ attest	□ attribute	□ attrition	□ attune
☑ audacious	□ audible	□ audience	□ audit	□ augment	□ auspices
□ auspicious	□ austere	□ authentic	□ authenticate		

18

authoritative	*adj.* 权威的，官方的（having or proceeding from authority）；专断的（dictatorial）
[ə'θɑːrəteɪtɪv]	
autobiographical	*adj.* 自传的，自传体的
[ˌɔːtəˌbaɪə'græfɪkl]	记 词根记忆：auto(自己的) + biography(传记) + ical → 自传的
autobiography	*n.* 自传（story of a person's life written by that person）
[ˌɔːtəbaɪ'ɑːgrəfi]	记 词根记忆：auto(自己) + bio(生命) + graphy(写) → 写自己的一生 → 自传
autograph	*n.* 亲笔稿，手迹（something written or made with one's own hand）*v.* 在…上亲笔签名（to write one's signature in or on）*adj.* 亲笔的（being in the writer's own handwriting）
['ɔːtəgræf]	
automated	*adj.* 自动的（using computers and machines to do a job, rather than people）
['ɔːtəmeɪtɪd]	
automotive	*adj.* 汽车的，自动的（of, relating to, or concerned with self-propelled vehicles or machines）
[ˌɔːtə'moʊtɪv]	
autonomous	*adj.* 自治的（marked by autonomy）；自主的（having the right or power of self-government）
[ɔː'tɑːnəməs]	
autonomy	*n.* 自治，自主（self-government；independent function）
[ɔː'tɑːnəmi]	记 词根记忆：auto(自己) + nomy(治理) → 自治
avarice	*n.* 贪财，贪婪（too great a desire to have wealth；cupidity）
['ævərɪs]	记 发音记忆："爱不释手" → 贪婪
avaricious	*adj.* 贪婪的，贪心的（full of avarice；greedy）
[ˌævə'rɪʃəs]	记 来自 avarice(*n.* 贪婪，贪心)
averse	*adj.* 反对的，不愿意的（not willing or inclined；opposed）
[ə'vɜːrs]	记 词根记忆：a + verse(转) → 转开 → 反对的，不愿意的
avid	*adj.* 渴望的（having an intense craving）；热心的（eager）
['ævɪd]	搭 be avid for 渴望
avocational	*adj.* 副业的，嗜好的（of or relating to an avocation）
[ˌævoʊ'keɪʃənl]	
avoid	*v.* 避开，躲避（to keep oneself away from）
[ə'vɔɪd]	记 词根记忆：a + void(空) → 使落空 → 避开
	搭 avoid (doing) sth. 避开(做)某事
	同 elude, eschew, evade, shun
awe	*n./v.* 敬畏（to cause a mixed feeling of reverence and fear）
[ɔː]	记 发音记忆：发音像"噢" → 表示敬畏的声音 → 敬畏
	搭 be in awe of... 对…望而生畏；对…感到害怕
awe-inspiring	*adj.* 令人敬畏的（inspiring awe from others）
[ˌɔːɪn'spaɪərɪŋ]	记 组合词：awe(敬畏) + inspiring(鼓舞人心的) → 令人敬畏的
awe-struck	*adj.* 充满敬畏的（filled with awe）
['ɔːstrʌk]	记 组合词：awe(敬畏) + struck(打动) → 充满敬畏的

awkward [ˈɔːkwərd]	*adj.* 笨拙的（ungainly）；难用的（difficult to use）；不便的（causing inconvenience） 记 发音记忆："拗口的" → 笨拙的，难用的 同 clumsy, gawky, lumbering, lumpish
axiom [ˈæksiəm]	*n.* 公理（maxim）；定理（an established principle） 记 联想记忆：ax(斧子) + iom → 斧子之下出公理 → 公理
bacterium [bækˈtɪriəm]	*n.* 细菌（any of a domain of prokaryotic round, spiral or rod shaped single celled microorganisms）
baffle [ˈbæfl]	*v.* 使困惑，难倒（to confuse; puzzle; confound） 记 发音记忆："拜服了" → 被难倒了，所以拜服了 → 难倒
balk [bɔːk]	*n.* 梁木，大梁（thick, roughly squared wooden beam）*v.* 妨碍；畏缩不前（be reluctant to tackle sth. because it is difficult） 同 baffle, bilk, foil, thwart
ballad [ˈbæləd]	*n.* 歌谣，小曲（a song or poem that tells a story in short stanzas） 记 联想记忆：ball(球) + ad → 像球一样一代代传下来 → 歌谣
balm [bɑːm]	*n.* 香油，药膏（any fragrant ointment or aromatic oil）；镇痛剂，安慰物 记 来自 balsam（*n.* 风仙花；香脂）
balmy [ˈbɑːmi]	*adj.* 芳香的；(指空气)温和的（soothing; mild; pleasant）；止痛的
banal [bəˈnɑːl]	*adj.* 乏味的，陈腐的（dull or stale; commonplace; insipid） 记 联想记忆：ban(禁止) + al → 应该禁止的 → 陈腐的 同 bland, flat, sapless, vapid
bane [beɪn]	*n.* 祸根（the cause of distress, death, or ruin） 记 发音记忆："背运" → 因为有祸根而背运 → 祸根
banish [ˈbænɪʃ]	*v.* 放逐（to send sb. out of the country as a punishment） 记 发音记忆："把你死" → 通过放逐把你弄死 → 放逐
banter [ˈbæntər]	*n.* 打趣，玩笑（playful, good-humoured joking） 记 发音记忆：绊他 → 打趣，玩笑
barbarous [ˈbɑːrbərəs]	*adj.* 野蛮的（uncultured; crude）；残暴的（cruel; brutal） 记 发音记忆："把爸勒死" → 残暴的
baroque [bəˈroʊk]	*adj.* 过分装饰的（gaudily ornate） 记 由 17 世纪"巴洛克"艺术而来，以古怪精巧为特色
barren [ˈbærən]	*adj.* 不育的；贫瘠的；不结果实的（sterile; bare） 记 发音记忆："拔了" → 拔了所有植物 → 贫瘠的
barrier [ˈbæriər]	*n.* 路障；障碍（obstruction as of a fence; obstacle） 记 联想记忆：bar(栅栏) + rier → 路障；障碍 同 bar, barricade, block, blockade
base [beɪs]	*adj.* 卑鄙的（devoid of high values or ethics）

bashfulness [ˈbæʃflnəs]	*n.* 害怯(shyness, timidity) 记 来自 bashful(*adj.* 羞怯的，忸怩的)
bask [bæsk]	*v.* 晒太阳，取暖(to warm oneself pleasantly in the sunlight) 记 联想记忆：把 basket 去掉 et，就是 bask → 拎着篮子晒太阳 → 取暖
bastion [ˈbæstiən]	*n.* 保垒，防御工事(a projecting part of a fortification)
beaded [ˈbiːdɪd]	*adj.* 以珠装饰的(decorated with beads)，珠状的 搭 beaded with sth. 带着…，缀着…
befriend [bɪˈfrend]	*v.* 以朋友态度对待(to become or act as a friend to) 记 词根记忆：be + riend(朋友) → 当作朋友 → 以朋友态度对待
beleaguer [bɪˈliːɡə]	*v.* 围攻(to besiege by encircling)，骚扰(to harass) 记 联想记忆：be + leaguer(围攻的部队或兵营) → 围攻 同 beset
belie [bɪˈlaɪ]	*v.* 掩饰(to disguise or misrepresent)，证明为假(to prove false) 记 联想记忆：be + lie(谎言) → 使…成谎言 → 证明为假 同 distort, falsify, garble, misstate
believable [bɪˈliːvəbl]	*adj.* 可信的 (capable of being believed especially as within the range of known possibility or probability)
belittle [bɪˈlɪtl]	*v.* 轻视，贬低(to speak slightingly of) 记 联想记忆：be + little(小) → 把(人)看小 → 轻视
bellicose [ˈbelɪkoʊs]	*adj.* 好战的，好斗的(eager to fight; warlike; belligerent) 记 词根记忆：bell(战争) + icose(形容词后缀) → 好斗的

Every day I remind myself that my inner and outer life are based on the labors of other men, living and dead, and that I must exert myself in order to give in the same measure as I have received and am still receiving.

每天我都提醒着自己：我的精神生活和物质生活都是以别人的劳动为基础的，我必须尽力以同样的分量来报偿我所获得的和至今仍在接受着的东西。

———美国科学家 爱因斯坦(Albert Einstein, American scientist)

Word List 3  MP3 - 03

belligerent [bə'lɪdʒərənt]	*adj.* 发动战争的（waging war）；好斗的，好挑衅的（inclined to or exhibiting assertiveness, hostility, or combativeness）
bemuse [bɪ'mjuːz]	*v.* 使昏头昏脑，使迷惑（to puzzle, distract, absorb） 同 bedaze, daze, paralyze, petrify, stun
benefactor ['benɪfæktər]	*n.* 行善者，捐助者（a person who has given financial help；patron） 记 词根记忆：bene(好) + fact(做) + or → 做好事的人 → 行善者
beneficent [bɪ'nefɪsnt]	*adj.* 慈善的，仁爱的（doing or producing good）；有益的（beneficial） 记 词根记忆：bene(好) + fic(做) + ent(的) → 做好事的 → 慈善的
beneficiary [ˌbenɪ'fɪʃieri]	*n.* 受益人（one that benefits from sth.） 记 来自benefit（*n.* 益处，好处）
benevolent [bə'nevələnt]	*adj.* 善心的，仁心的（kindly；charitable） 记 词根记忆：bene(好) + vol(意志) + ent → 好意的 → 善心的，仁心的 同 altruistic, humane, philanthropic
benign [bɪ'naɪn]	*adj.* （病）良性的（of a mild type or character that does not threaten health or life）；亲切和蔼的（showing kindness and gentleness）；慈祥的（good natured；kindly） 记 词根记忆：ben(好) + ign(形容词后缀) → 好的 → 亲切和蔼的
bereave [bɪ'riːv]	*v.* 夺去，丧亲（to deprive；dispossess） 记 词根记忆：be + reave(抢夺) → 抢夺掉 → 丧亲；reave 本身是一个单词 同 disinherit, divest, oust
beset [bɪ'set]	*v.* 镶嵌（to set or stud with or as if with ornaments）；困扰（to harass from all directions）
besiege [bɪ'siːdʒ]	*v.* 围攻；困扰（to overwhelm, harass, or beset） 记 词根记忆：be + siege(围攻，siege 本身是一个单词) → 围攻
bestow [bɪ'stoʊ]	*v.* 给予，赐赠（to give or present） 记 联想记忆：be + stow(收藏) → 给予以便收藏 → 赐赠
betray [bɪ'treɪ]	*v.* 背叛（to deliver to an enemy by treachery）；暴露（to reveal） 记 词根记忆：be + tray(背叛) → 背叛；联想记忆：bet(打赌) + ray(光线) → 打赌打到了光线下 → 暴露 同 disclose, divulge, uncover, unveil

bewilder [bɪ'wɪldər]	v. 使迷惑，混乱（to confuse） 记 词根记忆：be（使…成为）+ wilder（迷惑）→ 使迷惑 同 befog, confound, perplex
bias ['baɪəs]	n. 偏见（bent, tendency, prejudice）v. 使有偏见（to give a settled and often prejudiced outlook to） 记 联想记忆：bi(两) + as → 两者只取其一 → 偏见 搭 bias toward... 对…有偏见 同 leaning, disposition, partiality, penchant
bibliomania [ˌbɪblɪə'menɪə]	n. 藏书癖（extreme preoccupation with collecting books）
bilateral [ˌbaɪ'lætərəl]	adj. 两边的（having two sides）；双边的（affecting reciprocally two nations or parties）
bilingual [ˌbaɪ'lɪŋgwəl]	adj.（说）两种语言的（of two languages） 记 词根记忆：bi(两个) + lingu(语言) + al → （说）两种语言的
billion ['bɪljən]	num. 十亿（one thousand million）
birthright ['bɜːrθraɪt]	n. 与生俱来的权利（a right, privilege, or possession to which a person is entitled by birth）
bizarre [bɪ'zɑːr]	adj. 奇异的，古怪的（grotesque; fantastic） 记 比较记忆：bazaar(n. 集市)，集市上有各种古怪的东西 同 oddball, outlandish, peculiar, queer, weird
blackmail ['blækmeɪl]	v./n. 敲诈，勒索（payment extorted by threatening） 记 组合词：black(黑) + mail(寄信) → 寄黑信 → 敲诈
blameworthy ['bleɪmwɜːrði]	adj. 该责备的，有过失的（deserving blame） 同 blamable, blameful, censurable, culpable, reprehensible
bland [blænd]	adj.（人）情绪平稳的（pleasantly smooth）；（食物）无味的（insipid） 记 发音记忆："布蓝的" → 布是清淡的蓝色的 → 无味的
blatant ['bleɪtnt]	adj. 厚颜无耻的（brazen）；显眼的（completely obvious; conspicuous）；炫耀的（showy） 记 词根记忆：blat(闲聊) + ant → 侃大山 → 喧哗的 → 炫耀的
blazing ['bleɪzɪŋ]	adj. 炽烧的，闪耀的（of outstanding power, speed, heat, or intensity） 记 来自blaze(v. 燃烧；照耀)
bleach [bliːtʃ]	v. 去色，漂白（to cause sth. to become white）n. 漂白剂；漂白的行为 记 分析联想：b + leach(过滤) → 将其他颜色滤去 → 去色
blighted ['blaɪtɪd]	adj. 枯萎的（withered） 记 来自blight（v. 使枯萎）
blindness ['blaɪndnəs]	n. 失明（loss of sight） 搭 cultural blindness 文化盲目性

喵喵

bewilder

3

blissful [ˈblɪsfl]	*adj.* 极幸福的(extremely happy) 记 来自 bliss(*n.* 天赐之福)
blithe [blaɪð]	*adj.* 快乐的，无忧无虑的(cheerful; carefree)
blockbuster [ˈblɑːkbʌstər]	*n.* 巨型炸弹(a very large high-explosive bomb)；一鸣惊人的事物；非常成功的书或电影
blueprint [ˈbluːprɪnt]	*n.* 蓝图(photographic print of building plans)；方案(detailed plan) 记 组合词：blue(蓝) + print(印刷的图) → 蓝图
bluff [blʌf]	*n.* 虚张声势(pretense of strength)；悬崖峭壁(high cliff) 记 联想记忆：和 buffalo(美洲野牛) 一起记，buffalo bluffs(野牛虚张声势)
blur [blɜːr]	*n.* 模糊不清的事物(anything indistinct or hazy) *v.* 使…模糊(to make or become hazy or indistinct) 记 比较记忆：slur(*v.* 含糊不清地说)
boastfulness [ˈboʊstflnəs]	*n.* 自吹自擂；浮夸(the act or an instance of boasting) 记 来自 boast(*v.* 自夸，自吹自擂)
boisterous [ˈbɔɪstərəs]	*adj.* 喧闹的(noisy and unruly)；猛烈的(violent) 记 词根记忆：boister(喧闹) + ous → 喧闹的 同 disorderly, rambunctious, tumultuous, turbulent
bolster [ˈboʊlstər]	*n.* 枕垫(cushion or pillow) *v.* 支持，鼓励(to support, strengthen, or reinforce) 记 联想记忆：bol(倒着看 lob) + ster → lobster(龙虾)，拿龙虾当枕垫 → 枕垫
bombastic [bɑːmˈbæstɪk]	*adj.* 夸夸其谈的(full of important-sounding insincere words with little meaning)
bonanza [bəˈnænzə]	*n.* 富矿脉，贵金属矿(an exceptionally large and rich mineral deposit) 同 eldorado, golconda
boon [buːn]	*n.* 恩惠，天赐福利(a timely blessing or benefit) 记 联想记忆：从月亮(moon)得到恩惠(boon) → 天赐福利 搭 be a boon to 对…来说大有裨益
boost [buːst]	*v.* 增加，提高(to make higher)；促进(to promote the cause or interests)；往上推(to raise by a push) 记 联想记忆：boo(看作 boot, 靴子) + st → 穿上靴子往高处走 → 提高
bootless [ˈbuːtlɪs]	*adj.* 无益处的(without advantage or benefit)；无用的(useless) 同 futile, otiose, unavailing
boredom [ˈbɔːrdəm]	*n.* 厌烦(the state of being weary)；令人厌烦的事物(sth. boring) 记 词根记忆：bore(厌烦) + dom(表名词，参考 kingdom) → 厌烦
boundless [ˈbaʊndləs]	*adj.* 无限的，无边无际的(having no boundaries) 记 组合词：bound(边界，范围) + less(较少的) → 无边无际的
bowlegged [ˌboʊˈlegɪd]	*adj.* 弯脚的，弓形腿的

□ blissful	□ blithe	□ blockbuster	□ blueprint	□ bluff	□ blur
□ boastfulness	□ boisterous	□ bolster	□ bombastic	□ bonanza	□ boon
□ boost	□ bootless	□ boredom	□ boundless	□ bowlegged	

braggart [ˈbræɡərt]	*n.* 吹牛者（the person who brags）
braid [breɪd]	*v.* 编织（to form into a braid）*n.* 辫子；发辫（plait） 同 plait, twine, weave
brassy [ˈbræsi]	*adj.* 厚脸皮的，无礼的（brazen; insolent） 记 联想记忆：brass(黄铜) + y → 脸皮像黄铜一样厚 → 厚脸皮的
bravado [brəˈvɑːdoʊ]	*n.* 故作勇敢，虚张声势（pretended courage） 记 来自 bravo(*interj.* 欢呼；好极了)；词根记忆：brav(勇敢) + ado(状态) → 故作勇敢
brazen [ˈbreɪzn]	*adj.* 厚脸皮的（showing no shame; impudent） 记 词根记忆：braz(=brass 黄铜) + en → 像黄铜一样 → 厚脸皮的
breach [briːtʃ]	*v.* 打破，突破（to make a breach in）；违背（to break, violate）*n.* 裂缝，缺 □（a broken or torn place） 记 来自 break(*v.* 打破)
breed [briːd]	*v.* 繁殖（to produce offspring by hatching or gestation）；教养（to bring up） *n.* 品种，种类（class; kind）
brevity [ˈbrevəti]	*n.* 短暂（shortness of duration） 记 词根记忆：brev(短的) + i + ty → 短暂
brilliant [ˈbrɪliənt]	*adj.* 卓越的，出众的（striking distinctive）；辉煌的，壮丽的（glorious; magnificent） 记 词根记忆：brilli(发光) + ant(…的) → 发光的 → 辉煌的 搭 a brilliant painter 一位杰出的画家
brink [brɪŋk]	*n.* （峭壁的）边沿，边缘（the edge of a steep place; verge; border） 记 比较记忆：blink(*v.* 眨眼睛)
briny [ˈbraɪni]	*adj.* 盐水的，咸的（of, relating to, or resembling brine or the sea; salty） 记 来自 brine(*n.* 盐水)
brook [brʊk]	*n.* 小河（a small stream）
brownish [ˈbraʊnɪʃ]	*adj.* 成褐色的 记 来自 brown(*n.* 褐色)
brusqueness [ˈbrʌsknəs]	*n.* 唐突（abruptness）；直率（candor） 记 来自 brusque(*adj.* 寡言而无礼的)
brutality [bruːˈtæləti]	*n.* 野蛮（the quality or state of being brutal）；暴行（a brutal act or course of action）
brute [bruːt]	*n./adj.* 野兽(的)（beast）；残忍的(人)（(a person who is) brutal） 同 bestial, beastly
buckle [ˈbʌkl]	*n.* 皮带扣环 *v.* 扣紧（to fasten or join with a buckle） 搭 buckle up 扣紧安全带
bulky [ˈbʌlki]	*adj.* 庞大的（large of its kind）；笨重的（corpulent） 记 来自 bulk(*n.* 巨大的体重（或重量，形状，身体等）)

3

bumper [ˈbʌmpər]	*adj.* 特大的(unusually large) *n.* 保险杠(a device for absorbing shock or preventing damage)
buoyant [ˈbuːjənt]	*adj.* 有浮力的(showing buoyancy); 快乐的(cheerful)
burdensome [ˈbɜːrdnsəm]	*adj.* 繁重的, 劳累的(imposing or constituting a burden) 记 来自 burden(*n.* 负担, 重担)
burgeon [ˈbɜːrdʒən]	*v.* 迅速成长, 发展(to grow rapidly; proliferate) 记 词根记忆: burg(=bud 花蕾) + eon → 迅速成长; burg 本身是单词, 意为"城, 镇" → 成长的地方 → 发展 同 blossom, bloom, effloresce, flower, outbloom
burning [ˈbɜːrnɪŋ]	*adj.* 燃烧的(being on fire); 强烈的(ardent; intense)
burst [bɜːrst]	*v.* 爆炸; 爆裂(to break open, apart, or into pieces); 突然发生(to emerge or spring suddenly)
buttress [ˈbʌtrəs]	*n.* 拱墙, 拱壁(a projecting structure built against a wall to support or reinforce it) *v.* 支持(to prop up; bolster)
bygone [ˈbaɪɡɔːn]	*adj.* 过去的(gone by) 搭 a bygone age 过去的年代
byproduct [ˈbaɪˌprɑːdʌkt]	*n.* 副产品; 副作用(side effect) 记 词根记忆: by(在旁边; 副的) + product(产品) → 副产品
byzantine [ˈbɪzəntiːn]	*adj.* 错综复杂的(complicated) 记 来自 Byzantine (*adj.* 拜占庭帝国的)拜占庭帝国以政治错综复杂而著名
cabinet [ˈkæbɪnət]	*n.* 橱柜(a case or cupboard usu. having doors and shelves); 内阁(group of the most important government ministers)
cacophonous [kəˈkɑːfənəs]	*adj.* 发音不和谐的, 不协调的(marked by cacophony) 记 词根记忆: caco(不好的) + phon(声音) + ous → 发音不和谐的
calamity [kəˈlæməti]	*n.* 大灾祸, 不幸之事(any extreme misfortune) 记 词根记忆: calam(=destruction 破坏) + ity → 大灾祸
calculable [ˈkælkjələbl]	*adj.* 可计算的(subject to or ascertainable by calculation); 可信赖的(that may be counted on)
callous [ˈkæləs]	*adj.* 结硬块的(thick and hardened); 无情的(lacking pity; unfeeling) 记 来自 callus(*n.* 老茧)
calumny [ˈkæləmni]	*n.* 诽谤, 中伤(a false and malicious statement) 记 词根记忆: calumn(=beguile 欺诈) + y → 欺诈性的话 → 诽谤
camaraderie [ˌkɑːməˈrɑːdəri]	*n.* 同志之情, 友情(a spirit of friendly good-fellowship)
candid [ˈkændɪd]	*adj.* 率直的(not hiding one's thoughts) 记 词根记忆: cand(白, 发光) + id → 白的 → 坦白的 → 率直的 同 frank, openhearted, plain, straightforward, unconcealed

candor [ˈkændər]	*n.* 坦白，率直（frankness） 记 词根记忆：cand（白）+ or（表状态）→ 坦白 例 *Candor* may actually enhance one's standing.
cannily [ˈkænɪli]	*adv.* 机灵地
canny [ˈkæni]	*adj.* 精明仔细的（shrewd and careful） 记 联想记忆：can（能）+ ny → 能干的 → 精明仔细的
cantankerous [kænˈtæŋkərəs]	*adj.* 脾气坏的（bad tempered）；好争吵的（quarrelsome） 记 联想记忆：cant（黑话）+ anker（看作 anger，愤怒）+ ous → 用黑话愤怒地争吵 → 脾气坏的 搭 a cantankerous man 脾气坏的人 同 bearish, cranky, irascible, irritable, ornery
capitulate [kəˈpɪtʃuleɪt]	*v.*（有条件地）投降（to surrender conditionally） 记 词根记忆：capit（头）+ ulate → 低头 → 投降
capricious [kəˈprɪʃəs]	*adj.* 变化无常的，任性的（erratic；flighty） 同 inconstant, lubricious, mercurial, whimsical, whimsied
captious [ˈkæpʃəs]	*adj.* 吹毛求疵的（quick to find fault；carping） 记 联想记忆：capt（拿）+ ious → 拿（别人的缺点）→ 吹毛求疵的
captivating [ˈkæptɪveɪtɪŋ]	*adj.* 吸引人的（very attractive and interesting, in a way that holds your attention）
capture [ˈkæptʃər]	*v.* 俘获（to take as a prisoner）；夺取或赢得（to take or win）*n.* 战利品 记 词根记忆：capt（抓）+ ure → 抓住的状态 → 俘获
cardiac [ˈkɑːrdiæk]	*adj.* 心脏的（of, relating to, situated near, or acting on the heart） 记 词根记忆：card（心）+ iac → 心脏的
cardinal [ˈkɑːrdnl]	*adj.* 首要的，主要的（of basic importance）*n.* 红衣主教 记 词根记忆：card（心）+ inal → 心一样的 → 首要的，主要的
caricature [ˈkærɪkətʃər]	*n.* 讽刺画；滑稽模仿（art that has the qualities of caricature） 记 联想记忆：car（汽车）+ i（我）+ cat（猫）+ ure → 我在汽车和猫之间 → 很滑稽的样子 → 滑稽模仿 同 burlesque, mock, mockery, travesty
carnage [ˈkɑːrnɪdʒ]	*n.* 大屠杀，残杀（bloody and extensive slaughter） 记 联想记忆：carn（肉）+ age → 大堆的肉 → 大屠杀 同 bloodbath, massacre
carnivorous [kɑːrˈnɪvərəs]	*adj.* 肉食动物的（flesh-eating） 记 词根记忆：carn（肉）+ i + vor（吃）+ ous → 肉食动物的
carve [kɑːrv]	*v.* 雕刻（to shape by cutting, chipping and hewing）；（把肉等）切成片（to slice） 同 cleave, dissect, dissever, sever, split
cast [kæst]	*n.* 演员阵容；剧团（troupe）*v.* 扔（to throw）；铸造（to give a shape to（a substance）by pouring in liquid into a mold）

□ candor	□ cannily	□ canny	□ cantankerous	□ capitulate	□ capricious
□ captious	□ captivating	□ capture	□ cardiac	□ cardinal	□ caricature
□ carnage	□ carnivorous	□ carve	□ cast		

27

caste	*n.* 社会等级，等级（class distinction）
[kæst]	记 原指印度教的种姓制度；发音记忆："卡死他" → 在一个等级上卡死他，不让他上来 → 社会等级
	搭 a caste system 等级体系

castigate	*v.* 惩治，严责（to punish or rebuke severely）
['kæstɪgeɪt]	记 联想记忆：cast(扔) + i(我) + gate(门) → 向我的门扔东西 → 惩治，严责
	同 chasten, chastise, discipline

catalyze	*v.* 促使（to bring about）；激励（to inspire）
['kætəlaɪz]	

catastrophe	*n.* 突如其来的大灾难（sudden great disaster）
[kə'tæstrəfi]	记 词根记忆：cata(向下) + strophe(转) → 天地向下转 → 突如其来的大灾难
	搭 a major catastrophe 一次严重的灾难

category	*n.* 类别，范畴（a class or division in a scheme of classification）
['kætəgɔːri]	记 联想记忆：cat(猫) + ego(自我) + ry → 猫和我是两类生物 → 类别

cater	*v.* 迎合；提供饮食及服务（to provide food and services）
['keɪtər]	记 联想记忆：毛毛虫 caterpillar 的前半部分为 cater，原意为"猫"，引申为"迎合"
	搭 cater to 迎合

caterpillar	*n.* 毛毛虫，蝴蝶的幼虫（the elongated wormlike larva of a butterfly or moth）
['kætərpɪlər]	记 来自中古英语：cater(猫) + pillar(毛) → 原意为有毛的猫 → 毛毛虫

causal	*adj.* 原因的，因果关系的（implying a cause and effect relationship）
['kɔːzl]	记 来自 cause(*n.* 原因)

caustic	*adj.* 腐蚀性的（corrosive）；刻薄的（biting; sarcastic） *n.* 腐蚀剂
['kɔːstɪk]	记 词根记忆：caus(烧灼) + tic → 腐蚀性的
	搭 caustic responses 刻薄的反应

cautionary	*adj.* 劝人谨慎的，警戒的（giving advice or a warning）
['kɔːʃəneri]	记 词根记忆：caution(小心，谨慎) + ary → 劝人谨慎的，警戒的
	同 admonishing, admonitory, cautioning, monitory

cautious	*adj.* 小心的，谨慎的（marked by or given to caution）
['kɔːʃəs]	记 联想记忆：caut(看作 cat) + ious(…的) → 像猫一样的 → 小心的，谨慎的
	同 chary, circumspect, discreet, gingerly, wary

cavil	*v.* 挑毛病，吹毛求疵（to object when there is little reason to do so; quibble）
['kævl]	搭 cavil at 在…方面挑毛病

cavity	*n.* (牙齿等的)洞，腔（a hollow place in a tooth）
['kævəti]	

celestial	*adj.* 天体的，天上的（of or in the sky or universe）
[sə'lestʃl]	记 词根记忆：celest(天空) + ial → 天上的

celibate	*n.* 独身者（an unmarried person） *adj.* 不结婚的
['selɪbət]	记 词根记忆：celib(独身) + ate → 独身者

28

cellular [ˈseljələr]	*adj.* 细胞的（of, relating to, or consisting of cells）；蜂窝式的（containing cavities） 搭 cellular organization 细胞组织
censorious [senˈsɔːriəs]	*adj.* 挑剔的（marked by or given to censure） 记 词根记忆：cens(评价) + orious → 爱评价他人的 → 挑剔的
censure [ˈsenʃər]	*n.* 指责，谴责（a judgment involving condemnation）*v.* 指责，谴责（to find fault with and criticize as blameworthy） 同 denounce, denunciate, reprehend, reprobate
centralization [ˌsentrələˈzeɪʃn]	*n.* 集中；集权化（concentration） 记 来自 centralize(*v.* 集中)
ceramic [səˈræmɪk]	*adj.* 陶器的（made of clay and perrnanently hardened by heat）*n.* 陶瓷制品（the making of pots or tiles by shaping pieces of clay and baking them） 记 词根记忆：ceram(陶瓷) + ic → 陶器的
cerebral [səˈriːbrəl]	*adj.* 大脑的（of the brain）；深思的（of the intellect rather than the emotions） 记 词根记忆：cerebr(脑) + al → 大脑的 搭 cerebral cortex 大脑皮层
ceremonious [ˌserəˈmoʊniəs]	*adj.* 仪式隆重的（very formal） 记 来自 ceremony(*n.* 典礼，仪式)
certainty [ˈsɜːrtnti]	*n.* 确定的事情（thing that is certain） 记 来自 certain(*adj.* 确定的，必然的)
certitude [ˈsɜːrtɪtuːd]	*n.* 确定无疑（certainty of act or event） 记 词根记忆：cert(确定) + itude(状态) → 确定的状态 → 确定无疑
cessation [seˈseɪʃn]	*n.* 中止，(短暂的)停止（a short pause or a stop） 记 词根记忆：cess(走) + ation → 不走的状态 → 中止
chafe [tʃeɪf]	*v.* (将皮肤等)擦热，擦破（to warm by rubbing）；激怒（to annoy） 记 联想记忆：在 cafe 中加了一个 h(看作 hot) → 热咖啡 → 擦热
chagrin [ʃəˈɡrɪn]	*n.* 失望，懊恼（a feeling of annoyance because one has been disappointed） 记 联想记忆：cha(拼音：茶) + grin(苦笑) → 喝茶苦笑 → 失望，懊恼
chancy [ˈtʃænsi]	*adj.* 不确定的，不安的（uncertain in outcome or prospect, occurring by chance）
chantey [ˈʃæntɪ]	*n.* 船歌（a song sung by sailors in rhythm with their work）
chaotic [keɪˈɑːtɪk]	*adj.* 混乱的（in a state of complete disorder and confusion） 例 The traffic in the city is *chaotic* in the rush hour.
characteristic [ˌkærəktəˈrɪstɪk]	*adj.* 有特色的；典型性的 *n.* 与众不同的特征 记 来自 character(*n.* 性格；特征)

□ cellular	□ censorious	□ censure	□ centralization	□ ceramic	□ cerebral
□ ceremonious	□ certainty	□ certitude	□ cessation	□ chafe	□ chagrin
□ chancy	□ chantey	□ chaotic	□ characteristic		

29

characterize [ˈkærəktəraɪz]	*v.* 表现…的特色，刻画…的性格（to describe the character or quality of） 记 来自 character（*n.* 人或事物的特点、特征）
charismatic [ˌkærɪzˈmætɪk]	*adj.* 有魅力的（having, exhibiting, or based on charisma or charism） 搭 characterize... as... 将…的特点描述成…
charitable [ˈtʃærətəbl]	*adj.* 行善的（full of love for and goodwill toward others）；仁爱的（liberal in benefactions to the needy） 同 benevolent, clement, humanitarian, lenient, philanthropic
charlatan [ˈʃɑːrlətən]	*n.* 江湖郎中，骗子（fake; mountebank; quack） 记 联想记忆：意大利有个地方叫 Charlat，专卖假药并出江湖郎中（quack），所以叫 charlatan 同 quacksalver, quackster, saltimbanque
chart [tʃɑːrt]	*n.* 图表（map; a sheet）*v.* 绘制地图，制订计划（to make a map or chart） 同 graph, tabulation
charter [ˈtʃɑːrtər]	*n.* 特权或豁免权（special privilege or immunity）
chary [ˈtʃeri]	*adj.* 小心的，审慎的（careful; cautious） 搭 be chary of/about... 对…小心的 同 calculating, circumspect, discreet, gingerly, wary
chastisement [tʃæˈstaɪzmənt]	*n.* 惩罚（punishment） 同 castigation, penalty
chip [tʃɪp]	*n.* 薄片，碎片（shard; fragment）；集成电路片
chivalrous [ˈʃɪvlrəs]	*adj.* 骑士精神的（of, relating to, or characteristic of chivalry and knight-errantry）；对女人彬彬有礼的（gallant; courteous） 记 词根记忆：chival（=caval 骑马）+ rous → 骑马的 → 骑士精神的
choppy [ˈtʃɑːpi]	*adj.* 波浪起伏的（rough with small waves）；（风）不断改变方向的（changeable; variable）
chorale [kəˈræl]	*n.* 赞美诗（a hymn or psalm sung to a traditional or composed melody in church）；合唱队（chorus; choir）
choreographic [ˌkɔːriəˈɡræfɪk]	*adj.* 舞蹈术的，舞台舞蹈的 记 来自 choreography（*n.* 编舞设计，舞蹈设计）
chorus [ˈkɔːrəs]	*n.* 合唱队，歌舞团（a group of dancers and singers） 记 词根记忆：chor（跳舞）+ us → 跳舞的人 → 歌舞团
chromatic [krəˈmætɪk]	*adj.* 彩色的，五彩的（having colour or colours） 记 词根记忆：chrom（颜色）+ atic → 彩色的
chromosome [ˈkroʊməsoʊm]	*n.* 染色体 记 词根记忆：chrom（颜色）+ o + some（体）→ 染色体
chronological [ˌkrɑːnəˈlɑːdʒɪkl]	*adj.* 按年代顺序排列的（of, relating to, or arranged in or according to the order of time）

chubby [ˈtʃʌbi]	*adj.* 丰满的，圆胖的（plump） 搭 chubby checks 胖乎乎的脸
circuitous [sərˈkjuːɪtəs]	*adj.* 迂回的，绕圈子的（roundabout; indirect; devious） 记 词根记忆：circu（绕圈）+ it（走）+ ous → 迂回的；circuit 本身是个单词，意为"圆，电路"
circulate [ˈsɜːrkjəleɪt]	*v.* 循环；流通（to move around）；发行（to distribute） 记 词根记忆：circ（圆，环）+ ulate → 绕圈走 → 循环
circulation [ˌsɜːrkjəˈleɪʃn]	*n.* 循环，流通（going around continuously）；发行量（the average number of copies of a publication sold over a given period）
circumlocution [ˌsɜːrkəmləˈkjuːʃn]	*n.* 迂回累赘的陈述（a roundabout, lengthy way of expressing sth.） 记 词根记忆：circum（绕圈）+ locu（说话）+ tion → 说话绕圈子 → 迂回累赘的陈述

3

A man is not old as long as he is seeking something. A man is not old until regrets take the place of dreams.

只要一个人还有所追求，他就没有老。直到后悔取代了梦想，一个人才算老。

——美国演员 巴里穆尔（J. Barrymore, American actor）

Word List 4

circumscribe [ˈsɜːrkəmskraɪb]	*v.* 划界限；限制（to restrict; restrain; limit） 记 词根记忆：circum(绕圈) + scribe(画) → 画地为牢 → 限制
circumspect [ˈsɜːrkəmspekt]	*adj.* 慎重的（careful to consider all circumstances and possible consequences）
circumstantial [ˌsɜːrkəmˈstænʃl]	*adj.* 不重要的，偶然的（incidental）；描述详细的（marked by careful attention to detail） 记 词根记忆：circum(绕圈) + stant(站，立) + ial → 处于周围 → 不重要的
circumvent [ˌsɜːrkəmˈvent]	*v.* 回避（to bypass）；用计谋战胜或回避（to get the better of or prevent from happening by craft or ingenuity） 记 词根记忆：circum(绕圈) + vent(来) → 绕着圈过来 → 回避
cite [saɪt]	*v.* 引用，引述（to speak or write words taken from a passage） 记 词根记忆：cit(引用；唤起) + e → 引用，引述
civil [ˈsɪvl]	*adj.* 国内的（relating to the state）；公民的（relating to the citizens of a country）；文明的（adequate in courtesy and politeness）
civility [səˈvɪləti]	*n.* 彬彬有礼，斯文（politeness） 记 词根记忆：civil(文明的，市民的) + ity → 彬彬有礼
claim [kleɪm]	*v.* 要求或索要（to request sth.） *n.* 声称拥有的权利 记 本身为词根，意为"大叫" → 要求或索要 搭 claim against 对…要求赔偿；claim that... 要求… 同 argue, assert, contend, justify, maintain
clamber [ˈklæmbər]	*v.* 吃力地爬上，攀登（to climb awkwardly）
clamor [ˈklæmər]	*n.* 吵闹，喧哗（a loud, sustained noise） 记 词根记忆：clam(喊) + or → 吵闹，喧哗
clannish [ˈklænɪʃ]	*adj.* 排他的，门户之见的（tending to associate closely with one's own group and to avoid others） 记 词根记忆：clan(宗派，家族) + nish → 门户之见的
clarification [ˌklærəfɪˈkeɪʃn]	*n.* 解释，澄清（an interpretation that removes obstacles to understanding） 记 来自 clarify(*v.* 澄清)

□ circumscribe	□ circumspect	□ circumstantial	□ circumvent	□ cite	□ civil
□ civility	□ claim	□ clamber	□ clamor	□ clannish	□ clarification

clarify [ˈklærəfaɪ]	*v.* 澄清（to cause sth. to become clear to understand）
	记 词根记忆：clar（清楚，明白）+ ify（…化）→ 澄清
	同 elucidate, illuminate, illustrate
clause [klɔːz]	*n.* 从句；（法律等）条款（a stipulation in a document）
	记 联想记忆：cause（原因，事业）中加"l"，有事业必有条款加以限制
claustrophobic [ˌklɔːstrəˈfəʊbɪk]	*adj.* （患）幽闭恐怖症的，导致幽闭恐怖症的（affected with or inclined to claustrophobia）
cleave [kliːv]	*v.* 劈开（to divide with an axe）；分裂（to split; separate）
	记 联想记忆：c + leave（分开）→ 把 c 分开 → 劈开
clemency [ˈklemənsi]	*n.* 温和（mildness, esp. of weather）；仁慈，宽厚（mercy）
	记 和 cement（水泥）一起记
	同 caritas, charity, lenity
cliche [kliːˈʃeɪ]	*n.* 陈词滥调（a trite phrase or expression）
climactic [klaɪˈmæktɪk]	*adj.* 高潮的（of, relating to, or constituting a climax）
	记 来自 climax（*n.* 高潮）
climate [ˈklaɪmət]	*n.* 气候；风气（the prevailing set of conditions）
	同 atmosphere, clime
climax [ˈklaɪmæks]	*n.* 顶点，高潮（most significant event or point in time; summit）
	记 联想记忆：cli(m)（看作 climb）+ max（最大）→ 爬到最大值 → 顶点
clinical [ˈklɪnɪkl]	*adj.* 临床的（of, relating to, or conducted in or as if in a clinic）；冷静客观的（coldly objective）
	记 词根记忆：clinic（医疗诊所）+ al → 临床的
	搭 clinical practice 临床实践
clog [klɑːg]	*v.* 阻塞（to obstruct）*n.* 障碍（an obstruction）
	记 联想记忆：c + log（木头）→ 放上木头 → 阻塞
closet [ˈklɑːzət]	*adj.* 秘密的（closely private）*n.* 壁橱（a small room where clothing and personal objects are kept）
clumsy [ˈklʌmzi]	*adj.* 笨拙的（lacking grace; awkward）；拙劣的（ill-constructed）
	记 联想记忆：c + lum（亮度）+ sy → 没有亮光，不灵光 → 笨拙的
	同 gawky, lumbering, lumpish
clutter [ˈklʌtər]	*v.* 弄乱（to run in disorder）*n.* 零乱（a crowded or confused mass or collection）
	clumsy
coalesce [ˌkoʊəˈles]	*v.* 联合，合并（to unite or merge into a single body; mix）
	记 词根记忆：co + al（=ally 联盟）+ esce → 一起联盟 → 联合
	同 associate, bracket, combine, conjoin
coarse [kɔːrs]	*adj.* 粗糙的，低劣的（of low quality）；粗俗的（not refined）
	记 联想记忆：coar（看作 coal，煤炭）+ se → 煤炭是很粗糙的 → 粗糙的

4

□ clarify	□ clause	□ claustrophobic	□ cleave	□ clemency	□ cliche
□ climactic	□ climate	□ climax	□ clinical	□ clog	□ closet
□ clumsy	□ clutter	□ coalesce	□ coarse		

coax	*v.* 哄诱，巧言诱哄（to induce；persuade by soothing words；wheedle）
[koʊks]	搭 coax sth. out of/from sb. 哄劝；哄诱得到
code	*n.* 密码；法典 *v.* 将某事物编写成密码（to put in or into the form or symbols
[koʊd]	of a code）
codify	*v.* 编成法典，编辑成书
[ˈkɑːdɪfaɪ]	记 来自 code（*n.* 法典）
coerce	*v.* 强迫（to force or compel to do sth.）；压制（to restrain or constrain by
[koʊˈɜːrs]	force）
	记 发音记忆："可扼死" → 可以扼死 → 压制
coercion	*n.* 强制，高压统治（the act, process, or power of coercing）
[koʊˈɜːrʒn]	同 compulsion, constraint, enforcement
coercive	*adj.* 强制的，强迫性的（serving or intended to coerce）
[koʊˈɜːrsɪv]	
cogent	*adj.* 有说服力的（compelling；convincing；valid）
[ˈkoʊdʒənt]	记 联想记忆：cog（齿轮牙）+ ent → 像齿轮牙咬合一样严谨 → 有说服力的
	搭 cogent arguments 有说服力的争辩
cognitive	*adj.* 认知的；感知的（of, relating to, being, or involving conscious
[ˈkɑːgnətɪv]	intellectual activity）
	记 词根记忆：cognit（看作 cognis，知道）+ ive → 认知的
cognizant	*adj.* 知道的，认识的（having knowledge of sth.）
[ˈkɑːgnɪzənt]	记 词根记忆：co + gn（知道）+ izant → 知道的
coherence	*n.* 条理性，连贯性（the quality or state of cohering）
[koʊˈhɪrəns]	同 adherence, adhesion, bond, cohesion
coherent	*adj.* 连贯的，一致的（consistent；clearly articulated）
[koʊˈhɪrənt]	记 词根记忆：co + her（粘连）+ ent → 粘连在一起 → 连贯的，一致的
cohesive	*adj.* 凝聚的（sticking together）
[koʊˈhiːsɪv]	记 词根记忆：co + hes（粘着）+ ive → 有粘合力的 → 凝聚的
coincidental	*adj.* 巧合的（resulting from a coincidence）；同时发生的（occurring or
[koʊˌɪnsɪˈdentl]	existing at the same time）
coincidentally	*adv.* 巧合地（by coincidence）
[koʊˌɪnsɪˈdentəli]	记 来自 coincident（*adj.* 巧合的）
cold-blooded	*adj.* 冷血的；残酷的（without pity）
[ˌkoʊld ˈblʌdɪd]	
collaborate	*v.* 合作，协作（to work together with sb.）；通敌（to help enemy occupying
[kəˈlæbəreɪt]	one's country）
	记 词根记忆：col（共同）+ labor（劳动）+ ate → 共同劳动 → 合作
collaborative	*adj.* 协作的（characterized or accomplished by collaboration）
[kəˈlæbəreɪtɪv]	

collateral	*adj.* 平行的 (side by side; parallel); 附属的 (subordinate); 旁系的 (having
[kə'lætərəl]	an ancestor in common but descended from a different line) *n.* 担保品
	(property pledged by a borrower to protect the interests of the lender)
	记 词根记忆：col(共同) + later(边缘) + al → 共同的边 → 平行的
colloquial	*adj.* 口语的，口头的 (conversational)
[kə'loʊkwiəl]	记 词根记忆：col(共同) + loqu(说) + ial → 两人一起说 → 口语的
collusion	*n.* 共谋，勾结 (secret agreement or cooperation)
[kə'lu:ʒn]	搭 collusion with 与…勾结
collusive	*adj.* 共谋的 (having secret agreement or cooperation)
[kə'lu:sɪv]	记 词根记忆：col(共同) + lus(大笑，玩) + ive → 一起玩 → 共谋的
colonize	*v.* 建立殖民地，拓殖 (to establish a colony in an area); 定居，居于
['kɑ:lənaɪz]	
colony	*n.* 菌群 (a group of the same kind of one-celled organisms living or
['kɑ:ləni]	growing together); 殖民地
coloration	*n.* 着色法，染色法 (the method of dyeing); 颜色，色泽 (color)
[ˌkʌlə'reɪʃn]	记 来自color(*n.* 颜色)
colorful	*adj.* 富有色彩的 (having striking colors); 有趣的 (full of variety or interest)
['kʌlərfl]	
colossal	*adj.* 巨大的，庞大的 (like a colossus in size; huge; gigantic)
[kə'lɑ:sl]	记 词根记忆：coloss(大) + al → 巨大的
combative	*adj.* 好斗的 (marked by eagerness to fight or contend)
[kəm'bætɪv]	记 来自combat(*v.* 与…博斗)
combine	*v.* (使)联合，结合 (to merge, intermix, blend; possess in combination); 协
[kəm'baɪn]	力 (to act together)
	记 词根记忆：com(共同) + bi(两个) + ne → 使两个在一起 → (使)联合
	同 associate, bracket, coalesce, conjoin
combustible	*adj.* 易燃的 (flammable); 易激动的 (easily aroused)
[kəm'bʌstəbl]	记 词根记忆：com + bust(燃烧) + ible → 易燃的
cometary	*adj.* 彗星的，彗星似的
['kɒmɪtəri]	记 来自comet(*n.* 彗星)
comic	*adj.* 可笑的；喜剧的 (using comedy) *n.* 喜剧演员 (comedian)
['kɑ:mɪk]	搭 an inventive comic actor 一位有创造力的喜剧演员
commend	*v.* 推荐；举荐 (to recommend as worthy of confidence or notice); 表扬；
[kə'mend]	称赞 (to praise)
	同 acclaim, applaud, compliment, praise, recommend
commensurate	*adj.* 同样大小的 (equal in measure); 相称的 (proportionate)
[kə'menʃərət]	记 词根记忆：com(共同) + mensur(测量) + ate → 测量结果相同 → 同样
	大小的
	搭 be commensurate with 与…相称

commentary [ˈkɑːmənteri]	*n.* 实况报道(spoken description of an event as it happens)；（对书等的）集注(set of explanatory notes on a book) 记 词根记忆：comment(评论) + ary → 集注
commentator [ˈkɑːmənteɪtər]	*n.* 评论员(one who gives a commentary)
commercialize [kəˈmɜːrʃlaɪz]	*v.* 使商业化，使商品化(to manage on a business basis for profit)
commingle [kəˈmɪŋgl]	*v.* 掺和，混合(to mix up) 记 词根记忆：com(共同) + mingle(结合，混合) → 掺和，混合 同 commix, compound, immingle, immix, intermingle
commiserate [kəˈmɪzəreɪt]	*v.* 同情，怜悯(to feel or show sorrow or pity for sb.) 记 词根记忆：com + miser(可怜) + ate → 同情，怜悯
commission [kəˈmɪʃn]	*n.* 委托(piece of work given to sb. to do)；佣金(payment to sb. for selling goods) 记 词根记忆：com + miss(送，放出) + ion → 共同送出 → 委托
commitment [kəˈmɪtmənt]	*n.* 承诺，许诺(an agreement or pledge to do sth. in the future)
committed [kəˈmɪtɪd]	*adj.* （对事业，本职工作等)尽忠的(devoted to a cause) 记 来自 commit(*v.* 忠于某个人或机构等)
commodious [kəˈmoʊdiəs]	*adj.* 宽敞的(offering plenty of room; spacious; roomy) 记 词根记忆：com + mod(=code 方式，范围) + ious → 大的范围 → 宽敞的
commodity [kəˈmɑːdəti]	*n.* 商品(any article of commerce) 搭 a drop in commodity prices 商品价格的下跌
communal [kəˈmjuːnl]	*adj.* 全体共用的，共享的(held in common) 记 词根记忆：com + mun(公共) + al → 公共的 → 全体共用的，共享的
comparison [kəmˈpærɪsn]	*n.* 比较，对照(act of comparing)；比喻 记 来自 compare(*v.* 比较) 搭 by comparison 通过比较；in comparison with/to 与…比较
compass [ˈkʌmpəs]	*n.* 指南针，罗盘；界限，范围(scope; range) 记 词根记忆：com(共同) + pass(通过) → 共同通过的地方 → 界限
compassion [kəmˈpæʃn]	*n.* 同情，怜悯(sorrow for the sufferings or trouble of others) 记 词根记忆：com + pass(感情) + ion → 共同的感情 → 同情
compassionate [kəmˈpæʃənət]	*adj.* 有同情心的(sympathetic) 搭 compassionate nature 怜悯的性格
compel [kəmˈpel]	*v.* 强迫(to force or constrain) 记 词根记忆：com + pel(推) → 一起推 → 强迫 同 coerce, concuss, oblige
compelling [kəmˈpelɪŋ]	*adj.* 引起兴趣的(keenly interesting; captivating) 搭 a compelling subject 感兴趣的学科

compendium	*n.* 简要，概略（summary; abstract）
[kəmˈpendiəm]	同 digest, pandect, sketch, syllabus
compensatory	*adj.* 补偿性的，报酬的（compensating）
[kəmˈpensətɔːri]	例 He received a *compensatory* payment of £20000.
competence	*n.* 胜任，能力（the quality or state of being competent）
[ˈkɑːmpɪtəns]	记 compete（竞争）+ nce → 竞争需要能力 → 胜任，能力
competing	*adj.* 有竞争性的（rivalrous）；不相上下的
[kəmˈpiːtɪŋ]	记 来自 compete（*v.* 竞争，对抗）
complacence	*n.* 自满（satisfaction with oneself）
[kəmˈpleɪsns]	
complacency	*n.* 满足，安心（self-satisfaction）
[kəmˈpleɪsnsi]	记 词根记忆：com + plac（平静，满足）+ ency → 满足，安心
complacent	*adj.* 自满的，得意的（self-satisfied; smug）
[kəmˈpleɪsnt]	记 注意不要和 complaisant（*adj.* 随和的）相混
complementary	*adj.* 互补的（combining well to form a whole）
[ˌkɑːmplɪˈmentri]	记 来自 complement（*n.* 补充物）
	搭 be complementary to 与…互补
compliance	*n.* 顺从，遵从（obedience to a rule, agreement or demand）
[kəmˈplaɪəns]	记 来自 comply（*v.* 顺从）
compliant	*adj.* 服从的，顺从的（complying; yielding; submissive）
[kəmˈplaɪənt]	记 词根记忆：com + pliant（柔顺的）→ 顺从的
complicate	*v.* 使复杂化（to make sth. more difficult to do）
[ˈkɑːmplɪkeɪt]	记 词根记忆：com（全部）+ plic（重叠）+ ate → 全部重叠起来 → 使复杂化
	同 entangle, muddle, perplex, ravel, snarl
compliment	*n./v.* 恭维，称赞（praise; flattery）
[ˈkɑːmplɪmənt]	同 congratulate, felicitate, laud
component	*n.* 成分，零部件（any of the parts of which sth. is made）
[kəmˈpoʊnənt]	记 词根记忆：com（共同）+ pon（放）+ ent → 放到一起（的东西）→ 成分
composed	*adj.* 镇定的，沉着的（tranquil; self-possessed）；由…组成的（be made or formed from several parts）
[kəmˈpoʊzd]	搭 be composed of sth. 由…组成的
composure	*n.* 镇静，沉着；自若（tranquillity; equanimity）
[kəmˈpoʊʒər]	记 词根记忆：com + pos（放）+ ure（状态）→ 放在一起的状态 → 沉着
	同 calmness, coolness, phlegm, sangfroid, self-possession
compound	*n.* 复合物（sth. formed by a union of elements or parts especially）*v.* 掺和（to mix sth. together）
[kəmˈpaʊnd]	记 词根记忆：com + pound（放）→ 放到一起 → 掺和

compliment

comprehend [ˌkɑ:mprɪˈhend]	v. 理解(to understand sth. fully); 包括(to include) 记 词根记忆: com(全部) + prehend(抓住) → 全部抓住 → 理解; 包括
comprehensible [ˌkɑ:mprɪˈhensəbl]	adj. 可理解的, 易于理解的(that can be understood) 记 词根记忆: comprehen(=comprehend 理解) + sible(能够) → 能够理解 的 → 可理解的
comprehensively [ˌkɑ:mprɪˈhensɪvli]	adv. 包括地; 全面地 记 词根记忆: comprehen(=comprehend 理解) + sive + ly → 完全理解地 → 全面地
compromise [ˈkɑ:mprəmaɪz]	v. 妥协(to settle by concessions); 危害(to lay open to danger or disrepute) 记 词根记忆: com(共同) + promise(保证) → 相互保证 → 妥协
concede [kənˈsiːd]	v. 承认(to admit); 让步(to make a concession) 记 词根记忆: con + ced(割让) + e → 让出去 → 让步
conceive [kənˈsiːv]	v. 想象, 构想(to imagine); 怀孕(to become pregnant) 记 词根记忆: con(共同) + ceiv(抓) + e → 一起抓(思想) → 构想
concentrate [ˈkɑ:nsntreɪt]	v. 聚集, 浓缩(to bring into one main body) 记 词根记忆: con(加强) + centr(中心) + ate(做) → 重点放在一个中心 → 聚集 同 compress, condense, converge, concenter
concentration [ˌkɑ:nsnˈtreɪʃn]	n. 专心, 专注 (the act or process of concentra- ting); 集中(a concentrated mass or thing); 浓度 (the amount of a component in a given area or volume) concentration
concentric [kənˈsentrɪk]	adj. 同心的(having a common center) 记 词根记忆: con + centr (中心) + ic → 共同的 中心 → 同心的
conceptual [kənˈseptʃuəl]	adj. 概念上的(of, relating to, or consisting of concepts) 记 词根记忆: concept(n. 概念) + ual → 概念上的
conciliatory [kənˈsɪliətɔːri]	adj. 抚慰的, 调和的(intended or likely to conciliate) 记 来自 conciliate(v. 调和, 安慰)
conclusive [kənˈkluːsɪv]	adj. 最后的, 结论的, 决定性的(of, relating to, or being a conclusion); 确 凿的, 消除怀疑的(convincing) 记 来自 conclude(v. 作结论)
concoction [kənˈkɑ:kʃn]	n. (古怪或少见的)混合(物)(a strange or unusual mixture of things)
concomitant [kənˈkɑ:mɪtənt]	adj. 伴随的(accompanying; attendant) 记 联想记忆: con(共同) + com(看作 come) + itant → 一起来 → 伴随的
concurrent [kənˈkɜːrənt]	adj. 并发的(operating or occurring at the same time); 协作的, 一致的 (acting in conjunction)

condemnation [ˌkɑːndemˈneɪʃn]	*n.* 谴责（censure; blame） 同 conviction, damnation, denunciation
condense [kənˈdens]	*v.* 浓缩（to cause sth. to become thicker） 记 词根记忆：con + dense(浓密) → 浓缩 同 compress, constrict
condescending [ˌkɑːndɪˈsendɪŋ]	*adj.* 谦逊的，故意屈尊的（behaving as though one is better or more important than others）
condone [kənˈdoʊn]	*v.* 宽恕，原谅（to treat an offence as if it were not serious） 记 词根记忆：con(共同) + done(给予) → 全部给予 → 大度，宽容 → 宽恕
cone [koʊn]	*n.* 松果；圆锥体（solid body that narrows to a point from a circular flat base）
confide [kənˈfaɪd]	*v.* 吐露（心事）（to show confidence by imparting secrets）；倾诉（to tell confidentially） 记 词根记忆：con + fid(相信) + e → 相信别人 → 吐露
confidently [ˈkɑːnfɪdəntli]	*adv.* 确信地；肯定地（certainly） 记 来自 confident（*n.* 信心）
configuration [kənˌfɪɡjəˈreɪʃn]	*n.* 结构，配置（arrangement of parts; form）；轮廓（contour; outline） 记 来自 configure（*v.* 配置，使成型）
confine [kənˈfaɪn]	*v.* 限制，禁闭（to keep a person or an animal in a restricted space; restrain） 记 词根记忆：con(全部) + fin(限制) + e → 全限制 → 禁闭 同 circumscribe, delimit
conflagration [ˌkɑːnfləˈɡreɪʃn]	*n.* （建筑物或森林）大火（a big, destructive fire） 记 词根记忆：con + flagr(烧) + ation → 大火
conflate [kənˈfleɪt]	*v.* 合并（to combine or mix） 记 联想记忆：con(共同) + flat(吹气) + e → 吹到一起 → 合并
conflict	[kənˈflɪkt] *v.* 斗争，冲突，抵触 [ˈkɑːnflɪkt] *n.* 冲突（a clash between ideas; opposition） 记 词根记忆：con(共同) + flict(打击) → 共同打击 → 冲突 搭 conflict with sb./sth. 与某人/某事有冲突
conformity [kənˈfɔːrməti]	*n.* 一致，遵从；顺从（action in accordance with some specified standard or authority）
confound [kənˈfaʊnd]	*v.* 使迷惑，搞混（to puzzle and surprise sb.） 记 词根记忆：con + found(基础) → 把基础的东西全放到一起了 → 搞混
confront [kənˈfrʌnt]	*v.* 面临（to face）；对抗（to face or oppose defiantly or antagonistically） 记 词根记忆：con + front(面，前面) → 面对面 → 对抗
confrontation [ˌkɑːnfrənˈteɪʃn]	*n.* 对抗（the clashing of forces or ideas） 记 来自 confront（*v.* 面临，对抗）

conflict

□ condemnation	□ condense	□ condescending	□ condone	□ cone	□ confide
□ confidently	□ configuration	□ confine	□ conflagration	□ conflate	□ conflict
□ conformity	□ confound	□ confront	□ confrontation		

confusion [kənˈfjuːʒn]	*n.* 困惑，糊涂（an act or instance of confusing）；混乱，骚乱（a confused mass or mixture） 搭 be in confusion about... 对…有困惑 同 clutter, disarray
congenial [kənˈdʒiːniəl]	*adj.* 意气相投的，趣味相投的（having the same tastes and temperament; companionable）；性情好的（amiable）；适意的（agreeable） 记 词根记忆：con + geni（=genius 才能）+ al → 有共同才能的 → 意气相投的，趣味相投的
congenital [kənˈdʒenɪtl]	*adj.* 先天的，天生的（existing as such at birth; innate） 记 词根记忆：con + gen（产生）+ ital → 与生俱来的 → 天生的
congruent [ˈkɑːŋgruənt]	*adj.* 全等的，一致的（having identical shape and size） 记 词根记忆：con + gru（=gree 一致）+ ent → 全等的，一致的
congruity [kənˈgruɪti]	*n.* 一致性，适合性（the quality or state of being congruent or congruous）；共同点（a point of agreement）
congruous [ˈkɔŋgruːəs]	*adj.* 一致的，符合的（being in agreement, harmony, or correspondence）；[数] 全等的
conifer [ˈkɑːnɪfər]	*n.* 针叶树（a tree that has leaves like needles） 记 联想记忆：con（=cone 圆锥，松果）+ i + fer（带来）→ 带来松果的树 → 针叶树
conjecture [kənˈdʒektʃər]	*v./n.* 推测，臆测 记 词根记忆：con + ject（推，扔）+ ure → 全部是推出来的 → 臆测 同 presume, suppose, surmise
conjure [ˈkʌndʒər]	*v.* 召唤，想起（to call or bring to mind; evoke）；变魔术，变戏法（to practise magic or legerdemain） 搭 conjure for 召唤
connive [kəˈnaɪv]	*v.* 默许；纵容（to feign ignorance of another's wrongdoing）；共谋（to conspire） 记 词根记忆：con + nive（眨眼睛）→ 互相眨眼睛 → 共谋
connoisseur [ˌkɑːnəˈsɜːr]	*n.* 鉴赏家，行家（a person who has expert knowledge and keen discrimination in some field in the fine arts or in matters of taste） 记 词根记忆：con + nois（知道）+ s + eur（人）→ 什么都知道的人 → 行家
connotation [ˌkɑːnəˈteɪʃn]	*n.* 言外之意，内涵（idea or notion suggested in addition to its explicit meaning or denotation） 记 词根记忆：con + not（注意）+ ation → 全部注意到的内容 → 言外之意
conquer [ˈkɑːŋkər]	*v.* 以武力征服（to take possession of sth. by force） 记 词根记忆：con（全部）+ quer（寻求；询问）→ 全部寻求到 → 以武力征服
conscientious [ˌkɑːnʃiˈenʃəs]	*adj.* 尽责的（careful to do what one ought to do）；小心谨慎的（scrupulous） 记 词根记忆：con + sci（知道）+ entious（多…的）→ 所有事情都了解 → 尽责的 搭 be conscientious of... 对…尽责

consciousness [ˈkɑːnʃəsnəs]	*n.* 意识，观念（awareness; mind）；清醒状态；知觉（the normal state of conscious life） 同 concern, heed, heedfulness, regard
consecutive [kənˈsekjətɪv]	*adj.* 连续的（following one after the other in order） 例 She was absent for nine *consecutive* days.
conserve [kənˈsɜːrv]	*v.* 保存，保藏（to keep in a safe or sound state） 记 词根记忆：con(全部) + serv(服务，保持) + e → 全都保持下去 → 保存
considerable [kənˈsɪdərəbl]	*adj.* 相当多的（great in amount or size）；重要的；值得考虑的（worth consideration） 记 来自 consider(*v.* 考虑) 同 respectable, sensible, sizable, consequential, momentous
consign [kənˈsaɪn]	*v.* 托运；托人看管（to give over to another's care） 记 词根记忆：con + sign(签名) → 签完名后交托运 → 托运
consort	[kənˈsɔːrt] *v.* 陪伴（to keep company）；结交（to associate with） [ˈkɑːnsɔːrt] *n.* 配偶（husband or wife） 记 词根记忆：con(共同) + sort(类型) → 同类相聚 → 结交
conspiracy [kənˈspɪrəsi]	*n.* 共谋，阴谋（plan made by conspiring） 搭 conspiracy against 共谋反对
constant [ˈkɑːnstənt]	*adj.* 稳定的，不变的（unchanging）*n.* 常数（a figure, quality, or measurement that stays the same） 记 词根记忆：con(始终) + stant(站，立) → 始终站立 → 不变的 同 inflexible, immovable, immutable, inalterable, invariable
consternation [ˌkɑːnstərˈneɪʃn]	*n.* 大为吃惊，惊骇（great fear or shock） 记 词根记忆：con + stern(僵硬) + ation → 全身僵硬 → 惊骇
constituent [kənˈstɪtʃuənt]	*n.* 成分（component; element）；选区内的选民（a member of a constituency） 记 词根记忆：con + stit(=stat 站) + uent → 站在一起投票 → 选区内的选民
constitute [ˈkɑːnstətuːt]	*v.* 组成，构成（to form a whole）；建立（to establish） 记 词根记忆：con + stitut(建立，放) + e → 建立 同 compose, comprise, institute

□ consciousness □ consecutive □ conserve □ considerable □ consign □ consort
□ conspiracy □ constant □ consternation □ constituent □ constitute

41

Word List 5

MP3 - 05

constitution [ˌkɑːnstəˈtuːʃn]	*n.* 宪法(system of laws and principles according to which a state is governed); 体质(physical makeup of a person) 记 词根记忆：con + stitut(建立，放) + ion → 国无法不立 → 宪法
constrain [kənˈstreɪn]	*v.* 束缚，强迫(to make sb. do sth. by strong moral persuasion or force); 限制(to inhibit) 记 词根记忆：con + strain(拉紧) → 拉到一起 → 束缚，强迫 同 bridle, check, curb, withhold
constraint [kənˈstreɪnt]	*n.* 强制，强迫；对感情的压抑(sth. that limits one's freedom of action or feelings)
constrict [kənˈstrɪkt]	*v.* 约束(to inhibit); 收缩(to make sth. tighter, smaller or narrower) 记 词根记忆：con + strict(拉紧) → 拉到一起 → 收缩
construction [kənˈstrʌkʃn]	*n.* 结构，句法关系(syntactical arrangement); 解释，理解 同 construal, explanation, explication, exposition, interpretation
constructive [kənˈstrʌktɪv]	*adj.* 建设性的(promoting improvement or development) 搭 constructive suggestions 建设性的提议
construe [kənˈstru]	*v.* 解释(to explain or interpret); 翻译(to translate orally) 记 词根记忆：con + strue(=struct 结构) → 弄清结构 → 解释
consult [kənˈsʌlt]	*v.* 请教，咨询，商量(to consider; ask the advice or opinion of; refer to; confer) *n.* 咨询(consultation) 记 联想记忆：不顾侮辱(insult)，不耻请教(consult)
consummate [ˈkɑːnsəmət]	*adj.* 完全的，完善的(complete or perfect) *v.* 完成(to finish; accomplish) 记 词根记忆：con + sum(总数) + mate → 总数的，全数的 → 完全的
consumption [kənˈsʌmpʃn]	*n.* 消费，消耗(the act or process of consuming) 记 来自 consume(*v.* 消耗，耗费)
contact [ˈkɑːntækt]	*v.* 接触(to touch); 互通信息(to get in communication with) 记 词根记忆：con + tact(接触) → 接触 同 contingence, commerce, communion, intercourse
contagious [kənˈteɪdʒəs]	*adj.* 传染的，有感染力的(easily passed from person to person; communicable) 记 词根记忆：con + tag(接触) + ious → 接触(疾病的) → 传染的

42

☐ constitution   ☐ constrain   ☐ constraint   ☐ constrict   ☐ construction   ☐ constructive
☐ construe   ☐ consult   ☐ consummate   ☐ consumption   ☐ contact   ☐ contagious

containment	*n.* 阻止, 遏制(keeping sth. within limits)
[kənˈteɪnmənt]	搭 a policy of containment 遏制政策

contemplate	*v.* 深思(to think about intently); 凝视
[ˈkɑːntəmpleɪt]	记 词根记忆: con + templ(看作 temple, 庙) + ate → 像庙中人一样 → 深思
	搭 contemplate doing sth. 考虑做某事
	同 excogitate, perpend, ponder, view, gaze

contemplation	*n.* 注视; 凝视(an act of considering with attention); 意图; 期望(intention;
[ˌkɑːntəmˈpleɪʃn]	expectation)

contemplative	*adj.* 沉思的(marked by or given to contemplation) *n.* 沉思者(a person
[kənˈtemplətɪv]	who practices contemplation)

contemporary	*adj.* 同时代的(simultaneous); 当代的; 现代的(modern; current)
[kənˈtempəreri]	记 词根记忆: con(共同) + tempor(时间) + ary(人) → 同时代的人 → 同时代的
	搭 contemporary art 现代艺术

contempt	*n./v.* 轻视, 鄙视
[kənˈtempt]	记 联想记忆: con + tempt(尝试) → 大家都敢尝试 → 小意思 → 轻视
	搭 contempt for... 轻视…
	同 disdain, disparagement, defiance

contemptible	*adj.* 令人轻视的(despicable)
[kənˈtemptəbl]	记 来自 contempt(*n.* 蔑视, 轻视)

contemptuous	*adj.* 鄙视的, 表示轻蔑的(showing contempt)
[kənˈtemptʃuəs]	记 注意 contemptible 和 contemptuous 都来自 contempt; contemptible 是指做的事令人轻视, 而 contemptuous 是指人轻视的态度

content	[kənˈtent] *adj.* 知足的, 满意的(satisfied) *v.* (使)满意; (使)满足 *n.* 满意
	(the state of being content)
	[ˈkɑːntent] *n.* 内容(what is contained)
	记 词根记忆: con + tent(拉) → 全部拉开 → 全身舒展 → 满意的

contention	*n.* 争论(the act of dispute; discord); 论点(a statement one argues for as
[kənˈtenʃn]	valid)
	记 词根记忆: con + tent(拉) + ion → 你拉我夺 → 争论

contentious	*adj.* 好争吵的(argumentative; belligerent); 有争议的(controversial)
[kənˈtenʃəs]	搭 a contentious issue 有争议的问题

context	*n.* (语句等的)上下文(words that come before and after a word, phrase,
[ˈkɑːntekst]	or statement)
	记 词根记忆: con(共同) + text(编织) → 共同编织在一起的 → 上下文

continental	*adj.* 大陆的, 大陆性的(of, relating to, or characteristic of a continent)
[ˌkɑːntɪˈnentl]	搭 continental drift 大陆漂移(说)

continuation	*n.* 继续, 延续(a resumption after an interruption; without stopping)
[kənˌtɪnjuˈeɪʃn]	记 来自 continue(*v.* 继续)

contradict	*v.* 反驳, 驳斥(to affirm the contrary of a statement, etc.)
[ˌkɑːntrəˈdɪkt]	记 词根记忆: contra(反) + dict(说话, 断言) → 反说 → 反驳

□ containment	□ contemplate	□ contemplation	□ contemplative	□ contemporary	□ contempt
□ contemptible	□ contemptuous	□ content	□ contention	□ contentious	□ context
□ continental	□ continuation	□ contradict			

contradictory [ˌkɑːntrə'dɪktəri]	*adj.* 反驳的，反对的，抗辩的（involving, causing, or constituting a contradiction）
contrary ['kɑːntreri]	*adj.* 相反的（being so different as to be at opposite extremes）；对抗的（being opposite to or in conflict with each other） 记 词根记忆：contra(相反) + ry → 相反的 搭 be contrary to 与…相反
contravene [ˌkɑːntrə'viːn]	*v.* 违背(法规、习俗等)（to conflict with; violate） 记 词根记忆：contra(反) + ven(走) + e → 反着走 → 违背 同 breach, infract, infringe, offend, transgress
contrite [kən'traɪt]	*adj.* 悔罪的，痛悔的（feeling contrition; repentant） 记 词根记忆：con + trit(摩擦) + e → (心灵)摩擦 → 痛悔的
contrition [kən'trɪʃn]	*n.* 悔罪，痛悔（remorse for having done wrong） 记 来自 contrite(*adj.* 痛悔的)
contrive [kən'traɪv]	*v.* 计划，设计（to think up; devise; scheme） 记 词根记忆：contri(反) + ve(=ven 走) → (和普通人)反着走 → 设计(新东西) → 计划，设计 同 connive, intrigue, machinate, plot
control [kən'troʊl]	*n.* (科学实验的)对照标准，对照物（sth. used as a standard against which the results of a study can be measured） 记 control 的基本意思是"控制"
controversial [ˌkɑːntrə'vɜːrʃl]	*adj.* 引起或可能引起争论的（causing controversy） 记 词根记忆：contro(相反) + vers(转) + ial → 反着转 → 引起或可能引起争论的
controversy ['kɑːntrəvɜːrsi]	*n.* 公开辩论，论战（dispute; quarrel; strife） 记 词根记忆：contro（相反） + vers（转） + y → 意见转向相反的方向 → 论战 同 altercation, bickering, contention, hurrah
conventional [kən'venʃənl]	*adj.* 因循守旧的，传统的（based on convention） 记 来自 convention(*n.* 习俗，惯例) 同 orthodox
conventionalize [kən'venʃənəlaɪz]	*v.* 使按惯例，使习俗化（to make conventional） 记 词根记忆：convention(*n.* 习俗) + alize(使…) → 使习俗化
converge [kən'vɜːrdʒ]	*v.* 聚合，集中于一点（to come together at a point）；汇聚（to come together and unite in a common interest or focus） 记 词根记忆：con + verg(转) + e → 转到一起 → 汇聚
conversant [kən'vɜːrsnt]	*adj.* 精通的，熟悉的（familiar or acquainted; versed） 记 词根记忆：con + vers(转) + ant → 全方位转 → 精通的
converse	[kən'vɜːrs] *v.* 谈话，交谈（to exchange thoughts and opinions in speech） ['kɑːnvɜːrs] *adj.* 逆向的（opposite）*n.* 相反的事物（an opposite） 记 词根记忆：con + vers(转) + e → 全部转换方向 → 逆向的

convertible [kənˈvɜːrtəbl]	*adj.* 可转换的 (capable of being converted) *n.* 敞篷车 (an automobile with a canvas top that can be folded back or removed) 记 词根记忆：con + vert(转) + ible → 能够转动的 → 可转换的
convex [ˈkɑːnveks]	*adj.* 凸出的 (curving outward) 记 对比：concave (*adj.* 凹的)
convince [kənˈvɪns]	*v.* 使某人确信 (to make sb. feel certain)；说服 (to persuade) 记 词根记忆：con(全部) + vinc(征服，克服) + e → 彻底征服对方 → 使某人确信
convivial [kənˈvɪviəl]	*adj.* 欢乐的，快乐的 (having sth. to do with a feast or festive activity) 记 词根记忆：con + viv(活) + ial → 一起活跃 → 欢乐的
convoluted [ˈkɑːnvəluːtɪd]	*adj.* 旋绕的 (coiled；spiraled)；费解的 (extremely involved；intricate；complicated) 记 词根记忆：con + volut(转) + ed → 全部转 → 旋绕的
coordinate	[koʊˈɔːrdɪneɪt] *v.* 使各部分协调 (to cause different parts, limbs to function together efficiently) [koʊˈɔːrdɪnət] *adj.* 同等的 (of equal importance, rank, or degree) 记 词根记忆：co + ordin(顺序) + ate → 顺序一样 → 同等的
copious [ˈkoʊpiəs]	*adj.* 丰富的，多产的 (very plentiful；abundant) 记 联想记忆：copi(看作 copy) + ous → 能拷贝很多 → 丰富的
cordiality [ˌkɔːrˈdʒiləti]	*n.* 诚恳，热诚 (sincere affection and kindness) 同 heartiness, geniality, warmth
core [kɔːr]	*n.* 果心 (centre of fruits)；核心 (the most important part) *v.* 去掉某物的中心部分 (to take out the core of sth.)
correlate [ˈkɔːrəleɪt]	*v.* 使相互关联；使相互影响 (to establish a mutual or reciprocal relation) 搭 correlate...with... 使…与…相互关联
correlated [ˈkɔːrəleɪtɪd]	*adj.* 有相互关系的 (mutually or reciprocally related) 同 correlative
corroborate [kəˈrɑːbəreɪt]	*v.* 支持或证实 (to bolster；make more certain)；强化 (to strengthen) 记 词根记忆：cor + robor(力量) + ate → 加强力量 → 强化
corroboration [kəˌrɑːbəˈreɪʃn]	*n.* 证实，支持 (the act of corroborating) 记 来自 corroborate (*v.* 支持；强化)
corrosive [kəˈroʊsɪv]	*adj.* 腐蚀性的，腐蚀的，蚀坏的 (tending or having the power to corrode) 同 caustic, erosive
corruption [kəˈrʌpʃn]	*n.* 腐败，堕落 (impairment of integrity, virtue or moral principle) 记 来自 corrupt(*v.* 使腐化)
cosmic [ˈkɑːzmɪk]	*adj.* 宇宙的 (of or relating to the cosmos) 记 词根记忆：cosm(宇宙) + ic → 宇宙的
cosmopolitan [ˌkɑːzməˈpɑːlɪtən]	*adj.* 世界性的，全球的 (having worldwide rather than limited or provincial scope or bearing) *n.* 世界主义者，四海为家的人 (a person who has traveled widely and feels equally at home everywhere)

5

□ convertible	□ convex	□ convince	□ convivial	□ convoluted	□ coordinate
□ copious	□ cordiality	□ core	□ correlate	□ correlated	□ corroborate
□ corroboration	□ corrosive	□ corruption	□ cosmic	□ cosmopolitan	

coterie [ˈkoʊtəri]	*n.* （有共同兴趣的）小团体（a close circle of friends who share a common interest or background；clique） 记 来自 cote（小屋，笼）+ rie → 一个屋子里的人 → 小团体
countenance [ˈkaʊntənəns]	*v.* 支持，赞成（to sanction）*n.* 表情（the look on a person's face） 同 advocate, approve, approbate, encourage, favor
counteract [ˌkaʊntərˈækt]	*v.* 消除，抵消（to act directly against；neutralize, or undo the effect of opposing action） 记 词根记忆：counter（反）+ act（动作）→ 做相反的动作 → 消除，抵消
counterbalance [ˌkaʊntərˈbæləns]	*v.* 起平衡作用（to act as a balance to sb./sth.） 记 组合词：counter（反对，相反）+ balance（平衡）→ 相反的两边保持平衡 → 起平衡作用
counterclockwise [ˌkaʊntərˈklɑːkwaɪz]	*adj./adv.* 逆时针方向的（地）（in a direction opposite to that in which the hands of a clock rotate as viewed from in front）
counterfeit [ˈkaʊntərfɪt]	*v.* 伪造，仿造（to make an imitation of money, picture, etc. usually in order to deceive or defraud）*adj.* 伪造的，假冒的（made in imitation of sth. else with intent to deceive） 记 词根记忆：counter（反）+ feit（=fact 做）→ 和真的对着干 → 伪造
counterpart [ˈkaʊntərpɑːrt]	*n.* 相对应或具有相同功能的人或物（a person or thing that corresponds to or has the same function as） 记 组合词：counter（相反地）+ part（部分）→ 相对物 → 相对应或具有相同功能的人或物
counterproductive [ˌkaʊntərprəˈdʌktɪv]	*adj.* 事与愿违的（having the opposite effect to that intended） 记 组合词：counter（相反的）+ productive（有成效的）→ 与想象有相反效果的 → 事与愿违的
countless [ˈkaʊntləs]	*adj.* 无数的（too numerous to be counted） 同 incalculable, innumerable, numberless, uncountable
court [kɔːrt]	*n.* 法庭；宫廷 *v.* 献殷勤（to seek the affections of）；追求（to seek to gain or achieve）
courteous [ˈkɜːrtiəs]	*adj.* 有礼貌的（marked by respect for and consideration of others） 同 complaisant, goallant, polite, mannerty
covet [ˈkʌvət]	*v.* 贪求，妄想（to want ardently） 记 联想记忆：covert 去掉一个 r 变成 covet, 由秘密变成公开的贪求
cozy [ˈkoʊzi]	*adj.* 舒适的，惬意的（marked by or providing contentment or comfort）；亲切友好的（friendly）
craft [kræft]	*n.* 行业，手艺（occupation, especially one that needs skill） 搭 arts and crafts 手工艺
crash [kræʃ]	*v.* 猛撞（to break violently and noisily）；猛冲直闯（to enter or attend without invitation or paying）；撞碎（to break or go to pieces with or as if with violence and noise） 记 象声词：破裂声 → 撞碎

crater [ˈkreɪtər]	*n.* 火山口 (a bowl-shaped cavity at the mouth of a volcano); 弹坑 (a pit made by an exploding bomb)
crawl [krɔːl]	*v.* 爬, 爬行 (to move slowly in a prone position without or as if without the use of limbs) 记 联想记忆: c + raw(生疏的) + l → 对地形生疏, 就要缓慢地行进 → 爬行
credible [ˈkredəbl]	*adj.* 可信的, 可靠的 (offering reasonable grounds for being believed) 记 词根记忆: cred(相信) + ible(能…的) → 可靠的 同 authentic, convincing, creditable, trustworthy, trusty
credulous [ˈkredʒələs]	*adj.* 轻信的, 易上当的 (tending to believe too readily; easily convinced) 记 词根记忆: cred + ulous(多…的) → 太过信任别人的 → 轻信的
creed [kriːd]	*n.* 教义 (a brief authoritative formula of religious belief); 信条 (a set of fundamental beliefs)
crestfallen [ˈkrestfɔːlən]	*adj.* 挫败的, 失望的 (dejected, disheartened, or humbled) 记 联想记忆: crest(鸡冠) + fallen → 鸡冠下垂 → 斗败了的 → 挫败的
crimson [ˈkrɪmzn]	*n.* 绯红色 (any of several deep purplish reds) *adj.* 绯红色的 (of the color crimson) *v.* (使)变得绯红 (to make crimson; to become crimson)
cringe [krɪndʒ]	*v.* 畏缩 (to shrink from sth. dangerous or painful); 谄媚 (to act in a timid, servile manner; fawn) 记 联想记忆: c + ring(响铃) + e → 一响铃就退缩 → 畏缩 搭 cringe from 因…畏缩
criss-cross [ˈkrɪs krɔːs]	*v.* 交叉往来 (to go or pass back and forth) 例 The city is *criss-crossed* with canals.
criterion [kraɪˈtɪriən]	*n.* 评判的标准, 尺度 (standard by which sth. is judged) 记 词根记忆: crit(判断) + er(看作 err, 错误) + ion → 判断对错的标准 → 尺度; 注意其复数形式为 criteria
critic [ˈkrɪtɪk]	*n.* 批评者 (one who expresses a reasoned opinion on any matter especially involving a judgment of its value, truth, etc.)
critical [ˈkrɪtɪkl]	*adj.* 挑毛病的 (looking for faults); 关键的; 危急的 (of or at a crisis) 搭 be critical of... 对…挑毛病
criticize [ˈkrɪtɪsaɪz]	*v.* 评论, 批评; 挑剔 (to evaluate; find fault with) 同 blame, censure, condemn, denounce, reprehend, reprobate
critique [krɪˈtiːk]	*n.* 批评性的分析 (critical analysis) 例 The book provides a radical *critique* of modern workplace structure.
crooked [ˈkrʊkɪd]	*adj.* 不诚实的 (dishonest); 弯曲的 (not straight) 记 来自 crook(*v.* 弯曲)
crossfire [ˈkrɔːsfaɪər]	*n.* 交叉火力 (the firing of guns from two or more directions at the same time, so that the bullets cross) 记 组合词: cross(交叉) + fire(火) → 交叉火力
crumple [ˈkrʌmpl]	*v.* 把…弄皱; 起皱 (to crush together into creases or wrinkles); 破裂 (to fall apart)

5

□ crater	□ crawl	□ credible	□ credulous	□ creed	□ crestfallen
□ crimson	□ cringe	□ criss-cross	□ criterion	□ critic	□ critical
□ criticize	□ critique	□ crooked	□ crossfire	□ crumple	

47

cryptic	*adj.* 秘密的，神秘的(mysterious; baffling)
[ˈkrɪptɪk]	记 词根记忆：crypt(秘密) + ic → 秘密的
crystalline	*adj.* 水晶的(resembling crystal)；透明的(strikingly clear or sparkling)
[ˈkrɪstəlaɪn]	记 来自crystal(*n.* 水晶)
culinary	*adj.* 厨房的(of the kitchen)；烹调的(of cooking)
[ˈkʌlɪneri]	搭 culinary skills 烹饪技巧
culminate	*v.* 达到顶点(to rise to or form a summit)；使达到最高点(to bring to a head or to the highest point)
[ˈkʌlmɪneɪt]	
culpable	*adj.* 有罪的，该受谴责的(deserving blame; blameworthy)
[ˈkʌlpəbl]	记 词根记忆：culp(罪行) + able → 有罪的
cumbersome	*adj.* 笨重的，难处理的(hard to handle or deal with; clumsy)
[ˈkʌmbərsəm]	记 联想记忆：cumber(阻碍) + some → 受到阻碍的 → 笨重的
cursory	*adj.* 粗略的(superficial)；草率的(hasty)
[ˈkɜːrsəri]	记 词根记忆：curs(跑) + ory → 匆忙地跑过去 → 草率的
	例 A *cursory* glance pays little attention to details.
curt	*adj.* (言词、行为)简略而草率的(brief, esp. to the point of rudeness; terse)
[kɜːrt]	
curtail	*v.* 削减，缩短(to make sth. shorter or less)
[kɜːrˈteɪl]	记 联想记忆：cur(看作 curt, 短) + tail(尾巴) → 短尾巴 → 缩短
	同 abridge, diminish, lessen, minify
custodian	*n.* 管理员，监护人(a person who has the custody or care of sth.; caretaker)
[kʌˈstoʊdiən]	记 发音记忆："卡死偷电" → 管理比较严，卡死偷电的 → 管理员
customary	*adj.* 合乎习俗的(according to custom)
[ˈkʌstəmeri]	记 来自custom(*n.* 习俗)
cyclical	*adj.* 循环的(recurring in cycles)
[ˈsaɪklɪkl]	记 来自cycle(*n.* 循环)
cynical	*adj.* 愤世嫉俗的(captious, peevish, having or showing the attitude or temper of a cynic)
[ˈsɪnɪkl]	
damped	*adj.* 潮湿的；减震的，压低(声音)的
[dæmpt]	
dampen	*v.* (使)潮湿(to make damp; moisten)；使沮丧，泼凉水(to deaden; depress)
[ˈdæmpən]	记 来自damp(*adj.* 潮湿的)
dappled	*adj.* 有斑点的，斑驳的(covered with spots of a different color)
[ˈdæpld]	记 联想记忆：d + apple + d → 苹果上有斑点 → 有斑点的
daunt	*v.* 使胆怯，使畏缩(to dishearten; dismay)
[dɔːnt]	记 联想记忆：d(看作 devil, 魔鬼) + aunt(姑奶奶) → 像鬼一样的姑奶奶 → 使胆怯

cyclical

dearth [dɜːθ]	*n.* 缺乏，短缺(scarcity) 记 联想记忆：dear(珍贵的) + th → 物以稀为贵 → 缺乏，短缺
debase [dɪˈbeɪs]	*v.* 贬低，贬损(to make lower in value, quality or dignity) 记 词根记忆：de + base(低) → 使低下去 → 贬低
debatable [dɪˈbeɪtəbl]	*adj.* 未决定的，有争执的(open to dispute) 记 来自 debate(*v.* 辩论)
debate [dɪˈbeɪt]	*n.* 正式的辩论，讨论(formal argument of a question) *v.* 讨论，辩论 记 词根记忆：de(加强) + bat(打，击) + e → 加强打击 → 正式的辩论
debauch [dɪˈbɔːtʃ]	*v.* 使堕落，败坏(to lead away from virtue or excellence) *n.* 堕落(an act or occasion of debauchery) 同 corrupt, deprave, pervert
debilitate [dɪˈbɪlɪteɪt]	*v.* 使衰弱(to make weak or feeble; weaken) 同 depress, enervate
decadence [ˈdekədəns]	*n.* 衰落，颓废(the process of becoming decadent) 记 词根记忆：de(=down) + cad(落) + ence → 往下落 → 衰落，颓废
decelerate [ˌdiːˈseləreɪt]	*v.* (使)减速(to reduce the speed; to decrease the rate of progress) 同 delay, detain, embog
deceptive [dɪˈseptɪv]	*adj.* 欺骗的，导致误解的 (tending or having power to deceive) 搭 a deceptive advertisement 虚假广告
deciduous [dɪˈsɪdʒuəs]	*adj.* 非永久的，短暂的(not lasting; ephemeral)；脱落的(falling off or out)；落叶的(shedding leaves annually) 记 词根记忆：de + cid(落下) + uous → 脱落的
decimate [ˈdesɪmeɪt]	*v.* 毁掉大部分；大量杀死(to destroy or kill a large part) 记 词根记忆：decim(十分之一) + ate → 杀…十分之一 → 大量杀死
decipher [dɪˈsaɪfər]	*v.* 破译(to decode)；解开(疑团)(to make out the meaning) 记 词根记忆：de(去掉) + cipher(密码) → 解开密码 → 破译 同 crack, decrypt
decisive [dɪˈsaɪsɪv]	*adj.* 决定性的(having the power or quality of deciding)；坚定的，果断的(resolute; unquestionable) 同 bent, decided, determined, resolved
decisiveness [dɪˈsaɪsɪvnəs]	*n.* 坚决，果断 记 来自 decisive(*adj.* 坚决的，果断的)
decline [dɪˈklaɪn]	*v.* 拒绝；变弱，变小(to become smaller, weaker, fewer) *n.* 消减(gradual and continuous loss of strength, power or numbers) 记 词根记忆：de(向下) + clin(倾斜，斜坡) + e → 向下斜 → 消减
decompose [ˌdiːkəmˈpoʊz]	*v.* (使)腐烂(to rot; decay) 记 词根记忆：de(否定) + compose(组成) → 腐烂

5

deceptive

□ dearth	□ debase	□ debatable	□ debate	□ debauch	□ debilitate
□ decadence	□ decelerate	□ deceptive	□ deciduous	□ decimate	□ decipher
□ decisive	□ decisiveness	□ decline	□ decompose		

49

decorous	*adj.* 合宜的，高雅的（marked by propriety and good taste）
[ˈdekərəs]	记 词根记忆：decor(*n.* 装饰布局) + ous → 经过装饰的 → 合宜的，高雅的
decorum	*n.* 礼节，礼貌（propriety and good taste in behavior, dress; etiquette）
[dɪˈkɔːrəm]	记 词根记忆：decor(美，装饰) + um → 美的行为 → 礼节
decrepit	*adj.* 衰老的，破旧的（broken down or worn out by old age, illness, or long use）
[dɪˈkrepɪt]	记 词根记忆：de + crepit(破裂声) → 破旧的
decry	*v.* 责难(to denounce)；贬低(to depreciate officially; disparage)
[dɪˈkraɪ]	记 de + cry(喊) → 向下喊 → 贬低；注意不要和 descry(看见，望到)相混
defamation	*n.* 诽谤，中伤(the act of defaming another)
[ˌdefəˈmeɪʃn]	同 aspersion, calumniation, denigration, vilification
default	*n.* 违约（failure to perform a task or fulfill an obligation）；未履行的责任(failure to do sth. required by duty or law)；拖欠(a failure to pay financial debts) *v.* 不履行(to fail to fulfill a contract, agreement, or duty)
[dɪˈfɔːlt]	记 联想记忆：de + fault(错误) → 错下去 → 不履行
defecate	*v.* 澄清(to clarify)；净化
[ˈdefəkeɪt]	
defect	*n.* 缺点，瑕疵（fault; flaw）*v.* 变节，脱党(to forsake a cause or party)
[ˈdiːfekt]	记 词根记忆：de + fect(做) → 没做好 → 缺点
	同 blemish

defect

defense	*n.* 防御，防护（the action of fighting against attack）
[dɪˈfens]	记 来自 defend(*v.* 防御，防护)
defensive	*adj.* 自卫的(devoted to resisting or preventing aggression or attack) *n.* 戒备；防御
[dɪˈfensɪv]	搭 on/onto the defensive 处于防御姿态；采取守势
defer	*v.* 遵从，听从（to yield with courtesy）；延期（to put off to a future time; delay）
[dɪˈfɜːr]	
deference	*n.* 敬意，尊重(courteous regard or respect)
[ˈdefərəns]	搭 deference to 对⋯尊重
deferential	*adj.* 顺从的，恭顺的(showing deference)
[ˌdefəˈrenʃl]	同 duteous, dutiful
defiance	*n.* 挑战；违抗，反抗(open disobedience)
[dɪˈfaɪəns]	记 来自 defy(*v.* 公然反抗)
	搭 defiance against 对⋯的反抗或挑战
	同 contempt, contumacy, recalcitrance, stubbornness
defiant	*adj.* 反抗的，挑衅的(bold, impudent)
[dɪˈfaɪənt]	搭 a defiant teenager 一个具有反叛性格的少年
deficiency	*n.* 缺陷(absence of sth. essential; incompleteness)；不足(shortage)
[dɪˈfɪʃnsi]	记 词根记忆：de + fic(做) + iency → 没做好 → 缺陷

deficient [dɪˈfɪʃnt]	*adj.* 有缺点的(lacking in some necessary quality or element);缺少的;不足的(not up to a normal standard or complement) 记 词根记忆：de(变坏) + fic(做) + ient → 做得不好的 → 有缺点的;不足的 同 defective, inadequate, insufficient, scant, scarce
definite [ˈdefɪnət]	*adj.* 清楚的,明确的(clear; not doubtful) 记 来自define(*v.* 下定义)
definitive [dɪˈfɪnətɪv]	*adj.* 明确的,有权威的(clear and having final authority);最终的(conclusive)
defrost [diːˈfrɔːst]	*v.* 解冻(to release from a frozen state);将…除霜(to free from ice) 记 分拆记忆：de + frost(霜冻) → 将霜除去 → 解冻
deft [deft]	*adj.* 灵巧的,熟练的(skillful in a quick, sure, and easy way; dexterous) 同 adroit, handy, nimble
defunct [dɪˈfʌŋkt]	*adj.* 死亡的(dead or extinct) 记 词根记忆：de + funct(功能) → 无功能的 → 死亡的
defy [dɪˈfaɪ]	*v.* 违抗,蔑视(to refuse to respect sb. as an authority) 例 Hundreds of people today *defied* the ban on political gatherings.
dehumanize [diːˈhjuːmənaɪz]	*v.* 使失掉人性(to deprive of human qualities, personality, or spirit) 记 分拆记忆：de + humanize(使人性化) → 使失掉人性
dehydrate [diːˈhaɪdreɪt]	*v.* 使脱水(to remove water from) 记 词根记忆：de(去除) + hydr(水) + ate → 使脱水
deign [deɪn]	*v.* 惠允(做某事)(to condescend to do sth.; stoop);施惠于人(to condescend to give or grant) 记 参考：condescend(*v.* 屈尊)
deleterious [ˌdeləˈtɪriəs]	*adj.* 有害的,有毒的(harmful often in a subtle or unexpected way; injurious) 记 词根记忆：delete(删除) + rious → 要删除的东西 → 有害的 同 damaging, detrimental, hurtful, mischievous

5

Word List 6

deliberate	[dɪ'lɪbərət] *adj.* 深思熟虑的 (carefully thought out and formed); 故意的 (done on purpose) [dɪ'lɪbəreɪt] *v.* 慎重考虑 (to think or consider carefully and fully) 记 词根记忆: de(表加强) + liber(权衡) + ate → 反复权衡 → 深思熟虑的
deliberation [dɪ͵lɪbə'reɪʃn]	*n.* 细想, 考虑 (the act of deliberating) 同 cogitation, consideration, speculation
delight [dɪ'laɪt]	*n.* 快乐, 高兴, 乐事 (joy, sth. that gives great pleasure) *v.* 使高兴, 使欣喜 (to take great pleasure) 记 联想记忆: de(向下) + light(阳光) → 沐浴在阳光下 → 使高兴 同 exult, jubilate
delimit [di'lɪmɪt]	*v.* 定界, 划界 (to fix the limits of) 记 联想记忆: de + limit(界限) → 划界
delineate [dɪ'lɪnieɪt]	*v.* 勾画, 描述 (to sketch out; draw; describe) 记 联想记忆: de(加强) + line(线条) + ate → 加强线条 → 勾画
delude [dɪ'luːd]	*v.* 欺骗, 哄骗 (to mislead; deceive; trick) 记 词根记忆: de + lud(玩弄) + e → 玩弄别人 → 欺骗 同 beguile, bluff
deluge ['deljuːdʒ]	*n.* 大洪水 (a great flood); 暴雨 (heavy rainfall) 记 词根记忆: de + lug(=luv 冲洗) + e → 冲掉 → 大洪水
demagnetize [diː'mægnətaɪz]	*v.* 消磁, 使退磁 (to deprive of magnetic properties)
demean [dɪ'miːn]	*v.* 贬抑, 降低 (to degrade; humble) 记 联想记忆: de(加强) + mean(低下的) → 使低下 → 贬抑
demobilize [diː'moʊbəlaɪz]	*v.* 遣散, 使复员 (to discharge from military service) 同 disband
demolish [dɪ'mɑːlɪʃ]	*v.* 破坏, 摧毁 (to destroy; ruin); 拆除 (to break to pieces) 记 词根记忆: de(加强) + mol(碾碎) + ish → 摧毁

□ deliberate	□ deliberation	□ delight	□ delimit	□ delineate	□ delude
□ deluge	□ demagnetize	□ demean	□ demobilize	□ demolish	

demonstrate [ˈdemənstreɪt]	*v.* 证明，论证（to prove or make clear by reasoning or evidence）；示威（to make a demonstration） 记 词根记忆：de(加强) + monstr(显示) + ate → 加强显示 → 证明 同 evince, illustrate
demotic [dɪˈmɑːtɪk]	*adj.* 民众的，通俗的（of or pertaining to the people） 记 词根记忆：demo(人民) + tic(…的) → 民众的
demur [dɪˈmɜːr]	*v.* 表示异议，反对（to object） 记 词根记忆：de(加强) + mur(延迟) → 一再拖延 → 反对
demystify [ˌdiːˈmɪstɪfaɪ]	*v.* 减少…的神秘性（to make sth. less mysterious） 记 联想记忆：de(去掉) + mystify(使迷惑) → 去掉迷惑 → 减少…的神秘性
denigrate [ˈdenɪɡreɪt]	*v.* 污蔑，诽谤（to disparage the character or reputation of; defame; blacken） 记 词根记忆：de + nigr(黑色的) + ate → 弄黑 → 诽谤
denote [dɪˈnoʊt]	*v.* 指示，表示（to mark, indicate; signify） 记 词根记忆：de + not(知道) + e → 让人知道 → 表示
denounce [dɪˈnaʊns]	*v.* 指责（to accuse publicly） 记 词根记忆：de + nounc(报告) + e → 坏报告 → 指责 例 Although it is unusual to *denounce* museum-goers for not painting, it is quite common, even for those, who are unenthusiastic about sports, to criticize spectators for athletic inactivity.
dense [dens]	*adj.* 密集的，浓密的（marked by compactness or crowding together of parts） 记 联想记忆：和 sense(*n.* 感觉) 一起记
density [ˈdensəti]	*n.* 密集，稠密（the quality or state of being dense） 搭 population density 人口密度
dental [ˈdentl]	*adj.* 牙齿的，牙科的（of or relating to the teeth or dentistry） 记 词根记忆：dent(牙齿) + al(…的) → 牙齿的
dependable [dɪˈpendəbl]	*adj.* 可靠的，可信赖的（capable of being depended on） 记 来自 depend(*v.* 依靠；信任)
depict [dɪˈpɪkt]	*v.* 描绘（to represent by or as if by a picture）；描写，描述（to describe） 记 词根记忆：de(加强) + pict(描画) → 描绘
deplete [dɪˈpliːt]	*v.* 大量减少；耗尽，使枯竭（to exhaust） 记 词根记忆：de + plet(满) + e → 不满 → 倒空 → 使枯竭 同 drain, impoverish
deplore [dɪˈplɔːr]	*v.* 悲悼，哀叹（to express or feel grief for）；谴责（to condemn） 记 词根记忆：de(向下) + plor(喊) + e → 哀叹 同 bemoan, bewail, grieve, lament, moan

6

demonstrate

STOP THE WAR PEACE

deploy	*v.* 部署（to place in battle formation or appropriate positions）；拉长（战
[dɪˈplɔɪ]	线），展开（to extend (a military unit) especially in width）
deprave	*v.* 使堕落，使恶化（to make bad）
[dɪˈpreɪv]	记 词根记忆：de(向下) + prav(弯曲的) + e → 使弯曲 → 使堕落
deprecate	*v.* 反对（to express disapproval of）；轻视（to belittle）
[ˈdeprəkeɪt]	记 词根记忆：de(去掉) + prec(价值) + ate → 去掉价值 → 轻视
deprecation	*n.* 反对（disapproval）
[ˌdeprɪˈkeɪʃn]	记 来自 deprecate(*v.* 反对)
deprecatory	*adj.* 不赞成的，反对的（disapproving）
[ˈdeprɪkətɔːri]	搭 be deprecatory about... 反对…
depreciate	*v.* 轻视（to make seem less important; belittle; disparage）；贬值（to
[dɪˈpriːʃieɪt]	reduce or drop in value or price）
	记 词根记忆：de + prec(价值) + iate → 贬值
deprive	*v.* 剥夺，使丧失（to take sth. away from）
[dɪˈpraɪv]	记 词根记忆：de(去掉) + priv(单个) + e → 从个人身边拿走 → 剥夺
	同 denude, dismantle, divest, strip
derelict	*adj.* 荒废的（deserted by the owner; abandoned）；玩忽职守的（neglectful
[ˈderəlɪkt]	of duty; remiss）；疏忽的（negligent）*n.* 被遗弃的人（sb. abandoned by
	family and society）
	记 词根记忆：de + re(向后) + lict(=linqu 留下) → 完全置后 → 被遗弃的人
deride	*v.* 嘲笑，愚弄（to laugh at in contempt or scorn; ridicule）
[dɪˈraɪd]	记 词根记忆：de + rid(笑) + e → 嘲笑
derivative	*adj.* 派生的（derived）；无创意的（not original）
[dɪˈrɪvətɪv]	同 derivate, derivational
derogatory	*adj.* 不敬的，贬损的（disparaging; belittling）
[dɪˈrɑːɡətɔːri]	记 词根记忆：de（向下）+ rog（询问）+ at + ory → 为贬低某人而询问 →
	贬损的
descend	*v.* 下降（to pass from a higher place or level to a lower one）；降格，屈尊
[dɪˈsend]	(to lower oneself in status or dignity)
	记 词根记忆：de(向下) + scend(爬) → 向下爬 → 下降
	例 The critics were distressed that an essayist of such glowing promise
	could *descend* to writing such dull, uninteresting prose.
	同 decline, degenerate, deteriorate, sink
descriptive	*adj.* 描述的（serving to describe）
[dɪˈskrɪptɪv]	记 词根记忆：de(加强) + script(写) + ive → 描述的
descry	*v.* 看见，察觉（to catch sight of; discern）
[dɪˈskraɪ]	记 词根记忆：de(向下) + scry(写) → 写下 → 看见；不要和 decry(*v.* 谴
	责)或 outcry(*v.* 呐喊)相混
desecrate	*v.* 玷辱，亵渎（to treat as not sacred; profane）
[ˈdesɪkreɪt]	记 词根记忆：de(向下) + secr(神圣) + ate → 玷辱

□ deploy	□ deprave	□ deprecate	□ deprecation	□ deprecatory	□ depreciate
□ deprive	□ derelict	□ deride	□ derivative	□ derogatory	□ descend
□ descriptive	□ descry	□ desecrate			

designate ['dezɪgneɪt]	*v.* 指定，任命（to indicate and set apart for a specific purpose, office, or duty）；指明，指出 *adj.*《已受委派》尚未上任的（appointed to a job but not yet having officially started it） 记 词根记忆：de + sign（标出）+ ate → 标出来 → 指定
desirable [dɪ'zaɪərəbl]	*adj.* 值得要的（advisable; worthwhile; beneficial） 记 来自 desire（*v./n.* 渴望）
despicable [dɪ'spɪkəbl]	*adj.* 可鄙的，卑劣的（deserving to be despised; contemptible） 记 词根记忆：de + spic（看）+ able → 不值得看的 → 卑劣的
despondent [dɪ'spɑndənt]	*adj.* 失望的，意气消沉的（disheartened; depressed; hopeless） 记 词根记忆：de + spond（允诺）+ ent → 没有得到允诺 → 失望的
destine ['destɪn]	*v.* 命运注定，预定（to decree beforehand） 同 foreordain, predestine
desultory ['desəltɔːri]	*adj.* 不连贯的（disconnected）；散漫的（not methodical; random） 记 词根记忆：de + sult（跳）+ ory → 跳来跳去 → 散漫的
detect [dɪ'tekt]	*v.* 洞察（to discover the true character of）；查明，探测（to discover or determine the existence） 记 词根记忆：de（去掉）+ tect（=cover 遮盖）→ 去除遮盖 → 查明
detection [dɪ'tekʃn]	*n.* 查明，探测（the act of detecting） 记 来自 detect（*v.* 洞察；查明）
deter [dɪ'tɜːr]	*v.* 威慑，吓住（to discourage）；阻止（to inhibit） 记 词根记忆：de + ter（=terr 吓唬）→ 威慑，吓住 例 A major goal of law, to *deter* potential criminals by punishing wrongdoers, is not served when the penalty is so seldom invoked that it ceases to be a credible threat.
deteriorate [dɪ'tɪriəreɪt]	*v.* （使）变坏，恶化（to make inferior in quality or value） 记 词根记忆：de（向下）+ ter（=terr 地）+ iorate → 向着地面下降 →（使）变化，恶化 同 degenerate, descend, languish, weaken
determinant [dɪ'tɜːrmɪnənt]	*n.* 决定因素（sth. that determines or decides how sth. happens）*adj.* 决定性的（decisive） 记 来自 determine（*v.* 决定，下决心）
deterrent [dɪ'tɜːrənt]	*adj.* 威慑的，制止的（serving to deter） 记 来自 deter（*v.* 威慑，吓住）
detest [dɪ'test]	*v.* 厌恶，憎恨（to dislike intensely; hate; abhor） 记 联想记忆：de + test（测试）→ 有的学生十分憎恶测试 → 厌恶
detour ['diːtʊr]	*v.* 绕道，迂回 *n.* 弯路（a roundabout way）；绕行之路（a route used when the direct or regular route is not available） 记 联想记忆：de + tour（旅行，走）→ 绕着走 → 绕道 搭 detour around 绕行

6

detect

□ designate	□ desirable	□ despicable	□ despondent	□ destine	□ desultory
□ detect	□ detection	□ deter	□ deteriorate	□ determinant	□ deterrent
□ detest	□ detour				

detriment [ˈdetrɪmənt]	*n.* 损害，伤害(injury, damage) 记 词根记忆：de(加强) + tri(擦) + ment → 用力擦 → 损害
detrimental [ˌdetrɪˈmentl]	*adj.* 损害的，造成伤害的(causing detriment; harmful) 记 来自 detriment(*n.* 损害，伤害) 同 damaging, deleterious, injurious, mischievous, nocuous
devastate [ˈdevəsteɪt]	*v.* 摧毁，破坏(to ravage; destroy) 记 联想记忆：de(变坏) + vast(大量的) + ate → 大量弄坏 → 破坏 同 depredate, wreck
deviant [ˈdiːviənt]	*adj.* 越出常规的(deviating especially from an accepted norm) 记 词根记忆：de(偏离) + vi(路) + ant → 偏离道路 → 越轨 → 越出常规的
deviation [ˌdiːviˈeɪʃn]	*n.* 背离 (noticeable or marked departure from accepted norms of behavior) 同 aberration, deflection, divergence, diversion
devious [ˈdiːviəs]	*adj.* 不坦诚的(not straightforward or frank)；弯曲的，迂回的(roundabout; winding) 记 词根记忆：de(偏离) + vi(道路) + ous → 偏离正常道路的 → 弯曲的
devoid [dɪˈvɔɪd]	*adj.* 空的，全无的(empty or destitute of) 记 词根记忆：de + void(空的) → 空的 搭 be devoid of... 缺乏…
devour [dɪˈvaʊər]	*v.* 狼吞虎咽地吃，吞食(to eat or eat up hungrily)；贪婪地看(或听、读等) (to enjoy avidly) 记 词根记忆：de + vour(吃) → 吞食
devout [dɪˈvaʊt]	*adj.* 虔诚的(seriously concerned with religion)；忠诚的，忠心的(totally committed to a cause or a belief) 记 可能来自 devote(*v.* 投身于，献身)
dexterous [ˈdekstrəs]	*adj.* 灵巧的，熟练的(adroit; handy) 记 词根记忆：dexter(右手) + ous → 如右手般灵活的 → 灵巧的
diagnostic [ˌdaɪəɡˈnɑːstɪk]	*adj.* 诊断的(of, relating to, or used in diagnosis) *n.* 诊断(the art or practice of diagnosis)
dialect [ˈdaɪəlekt]	*n.* 方言(a form of a language used in a part of a country) 记 词根记忆：dia(对面) + lect(讲) → 对面讲话 → 方言
dichotomy [daɪˈkɑːtəmi]	*n.* 两分法；矛盾对立，分歧 (bifurcation)；具有两分特征的事物(sth. with seemingly contradictory qualities)
dictate [ˈdɪkteɪt]	*v.* 口述 (to speak or read aloud for sb. else to write down)；命令(to prescribe or command forcefully) 记 词根记忆：dict(讲话；命令) + ate → 口述；命令
didactic [daɪˈdæktɪk]	*adj.* 教诲的(morally instructive)；说教的(boringly pedantic or moralistic) 记 联想记忆：did(做) + act(行动) + ic → 教人如何做或行动 → 教诲的
die [daɪ]	*n.* 金属模子，金属印模(a block of hard metal with a design, etc. cut into it) 记 注意不是"死亡"的意思

diehard [ˈdaɪhɑːrd]	*n.* 顽固分子(a fanatically determined person) 记 组合词：die(死) + hard(硬的) → 死硬(分子) → 顽固分子
dietary [ˈdaɪəteri]	*adj.* 饮食的(of or relating to a diet or to the rules of a diet) 记 来自 diet(*n.* 饮食)
diffident [ˈdɪfɪdənt]	*adj.* 缺乏自信的(not showing much belief in one's own abilities) 同 bashful, coy, demure, modest, self-effacing
diffusion [dɪˈfjuːʒn]	*n.* 扩散，弥漫(diffuseness)；冗长(prolixity)；反射(reflection of light by a rough reflecting surface)；漫射(transmission of light through a translucent material; scattering)
digressive [daɪˈgresɪv]	*adj.* 离题的，枝节的(characterized by digressions) 搭 digressive remarks 离题的言论
dilapidated [dɪˈlæpɪdeɪtɪd]	*adj.* 破旧的，毁坏的(broken down; shabby and neglected) 记 词根记忆：di (=dis 分离) + lapid (石头) + ated → 石头裂或碎片的 → 毁坏的
dilate [daɪˈleɪt]	*v.* 使膨胀，使扩大(to swell; expand) 记 词根记忆：di + lat(搬运) + e → 分开搬运 → 使扩大；注意不要和 dilute(*v.* 冲淡，稀释)相混
dilatory [ˈdɪlətɔːri]	*adj.* 慢吞吞的，磨蹭的(inclined to delay; slow or late in doing things) 记 词根记忆：di + lat(搬运) + ory → 分开搬运 → 慢吞吞的
dilettante [ˌdɪləˈtænti]	*n.* 一知半解者，业余爱好者(dabbler; amateur) 记 词根记忆：di + let(=delect 引诱) + tante → 受到了诱惑 → 业余爱好者
diligent [ˈdɪlɪdʒənt]	*adj.* 勤奋的，勤勉的(characterized by steady, earnest, and energetic effort)
dilute [daɪˈluːt]	*v.* 稀释，冲淡(to thin down or weaken by mixing with water or other liquid) 记 词根记忆：di + lut(冲洗) + e → 冲开 → 稀释
diminish [dɪˈmɪnɪʃ]	*v.* (使)减少，缩小(to make less or cause to appear less, belittle, dwindle) 记 词根记忆：di + mini(小) + sh → 缩小
diminution [ˌdɪmɪˈnuːʃn]	*n.* 减少，缩减(a case or the state of diminishing or being diminished) 记 词根记忆：di + minu(变小，减少) + tion → 减少，缩减
diplomatic [ˌdɪpləˈmætɪk]	*adj.* 外交的；圆滑的(tactful and adroit; suave) 记 词根记忆：di(双，两) + plo(折叠) + matic → 有着双重手段的 → 外交的
disabuse [ˌdɪsəˈbjuːz]	*v.* 打消(某人的)错误念头，使醒悟(to rid of false ideas; undeceive) 记 联想记忆：dis(分离) + abuse(滥用，误用) → 解除错误 → 使醒悟 例 Although he attempted repeatedly to *disabuse* her of her conviction of his insincerity, he was not successful; she remained adamant in her judgment.

6

disarm [dɪsˈɑːrm]	*v.* 使缴械（to take weapons away from sb.）；使缓和（to make sb. less angry, hostile, etc） 记 联想记忆：dis(除去) + arm(武器) → 除去某人的武器 → 使缴械
disarray [ˌdɪsəˈreɪ]	*n.* 混乱，无秩序（an untidy condition；disorder；confusion） 记 联想记忆：dis(离开) + array(排列) → 没有进行排列 → 无秩序 例 Because of their frequent *disarray*, confusion, and loss of memory, those hit by lightning while alone are sometimes mistaken for victims of assault.
disavowal [ˌdɪsəˈvaʊəl]	*n.* 否认（repudiation） 记 词根记忆：dis(不) + a(=ad 向) + vow(=voc 叫喊) + al → 向人们大喊说不是 → 否认
discernible [dɪˈsɜːnəbl]	*adj.* 可识别的，可辨的（being recognized or identified） 记 联想记忆：discern(洞悉，辨别) + ible(可…的) → 可识别的，可辨的 例 Many of the earliest colonial houses that are still standing have been so modified and enlarged that the initial design is no longer *discernible*.
discharge [dɪsˈtʃɑːrdʒ]	*v.* 排出，流出（to emit）；释放（to officially allow sb. to leave）；解雇(to dismiss from employment)；履行义务(to carry out duty)；放电(to release electrical energy) 记 联想记忆：dis(离开) + charge(充电) → 放电
disciple [dɪˈsaɪpl]	*n.* 信徒，弟子（a convinced adherent of a school or individual） 记 和 discipline(*n.* 纪律)一起记；信徒(disciple)必须遵守纪律(discipline)
discipline [ˈdɪsəplɪn]	*n.* 纪律（a rule or system of rules governing conduct or activity)；惩罚，处分(punishment) *v.* 训练，训导(to train or develop by instruction and exercise especially in self-control) 记 联想记忆：dis(不) + cip + line(线) → 不站成一线就要受惩罚 → 惩罚 同 educate
discomfit [dɪsˈkʌmfɪt]	*v.* 使难堪，使困惑（to make uneasy；disconcert；embarrass） 记 联想记忆：dis(不) + comfit(看作 comfort，舒适) → 使不舒服 → 使难堪
discomfited [dɪsˈkʌmfɪtɪd]	*adj.* 困惑的，尴尬的（frustrated；embarrassed） 例 While not completely nonplussed by the unusually caustic responses from members of the audience, the speaker was nonetheless visibly *discomfited* by their lively criticism.
discomfort [dɪsˈkʌmfərt]	*v.* 使不适（to make uncomfortable or uneasy） *n.* 不适（mental or physical uneasiness）
disconsolate [dɪsˈkɑːnsələt]	*adj.* 闷闷不乐的，郁郁寡欢的（cheerless, dejected, downcast） 记 词根记忆：dis(不) + con + sol(安慰) + ate → 没有安慰的 → 闷闷不乐的
discontent [ˌdɪskənˈtent]	*n.* 不满（lack of contentment） *v.* 使不满（to make discontented） *adj.* 不满的（discontented）

discount [ˈdɪskaʊnt]	*n.* 折扣 (amount of money taken off the cost of sth.) 记 词根记忆：dis (除去) + count (数量) → 除去一定的数 → 打折 → 折扣
discourage [dɪsˈkɜːrɪdʒ]	*v.* 使气馁，使沮丧 (to deprive of courage or confidence)；阻碍 (to dissuade or attempt to dissuade from doing sth.) 记 联想记忆：dis (消失) + courage (精神) → 使精神消失 → 使沮丧
discouraging [dɪsˈkɜːrɪdʒɪŋ]	*adj.* 令人气馁的 (making sb. lose the confidence or determination)
discourse [ˈdɪskɔːrs]	*n.* 演讲，论述 (a long and formal treatment of a subject, in speech or writing; dissertation) 记 联想记忆：dis + course (课程) → 进行课堂演讲 → 演讲
discourteous [dɪsˈkɜːrtiəs]	*adj.* 失礼的，粗鲁的 (lacking courtesy) 记 联想记忆：dis (离开) + court (宫庭) + eous → 远离宫庭的 → 村野匹夫的 → 失礼的，粗鲁的
discredit [dɪsˈkredɪt]	*v.* 怀疑 (to reject as untrue; disbelieve) *n.* 丧失名誉 (disgrace; dishonor) 记 词根记忆：dis (不) + cred (相信) + it → 不相信 → 怀疑
discreet [dɪˈskriːt]	*adj.* 小心的，言行谨慎的 (prudent; modest) 记 词根记忆：dis + creet (分辨) → 分辨出不同来 → 小心的；注意不要和 discrete (*adj.* 个别的) 相混 同 calculating, cautious, chary, circumspect, gingerly
discrete [dɪˈskriːt]	*adj.* 个别的，分离的 (individual; separate)；不连续的 (made up of distinct parts; discontinuous) 记 词根记忆：dis (分离) + cre (生产) + te → 个别的，分离的 同 different, diverse, several, various
discretion [dɪˈskreʃn]	*n.* 谨慎，审慎 同 circumspection, prudence
discriminatory [dɪˈskrɪmɪnətɔːri]	*adj.* 歧视的，差别对待的，偏见的 (showing prejudice) 记 来自 discriminate (*v.* 歧视，差别对待)
discursive [dɪsˈkɜːrsɪv]	*adj.* 散漫的，不得要领的 (rambling or wandering from topic to topic without order) 记 词根记忆：dis + curs (跑) + ive → 到处乱跑 → 散漫的
disdain [dɪsˈdeɪn]	*v.* 轻视，鄙视 (to refuse or reject with aloof contempt or scorn) *n.* 轻视，鄙视 (contempt) 记 词根记忆：dis (不) + dain (=dign 高贵) → 把人弄得不高贵 → 轻视 搭 disdain for 轻视 同 contemn, despise
disenfranchise [ˌdɪsɪnˈfræntʃaɪz]	*v.* 剥夺…的权利 (to deprive of a franchise, of a legal right, or of some privilege or immunity)

discount

50% off 30% off

6

disgruntled [dɪs'ɡrʌntld]	*adj.* 不悦的，不满意的(annoyed or disappointed) 记 联想记忆：dis(不) + gruntle(使高兴) + d → 使不高兴的 → 不悦的
disillusion [ˌdɪsɪ'luːʒn]	*v.* 使梦想破灭，使醒悟(to cause to lose naive faith and trust) 记 联想记忆：dis(不)+illusion(幻想) → 不再有幻想 → 使梦想破灭，使醒悟
disinclination [ˌdɪsɪnklɪ'neɪʃn]	*n.* 不愿意，不情愿(a preference for avoiding sth.) 同 aversion, disfavor, dislike, disrelish, dissatisfaction
disingenuous [ˌdɪsɪn'dʒenjuəs]	*adj.* 不坦率的(lacking in candor) 记 词根记忆：dis(不) + in + gen(出生) + uous → 失去刚出生时的状态 → 不坦率的
disinterest [dɪs'ɪntrəst]	*v.* 使失去兴趣(to cause to regard sth. with no interest or concern) *n.* 无兴趣(lack of interest) 搭 disinterest in... 对…无兴趣
disinterested [dɪs'ɪntrəstɪd]	*adj.* 公正的，客观的(impartial; unbiased) 记 注意区别 uninterested(*adj.* 不感兴趣的) 搭 be disinterested in... 对…客观的、公正的；disinterested attitude 公正的态度 同 detached, dispassionate, neutral
disjunctive [dɪs'dʒʌŋktɪv]	*adj.* 分离的；转折的，反意的(showing opposition or contrast between two ideas) 记 词根记忆：dis(分离) + junct(捆绑) + ive → 分开绑的 → 分离的；转折的
dismal ['dɪzməl]	*adj.* 沮丧的，阴沉的(showing sadness) 记 来自拉丁文 dies mail，意为"不吉利的日子"，后转变为"沮丧的，阴沉的"的意思 例 Despite a string of *dismal* earnings reports, the two-year-old strategy to return the company to profitability is beginning to work.
dismember [dɪs'membər]	*v.* 肢解(to cut off or disjoin the limbs, members, or parts of)；分割(to break up or tear into pieces)
dismiss [dɪs'mɪs]	*v.* 解散(to permit or cause to leave)；解雇(to remove from position or service) 记 词根记忆：dis(分开) + miss(送，放出) → 解散
disorganize [dɪs'ɔːɡənaɪz]	*v.* 扰乱，使混乱(to destroy or interrupt the orderly structure or function of)
disparage [dɪ'spærɪdʒ]	*v.* 贬低，轻蔑(to speak slightingly of; depreciate; decry) 记 词根记忆：dis(除去) + par(平等) + age → 剥夺平等 → 贬低 同 belittle, derogate
disparate ['dɪspərət]	*adj.* 迥然不同的(essentially not alike; distinct or different in kind) 记 dis(不) + par(平等) + ate → 不等的 → 迥然不同的
dispassionate [dɪs'pæʃənət]	*adj.* 平心静气的(free from passion, emotion, or bias) 记 联想记忆：dis(不) + passionate(激情的) → 不表现激情的 → 平心静气的

dispel [dɪˈspel]	*v.* 驱散，消除 (to scatter and drive away；disperse) 记 词根记忆：dis(分开) + pel(推) → 推开 → 驱散
dispensable [dɪˈspensəbl]	*adj.* 不必要的，可有可无的 (capable of being dispensed with) 记 词根记忆：dis(分离) + pens(重量) + able → 重量可被分割的 → 不必要的
disperse [dɪˈspɜːrs]	*v.* 消散，驱散 (to spread or distribute from a fixed or constant source) 记 词根记忆：di(分开) + spers(散开) + e → 分散开 → 驱散 同 dispel, dissipate, scatter
disposable [dɪˈspoʊzəbl]	*adj.* 一次性的 (made to be thrown away after use)；可自由使用的 (available for use)
disproportionate [ˌdɪsprəˈpɔːrʃənət]	*adj.* 不成比例的 (being out of proportion) 记 联想记忆：dis(不) + proportion(比例) + ate → 不成比例的
disprove [ˌdɪsˈpruːv]	*v.* 证明…有误 (to show that sth. is wrong) 记 词根记忆：dis(分离) + prov(试验) + e → 经试验后被否定 → 证明…有误
disputable [dɪˈspjuːtəbl]	*adj.* 有争议的 (not definitely true or right, arguable) 同 debatable
dispute [dɪˈspjuːt]	*v.* 争论 (to argue about；debate) 记 词根记忆：dis + put (思考) + e → 思考相悖 → 争论
disrupt [dɪsˈrʌpt]	*v.* 使混乱 (to cause disorder in sth.)；使中断 (to break apart) 记 词根记忆：dis(分开) + rupt(断) → 使断裂开 → 使中断
dissect [dɪˈsekt]	*v.* 解剖 (to cut up a dead body)；剖析 (to analyze and interpret minutely) 记 词根记忆：dis(分开) + sect(切) → 切开 → 解剖 同 dichotomize, disjoin, disjoint, dissever, separate
disseminate [dɪˈsemɪneɪt]	*v.* 传播，宣传 (to spread abroad；promulgate widely) 记 词根记忆：dis(分开) + semin(种子) + ate → 散布(种子) → 传播
dissent [dɪˈsent]	*n.* 异议 (difference of opinion) *v.* 不同意，持异议 (to differ in belief or opinion；disagree) 记 词根记忆：dis(分开) + sent(感觉) → 感觉不同 → 不同意 例 Even though political editorializing was not forbidden under the new regime, journalists still experienced discreet, though perceptible, governmental pressure to limit *dissent*.
dissident [ˈdɪsɪdənt]	*n.* 唱反调者 (a person who disagrees；dissenter) 记 词根记忆：dis(分开) + sid(坐) + ent → 分开坐的人 → 唱反调者
dissimilar [dɪˈsɪmɪlər]	*adj.* 不同的，不相似的 (unlike) 同 different, disparate, distant, divergent, diverse
dissipate [ˈdɪsɪpeɪt]	*v.* (使)消失，(使)消散 (to break up and scatter or vanish)；浪费 (to waste or squander) 记 联想记忆：dis (表加强) + sip (喝，饮) + ate → 到处吃喝 → 浪费；sip 本身是一个常考单词

6

dispute

□ dispel	□ dispensable	□ disperse	□ disposable	□ disproportionate	□ disprove
□ disputable	□ dispute	□ disrupt	□ dissect	□ disseminate	□ dissent
□ dissident	□ dissimilar	□ dissipate			

61

dissolve [dɪˈzɑːlv]	*v.* （使）溶解（to make a solid become liquid） 记 词根记忆：dis（分开）+ solv（松开）+ e → 松开 →（使）溶解
dissonant [ˈdɪsənənt]	*adj.* 不和谐的，不一致的（opposing in opinion, temperament; discordant） 记 词根记忆：dis（分开）+ son（声音）+ ant → 声音分散的 → 不和谐的
distant [ˈdɪstənt]	*adj.* 疏远的，冷淡的（reserved or aloof in personal relationship） 记 词根记忆：dis（分开）+ tant → 分开了的 → 疏远的 同 insociable, unsociable
distasteful [dɪsˈteɪstfl]	*adj.* （令人）不愉快的，讨厌的（unpleasant; disagreeable） 记 联想记忆：dis（不）+ tasteful（好吃的）→ 不好吃的 → 讨厌的
distent [dɪsˈtent]	*adj.* 膨胀的（swollen）；扩张的（expanded） 记 词根记忆：dis（分开）+ tent（延伸）→ 向外延伸的 → 扩张的
distinct [dɪˈstɪŋkt]	*adj.* 清楚的，明显的（definite; evident） 记 词根记忆：di（分开）+ stinct（刺）→ 把刺分开 → 与众不同的 → 明显
distinctive [dɪˈstɪŋktɪv]	*adj.* 出众的，有特色的（distinguishing; characteristic or typical）
distinguish [dɪˈstɪŋgwɪʃ]	*v.* 成为…的特征，使有别于（to mark as separate or different）；把…分类（to separate into kinds, classes, or categories）；区别，辨别（to discern） 记 词根记忆：di（分开）+ sting（刺）+ uish → 将刺挑出来 → 区别，辨别
distort [dɪˈstɔːrt]	*v.* 扭曲，弄歪（to twist sth. out of its usual shape） 记 词根记忆：dis（坏）+ tort（扭曲）→ 扭坏了 → 弄歪 同 contort, deform, misshape, torture, warp
distortion [dɪˈstɔːrʃn]	*n.* 扭曲（the act of distorting）；曲解（a statement that twists fact; misrepresentation）
distraught [dɪˈstrɔːt]	*adj.* 心神狂乱的，发狂的（mentally confused）；心烦意乱的（distressed） 记 由 distract（*v.* 分散注意力；使不安）变化而来

dissolve

Word List 7

distribute [dɪˈstrɪbjuːt]	*v.* 分发，分配（to separate sth. into part and give a share to each person） 记 词根记忆：dis(分开) + tribut(给予) + e → 分开给 → 分发
diurnal [daɪˈɜːrnl]	*adj.* 白昼的，白天的（of daytime） 记 词根记忆：di(白天) + urnal(…的) → 白天的
diverge [daɪˈvɜːrdʒ]	*v.* 分歧，分开（to go or move in different directions；deviate） 记 词根记忆：di(离开) + verg(转向) + e → 转开 → 分歧
divergent [daɪˈvɜːrdʒənt]	*adj.* 分叉的，叉开的（diverging from each other）；发散的，扩散的；不同的 记 词根记忆：di(二) + verg(倾斜) + ent → 向两边倾斜的 → 发散的 同 disparate, dissimilar, distant, diverse
diverse [daɪˈvɜːrs]	*adj.* 不同的（different；dissimilar）；多样的（diversified） 记 词根记忆：di（离开）+ vers（转）+ e → 转开 → 不同的 同 disparate, distant, divergent diverse
diversify [daɪˈvɜːrsɪfaɪ]	*v.* (使)多样化（to give variety to） 记 来自 diverse(*adj.* 多样的)
divert [daɪˈvɜːrt]	*v.* 转移，(使)转向（to turn from one course to another）；使娱乐（to entertain） 记 词根记忆：di(离开) + vert(转) → (使)转向
dividend [ˈdɪvɪdend]	*n.* 红利，股利（bonus） 记 词根记忆：di(分开) + vid(看) + end → 往不同方向看 → 红利
divisive [dɪˈvaɪsɪv]	*adj.* 引起分歧的，导致分裂的（creating disunity or dissension） 记 词根记忆：di(分开) + vis(看) + ive → 往不同方向看的 → 引起分歧的
divulge [daɪˈvʌldʒ]	*v.* 泄露，透露（to make known；disclose） 记 词根记忆：di(分离) + vulg(人们) → 使从秘密状态中脱离并被人们知道 → 透露 同 betray, reveal
docile [ˈdɑːsl]	*adj.* 驯服的，听话的（(of a person or an animal) easy to control） 记 词根记忆：doc(教导) + ile(能…的) → 能教的 → 听话的

☐ distribute	☐ diurnal	☐ diverge	☐ divergent	☐ diverse	☐ diversify
☐ divert	☐ dividend	☐ divisive	☐ divulge	☐ docile	

	例 He was habitually so *docile* and accommodating that his friends could not understand his sudden outburst against his employers.
doctrinaire [ˌdɑːktrə'ner]	*n.* 教条主义者(one who attempts to put into effect an abstract doctrine) *adj.* 教条的，迂腐的(stubbornly adhering to a doctrine) 记 来自 doctrine(*n.* 教条) 同 authoritarian, authoritative, dictatorial, dogmatic
doctrine ['dɑːktrɪn]	*n.* 教义，教条，主义，学说(a set of beliefs held by a church, political party, group of scientists, etc.) 记 词根记忆：doc(教导) + trine → 教义
document	['dɑːkjumənt] *n.* 文件(an original or official paper) ['dɑːkjument] *v.* 为…提供书面证明(to prove or support with documents) 同 certification, documentation, monument
dogged ['dɔːgɪd]	*adj.* 顽强的(stubborn; tenacious) 记 联想记忆：dog(狗) + ged → 像狗一样顽强 → 顽强的
dogma ['dɔːgmə]	*n.* 教条，信条(doctrine; principle)
dogmatist ['dɔːgmətɪst]	*n.* 独断家，独断论者(one who dogmatizes) 记 来自 dogma(*n.* 教条，信条)
domain [douˈmeɪn]	*n.* 领土(territory; dominion)；领域(field or sphere of activity or influence) 记 词根记忆：dom(家) + ain → 领土；领域
domesticated [dəˈmestɪkeɪtɪd]	*adj.* 驯养的，家养的 记 词根记忆：dom(家) + esticated → 家养的
dominate ['dɑːmɪneɪt]	*v.* 控制，支配(to control, govern or rule) 记 词根记忆：domin(支配) + ate → 控制，支配 同 direct, handle, manage, predominate
domination [ˌdɑːmɪˈneɪʃn]	*n.* 控制，支配，管辖(exercise of mastery or ruling power) 记 词根记忆：domin(支配) + ation → 控制，支配，管辖
domineer [ˌdɑːmɪˈnɪə]	*v.* 压制(to exercise arbitrary or overbearing control; tyrannize over) 同 dominate, predominate, preponderate, prevail, reign
dormant ['dɔːrmənt]	*adj.* 冬眠的(torpid in winter)；静止的(quiet; still) 记 词根记忆：dorm(睡眠) + ant → 冬眠的
dorsal ['dɔːrsl]	*adj.* 背部的，背脊的(of, on, or near the back) 记 词根记忆：dors(背) + al → 背部的
dose [dous]	*n.* 剂量，(一)剂(an exact amount of a medicine) 记 词根记忆：dos(给予) + e → 给予力量 → 剂量
dossier ['dɔːsieɪ]	*n.* 卷宗，档案(a collection of documents and reports) 记 发音记忆："东西压" → 被东西压着的东西 → 堆在一起的档案 → 档案
down [daʊn]	*n.* 绒毛(a covering of soft fluffy feathers)；软毛(fine soft hair)

downfall ['daʊnfɔːl]	*n.* 垮台(a sudden fall) 同 overthrow, upset
downplay [ˌdaʊn'pleɪ]	*v.* 贬低，不予重视(to belittle) 记 组合词：down(向下) + play(玩) → 玩下去 → 不予重视
drab [dræb]	*adj.* 黄褐色的(of a dull yellowish brown)；单调的，乏味的(not bright or lively; monotonous) 例 Thomas Paine, whose political writing was often flamboyant, was in private life a surprisingly simple man: he lived in rented rooms, ate little, and wore *drab* clothes.
draft [dræft]	*n.* 草稿，草案(preliminary written version of sth.)；汇票(written order to a bank to pay money to sb.)
dramatic [drə'mætɪk]	*adj.* 戏剧的 (of or relating to the drama)；引人注目的 (striking in appearance or effect)；戏剧般的(of an opera singer) 记 来自 drama(*n.* 戏剧) 同 dramaturgic, histrionic, theatric, theatrical, thespian
drastic ['dræstɪk]	*adj.* 猛烈的，激烈的(strong; violent and severe) 搭 a drastic change 剧烈的变化
drizzly ['drɪzli]	*adj.* 毛毛细雨的 记 注意该单词虽以-ly 结尾，但不是副词，而是形容词
drollery ['droʊləri]	*n.* 滑稽(quaint or wry humor) 记 来自 droll(*adj.* 滑稽的)
drone [droʊn]	*v.* 嗡嗡地响(to make monotonous humming or buzzing sound)；单调地说 (to speak in a monotonous tone) *n.* 单调的低音(a bass voice)
drowsy ['draʊzi]	*adj.* 昏昏欲睡的(ready to fall asleep) 记 来自 drowse(*v.* 打瞌睡)
drudgery ['drʌdʒəri]	*n.* 苦工，苦活(dull and fatiguing work) 记 来自 drudge(*v.* 做苦工)
dual ['duːəl]	*adj.* 双重的(having or composed of two parts) 记 词根记忆：du(二，双) + al → 两个的 → 双重的
dubious ['duːbiəs]	*adj.* 可疑的(slightly suspicious about)；有问题的，靠不住的(questionable or suspect as to true nature or quality) 记 词根记忆：dub (二，双) + ious → 两种状态 → 不肯定的，怀疑的 → 可疑的 同 disputable, dubitable, equivocal, problematic dubious
ductile ['dʌktaɪl]	*adj.* 易延展的(capable of being stretched)；可塑的(easily molded; pliable) 记 词根记忆：duct(引导) + ile → 易引导的 → 可塑的

7

dull	*adj.* 不鲜明的(not bright)；迟钝的 (mentally slow)；乏味的 *v.* 变迟钝(to become dull)
[dʌl]	记 联想记忆：和充实的(full)相反的是乏味的(dull)
	同 blunt, doltish, imbecile, moronic, obtuse
dumbbell-like	*adj.* 哑铃状的
[ˈdʌmbelˌlaɪk]	记 组合词：dumbell(哑铃) + like(像) → 哑铃状的
dumbfound	*v.* 使…惊讶(to astonish)
[dʌmˈfaʊnd]	记 组合词：dumb(哑) + found(被发现) → 惊讶得说不出话来 → 使…惊讶
	同 amaze, astound
dupe	*n.* 易上当者(a person easily tricked or fooled)
[duːp]	记 发音记忆："丢谱" → 瞎摆谱，结果上了当，丢了面子 → 易上当者
duplicate	[ˈduːplɪkət] *adj.* 复制的，两重的(consisting of or existing in two corresponding or identical parts or examples)
	[ˈduːplɪkeɪt] *v.* 复制(to make double) *n.* 复制品，副本(an additional copy of sth. already in a collection; counterpart)
	同 reduplicate, replicate, reproduce
duplicity	*n.* 欺骗，口是心非(hypocritical cunning or deception)
[duːˈplɪsəti]	记 词根记忆：du(二) + plic(重叠) + ity → 有两种(态度) → 口是心非
	同 deceit, dissemblance, dissimulation, guile
durable	*adj.* 持久的(lasting)；耐用的 (able to exist for a long time without significant deterioration)
[ˈdʊrəbl]	记 词根记忆：dur(持续) + able → 持久的
dutiful	*adj.* 尽职的(filled with a sense of duty)
[ˈduːtɪfl]	记 来自duty(*n.* 责任)
dwindle	*v.* 变小，减少(to diminish; shrink; decrease)
[ˈdwɪndl]	记 联想记忆：d + wind(风) + le → 随风而去，越来越小 → 变小；注意不要和swindle(*n./v.* 欺骗，诈骗)相混
	同 abate, bate, wane
dynamic	*adj.* 动态的(opposed to static)；有活力的(energetic; vigorous)
[daɪˈnæmɪk]	记 词根记忆：dynam(力量) + ic → 有活力的
dysfunctional	*adj.* 功能失调的(functioning abnormally)
[dɪsˈfʌŋkʃənl]	记 联想记忆：dys(坏) + function(功能) + al → 功能坏了的 → 功能失调的
earnest	*adj.* 诚挚的，认真的(showing deep sincerity or seriousness)
[ˈɜːrnɪst]	记 联想记忆：earn(挣钱) + est → 要想挣钱就得认真地干 → 认真的
earthiness	*n.* 土质，土性(the state of earth)
[ˈɜːrθinəs]	记 来自earthy(*adj.* 泥土的，土的)
ebb	*v.* 退潮(to recede from the flood)；衰退(to decline; wane)
[eb]	记 发音记忆："二步" → 退后一步 → 衰退
eccentric	*adj.* 古怪的，反常的(deviating from the norm; unconventional)；(指圆形)没有共同圆心的 *n.* 古怪的人(an eccentric person)
[ɪkˈsentrɪk]	记 词根记忆：ec(出) + centr(中心) + ic → 离开中心 → 古怪的

□ dull	□ dumbbell-like	□ dumbfound	□ dupe	□ duplicate	□ duplicity
□ durable	□ dutiful	□ dwindle	□ dynamic	□ dysfunctional	□ earnest
□ earthiness	□ ebb	□ eccentric			

	例 In Germany her startling powers as a novelist are widely admired, but she is almost unknown in the English-speaking world because of the difficulties of translating her *eccentric* prose.
echo [ˈekoʊ]	*n.* 回声(the repetition of a sound caused by reflection of sound waves); 反响(reflection, repercussion, result, response); 共鸣(a sympathetic response) *v.* 回响, 回荡(to resound with echoes); 重复, 模仿(to repeat; imitate) 搭 an echo of... 对…共鸣 同 reverberate
eclectic [ɪˈklektɪk]	*adj.* 折衷的; 兼容并蓄的(selecting the best from various systems, doctrines, or sources) 记 词根记忆: ec(出) + lect(选) + ic → 选出的 → 折衷的 例 Although *eclectic* in her own responses to the plays she reviewed, the theatre critic was, paradoxically, suspicious of those who would deny that a reviewer must have a single method of interpretation.
eclipse [ɪˈklɪps]	*n.* 日食, 月食; 黯然失色, 衰退(a fall into obscurity or disuse; a decline) 记 联想记忆: ec + lipse(看作 lapse, 滑走) → 日月的光华滑走 → 日食, 月食
ecological [ˌiːkəˈlɑːdʒɪkl]	*adj.* 生态的; 生态学的 例 With the evolution of wings, insects were able to disperse to the far *ecological* comers, across deserts and bodies of water, to reach new food sources and inhabit a wider variety of promising environmental niches.
economize [ɪˈkɑːnəmaɪz]	*v.* 节约, 节省(to save) 记 来自 economy(*adj.* 经济的 *n.* 节约)
economy [ɪˈkɑːnəmi]	*n.* 节约(thrifty and efficient use of material resources); 经济(the structure or conditions of economic life) *adj.* 经济的(designed to save money) 记 发音记忆: "依靠农民" → 中国是农业大国, 经济发展离不开农民 → 经济 同 frugality
edifice [ˈedɪfɪs]	*n.* 宏伟的建筑(如宫殿、教堂等)(a large, imposing building) 记 词根记忆: edi(建筑) + fic(做) + e → 宏伟的建筑
edify [ˈedɪfaɪ]	*v.* 陶冶, 启发(to enlighten, or uplift morally or spiritually) 记 词根记忆: ed(吃) + ify(表动作) → 吃下去 → 陶冶, 启发 同 illume, illuminate, illumine
efface [ɪˈfeɪs]	*v.* 擦掉, 抹去(to wipe out; erase) 记 词根记忆: ef + fac(脸, 表面) + e → 从表面去掉 → 擦掉
effective [ɪˈfektɪv]	*adj.* 有效的, 生效的(producing a decided, decisive, or desired effect); 给人印象深刻的(impressive; striking) 记 来自 effect(*n.* 影响, 效果)
effervescence [ˌefərˈvesns]	*n.* 冒泡(bubbling, hissing, and foaming as gas escapes); 活泼(liveliness or exhilaration) 同 buoyancy, ebullience, exuberance, exuberancy

7

effete	*adj.* 无生产力的(spent and sterile); 虚弱的(lacking vigor)
[ɪˈfiːt]	记 词根记忆：ef(没有) + fet(生产性的) + e → 无生产力的
efficacious	*adj.* 有效的(producing the desired result)
[ˌefɪˈkeɪʃəs]	例 If *efficacious* new medicines have side effects that are commonly observed and unremarkable, such medicines are too often considered safe, even when laboratory tests suggest caution.
efficacy	*n.* 功效, 有效性(the power to produce an effect)
[ˈefɪkəsi]	记 词根记忆：ef(出) + fic(做) + acy → 做出了成绩 → 功效, 有效性
	同 capability, effectiveness, efficiency
egalitarian	*adj.* 主张人人平等的(advocating the belief that all people should have equal rights)
[iˌgælɪˈteriən]	记 词根记忆：egalit(平等的) + arian → 主张人人平等的；该词等同于 equalitarian(*adj.* 平等主义的)
egocentric	*adj.* 利己的(self-centered)
[ˌiːgoʊˈsentrɪk]	记 词根记忆：ego(我) + centr(中心) + ic → 以自我为中心的 → 利己的
egoist	*n.* 自我主义者(a believer in egoism)
[ˈiːgoʊɪst]	记 来自 ego(*n.* 自我)
egoistic(al)	*adj.* 自我中心的, 自私自利的(of or relating to the self)
[ˌegoʊˈɪstɪk(l)]	同 egocentric, egomaniacal, self-centered, selfish
egregious	*adj.* 极端恶劣的(conspicuously bad; flagrant)
[ɪˈgriːdʒiəs]	记 词根记忆：e(出) + greg(团体) + ious → 超出一般人 → 极端恶劣的
elaborate	[ɪˈlæbərət] *adj.* 精致的, 复杂的(marked by complexity, fullness of detail, or ornateness)
	[ɪˈlæbəreɪt] *v.* 详尽地说明, 阐明(to describe in detail)
	记 联想记忆：e(出) + labor(劳动) + ate(使) → 辛苦劳动做出来的 → 精心制作的 → 精致的
elapse	*v.* 消逝, 过去(to pass; go by) *n.* 消逝(passage)
[ɪˈlæps]	记 词根记忆：e(出) + laps(落下) + e → 滑落 → 消逝
elate	*v.* 使高兴, 使得意(to fill with joy or pride)
[iˈleɪt]	同 commove, exhilarate, intoxicate
electromagnetic	*adj.* 电磁的(of, relating to, or produced by electromagnetism)
[ɪˌlektroʊmægˈnetɪk]	记 词根记忆：electr(电) + o + magnetic(磁的) → 电磁的
elegiac	*adj.* 哀歌的, 挽歌的(of, relating to, or involving elegy or mourning or expressing sorrow for that which is irrecoverably past) *n.* 哀歌, 挽歌(elegy)
[ˌelɪˈdʒaɪək]	
elementary	*adj.* 初级的(in the beginning stages of a course of study)
[ˌelɪˈmentri]	同 basal, elemental, fundamental, primitive, rudimental
elicit	*v.* 得出, 引出(to draw forth or bring out)
[iˈlɪsɪt]	记 词根记忆：e(出) + licit(引导) → 引出

eligible [ˈelɪdʒəbl]	*adj.* 合格的，有资格的（qualified to be chosen; suitable） 记 词根记忆：e + lig(=lect 选择) + ible → 能被选出来的 → 合格的
eliminate [ɪˈlɪmɪneɪt]	*v.* 除去，淘汰（to remove; eradicate） 记 联想记忆：e(出) + limin(看作 limit，界限) + ate → 划到界限之外 → 除去，淘汰 同 debar, exclude, purge
elite [eɪˈliːt]	*n.* 精英；主力，中坚（the group regarded as the best and most powerful） 记 词根记忆：e + lit(=lig 选择) + e → 选出来的 → 精英
elongate [ɪˈlɔːŋgeɪt]	*v.* 延长，伸长（to extend the length of） 记 词根记忆：e + long(长的) + ate → 向外变长 → 伸长
eloquent [ˈeləkwənt]	*adj.* 雄辩的，流利的（marked by forceful and fluent expression） 记 词根记忆：e + loqu(说) + ent(…的) → 能说会道的 → 雄辩的 同 articulate
elucidate [iˈluːsɪdeɪt]	*v.* 阐明，说明（to give a clarifying explanation） 记 词根记忆：e + luc(清晰的) + id + ate → 弄清晰 → 阐明
elude [iˈluːd]	*v.* 逃避（to avoid adroitly）；搞不清，理解不了（to escape the perception or understanding） 记 词根记忆：e + lud(玩弄) + e → 通过玩弄的方式出去 → 逃避 同 eschew, evade, shun
elusive [iˈluːsɪv]	*adj.* 难懂的，难以描述的（hard to comprehend or define）；不易被抓获的（tending to evade grasp or pursuit） 记 词根记忆：e(出) + lus(光) + ive → 没有灵光出来的 → 难懂的 例 The guerrillas were so *elusive* that the general had to develop various strategies to trap them.
emancipate [ɪˈmænsɪpeɪt]	*v.* 解放，释放（to free from restraint） 记 词根记忆：e + man(手) + cip(落下) + ate → 使从手中落下 → 解放
embed [ɪmˈbed]	*v.* 牢牢插入，使嵌入（to set or fix firmly in a surrounding mass; wedge） 记 联想记忆：em(进入) + bed(床) → 深深进入内部 → 牢牢插入
embellish [ɪmˈbelɪʃ]	*v.* 装饰，美化（to make beautiful with ornamentation; decorate） 记 词根记忆：em + bell(美的) + ish → 使…美丽 → 装饰，美化
embellishment [ɪmˈbelɪʃmənt]	*n.* 装饰；装饰品（ornament） 同 decoration
embezzlement [ɪmˈbezlmənt]	*n.* 贪污，盗用（act of using money that is placed in one's care in a wrong way to benefit oneself） 记 联想记忆：em + bezzle(看作 bezzant，金银币) + ment → 将金钱据为己有 → 贪污，盗用 例 The bank teller's *embezzlement* of the funds was not discovered until the auditors examined the accounts.

eloquent

| **emblematic** | *adj.* 作为象征的(symbolic; representative) |
| [ˌembləˈmætɪk] | 记 来自 emblem(*n.* 象征) |

| **embrace** | *v.* 拥抱 (to take a person into one's arms as a sign of affection); 包含(to take in or include as a part) |
| [ɪmˈbreɪs] | 记 词根记忆:em(进入) + brac(胳膊) + e → 进入怀抱 → 拥抱 |

| **embroider** | *v.* 刺绣, 镶边(to ornament with needlework); 装饰(to provide embellishments) |
| [ɪmˈbrɔɪdər] | 记 联想记忆:em + broider(刺绣) → 刺绣 |

| **embryological** | *adj.* 胚胎学的 |
| [ˌembriəˈlɑːdʒɪkl] | 记 联想记忆:embryo(胚胎) + olog(y)(…学) + ical → 胚胎学的 |

| **embryonic** | *adj.* 胚胎的; 萌芽期的(incipient; rudimentary) |
| [ˌembriˈɑːnɪk] | 记 来自 embryo(*n.* 胚胎); em + bryo(变大) → (种子)变大 → 胚胎 |

| **emend** | *v.* 订正, 校订(to make scholarly corrections) |
| [iˈmend] | 记 词根记忆:e(出) + mend(错误) → 找出错误 → 订正 |

| **eminence** | *n.* 卓越, 显赫, 杰出(a position of prominence or superiority) |
| [ˈemɪnəns] | 同 distinction, illustriousness, preeminence |

eminent	*adj.* 显赫的, 杰出的(prominent; conspicuous)
[ˈemɪnənt]	记 词根记忆:e + min(突出) + ent → 突出来 → 显赫的
	例 The *eminent* ambassador was but an indifferent linguist; yet he insisted on speaking to foreign dignitaries in their own tongues without resorting to a translator's aid.

| **empathy** | *n.* 同感, 移情(作用)(the mental ability of sharing other people's ideas and feelings); 全神贯注 |
| [ˈempəθi] | 记 词根记忆:em + path(感情) + y → 感情移入 → 移情 |

| **emphatic** | *adj.* 重视的, 强调的(showing or using emphasis) |
| [ɪmˈfætɪk] | 记 词根记忆:em(表加强) + pha(说话) + tic → 用力说话的 → 重视的, 强调的 |

| **empirically** | *adv.* 凭经验地(in an empirical manner) |
| [ɪmˈpɪrɪkli] | 记 词根记忆:em(在里面) + pir(实验) + ical + ly → 在内部进行严密的实验 → 凭经验地 |

| **empiricism** | *n.* 经验主义(the practice of relying on observation and experiment) |
| [ɪmˈpɪrɪsɪzəm] | 记 来自 empiric(*n.* 经验主义者) |

| **empty** | *adj.* 空的, 缺乏的(containing nothing; null; hollow) *v.* (使)变空, 把…弄空(to make empty; become empty) |
| [ˈempti] | 同 idle, vacant, vacuous, void |

| **emulate** | *v.* 与…竞争, 努力赶上(to strive to equal or excel) |
| [ˈemjuleɪt] | 记 词根记忆:em(模仿) + ulate → 与…竞争 |

enamored	*adj.* 倾心的, 被迷住(inflamed with love; fascinated)
[ɪˈnæmərd]	记 词根记忆:en + amor(爱) + ed → 珍爱的 → 倾心的
	搭 be enamored of... 珍爱…, 喜爱…
	同 bewitched, captivated, charmed, enchanted, infatuated

□ emblematic	□ embrace	□ embroider	□ embryological	□ embryonic	□ emend
□ eminence	□ eminent	□ empathy	□ emphatic	□ empirically	□ empiricism
□ empty	□ emulate	□ enamored			

encapsulation [ɪnˈkæpsjuleɪʃən]	*n.* 包装(packing) 记 来自 encapsulate(*v.* 封装)
encounter [ɪnˈkaʊntər]	*v.* 遭遇；邂逅(to come upon face-to-face) 记 联想记忆：en(使) + counter(相反的) → 使从两个相反的方向而来 → 邂逅
encroach [ɪnˈkroʊtʃ]	*v.* 侵占，蚕食(to enter by gradual steps or by stealth into the possessions or rights of another) 记 词根记忆：en(进入) + croach(钩) → 钩进去 → 侵占
encumber [ɪnˈkʌmbər]	*v.* 妨碍，阻碍(to impede or hamper) 记 联想记忆：en + cumber(妨碍) → 妨碍
endear [ɪnˈdɪr]	*v.* 使受喜爱(to cause to become beloved or admired) 记 联想记忆：en(使) + dear(珍爱的) → 使受喜爱
endemic [enˈdemɪk]	*adj.* 地方性的(restricted to a locality or region; native) 记 词根记忆：en + dem(人民) + ic → 在人民之内 → 地方性的
endorse [ɪnˈdɔːrs]	*v.* 赞同(to approve openly)；背书(to write one's name on the back) 记 词根记忆：en + dors(背) + e → 在背后签字 → 背书
endow [ɪnˈdaʊ]	*v.* 捐赠(to give money or property to)；赋予(to equip or supply with a talent or quality) 同 bequeath, contribute
endure [ɪnˈdʊr]	*v.* 忍受，忍耐(to suffer sth. painful or uncomfortable patiently) 记 联想记忆：end(结束) + ure → 坚持到结束 → 忍受，忍耐 同 abide, bear, brook, swallow
enduring [ɪnˈdʊrɪŋ]	*adj.* 持久的(lasting)；不朽的 记 词根记忆：en + dur(持续) + ing → 持久的
energize [ˈenərdʒaɪz]	*v.* 给予…精力、能量(to make energetic, vigorous, or active) 同 activize, invigorate, reinforce, vitalize
enervate [ˈenərveɪt]	*v.* 使虚弱，使无力(to lessen the vitality or strength of) 记 词根记忆：e + nerv(力量；神经) + ate → 力量出去 → 使无力
engage [ɪnˈɡeɪdʒ]	*v.* 从事，参加(to involve)；雇用，聘用(to hire)；使参与(to induce to participate; participate)；引起…的注意(to hold the attention of) 记 联想记忆：en(使…) + gage(挑战) → 使接受挑战 → 从事
engender [ɪnˈdʒendər]	*v.* 产生，引起(to produce; beget) 记 词根记忆：en + gen(出生) + der → 使出生 → 产生，引起 同 cause, generate, induce, provoke
engrave [ɪnˈɡreɪv]	*v.* 雕刻，铭刻(to cut or carve words or designs on a hard surface)；牢记，铭记(to impress sth. deeply on the memory or mind)
enigma [ɪˈnɪɡmə]	*n.* 谜一样的人或事物(sth. hard to understand or explain; an inscrutable or mysterious person) 例 To astronomers, the moon has long been an *enigma*, its origin escaping simple solution.

7

endure

☐ encapsulation	☐ encounter	☐ encroach	☐ encumber	☐ endear	☐ endemic
☐ endorse	☐ endow	☐ endure	☐ enduring	☐ energize	☐ enervate
☐ engage	☐ engender	☐ engrave	☐ enigma		

enmity	*n.* 敌意，仇恨（hostility；antipathy）
[ˈenməti]	记 来自 enemy（*n.* 敌人）
	搭 enmity toward 对…的敌意

enormous	*adj.* 极大的，巨大的（shockingly large）
[ɪˈnɔːrməs]	记 词根记忆：e(出) + norm(规范) + ous(…的) → 超出规范的 → 巨大的
	同 colossal, gargantuan, immense, titanic, tremendous

enrage	*v.* 激怒，触怒（to make sb. very angry）
[ɪnˈreɪdʒ]	记 联想记忆：en(进入) + rage(狂怒) → 进入狂怒 → 激怒

entangle	*v.* 使卷入（to involve in a perplexing or troublesome situation）
[ɪnˈtæŋgl]	记 联想记忆：en + tangle(纠缠，混乱) → 使卷入

enterprise	*n.* 公司，企业（business company or firm）；进取心（willingness to take risks and do difficult or new things）
[ˈentərpraɪz]	

entertain	*v.* 款待，招待（to show hospitality to）；使欢乐，娱乐（to provide entertainment for）
[ˌentərˈteɪn]	记 联想记忆：enter(进入) + tain(拿住) → 拿着东西进去 → 款待，招待

OH!! LOVE!! AH!!

entertain

enthral	*v.* 迷惑（to hold spellbound）
[ɪnˈθrɔːl]	记 词根记忆：en(使) + thral(奴隶) → 使成为奴隶 → 迷惑

entice	*v.* 诱使，引诱（to attract artfully or adroitly；lure）
[ɪnˈtaɪs]	记 联想记忆：ent(看作 enter，进入) + ice(冰) → 引诱人进入冰中 → 引诱

entitle	*v.* 使有权(做某事)（to give sb. the right to do sth.）
[ɪnˈtaɪtl]	记 联想记忆：en(使) + title(权力) → 使有权

entrenched	*adj.* (权利、传统)确立的，牢固的（strongly established and not likely to change）
[ɪnˈtrentʃt]	

entrepreneur	*n.* 企业家，创业人（a person who organizes and manages a business undertaking）
[ˌɑːntrəprəˈnɜːr]	记 来自法语，等同于 enterpriser

enumerate	*v.* 列举，枚举（to name one by one）
[ɪˈnuːməreɪt]	记 词根记忆：e + numer(数字) + ate → 用数字表示出来 → 列举

enviable	*adj.* 令人羡慕的（highly desirable）
[ˈenviəbl]	记 来自 envy（*n./v.* 羡慕）

envision	*v.* 想象，预想（to picture to oneself）
[ɪnˈvɪʒn]	记 词根记忆：en + vis(看) + ion → 想象，预想

enzyme	*n.* 酵素，酶（biochemical catalyst）
[ˈenzaɪm]	记 词根记忆：en(在…里) + zym(发酵) + e → 酵素，酶

ephemeral	*adj.* 朝生暮死的（lasting only for a day）；生命短暂的（transitory；transient）
[ɪˈfemərəl]	记 词根记忆：e + phem(出现) + eral → 一出现就消失 → 生命短暂的
	同 evanescent, fleeting, fugacious, momentary

□ enmity	□ enormous	□ enrage	□ entangle	□ enterprise	□ entertain
□ enthral	□ entice	□ entitle	□ entrenched	□ entrepreneur	□ enumerate
□ enviable	□ envision	□ enzyme	□ ephemeral		

epic ['epɪk]	*n.* 叙事诗，史诗（a long narrative poem）*adj.* 史诗的，叙事诗的；英雄的；大规模的（of great size） 例 Telling gripping tales about a central character engaged in a mighty struggle with events, modern biographies satisfy the American appetite for *epic* narratives.
epidemic [,epɪ'demɪk]	*adj.* 传染性的，流行性的（prevalent and spreading rapidly in a community） 记 词根记忆：epi(在…中) + dem(人民) + ic → 在一群人之中 → 流行性的
episodic [,epɪ'sɑːdɪk]	*adj.* 偶然发生的（occurring irregularly）；分散性的 记 来自 episode(*n.* 片断)
epitome [ɪ'pɪtəmi]	*n.* 典型（sb./sth. showing all the typical qualities of sth.）；梗概（abstract; summary; abridgment） 记 词根记忆：epi(在…上) + tom(切) + e → 切下来放在最上面 → 梗概；单词 tome 意为"卷，册"
epoch ['epək]	*n.* 新纪元（the beginning of a new and important period in the history）；重大的事件（a noteworthy and characteristic event）
equate [i'kweɪt]	*v.* 认为…相等或相仿（to consider sth. as equal to sth. else） 记 词根记忆：equ(相等的) + ate(表动作) → 使相等 → 认为…相等或相仿
equation [ɪ'kweɪʒn]	*n.* 等式（two expressions connected by the sign"="）；等同，相等（action of making equal）

If you would go up high, then use your own legs! Do not let yourselves carried aloft; do not seat yourselves on other people's backs and heads.

如果你想要走到高处，就要使用自己的两条腿！不要让别人把你抬到高处；不要坐在别人的背上和头上。

——德国哲学家 尼采（F. W. Nietzsche, German philosopher）

□ epic □ epidemic □ episodic □ epitome □ epoch □ equate
□ equation

Word List 8 MP3 - 08

equator [ɪˈkweɪtər]	*n.* 赤道（the imaginary line around the earth at an equal distance from the North and South poles） 记 词根记忆：equ（相等的）+ ator → 使（地球）平分 → 赤道
equestrian [ɪˈkwestrɪən]	*adj.* 骑马的（of horse riding）；骑士阶层的（of, relating to, or composed of knights）*n.* 骑师（one who rides on horseback） 记 词根记忆：equ（古意：马）+ estrian（人）→ 骑在马上的人 → 骑师
equilibrium [ˌekwɪˈlɪbrɪəm]	*n.* 平衡（a state of balance or equality between opposing forces） 记 词根记忆：equi（平等的）+ libr（平衡）+ ium → 平衡
equitable [ˈekwɪtəbl]	*adj.* 公正的，合理的（dealing fairly） 例 I am seeking an *equitable* solution to this dispute, one that will be fair and acceptable to both sides. 同 dispassionate, impartial, impersonal, nondiscriminatory, objective
equivalent [ɪˈkwɪvələnt]	*adj.* 相等的，等值的（equal in quantity, value, meaning, etc.） 记 词根记忆：equi（平等的）+ val（力量）+ ent → 力量平等的 → 相等的 搭 be equivalent to... 与…相等或等值
equivocal [ɪˈkwɪvəkl]	*adj.* 模棱两可的（subject to two or more interpretations and usually used to mislead or confuse）；不明确的，不确定的（of uncertain nature or classification, undecided） 同 ambiguous, obscure
equivocator [ɪˈkwɪvəkeɪtər]	*n.* 说模棱话的人，说话支吾的人 记 词根记忆：equi（相同的）+ voc（叫喊）+ at + or → 发出相同声音的人 → 说模棱话的人
eradicate [ɪˈrædɪkeɪt]	*v.* 根除（to tear out by the roots; uproot）；扑灭（to exterminate） 记 词根记忆：e（出）+ radic（根）+ ate → 根除 同 abolish, annihilate, extirpate
erode [ɪˈroʊd]	*v.* 侵蚀（to eat into or away by slow destruction of substance）；受到侵蚀（to undergo erosion） 记 词根记忆：e + rod（咬）+ e → 咬掉 → 侵蚀

erratic	*adj.* 无规律的，不稳定的(irregular; random; wandering)；古怪的(eccentric; queer)
[ɪˈrætɪk]	记 联想记忆：err(出错) + atic → 性格出错 → 古怪的
	同 bizarre, idiosyncratic, oddball
erratically	*adv.* 不规律地，不定地(in an erratic and unpredictable manner)
[ɪˈrætɪkli]	记 来自 erratic(*adj.* 无规律的)
erudite	*adj.* 博学的，饱学的(learned; scholarly)
[ˈerudaɪt]	记 词根记忆：e(出) + rud(原始的，无知的) + ite → 走出无知 → 博学的
erudition	*n.* 博学(extensive knowledge acquired chiefly from books)
[ˌeruˈdɪʃn]	同 eruditeness, scholarship
escalate	*v.* (战争等)升级(to make a conflict more serious)；扩大，上升，增强(to grow or increase rapidly)
[ˈeskəleɪt]	例 The mayor and school superintendent let their dispute over budget cuts *escalate* to ugly and destructive proportions.
escapism	*n.* 逃避现实(的习气)(the tendency to escape from daily realities by means of entertainment)
[ɪˈskeɪpɪzəm]	
eschew	*v.* 避开，戒绝(to shun; avoid; abstain from)
[ɪsˈtʃuː]	记 联想记忆：es(出) + chew(咀嚼；深思) → 通过深思而去掉 → 戒绝
esoteric	*adj.* 秘传的，机密的，隐秘的(beyond the understanding or knowledge of most people)
[ˌesəˈterɪk]	记 联想记忆：es(出) + oter(看作 outer，外面的) + ic → 不出外面的 → 秘传的
	同 abstruse, occult, recondite
espouse	*v.* 支持，拥护(to take up; support; advocate)
[ɪˈspaʊz]	记 词根记忆：e(出) + spous(约定) + e → 给出约定 → 支持
essentially	*adv.* 本质上；基本上(basically)
[ɪˈsenʃəli]	记 来自 essential(*adj.* 本质的；基本的)
estimable	*adj.* 值得尊敬的(worthy of great respect)；可估计的(capable of being estimated)
[ˈestɪməbl]	记 来自 estimate(*v.* 估计；评价)
estrange	*v.* 使疏远(to alienate the affections)
[ɪˈstreɪndʒ]	记 联想记忆：e + strange(陌生的) → 使…陌生 → 使疏远
estranged	*adj.* 疏远的，不和的(alienated)
[ɪˈstreɪndʒd]	记 联想记忆：e + strange(陌生的) + d → 使…陌生的 → 疏远的
	例 In attempting to reconcile *estranged* spouses, counselors try to foster a spirit of compromise rather than one of stubborn implacability.
ethereal	*adj.* 太空的(of or like the ether)；轻巧的，轻飘飘的(very light; airy)
[iˈθɪriəl]	记 来自 ether(*n.* 太空；苍天)
ethnic	*adj.* 民族的，种族的(of a national, racial or tribal group that has a common culture tradition)
[ˈeθnɪk]	记 词根记忆：ethn(民族，种族) + ic → 民族的，种族的

8

ethos	*n.* (个人、团体或民族)风貌，气质(the characteristic and distinguishing attitudes, habits, beliefs of an individual or of a group)
['i:θɑːs]	记 词根记忆：eth(=ethn 民族，种族) + os → 风貌
eulogistic	*adj.* 颂扬的，歌功颂德的(praising highly; laudatory)
[ˌjuːlə'dʒɪstɪk]	记 词根记忆：eu(好的) + log(说) + istic → 说好话的 → 颂扬
eulogize	*v.* 称赞，颂扬(to praise highly in speech or writing)
['juːlədʒaɪz]	记 词根记忆：eu(好的) + log(说) + ize → 说好话 → 称赞
euphemism	*n.* 婉言，委婉的说法(the act or example of substituting a mild, indirect, or vague term for one considered harsh, blunt, or offensive)
['juːfəmɪzəm]	记 词根记忆：eu(好的) + phem(出现) + ism → 以好的语言出现 → 委婉的说法
euphemistic	*adj.* 委婉的
[ˌjuːfə'mɪstɪk]	同 inoffensive
euphonious	*adj.* 悦耳的(having a pleasant sound; harmonious)
[juː'fəʊniəs]	记 词根记忆：eu(好的) + phon(声音) + ious → 声音好听的 → 悦耳的
euphoric	*adj.* 欢欣的(feeling very happy and excited)
[juː'fɔːrɪk]	例 Our mood swings about the economy grow more extreme: when things go well, we become *euphoric*; when things go poorly, gloom descends.
evade	*v.* 躲避，逃避(to avoid or escape by deceit or cleverness; elude); 规避(to avoid facing up to)
[ɪ'veɪd]	记 词根记忆：e + vad(走) + e → 走出去 → 逃避
	同 duck, eschew, shun
evaluation	*n.* 评价，评估(the determined or fixed value of)
[ɪˌvæljuˈeɪʃn]	记 来自 evaluate(*v.* 评价，评估)
evanescent	*adj.* 易消失的，短暂的(vanishing; ephemeral; transient)
[ˌevə'nesnt]	记 词根记忆：e + van(空) + escent(开始…的) → 一出现就空了的 → 短暂的
evasive	*adj.* 回避的，逃避的，推脱的(tending or intended to evade)
[ɪ'veɪsɪv]	记 来自 evade(*v.* 躲避，逃避)
	例 In the midst of so many *evasive* comments, this forthright statement, whatever its intrinsic merit, plainly stands out as an anomaly.
evenhanded	*adj.* 公平的，不偏不倚的(fair and impartial)
['iːvn'hændɪd]	记 组合词：even(平的) + hand(手) + ed → 两手放得一样平 → 公平的
eventful	*adj.* 多事的(full of or rich in events); 重要的(momentous)
[ɪ'ventfl]	记 来自 event(*n.* 事件)
eventual	*adj.* 最终的(ultimately resulting)
[ɪ'ventʃuəl]	同 final, last, terminal
evergreen	*adj.* 常绿的(having foliage that remains green and functional through more than one growing season)
['evərgriːn]	你树老珠黄咯

evergreen

76

□ ethos □ eulogistic □ eulogize □ euphemism □ euphemistic □ euphonious
□ euphoric □ evade □ evaluation □ evanescent □ evasive □ evenhanded
□ eventful □ eventual □ evergreen

evil [ˈiːvl]	*adj.* 邪恶的，罪恶的(sinful; wicked) *n.* 坏事，恶行(sth. that brings sorrow, distress, or calamity) 记 联想记忆：live → evil, 位置颠倒 → 黑白颠倒，罪恶丛生 → 邪恶的 同 atrocious, foul, malicious, vile
evince [ɪˈvɪns]	*v.* 表明，表示(to show plainly; indicate; make manifest) 记 词根记忆：e + vinc(展示) + e → 向外展示 → 表明
eviscerate [ɪˈvɪsəreɪt]	*v.* 取出内脏(to remove the viscera from; disembowel); 除去主要部分(to deprive of vital content or force) 记 联想记忆：e + viscera(内脏) + te → 取出内脏
evocative [ɪˈvɑːkətɪv]	*adj.* 唤起的，激起的(tending to evoke) 例 The documentary film about high school life was so realistic and *evocative* that feelings of nostalgia flooded over the college-age audience.
evoke [ɪˈvoʊk]	*v.* 引起(to draw forth or elicit); 唤起(to call forth or summon a spirit) 记 词根记忆：e + vok(喊) + e → 喊出来 → 唤起 同 educe, induce
exacerbate [ɪɡˈzæsərbeɪt]	*v.* 使加重，使恶化(to aggravate disease, pain, annoyance, etc.) 记 词根记忆：ex(表加强) + acerb(苦涩的) + ate → 非常苦涩 → 使恶化
exaggerate [ɪɡˈzædʒəreɪt]	*v.* 夸大，夸张 (to overstate); 过分强调(to overemphasize; intensify) 记 词根记忆：ex(出) + ag(表加强) + ger(搬运) + ate → 全部运出 → 夸张 同 magnify
exaggeration [ɪɡˌzædʒəˈreɪʃn]	*n.* 夸张(overstatement) 记 来自 exaggerate(*v.* 夸张，夸大)
exalted [ɪɡˈzɔːltɪd]	*adj.* 崇高的，高贵的 (having a very high rank and highly respected) 记 词根记忆：ex + alt(高的) + ed → 崇高的
exasperate [ɪɡˈzæspəreɪt]	*v.* 激怒，使恼怒(to make angry; vex) 记 词根记忆：ex + asper(粗鲁的) + ate → 显出粗鲁 → 激怒 同 huff, irritate, peeve, pique, rile, roil
exasperation [ɪɡˌzæspəˈreɪʃn]	*n.* 激怒，恼怒(the state of being exasperated; the act or an instance of exasperating)
excavate [ˈekskəveɪt]	*v.* 开洞，凿洞(to make a hole or cavity in); 挖掘，发掘(to uncover or expose) 记 词根记忆：ex + cav(洞) + ate → 挖出洞 → 凿洞 同 scoop, shovel, unearth
excess [ɪkˈses]	*n.* 过分，过度(lack of moderation; intemperance) 记 词根记忆：ex + cess(走) → 走出常规 → 过分 例 Perhaps because he feels confined by an *excess* of parental restrictions and rules, at adolescence the repressd child may break out dramatically.

8

exaggerate

excessive [ɪkˈsesɪv]	*adj.* 过度的，过分的（exceeding what is usual, proper, necessary, or normal） 例 Unfortunately, *excessive* care in choosing one's words often results in a loss of spontaneity. 同 exorbitant, extravagant, extreme, immoderate, inordinate
excessively [ɪkˈsesɪvli]	*adv.* 过度地（overly） 例 Helen valued people who behaved as if they respected themselves; nothing irritated her more than an *excessively* obsequious waiter or a fawning salesclerk.
excise [ˈeksaɪz]	*v.* 切除，删去（to remove by cutting out or away） 记 词根记忆：ex + cis(切) + e → 切出去 → 切除
excite [ɪkˈsaɪt]	*v.* 激发（to call to activity）；使动感情，使激动（to rouse to an emotional response）；使增加能量（to energize） 同 galvanize, innervate, innerve, motivate, provoke
exclusive [ɪkˈskluːsɪv]	*adj.* （人）孤僻的（single and sole）；（物）专用的（not shared or divided） 记 词根记忆：ex(出) + clus(关闭) + ive → 关在外面的 → 孤僻的
execute [ˈeksɪkjuːt]	*v.* 执行，履行（to carry out）；将（某人）处死（to kill sb. as a legal punishment） 记 联想记忆：exe(电脑中的可执行文件) + cute → 执行，履行 例 Totem craftsmanship reached its apex in the 19th century, when the introduction of metal tools enabled carvers to *execute* more sophisticated designs. 同 administer, administrate, implement, perform
exemplar [ɪgˈzemplɑːr]	*n.* 模范，榜样（one that serves as a model or example） 同 ideal
exemplary [ɪgˈzempləri]	*adj.* 模范的，典范的（serving as an example）；可仿效的（deserving imitation） 记 来自 exemplar(*n.* 模范，榜样)
exemplify [ɪgˈzemplɪfaɪ]	*v.* 是…的典型，作为…例子（to be a typical example of sth.） 同 demonstrate, illustrate
exempt [ɪgˈzempt]	*adj.* 被免除的，被豁免的（not subject to a rule or obligation）*v.* 免除，豁免（to free from a rule or obligation） 记 词根记忆：ex + empt(拿；买) → 拿出去 → 被免除的
exert [ɪgˈzɜːrt]	*v.* 运用，行使，施加（to apply with great energy or straining effort） 记 词根记忆：ex(出) + ert(=sert 放置) → 将力量等放出来 → 运用
exhale [eksˈheɪl]	*v.* 呼出（to breathe out）；呼气；散发 记 词根记忆：ex(出) + hale(呼吸) → 呼出
exhaust [ɪgˈzɔːst]	*v.* 耗尽；使筋疲力尽（to make sb. very tired）*n.* （机器排出的）废气 记 词根记忆：ex(出) + haust(抽) → 把水全部抽出 → 耗尽

学习雷锋好榜样

exemplary

□ excessive	□ excessively	□ excise	□ excite	□ exclusive	□ execute
□ exemplar	□ exemplary	□ exemplify	□ exempt	□ exert	□ exhale
□ exhaust					

exhaustiveness [ɪɡˈzɔːstɪvnəs]	*n.* 全面, 详尽, 彻底
exhilarate [ɪɡˈzɪləreɪt]	*v.* 使兴奋, 使高兴(to make cheerful); 使振作, 鼓舞(to animate) 记 词根记忆: ex + hilar(高兴的) + ate → 使高兴
exhilaration [ɪɡˌzɪləˈreɪʃn]	*n.* 高兴, 兴奋(the feeling or the state of being exhilarated) 搭 the exhilaration of …的兴奋之情
exigency [ˈeksɪdʒənsi]	*n.* 紧急要求, 迫切需要(that which is required in a particular situation) 记 词根记忆: ex(外) + ig(驱赶) + ency → 赶到外边 → 紧急要求
exodus [ˈeksədəs]	*n.* 大批离去, 成群外出(a mass departure or emigration) 记 词根记忆: ex(外面) + od(=hod 路) + us → 走上外出的道路 → 成群外出 例 For many young people during the Roaring Twenties, a disgust with the excesses of American culture combined with a wanderlust to provoke an *exodus* abroad.
exonerate [ɪɡˈzɑːnəreɪt]	*v.* 免除责任(to relieve from an obligation); 确定无罪(to clear from guilt; absolve) 记 词根记忆: ex + oner(负担) + ate → 走出负担 → 免除责任
exoneration [ɪɡˌzɑːnəˈreɪʃn]	*n.* 免除(责任、义务、苦难等)(a freeing or clearing from a responsibility, obligation, or hardship)
exorbitant [ɪɡˈzɔːrbɪtənt]	*adj.* 过分的, 过度的 (exceeding the bounds of custom, propriety, or reason) 记 联想记忆: ex + orbit(轨道, 常规) + ant → 走出常规 → 过分的 搭 exorbitant fees 过度收费 同 excessive, extravagant, extreme, immoderate, inordinate
exorcise [ˈeksɔːrsaɪz]	*v.* 驱除妖魔(to expel by adjuration; free of an evil spirit); 去除(坏念头等)(to get rid of) 记 词根记忆: ex + or(说) + cise → 通过说话把不好的东西赶出 → 驱除妖魔
exotic [ɪɡˈzɑːtɪk]	*adj.* 异国的, 外来的 (not native; foreign); 奇异的, 珍奇的(strikingly unusual) 记 词根记忆: exo(外面) + tic → 外来的 例 Surprisingly enough, it is more difficult to write about the commonplace than about the *exotic* and strange.
expand [ɪkˈspænd]	*v.* 扩大, 膨胀 (to increase in extent, scope, or volume) 记 词根记忆: ex + pand(分散) → 分散出去 → 扩大
expediency [ɪkˈspiːdiənsi]	*n.* 方便(advantageousness); 权宜之计 (a regard for what is politic or advantageous rather than for what is right or just) 记 词根记忆: ex + ped(脚) + iency → 把脚迈出去 → 权宜之计
expedient [ɪkˈspiːdiənt]	*n.* 权宜之计, 临时手段(a temporary means to an end) *adj.* (指行动)有用的(useful, helpful or advisable)

8

expeditiously [ˌekspəˈdɪʃəsli]	*adv.* 迅速地，敏捷地(promptly and efficiently) 同 rapidly, speedily, swiftly
expertise [ˌekspɜːrˈtiːz]	*n.* 专门技术，专业知识(the skill, knowledge, judgment of an expert) 记 来自 expert(*n.* 专家)
explanatory [ɪkˈsplænətɔːri]	*adj.* 说明的，解释的(serving to explain)
explicate [ˈeksplɪkeɪt]	*v.* 详细解说(to make clear or explicit; explain fully) 同 elucidate, illustrate, interpret
explicit [ɪkˈsplɪsɪt]	*adj.* 明白的，清楚的(distinctly expressed; definite)；不含糊的，明确的 (fully developed and formulated) 记 词根记忆：ex + plic(重叠) + it → 把重叠在一起的弄清楚 → 清楚的
explicitly [ɪkˈsplɪsɪtli]	*adv.* 明白地；明确地 同 definitely, distinctly, expressly
exploit	[ɪkˈsplɔɪt] *v.* 剥削 (to make use of meanly or unfairly for one's own advantage)；充分利用(to utilize productively) [ˈeksplɔɪt] *n.* 英勇行为 (a notable or heroic act) 记 词根记忆：ex + plo (折) + it → 向外折 → 充分利用 exploit
explore [ɪkˈsplɔːr]	*v.* 探究 (to investigate, study, or analyze)；勘探 (to travel over for adventure or discovery)；考察(to make or conduct a systematic search) 记 联想记忆：ex + pl + ore(矿石) → 把矿石挖出来 → 勘探 例 One reason why pertinent fossils are uncommon is that crucial stages of evolution occurred in the tropics where it is difficult to *explore* for fossils, and so their discovery has lagged.
exposition [ˌekspəˈzɪʃn]	*n.* 阐释(detailed explanation)；博览会(a public exhibition or show) 记 词根记忆：ex + pos(放) + ition → 放出来(让人看) → 博览会
expository [ɪkˈspɑːzətɔːri]	*adj.* 说明的(explanatory; serving to explain) 记 来自 exposit(*v.* 解释，说明)
exposure [ɪkˈspoʊʒər]	*n.* 暴露，显露；曝光(action of exposing or state of being exposed) 记 词根记忆：ex(出) + pos(放) + ure → 放出来 → 暴露，显露
expressly [ɪkˈspresli]	*adv.* 清楚地(explicitly)；特意地(particularly) 记 来自 express(*v.* 表达 *adj.* 特别的；清楚的)
exquisite [ɪkˈskwɪzɪt]	*adj.* 精致的 (elaborately made; delicate)；近乎完美的(consummate; perfected) 记 词根记忆：ex + quis(要求，寻求) + ite → 按要求做出的 → 精致的
extant [ekˈstænt]	*adj.* 现存的，现有的(currently or actually existing) 记 联想记忆：ex + tant(看作 stand，站) → 站出来 → 现存的

□ expeditiously	□ expertise	□ explanatory	□ explicate	□ explicit	□ explicitly
□ exploit	□ explore	□ exposition	□ expository	□ exposure	□ expressly
□ exquisite	□ extant				

extend [ɪkˈstend]	*v.* 延伸，扩大(to make sth. longer or larger)；舒展(肢体)(to stretch out the body or a limb at full length)；宽延，延缓(to streth out in time) 记 词根记忆：ex(出) + tend(伸展) → 伸出去 → 延伸 例 The primary criterion for judging a school is its recent performance: critics are reluctant to *extend* credit for earlier victories. 同 expand, outspread, outstretch, unfold
extension [ɪkˈstenʃn]	*n.* 延伸，扩展(the action of extending; an enlargement in scope or operation) 同 elongation, prolongation, protraction
extensive [ɪkˈstensɪv]	*adj.* 广大的，广阔的；多方面的，广泛的 (having wide or considerable extent) 例 The development of containers, possibly made from bark or the skins of animals, although this is a matter of conjecture, allowed the *extensive* sharing of forage foods in prehistoric human societies.
exterminate [ɪkˈstɜːrmɪneɪt]	*v.* 消灭，灭绝(to wipe out; eradicate) 记 词根记忆：ex + termin(范围；结束) + ate → 从范围中消除 → 消灭 同 abolish, annihilate, extirpate
extinct [ɪkˈstɪŋkt]	*adj.* 绝种的，不存在的(no longer in existence) 记 词根记忆：ex + tinct(刺) → 用针刺使…失去 → 绝种的 例 Given the ability of modern technology to destroy the environment, it is clear that if we are not careful, the human race may soon be as *extinct* as the dinosaur.
extinction [ɪkˈstɪŋkʃn]	*n.* 消灭，废除 (the process of eliminating or reducing a conditioned response by not reinforcing it)
extol [ɪkˈstoʊl]	*v.* 赞美(to praise highly; laud) 记 词根记忆：ex + tol(举起) → 举起来 → 赞美
extract [ɪkˈstrækt]	*v.* 拔出(to take sth. out with effort or by force)；强索(to forcefully obtain money or information) 记 词根记忆：ex(出) + tract(拉) → 拉出 → 拔出
extraneous [ɪkˈstreɪniəs]	*adj.* 外来的(coming from outside)；无关的(not pertinent) 记 词根记忆：extra(外面) + neous → 外来的
extrapolate [ɪkˈstræpəleɪt]	*v.* 预测，推测(to speculate) 记 词根记忆：extra(外面) + pol(放) + ate → 放出想法 → 预测，推测
extravagance [ɪkˈstrævəgəns]	*n.* 奢侈，挥霍(the quality or fact of being extravagant) 记 词根记忆：extra(外面) + vag(走) + ance → 走到外面，超过限度 → 奢侈
extremity [ɪkˈstreməti]	*n.* 极度 (the utmost degree)；绝境，险境，临终(a moment marked by imminent destruction or death)
extricable [ˈekstrɪkəbl]	*adj.* 可解救的，能脱险的(capable of being freed from difficulty) 记 词根记忆：ex(外面) + tric(小障碍物) + able → 能摆脱小障碍物的 → 可解救的

8

□ extend	□ extension	□ extensive	□ exterminate	☑ extinct	□ extinction
□ extol	□ extract	□ extraneous	□ extrapolate	☑ extravagance	□ extremity
□ extricable					

81

exuberant [ɪɡ'zuːbərənt]	*adj.* (人)充满活力的 (very lively and cheerful)；(植物)茂盛的 (of plant produced in extreme abundance) 词根记忆：ex(出) + uber(=udder 乳房，引申为"果实") + ant → 出果实的 → 充满活力的；茂盛的
fabricate ['fæbrɪkeɪt]	*v.* 捏造 (to make up for the purpose of deception)；制造 (to construct; manufacture) 来自 fabric(*n.* 构造) 同 frame
facetious [fə'siːʃəs]	*adj.* 滑稽的，好开玩笑的 (joking or jesting often inappropriately) 联想记忆：face(脸) + tious → 做鬼脸 → 好开玩笑的
facile ['fæsl]	*adj.* 易做到的 (easily accomplished or attained)；肤浅的 (superficial) 词根记忆：fac(做) + ile(能…的) → 能做的 → 易做到的
facilitate [fə'sɪlɪteɪt]	*v.* 使容易，促进 (to make easy or easier) 同 assist, ease, speed
factorable ['fæktərəbl]	*adj.* 能分解成因子的 (capable of being factored) 联想记忆：factor(因素) + able(能…的) → 能分解成因素 → 能分解成因子的
factual ['fæktʃuəl]	*adj.* 事实的，实际的 (restricted to or based on fact) 来自 fact(*n.* 事实)
faddish ['fædɪʃ]	*adj.* 流行一时的，时尚的 (having the nature of a fad) 来自 fad(*n.* 时尚)
fade [feɪd]	*v.* 变暗，褪色，枯萎，凋谢 (to lose brightness, color, vigor or freshness) 同 dim, wither
fallacious [fə'leɪʃəs]	*adj.* 欺骗性的，误导的 (misleading or deceptive)；谬误的 (erroneous) 词根记忆：fall(错误) + aci + ous(多…的) → 谬误的
fallible ['fæləbl]	*adj.* 易犯错的 (liable to be erroneous) 例 For those who admire realism, Louis Malle's recent film succeeds because it consciously shuns the stuff of legend and tells an unembellished story as it might actually unfold with *fallible* people in earthly time.
fallow ['fæloʊ]	*n.* 休耕地 (cultivated land that is allowed to lie idle during the growing season) *adj.* 休耕的 (left uncultivated or unplanted) 记 和 fellow(*n.* 伙伴，同伙)一起记
falsify ['fɔːlsɪfaɪ]	*v.* 篡改 (to alter a record, etc. fraudulently)；说谎 (to tell falsehoods; lie) 词根记忆：fals(假的) + ify → 造假 → 篡改
falter ['fɔːltər]	*v.* 蹒跚 (to walk unsteadily; stumble)；支吾地说 (to stammer) 同 flounder, stagger, tumble
fanatic [fə'nætɪk]	*adj.* 狂热的，盲信的 (marked by excessive enthusiasm and often intense uncritical devotion) *n.* 狂热者 (a person marked or motivated by an extreme, unreasoning enthusiasm) 来自 fan(*n.* 入迷者)

fanciful [ˈfænsɪfl]	*adj.* 幻想的，奇特的(marked by fancy or unrestrained imagination) 例 In discussing Rothko's art, Breslin is scrupulous in keeping to the facts and resisting the temptation of *fanciful* interpretation.
fantasy [ˈfæntəsi]	*n.* 想象，幻想(imagination or fancy) 记 发音记忆："范特西" → 听着周杰伦的范特西，陷入无限的想象 → 想象，幻想
farce [fɑːrs]	*n.* 闹剧，滑稽剧(an exaggerated comedy)；可笑的行为，荒唐的事情(sth. ridiculous or absurd)
far-reaching [ˌfɑː ˈriːtʃɪŋ]	*adj.* 影响深远的(having a wide influence) 记 组合词：far(远的) + reaching(到达) → 影响到达很远的地方 → 影响深远的
fascinate [ˈfæsɪneɪt]	*v.* 迷惑，迷住(to charm; captivate; attract) 记 词根记忆：fas(说话) + cin + ate → 巫婆通过说话把人迷住 → 迷住
fascinating [ˈfæsɪneɪtɪŋ]	*adj.* 迷人的，醉人的(extremely interesting or charming) 例 Walpole's art collection was huge and *fascinating*, and his novel *The Castle of Otranto* was never out of print; none of this mattered to the Victorians, who dismissed him as, at best, insignificant.
fast [fæst]	*n.* 禁食，斋戒(the practice of very) *adv.* 很快地；紧紧地；深沉地
fastidious [fæˈstɪdiəs]	*adj.* 难取悦的，挑剔的(not easy to please; very critical or discriminating) 记 联想记忆：fast(绝食) + idious(看作 tedious, 乏味的) → 因乏味而绝食 → 挑剔的
fault [fɔːlt]	*n.* 错误(mistake)；【地质】断层(a fracture in the crust of a planet) 同 deficiency, demerit, foible, imperfection
favorable [ˈfeɪvərəbl]	*adj.* 有利的(helpful)；赞成的(showing approval) 记 来自 favor(*n.* 好意；喜爱)
fearsome [ˈfɪrsəm]	*adj.* 吓人的，可怕的(causing fear) 记 来自 fear(*n./v.* 害怕)
feckless [ˈfekləs]	*adj.* 无效的，效率低的(inefficient)；不负责任的(irresponsible) 记 联想记忆：feck(效果) + less(无…的) → 没有效果 → 无效的；注意不要和 reckless(*adj.* 轻率的)相混
fecund [ˈfekənd]	*adj.* 肥沃的，多产的(fruitful in offspring or vegetation)；创造力旺盛的(intellectually productive or inventive to a marked degree) 记 发音记忆："翻垦" → 可翻垦的土地 → 肥沃的 同 fertile, prolific
feign [feɪn]	*v.* 假装，装作(to make a false show of; pretend) 同 counterfeit, fake, sham, simulate 例 Although Johnson *feigned* great enthusiasm for his employees' project, in reality his interest in the project was so perfunctory as to be almost non-existent.

8

fantasy

□ fanciful	□ fantasy	□ farce	□ far-reaching	□ fascinate	□ fascinating
□ fast	□ fastidious	□ fault	□ favorable	□ fearsome	□ feckless
□ fecund	□ feign				

feigned [feɪnd]	*adj.* 假装的(pretended; simulated); 假的; 不真诚的 记 和 feint(*n.* 佯攻)一起记; A feint is a feigned attack. 佯攻是假装进攻。
feminist [ˈfemənɪst]	*n.* 女权运动者(a person who supports and promotes women's rights) 记 词根记忆: femin(女人) + ist → 女权运动者
ferment	[fərˈment] *v.* 使发酵(to cause fermentation in); (使)激动, (使)动乱(to excite; agitate) [ˈfɜːrment] *n.* 发酵(a living organism that causes fermentation); 骚动(a state of unrest) 记 词根记忆: ferm(=ferv 热) + ent → 生热 → 发酵
ferocity [fəˈrɑːsəti]	*n.* 凶猛, 残暴(the quality or state of being ferocious) 同 fierceness, furiousness, vehemence, wildness
ferromagnetic [ˌferoʊmægˈnetɪk]	*adj.* 铁磁的, 铁磁体的 记 联想记忆: ferr(铁) + o + magnetic(磁的) → 铁磁的
fertilize [ˈfɜːrtəlaɪz]	*v.* 使受精; 使肥沃(to make soil productive) 记 词根记忆: fer(带来) + il + ize → 带来果实 → 使受精
fertilizer [ˈfɜːrtəlaɪzər]	*n.* 肥料, 化肥(natural or artificial substance added to soil to make it more productive)
fervent [ˈfɜːrvənt]	*adj.* 炎热的(very hot); 热情的(exhibiting or marked by great intensity of feeling)
fervid [ˈfɜːrvɪd]	*adj.* 炽热的(extremely hot); 热情的(marked by great passion) 记 词根记忆: ferv(沸腾) + id → 炽热的; 热情的
fervor [ˈfɜːrvər]	*n.* 热诚, 热烈(great warmth of emotion; ardor) 同 enthusiasm, fury, passion
festive [ˈfestɪv]	*adj.* 欢宴的, 节日的(of, relating to, or suitable for a feast or festival) 记 词根记忆: fest(=feast 盛宴) + ive → 欢宴的
fetid [ˈfetɪd]	*adj.* 有恶臭的(having a heavy offensive smell) 同 foul, noisome, smelly
fickle [ˈfɪkl]	*adj.* (尤指在感情方面)易变的, 变化无常的, 不坚定的(changeable or unstable especially in affection; inconstant) 记 和 tickle(*v.* 呵痒)一起记 例 Though dealers insist that professional art dealers can make money in the art market, even an insider's knowledge is not enough: the art world is so *fickle* that stock-market prices are predictable by comparison.
fickleness [ˈfɪklnəs]	*n.* 浮躁; 变化无常 同 inconstancy
fictitious [fɪkˈtɪʃəs]	*adj.* 假的(not real; false); 虚构的(imaginary; fabulous) 记 词根记忆: fict(做) + itious → 做出来的 → 假的
figment [ˈfɪgmənt]	*n.* 虚构的事(sth. merely imagined) 记 词根记忆: fig(做) + ment → 做出来的 → 虚构的事

□ feigned	□ feminist	□ ferment	□ ferocity	□ ferromagnetic	□ fertilize
□ fertilizer	□ fervent	□ fervid	□ fervor	□ festive	□ fetid
□ fickle	□ fickleness	□ fictitious	□ figment		

financial	*adj.* 财政的，金融的 (relating to finance or financiers)
[faɪˈnænʃl]	搭 financial scandal 金融丑闻
finicky	*adj.* 苛求的，过分讲究的 (too particular or exacting; fussy)
[ˈfɪnɪki]	记 单词 finical 的变体; fin (fine, 精细的) + ical → 精细的 → 过分讲究的
	同 dainty, fastidious, finicking
fireproof	*adj.* 耐火的，防火的 (proof against or resistant to fire)
[ˈfaɪərpruːf]	
flabby	*adj.* (肌肉等)不结实的，松弛的 (limp and soft; flaccid);意志薄弱的 (lacking force; weak)
[ˈflæbi]	参 flaggy (*adj.* 枯萎的), floppy (*adj.* 松软的)
flag	*v.* 减弱，衰退 (to lose strength);枯萎 (to droop)
[flæg]	记 flag "旗，国旗" 之意众所周知
	同 deteriorate, languish, wilt
flagging	*adj.* 下垂的;衰弱的 (drooping; weakening)
[ˈflægɪŋ]	同 languid, languorous, limp, listless, lymphatic, spiritless
flaggy	*adj.* 枯萎的;松软无力的 (lacking vigor or force)
[ˈflægi]	
flagrant	*adj.* 罪恶昭彰的;公然的 (conspicuously offensive)
[ˈfleɪgrənt]	记 不要和 fragrant (*adj.* 芳香的)相混
flake	*v.* 使成薄片 (to form or break into flakes)
[fleɪk]	记 联想记忆: f(看作 fly, 飞) + lake(湖) → 飞向湖中的薄片 → 使成薄片
flamboyant	*adj.* 艳丽的，显眼的，炫耀的 (too showy or ornate; florid; extravagant)
[flæmˈbɔɪənt]	记 联想记忆: flam(火) + boy(男孩) + ant(蚂蚁) → 男孩和蚂蚁高举火把 → 显眼的
	例 Thomas Paine, whose political writing was often *flamboyant*, was in private life a surprisingly simple man: he lived in rented rooms, ate little, and wore drab clothes.
flatter	*v.* 恭维，奉承 (to praise sb. too much)
[ˈflætər]	同 adulate, blandish, honey, slaver

flag

□ financial	□ finicky	□ fireproof	□ flabby	□ flag	□ flagging
□ flaggy	□ flagrant	□ flake	□ flamboyant	□ flatter	

85

flaunt [flɔ:nt]	*v.* 炫耀，夸耀(to display or obtrude oneself to public notice) 记 联想记忆：fl(看作 fly，飞) + aunt(姑姑) → 到处飞的姑姑 → 炫耀 例 Fortunately, she was deprecatory about her accomplishments, properly unwilling to *flaunt* them before her friends. 同 flash, parade, show off
flaunty [ˈflɔ:nti]	*adj.* 炫耀的，虚华的(ostentatious) 记 来自 flaunt(*v.* 炫耀，夸耀)
flaw [flɔ:]	*n.* 瑕疵(imperfection；defect) *v.* 生裂缝；变得有缺陷(to become defective) 同 blemish, bug, fault, shortcoming
flawed [flɔ:d]	*adj.* 有缺点的；错误的(spoiled by having mistakes, weaknesses, or by being damaged)
fleeting [ˈfliːtɪŋ]	*adj.* 短暂的；飞逝的(transient；passing swiftly) 记 来自 fleet(*v.* 疾飞，掠过)
flexible [ˈfleksəbl]	*adj.* 易弯曲的(easily bent)；灵活的(adjustable to change) 记 词根记忆：flex(弯曲) + ible(能…的) → 易弯曲的
flickering [ˈflɪkərɪŋ]	*adj.* 闪烁的，摇曳的，忽隐忽现的(glittery, twinkling) 记 来自 flicker(*v.* 闪烁，摇曳)
flimsy [ˈflɪmzi]	*adj.* 轻而薄的 (thin and easily broken or damaged)；易损坏的(poorly made and fragile) 记 联想记忆：flim(看作 film，胶卷) + sy → 像胶卷一样的东西 → 易损坏的
flip [flɪp]	*v.* 用指轻弹(to strike quickly or lightly)；蹦蹦跳跳(to move with a small quick motion) *adj.* 无礼的；冒失的；轻率的(rude；glib；flippant)
flippant [ˈflɪpənt]	*adj.* 无礼的 (frivolous and disrespectful)；轻率的 (lacking proper respect or seriousness)
flock [flɑːk]	*n.* 羊群；鸟群(a group of certain animals, as goats or sheep, or of birds) 同 crowd, drove, horde, host, legion, mass
floral [ˈflɔːrəl]	*adj.* 花的，植物的(of or relating to a flora) 搭 a floral arrangement/display 插花，花展
florid [ˈflɒrɪd]	*adj.* 华丽的(highly decorated；showy)；(脸)红润的(rosy；ruddy) 记 词根记忆：flor(花) + id → 像花一样的 → 华丽的
flounder [ˈflaʊndər]	*v.* 挣扎(to plunge about in a stumbling manner)；艰苦地移动(to struggle awkwardly to move) *n.* 比目鱼(flatfish) 记 联想记忆：flo(看作 flow，流) + under(在…下面) → 在下面流动 → 挣扎
flourish [ˈflɜːrɪʃ]	*v.* 繁荣，兴旺(to develop well and be successful)；活跃而有影响力(to be very active and influential) 记 词根记忆：flour(=flor 花) + ish → 花一样开放 → 繁荣，兴旺
flout [flaʊt]	*v.* 蔑视(to mock or scoff at；show scorn or contempt for)；违抗 记 联想记忆：fl(=fly，飞) + out(出去) → 飞出去 → 不再服从命令 → 违抗 同 fleer, gibe, jeer, jest, sneer

fluctuate [ˈflʌktʃueɪt]	*v.* 波动(to undulate as waves); 变动(to be continually changing)
	记 词根记忆: fluct(=flu, 流动) + uate → 波动; 变动
fluctuation [ˌflʌktʃuˈeɪʃn]	*n.* 波动, 起伏, 涨落(undulation, waving)
	记 来自fluctuate(*v.* 波动; 变动)
fluffy [ˈflʌfi]	*adj.* 有绒毛的(covered with fluff); 无聊的, 琐碎的(light or frivolous)
	记 来自fluff(*n.* 绒毛)
fluid [ˈfluːɪd]	*adj.* 流体的, 流动的 (capable of flowing); 易变的, 不固定的 (subject to change or movement)
	记 词根记忆: flu(流动) + id → 流动的
fluorescent [ˌflɔːˈresnt]	*adj.* 荧光的, 发亮的(producing light)
	记 词根记忆: fluor(荧光) + escent(发生…的) → 荧光的, 发亮的
flustered [ˈflʌstərd]	*adj.* 慌张的, 激动不安的(nervous or upset)
	同 perturbed, rattled
foible [ˈfɔɪbl]	*n.* 小缺点, 小毛病(a small weakness; fault)
	记 与feeble(*adj.* 虚弱的, 衰弱的)一起记
foliage [ˈfoʊliɪdʒ]	*n.* 叶子(mass of leaves; leafage)
	记 词根记忆: foli(树叶) + age → 叶子
folklore [ˈfoʊklɔːr]	*n.* 民间传说; 民俗学
	记 组合词: folk(乡民) + lore(传说, 学问) → 民间传说
folly [ˈfɑːli]	*n.* 愚蠢(lack of wisdom); 愚蠢的想法或做法(a foolish act or idea)
	同 foolery, idiocy, insanity
foodstuff [ˈfuːdstʌf]	*n.* 食料, 食品(any substance used as food)
	记 组合词: food(食物) + stuff(东西) → 食品
forbear [fɔːrˈber]	*v.* 克制 (to hold oneself back from especially with an effort); 忍耐(to control oneself when provoked)
forebode [fɔːˈboʊd]	*v.* 预感, 预示(灾祸等), 预兆(to foretell; predict)
	记 组合词: fore(提前) + bode(兆头) → 预兆
foreknowledge [fɔːrˈnɑːlɪdʒ]	*n.* 预知, 先见之明(knowledge of sth. before it happens or exists)
	记 组合词: fore(预先) + knowledge(知道) → 预知
foreshadow [fɔːrˈʃædoʊ]	*v.* 成为先兆, 预示(to represent, indicate, or typify beforehand)
	记 组合词: fore(预先) + shadow(影子) → 影子先来 → 预示
foresight [ˈfɔːrsaɪt]	*n.* 远见, 深谋远虑(an act or the power of foreseeing)
	记 组合词: fore(预先) + sight(看见) → 远见
forestall [fɔːrˈstɔːl]	*v.* 预先阻止, 先发制人(to hinder by doing sth. ahead of time; prevent)
	记 组合词: fore(前面) + stall(停止) → 预先阻止
	同 deter, forfend, obviate, preclude
forested [ˈfɔːrɪstɪd]	*adj.* 树木丛生的(wooded)
	记 来自forest(*n.* 森林)

9

forfeit [ˈfɔːrfət]	*v.* 丧失，被罚没收（to lose, or be deprived of） *n.* 丧失的东西（sth. one loses） 记 词根记忆：for(出去) + feit(=fect，做) → 做出去 → 丧失
forlorn [fərˈlɔːrn]	*adj.* 孤独的（abandoned or deserted）；凄凉的（wretched; miserable） 记 词根记忆：for(出去) + lorn(被弃的) → 抛弃 → 孤独的
formalized [ˈfɔːrməlaɪzd]	*adj.* 形式化的，正式的 记 来自 formalize(*v.* 使形式化，使正式)
formation [fɔːrˈmeɪʃn]	*n.* 组成，形成（thing that is formed）；编队，排列（an arrangement of a group of persons in some prescribed manner or for a particular purpose） 记 词根记忆：form(形状) + ation → 形成形状 → 形成
formidable [ˈfɔːrmɪdəbl]	*adj.* 令人畏惧的，可怕的（causing fear or dread）；难以克服的（hard to handle or overcome） 例 Even though *formidable* winters are the norm in the Dakotas, many people were unprepared for the ferocity of the blizzard of 1888.
formidably [ˈfɔːrmɪdəbli]	*adv.* 可怕地，难对付地，强大地（strongly） 记 来自 formidable(*adj.* 可怕的，难对付的)
formulaic [ˌfɔːrmjuˈleɪɪk]	*adj.* 公式的，刻板的（containing or made from ideas or expressions that have been used many times before and are therefore not very new or interesting）
forsake [fərˈseɪk]	*v.* 遗弃（to leave; abandon），放弃（to give up; renounce） 记 联想记忆：for(出去) + sake(缘故) → 为了某种缘故而抛出去 → 遗弃
forte [fɔːrt]	*n.* 长处，特长（special accomplishment or strong point） *adj.* (音乐)强音的（used as a direction in music）
forthright [ˈfɔːrθraɪt]	*adj.* 直率的（clear and honest in manner and speech） 同 candid, frank, straightforward
fortify [ˈfɔːrtɪfaɪ]	*v.* 加强，巩固（to make strong） 记 词根记忆：fort(强大) + ify → 力量化 → 巩固
fortitude [ˈfɔːrtətuːd]	*n.* 坚毅，坚忍不拔（strength of mind that enables a person to encounter danger or bear pain） 记 词根记忆：fort(强) + itude(状态) → 坚毅
fortuitous [fɔːrˈtuːɪtəs]	*adj.* 偶然发生的，偶然的（happening by chance; accidental）；幸运的（lucky） 记 词根记忆：fortun(看作 fortune，运气) + itous → 运气的 → 偶然发生的 例 Although he had spent many hours at the computer trying to solve the problem, he was the first to admit that the final solution was *fortuitous* and not the result of his labor. 同 casual, contingent, incidental

forfeit 随地吐痰罚款十元

fossilized [ˈfɑːsəlaɪzd]	*adj.* 变成化石的 记 来自 fossilize(*v.* 变成化石)
foster [ˈfɔːstər]	*v.* 鼓励，促进 (to promote the growth or development of sth.)；养育，抚养 (to give parental care to) 记 联想记忆：fost(看作 fast，快速的) + er → 鼓励，促进 例 In attempting to reconcile estranged spouses, counselors try to ***foster*** a spirit of compromise rather than one of stubborn implacability.
foul [faʊl]	*adj.* 污秽的，肮脏的 (full of dirt or mud)；恶臭的 (stinking; loathsome)；邪恶的 (very wicked) *v.* 弄脏 (to soil; defile) *n.* (体育等)犯规 (an infraction of the rules, as of a game or sport)
founder [ˈfaʊndər]	*v.* (船)沉没 (to sink)；(计划)失败 (to collapse; fail) 记 founder "创建者"之意众所周知
fractious [ˈfrækʃəs]	*adj.* (脾气)易怒的，好争吵的 (peevish; irritable) 记 词根记忆：fract(碎裂) + ious(易…的) → 脾气易碎 → (脾气)易怒的
fragile [ˈfrædʒl]	*adj.* 易碎的，易损坏的 (brittle; crisp; friable) 记 词根记忆：frag(=fract 断裂) + ile(易…的) → 易碎的 同 breakable, delicate, frail, frangible, shatterable
fragment [ˈfrægmənt]	*n.* 碎片 (small part or piece)；片段 (an incomplete or isolated portion) 记 词根记忆：frag(打碎) + ment(表名词) → 碎片 同 scrap, shred
fragmentary [ˈfrægmənteri]	*adj.* 碎片的，片段的 (consisting of fragments) 例 Although the records of colonial New England are sketchy in comparison with those available in France or England, the records of other English colonies in America are even more ***fragmentary***.
frail [freɪl]	*adj.* 脆弱的 (fragile; delicate)；不坚实的 (slender and delicate) 记 可能是 fragile(*adj.* 易碎的)的变体 例 A human being is quite a ***frail*** creature, for the gloss of rationality that covers his or her fears and insecurity is thin and often easily breached. 同 feeble, flimsy
frantic [ˈfræntɪk]	*adj.* 疯狂的，狂乱的 (wild with anger; frenzied) 记 联想记忆：fr(看作 fry，炸) + ant(蚂蚁) + ic(看作 ice，冰) → 在冰上炸蚂蚁吃 → 疯狂的
fraternity [frəˈtɜːrnəti]	*n.* 同行 (a group of people with the same beliefs, interests, work, etc.)；友爱 (fraternal relationship or spirit)

9

□ fossilized	□ foster	□ foul	□ founder	□ fractious	□ fragile
□ fragment	□ fragmentary	□ frail	□ frantic	□ fraternity	

89

fraud	*n.* 欺诈，欺骗 (deceit; trickery)；骗子 (impostor;
[frɔːd]	cheat)
	记 frau 是德语"妻子，太太"之意；如果妻子 (frau)
	欺骗丈夫，那就是欺骗 (fraud)
	例 Paradoxically, while it is relatively easy to
	prove a fraudulent work of art is a *fraud*, it is
	often virtually impossible to prove that an
	authentic one is genuine.

现在投资就有
100倍回报！

fraud

fraudulent	*adj.* 欺骗的，不诚实的 (acting with fraud; deceitful)
[ˈfrɔːdʒələnt]	例 Paradoxically, while it is relatively easy to prove a *fraudulent* work of
	art is a fraud, it is often virtually impossible to prove that an authentic one
	is genuine.
fraught	*adj.* 充满的 (filled; charged; loaded)
[frɔːt]	记 和 freight (*n.* 货物)一起记
	例 Their married life was not tranquil since it was *fraught* with bitter
	fighting and arguments.
fray	*n.* 吵架，打斗 (a noisy quarrel or fight) *v.* 磨破 (to become worn, ragged
[freɪ]	or raveled by rubbing)
	记 联想记忆：f + ray (光线) → 时光催人老 → 磨破
frenetic	*adj.* 狂乱的，发狂的 (frantic; frenzied)
[frəˈnetɪk]	记 联想记忆：fren (=phren 心灵) + etic → 心灵承受不了的 → 狂乱的，发
	狂的
frequency	*n.* 频率 (rate of occurrence or repetition of sth.)
[ˈfriːkwənsi]	记 来自 frequent (*adj.* 频繁的)
fret	*v.* (使)烦躁，焦虑 (to irritate; annoy) *n.* 烦躁，焦虑 (an agitation of mind)
[fret]	同 cark, pother, ruffle, vex
friend	*n.* 赞助者，支持者 (one who supports, sympathizes with, or patronizes a
[frend]	group, cause, or movement)
	例 Queen Elizabeth I has quite correctly been called a *friend* of the arts,
	because many young artists received her patronage.
frigid	*adj.* 寒冷的 (very cold)；冷漠的，冷淡的 (lacking in warmth and life)
[ˈfrɪdʒɪd]	记 词根记忆：frig (冷) +id (…的) → 寒冷的
frisky	*adj.* 活泼的，快活的 (playful; frolicsome; merry)
[ˈfrɪski]	同 impish, mischievous, sportive, waggish
frivolity	*n.* 轻浮的行为 (a frivolous act or thing)
[frɪˈvɑːləti]	例 Despite an affected nonchalance which convinced casual observers
	that he was indifferent about his painting and enjoyed only *frivolity*,
	Warhol cared deeply about his art and labored at it diligently.
frivolous	*adj.* 轻薄的，轻佻的 (marked by unbecoming levity)
[ˈfrɪvələs]	记 词根记忆：friv (愚蠢) + olous → 愚蠢的 → 轻佻的

□ fraud	□ fraudulent	□ fraught	□ fray	□ frenetic	□ frequency
□ fret	□ friend	□ frigid	□ frisky	□ frivolity	□ frivolous

frugal [ˈfruːɡl]	*adj.* 节约的，节俭的(careful and thrifty) 记 发音记忆："腐乳过日" → 吃腐乳过日子 → 节约的
frugality [fruˈɡæləti]	*n.* 朴素；节俭(prudence in avoiding waste) 例 Her *frugality* should not be confused with miserliness; as long as I have known her, she has always been willing to assist those who are in need. 同 economy, thriftiness
fruitlessly [ˈfruːtləsli]	*adv.* 徒劳地，无益地(unproductively) 同 unprofitably
frustrate [ˈfrʌstreɪt]	*v.* 挫败，使沮丧(to baffle; defeat) 记 联想记忆：frust(一部分) + rate(费用) → 买东西只带了一部分钱，买不成 → 挫败 同 foil, thwart
fulsome [ˈfʊlsəm]	*adj.* 虚情假意的(disgustingly insincere)；充足的(full; ample; abundant) 记 组合词：ful(l)(满) + some(带有…的) → 充足的
fumigate [ˈfjuːmɪɡeɪt]	*v.* 用烟熏消毒(to expose to the action of fumes in order to disinfect or kill the vermin) 记 词根记忆：fum(=fume 烟) + igate(用…的) → 用烟熏消毒
function [ˈfʌŋkʃn]	*v.* 运行(to serve; operate) *n.* 功能；职责(professional or official position) 记 发音记忆："放颗心" → 公务员的职责就是让人民放心 → 职责
fundamental [ˌfʌndəˈmentl]	*adj.* 根本的，基本的(of or forming the basis or foundation of sth.)；十分重要的(essential) 记 来自 fundament(*n.* 基础)
furtive [ˈfɜːrtɪv]	*adj.* 偷偷的，秘密的(done or acting in a stealthy manner; sneaky) 例 The teacher suspected cheating as soon as he noticed the pupil's *furtive* glances at his classmate's paper. 同 catlike, clandestine, covert, secret, surreptitious
fuse [fjuːz]	*v.* 熔化；融合(to reduce to a liquid or plastic state by heat; combine; become blended or joined)
fused [fjuːzd]	*adj.* 熔化的 记 来自 fuse(*v.* 熔化；融合)
fusion [ˈfjuːʒn]	*n.* 融合(a union by or as if by melting)；核聚变(union of atomic nuclear) 同 admixture, amalgam, blend, merger, mixture
fussy [ˈfʌsi]	*adj.* 爱挑剔的，难取悦的(overly exacting and hard to please) 同 dainty, exacting, fastidious, finicky, meticulous
futile [ˈfjuːtl]	*adj.* 无效的，无用的(completely ineffective)；(人)没出息的；琐细的(occupied with trifles) 记 联想记忆：f(看作 fail, 失败) + uti(用)+le → 无法利用的 → 无效的，无用的 同 abortive, bootless, ineffectual, unavailing, vain

□ frugal	□ frugality	□ fruitlessly	□ frustrate	□ fulsome	□ fumigate
□ function	□ fundamental	□ furtive	□ fuse	□ fused	□ fusion
□ fussy	□ futile				

gain [geɪn]	*n.* 利润，收获（profit, the act or process of gaining） 同 earnings, lucre
gainsay [ˌɡeɪn'seɪ]	*v.* 否认（to deny） 记 联想记忆：gain(=against 反) + say(说) → 反着说 → 否认 同 contradict, disaffirm, negate
galaxy ['ɡæləksi]	*n.* 星系；一群(杰出人物)（an assemblage of brilliant or notable persons）
gall [ɡɔːl]	*n.* 胆汁（bile）；怨恨（hatred; bitter feeling） 记 和 wall(*n.* 墙)一起记
gallant ['ɡælənt]	*adj.* 勇敢的，英勇的（brave and noble）；(对女人)献殷勤的（polite and attentive to women） 记 词根记忆：gall(胆) + ant → 有胆量的 → 勇敢的，英勇的
galvanize ['ɡælvənaɪz]	*v.* 刺激，激起（to stimulate）；电镀（to plate metal with zinc, originally by galvanic action）；通电（to apply an electric current to） 记 来自 galvanic(*adj.* 电流的)
garble ['ɡɑːbl]	*v.* 曲解，窜改（to alter or distort as to create a wrong impression or change the meaning） 记 联想记忆：美国女影星嘉宝（Garbo）
garish ['ɡerɪʃ]	*adj.* 俗丽的，过于艳丽的（too bright or gaudy; tastelessly showy） 记 词根记忆：gar(花) + ish → 花哨的 → 俗丽的；注意不要和 garnish (*v.* 装饰)相混
garrulous ['ɡærələs]	*adj.* 唠叨的，多话的（loquacious; talkative） 同 chatty, conversational, voluble
gaudy ['ɡɔːdi]	*adj.* 俗丽的（bright and showy） 记 发音记忆："高低" → 花衣服穿得高高低低 → 俗丽的
gene [dʒiːn]	*n.* 基因（unit in a chromosome which controls heredity）
generalize ['dʒenrəlaɪz]	*v.* 概括，归纳（to draw a general conclusion from particular examples） 记 联想记忆：general(概括的) + ize → 概括，归纳
generate ['dʒenəreɪt]	*v.* 造成（to bring into being）；产生（to originate or produce） 记 词根记忆：gener(种属；产生) + ate → 产生
generation [ˌdʒenə'reɪʃn]	*n.* 一代人（a group of individuals born and living at about the same time）；(产品类型的)代（single stage in the development of a type of product）；产生，发生（production）
generic [dʒə'nerɪk]	*adj.* 种类的，类属的（of or characteristic of a genus） 记 来自 genus(*n.* 种类)；注意不要和 genetic(*adj.* 遗传的；起源的)相混
generosity [ˌdʒenə'rɑːsəti]	*n.* 慷慨，大方（willingness to share; unselfishness） 例 Although ordinarily skeptical about the purity of Robinson's motives, in this instance Jenkins did not consider Robinson's *generosity* to be alloyed with consideration of personal gain.

generous [ˈdʒenərəs]	*adj.* 慷慨的(liberal in giving)；大量的(marked by abundance or ample proportions) 记 词根记忆：gener(产生) + ous → 产生很多的 → 大量的 例 Famous among job seekers for its largesse, the company, quite apart from *generous* salaries, bestowed on its executives annual bonuses and such perquisites as low-interest home mortgages and company cars.
genetic [dʒəˈnetɪk]	*adj.* 遗传的(having to do with genetic)；起源的(of the genesis) 例 Ethologists are convinced that many animals survive through learning—but learning that is dictated by their *genetic* programming, learning as thoroughly stereotyped as the most instinctive of behavioral responses.
genial [ˈdʒiːniəl]	*adj.* 友好的，和蔼的(cheerful, friendly and amiable) 记 联想记忆：做个和蔼的(genial)天才(genius)
genre [ˈʒɑːnrə]	*n.* (文学、艺术等的)类型，体裁(a kind of works of literature, art, etc.) 记 词根记忆：gen(种属) + re → 类型，体裁
genus [ˈdʒiːnəs]	*n.* (动植物的)属，类(division of animals or plants, below a family and above a species)
geomagnetic [ˌdʒiːoʊmægˈnetɪk]	*adj.* 地磁的(of or relating to terrestrial magnetism) 记 和 geomagnetism(*n.* 地磁学)一起记
germinate [ˈdʒɜːrmɪneɪt]	*v.* 发芽(to sprout or cause to sprout)；发展(to start developing or growing) 记 词根记忆：germ(种子，幼芽) + inate → 发芽
gibe [dʒaɪb]	*v.* 嘲弄，讥笑(to jeer or taunt; scoff) *n.* 嘲笑，讥笑 记 联想记忆：也写作 jibe，但 jibe 还有另一个意思"与…一致"，是 GRE 常考的释义
giddy [ˈgɪdi]	*adj.* 轻浮的，轻率的(not serious; frivolous) 同 flighty, frothy
glacial [ˈgleɪʃl]	*adj.* 冰河期的(of the Ice Age)；寒冷的(very cold) 记 词根记忆：glaci(冰) + al → 冰河期的
glamorous [ˈglæmərəs]	*adj.* 迷人的，富有魅力的(full of glamour; fascinating; alluring) 记 来自苏格兰语 glamour(魔法)，因作家司各特常用 cast the glamour(施魔法)这一习语而成为人所共知的单词
glance [glæns]	*v.* 瞥见(to take a quick look at) *n.* 一瞥 搭 at first glance 乍一看
glandular [ˈglændʒələr]	*adj.* 腺状的，腺的(of, relating to, or involving glands, gland cells, or their products)
glaze [gleɪz]	*v.* 上釉于(to apply a glaze to)；使光滑(to give a smooth glossy surface to) *n.* 釉
gloat [gloʊt]	*v.* 幸灾乐祸地看，心满意足地看(to gaze or think with exultation, or malicious pleasure) 搭 gloat over 幸灾乐祸地看

□ generous □ genetic □ genial □ genre □ genus □ geomagnetic
□ germinate □ gibe □ giddy □ glacial □ glamorous □ glance
□ glandular □ glaze □ gloat

93

gloom [gluːm]	*n.* 昏暗 (darkness; dimness; obscurity); 忧郁 (deep sadness or hopelessness) 例 Our mood swings about the economy grow more extreme: when things go well, we become euphoric; when things go poorly, *gloom* descends.
glossary [ˈɡlɑːsəri]	*n.* 词汇表; 难词表 (a list of difficult, technical, or foreign terms with definitions or translations) 记 词根记忆: gloss(舌头，语言) + ary → 词汇表
glossy [ˈɡlɔːsi]	*adj.* 有光泽的, 光滑的 (having a smooth, shiny appearance) 同 glassy, glistening, lustrous, polished
glucose [ˈɡluːkoʊs]	*n.* 葡萄糖 (a form of sugar)
glutinous [ˈɡluːtənəs]	*adj.* 黏的, 胶状的 (gluey; sticky) 记 来自 glue(*n.* 胶，胶水)
gluttonous [ˈɡlʌtənəs]	*adj.* 贪吃的, 暴食的 (very greedy for food) 同 edacious, hoggish, ravenous, voracious
gorgeous [ˈɡɔːrdʒəs]	*adj.* 华丽的; 极好的 (brilliantly showy; splendid) 记 联想记忆: gorge(峡谷) + ous → 峡谷是美丽的 → 华丽的
gospel [ˈɡɑːspl]	*n.* 教义, 信条 (any doctrine or rule widely or ardently maintained) 记 来自《圣经·新约》中的福音书(Gospel); Go(看作 God, 上帝) + spel(看作 spell, 符咒、咒语) → 上帝的话 → 教义, 信条
gouge [ɡaʊdʒ]	*v.* 挖出 (to scoop out); 敲竹杠 (to cheat out of money) *n.* 半圆凿(a semicircular chisel) 记 不要和 gauge(*n.* 准则, 规范)相混
graft [ɡræft]	*v.* 嫁接 (to cause a scion to unite with a stock), 结合 (to be or become joined); 贪污(to get by graft) *n.* 嫁接, 结合; 贪污 记 联想记忆: g(看作 go) + raft(木筏) → 用木筏运送嫁接的树苗 → 嫁接
grain [ɡreɪn]	*n.* 谷物 (small hard seeds of food plants); 小的硬粒 (tiny hard bit)
grandeur [ˈɡrændʒər]	*n.* 壮丽, 宏伟 (splendor; magnificence) 记 来自 grand(*adj.* 宏伟的, 壮丽的)
grandiloquence [ɡrænˈdɪləkwəns]	*n.* 豪言壮语, 夸张之言 (a lofty, extravagantly colorful, pompous, or bombastic style, manner, or quality especially in language)
grandiose [ˈɡrændioʊs]	*adj.* 宏伟的 (impressive because of uncommon largeness); 浮夸的 (characterized by affectation or exaggeration) 记 词根记忆: grandi(大的) + ose(多…的) → 多大(话)的 → 浮夸的
graphic [ˈɡræfɪk]	*adj.* 图表的 (of graphs); 生动的 (vivid) 记 来自 graph(*n.* 图表, 图解) 同 pictorial
grateful [ˈɡreɪtfl]	*adj.* 感激的, 感谢的 (expressing gratitude; appreciative) 记 不要和 grate(*v.* 磨碎)相混

gratify [ˈɡrætɪfaɪ]	*v.* 使高兴，使满足（to give pleasure or satisfaction） 记 词根记忆：grat（高兴）+ ify → 使高兴 同 arride, delectate, gladden, happify
grating [ˈɡreɪtɪŋ]	*adj.* （声音）刺耳的（harsh and rasping）；恼人的（irritating or annoying） 同 hoarse, raucous
gratuitous [ɡrəˈtuːɪtəs]	*adj.* 无缘无故的（without cause or justification）；免费的（free） 记 来自gratuity（*n.* 小费）；付小费严格说不是义务，所以有"无缘无故"之意
grave [ɡreɪv]	*adj.* 严肃的，庄重的（serious）*n.* 墓穴 记 词根记忆：grav（重）+e → 庄重的
gravitational [ˌɡrævɪ ˈteɪʃnl]	*adj.* 万有引力的，重力的（of or relating to gravitational force） 记 来自gravitation（*n.* 引力；倾向） 例 Clearly refuting sceptic, researchers have demonstrated not only that *gravitational* radiation exists but that it also does exactly what theory predicted it should do.
gravity [ˈɡrævəti]	*n.* 严肃，庄重（solemnity or sedateness；seriousness） 记 词根记忆：grav（重）+ ity → 庄重 例 At first, I found her *gravity* rather intimidating；but, as I saw more of her, I found that laughter was very near the surface.
graze [ɡreɪz]	*v.* （让动物）吃草（to feed on growing grass）；放牧（to put livestock to eat grass） 记 来自grass（*n.* 草）；和glaze（*v.* 装玻璃，上釉于）一起记
gregarious [ɡrɪ ˈɡeriəs]	*adj.* 群居的（living in herds or flocks）；爱社交的（sociable） 记 词根记忆：greg（群体）+ arious → 群居的 例 Contrary to her customary *gregarious* behavior, Susan began leaving parties early to seek the solitude of her room.

9

Word List 10  MP3-10

grief [griːf]	*n.* 忧伤，悲伤(deep or violent sorrow) 例 Because he had assumed that the child's first, fierce rush of *grief* would quickly subside, Murdstone was astonished to find him still disconsolate.
grieve [griːv]	*v.* 使某人极为悲伤(to cause great sorrow to sb.) 搭 grieve over 因为…而悲伤 同 aggrieve, bemoan, deplore, distress, mourn
grim [grɪm]	*adj.* 冷酷的，可怕的(appearing stern; forbidding) 同 ghastly
grind [graɪnd]	*v.* 磨碎，碾碎(to crush into bits or fine particles) *n.* 苦差事(long, difficult, tedious task) 记 联想记忆：将一块大(grand)石头磨碎(grind)
gripping ['grɪpɪŋ]	*adj.* 吸引注意力的，扣人心弦的(holding the interest strongly) 例 Telling *gripping* tales about a central character engaged in a mighty struggle with events, modern biographies satisfy the American appetite for epic narratives.
grope [groʊp]	*v.* 摸索，探索(to feel or search about blindly) 记 联想记忆：g(看作 grasp, 抓住) + rope(绳子) → 抓住绳子 → 摸索，探索
groundless ['graʊndləs]	*adj.* 无理由的，无根据的(having no ground or foundation) 搭 groundless fear 没由来的恐惧
grudge [grʌdʒ]	*v.* 吝惜，勉强给或承认(to be reluctant to give or admit); 不满，怨恨(to feel resentful about sth.) 记 联想记忆：去做苦工 (drudge) 肯定会怨恨 (grudge)
grumble ['grʌmbl]	*v.* 嘟囔，抱怨，发牢骚 (to utter or mumble in discontent) 搭 grumble at 抱怨
guile [gaɪl]	*n.* 欺骗，欺诈；狡猾(deceit; cunning) 记 发音记忆："贵了" → 东西买贵了 → 被欺骗了 → 欺骗

可恶 干不完没饭吃

grudge

□ grief　　□ grieve　　□ grim　　□ grind　　□ gripping　　□ grope
□ groundless　　□ grudge　　□ grumble　　□ guile

guilt [gɪlt]	*n.* 罪行(crime; sin); 内疚(a painful feeling of self-reproach) 搭 be free of guilt 无罪的
gullible [ˈgʌləbl]	*adj.* 易受骗的(easily cheated or deceived; credulous) 记 来自 gull(*v.* 欺骗)
gush [gʌʃ]	*v.* 涌出, 迸出(to pour out; spout); 滔滔不绝地说(to talk effusively) *n.* 涌出, 迸发(a sudden copious outflow)
gymnastic [dʒɪmˈnæstɪk]	*adj.* 体操的, 体育的(of or relating to gymnastics) 同 athletic
habituate [həˈbɪtʃueɪt]	*v.* 使习惯于(to make used to; accustom) 记 词根记忆: habit(住; 习惯) + uate → 使习惯于
hackneyed [ˈhæknɪd]	*adj.* 陈腐的, 老一套的(overfamiliar through overuse; trite) 记 来自 Hackney(*n.* 伦敦近郊城镇), 以养马闻名, hack 的意思是"出租的老马", 引申为"陈腐的"
haggle [ˈhægl]	*v.* 讨价还价(to bargain, as over the price of sth.) 同 dicker, wrangle
hale [heɪl]	*adj.* 健壮的, 矍铄的(free from defect, disease, or infirmity sound; healthy) 记 词根记忆: hal(呼吸) + e → 呼吸得很好的 → 精神矍铄的
halfhearted [ˌhæfˈhɑːrtɪd]	*adj.* 不认真的, 不热心的(showing little interest, enthusiasm, or heart) 记 组合词: half(半) + heart(心) + ed → 只花一半心思的 → 不认真的
hallow [ˈhæləu]	*v.* 把…视为神圣(to make or set apart as holy); 尊敬, 敬畏(to respect or honor greatly; revere) 记 注意不要和 hollow(*adj.* 空洞的)相混
halting [ˈhɔːltɪŋ]	*adj.* 踌躇的, 迟疑不决的(marked by hesitation or uncertainty) 记 来自 halt(*v.* 停住, 停顿)
hamper [ˈhæmpər]	*v.* 妨碍, 阻挠(to hinder, impede, encumber) *n.* (有盖的)大篮子(a large basket, especially with a cover)
haphazardly [hæpˈhæzərdli]	*adv.* 偶然地(accidentally); 随意地(randomly); 杂乱地(in a jumble) 记 联想记忆: hap(机会, 运气) + hazard(危险; 意外) + ly → 偶然地; 随意地
harass [ˈhærəs]	*v.* 侵扰, 烦扰(to annoy persistently) 搭 harass the border area 骚扰边境
hardheaded [ˌhɑːrdˈhedɪd]	*adj.* (尤指做生意时)讲究实际的, 冷静的, 精明的 (shrewd and unsentimental; practical) 记 组合词: hard(硬的) + head(头) + ed → 头脑坚硬的 → 冷静的
hardship [ˈhɑːrdʃɪp]	*n.* 困苦, 拮据(privation, suffering) 记 联想记忆: hard(艰苦的) + ship(表状态) → 困苦 同 asperity, difficulty, hardness, rigor
harmonic [hɑːrˈmɑːnɪk]	*adj.* 和声的; 和谐的(pleasing to the ear) 记 来自 harmony(*n.* 和声, 和谐)

10

harsh [hɑːrʃ]	*adj.* 严厉的 (stern)；粗糙的 (rough)；刺耳的 (sharp) 记 联想记忆：har (看作 hard，坚硬的) + sh → 态度强硬 → 严厉的 同 rugged, scabrous
hatch [hætʃ]	*n.* 船舱盖 (a covering for a ship's hatchway) *v.* 孵化 (to produce young by incubation)；策划 (to bring into being; originate) 搭 hatch a plot 策划阴谋
haughty [ˈhɔːti]	*adj.* 傲慢的，自大的 (blatantly and disdainfully proud) 记 词根记忆：haught (=haut 高的) + y → 自视甚高的 → 傲慢的
haunt [hɔːnt]	*v.* (思想，回忆等) 萦绕心头 (to remain in one's thoughts)；经常去 (某地) (to visit often)；(鬼魂) 常出没于 (to visit or inhabit as a ghost) *n.* 常去的地方 记 联想记忆：姑妈 (aunt) 常去的地方 (haunt) 是商店
hazard [ˈhæzərd]	*n.* 危险 (risk; peril; danger) 搭 at hazard 在危急关头
hazardous [ˈhæzərdəs]	*adj.* 危险的，冒险的 (marked by danger; perilous; risky) 例 Given the inconclusive state of the published evidence, we do not argue here that exposure to low-level microwave energy is either *hazardous* or safe.
headstrong [ˈhedstrɔːŋ]	*adj.* 刚愎自用的 (determined to have one's own way; obstinate; unruly) 记 组合词：head (头) + strong (强的) → 头很强 → 刚愎自用的
hearten [ˈhɑːrtn]	*v.* 鼓励，激励 (to make sb. feel cheerful and encouraged) 记 联想记忆：heart (心) + en → 鼓励别人的心 → 鼓励
heartfelt [ˈhɑːrtfelt]	*adj.* 衷心的，诚挚的 (deeply felt) 记 组合词：heart (心) + felt (感觉到的) → 能感觉到心意的 → 衷心的，诚挚的
heavenly [ˈhevnli]	*adj.* 天空的，天上的 (of or relating to heaven or the heavens) 同 celestial
hedonist [ˈhiːdənɪst]	*n.* 享乐主义者 (believer in hedonism) 记 联想记忆：he (他) + don (看作 done，做) + ist → 他做了自己想做的一切 → 享乐主义者
heed [hiːd]	*v.* 注意，留心 (to give attention to) *n.* 注意，留心 (careful attention) 记 和 need (*n.* 需要) 一起记；需要 (need) 的东西格外注意、留心 (heed) 例 Students of the Great Crash of 1929 have never understood why even the most informed observers did not recognize and *heed* the prior economic danger signals that in retrospect seem so apparent.
heinous [ˈheɪnəs]	*adj.* 十恶不赦的，可憎的 (grossly wicked or reprehensible; abominable) 记 联想记忆：he (他) + in + ous (音似：恶死) → 他在恶死中 → 十恶不赦的

□ harsh	□ hatch	□ haughty	□ haunt	□ hazard	□ hazardous
□ headstrong	□ hearten	□ heartfelt	□ heavenly	□ hedonist	□ heed
□ heinous					

herald [ˈherəld]	*v.* 宣布…的消息(to give notice of); 预示…的来临(to signal the approach of) *n.* 传令官; 信使; 先驱(forerunner) 记 联想记忆: her(她) + ald(看作 old, 老的) → 她带来老人的告诫 → 信使
herbaceous [ɜːrˈbeɪʃəs]	*adj.* 草本的(of, relating to, or having the characteristics of an herb) 记 词根记忆: herb(草) + aceous → 草本的
hereditary [həˈredɪteri]	*adj.* 祖传的, 世袭的 (passed on from one generation to following generations); 遗传的 记 词根记忆: her(=heir, 继承人) + editary → 祖传的 例 Natural selection tends to eliminate genes that cause inherited diseases, acting most strongly against the most severe diseases; consequently, *hereditary* diseases that are lethal would be expected to be very rare, but, surprisingly, they are not.
heretical [həˈretɪkl]	*adj.* 异端的, 异教的(of or relating to heresy or heretics) 同 dissident, heterodox, unorthodox
hesitant [ˈhezɪtənt]	*adj.* 犹豫的(tending to hesitate) 搭 be hesitant to 犹豫, 不愿意 同 faltering, halting, irresolute, vacillating
heterodox [ˈhetərədɑːks]	*adj.* 异端的, 非正统的(unorthodox) 记 词根记忆: hetero(其他的; 相异的) + dox(思想) → 持异端思想的 → 异端的 同 dissident, heretical
heterogeneous [ˌhetərəˈdʒiːniəs]	*adj.* 异类的, 多样化的(dissimilar; incongruous; foreign) 记 词根记忆: hetero(其他的; 相异的) + gene(产生, 基因) + ous → 异类的
hiatus [haɪˈeɪtəs]	*n.* 空隙, 裂缝(a gap or interruption in space, time, or continuity; break) 记 联想记忆: hi(音似: "嗨") + at + us → 对我们喊"嗨", 我们能听到, 说明有空隙 → 空隙
hibernate [ˈhaɪbərneɪt]	*v.* 冬眠(to spend the winter in a dormant or torpid state) 记 词根记忆: hibern(冬天) + ate → 冬眠
hierarchy [ˈhaɪərɑːrki]	*n.* 阶层; 等级制度(a system of ranks) 记 词根记忆: hier(神圣的) + archy(统治) → 神圣的统治 → 等级制度
hieroglyph [ˈhaɪərəɡlɪf]	*n.* 象形文字, 神秘符号(a picture or symbol used in hieroglyphic writing) 记 词根记忆: hier(神圣的) + o + glyph(写, 刻) → 神写的字 → 神秘符号
hilarity [hɪˈlærəti]	*n.* 欢闹, 狂欢 (boisterous and high-spirited merriment or laughter) 同 glee, jocularity, jocundity, jollity, mirth
histrionic [ˌhɪstriˈɑːnɪk]	*adj.* 做作的(deliberately affected); 戏剧的(of or relating to actors, acting, or the theater) 记 词根记忆: histrion(演员) + ic → 戏剧的; 注意不要和 historic(*adj.* 历史的)相混 同 theatrical; dramatic

hieroglyph

hitherto [ˌhɪðər ˈtuː]	*adv.* 到目前为止（until this or that time） 摺 a hither to unknown fact 至今无人知道的事实
hive [haɪv]	*n.* 蜂房，蜂巢（a container for housing honeybees）；热闹的场所（a place swarming with activity）
hoard [hɔːrd]	*v.* 贮藏，秘藏（to accumulate and hide or keep in reserve）*n.* 贮藏，秘藏 记 把东西藏（hoard）在木板（board）后
homemade [ˌhəʊm ˈmeid]	*adj.* 自制的，家里做的（made in the home, on the premises, or by one's own efforts）
homespun [ˈhəʊmspʌn]	*adj.* 朴素的（simple）；家织的（spun or made at home） 同 homely
homogeneity [ˌhɑːmədʒə ˈniːɪti]	*n.* 同种，同质（quality of being homogeneous） 记 词根记忆：homo(同类的) + gene(基因) + ity(表性质) → 具有同种基因 → 同种，同质
homogeneous [ˌhəʊmə ˈdʒiːniəs]	*adj.* 同类的，相似的（of the same or similar kind or nature） 摺 a homogeneous grouping of students 一组同类的学生
homogenize [hə ˈmɑːdʒənaɪz]	*v.* 使均匀（to reduce to small particles of uniform size and distribute evenly usually in a liquid）
hormone [ˈhɔːrmoʊn]	*n.* 荷尔蒙，激素 记 发音记忆："荷尔蒙"
horrific [hə ˈrɪfɪk]	*adj.* 可怕的（causing horror） 同 terrifying
hospitable [hɑː ˈspɪtəbl]	*adj.* 热情好客的（disposed to treat guests with warmth and generosity）；易接受的（having an open mind; receptive） 记 联想记忆：hospita(l)(医院) + (a)ble(能…的) → 在医院治疗要接受医生的安排 → 易接受的 例 Our times seem especially *hospitable* to bad ideas, probably because in throwing off the shackles of tradition, we have ended up being quite vulnerable to untested theories and untried remedies.
host [hoʊst]	*n.* 东道主（one that receives or entertains guests socially）；(寄生动植物的)寄主，宿主（a living animal or plant on or in which a parasite lives）
hostile [ˈhɑːstl]	*adj.* 敌对的，敌意的（of or relating to an enemy; antagonistic） 记 联想记忆：host(主人) + ile → 反客为主 → 敌对的 摺 be hostile to/towards... 对…有敌意的 同 inimicable, inimical
hostility [hɑː ˈstɪləti]	*n.* 敌意，敌对状态（enmity） 例 He had expected gratitude for his disclosure, but instead he encountered indifference bordering on *hostility*.

hot-tempered [ˌhɒt ˈtempərd]	*adj.* 性急的，易怒的，暴躁的（tending to become very angry easily） 同 irascible
hover [ˈhʌvər]	*v.* 翱翔（to remain fluttering in the air）；（人）徘徊（to linger near a place） 记 联想记忆：爱人（lover）在自己身边徘徊（hover）
huckster [ˈhʌkstə]	*n.* 叫卖小贩，零售商（a peddler or hawker） 记 词根记忆：huck（=back，背）+ ster（人）→ 背东西卖的人 → 叫卖小贩
huddle [ˈhʌdl]	*v.* 挤成一团（to crowd or nestle close together） *n.* 一堆人（或物） 记 联想记忆：聚集在一起（huddle）处理（handle）问题
humane [hjuː ˈmeɪn]	*adj.* 人道的，慈悲的（marked by compassion, sympathy, or consideration for humans or animals）；人文主义的（humanistic） 搭 human treatment 人道的待遇
humanistic [ˌhjuːmə ˈnɪstɪk]	*adj.* 人性的；人文主义的 例 Even after safeguards against the excesses of popular sovereignty were included, major figures in the *humanistic* disciplines remained skeptical about the proposal to extend suffrage to the masses.
humanitarian [hjuːˌmænɪ ˈteriən]	*n.* 人道主义者（a person promoting human welfare and social reform） 同 philanthropist
humble [ˈhʌmbl]	*adj.* 卑微的（ranking low in a hierarchy or scale）；谦虚的（not proud or haughty）*v.* 使谦卑（to make humble） 记 词根记忆：hum（地面）+ ble → 接近地面的 → 低下的 → 卑微的
humdrum [ˈhʌmdrʌm]	*adj.* 单调的，乏味的（dull; monotonous; boring） 记 组合词：hum（嗡嗡声）+ drum（鼓声）→ 单调的
humidity [hjuː ˈmɪdəti]	*n.* 湿度，湿气（moistness，dampness） 记 来自 humid（*adj.* 潮湿的）
humiliate [hjuː ˈmɪlieɪt]	*v.* 羞辱，使丢脸（to hurt the pride or dignity; mortify; degrade） 记 词根记忆：hum（地）+ iliate（使…）→ 使人靠近地面 → 羞辱
humility [hjuː ˈmɪləti]	*n.* 谦逊，谦恭（the quality or state of being humble） 同 modesty
hunch [hʌntʃ]	*n.* 直觉，预感（an intuitive feeling or a premonition） 搭 have a hunch (that) 有预感（将发生…）
hurl [hɜːrl]	*v.* 用力投掷（to throw with force）；大声叫骂（to shout out violently） 同 fling, yell
hydrate [ˈhaɪdreɪt]	*n.* 水合物 *v.*（使）水合（to cause to take up or combine with water） 记 词根记忆：hydr（水）+ ate → 水合

□ hot-tempered	□ hover	□ huckster	□ huddle	□ humane	□ humanistic
□ humanitarian	□ humble	□ humdrum	□ humidity	□ humiliate	□ humility
□ hunch	□ hurl	□ hydrate			

101

hyperbole [haɪˈpɜːrbəli]	*n.* 夸张法（extravagant exaggeration） 记 词根记忆：hyper（过度）+ bole（扔）→ 扔得过度 → 夸张法 例 Rhetoric often seems to triumph over reason in a heated debate, with both sides engaging in *hyperbole*. 同 overstatement
hypersensitive [ˌhaɪpərˈsensətɪv]	*adj.* 非常敏感的（excessively or abnormally sensitive） 搭 hypersensitive to pollen 花粉过敏
hypnotic [hɪpˈnɑːtɪk]	*adj.* 催眠的（tending to produce sleep）*n.* 催眠药（a sleep-inducing agent）
hypochondriac [ˌhaɪpəˈkɑːndriæk]	*n.* 忧郁症患者（a person affected with hypochondria）*adj.* 忧郁症的（relating to or affected with hypochondria）
hypocrisy [hɪˈpɑːkrəsi]	*n.* 伪善，虚伪（a feigning to be what one is not or to believe what one does not） 同 cant, pecksniff, sanctimony, sham
hypocritical [ˈhɪpəkrɪtɪkl]	*adj.* 虚伪的，伪善的（characterized by hypocrisy or being a hypocrite） 搭 hypocritical affection 虚假的情谊
hypothesis [haɪˈpɑːθəsɪs]	*n.* 假设，假说（an unproved theory） 记 词根记忆：hypo（在…下面）+ thesis（论点）→ 下面的论点 → 假说
hypothetical [ˌhaɪpəˈθetɪkl]	*adj.* 假设的（based on a hypothesis） 同 conjectual
hysteria [hɪˈstɪriə]	*n.* 歇斯底里症（a psychoneurosis marked by emotional excitability）；过度兴奋（behavior exhibiting emotional excess） 记 联想记忆：hyster（=hystero，子宫；癔症）+ ia → 像患了癔症一样 → 歇斯底里症 例 During the Battle of Trafalgar, Admiral Nelson remained imperturbable and in full command of the situation in spite of the *hysteria* and panic all around him.
iconoclasm [aɪˈkɑːnəklæzəm]	*n.* 破坏偶像的理论，打破旧习（the doctrine, practice, or attitude of an iconoclast）
iconoclastic [aɪˌkɑːnəˈklæstɪk]	*adj.* 偶像破坏的，打破旧习的 搭 iconoclastic ideas 打破旧习的思想
iconographic [aɪˌkɑːnəˈgræfik]	*adj.* 肖像的，肖像学的；图解的（representing something by pictures or diagrams）
idealism [aɪˈdiːəlɪzəm]	*n.* 理想主义（the act or practice of envisioning things in an ideal form）；唯心主义（a theory that only the perceptible is real） 例 In sharp contrast to the intense *idealism* of the young republic, with its utopian faith in democracy and hopes for eternal human progress, recent developments suggest a mood of almost unrelieved cynicism.

□ hyperbole □ hypersensitive □ hypnotic □ hypochondriac □ hypocrisy □ hypocritical
□ hypothesis □ hypothetical □ hysteria □ iconoclasm □ iconoclastic □ iconographic
□ idealism

identifiable	*adj.* 可辨认的（acknowledgeable）
[aɪˌdentɪˈfaɪəbl]	例 Longdale and Stern discovered that mitochondria and chloroplasts share a long, *identifiable* sequence of DNA; such a coincidence could be explained only by the transfer of DNA between the two systems.
ideological	*adj.* 意识形态的，思想体系的（of, relating to, or based on ideology）；思想上的（of or concerned with ideas）
[ˌaɪdɪəˈlɑːdʒɪkl]	
ideology	*n.* 思想体系，思想意识（a systematic body of concepts）
[ˌaɪdiˈɑːlədʒi]	记 联想记忆：ide(看作 idea，思想) + ology(学科) → 思想体系
idiomatic	*adj.* 符合语言习惯的（of, relating to, or conforming to idiom）；惯用的（peculiar to a particular group, individual, or style）
[ˌɪdiəˈmætɪk]	
idiosyncracy	*n.* 特质
[ˌɪdiːəʊˈsɪŋkrəsi]	搭 innate idiosyncracy 内在特质
idiosyncratic	*adj.* 特殊物质的，特殊的，异质的（peculiar to the individual）
[ˌɪdiəsɪŋˈkrætɪk]	例 To have true disciples, a thinker must not be too *idiosyncratic*: any effective intellectual leader depends on the ability of other people to reenact thought processes that did not originate with them.
	同 characteristic, distinctive
idyllic	*adj.* 田园诗的（of, relating to, or being an idyll）
[aɪˈdɪlɪk]	搭 an idyllic vacation 田园诗般的假日
igneous	*adj.* 火的，似火的（having the nature of fire; fiery）
[ˈɪgniəs]	记 词根记忆：ign(点燃) + eous → 火的
ignoble	*adj.* 卑鄙的（dishonorable; base; mean）
[ɪgˈnoʊbl]	记 词根记忆：ig(不) + noble(高贵) → 不高贵的 → 卑鄙的
ignominious	*adj.* 可耻的（despicable）；耻辱的（dishonorable）
[ˌɪgnəˈmɪniəs]	同 disgraceful, humiliating
ignominy	*n.* 羞耻，耻辱（shame and dishonor; infamy）
[ˈɪgnəmɪni]	记 词根记忆：ig(不) + nomin(名声) + y → 名声不好 → 耻辱
	同 disgrace, disrepute, opprobrium
ignorance	*n.* 无知，愚昧（lack of knowledge, education, or awareness）
[ˈɪgnərəns]	记 词根记忆：ig(不) + (g)nor(知道) + ance → 什么都不知道 → 无知，愚昧
	同 benightedness, illiteracy, unacquaintance
ignore	*v.* 不顾，不理，忽视（to refuse to take notice of）
[ɪgˈnɔːr]	记 联想记忆：ig+nore(看作 nose, 鼻子) → 翘起鼻子不理睬 → 不理
	例 Johnson never scrupled to *ignore* the standards of decent conduct mandated by company policy if literal compliance with instructions from his superiors enabled him to do so, whatever the effects on his subordinates.

illegitimate [ˌɪlə'dʒɪtəmət]	*adj.* 不合法的(illegal; unlawful); 私生的(born of parents not married) 记 联想记忆: il(不) + legitimate(合法的) → 不合法的 例 An example of an *illegitimate* method of argument is to lump dissimilar cases together deliberately under the pretense that the same principles apply to each.
illicit [ɪ'lɪsɪt]	*adj.* 违法的(unlawful; prohibited) 记 词根记忆: il(不) + licit(合法的) → 违法的
illiterate [ɪ'lɪtərət]	*adj.* 文盲的(ignorant; uneducated) 记 联想记忆: il(不) + literate(识字的) → 不识字的 → 文盲的
ill-paying [ˌɪl'peɪɪŋ]	*adj.* 工资低廉的
ill-prepared [ˌɪlprɪ'peəd]	*adj.* 准备不足的(not ready for sth.) 例 As former Supreme Court Justice Warren Burger was fond of pointing out, many lawyers are not legal hotshots; they often come to court *illprepared* and lacking professional skills.
ill-repute [ˌɪlrɪ'pjuːt]	*n.* 名誉败坏(bad fame) 同 notoriousness
illusory [ɪ'luːsəri]	*adj.* 虚幻的(deceptive; unreal; illusive) 例 The trick for Michael was to conjure for his son an *illusory* orderliness; only alone at night, when the boy was asleep, could Michael acknowledge the chaos he kept hidden from his son. 同 chimerical, fanciful, fictive, imaginary
illustrative [ɪ'lʌstrətɪv]	*adj.* 解说性的, 用作说明的(serving, tending, or designed to illustrate) 搭 for illustrative purposes 为了便于说明
ill-will [ˌɪl'wɪl]	*n.* 敌意, 仇视, 恶感(enmity) 同 malice
imbue [ɪm'bjuː]	*v.* 浸染, 浸透 (to permeate or influence as if by dyeing); 使充满, 灌输, 激发(to endow)
imitate ['ɪmɪteɪt]	*v.* 模仿(to mimic, counterfeit) 记 联想记忆: im + it(它) + ate(eat 的过去式, 吃) → 它照着别人的样子吃 → 模仿 同 ape, burlesque
immaculate [ɪ'mækjələt]	*adj.* 洁净的, 无瑕的(perfectly clean; unsoiled; impeccable) 记 词根记忆: im(不) + macul(斑点) + ate → 无斑点的 → 洁净的, 无瑕的
immature [ˌɪmə'tʃʊr]	*adj.* 未充分成长的, 未完全发展的(lacking complete growth, differentiation, or development); (行为等)不成熟的 (exhibiting less than an expected degree of maturity) 记 联想记忆: im(不) + mature(成熟的) → 不成熟的
immense [ɪ'mens]	*adj.* 极大的(very large); 无限的(limitless; infinite) 记 词根记忆: im(不) + mense(=measure 测量) → 不能测量的 → 极大的 搭 have an immense influence on... 对…有极大的影响 同 colossal, monstrous, prodigious, titanic

imminent [ˈɪmɪnənt]	*adj.* 即将发生的，逼近的(about to occur)
	记 词根记忆：im(进入) + min(突出) + ent → 突进来 → 逼近的
	例 Rosa was such a last-minute worker that she could never start writing a paper till the deadline was *imminent*.
	同 close, impending, proximate
immobile [ɪˈmoʊbl]	*adj.* 稳定的，不动的，静止的(fixed, motionless)
immodest [ɪˈmɑːdɪst]	*adj.* 不谦虚的 (not modest)；不正派的
	搭 immodest behavior 不雅的举动
immutability [ˌɪmjuːtəˈbɪləti]	*n.* 不变，不变性(the quality of being incapable of mutation)
impair [ɪmˈper]	*v.* 损害，削弱(to damage; reduce; injure)
	记 词根记忆：im(进入) + pair(坏) → 使…变坏 → 损害
	例 Exposure to sustained noise has been claimed to *impair* blood pressure regulation in human beings and, particularly, to increase hypertension, even though some researchers have obtained inconclusive results that obscure the relationship.
	同 blemish, mar, prejudice, tarnish, vitiate
impart [ɪmˈpɑːrt]	*v.* 传授，赋予(bestow)；传递(transmit)；告知，透露(to make known)
	记 词根记忆：im(进入) + part(部分) → 使成为一部分 → 告知
impartial [ɪmˈpɑːrʃl]	*adj.* 公平的，无私的(without prejudice or bias)
	记 联想记忆：im(不) + partial(偏见的) → 没有偏见的 → 公平的
	例 New judges often fear that the influence of their own backgrounds will condition their verdicts, no matter how sincere they are in wanting to be *impartial*.
	同 dispassionate, equitable, nondiscriminatory, unbiased, unprejudiced
impartiality [ˌɪmˌpɑːrʃiˈæləti]	*n.* 公平，公正(the quality or state of being just and unbiased)
	同 fair
impassable [ɪmˈpæsəbl]	*adj.* 不能通行的，无法通过的 (incapable of being passed, traveled, crossed, or surmounted)
impassioned [ɪmˈpæʃnd]	*adj.* 充满激情的，慷慨激昂的(filled with passion or zeal)
	记 联想记忆：im(进入) + passion(激情) + ed → 投入激情的 → 慷慨激昂的
impassive [ɪmˈpæsɪv]	*adj.* 无动于衷的，冷漠的(stolid; phlegmatic)
	记 词根记忆：im (没有) + passi (感情) + ve → 没有感情的；注意不要和 impassioned(*adj.* 充满激情的)相混
impatience [ɪmˈpeɪʃns]	*n.* 不耐烦，焦躁(the quality or state of being impatient)
	记 来自 patient (*adj.* 有耐心的)
impeccable [ɪmˈpekəbl]	*adj.* 无瑕疵的(faultless; flawless)
	记 词根记忆：im(无) + pecc(斑点) + able → 无斑点的 → 无瑕疵的
	同 fleckless, immaculate, indefectible, irreproachable, perfect

10

□ imminent　　□ immobile　　□ immodest　　□ immutability　　□ impair　　□ impart
□ impartial　　□ impartiality　　□ impassable　　□ impassioned　　□ impassive　　□ impatience
□ impeccable

105

impecunious [ˌɪmpɪˈkjuːniəs]	*adj.* 不名一文的，没钱的（having very little or no money） 记 词根记忆：im(无) + pecun(钱) + ious → 没钱的
impede [ɪmˈpiːd]	*v.* 妨碍（to bar or hinder the progress of; obstruct） 记 词根记忆：im(进入) + ped(脚) + e → 把脚放入 → 妨碍
impediment [ɪmˈpedɪmənt]	*n.* 妨碍，阻碍物（obstacle） 搭 an impediment to reform 改革的障碍
impending [ɪmˈpendɪŋ]	*adj.* 即将发生的，逼近的（imminent） 记 词根记忆：im(进入) + pend(挂) + ing → 挂到眼前 → 即将发生的，逼近的 例 William James lacked the usual awe of death; writing to his dying father, he spoke without inhibition about the old man's *impending* death.
impenetrable [ɪmˈpenɪtrəbl]	*adj.* 不能穿透的（incapable of being penetrated）；不可理解的（unfathomable; inscrutable） 记 联想记忆：im(不) + penetrable(可刺穿的) → 不能穿透的 例 The First World War began in a context of jargon and verbal delicacy and continued in a cloud of euphemism as *impenetrable* as language and literature, skillfully used, could make it. 同 impassable, impermeable, imperviable, impervious
imperative [ɪmˈperətɪv]	*adj.* 紧急的（urgent; pressing） 记 词根记忆：imper(命令) + ative → 命令的，紧急的 → 紧急的 例 Although strong legal remedies for nonpayment of child support are available, the delay and expense associated with these remedies make it *imperative* to develop other options. 同 exigent, importunate
imperial [ɪmˈpɪriəl]	*adj.* 帝王的，至尊的（of, relating to, or suggestive of an empire or a sovereign） 例 The sale of Alaska was not so much an American coup as a matter of expediency for an *imperial* Russia that was short of cash and unable to defend its own continental coastline.
imperious [ɪmˈpɪriəs]	*adj.* 傲慢的，专横的（overbearing; arrogant） 记 词根记忆：imper(命令) + ious → 命令的 → 专横的 搭 imperious manner 专横的态度 同 magisterial, peremptory
impermanent [ɪmˈpɜːrmənənt]	*adj.* 暂时的（temporary） 记 联想记忆：im(不) + permanent(永久的) → 不能永久的 → 暂时的
impermeable [ɪmˈpɜːrmiəbl]	*adj.* 不可渗透的，不透水的（not allowing a liquid to pass through） 记 联想记忆：im(不) + permeable(可渗透的) → 不可渗透的
impermissible [ˌɪmpɜːrˈmɪsəbl]	*adj.* 不容许的（not permissible） 搭 impermissible behavior 越轨行为
impersonal [ɪmˈpɜːrsənl]	*adj.* 不受个人感情影响的（having no personal reference or connection） 记 联想记忆：im(不) + personal(个人的) → 不投入个人感情的 → 不受个人感情影响的

impersonate [ɪmˈpɜːrsəneɪt]	*v.* 模仿(to mimic); 扮演(to act the part of) 记 联想记忆: im(进入) + person(人, 角色) + ate → 进入角色 → 扮演
impertinent [ɪmˈpɜːrtnənt]	*adj.* 不切题的 (irrelevant); 无礼的, 莽撞的 (exceeding the limits of propriety or good manners)
imperturbable [ˌɪmpərˈtɜːrbəbl]	*adj.* 冷静的, 沉着的(unshakably calm and collected) 记 联想记忆: im(不) + perturb(打扰) + able → 不能被打扰的 → 冷静的, 沉着的 例 During the Battle of Trafalgar, Admiral Nelson remained *imperturbable* and in full command of the situation in spite of the hysteria and panic all around him. 同 cool, disimpassioned, unflappable, unruffled

10

When an end is lawful and obligatory, the indispensable means to it are also lawful and obligatory.

如果一个目的是正当而必须做的,则达到这个目的的必要手段也是正当而必须采取的。

——美国政治家 林肯(Abraham Lincoln, American statesman)

Word List 11

impervious [ɪmˈpɜːrvɪəs]	*adj.* 不能渗透的（not allowing entrance or passage）；不为所动的（not capable of being affected or disturbed） 记 联想记忆：im（不）+ pervious（渗透的）→ 不能渗透的
impetuous [ɪmˈpetʃuəs]	*adj.* 冲动的，鲁莽的（impulsive; sudden） 搭 an impetuous decision 草率的决定
impiety [ɪmˈpaɪəti]	*n.* 不虔诚，无信仰（the quality or state of being impious）
implausible [ɪmˈplɔːzəbl]	*adj.* 难以置信的（not plausible） 记 联想记忆：im（不）+ plausible（可信的）→ 难以置信的
implement	[ˈɪmplɪmənt] *n.* 工具，器具 [ˈɪmplɪment] *v.* 实现，实施（fulfill; accomplish） 记 词根记忆：im（进入）+ ple（满的）+ ment → 进入圆满 → 实现 例 The political success of any government depends on its ability to *implement* both foreign and domestic policies.
implication [ˌɪmplɪˈkeɪʃn]	*n.* 暗示（something that is not openly stated） 记 来自 imply（*v.* 暗示，暗指）
imply [ɪmˈplaɪ]	*v.* 暗示，暗指（to express indirectly） 记 词根记忆：im（进入）+ ply（重叠）→ 重叠表达 → 暗示 例 Although the revelation that one of the contestants was a friend left the judge open to charges of lack of disinterestedness, the judge remained adamant in her assertion that acquaintance did not necessarily *imply* partiality. 同 connote, indicate, insinuate, intimate
impolitic [ɪmˈpɑːlətɪk]	*adj.* 不明智的，失策的（unwise; injudicious） 记 联想记忆：im（不）+ politic（有手腕的，有策略的）→ 失策的 例 Although Tom was aware that it would be *impolitic* to display annoyance publicly at the sales conference, he could not hide his irritation with the client's unreasonable demands. 同 imprudent, indiscreet

☐ impervious ☐ impetuous ☐ impiety ☐ implausible ☐ implement ☐ implication
☑ imply ☐ impolitic

imponderable [ɪmˈpɑːndərəbl]	*adj.* (重量等)无法衡量的(incapable of being weighed or measured) 记 联想记忆：im(不) + ponder(仔细考量) + able → 无法衡量的 同 impalpable, imperceptible, indiscernible, insensible, unmeasurable
imposing [ɪmˈpoʊzɪŋ]	*adj.* 给人深刻印象的(impressive)；壮丽的，雄伟的(grand)
impostor [ɪmˈpɑːstər]	*n.* 冒充者，骗子(a person who deceives under an assumed name) 记 词根记忆：im(进入) + pos(放) + tor → 把自己放入别人的角色 → 冒充者 例 The "*impostor* syndrome" often afflicts those who fear that true self-disclosure will lower them in others' esteem; rightly handled, however, candor may actually enhance one's standing.
imposture [ɪmˈpɑːstʃər]	*n.* 冒充(being an impostor; fraud) 记 词根记忆：im(进入) + pos(放) + ture → 把别的东西放进去 → 冒充
impound [ɪmˈpaʊnd]	*v.* 限制(to confine)；依法没收，扣押(to seize and hold in the custody of the law; take possession of)
impracticability [ɪmˌpræktɪkəˈbɪləti]	*n.* 无法实施；不能实施的事项 例 The *impracticability* of such utopian notions is reflected by the quick disintegration of the idealistic community at Brooke Farm.
impractical [ɪmˈpræktɪkl]	*adj.* 不切实际的(not wise to put into or keep in practice or effect) 例 Though one cannot say that Michelangelo was an *impractical* designer, he was, of all nonprofessional architects known, the most adventurous in that he was the least constrained by tradition or precedent.
imprecise [ˌɪmprɪˈsaɪs]	*adj.* 不精确的(not precise) 记 联想记忆：im(不) + precise(精确的) → 不精确的 例 A leading chemist believes that many scientists have difficulty with stereochemistry because much of the relevant nomenclature is *imprecise*, in that it combines concepts that should be kept discrete.
impressed [ɪmˈprest]	*adj.* 被打动的，被感动的 搭 be impressed by (对…)钦佩，有深刻的好印象
impressionable [ɪmˈpreʃənəbl]	*adj.* 易受影响的(easily affected by impressions) 例 We realized that John was still young and *impressionable*, but were nevertheless surprised at his naivete.
impressive [ɪmˈpresɪv]	*adj.* 给人印象深刻的，感人的 (making or tending to make a marked impression) 例 A born teller of tales, Olsen used her *impressive* narrative skills to advantage in her story "I Stand Here Ironing." 同 gorgeous, lavish, poignant, splendid, sumptuous
impromptu [ɪmˈprɑːmptuː]	*adj.* 即席的，即兴的(without preparation; offhand) 记 联想记忆：im(不) + prompt(按时的) + u → 不按照时间来的 → 即席的
improper [ɪmˈprɑːpər]	*adj.* 不合适的，不适当的(incorrect; not regularly or normally formed) 同 indecorous, malapropos, undue, unfitting, unseasonable

impropriety [ˌɪmprəˈpraɪəti]	*n.* 不得体的言行举止（an improper or indecorous act or remark）；不合适，不适当（the quality or state of being improper）
improvident [ɪmˈprɑːvɪdənt]	*adj.* 无远见的，不节俭的（lacking foresight or thrift） 记 联想记忆：im（不）+ provident（有远见的；节俭的）→ 无远见的，不节俭的 例 Left to endure a penniless old age, the *improvident* man lived to regret his prodigal youth.
improvise [ˈɪmprəvaɪz]	*v.* 即席创作（to extemporize） 记 词根记忆：im（不）+ pro（在…前面）+ vis（看）+ e → 没有预先看过 → 即席创作
improvised [ˈɪmprəvaɪzd]	*adj.* 临时准备的，即席而作的（making offhand） 例 The villagers fortified the town hall, hoping this *improvised* bastion could protect them from the guerrilla raids.
imprudent [ɪmˈpruːdnt]	*adj.* 轻率的（indiscreet）；不理智的（not wise） 例 It would be *imprudent* to invest all your money in one company.
impudent [ˈɪmpjədənt]	*adj.* 鲁莽的，无礼的（marked by contemptuous or cocky boldness or disregard of others）
impugn [ɪmˈpjuːn]	*v.* 提出异议，对…表示怀疑（to challenge as false or questionable） 记 词根记忆：im（进入）+ pugn（打斗）→ 马上就要进入打斗状态 → 提出异议
impulse [ˈɪmpʌls]	*n.* 动力，刺激（an impelling or motivating force） 记 词根记忆：im（在内）+ puls（推）+ e → 在内推 → 动力
impulsive [ɪmˈpʌlsɪv]	*adj.* 冲动的，由冲动引起的（arising from an impulse）；易冲动的（prone to act on impulse） 例 Though *impulsive* in her personal life, Edna St. Vincent Millay was nonetheless disciplined about her work, usually producing several pages of complicated rhyme in a day. 同 automatic, instinctive, involuntary, spontaneous
impunity [ɪmˈpjuːnəti]	*n.* 免受惩罚（exemption from punishment） 记 词根记忆：im（不）+ pun（惩罚）+ ity → 免受惩罚 例 Because outlaws were denied protection under medieval law, anyone could raise a hand against them with legal *impunity*.
impute [ɪmˈpjuːt]	*v.* 归咎于（to charge with fault）；归于（to attribute） 记 词根记忆：im（进入）+ put（认为）+ e → 认为某人有罪 → 归咎于
inadvertent [ˌɪnədˈvɜːrtənt]	*adj.* 疏忽的（not focusing the mind on a matter）；不经意的，无心的（unintentional） 例 Professional photographers generally regard *inadvertent* surrealism in a photograph as a curse rather than a blessing; magazine photographers, in particular, consider themselves fortunate to the extent that they can minimize its presence in their photographs.

□ impropriety □ improvident □ improvise □ improvised □ imprudent □ impudent
□ impugn □ impulse □ impulsive □ impunity □ impute □ inadvertent

inadvisable [ˌɪnəd'vaɪzəbl]	*adj.* 不明智的，不妥当的(not wise or prudent)
	例 It would be beneficial if someone so radical could be brought to believe that old customs need not necessarily be worthless and that change may possibly be *inadvisable*.
	同 impolitic, inexpedient, unadvisable
inalienable [ɪn'eɪlɪənəbl]	*adj.* 不能转让的；不可剥夺的 (not transferable to another or capable of being repudiated)
	记 联想记忆：in(不) + alien(转让) + able → 不能转让的
inane [ɪ'neɪn]	*adj.* 无意义的，空洞的(empty; lacking sense; void)；愚蠢的(silly)
	例 Just as an insipid dish lacks flavor, an *inane* remark lacks sense.
	同 innocuous, insipid, jejune, sapless, vapid
inappropriate [ˌɪnə'proʊprɪət]	*adj.* 不恰当的，不适宜的(unsuitable)
	例 Because the majority of the evening cable TV programs available dealt with violence and sex, the parents decided that the programs were *inappropriate* for the children to watch.
	同 inapt, inept, malapropos, unfitted, unmeet
inaugurate [ɪ'nɔːgjəreɪt]	*v.* 举行就职典礼(to induct into an office with suitable ceremonies)；创始，开创(to initiate; commence)
	记 联想记忆：in(进入) + augur(预示) + ate → 通过预示创新 → 开创
	同 instate, institute, launch, originate
inborn [ˌɪn'bɔːrn]	*adj.* 天生的，先天的(naturally present at birth; innate)
	记 联想记忆：in(内) + born(出生) → 与生俱来的 → 天生的
incandescent [ˌɪnkæn'desnt]	*adj.* 遇热发光的，发白热光的 (white, glowing, or luminous with intense heat)
incapacitate [ˌɪnkə'pæsɪteɪt]	*v.* 使无能力，使不适合(disable)
incarnate [ɪn'kɑːrnət]	*adj.* 具有人体的(given a bodily form)；化身的，拟人化的(personified)
	记 词根记忆：in(进入) + carn(肉体) + ate → 变成肉体的 → 具有人体的
incendiary [ɪn'sendieri]	*adj.* 放火的，纵火的(pertaining to the criminal setting on fire of property)
	记 词根记忆：in(进入) + cend(=cand 发光) + iary → 燃烧发光 → 放火的
incense	['ɪnsens] *n.* 香味(any pleasant fragrance)
	[ɪn'sens] *v.* 激怒(to arouse the wrath of)
	记 词根记忆：in(进入) + cens(=cand 发光) + e → 焚烧 → 点燃怒气 → 激怒
	同 enrage, infuriate, madden
incentive [ɪn'sentɪv]	*n.* 刺激，诱因，动机(motive)；刺激因素(sth. that incites to determination or action)
	记 词根记忆：in(进入) + cent(=cant 唱，说) + ive → 说服他人做某事 → 刺激，诱因
	例 Imposing steep fines on employers for on-the-job injuries to workers could be an effective

11

incentive to creating a safer workplace, especially in the case of employers with poor safety records.

同 goad, impetus, impulse, stimulus

| **incessant** | *adj.* 不停的，不断的（continuing without interruption） |
| [ɪnˈsesnt] | 记 词根记忆：in(不) + cess(走) + ant → 不停的 |

| **incidence** | *n.* 发生，出现（an instance of happening）；发生率（rate of occurrence or influence） |
| [ˈɪnsɪdəns] | 记 词根记忆：in + cid(落下) + ence → 落下来的事 → 发生，出现 |

| **incidental** | *adj.* 作为自然结果的，伴随而来的（being likely to ensue as a chance or minor consequence）；偶然发生的（occurring merely by chance） |
| [ˌɪnsɪˈdentl] | 例 Because we have completed our analysis of the major components of the proposed project, we are free to devote the remainder of this session to a study of the project's *incidental* details. |

incipient	*adj.* 初期的，起初的（beginning to exist or appear）
[ɪnˈsɪpiənt]	记 词根记忆：in + cip(掉) + ient → 掉进来的 → 初期的
	例 It is wise to begin to treat a progressive disease while it is still in its *incipient* stage.
	同 inceptive, initial, initiatory, introductory, nascent

incise	*v.* 切入，切割（to cut into）
[ɪnˈsaɪz]	记 词根记忆：in(进入) + cis(切) + e → 切入
	同 gash, pierce, slash, slice, slit

| **incisive** | *adj.* 尖锐的，深刻的（keen; penetrating; sharp） |
| [ɪnˈsaɪsɪv] | 搭 incisive comments 深刻的评论 |

| **incoherent** | *adj.* 不连贯的（lacking coherence）；语无伦次的 |
| [ˌɪnkoʊˈhɪrənt] | |

| **incommensurate** | *adj.* 不成比例的，不相称的（not proportionate; not adequate） |
| [ˌɪnkəˈmenʃərət] | 记 联想记忆：in(不) + commensurate(成比例的，相称的) → 不成比例的，不相称的 |

| **incompatibility** | *n.* 不相容(性)（the quality or state of being incompatible） |
| [ˈɪnkəmˌpætəˈbɪləti] | |

incompatible	*adj.* 无法和谐共存的，不相容的（not able to exist in harmony or agreement）
[ˌɪnkəmˈpætəbl]	记 联想记忆：in(不) + compatible(和谐共存的) → 无法和谐共存的，不相容的
	搭 be incompatible with 与…不相容
	同 disconsonant, dissonant, incongruent, incongruous, inconsonant

| **incompetent** | *adj.* 无能力的，不胜任的（lacking the qualities needed for effective action） |
| [ɪnˈkɑːmpɪtənt] | 记 联想记忆：in(不) + competent(有能力的) → 无能力的 |

| **incomplete** | *adj.* 不完全的，不完整的（not complete） |
| [ˌɪnkəmˈpliːt] | |

112

□ incessant   □ incidence   □ incidental   □ incipient   □ incise   □ incisive
□ incoherent   □ incommensurate   □ incompatibility   □ incompatible   □ incompetent   □ incomplete

incomprehensible [ˌɪnˌkɑːmprɪˈhensəbl]	*adj.* 难以理解的，难懂的（impossible to comprehend）
inconclusive [ˌɪnkənˈkluːsɪv]	*adj.* 非决定性的；无定论的（leading to no conclusion or definite result） 例 Given the *inconclusive* state of the published evidence, we do not argue here that exposure to low-level microwave energy is either hazardous or safe.
incongruity [ˌɪnkɑːnˈgruːəti]	*n.* 不协调，不相称（the quality or state of being incongruous） 记 联想记忆：in(不) + congruity(一致，和谐) → 不协调，不相称
incongruous [ɪnˈkɑːŋgruəs]	*adj.* 不协调的，不一致的（incompatible, disagreeing, inconsistent within itself; unsuitable）
inconsequential [ɪnˌkɑːnsɪˈkwenʃl]	*adj.* 不重要的，微不足道的（unimportant；trivial） 记 联想记忆：in(不) + consequential(重要的) → 不重要的 例 While admitting that the risks incurred by use of the insecticide were not *inconsequential*, the manufacturer's spokesperson argued that effective substitutes were simply not available.
inconsolable [ˌɪnkənˈsoʊləbl]	*adj.* 无法慰藉的（incapable of being consoled），悲痛欲绝的 例 In the poem *Annabel Lee*, the speaker reveals that he is not resigned to the death of his beloved；on the contrary, he is *inconsolable*.
incontrovertible [ˌɪnkɑːntrəˈvɜːrtəbl]	*adj.* 无可辩驳的（incapable of being disputed），不容置疑的 记 联想记忆：in(不) + controvertible(可辩论的) → 无可辩驳的
inconvenient [ˌɪnkənˈviːniənt]	*adj.* 不便的，打扰的，造成麻烦的（not convenient especially in giving trouble or annoyance）
incorporate [ɪnˈkɔːrpəreɪt]	*v.* 合并，并入（to combine or join with sth. already formed；embody） 记 词根记忆：in(进入) + corp(身体) + orate → 进入体内 → 合并 搭 incorporate...into... 使并入；将…包括在内 同 assimilate, imbibe, inhaust, insorb, integrate
incorrigible [ɪnˈkɔːrɪdʒəbl]	*adj.* 积习难改的，不可救药的（incapable of being corrected） 记 联想记忆：in(不) + corrigible(可改正的) → 积习难改的
incorruptible [ˌɪnkəˈrʌptəbl]	*adj.* 廉洁的，不腐败的（unable to be corrupted morally） 记 联想记忆：in(不) + corrupt(变腐败) + ible → 不会腐败的 → 廉洁的
incredulity [ˌɪnkrəˈduːləti]	*n.* 怀疑，不相信（disbelief） 记 词根记忆：in(不) + cred(信任) + ulity → 怀疑，不相信
incumbent [ɪnˈkʌmbənt]	*n.* 在职者，现任者（the holder of an office or benefice） *adj.* 义不容辞的（obligatory） 记 词根记忆：in + cumb(躺) + ent → 躺在(职位)上的人 → 在职者
indebted [ɪnˈdetɪd]	*adj.* 感激的，蒙恩的（owing gratitude） 记 联想记忆：in(进入) + debt(债务) + ed → 欠人情债的 → 感激的，蒙恩的
indecipherable [ˌɪndɪˈsaɪfrəbl]	*adj.* 无法破译的（incapable of being deciphered） 记 联想记忆：in(不) + decipher(破解，破译) + able → 无法破译的

11

indefatigable [ˌɪndɪˈfætɪɡəbl]	*adj.* 不知疲倦的(not yielding to fatigue; untiring) 记 联想记忆：in(不) + de(表强调) + fatigable(易疲倦的) → 不知疲倦的
indent [ɪnˈdent]	*v.* 切割成锯齿状(to cut tooth-like points; notch) 记 联想记忆：in(进入) + dent(牙齿) → 切割成锯齿状
indented [ɪnˈdentɪd]	*adj.* 锯齿状的；高低不平的
indenture [ɪnˈdentʃər]	*n.* 契约，合同(a written contract or agreement) *v.* 以契约约束(to bind (as an apprentice) by or as if by indentures) 记 来自indent(*v.* 切割成锯齿状)，原指古代师徒间分割成锯齿状的契约
indestructible [ˌɪndɪˈstrʌktəbl]	*adj.* 不能破坏的，不可毁灭的 (incapable of being destroyed, ruined, or rendered ineffective)
indicate [ˈɪndɪkeɪt]	*v.* 指示，指出(to show sth.)；象征，显示(to be a sign of) 记 词根记忆：in + dic(说) + ate → 指示，指出 例 These sporadic raids seem to *indicate* that the enemy is waging a war of attrition rather than attacking us directly. 同 attest, bespeak, betoken, signify

Meeting Room
indicate

indict [ɪnˈdaɪt]	*v.* 控诉，起诉 (to make a formal accusation against; accuse) 记 词根记忆：in(进入) + dict(说) → (在法庭上)把…说出来 → 控诉 同 criminate, impeach, incriminate, inculpate
indigence [ˈɪndɪdʒəns]	*n.* 贫穷，贫困(poverty; lacking money and goods) 记 联想记忆：in(无) + dig(挖) + ence → 挖不出东西 → 贫穷 例 Micawber's habit of spending more than he earned left him in a state of perpetual *indigence*, but he persevered in hoping to see a more affluent day. 同 destitution, impecuniousness, impoverishment, penury, privation
indigenous [ɪnˈdɪdʒənəs]	*adj.* 土产的，本地的(native)；生来的，固有的(innate) 记 词根记忆：indi(内部) + gen(产生) + ous → 产生于内部的 → 本地的
indigent [ˈɪndɪdʒənt]	*adj.* 贫穷的，贫困的(deficient; impoverished) 记 联想记忆：in(无) + dig(挖) + ent → 挖不出东西 → 贫穷的
indignation [ˌɪndɪɡˈneɪʃn]	*n.* 愤慨，义愤(anger or scorn; righteous anger) 搭 to be full of righteous indignation 义愤填膺
indiscriminate [ˌɪndɪˈskrɪmɪnət]	*adj.* 不加选择的 (not marked by careful distinction)；随意的，任意的 (haphazard; random)
indiscriminately [ˌɪndɪˈskrɪmɪnətli]	*adv.* 随意地，任意地(in a random manner; promiscuously) 例 Although most worthwhile criticism concentrates on the positive, one should not *indiscriminately* praise everything. 同 arbitrarily

☑ indefatigable	□ indent	□ indented	□ indenture	□ indestructible	□ indicate
□ indict	□ indigence	□ indigenous	□ indigent	□ indignation	□ indiscriminate
□ indiscriminately					

indistinguishable	*adj.* 无法区分的，难以分辨的（not distinguishable）
[ˌɪndɪˈstɪŋgwɪʃəbl]	搭 be indistinguishable from 无法从…中区分
individual	*adj.* 单独的，单个的（single; separate）；特有的（particular）；个人的，个体
[ˌɪndɪˈvɪdʒuəl]	的 *n.* 个人，个体（single human being）
	记 联想记忆：in + divid(e)(分割) + ual → 分割开的 → 单独的，单个的
	例 Unlike a judge, who must act alone, a jury discusses a case and then reaches its decision as a group, thus minimizing the effect of *individual* bias.
	同 distinctive, idiosyncratic
individualism	*n.* 个人主义（a doctrine that the interests of the individual are or ought to
[ˌɪndɪˈvɪdʒuəlɪzəm]	be ethically paramount）
indolent	*adj.* 懒惰的（idle; lazy）
[ˈɪndələnt]	记 词根记忆：in(不) + dol(悲痛) + ent → 不悲痛的 → 不因时间的流逝而
	悲痛的 → 懒惰的
	同 faineant, slothful, slowgoing, work-shy
indubitable	*adj.* 不容置疑的（unquestionable）
[ɪnˈduːbɪtəbl]	记 词根记忆：in(不) + dub(不确定的) + it + able → 不容置疑的
indubitably	*adv.* 无疑地，确实地（certainly or without doubt）
[ɪnˈduːbɪtəbli]	例 Before the inflation spiral, one could have had a complete meal in a restaurant for a dollar, including the tip, whereas today a hot dog, coffee, and dessert would *indubitably* add up to two or three times that much.
inducement	*n.* 引诱；引诱物，诱因，动机
[ɪnˈduːsmənt]	记 来自 induce(*v.* 引诱)
inducible	*adj.* 可诱导的（capable of being induced）
[ɪnˈduːsəbl]	
indulge	*v.* 放纵，纵容（to allow to have whatever one likes or wants）；满足（to
[ɪnˈdʌldʒ]	satisfy a perhaps unwarranted desire）
	同 cosset, pamper, spoil
indulgent	*adj.* 放纵的，纵容的（indulging or characterized by indulgence）
[ɪnˈdʌldʒənt]	搭 indulgent parents 纵容子女的父母
inedible	*adj.* 不能吃的，不可食的（not fit to be eaten）
[ɪnˈedəbl]	
inefficient	*adj.* 无效率的（not efficient）；无能的，不称职的（incapable; incompetent）
[ˌɪnɪˈfɪʃnt]	搭 an inefficient heating system 效率不佳的暖气系统
inelastic	*adj.* 无弹性的（inflexible）
[ˌɪnɪˈlæstɪk]	记 联想记忆：in(不) + elastic(有弹性的) → 无弹性的
ineligible	*adj.* 不合格的（not legally or morally qualified）
[ɪnˈelɪdʒəbl]	记 联想记忆：in(不) + eligible(合格的) → 不合格的
inept	*adj.* 无能的（inefficient）；不适当的（not suitable）
[ɪˈnept]	记 联想记忆：in(不) + ept(能干的) → 无能的

11

□ indistinguishable	□ individual	□ individualism	□ indolent	□ indubitable	□ indubitably
□ inducement	□ inducible	□ indulge	□ indulgent	□ inedible	☑ inefficient
□ inelastic	□ ineligible	□ inept			

ineptitude [ɪˈneptɪtuːd]	*n.* 无能；不适当（the quality or state of being inept）
inert [ɪˈnɜːrt]	*adj.* 惰性的（having few or no active chemical or other properties）；呆滞的，迟缓的（dull; slow） 记 词根记忆：in(不) + ert(动) → 不动的 → 惰性的
inestimable [ɪnˈestɪməbl]	*adj.* 无法估计的（incapable of being estimated or computed）；无价的，极有价值的（too valuable or excellent to be measured or appreciated）
inevitable [ɪnˈevɪtəbl]	*adj.* 不可避免的，必然的（incapable of being avoided or evaded） 记 联想记忆：in(不) + evitable(可避免的) → 不可避免的 例 Because vast organizations are an *inevitable* element in modern life, it is futile to aim at their abolition. 同 ineluctable, ineludible, inescapable, inevasible
inexcusable [ˌɪnɪkˈskjuːzəbl]	*adj.* 不可原谅的，不可宽恕的（impossible to excuse or justify）
inexhaustible [ˌɪnɪɡˈzɔːstəbl]	*adj.* 用不完的，无穷无尽的（incapable of being used up or emptied） 记 联想记忆：in(不) + exhaust(耗尽) + ible → 用不完的 例 The sheer diversity of tropical plants represents a seemingly *inexhaustible* source of raw materials, of which only a few have been utilized.
inexorable [ɪnˈeksərəbl]	*adj.* 不为所动的（incapable of being moved or influenced）；无法改变的（that cannot be altered） 记 词根记忆：in(不) + ex(出) + or(说) + able → 不可被说服的 → 不为所动的
inexpensive [ˌɪnɪkˈspensɪv]	*adj.* 廉价的，便宜的（reasonable in price） 例 Because many of the minerals found on the ocean floor are still plentiful on land, where mining is relatively *inexpensive*, mining the ocean floor has yet to become a profitable enterprise.
inexplicable [ˌɪnɪkˈsplɪkəbl]	*adj.* 无法解释的（incapable of being explained or accounted for） 记 联想记忆：in(不) + explicable(可解释的) → 无法解释的 例 There were contradictions in her nature that made her seem an *inexplicable* enigma: she was severe and gentle; she was modest and disdainful; she longed for affection and was cold.
infamous [ˈɪnfəməs]	*adj.* 臭名昭著的（having a reputation of the worst kind） 同 notorious
infant [ˈɪnfənt]	*n.* 婴儿（a child in the first period of life） 记 联想记忆：in + fant(看作 faint, 虚弱的) → 尚处于无力虚弱的状态 → 婴儿
infantile [ˈɪnfəntaɪl]	*adj.* 幼稚的，孩子气的（like or typical of a small child） 记 来自 infant(*n.* 婴儿)
infect [ɪnˈfekt]	*v.* 传染（to contaminate with a disease-producing substance or agent）；使感染，侵染（to communicate a pathogen or a disease）；污染（to contaminate）

☐ ineptitude ☐ inert ☐ inestimable ☑ inevitable ☐ inexcusable ☐ inexhaustible
☐ inexorable ☑ inexpensive ☐ inexplicable ☑ infamous ☐ infant ☐ infantile
☐ infect

	例 No computer system is immune to a virus, a particularly malicious program that is designed to *infect* and electronically damage the disks on which data are stored.
infection [ɪnˈfekʃn]	*n.* 传染；感染（an act or process of infecting） 记 词根记忆：in(进入) + fect(做) → 在里面做 → 传染
infectious [ɪnˈfekʃəs]	*adj.* 传染的，有传染性的（capable of causing infection; communicable by infection）
infer [ɪnˈfɜːr]	*v.* 推断，推论，推理（to reach an opinion from reasoning） 记 词根记忆：in(进入) + fer(带来) → 带进(意义) → 推断
inferable [ɪnˈfɜːrəbl]	*adj.* 能推理的，能推论的
inferior [ɪnˈfɪriər]	*adj.* 下级的，下属的；低等的，较差的（lower in rank, importance, etc.） 搭 to make sb. feel inferior 使某人自惭形秽
infertile [ɪnˈfɜːrtl]	*adj.* 贫瘠的，不结果实的（not fertile or productive）
infest [ɪnˈfest]	*v.* 大批出没于，骚扰（to spread or swarm in or over in a troublesome manner）；寄生于（to live in or on as a parasite） 记 联想记忆：in(进入) + fest(集会) → 全部来参加集会 → 大批出没于，骚扰
infiltrate [ˈɪnfɪltreɪt]	*v.* 渗透，渗入（to pass through） 记 词根记忆：in(进入) + filtr(过滤) + ate → 过滤进去 → 渗透，渗入
infinitesimal [ˌɪnfɪnɪˈtesɪml]	*adj.* 极微小的（infinitely small）*n.* 极小量 记 词根记忆：in(不) + fin(边界) + ite + sim(百分之一) + al → 无穷小的 → 极微小的
infirm [ɪnˈfɜːrm]	*adj.* 虚弱的（physically weak） 记 联想记忆：in(不) + firm(坚定的) → 不坚定的 → 虚弱的
inflamed [ɪnˈfleɪmd]	*adj.* 发炎的，红肿的（red and swollen because of infection） 记 联想记忆：in(在…里面) + flame(火焰) + d → 像有火焰在里面烧 → 发炎的，红肿的
inflate [ɪnˈfleɪt]	*v.* 使充气，使膨胀（to fill with air） 记 词根记忆：in(朝内) + flat(吹气) + e → 朝内吹气 → 使充气
inflexible [ɪnˈfleksəbl]	*adj.* 坚定的，不屈不挠的（rigidly firm in will or purpose）
inflict [ɪnˈflɪkt]	*v.* 使遭受(痛苦、损伤等)（to cause a blow, penalty to be suffered by sb.） 记 词根记忆：in(进入) + flict(击，打) → 使进入打斗状态 → 使遭受(痛苦、损伤等)
influence [ˈɪnfluəns]	*n.* 影响 *v.* 影响（to affect or alter by indirect or intangible means） 记 联想记忆：in(进入) + flu(流感) + ence → 患上流感容易影响别人 → 影响 搭 influence on 对…产生影响

别喝，我有肝炎

infectious

11

influential [ˌɪnflu'enʃl]	*adj.* 有影响力的（exerting or possessing influence）
inform [ɪn'fɔːrm]	*v.* 对…有影响（to have an influence on sth.）；使活跃，使有生气（to animate）；告诉，通知（to impart information or knowledge） 记 词根记忆：in(进入) + form(形成) → 形成文字，进行通知 → 通知 例 Just as the authors' book on eels is often a key text for courses in marine vertebrate zoology, their ideas on animal development and phylogeny *inform* teaching in this area. 同 acquaint, apprise
informal [ɪn'fɔːrml]	*adj.* 随便的，日常的（characteristic of or appropriate to ordinary, casual, or familiar use）；不拘礼节的，非正式的（marked by the absence of formality or ceremony）
informality [ˌɪnfɔːr'mæləti]	*n.* 非正式，不拘礼节
informative [ɪn'fɔːrmətɪv]	*adj.* 提供信息的（imparting knowledge; instructive）；见闻广博的
infrared [ˌɪnfrə'red]	*adj.* 红外线的
infrequently [ɪn'friːkwəntli]	*adv.* 稀少地，罕见地 同 rarely, seldom
infuriate [ɪn'fjʊrieɪt]	*v.* 使恼怒，激怒（to enrage） 记 词根记忆：in(进入) + furi(=fury 狂怒) + ate → 进入狂怒 → 使恼怒，激怒
infuse [ɪn'fjuːz]	*v.* 注入，灌输（to instill; impart）；鼓励（to inspire） 记 词根记忆：in(进入) + fus(流) + e → 流进去 → 注入，灌输
ingenious [ɪn'dʒiːniəs]	*adj.* 聪明的（clever）；善于创造发明的，心灵手巧的（original; inventive） 记 词根记忆：in(在里面) + gen(产生) + ious → 聪明产生于内 → 聪明的；注意不要和 ingenuous(*adj.* 纯真的，纯朴的；坦率的)相混
ingeniousness [ɪn'dʒiːniəsnəs]	*n.* 独创性（ingenuity）
ingenuity [ˌɪndʒə'nuːəti]	*n.* 聪明才智（cleverness）；独创性（originality）
ingenuous [ɪn'dʒenjuəs]	*adj.* 纯真的，纯朴的（simple; artless）；坦率的（frank） 同 natural, unsophisticated
ingenuously [ɪn'dʒenjuəsli]	*adv.* 纯真地；坦率地
ingest [ɪn'dʒest]	*v.* 咽下，吞下（to take into the body by swallowing） 记 词根记忆：in(进入) + gest(搬运) → 搬进去 → 咽下，吞下

☑ influential ☐ inform ☑ informal ☐ informality ☐ informative ☐ infrared
☐ infrequently ☑ infuriate ☐ infuse ☐ ingenious ☐ ingeniousness ☐ ingenuity
☐ ingenuous ☐ ingenuously ☐ ingest

ingrain [ɪnˈɡreɪn]	*adj.* 根深蒂固的（thoroughly worked in）*n.* 本质（innate quality or character） 记 联想记忆：in（进入）+ grain（木头的纹理）→ 进入纹理 → 根深蒂固的
ingrained [ɪnˈɡreɪnd]	*adj.* 根深蒂固的（firmed, fixed or established） 搭 ingrained prejudices 很深的成见
ingrate [ɪnˈɡreɪt]	*n.* 忘恩负义的人（an ungrateful person） 记 词根记忆：in（不）+ grat（感激）+ e → 不知感激 → 忘恩负义的人

If you put out your hands, you are a laborer; if you put out your hands and mind, you are a craftsperson; if you put out your hands, mind, heart and soul, you are an artist.

如果你用双手工作，你是一个劳力；如果你用双手和头脑工作，你是一个工匠；如果你用双手和头脑工作，并且全身心投入，你就是一个艺术家。

——美国电影 *American Heart and Soul*

Word List 12  MP3 - 12

ingratiating [ɪnˈɡreɪʃieɪtɪŋ]	*adj.* 讨人喜欢的，迷人的（capable of winning favor）；讨好的，献媚的（calculated to please or win favor）
inhabit [ɪnˈhæbɪt]	*v.* 居住于（to live in; occupy）；占据 记 词根记忆：in(进入) + hab(拥有) + it → 在里面拥有 → 居住于；占据 例 With the evolution of wings, insects were able to disperse to the far ecological corners, across deserts and bodies of water, to reach new food sources and *inhabit* a wider variety of promising environmental niches.
inherent [ɪnˈhɪrənt]	*adj.* 固有的，内在的（involved in the constitution or essential character of sth.; belonging by nature or habit） 记 词根记忆：in(在里面) + her(黏附) + ent → 黏附在内的 → 固有的，内在的 搭 be inherent in 为…所固有
inherently [ɪnˈhɪrəntli]	*adv.* 固有地，天性地（intrinsically） 例 Although scientists claim that the seemingly literal language of their reports is more precise than the figurative language of fiction, the language of science, like all language, is *inherently* allusive.
inhibit [ɪnˈhɪbɪt]	*v.* 阻止（to prohibit from doing something）；抑制（to hold in check） 记 词根记忆：in(不) + hib(拿) + it → 不许拿 → 阻止；抑制 同 bridle, constrain, withhold
inhibition [ˌɪn(h)ɪˈbɪʃn]	*n.* 阻止；抑制（the act of inhibiting）；抑制物（sth. that forbids, debars, or restricts） 例 William James lacked the usual awe of death; writing to his dying father, he spoke without *inhibition* about the old man's impending death.
inimical [ɪˈnɪmɪkl]	*adj.* 敌意的，不友善的（hostile; unfriendly） 记 词根记忆：in(不) + im(爱) + ical → 不爱的 → 敌意的，不友善的
inimitable [ɪˈnɪmɪtəbl]	*adj.* 无法仿效的（incapable of being imitated or matched） 记 词根记忆：in(不) + imit(模仿) + able → 不可模仿的 → 无法仿效的
iniquitous [ɪˈnɪkwɪtəs]	*adj.* 邪恶的，不公正的（wicked; unjust） 记 词根记忆：in(不) + iqu(公正的) + itous → 不公正的

□ ingratiating	□ inhabit	□ inherent	□ inherently	□ inhibit	□ inhibition
□ inimical	□ inimitable	□ iniquitous			

initial	*adj.* 开始的，最初的（at the very beginning）
[ɪˈnɪʃl]	*n.* (姓名的)首字母（the first letter of a name）
	记 词根记忆：in（朝内）+ it（走）+ ial → 朝内走
	→ 开始的，最初的
	例 Many of the earliest colonial houses that are still standing have been so modified and enlarged that the *initial* design is no longer discernible.
	同 inceptive, incipient, initiative, initiatory, nascent

initial

initiate	*v.* 发起，开始（to set going by taking the first step; begin）；接纳（to admit into membership, as with ceremonies or ritual）
[ɪˈnɪʃieɪt]	记 词根记忆：in（朝内）+ it（走）+ ial → 朝内走 → 发起，开始
	同 commence, inaugurate, institute, originate

| **injurious** | *adj.* 有害的（harmful） |
| [ɪnˈdʒʊəriəs] | 记 来自 injury（n. 伤害） |

innate	*adj.* 天生的，固有的（inborn; inbred）
[ɪˈneɪt]	记 词根记忆：in（在内）+ nat（出生）+ e → 出生时带来的 → 天生的
	例 Unlike Sartre, who was born into a cultivated environment, receiving culture in his feeding bottle, so to speak, the child Camus had to fight to acquire a culture that was not *innate*.
	同 connate, connatural, indigenous

| **innermost** | *adj.* 最里面的（farthest inward） |
| [ˈɪnəməʊst] | 记 组合词：inner（里面的）+ most（最）→ 最里面的 |

innocence	*n.* 无辜，清白（the quality of being innocent）
[ˈɪnəsns]	记 词根记忆：in（无）+ noc（伤害）+ ence → 无辜，清白
	例 Melodramas, which presented stark oppositions between *innocence* and criminality, virtue and corruption, good and evil, were popular precisely because they offered the audience a world devoid of neutrality.

innocuous	*adj.* (行为、言论等)无害的（harmless）
[ɪˈnɑːkjuəs]	记 词根记忆：in（无）+ noc（伤害）+ uous → 无害的
	例 The articles that he wrote ran the gamut from the serious to the lighthearted, from objective to the argumentative, from the *innocuous* to the hostile.
	同 innocent, innoxious, inoffensive, unoffensive

| **innovative** | *adj.* 革新的，创新的（introducing or using new ideas or techniques） |
| [ˈɪnəveɪtɪv] | 记 来自 innovate（v. 革新，创新） |

| **inoffensive** | *adj.* 无害的（causing no harm or injury）；不讨厌的（not objectionable to the senses） |
| [ˌɪnəˈfensɪv] | 例 Because medieval women's public participation in spiritual life was not welcomed by the male establishment, a compensating involvement with religious writings, *inoffensive* to the members of the establishment because of its privacy, became important for many women. |

---

inordinate [ɪnˈɔːrdɪnət]	*adj.* 过度的, 过分的(immoderate; excessive) 记 词根记忆: in(不) + ordin(次序) + ate → 无序的 → 不正常的 → 过度的, 过分的 例 In the absence of native predators to stop their spread, imported deer thrived to such an *inordinate* degree that they overgrazed the countryside and threatened the native vegetation.
inquiry [ˈɪnkwəri]	*n.* 询问(a request for help or information) 同 interrogation, query, question
inquisitive [ɪnˈkwɪzətɪv]	*adj.* 好奇的, 好问的(inclined to ask questions; prying); 爱打听的 记 词根记忆: in(进入) + quis(询问) + itive → 进入询问 → 好奇的, 好问的 例 Excited and unafraid, the *inquisitive* child examined the stranger with bright-eyed curiosity.
insatiable [ɪnˈseɪʃəbl]	*adj.* 不知足的, 贪得无厌的(very greedy) 记 词根记忆: in(不) + sati(填满) + able → 填不满的 → 不知足的
insatiably [ɪnˈseɪʃəbli]	*adv.* 不知足地, 贪得无厌地(to an insatiable degree; with persistence but without satisfaction) 例 Most people are shameless voyeurs where the very rich are concerned, *insatiably* curious about how they get their money and how they spend it.
insecure [ˌɪnsɪˈkjʊr]	*adj.* 无保障的, 不安全的(not adequately guarded or sustained) 同 unprotected, unsafe
insider [ɪnˈsaɪdər]	*n.* 局内人, 圈内人(a person inside a given place or group) 例 Though dealers insist that professional art dealers can make money in the art market, even an *insider's* knowledge is not enough: the art world is so fickle that stock-market prices are predictable by comparison.
insidious [ɪnˈsɪdiəs]	*adj.* 暗中危害的, 阴险的(working or spreading harmfully in a subtle or stealthy manner) 记 词根记忆: in(在里面) + sid(坐) + ious → (祸害)坐在里面的 → 暗中危害的
insight [ˈɪnsaɪt]	*n.* 洞察力(the power or act of seeing into a situation); 洞悉 记 联想记忆: in(进入) + sight(眼光) → 眼光深入 → 洞察力 例 Marison was a scientist of unusual *insight* and imagination who had startling success in discerning new and fundamental principles well in advance of their general recognition. 同 discernment, intuition, penetration, perception
insightful [ˈɪnsaɪtfʊl]	*adj.* 富有洞察力的, 有深刻见解的(exhibiting or characterized by insight) 例 Although in his seventies at the time of the interview, Picasso proved alert and *insightful*, his faculties intact despite the inevitable toll of the years. 同 discerning, perceptive, sagacious, sage, sophic

insignificant [ˌɪnsɪgˈnɪfɪkənt]	*adj.* 无价值的，无意义的，无用的（lacking meaning or importance; unimportant） 例 The acts of vandalism that these pranksters had actually perpetrated were *insignificant* compared with those they had contemplated but had not attempted. 同 purposeless, trivial, unmeaning
insincere [ˌɪnsɪnˈsɪr]	*adj.* 不诚恳的，虚伪的（hypocritical） 例 Since she believed him to be both candid and trustworthy, she refused to consider the possibility that his statement had been *insincere*.
insinuate [ɪnˈsɪnjueɪt]	*v.* 暗指，暗示（to hint or suggest indirectly; imply） 记 词根记忆：in(进入) + sinu(弯曲) + ate → 绕弯说出来 → 暗指
insipid [ɪnˈsɪpɪd]	*adj.* 乏味的，枯燥的（banal; dull; vapid） 记 词根记忆：in(不) + sip(有味道) + id → 没味道的 → 乏味的 例 Just as an *insipid* dish lacks flavor, an inane remark lacks sense. 同 distasteful, savorless, unappetizing, unpalatable, unsavory
insolent [ˈɪnsələnt]	*adj.* 粗野的，无礼的（boldly disrespectful in speech or behavior; impudent）
insoluble [ɪnˈsɑːljəbl]	*adj.* 不能溶解的（incapable of being dissolved）；不能解决的（incapable of being solved） 记 词根记忆：in(不) + solu(溶解；解决) + ble → 不能溶解的；不能解决的
inspire [ɪnˈspaɪər]	*v.* 鼓舞，激励（to impel; motivate） 记 词根记忆：in(使) + spir(呼吸) + e → 使…呼吸澎湃 → 鼓舞 同 animate, elate, exalt, exhilarate
instantaneous [ˌɪnstənˈteɪniəs]	*adj.* 立即的，即刻的（immediate）；瞬间的（occurring, or acting without any perceptible duration of time） 记 来自 instant(*adj.* 立即的，即刻的 *n.* 瞬间，顷刻)
instantly [ˈɪnstəntli]	*adv.* 立即，即刻（with importunity）*conj.* 一…就（as soon as） 记 directly, forthwith, immediately
instigate [ˈɪnstɪgeɪt]	*v.* 怂恿，鼓动，煽动（to urge on; foment; incite） 记 词根记忆：in(进入) + stig(=sting 刺激) + ate → 刺激起来 → 怂恿，鼓动，煽动 同 abet, provoke, stir
instinctive [ɪnˈstɪŋktɪv]	*adj.* 本能的（prompted by natural instinct） 记 来自 instinct(*n.* 本能) 例 Ethologists are convinced that many animals survive through learning—but learning that is dictated by their genetic programming, learning as thoroughly stereotyped as the most *instinctive* of behavioral responses.

12

□ insignificant　□ insincere　□ insinuate　□ insipid　□ insolent　□ insoluble
□ inspire　□ instantaneous　□ instantly　□ instigate　□ instinctive

123

institute [ˈɪnstɪtuːt]	v. 设立，创立(社团等)；制定(政策等)(to set up; establish) n. 学院，学会，协会 记 词根记忆：in(进入) + stit(站) + ute → 站进去 → 设立，创立 例 Doreen justifiably felt she deserved recognition for the fact that the research *institute* had been returned to a position of preeminence, since it was she who had directed the transformation. 同 constitute, inaugurate, initiate, launch
institution [ˌɪnstɪˈtuːʃn]	n. 机构(an established organization or corporation)；制度 记 来自 institute(v. 设立，创立；制定) 例 During the 1960's assessments of the family shifted remarkably, from general endorsement of it as a worthwhile, stable *institution* to wide spread censure of it as an oppressive and bankrupt one whose dissolution was both imminent and welcome.
institutionalize [ˌɪnstɪˈtuːʃənəlaɪz]	v. 使制度化(to make into an institution) 记 和 institutionalization(n. 制度化)一起记
institutionalized [ˌɪnstɪˈtuːʃənəlaɪzd]	adj. 制度化的(making into an institution) 例 As the creation of new knowledge through science has become *institutionalized* resistance to innovation has become less aggressive taking the form of inertia rather than direct attack.
instructive [ɪnˈstrʌktɪv]	adj. 传授知识的(giving much useful information)，教育的；有益的(helpful) 记 来自 instruct(v. 教导，教授) 例 The parables in the *Bible* are both entertaining and *instructive*.
instrumental [ˌɪnstrəˈmentl]	adj. 作为手段的，有帮助的(serving as a crucial means, agent, or tool; helpful in bringing sth. about)；器械的(of, relating to, or accomplished with an instrument or a tool) 记 来自 instrument(n. 器械；手段)
insubordinate [ˌɪnsəˈbɔːrdɪnət]	adj. 不服从的，违抗的(disobedient) 记 联想记忆：in(不) + subordinate(服从的) → 不服从的 例 By idiosyncratically refusing to dismiss an *insubordinate* member of his staff, the manager not only contravened established policy, but he also jeopardized his heretofore good chances for promotion.
insubstantial [ˌɪnsəbˈstænʃl]	adj. 无实体的(immaterial)；脆弱的(frail) 记 联想记忆：in(不) + substantial(实体的；坚固的) → 无实体的；脆弱的
insular [ˈɪnsələr]	adj. 岛屿的；心胸狭窄的(illiberal; narrow-minded) 记 词根记忆：insul(岛) + ar → 岛屿的
insulting [ɪnˈsʌltɪŋ]	adj. 侮辱的，污蔑的(abusive) 记 来自 insult(v. 侮辱，辱骂)
insurgent [ɪnˈsɜːrdʒənt]	adj. 叛乱的，起义的(rebellious) n. 叛乱分子(a person engaged in insurgent activity) 记 联想记忆：in(内部) + surge(浪涛；升起) + nt → 内部起浪潮 → 叛乱的
insurmountable [ˌɪnsərˈmaʊntəbl]	adj. 不能克服的，不能超越的(incapable of being surmounted) 同 impassable, insuperable

intact [ɪnˈtækt]	*adj.* 完整的，完好无缺的(complete; unimpaired) 记 词根记忆：in(不) + tact(接触) → 未被接触过的 → 完整的 例 The hierarchy of medical occupations is in many ways a caste system; its strata remain *intact* and the practitioners in them have very little vertical mobility. 同 flawless, unblemished, unmarred
intangible [ɪnˈtændʒəbl]	*adj.* 触摸不到的(not tangible; impalpable)；无形的(incorporeal) 记 词根记忆：in(不) + tang(触摸) + ible → 触摸不到的 同 imperceptible, indiscernible, untouchable
integrate [ˈɪntɪɡreɪt]	*v.* 使成整体，使一体化(to make whole or complete) 记 词根记忆：in(不) + tegr(触摸) + ate → 未被触摸 → 使成整体
intellectual [ˌɪntəˈlektʃuəl]	*adj.* 智力的 (of or relating to the intellect)；理性的 (rational rather than emotional) *n.* 知识分子 记 词根记忆：intel(在…中间) + lect(选择) + ual → 能从中选择的 → 智力的 例 As painted by Constable, the scene is not one of bucolic serenity; rather it shows a striking emotional and *intellectual* tension. 同 cerebral, intellective, intelligent
intelligible [ɪnˈtelɪdʒəbl]	*adj.* 可理解的，易于理解的 (incapable of being understood; comprehensible) 记 词根记忆：intel (在…中间) + lig (选择) + ible → 能从中间选择出来的 → 可理解的
intemperance [ɪnˈtempərəns]	*n.* 放纵，不节制，过度(lack of temperance) 同 excess, overindulgence, surfeit
intensification [ɪnˌtensɪfɪˈkeɪʃn]	*n.* 增强，加剧，激烈化 记 来自 intensify(*v.* 增强，加剧)
intent [ɪnˈtent]	*adj.* 专心的，专注的(having the attention applied; engrossed)；热烈的，渴望的(directed with strained or eager attention; full of eager interest) *n.* 目的，意向(purpose) 记 来自 intend(*v.* 打算) 例 The idea that people are basically economic creatures, *intent* only upon their own material advantage, induces disbelief in the integrity of any unselfish motive.
intentional [ɪnˈtenʃənl]	*adj.* 存心的，故意的(on purpose) 同 deliberate, intended, purposeful, willful
interactive [ˌɪntərˈæktɪv]	*adj.* 交互式的(mutually or reciprocally active) 记 来自 interact(*v.* 相互作用，相互影响)
interchangeable [ˌɪntərˈtʃeɪndʒəbl]	*adj.* 可互换的(incapable of being interchanged) 记 来自 interchange(*v.* 互换)

12

interchangeably [ˌɪntərˈtʃeɪndʒəbli]	*adv.* 可互换地 例 Although newscasters often use the terms Chicano and Latino *interchangeably*, students of Hispanic-American culture are profoundly aware of the dissimilarities between the two.
interconnected [ˌɪntərkəˈnektɪd]	*adj.* 相互连接的(mutually joined or related) 记 联想记忆：inter(在···中间) + connect(连接) + ed → 在中间连接 → 相互连接的
interdependent [ˌɪntərdɪˈpendənt]	*adj.* 相互依赖的，互助的(mutually dependent) 记 联想记忆：inter(在···中间) + dependent(依赖的) → 在中间依赖的 → 相互依赖的
interlocking [ˌɪntərˈlɑːkɪŋ]	*adj.* 连锁；关联的 记 来自 interlock(v. 连锁；连结)
interminable [ɪnˈtɜːrmɪnəbl]	*adj.* 无止境的，没完没了的(without end; lasting) 记 词根记忆：in(不) + termin(尽头) + able → 无尽头的 → 无止境的
interplay [ˈɪntərpleɪ]	*v.* 相互影响(to interact) *n.* 相互影响(interaction) 记 联想记忆：inter（在···之间） + play（扮演角色） → 在两者中间扮演角色 → 相互影响
interpolate [ɪnˈtɜːrpəleɪt]	*v.* 插入(to insert between or among others)；（通过插入新语句)篡改(to alter by putting in new words) 记 词根记忆：inter + pol(修饰) + ate → 通过在中间放入某物来修饰 → 插入；篡改
interpret [ɪnˈtɜːrprɪt]	*v.* 解释，说明(to explain or tell the meaning of)；演绎(to represent by means of art) 记 词根记忆：inter(在···之间) + pret(传播) → 在两种语言中间说 → 解释 搭 interpret...as... 把···理解为··· 同 construe, explicate, expound
interpretation [ɪnˌtɜːrprɪˈteɪʃn]	*n.* 解释，说明（the act or the result of interpreting)；演绎（a particular adaptation or version of a work, method, or style) 例 Fossils may be set in stone, but their *interpretation* is not; a new find may necessitate the revision of a traditional theory.
interrelate [ˌɪntərɪˈleɪt]	*v.* 相互关联，相互影响(to bring into mutual relation; have mutual relationship)
interrogation [ɪnˌterəˈɡeɪʃn]	*n.* 审问，质问；疑问句 同 inquiry, query, question
interruption [ˌɪntəˈrʌpʃn]	*n.* 中断，打断 同 break, disruption, pause, suspension
intersect [ˌɪntərˈsekt]	*v.* 相交（to meet and cross at a point)；贯穿，横穿（to divide into two parts; cut across) 记 词根记忆：inter + sect(切，割) → 从中间切 → 横穿

Hello! 他说你好

interpret

intimate	[ˈɪntɪmət] *adj.* 亲密的(closely acquainted) *n.* 密友(an intimate friend or companion) [ˈɪntɪmeɪt] *v.* 暗示(to hint or imply; suggest) 记 词根记忆：intim(最深入的) + ate → 亲密的 例 Even those siblings whose childhood was dominated by familial feuding and intense rivalry for their parents' affection can nevertheless develop congenial and even *intimate* relationships with each other in their adult lives.
intimation [ˌɪntɪˈmeɪʃn]	*n.* 暗示 同 clue, cue, hint, suggestion
intimidate [ɪnˈtɪmɪdeɪt]	*v.* 恐吓(to make timid)；胁迫(to compel by or as if by threats) 记 词根记忆：in(使…) + timid(害怕) + ate → 使害怕 → 恐吓 例 Gaddis is a formidably talented writer whose work has been, unhappily, more likely to *intimidate* or repel his readers than to lure them into his fictional world.
intractable [ɪnˈtræktəbl]	*adj.* 倔强的，难以管理的(not easily managed; unruly or stubborn)；难以加工的，难以操作的(difficult to mold or manipulate) 记 词根记忆：in(不) + tract(拉) + able → 拉不动的 → 倔强的
intransigent [ɪnˈtrænzɪdʒənt]	*adj.* 不妥协的(uncompromising) 记 联想记忆：in(不) + transigent(妥协的) → 不妥协的 例 Always circumspect, she was reluctant to make judgments, but once arriving at a conclusion, she was *intransigent* in its defense. 同 incompliant, intractable, obstinate, pertinacious
intrepid [ɪnˈtrepɪd]	*adj.* 勇敢的，刚毅的(characterized by fearless-ness and fortitude) 记 词根记忆：in(不) + trep(害怕) + id → 不害怕 → 勇敢的
intricacy [ˈɪntrɪkəsi]	*n.* 错综复杂(the quality of being intricate) 记 词根记忆：in(在里面) + tric(小障碍物) + acy → 在里面放入很多小障碍物 → 错综复杂
intricate [ˈɪntrɪkət]	*adj.* 错综复杂的(having many complexly arranged elements; elaborate)；难懂的(complex; hard to follow or understand) 记 词根记忆：in(在里面) + tric(小障碍物) + ate → 在里面放入很多小障碍物 → 错综复杂的 例 Although the minuet appeared simple, its *intricate* steps had to be studied very carefully before they could be gracefully executed in public. 同 complicated, knotty, labyrinthine, sophisticated
intrigue [ɪnˈtriːg]	*v.* 密谋(to plot or scheme secretly)；引起…的兴趣(to arouse the interest or curiosity of) 记 词根记忆：in + trig(=tric 小障碍物) + ue → 在里面放入很多小障碍物 → 密谋

intrepid

12

intrinsic [ɪnˈtrɪnsɪk]	*adj.* 固有的，内在的，本质的（belonging to the essential nature） 例 In his address, the superintendent exhorted the teachers to discover and develop each student's *intrinsic* talents. 同 congenital, connate, elemental, inherent, innate
introspective [ˌɪntrəˈspektɪv]	*adj.* 内省的，自省的（characteristic of sb. who is inclined to introspect） 记 来自 introspect(*v.* 内省，反省) 例 Unlike many recent interpretations of Beethoven's piano sonatas, the recitalist's performance was a delightfully free and *introspective* one; nevertheless, it was also, seemingly paradoxically, quite controlled.
introvert [ˈɪntrəvɜːrt]	*n.* 性格内向的人（one whose thoughts and feelings are directed toward） 例 Because he was an *introvert* by nature, he preferred reading a book in the privacy of his own study to visiting a night club with friends.
intruding [ɪnˈtruːdɪŋ]	*adj.* 入侵的，入侵性的（intrusive） 记 来自 intrude(*v.* 侵入，侵扰)
intrusively [ɪnˈtruːsɪvli]	*adv.* 入侵地 记 来自 intrusive(*adj.* 入侵的，入侵性)
intuition [ˌɪntuˈɪʃn]	*n.* 直觉（the act or faculty of knowing or sensing without the use of rational processes; immediate cognition）；直觉知识（knowledge gained by this power） 记 来自 intuit(*v.* 由直觉知道)
intuitive [ɪnˈtuːɪtɪv]	*adj.* 直觉的（of, relating to, or arising from intuition） 例 She is an interesting paradox, an infinitely shy person who, in apparent contradiction, possesses an enormously *intuitive* gift for understanding people.
inure [ɪˈnjʊr]	*v.* 使习惯于（to accustom to accept something undesirable）；生效（to become of advantage）
invade [ɪnˈveɪd]	*v.* 侵略，侵入（to enter a country or territory with armed forces） 记 词根记忆：in(进入) + vad(走) + e → 走进(其他国家) → 侵略 同 encroach, foray, infringe, raid, trespass
invalidate [ɪnˈvælɪdeɪt]	*v.* 使无效，使作废（to make invalid） 例 Strindberg's plays are marked by his extreme misogyny; he felt modem woman needed to dominate man and by subordinating him *invalidate* his masculinity.
invariable [ɪnˈverəriəbl]	*adj.* 恒定的，不变的（not changing or capable of change） 同 changeless, consonant, equable, invariant
invention [ɪnˈvenʃn]	*n.* 发明，创造（the act or process of inventing）；发明才能，创造力（skill in inventing; inventiveness）；发现，找到（discovery; finding）
inventive [ɪnˈventɪv]	*adj.* 善于发明的，有创造力的（adept or prolific at producing inventions）；发明的（characterized by invention） 例 The reader has the happy impression of watching an extraordinarily *inventive* and intellectually fecund novelist working at the height of her powers.

□ intrinsic	□ introspective	□ introvert	□ intruding	□ intrusively	□ intuition
□ intuitive	□ inure	□ invade	□ invalidate	□ invariable	□ invention
□ inventive					

inverse [ˌɪnˈvɜːrs]	*adj.* 相反的(directly opposite); 倒转的(inverted) 记 词根记忆: in(反) + vers(转) + e → 反转 → 相反的; 倒转的
investigate [ɪnˈvestɪɡeɪt]	*v.* 调查(to examine in order to obtain the truth) 记 联想记忆: in + vest(背心) + i + gate(大门) → 穿上背心出大门去调查 → 调查
investigative [ɪnˈvestɪɡeɪtɪv]	*adj.* 调查的 记 来自 investigate(*v.* 调查)
investor [ɪnˈvestər]	*n.* 投资者 记 来自 invest(*v.* 投资)
invigorate [ɪnˈvɪɡəreɪt]	*v.* 鼓舞, 使精力充沛(to give life and energy to) 记 联想记忆: in(使…) + vigor(活力) + ate → 使 有活力 → 鼓舞, 使精力充沛
inviolate [ɪnˈvaɪələt]	*adj.* 不受侵犯的, 未受损害的(not violated or profaned) 记 联想记忆: in(不) + violate(侵犯, 妨碍) → 不受侵犯的
involuntary [ɪnˈvɑːlənteri]	*adj.* 无意的(done without intention) 记 词根记忆: in(无) + volunt(意识) + ary → 无意的
involve [ɪnˈvɑːlv]	*v.* 包含, 含有(to contain as a part; include); 参与(to engage as a participant); 牵涉, 牵连(to oblige to take part) 记 词根记忆: in(使…) + volv(卷) + e → 使卷入 → 牵涉, 牵连 例 When you learn archaeology solely from lectures, you get only an abstract sense of the concepts presented, but when you hold a five-thousand-year-old artifact in your hands, you have a chance to *involve* your senses, not just your intellect.
involvement [ɪnˈvɑːlvmənt]	*n.* 参与(participation); 连累; 投入(the feeling of excitement and satisfaction that you get from an activity) 例 Halls and audiences for lieder recitals tend to be smaller than for opera and thus more conducive to the intimacy and sense of close *involvement*, which is the recital's particular charm.
invulnerable [ɪnˈvʌlnərəbl]	*adj.* 不会受伤的, 刀枪不入的(incapable of being wounded or injured) 记 词根记忆: in(不) + vuln(伤害) + erable → 不易被伤害的 → 不会受伤害的
irascible [ɪˈræsəbl]	*adj.* 易怒的(easily angered) 记 词根记忆: ira(愤怒) + sc + ible → 易怒的
irate [aɪˈreɪt]	*adj.* 发怒的(angry; incensed) 记 联想记忆: i(我) + rate(责骂) → 我被责骂了 → 发怒的
iridescent [ˌɪrɪˈdesnt]	*adj.* 色彩斑斓的(producing a display of lustrous, rainbowlike colors) 记 词根记忆: irid(=iris 彩虹) + escent(开始…的) → 闪着彩虹般的光的 → 色彩斑斓的
ironic [aɪˈrɑːnɪk]	*adj.* 挖苦的, 讽刺的(sarcastic); 出乎意料的(directly opposite to what might be expected) 例 It is *ironic* that a critic of such overwhelming vanity now suffers from a measure of the oblivion to which he was forever consigning others, in the end, all his self-adulation has only worked against him.

麻烦您填个
调查问卷！

investigate

12

□ inverse	□ investigate	□ investigative	□ investor	□ invigorate	□ inviolate
□ involuntary	□ involve	□ involvement	□ invulnerable	□ irascible	□ irate
□ iridescent	□ ironic				

irony [ˈaɪrəni]	*n.* 反话(the use of words to express something other than and especially the opposite of the literal meaning); 讽刺意味(incongruity between what might be expected and what actually occurs); 出乎意料的结果(the opposite of what is expected) 记 联想记忆:iron(铁) + y → 像铁一样冷冰冰的话 → 反话 例 This final essay, its prevailing kindliness marred by occasional flashes of savage *irony*, bespeaks the dichotomous character of the author.

irony 您真苗条!

irradiate [ɪˈreɪdieɪt]	*v.* 照射(to cast rays of light upon); 照耀，照亮(to shine; light up) 记 词根记忆:ir(在里面) + rad(光线) + iate → 使在光线里面 → 照射;照耀
irradicable [ɪˈrædɪkəbl]	*adj.* 无法根除的，根深蒂固的(impossible to eradicate) 同 confirmed, entrenched, ineradicable, inveterate
irrational [ɪˈræʃnl]	*adj.* 不理智的(not endowed with reason or understanding); 失去理性的，不合理的(not governed by or according to reason) 例 In the seventeenth century, direct flouting of a generally accepted system of values was regarded as *irrational*, even as a sign of madness. 同 fallacious, illogical, unreasoned
irreconcilable [ɪˈrekənsaɪləbl]	*adj.* 无法调和的，矛盾的(incompatible; conflicting) 记 联想记忆:ir(不) + reconcilable(可调和的) → 无法调和的 例 The faculty senate warned that, if its recommendations were to go unheeded, the differences between the administration and the teaching staff would be exacerbated and eventually rendered *irreconcilable*.
irredeemable [ˌɪrɪˈdiːməbl]	*adj.* 无法挽回的，不可救药的(incapable of being remedied) 记 联想记忆:ir(不) + redeem(挽回，弥补) + able → 无法挽回的，不可救药的
irrefutable [ˌɪrɪˈfjuːtəbl]	*adj.* 无可辩驳的，毋庸置疑的(impossible to refute) 同 inarguable, incontestable, incontrovertible
irrelevant [ɪˈreləvənt]	*adj.* 不相关的;不切题的 搭 be irrelevant to 与…不相关
irreparable [ɪˈrepərəbl]	*adj.* 不能挽回的，无法弥补的(irremediable) 搭 irreparable damage 不可弥补的损害
irrepressible [ˌɪrɪˈpresəbl]	*adj.* 抑制不住的，压抑不住的(incapable of being controlled) 记 联想记忆:ir(不) + repress(抑制) + ible → 抑制不住的
irreproachable [ˌɪrɪˈprəʊtʃəbl]	*adj.* 无可指责的，无瑕疵的(blameless; impeccable) 例 One might dispute the author's handling of particular points of Kandinsky's interaction with his artistic environment, but her main theses are *irreproachable*.

□ irony　　　□ irradiate　　　□ irradicable　　　□ irrational　　　□ irreconcilable　　□ irredeemable
□ irrefutable　　□ irrelevant　　　□ irreparable　　　□ irrepressible　　□ irreproachable

irresistible [ˌɪrɪˈzɪstəbl]	*adj.* 无法抗拒的；不能压制的(impossible to resist) 记 联想记忆：ir(不) + resist(抵抗，抑制) + ible(能…的) → 无法抗拒的；不能压制
irresolute [ɪˈrezəluːt]	*adj.* 未决定的 (uncertain how to act or proceed)；犹豫不决的 (lacking in resolution; indecisive)
irresponsible [ˌɪrɪˈspɑːnsəbl]	*adj.* 不对更高一级负责(not answerable to higher authority)；不承担责任的 (said or done with no sense of responsibility)；无责任感的 (lacking a sense of responsibility)；无负责能力的 (unable especially mentally or financially to bear responsibility) *n.* 不负责任的人，无责任感的人(a person who is irresponsible) 例 It is *irresponsible* for a government to fail to do whatever it can to eliminate a totally preventable disease.
irreverent [ɪˈrevərənt]	*adj.* 不尊敬的(lacking proper respect or seriousness) 同 disrespectful
irreversible [ˌɪrɪˈvɜːrsəbl]	*adj.* 不能撤回的，不能取消的(not reversible) 同 irrevocable, unalterable
irrevocable [ɪˈrevəkəbl]	*adj.* 不能撤回的，无法取消的 (not possible to revoke) 记 词根记忆：ir(不) + re(向后) + voc(叫喊) + able → 不能向后叫喊的 → 不能撤回的，无法取消的
irrigate [ˈɪrɪɡeɪt]	*v.* 灌溉(to supply land with water)；冲洗(伤口)(to flush (a body part) with a stream of liquid) 记 词根记忆：ir(进入) + rig(水) + ate → 把水引进 → 灌溉
irritable [ˈɪrɪtəbl]	*adj.* 易怒的，急躁的(easily annoyed; choleric; fretful; irascible)；易受刺激的(responsive to stimuli) 记 词根记忆：irrit(痒) + able → 易怒的，急躁的
irritate [ˈɪrɪteɪt]	*v.* 激怒(to provoke anger)；刺激(to induce irritability in or of) 记 词根记忆：irrit(痒) + ate → 激怒；刺激 同 exasperate, peeve, pique, roil
irritating [ˈɪrɪteɪtɪŋ]	*adj.* 刺激的(irritative)；使人愤怒的，气人的(annoying) 例 His critical reviews were enjoyed by many of his audience, but the subjects of his analysis dreaded his comments; he was vitriolic, devastating, *irritating* and never constructive.
isolate [ˈaɪsəleɪt]	*v.* 孤立(to set apart from others) 记 词根记忆：isol(岛) + ate → 使成为孤岛 → 孤立 例 Some biologists argue that each specifically human trait must have arisen gradually and erratically, and that it is therefore difficult to *isolate* definite milestones in the evolution of the species. 同 enisle, insulate, segregate
iterate [ˈɪtəreɪt]	*v.* 重申，重做(to do or utter repeatedly) 记 词根记忆：iter(=again 再) + ate → 再来一次 → 重申，重做

12

irreverent

□ irresistible   □ irresolute   □ irresponsible   □ irreverent   □ irreversible   □ irrevocable
□ irrigate   □ irritable   □ irritate   □ irritating   □ isolate   □ iterate

131

itinerant [aɪˈtɪnərənt]	*adj.* 巡回的 (peripatetic; nomadic) 记 词根记忆: it(走) + iner + ant → 巡回的
jaded [ˈdʒeɪdɪd]	*adj.* 疲惫的 (wearied); 厌倦的 (dull or satiated) 搭 be jaded by 厌倦…
jeopardize [ˈdʒepərdaɪz]	*v.* 危及, 危害 (to endanger) 记 发音记忆: "皆怕打死" → 当危及到自身安全时, 谁都怕死 → 危及 同 compromise, hazard, imperil, jeopard
jest [dʒest]	*n.* 笑话, 俏皮话 (joke) *v.* 说笑, 开玩笑 (to joke; be playful in speech and actions) 同 fleer, flout, gibe, jeer, scoff
jocular [ˈdʒɑːkjələr]	*adj.* 滑稽的, 幽默的 (characterized by jesting; humorous); 爱开玩笑的 (given to jesting; playful) 记 词根记忆: joc(=joke 笑话) + ular → 爱开玩笑的
jolting [ˈdʒoʊltɪŋ]	*adj.* 令人震惊的 同 astonishing, astounding, startling, surprising
journalistic [ˌdʒɜːrnəˈlɪstɪk]	*adj.* 新闻业的, 新闻工作者的 (of, relating to, or characteristic of journalism or journalists)
jubilant [ˈdʒuːbɪlənt]	*adj.* 欢呼的, 喜气洋洋的 (elated; exultant) 记 词根记忆: jubil(大叫) + ant → 高兴得大叫的 → 欢呼的
judicious [dʒuˈdɪʃəs]	*adj.* 有判断力的 (having or showing sound judgment); 审慎的 (wise and careful) 记 词根记忆: jud(判断) + icious → 有判断力的 同 judgmatic, prudent, sane, sapient, sensible
jumble [ˈdʒʌmbl]	*v.* 使混乱, 混杂 (to mix in disorder) *n.* 混杂, 杂乱 (a disorderly mixture) 记 联想记忆: jum(看作 jump, 跳) + ble → 上蹿下跳, 群魔乱舞 → 混杂
juncture [ˈdʒʌŋktʃər]	*n.* 关键时刻, 危急关头 (a critical point); 结合处, 接合点 (a joining point) 例 The TV news magazine sits precisely at the *juncture* of information and entertainment, for while it is not a silly sitcom, it is not a documentary either.
justifiable [ˈdʒʌstɪfaɪəbl]	*adj.* 有理由的, 无可非议的 (capable of being justified or defended as correct) 记 来自 justify(*v.* 证明…是正当或合理的)
justify [ˈdʒʌstɪfaɪ]	*v.* 证明…是正当或合理的 (to show that sb./sth. is reasonable or just) 记 词根记忆: just(正确的) + ify(使…) → 证明…是正当或合理的 例 The accusations we bring against others should be warnings to ourselves; they should not *justify* complacency and easy judgments on our part concerning our own moral conduct. 同 confirm, corroborate, substantiate, validate, verify

juvenile [ˈdʒuːvənl]	*adj.* 青少年的（of or like young people）；孩子气的，幼稚的（marked by immaturity; childish） 记 词根记忆：juven(年轻的) + ile → 青少年的
keen [kiːn]	*adj.* 锋利的，锐利的（having a fine edge or point）；敏锐的，灵敏的（pungent to the sense; extremely sensitive in perception）；热心的（enthusiastic） 例 Our young people, whose *keen* sensitivities have not yet become calloused, have a purer and more immediate response than we do to our environment.
kidney [ˈkɪdni]	*n.* 肾 记 联想记忆：kid(孩子) + ney → 这个孩子爱吃腰花 → 肾

12

Jovons saw the kettle boil and cried out with the delighted voice of a child; Marshal too had seen the kettle boil and sat down silently to build an engine.

杰文斯看见壶开了, 高兴得像孩子似地叫了起来; 马歇尔也看见壶开了, 却悄悄地坐下来造了一部蒸气机。

——英国经济学家 凯恩斯(John Maynard Keynes, British economist)

Word List 13  MP3-13

misalliance [ˌmɪsə'laɪəns]	*n.* 不适当的结合(an improper alliance) 记 联想记忆: mis(坏) + alliance(结盟，联盟) → 坏的联盟 → 不适当的结合
misanthrope ['mɪsənθroʊp]	*n.* 厌恶人类者(a person who hates humankind) 记 词根记忆: mis(恨) + anthrop(人类) + e → 恨人类的人 → 厌恶人类者 例 Because he was a *misanthrope*, he shunned human society.
misapprehension [ˌmɪsæprɪ'henʃn]	*n.* 误会，误解(misunderstanding) 同 misconception, misinterpretation
mischievous ['mɪstʃɪvəs]	*adj.* 淘气的(playfully annoying); 有害的(harmful) 记 联想记忆: mis(坏) + chiev(看作 achieve, 完成，达到) + ous → 带来坏结果的 → 有害的
misconstrue [ˌmɪskən'struː]	*v.* 误解，曲解 同 misapprehend, misconceive, misinterpret, misunderstand
misdirect [ˌmɪsdə'rekt]	*v.* 误导(to give a wrong direction to) 记 联想记忆: mis(坏) + direct(指导) → 坏的指导 → 误导
miserable ['mɪzrəbl]	*adj.* 痛苦的，悲惨的(being in a pitiable state of distress or unhappiness); 少得可怜的(wretchedly inadequate or meager) 记 来自 misery(*n.* 痛苦; 悲惨的境遇) 例 Hoping for a rave review of his new show, the playwright was *miserable* when the critics panned it unanimously. 同 afflicted, doleful, dolorous, woeful
misery ['mɪzəri]	*n.* 悲惨的境遇 (a state of suffering); 痛苦，苦恼 (a state of great unhappiness and emotional distress) 同 agony, dolor, woe
misnomer [ˌmɪs'noʊmər]	*n.* 名称的误用 (an error in naming a person or place); 误用的名称(a name wrongly or unsuitably applied to a person or an object) 记 词根记忆: mis(错) + nom(名字) + er → 名称的误用 例 The term mole rat is a *misnomer*, for these small, furless rodents are neither moles nor rats.

misogyny [mɪˈsɑːdʒɪni]	*n.* 厌恶女人(hatred of women) 例 Strindberg's plays are marked by his extreme *misogyny*; he felt modem woman needed to dominate man and by subordinating him invalidate his masculinity.
mite [maɪt]	*n.* 极小量(a very little);小虫 记 mite 原指"螨虫"
mitigant [ˈmɪtəɡənt]	*adj.* 缓和的,减轻的 *n.* 缓和物 记 来自 mitigate(*v.* 使缓和,使减轻)
mitigate [ˈmɪtɪɡeɪt]	*v.* 使缓和,使减轻(to lessen in force or intensity) 记 词根记忆:miti(小的;轻的) + gat(=ag 做) + e → 弄轻 → 使缓和,使减轻
moderately [ˈmɑːdərətli]	*adv.* 适度地,有节制地 记 来自 moderate(*adj.* 适当的,有节制的)
modernize [ˈmɑːdərnaɪz]	*v.* 使现代化(to make modern (as in taste, style, or usage)) 同 update
modest [ˈmɑːdɪst]	*adj.* 谦虚的,谦逊的(humble; unassuming);适度的(not large in quantity or size) 记 词根记忆:mod(方式;风度) + est → 做事有风度 → 谦虚的;适度的 例 The corporation expects only *modest* increases in sales next year despite a yearlong effort to revive its retailing business.
modestly [ˈmɑːdɪstli]	*adv.* 谦虚地,谦逊地;适度地 记 来自 modest(*adj.* 谦虚的,谦逊的;适度的)
modifier [ˈmɑːdɪfaɪər]	*n.* 修改者(one that modifies);修饰语(a word or phrase that makes specific the meaning of another word or phrase)
modify [ˈmɑːdɪfaɪ]	*v.* 修改,更改(to alter partially; amend) 记 词根记忆:mod(方式) + ify → 使改变方式 → 修改,更改
modulate [ˈmɑːdʒəleɪt]	*v.* 调整,调节(to adjust to or keep in proper measure or proportion; regulate by or adjust to);调音(to tune to a key or pitch) 记 词根记忆:mod(方式) + ulate → 改变方式 → 调整
moisten [ˈmɔɪsn]	*v.* 弄湿,使湿润(to make moist) 记 来自 moist(*adj.* 潮湿的)
molecular [məˈlekjələr]	*adj.* 分子的(of, relating to, consisting of, or produced by molecules) 记 来自 molecule(*n.* 分子)
mollify [ˈmɑːlɪfaɪ]	*v.* 抚慰,安抚(to soothe in temper or disposition);使减轻,缓和(to reduce in intensity)
molten [ˈmoʊltən]	*adj.* 熔融的,熔化的(melted) 记 来自 melt(*v.* 融化,熔化)

13

过奖…

modest

momentarily [ˌmoʊmən'terəli]	*adv.* 暂时地(for a moment); 片刻，立刻(in a moment) 记 来自 momentary(*adj.* 短暂的，瞬间的)
momentous [moʊ'mentəs]	*adj.* 极为重要的，重大的(of great importance or consequence) 例 The failure of many psychotherapists to utilize the results of pioneering research could be due in part to the specialized nature of such findings: even *momentous* findings may not be useful. 同 consequential, considerable, significant, substantial
monetary ['mʌnɪteri]	*adj.* 金钱的(about money); 货币的(of or relating to a nation's currency or coinage) 记 来自 money(*n.* 金钱；货币) 例 He was indifferent to success, painting not for the sake of fame or *monetary* reward, but for the sheer love of art. 同 financial, fiscal, pecuniary
monochromatic [ˌmɑːnəkroʊ'mætɪk]	*adj.* 单色的(having only one color) 记 词根记忆: mono(单一) + chrom(颜色) + atic → 单色的 例 Most people who are color-blind actually can distinguish several colors; some, however, have a truly *monochromatic* view of a world all in shades of gray.
monolith ['mɑːnəlɪθ]	*n.* 单块巨石 (a single great stone often in the form of an obelisk or column); 单一的庞大组织 (an organized whole that acts as a single unified powerful or influential force) 例 Publishers have discovered that black America is not a *monolith* of attitudes and opinions but a rich mixture lending itself to numerous expressions in print.
monopolize [mə'nɑːpəlaɪz]	*v.* 垄断，独占(to assume complete possession or control of) 记 词根记忆: mono(单一) + pol(=poly 出售) + ize → 由一个人出售的 → 垄断，独占
monotony [mə'nɑːtəni]	*n.* 单调，千篇一律(tedious sameness) 同 humdrum, monotone
monumental [ˌmɑːnju'mentl]	*adj.* 极大的(massive; impressively large); 纪念碑的(built as a monument) 记 来自 monument(*n.* 纪念碑)
moralistic [ˌmɔːrə'lɪstɪk]	*adj.* 道学的，说教的(concerned with morals) 记 来自 moral(*n.* 道德)
moratorium [ˌmɔːrə'tɔːriəm]	*n.* 延缓偿付 (a legal authorization to delay payment of money); 活动中止 (a suspension of activity) 记 词根记忆: mor(推迟) + at + orium → 延缓偿付 例 The breathing spell provided by the *moratorium* on arms shipments should give all the combatants a chance to reevaluate their positions.

monumental

纪念碑

□ momentarily   □ momentous   □ monetary   □ monochromatic   □ monolith   □ monopolize
□ monotony   □ monumental   □ moralistic   □ moratorium

morbid [ˈmɔːrbɪd]	*adj.* 病态的，不健康的（diseased; unhealthy）
	记 词根记忆：morb(病) + id → 病态的
mordant [ˈmɔːrdnt]	*adj.* 讥讽的，尖酸的（biting or sarcastic in thought, manner, or style）
	记 词根记忆：mord(咬) + ant → 咬人的 → 尖酸的
morose [məˈrous]	*adj.* 郁闷的（sullen or gloomy）
	记 联想记忆：mo(音似"没") + rose(玫瑰) → 情人节没收到玫瑰 → 不高兴的 → 郁闷的
mortality [mɔːrˈtæləti]	*n.* 死亡率（the rate of deaths）
	记 词根记忆：mort(死亡) + ality(表性质) → 死亡率
mortify [ˈmɔːrtɪfaɪ]	*v.* 使丢脸，侮辱（to cause to experience humiliation and chagrin）
	记 词根记忆：mort(死) + ify → 让人想死 → 使丢脸，侮辱
motif [mouˈtiːf]	*n.* （文艺作品等的）主题，主旨（a main theme or idea）
	记 词根记忆：mot(动) + if → 促成移动的原因 → 主题，主旨
	例 If you listen carefully, you can hear this simple *motif* throughout the entire score.
	同 leitmotiv, subject
motivate [ˈmoutɪveɪt]	*v.* 激发，刺激（to provide with a motive）
	记 词根记忆：mot(动) + iv + ate(使…) → 激发
motley [ˈmɑːtli]	*adj.* 混杂的（heterogeneous）；多色的，杂色的（of many colors）
	记 词根记忆：mot(=mote 微粒) + ley → 各种微粒混合 → 混杂的
mournful [ˈmɔːrnfl]	*adj.* 悲伤的（feeling or expressing sorrow or grief）
	同 doleful, dolorous, plaintive, woeful
movement [ˈmuːvmənt]	*n.* 乐章（a principal division or section of a sonata or symphony）
muddle [ˈmʌdl]	*n.* 迷惑，困惑（a confused or disordered state）；混乱（mess）
	记 联想记忆：mud(泥浆) + dle → 混入泥浆 → 混乱
multicellular [ˌmʌltiˈseljələr]	*adj.* 多细胞的
	记 联想记忆：multi(多的) + cellular(细胞的；由细胞组成的) → 多细胞的
multifaceted [ˌmʌltiˈfæsɪtɪd]	*adj.* 多方面的（having many facets or aspects）
	同 protean, various, versatile
multiple [ˈmʌltɪpl]	*adj.* 多样的，多重的（various; including more than one）
	记 词根记忆：multi(多的) + ple(折叠) → 多次折叠 → 多样的，多重的
multiply [ˈmʌltɪplaɪ]	*v.* 乘；增加（to greatly increase）；繁殖（to breed）
	记 词根记忆：multi(多的) + ply(折叠) → 多次折叠 → 乘；增加
mundane [mʌnˈdeɪn]	*adj.* 现世的，世俗的（relating to the world; worldly）；平凡的，普通的（commonplace）
	记 词根记忆：mund(世界) + ane → 现世的，世俗的

13

motivate

连续工作 240小时 奖励：$1000000

□ morbid	□ mordant	□ morose	□ mortality	□ mortify	□ motif
□ motivate	□ motley	□ mournful	□ movement	□ muddle	□ multicellular
□ multifaceted	□ multiple	□ multiply	□ mundane		

munificence	*n.* 慷慨给予，宽宏大量（generosity）
[mjuːˈnɪfɪsns]	记 词根记忆：muni（公共）+ fic（做）+ ence → 为公共着想 → 慷慨给予，宽宏大量
	同 largess, liberality, magnanimity, openhandedness
munificent	*adj.* 慷慨的（very liberal in giving or bestowing）；丰厚的（characterized by
[mjuːˈnɪfɪsnt]	great liberality or generosity）
mural	*adj.* 墙壁的（of a wall）*n.* 壁画
[ˈmjʊrəl]	记 词根记忆：mur（墙）+ al → 墙壁的
murderous	*adj.* 蓄意谋杀的，凶残的（having the purpose or
[ˈmɜːrdərəs]	capability of murder）；极厉害的，要命的（having the ability or power to overwhelm）
murky	*adj.* 黑暗的，昏暗的（dark; gloomy）；朦胧的
[ˈmɜːrki]	（vague）
	记 来自 murk（*n.* 黑暗，昏暗）
mutable	*adj.* 可变的（capable of change or of being changed）；易变的（capable of
[ˈmjuːtəbl]	or liable to mutation）
	同 changeable, fluid, mobile, protean
myriad	*adj.* 许多的，无数的（innumerable）
[ˈmɪriəd]	同 legion, multitudinous, numerous
mystic	*adj.* 神秘的（having a spiritual meaning or reality that is neither apparent
[ˈmɪstɪk]	to the senses nor obvious to the intelligence）；谜样的，难解的（enigmatic; obscure）*n.* 神秘主义者
mysticism	*n.* 神秘主义（immediate consciousness of the transcendent or ultimate
[ˈmɪstɪsɪzəm]	reality）
	例 No longer sustained by the belief that the world around us was expressly designed for humanity, many people try to find intellectual substitutes for that lost certainty in astrology and in *mysticism*.
mythic	*adj.* 神话的；虚构的
[ˈmɪθɪk]	同 legendary, mythical, mythological
naivete	*n.* 天真的言行举止（a naive remark or action）；天真无邪（the quality or
[naɪˈiːvəti]	state of being naive）
	例 We realized that John was still young and impressionable, but were nevertheless surprised at his *naivete*.
narcotic	*n.* 麻醉剂 *adj.* 麻醉的，催眠的（having the properties of or yielding a
[nɑːrˈkɑːtɪk]	narcotic）
	记 词根记忆：narc（麻木；昏迷）+ ot + ic → 麻醉的；催眠的
narrative	*adj.* 叙述性的（of, or in the form of story-telling）
[ˈnærətɪv]	记 来自 narrate（*v.* 叙述）
	例 Because it has no distinct and recognizable typographical form and few recurring *narrative* conventions, the novel is, of all literary genres, the least susceptible to definition.

mural

□ munificence □ munificent □ mural □ murderous □ murky □ mutable
□ myriad □ mystic □ mysticism □ mythic □ naivete □ narcotic
□ narrative

narrow [ˈnæroʊ]	*adj.* 狭窄的(of slender width); 狭隘的(prejudiced) *v.* 变窄(to contract) 例 The well-trained engineer must understand fields as diverse as physics, economics, geology, and sociology; thus, an overly *narrow* engineering curriculum should be avoided.
natty [ˈnæti]	*adj.* 整洁的(trimly neat and tidy); 敏捷的，灵巧的(neatly or trimly smart) 同 dapper, dashing, jaunty, spruce
naturalistic [ˌnætʃrəˈlɪstɪk]	*adj.* 自然主义的(of, characterized by, or according with naturalism) 同 natural, realistic, true, truthful
navigate [ˈnævɪɡeɪt]	*v.* 驾驶(to direct the course of a ship or plane); 航行(to follow a planned course on, across, or through); 使通过 记 词根记忆: nav(船) + ig(走) + ate → 坐船走 → 航行 例 As more people try to *navigate* the legal system by themselves, representing themselves in court and drawing up their own wills and contracts, the question arises whether they will be able to avoid judicial quagmires without lawyers to guide them.
nebulous [ˈnebjələs]	*adj.* 模糊的(hazy; indistinct; vague); 云状的(cloudlike) 记 词根记忆: neb(云，雾) + bl + ous → 云状的
negate [nɪˈɡeɪt]	*v.* 取消(to nullify or invalidate); 否认(to deny) 记 词根记忆: neg(否认) + ate → 否认
negligent [ˈneɡlɪdʒənt]	*adj.* 疏忽的，粗心大意的(marked by or given to neglect especially habitually or culpably) 例 Because of his *negligent* driving, the other car was forced to turn off the road or be hit. 同 neglectful, regardless, remiss, slack
negligible [ˈneɡlɪdʒəbl]	*adj.* 可以忽略的，微不足道的(so small or unimportant or of so little consequence as to warrant little or no attention; trifling) 例 Because the damage to his car had been *negligible*, Michael decided he wouldn't bother to report the matter to his insurance company.
negligibly [ˈneɡlɪdʒəbli]	*adv.* 无足轻重地，不值一提地 记 来自 negligible(*adj.* 可以忽略的，微不足道的)
negotiable [nɪˈɡoʊʃiəbl]	*adj.* 可协商的(capable of being negotiated); 可通行的 同 navigable, passable
negotiate [nɪˈɡoʊʃieɪt]	*v.* 协商，商定，议定(to arrange for or bring about through conference, discussion, and compromise) 例 The actual rigidity of Wilson's position was always betrayed by his refusal to compromise after having initially agreed to *negotiate* a settlement.
neolithic [niːəˈlɪθɪk]	*adj.* 新石器时代的 记 词根记忆: neo(新的) + lith(石头) + ic → 新石头的 → 新石器时代的

13

neutron [ˈnuːtrɑːn]	*n.* 中子（a particle carrying no electric charge）
newsworthy [ˈnuːzwɜːrði]	*adj.* 有新闻价值的，有报道价值的（interesting enough to the general public to warrant reporting）
nibble [ˈnɪbl]	*v.* 一点点地咬，慢慢啃（to bite off small bits） 记 联想记忆：nib（笔尖）+ ble → 每次只咬笔尖那么多 → 一点点地咬；注意不要和 nipple（*n.* 乳头）相混
nocturnal [nɑːkˈtɜːrnl]	*adj.* 夜晚的，夜间发生的（of, relating to, or happening in the night） 记 词根记忆：noct（夜）+ urnal → 夜晚的
noisome [ˈnɔɪsəm]	*adj.* 有恶臭的（offensive to the senses and especially to the sense of smell）；令人作呕的，令人讨厌的（highly obnoxious or objectionable） 记 词根记忆：noi（=annoy 讨厌）+ some → 讨厌的 → 令人讨厌的
nomadic [noʊˈmædɪk]	*adj.* 游牧的（of nomad）；流浪的 同 itinerant, peripatetic, vagabond, vagrant
nominally [ˈnɑːmɪnəli]	*adv.* 名义上地；有名无实地 记 来自 nominal（*adj.* 名义上的；有名无实的）
nonchalance [ˌnɑːnʃəˈlɑːns]	*n.* 冷漠，冷淡（the quality or state of being nonchalant; casual lack of concern） 记 词根记忆：non（不）+ chal（关心）+ ance → 不关心 → 无动于衷 → 冷漠 例 Despite an affected *nonchalance* which convinced casual observers that he was indifferent about his painting and enjoyed only frivolity, Warhol cared deeply about his art and labored at it diligently.
nonchalant [ˌnɑːnʃəˈlɑːnt]	*adj.* 冷淡的，冷漠的（having an air of easy unconcern or indifference; not showing interest） 例 No real life hero of ancient or modern days can surpass James Bond with his *nonchalant* disregard of death and the fortitude with which he bears torture.
nonchalantly [ˌnɑːnʃəˈlɑːntli]	*adv.* 冷淡地，冷漠地（indifferently） 例 Instead of taking exaggerated precautions against touching or tipping or jarring the bottle of wine, the waitress handled it quite *nonchalantly*, being careful only to use a napkin to keep her hands from the cool bottle itself.
noncommittal [ˌnɑːnkəˈmɪtl]	*adj.* 态度暧昧的（giving no clear indication of attitude or feeling）；不承担义务的 记 联想记忆：non（不）+ committal（承担义务）→ 不承担义务的 例 The president was *noncommittal* about farm subsidies, nor did he say much about the even more vital topic of unemployment.
nonconformist [ˌnɑːnkənˈfɔːrmɪst]	*adj.* 不墨守成规的 *n.* 不墨守成规的人 记 联想记忆：non（不）+ conform（遵守）+ ist → 不墨守成规的人

140

□ neutron	□ newsworthy	□ nibble	□ nocturnal	□ noisome	□ nomadic
□ nominally	□ nonchalance	□ nonchalant	□ nonchalantly	□ noncommittal	□ nonconformist

nonentity [nɑːˈnentəti]	*n.* 无足轻重的人或事(a person or thing of no importance) 记 联想记忆：non(不) + entity(存在) → 不存在 → 无足轻重的人或事
nonflammable [ˌnɑːnˈflæməbl]	*adj.* 不易燃的(not flammable) 记 联想记忆：non（不） + flammable（易燃的） → 不易燃的；注意不要和 inflammable(*adj.* 易燃的)相混
nonplussed [ˌnɑːnˈplʌst]	*adj.* 不知所措的, 陷于困境的 记 来自 nonplus(*v.* 使迷惑)
nonporous [ˌnɑːnˈpɔːrəs]	*adj.* 无孔的；不渗透的 记 联想记忆：non(不) + porous(多孔的；能渗透的) → 无孔的；不渗透的
nonradioactive [ˌnɑːnˈreɪdioʊˈæktɪv]	*adj.* 非放射性的 记 联想记忆：non(不) + radioactive(放射性的) → 非放射性的 搭 nonradioactive labeling 非放射性标记
nonsensical [nɑːnˈsensɪkl]	*adj.* 无意义的 (having no meaning or conveying no intelligible ideas)；荒谬的(absurd)
nonthreatening [nɑːnˈθretnɪŋ]	*adj.* 不构成威胁的 记 联想记忆：non(不) + threatening(威胁的) → 不构成威胁的
nonviable [nɑːnˈvaɪəbl]	*adj.* 无法生存的, 不能成活的(not able to live) 记 联想记忆：non(不) + viable(能存活的) → 无法生存的
nostalgia [nəˈstældʒə]	*n.* 思乡(the state of being homesick)；怀旧之情 (a sentimental yearning for return to or of some past period) 记 词根记忆：nost(家) + alg(痛) + ia → 想家想到心痛 → 思乡 例 The documentary film about high school life was so realistic and evocative that feelings of *nostalgia* flooded over the college-age audience.
notable [ˈnoʊtəbl]	*adj.* 值得注意的, 显著的(deserving to be noticed; remarkable) 记 词根记忆：not(标示) + able → 能被标示的 → 值得注意的 例 Perhaps predictably, since an ability to communicate effectively is an important trait of any great leader, it has been the exceptional Presidents who have delivered the most *notable* inaugural addresses. 同 distinguished, eminent, famed, memorable, noteworthy
notate [ˈnoʊtɪt]	*v.* 以符号表示(to put into notation) 记 词根记忆：not(标示) + ate → (用符号)标示 → 以符号表示
notch [nɑːtʃ]	*n.* V 字形切口, 刻痕；等级, 档次 搭 top notch 大腕
notoriety [ˌnoʊtəˈraɪəti]	*n.* 臭名昭著 (the quality or state of being notorious)；臭名昭著的人(a notorious person)
notorious [noʊˈtɔːriəs]	*adj.* 臭名昭著的(widely and unfavorably known) 记 词根记忆：not (知道) + orious → 人所共知的 → 臭名昭著的

notch

notoriously [nouˈtɔːriəsli]	*adv.* 臭名昭著地(in a notorious manner) 例 The testimony of eyewitnesses is *notoriously* unreliable; emotion and excitement all too often cause our minds to distort what we see.
novelty [ˈnɑːvlti]	*n.* 新奇(the quality of being novel; newness); 新奇的事物(sth. new and unusual) 记 词根记忆: nov(新的) + el + ty → 新奇
novice [ˈnɑːvɪs]	*n.* 生手, 新手(apprentice; beginner) 记 联想记忆: no(不) + vice(副的) → 连副的都不是 → 新手
nuance [ˈnuːɑːns]	*n.* 细微差异(a subtle difference) 同 nicety, shade, subtlety, refinement
nubile [ˈnuːbaɪl]	*adj.* 适婚的(marriageable); 性感的(sexually attractive) 记 词根记忆: nub(结婚) + ile → 适婚的
null [nʌl]	*adj.* 无效的(having no legal or binding force); 等于零的(amounting to nothing)
numerous [ˈnuːmərəs]	*adj.* 许多的, 很多的 记 词根记忆: numer(计数) + ous → 不计其数的 → 许多的, 很多的 例 Known for his commitment to *numerous* worthy causes, the philanthropist deserved credit for his altruism. 同 abundant, multitudinous, myriad, various
nurture [ˈnɜːrtʃər]	*v.* 养育, 教养(to care for and educate) *n.* 养育(the act of bringing up); 营养物(sth. that nourishes) 记 联想记忆: 大自然(nature)像母亲一样养育(nurture)着人类 同 cultivate, foster
nutrient [ˈnuːtriənt]	*n.* 营养品, 滋养物(substance serving as or providing nourishment) 记 词根记忆: nutri(滋养) + ent(表物) → 滋养物 例 Biologists categorize many of the world's environments as deserts: regions where the limited availability of some key factor, such as water, sunlight, or an essential *nutrient*, places sharp constraints on the existence of living things.
nutritional [nuˈtrɪʃnl]	*adj.* 营养的, 滋养的 同 alimentary, nutritive
nutritious [nuˈtrɪʃəs]	*adj.* 有营养的, 滋养的(nourishing) 同 alimentary, nutrient, nutritive
obdurate [ˈɑːbdərət]	*adj.* 固执的, 顽固的(stubbornly persistent; inflexible) 记 词根记忆: ob(表加强) + dur(持续) + ate → 非常坚持的 → 固执的 例 If you come to the conference table with such an *obdurate* attitude, we cannot expect to reach any harmonious agreement. 同 adamant, dogged
obese [oʊˈbiːs]	*adj.* 极胖的(very fat; corpulent) 记 发音记忆: "O 必死" → 对怕胖的女人来说, O 形身材必死无疑 → 极胖的

142

□ notoriously □ novelty □ novice □ nuance □ nubile □ null
□ numerous □ nurture □ nutrient □ nutritional □ nutritious □ obdurate
□ obese

obfuscate [ˈɑːbfʌskeɪt]	*v.* 使困惑，使迷惑（to muddle; confuse; bewilder） 记 词根记忆：ob(在…之上) + fusc(黑暗的) + ate → 使变成全黑 → 使困惑，使迷惑
obligated [ˈɑːblɪgeɪtɪd]	*adj.* 有义务的，有责任的 同 beholden, indebted, obliged
obligatory [əˈblɪgətɔːri]	*adj.* 强制性的，义不容辞的（binding in law or conscience） 同 compulsory, imperative, mandatory
obliging [əˈblaɪdʒɪŋ]	*adj.* 乐于助人的（helpful; accommodating） 记 来自oblige(*v.* 施恩惠于，帮助)
obliqueness [əˈbliːknəs]	*n.* 斜度；倾斜 记 来自oblique(*adj.* 斜的，歪的)
obliterate [əˈblɪtəreɪt]	*v.* 涂掉，擦掉（to efface; erase） 记 词根记忆：ob(去掉) + liter(文字) + ate → 去掉(文字等) → 涂掉，擦掉
oblivious [əˈblɪviəs]	*adj.* 遗忘的，忘却的（lacking all memory; forgetful）；疏忽的（lacking conscious awareness; unmindful） 记 词根记忆：ob + liv（使光滑） + ious → 使记忆变得完全光滑 → 遗忘的；疏忽的
obscure [əbˈskjʊr]	*adj.* 难以理解的，含糊的（cryptic; ambiguous）；不清楚的，模糊的（not clear or distinct） *v.* 使变模糊（to make less conspicuous）；隐藏（to conceal） 记 词根记忆：ob(在…之上) + scur(覆盖) + e → 盖上一层东西 → 使变模糊；隐藏 例 The *New Yorker* short stories often include esoteric allusions to *obscure* people and events: the implication is, if you are in the in-crowd, you'll get the reference; if you come from Cleveland, you won't. 同 dislimn, haze, obfuscate, overcast
obscurity [əbˈskjʊrəti]	*n.* 费解（the quality of being obscure）；不出名 例 The civil rights movement did not emerge from *obscurity* into national prominence overnight; on the contrary, it captured the public's imagination only gradually.
obsequious [əbˈsiːkwiəs]	*adj.* 逢迎的，谄媚的（showing too great a willingness to serve or obey） 记 词根记忆：ob(在…后面) + sequ(跟随) + ious → 跟在后面的 → 逢迎的，谄媚的 例 Helen valued people who behaved as if they respected themselves; nothing irritated her more than an excessively *obsequious* waiter or a fawning salesclerk. 同 menial, servile, slavish, subservient
obsequiousness [əbˈsiːkwiəsnəs]	*n.* 谄媚（abject submissiveness） 同 servility, subservience

13

observant [əbˈzɜːrvənt]	*adj.* 密切注意的，警惕的(paying strict attention；watchful；mindful)；遵守的，遵从的(careful in observing (as rites, laws, or customs))；敏锐的(quick to perceive or apprehend；alert)
obsessed [əbˈsest]	*adj.* 着迷的，沉迷的(considering sb. or sth. as so important that you are always thinking about them) 记 来自 obsess (*v.* 迷住；困扰)
obsolescent [ˌɑːbsəˈlesnt]	*adj.* 逐渐荒废的(in the process of becoming obsolete) 记 和 obsolescence (*n.* 废弃，陈旧) 一起记
obstacle [ˈɑːbstəkl]	*n.* 障碍，妨碍物 记 词根记忆：ob(反) + sta(站) + (a)cle(表东西) → 反着站，挡住了去路 → 障碍 搭 obstacle to (doing) sth. (做)某事的障碍 同 hurdle, impediment, obstruction, snag
obstinacy [ˈɑːbstɪnəsi]	*n.* 固执，倔强，顽固(the state of being obstinate；stubbornness) 记 词根记忆：ob(反) + stin(=stand 站) + acy → 反着站 → 固执，倔强
obstinateness [ˈɑːbstɪnətnəs]	*n.* 固执，顽固 记 来自 obstinate(*adj.* 顽固的，固执的)
obstruct [əbˈstrʌkt]	*v.* 阻塞（道路、通道等）(to block or close up by an obstacle)；妨碍，阻挠(to hinder from passage, action, or operation) 记 词根记忆：ob(反) + struct(建造) → 反着建 → 阻塞
obtainable [əbˈteɪnəbl]	*adj.* 能得到的(capable of being obtained) 记 来自 obtain(*v.* 得到) 同 attainable, available, procurable, securable
obviate [ˈɑːbvieɪt]	*v.* 排除，消除(困难、危险等)(to remove；get rid of) 记 词根记忆：ob(反) + vi(路) + ate → 使障碍等离开道路 → 排除，消除 同 eliminate, exclude, preclude
obvious [ˈɑːbviəs]	*adj.* 明显的，显而易见的(easy to see and understand) 记 词根记忆：ob + vi(路) + ous → 在路上的，随处可见 → 明显的 例 While not teeming with the colorfully *obvious* forms of life that are found in a tropical rain forest, the desert is host to a surprisingly large number of species. 同 apparent, evident, manifest, palpable
occasional [əˈkeɪʒənl]	*adj.* 偶尔的(occurring from time to time)；特殊场合的(of or relating to a particular occasion)；不经常的(acting in a specified capacity from time to time) 记 来自 occasion(*n.* 场合；时机) 例 For all the hardships involved in the study of seals, we Arctic researchers have *occasional* moments of pure exhilaration over some new idea or discovery. 同 seldom, semioccasional, sporadic, uncommon
occupation [ˌɑːkjuˈpeɪʃn]	*n.* 工作，职业(a job；employment)；占有，占领(the act or process of taking possession of a place or area) 记 来自 occupy(*v.* 占有，占领；忙于)

odious [ˈoʊdiəs]	*adj.* 可憎的，令人作呕的（disgusting; offensive） 记 发音记忆："呕得要死" → 可憎的，令人作呕的
odorless [ˈoʊdərləs]	*adj.* 无嗅的，没有气味的 记 来自 odor（*n.* 气味，香气）
offhand [ˌɔːfˈhænd]	*adj.* 无准备的，即席的（performed or expressed without preparation or forethought）；随便的（casual）*adv.* 无准备地，即席地（without preparation or forethought）；随便地（casually）
officious [əˈfɪʃəs]	*adj.* 过于殷勤的，多管闲事的（too ready or willing to give orders or advice; meddlesome）；非官方的（informal; unofficial）
off-key [ˌɔːfˈkiː]	*adj.* 走调的，不和谐的（out of tune）
offspring [ˈɔːfsprɪŋ]	*n.* 〈总称〉后代（the progeny or descendants of a person, an animal, or a plant considered as a group）；儿女（children from particular parents）
offstage [ˌɔːfˈsteɪdʒ]	*adj.* 台后的，幕后的（not on the open stage） 记 组合词：off（离开…）+ stage（舞台）→ 离开舞台 → 台后的
oligarch [ˈɑːləɡɑːrk]	*n.* 寡头政治（a member of a form of government in which a small group of people hold all the power）；寡头统治集团（a member of a small governing faction） 记 词根记忆：olig（少数）+ arch（统治）→ 由少数人来统治 → 寡头政治
ominous [ˈɑːmɪnəs]	*adj.* 恶兆的，不祥的（portentous; of an evil omen） 记 米自 omen（*n.* 预兆，征兆）
omit [əˈmɪt]	*v.* 忽略，遗漏（to leave out）；不做，未能做（to leave undone） 记 联想记忆：om（音似："呕"）+ it（它）→ 把它呕出去 → 忽略 同 disregard, ignore, neglect
omnipotent [ɑːmˈnɪpətənt]	*adj.* 全能的，万能的（almighty; all-powerful） 记 词根记忆：omni（全）+ pot（有力的）+ ent → 全能的
onerous [ˈɑːnərəs]	*adj.* 繁重的，费力的（burdensome） 记 词根记忆：oner（负担）+ ous → 负担重的 → 繁重的
ongoing [ˈɑːnɡoʊɪŋ]	*adj.* 进行中的（being actually in process）；前进的；不间断的 同 ceaseless, continuous, endless, everlasting

13

□ odious	□ odorless	□ offhand	□ officious	□ off-key	□ offspring
□ offstage	□ oligarch	□ ominous	□ omit	□ omnipotent	□ onerous
□ ongoing					

145

Word List 14

opacity [oʊˈpæsəti]	*n.* 不透明性（the quality of being opaque）；晦涩（obscurity of sense） 例 The semantic *opacity* of ancient documents is not unique; even in our own time, many documents are difficult to decipher.
opalescent [ˌoʊpəˈlesnt]	*adj.* 发乳白色光的（reflecting an iridescent light）
operable [ˈɑːpərəbl]	*adj.* 可操作的，可使用的（fit, possible, or desirable to use）；可手术治疗的（likely to result in a favorable outcome upon surgical treatment）
operative [ˈɑːpərətɪv]	*adj.* （计划等）实施中的，运行着的（operating）；生效的（effective） 记 词根记忆：oper（做）+ ative → 在做的 → 实施中的
opinionated [əˈpɪnjəneɪtɪd]	*adj.* 固执己见的（holding obstinately to one's own opinions） 记 来自 opinion（n. 观点）
opponent [əˈpoʊnənt]	*n.* 对手，敌手（one that opposes another or others in a battle, contest, controversy, or debate） 记 词根记忆：op（反）+ pon（放）+ ent → 处于对立位置 → 对手 同 adversary, antagonist
opportune [ˌɑːpərˈtuːn]	*adj.* 合适的，适当的（right for a particular purpose） 记 词根记忆：op（向）+ port（搬运）+ une → 向着某物搬 → 合适的，适当的
opposed [əˈpoʊzd]	*adj.* 反对的（set or placed in opposition） 搭 be opposed to 反对…
opposite [ˈɑːpəzət]	*adj.* 相反的，对立的（contrary to one another or to a thing specified） 记 词根记忆：op（反）+ pos（放）+ ite（表形容词）→ 放在反面的 → 相反的，对立的
oppressive [əˈpresɪv]	*adj.* 高压的，压制性的（unreasonably burdensome or severe）；压抑的（overwhelming or depressing to the spirit or senses） 例 During the 1960's assessments of the family shifted remarkably, from general endorsement of it as a worthwhile, stable institution to wide spread censure of it as an *oppressive* and bankrupt one whose dissolution was both imminent and welcome.

☐ opacity ☐ opalescent ☐ operable ☐ operative ☐ opinionated ☐ opponent
☐ opportune ☐ opposed ☐ opposite ☐ oppressive

opprobrious [ə'prəʊbriəs]	*adj.* 辱骂的, 侮辱的(expressing scorn; abusive) 记 词根记忆: op(反) + pro(向前) + br(=fer 搬运) + ious → 以相反的方向往前搬运 → 辱骂的
optical ['ɑːptɪkl]	*adj.* 视觉的(of or relating to vision); 光学的(of or relating to the science of optics) 记 词根记忆: opt(眼睛) + ical → 视觉的
optimal ['ɑːptɪməl]	*adj.* 最佳的, 最理想的(most desirable or satisfactory) 同 optimum
optimism ['ɑːptɪmɪzəm]	*n.* 乐观主义(a tendency to expect the best possible outcome or dwell on the most hopeful aspects of a situation) 记 词根记忆: optim(最好的) + ism → 什么都往最好的一面想 → 乐观主义 例 While the delegate clearly sought to dampen the *optimism* that has emerged recently, she stopped short of suggesting that the conference was near collapse and might produce nothing of significance.
optimist ['ɑːptɪmɪst]	*n.* 乐观主义者(the person who is always hopeful and expects the best in all things) 例 Always trying to look on the bright side of every situation, she is a born *optimist*.
optimistic [ˌɑːptɪ'mɪstɪk]	*adj.* 乐观的(believing that good things will happen in the future) 记 词根记忆: optim(最好的) + istic → 最好的 → 乐观的 搭 be optimistic about 对…持乐观的心态
optimum ['ɑːptɪməm]	*adj.* 最有利的, 最理想的 (most favorable or desirable) 记 词根记忆: optim(最好的) + um → 最有利的
opulent ['ɑːpjələnt]	*adj.* 富裕的(very wealthy); 充足的(profuse; luxuriant) 记 词根记忆: opul(财富) + ent → 富裕的
orbital ['ɔːrbɪtl]	*adj.* 轨道的 记 来自 orbit(*n.* 轨道 *v.* 绕轨道运行)
orchestrate ['ɔːrkɪstreɪt]	*v.* 给…配管弦乐(to provide with orchestration); 精心安排, 组织(to arrange or combine so as to achieve a desired or maximum effect)
ordeal [ɔːr'diːl]	*n.* 严峻的考验(any difficult and severe trial) 记 发音记忆: "恶地儿" → 险恶之地 → 严峻的考验 例 The senator's reputation, though shaken by false allegations of misconduct, emerged from the *ordeal* unscathed. 同 affliction, tribulation
ordinary ['ɔːrdneri]	*adj.* 普通的, 平常的(routine; usual); 拙劣的, 质量差的(deficient in quality; of poor or inferior quality) *n.* 惯例, 寻常情况(the regular or customary condition or course of things) 同 commonplace, quotidian, unremarkable

天塌下来
高个顶着

optimistic

14

□ opprobrious　□ optical　□ optimal　□ optimism　□ optimist　□ optimistic
□ optimum　□ opulent　□ orbital　□ orchestrate　□ ordeal　□ ordinary

147

organism [ˈɔːrɡənɪzəm]	*n.* 生物，有机体（an individual form of life; a body made up of organs, organelles, or other parts that work together to carry on the various processes of life） 记 词根记忆：organ(器官) + ism → 生物，有机体
original [əˈrɪdʒənl]	*adj.* 最初的，最早的（first or earliest）；有创意的，有创造性的（able to produce new ideas; creative） 记 来自origin(*n.* 起源，由来） 例 We find it difficult to translate a foreign text literally because we cannot capture the connotations of the *original* passage exactly.
ornamental [ˌɔːrnəˈmentl]	*adj.* 装饰性的（of, relating to, or serving as ornament） 记 词根记忆：orn(装饰) + amental → 装饰性的
ossify [ˈɑːsɪfaɪ]	*v.* 骨化（to change or develop into bone）；僵化（to become hardened or conventional and opposed to change） 记 词根记忆：oss(骨头) + ify(…化) → 骨化；僵化
ostentation [ˌɑːstenˈteɪʃn]	*n.* 夸示，炫耀（showy display; pretentiousness） 记 词根记忆：os(在前面) + tent(伸展) + ation → 在他人面前伸展 → 显现出来 → 夸示，炫耀
ostentatious [ˌɑːstenˈteɪʃəs]	*adj.* 华美的；炫耀的（marked by or fond of conspicuous or vainglorious and sometimes pretentious display） 例 Compared with the *ostentatious* glamour of opera, classical song is a more subdued tradition. 同 flamboyant, peacockish, splashy, swank
ostracize [ˈɑːstrəsaɪz]	*v.* 排斥（to exclude from a group by common consent）；放逐（to exile by ostracism） 记 词根记忆：ostrac（贝壳) + ize → 用投贝壳的方法决定是否放逐某人 → 放逐 例 As news of his indictment spread through the town, the citizens began to *ostracize* him and to avoid meeting him. 同 banish, expatriate, expulse, oust
oust [aʊst]	*v.* 驱逐，把…赶走（to expel; force out） 记 联想记忆：out(出去)中加上 s → 死也要让他出去 → 驱逐
outburst [ˈaʊtbɜːrst]	*n.* 爆发，迸发（a violent expression of feeling; eruption）；激增（a surge of activity or growth） 例 He was habitually so docile and accommodating that his friends could not understand his sudden *outburst* against his employers. 同 burst, explosion, gust, sally
outdated [ˌaʊtˈdeɪtɪd]	*adj.* 过时的（no longer current） 同 outmoded
outgoing [ˈaʊtɡoʊɪŋ]	*adj.* 友善的（openly friendly; sociable）；即将离去的（going out; leaving） 例 Rebuffed by his colleagues, the initially *outgoing* young researcher became increasingly withdrawn.

148

□ organism □ original □ ornamental □ ossify □ ostentation □ ostentatious
□ ostracize □ oust □ outburst □ outdated □ outgoing

outgrow [ˌaʊtˈɡroʊ]	*vt.* 生长速度超过…，长得比…快(to grow or increase faster than) 记 组合词：out(向外；超越) + grow(生长) → 生长速度超过…
outgrowth [ˈaʊtɡroʊθ]	*n.* 结果(consequence)；副产品(by-product) 记 组合词：out(出来) + growth(生长) → 结果；副产品
outlast [ˌaʊtˈlæst]	*v.* 比…持久 记 组合词：out(超越) + last(坚持) → 比…持久
outline [ˈaʊtlaɪn]	*n.* 轮廓；概要(the main ideas or facts) 记 组合词：out(出来) + line(线条) → 划出线条 → 轮廓
outlying [ˈaʊtlaɪɪŋ]	*adj.* 边远的，偏僻的(remote from a center or main body)
outmoded [ˌaʊtˈmoʊdɪd]	*adj.* 过时的(no longer in fashion; obsolete) 记 联想记忆：out(出) + mode(时尚) + d → 不再时尚的 → 过时的
outspoken [aʊtˈspoʊkən]	*adj.* 坦率的，直言不讳的(direct and open in speech or expression) 记 组合词：out(出) + spoken(口头的，说的) → 说出来的 → 直言不讳的 例 While Parker is very *outspoken* on issues she cares about, she is not fanatical; she concedes the strength of opposing arguments when they expose weaknesses inherent in her own.
outstrip [ˌaʊtˈstrɪp]	*v.* 超过，超越(to excel; surpass)；比…跑得快(to run faster) 记 联想记忆：out(出) + strip(剥去，夺去) → 比别人夺得多 → 超过 同 exceed, outdo, transcend
outweigh [ˌaʊtˈweɪ]	*v.* 比…重，比…更重要(to exceed in weight, value, or importance)
oval [ˈoʊvl]	*adj.* 卵形的，椭圆形的(having the shape of an egg) 记 联想记忆：o(音似：喔) + val(音似：哇哦) → 发哇哦这些音时嘴要张成椭圆形 → 椭圆形的
overawe [ˌoʊvərˈɔː]	*v.* 威慑(to restrain or subdue by awe) 记 联想记忆：over(过度) + awe(敬畏) → 过度敬畏 → 威慑
overbalance [ˌoʊvərˈbæləns]	*v.* 使失去平衡(to cause to lose balance)
overbear [ˌoʊvərˈber]	*v.* 压倒(to bring down by superior weight or physical force)；镇压(to domineer over)；比…更重要，超过(to surpass in importance or cogency)
overblown [ˌoʊvərˈbloʊn]	*adj.* 盛期已过的，残败的(past the prime of bloom)；夸张的(inflated)
overcast [ˌoʊvərˈkæst]	*adj.* 阴天的，阴暗的 同 bleak, cloudy, gloomy, somber
overconfident [ˌoʊvərˈkɑːnfɪdənt]	*adj.* 过于自信的，自负的

outline

14

overcrowd [ˌoʊvərˈkraʊd]	*v.* (使)过度拥挤(to cause to be too crowded; crowd together too much)
overdraw [ˌoʊvərˈdrɔː]	*v.* 透支(to draw checks on (a bank account) for more than the balance; make an overgraft); 夸大(to exaggerate)
overdue [ˌoʊvərˈduː]	*adj.* 到期未付的(left unpaid too long); 晚来的, 延误的(coming or arriving after the scheduled or expected time; later than expected) 记 组合词: over(越过) + due(应付的; 约定的) → 过了应付或约定的时间的 → 到期未付的; 晚来的 例 The college librarian initiated a new schedule of fines for *overdue* books with the acquiescence, if not the outright encouragement, of the faculty library committee.
overemphasize [ˌoʊvərˈemfəsaɪz]	*v.* 过分强调(to give something more importance than it deserves or than is suitable) 同 magnify, overplay
overestimate [ˌoʊvərˈestɪmeɪt]	*v.* 评价过高 记 组合词: over(在…上) + estimate(估) → 评价过高
overinflated [ˌoʊvərɪnˈfleɪtɪd]	*adj.* 过度充气的(filled with too much air) 例 Like a balloon that is *overinflated*, aneurysms sometimes enlarge so much that they burst.
overlap [ˌoʊvərˈlæp]	*v.* 部分重叠(to coincide in part with) 记 组合词: over(在…上) + lap(大腿) → 把一条腿放在另一条腿上 → 部分重叠 同 lap, overlie, override
overload [ˌoʊvərˈloʊd]	*v.* 使超载
overlook [ˌoʊvərˈlʊk]	*v.* 俯视(to have a view from above); 忽视(not to notice) 记 组合词: over(在…上) + look(看) → 在上面看 → 俯视; 引申为"忽视"
overpower [ˌoʊvərˈpaʊər]	*v.* 压倒(to affect with overwhelming intensity) 例 The sheer bulk of data from the mass media seems to *overpower* us and drive us to synoptic accounts for an easily and readily digestible portion of news.
overpowering [ˌoʊvərˈpaʊərɪŋ]	*adj.* 压倒性的, 不可抗拒的(overwhelming) 记 来自 overpower(*v.* 压倒) 例 Charlotte Salomon's biography is a reminder that the currents of private life, however diverted, dislodged, or twisted by *overpowering* public events, retain their hold on the individual recording them.
overrate [ˌoʊvərˈreɪt]	*v.* 对…估价过高, 对…评价过高(to rate, value, or estimate too highly) 同 overesteem, overestimate, overprize, overvalue
override [ˌoʊvərˈraɪd]	*v.* 驳回(to disregard; overrule); 蹂躏, 践踏(to ride over or across; trample) 记 组合词: over(在…上) + ride(骑) → 骑在…之上 → 蹂躏

150

□ overcrowd □ overdraw □ overdue □ overemphasize □ overestimate □ overinflated
□ overlap □ overload □ overlook □ overpower □ overpowering □ overrate
□ override

overrule [ˌoʊvərˈruːl]	*v.* 驳回，否决(to decide against by exercising one's higher authority) 记 组合词：over(在…上) + rule(统治) → 凌驾于他人之上 → 驳回，否决
overshadow [ˌoʊvərˈʃædoʊ]	*v.* 使蒙上阴影(to cast a shadow over)；使黯然失色 记 组合词：over(在…上) + shadow(阴影) → 蒙上一层阴影 → 使蒙上阴影；使黯然失色
overstate [ˌoʊvərˈsteɪt]	*v.* 夸张，对…言过其实(to exaggerate) 记 组合词：over(过分) + state(陈述) → 夸张
overt [oʊˈvɜːrt]	*adj.* 公开的，非秘密的(apparent; manifest) 记 词根记忆：o(出) + vert(转) → 转出来 → 公开的 例 Such an *overt* act of hostility can only lead to war.
overtax [ˌoʊvərˈtæks]	*v.* 课税过重
overtire [ˌoʊvərˈtaɪər]	*v.* 使过度疲劳
overturn [ˌoʊvərˈtɜːrn]	*v.* 翻倒(to (cause to) turn over or capsize)；推翻，倾覆(to cause the ruin or destruction of; overthrow)
overwhelm [ˌoʊvərˈwelm]	*v.* 战胜，征服，压倒(to overcome by superior force or numbers; crush; overpower)；淹没，席卷(to surge over and submerge; engulf) 记 组合词：over(在…上) + whelm(淹没) → 压倒；淹没
overwrought [ˌoʊvərˈrɔːt]	*adj.* 紧张过度的，兴奋过度的(very nervous or excited)
pacifist [ˈpæsɪfɪst]	*n.* 和平主义者，反战主义者(a person who believes that all wars are wrong and refuses to fight in them) 记 词根记忆：pac(和平的，宁静的) + if(使) + ist → 和平主义者
pack [pæk]	*n.* 兽群(a number of wild animals living and hunting together) 记 该词的"包裹"一义大家应该比较熟悉
packed [pækt]	*adj.* 压紧的，压实的(compressed)；充满人的，拥挤的(crowded; crammed) 记 来自pack(*v.* 打包，包装)
paean [ˈpiːən]	*n.* 赞美歌，颂歌(a song of joy, praise, triumph) 记 参考：hymn(*n.* 赞美歌)
painstakingly [ˈpeɪnzteɪkɪŋli]	*adv.* 细心地，专注地(fastidiously)；辛苦地 例 The President reached a decision only after lengthy deliberation, *painstakingly* weighing the divergent opinions expressed by cabinet members. 同 assiduously, exhaustively, meticulously
palatable [ˈpælətəbl]	*adj.* 美味的(agreeable to the palate or taste) 同 appetizing, savory, tasty

palatable

14

paleolithic [ˌpælɪəˈlɪθɪk]	*adj.* 旧石器时代的(of or relating to the earliest period of the Stone Age characterized by rough or chipped stone implements) 记 词根记忆：paleo(古老的) + lith(石头) + ic → 旧石器的 → 旧石器时代的
palpable [ˈpælpəbl]	*adj.* 可触知的，可察觉的；明显的(tangible; perceptible; noticeable) 记 词根记忆：palp(摸) + able → 摸得到的 → 可触知的；明显的
paltry [ˈpɔːltri]	*adj.* 无价值的，微不足道的(trashy; trivial; petty) 记 联想记忆：pal(=pale 苍白的) + try(努力) → 白努力 → 无价值的
panacea [ˌpænəˈsiːə]	*n.* 万灵药(a remedy for all ills or difficulties) 记 词根记忆：pan(全部) + acea(治疗) → 包治百病 → 万灵药 例 Although the discovery of antibiotics led to great advances in clinical practice, it did not represent a *panacea* for bacterial illness, for there are some bacteria that cannot be effectively treated with antibiotics.
pancreas [ˈpæŋkriəs]	*n.* 胰腺(a large lobulated gland of vertebrates that secretes digestive enzymes and the hormones insulin and glucagon) 记 词根记忆：pan(全部) + cre(肉) + as → 给身体生长提供养分的器官 → 胰腺
pantomime [ˈpæntəmaɪm]	*n.* 哑剧(a performance done using gestures and postures instead of words) 记 词根记忆：panto(=pan 全部) + mim(模仿) + e → 模仿他人进行的表演 → 哑剧
parable [ˈpærəbl]	*n.* 寓言(a short fictitious story that illustrates a moral attitude or a religious principle) 记 词根记忆：para(旁边) + bl(扔) + e → 向旁边仍，能平行比较 → 寓言 例 In certain forms of discourse such as the *parable*, the central point of a message can be effectively communicated even though this point is not explicit.
paradigm [ˈpærədaɪm]	*n.* 范例，示范(a typical example or archetype) 记 词根记忆：para(旁边) + digm(显示) → 在一旁显示 → 范例，示范
paradox [ˈpærədɑːks]	*n.* 似非而是的理论(a statement that is seemingly contradictory or opposed to common sense and yet is perhaps true)；矛盾的人或物(one exhibiting inexplicable or contradictory aspects)；与通常的见解相反的观点 (a statement contrary to received opinion) 记 词根记忆：para(相反的) + dox(观点) → 与一般观点相反的观点 → 与通常见解相反的观点 例 She is an interesting *paradox*, an infinitely shy person who, in apparent contradiction, possesses an enormously intuitive gift for understanding people.

□ paleolithic   □ palpable   □ paltry   □ panacea   □ pancreas   □ pantomime
□ parable   □ paradigm   □ paradox

paradoxical	*adj.* 矛盾的（of the nature of a paradox）；不正常的（not being the normal or usual kind）
[ˌpærəˈdɑːksɪkl]	例 The concept of timelessness is *paradoxical* from the start, for adult consciousness is permeated by the awareness of duration.
paragon	*n.* 模范，典范（a model of excellence or perfection）
[ˈpærəgɑːn]	记 词根记忆：para（旁边）+ gon（比较）→ 放在旁边作为比较的对象 → 模范，典范
paramount	*adj.* 最重要的（of chief concern or importance）；最高权力的，至高无上的（supreme in rank, power, or authority; dominant）
[ˈpærəmaʊnt]	记 词根记忆：para（旁边）+ mount（山）→ 在山坡旁边的 → 最重要的
paraphrase	*n.* 释义，解释，改写（a restatement of a text, passage, or work giving the meaning in another form）*v.* 释义，解释，改写（to restate in a paraphrase）
[ˈpærəfreɪz]	记 词根记忆：para（旁边）+ phras（告诉）+ e → 在旁边说 → 释义，解释
parasite	*n.* 食客（a person who lives off others and gives nothing in return）；寄生物（an organism that grows, feeds, and is sheltered on or in a different organism while contributing nothing to the survival of its host）
[ˈpærəsaɪt]	记 词根记忆：para（旁边）+ sit（食物）+ e → 坐在旁边吃的人或物 → 食客；寄生物
parasitic	*adj.* 寄生的
[ˌpærəˈsɪtɪk]	例 The tapeworm is an example of a *parasitic* organism, one that lives within or on another creature, deriving some or all of its nutriment from its host.
parliamentary	*adj.* 议会（制）的（of or relating to a parliament; enacted, done, or ratified by a parliament）
[ˌpɑːrləˈmentri]	
parody	*n.* 拙劣的模仿（a feeble or ridiculous imitation）；滑稽模仿作品或表演（a literary or artistic work that imitates the characteristic style of an author or a work for comic effect or ridicule）
[ˈpærədi]	记 词根记忆：par（旁边）+ ody（=ode 唱）→ 在旁边唱 → 拙劣的模仿
parsimony	*n.* 过分节俭，吝啬（the quality of being stingy）
[ˈpɑːrsəmoʊni]	同 thrift
partiality	*n.* 偏袒，偏心（the state of being partial; bias）
[ˌpɑːrʃiˈæləti]	记 来自 partial（*adj.* 有偏见的）
	例 Although the revelation that one of the contestants was a friend left the judge open to charges of lack of disinterestedness, the judge remained adamant in her assertion that acquaintance did not necessarily imply *partiality*.
	同 prejudice, proclivity, propensity, tendency
participate	*v.* 分担（to possess some of the attributes of a person, thing, or quality）；参与（to take part in sth.）；分享（to have a part or share in sth.）
[pɑːrˈtɪsɪpeɪt]	记 联想记忆：parti（看作 party，晚会）+ cip（抓，拿）+ ate → 找人参加晚会 → 参与
	搭 participate in 参与…

14

participation	n. 参加，参与（the act of taking part or sharing in something）
[pɑːrˌtɪsɪˈpeɪʃn]	例 Because medieval women's public *participation* in spiritual life was not welcomed by the male establishment, a compensating involvement with religious writings, inoffensive to the members of the establishment because of its privacy, became important for many women.
particular	n. 细节，详情（an individual fact or detail；item）
[pərˈtɪkjələr]	同 fact
particularity	n. 独特性 （the quality or state of being particular as distinguished from universal）
[pərˌtɪkjuˈlærəti]	
particulate	adj. 微粒的（of or relating to minute separate particles）n. 微粒（a minute separate particle, as of a granular substance or powder）
[pɑːrˈtɪkjələt]	
partisan	n. 党派支持者，党羽（a firm adherent to a party）
[ˈpɑːrtəzn]	记 来自 party（n. 党，政党）
passionate	adj. 充满激情的（showing or filled with passion）
[ˈpæʃənət]	记 来自 passion（n. 激情）
	例 Though science is often imagined as a disinterested exploration of external reality, scientists are no different from anyone else: they are *passionate* human beings enmeshed in a web of personal and social circumstances.
	同 ardent, fervid, impassioned
passively	adv. 被动地，顺从地
[ˈpæsɪvli]	记 来自 passive（adj. 被动的）
pathological	adj. 病态的，不理智的（unreasonable, irrational）；病理学的（of or relating to pathology）
[ˌpæθəˈlɑːdʒɪkl]	
patience	n. 耐性（the capacity, habit, or fact of being patient）
[ˈpeɪʃns]	例 The diplomat, selected for her demonstrated *patience* and skill in conducting such delicate negotiations, declined to make a decision during the talks because any sudden commitment at that time would have been inopportune.
patriarchal	adj. 家长的，族长的（of, relating to, or being a patriarch）；父权制的（of, or relating to a patriarchy）
[ˌpeɪtriˈɑːrkl]	
patronage	n. 资助，赞助（the support, especially financial, that is given to a person or an organization by a patron）；惠顾（the trade given to a commercial establishment by its customers）
[ˈpætrənɪdʒ]	记 来自 patron（n. 赞助人）
	例 Queen Elizabeth I has quite correctly been called a friend of the arts, because many young artists received her *patronage*.
patronize	v. 屈尊俯就（to behave towards sb. as if one were better or more important than him）；光顾，惠顾（to be a frequent or regular customer or client of）
[ˈpeɪtrənaɪz]	记 来自 patron（n. 赞助人）

□ participation □ particular □ particulate □ partisan □ passionate □ passively
□ pathological □ patience □ patriarchal □ patronage □ patronize

patronizing [ˈpeɪtrənaɪzɪŋ]	*adj.* 以恩惠态度对待的，要人领情的 例 To take a *patronizing* attitude, looking down on others as one's inferiors, often is to eliminate any chance of favorable relations with them.
paucity [ˈpɔːsəti]	*n.* 少量(fewness)；缺乏(dearth) 记 词根记忆：pauc(少的) + ity → 少量；缺乏
peculiar [pɪˈkjuːliər]	*adj.* 独特的(distinctive)；古怪的(eccentric；queer) 同 characteristic, idiosyncratic, individual
pecuniary [pɪˈkjuːnieri]	*adj.* 金钱的(monetary；financial) 记 词根记忆：pecu(钱) + ni + ary → 金钱的 同 fiscal
pedagogic [ˌpedəˈɡɑːdʒɪk]	*adj.* 教育学的(of, relating to, or befitting a teacher or education) 记 词根记忆：ped(= child 儿童) + agog(引导) + ic → 教育学的
pedant [ˈpednt]	*n.* 迂腐之人，学究(one who unduly emphasizes minutiae in the use of knowledge) 记 词根记忆：ped(教育) + ant → 与儿童教育相关的人 → 学究
pedantry [ˈpedntri]	*n.* 迂腐(pedantic presentation or application of knowledge or learning) 例 Learned though she was, her erudition never degenerated into *pedantry*.
pedestrian [pəˈdestriən]	*adj.* 徒步的(going or performed on foot)；缺乏想象力的(unimaginative) *n.* 行人(a person traveling on foot) 记 词根记忆：ped(脚) + estr + ian(表人) → 用脚走路的人 → 行人 例 We were amazed that a man who had been heretofore the most *pedestrian* of public speakers could, in a single speech, electrify an audience and bring them cheering to their feet.
peerless [ˈpɪrləs]	*adj.* 出类拔萃的，无可匹敌的(matchless；incomparable) 记 联想记忆：peer(同等的人) + less(无) → 无可匹敌的
peevish [ˈpiːvɪʃ]	*adj.* 不满的，抱怨的(discontented；querulous)；暴躁的，坏脾气的，易怒的(fractious；fretful) 记 来自 peeve(*v.* 使气恼，使焦躁) 例 Safire as a political commentator is patently never satisfied; he writes *peevish* editorials about every action the government takes. 同 huffy, irritable, pettish
pejorative [pɪˈdʒɔːrətɪv]	*adj.* 轻视的，贬低的(tending to disparage；depreciatory) 记 词根记忆：pejor(坏的) + ative → 变坏的 → 轻视的，贬低的 例 The campus police who monitored the demonstrations had little respect for the student protesters, generally speaking of them in *pejorative* terms.
penal [ˈpiːnl]	*adj.* 惩罚的，刑罚的(of, relating to, or involving punishment, penalties, or punitive institutions)
penalize [ˈpiːnəlaɪz]	*v.* 置…于不利地位(to put at a serious disadvantage)；处罚(to inflict a penalty on) 记 来自 penal(*adj.* 惩罚的，刑罚的)

14

penchant	*n.* 爱好，嗜好(liking)
['pentʃənt]	记 词根记忆：pench(=pend 挂) + ant → 对…挂着一颗心 → 爱好
	例 Although retiring, almost self-effacing in his private life, he displays in his plays and essays a strong *penchant* for publicity and controversy.
pending	*adj.* 即将发生的(imminent; impending)；未决的(not yet decided)
['pendɪŋ]	记 词根记忆：pend(挂) + ing → 挂着的 → 未决的
penetrating	*adj.* (声音)响亮的，尖锐的；(气味)刺激的；(思想)敏锐的，有洞察力的(acute, discerning)
['penɪtreɪtɪŋ]	
penitent	*adj.* 悔过的，忏悔的(expressing regretful pain; repentant)
['penɪtənt]	记 词根记忆：pen(处罚) + it + ent → 受了处罚所以后悔 → 悔过的
pensive	*adj.* 沉思的(reflective; meditative)；忧心忡忡的(suggestive of sad thoughtfulness)
['pensɪv]	记 词根记忆：pens(挂) + ive → 挂在心上 → 沉思的；忧心忡忡的

pensive

perception	*n.* 感知，知觉(the process, act, or faculty of perceiving)；洞察力(quick, acute, and intuitive cognition)
[pər'sepʃn]	记 来自 percept(*n.* 感知；感知对象)
perceptive	*adj.* 感知的，知觉的(responsive to sensory stimuli)；有洞察力的，敏锐的(capable of or exhibiting keen perception)
[pər'septɪv]	
perennial	*adj.* 终年的，全年的(present all the year)；永久的，持久的(perpetual; enduring)
[pə'reniəl]	记 词根记忆：per(全部) + enn(年) + ial → 全年的；永久的
	例 A *perennial* goal in zoology is to infer function from structure, relating the behavior of an organism to its physical form and cellular organization.
	同 continuing, eternal, lifelong, permanent
perfervid	*adj.* 过于热心的(excessively fervent)
[pə'fɜːrvɪd]	记 词根记忆：per(十分，完全) + ferv(热的) + id → 十分热的 → 过于热心的
perfidious	*adj.* 不忠的，背信弃义的(faithless)
[pər'fɪdiəs]	记 词根记忆：per(假装) + fid(相信) + ious → 不相信的 → 不忠的，背信弃义的
perfume	*n.* 香味(the scent of sth. sweet-smelling)；香水(a substance that emits a pleasant odor)
[pər'fjuːm]	记 联想记忆：per(贯穿) + fume(气体) → 缭绕在身上的气体 → 香味
	例 His olfactory sense was so highly developed that he was often called in to judge *perfume*.
	同 aroma, balm, fragrance, redolence
perfunctory	*adj.* 例行公事般的，敷衍的(characterized by routine or superficiality)
[pər'fʌŋktəri]	例 Her first concert appearance was disappointingly *perfunctory* and derivative, rather than the inspired performance in the innovative style we had anticipated.

perilous	*adj.* 危险的，冒险的(full of peril; hazardous)
[ˈperələs]	记 来自 peril(*n.* 危险)
periodic	*adj.* 周期的，定期的(occurring or recurring at regular intervals)
[ˌpɪriˈɑːdɪk]	记 来自 period(*n.* 一段时间)
peripatetic	*adj.* 巡游的，流动的(travelling from place to place; itinerant)
[ˌperipəˈtetɪk]	记 词根记忆：peri(周围) + pat(走) + et + ic → 巡游的，流动的
peripheral	*adj.* 周边的，外围的(of a periphery or surface part)
[pəˈrɪfərəl]	记 词根记忆：peri(周围) + pher(带) + al → 带到周围 → 周边的，外围的
	例 One virus strain that may help gene therapists cure genetic brain diseases can enter the *peripheral* nervous system and travel to the brain, obviating the need to inject the therapeutic virus directly into the brain.
periphery	*n.* 次要部分(the less important part of sth.)；外围，周围(the outer edge of a particular area)；外表面(the external boundary or surface of a body)
[pəˈrɪfəri]	记 词根记忆：peri(周围) + pher(带) + y → 带到周围 → 外围，周围
perishable	*adj.* 易腐烂的，易变质的(likely to decay or go bad quickly) *n.* 易腐烂的东西(stuff subject to decay)
[ˈperɪʃəbl]	记 来自 perish(*v.* 毁灭；腐烂)
	例 Given the *perishable* nature of wood, the oldest totem poles of the Northwest Coast Indians eventually fell to decay; only a few still stand today.
permeable	*adj.* 可渗透的(penetrable)
[ˈpɜːrmiəbl]	记 词根记忆：per(贯穿) + mea(通过) + ble → 可通过的 → 可渗透的
permeate	*v.* 扩散，弥漫(to spread or diffuse through)；穿透(to pass through the pores or interstices)
[ˈpɜːrmieɪt]	记 词根记忆：per(贯穿) + mea(通过) + te → 通过 → 扩散；穿透
	同 impenetrate, penetrate, percolate
permissive	*adj.* 许可的，容许的(granting or inclined to grant permission; tolerant or lenient)；过分纵容的(indulgent)
[pərˈmɪsɪv]	
pernicious	*adj.* 有害的(noxious)；致命的(deadly)
[pərˈnɪʃəs]	记 词根记忆：per(表加强) + nic(伤害) + ious → 带来极大伤害的 → 有害的；致命的
perpendicular	*adj.* 垂直的，竖直的(exactly upright; vertical)
[ˌpɜːrpənˈdɪkjələr]	记 词根记忆：per(彻底) + pend(挂) + icular → 彻底挂着的 → 垂直的
perpetrate	*v.* 犯罪(to commit)；负责(to be responsible for)
[ˈpɜːrpətreɪt]	
perpetuate	*v.* 使永存(to make perpetual)
[pərˈpetʃueɪt]	记 词根记忆：per(贯穿) + pet(追求) + uate → 永远追求 → 使永存
perquisite	*n.* 额外收入，津贴(a payment or profit received in addition to a regular wage or salary)；小费(a tip)
[ˈpɜːrkwɪzɪt]	记 词根记忆：per(全部) + quis(要求) + ite → 要求全部得到 → 额外收入，津贴
	同 cumshaw, lagniappe, largess

14

persevere [ˌpɜːrsəˈvɪr]	**v.** 坚持不懈 (to persist in a state, enterprise, or undertaking in spite of counterinfluences, opposition, or discouragement)
persist [pərˈsɪst]	**v.** 坚持不懈，执意 (to go on resolutely or stubbornly in spite of opposition, importunity, or warning)；坚持问，不停地说 (to be insistent in the repetition or pressing of an utterance)；继续存在，长存 (to continue in existence; last) 记 词根记忆：per(始终) + sist(坐) → 始终坐着 → 坚持不懈 例 The chances that a species will *persist* are reduced if any vital function is restricted to a single kind of organ; redundancy by itself possesses an enormous survival advantage. 同 abide, endure, perdure, persevere

Man errs so long as he strives.

人只要奋斗就会犯错误。

——德国诗人、剧作家 歌德
(Johann Wolfgang Goethe, German poet and dramatist)

personally [ˈpɜːrsənəli]	*adv.* 亲自(in person); 作为个人(as a person) 例 Despite the daunting size of her undergraduate class, the professor made a point of getting to know as many as possible of the more than 700 students *personally*.
perspective [pərˈspektɪv]	*n.* 思考方法(a way of thinking about sth.); 观点, 看法(a point of view); 透视法 记 词根记忆: per(贯穿) + spect(看) + ive → 贯穿看 → 透视法
perspicacious [ˌpɜːrspɪˈkeɪʃəs]	*adj.* 独具慧眼的, 敏锐的(of acute mental vision or discernment) 记 词根记忆: per(全部) + spic(=spect 看) + acious → 全部都看到的 → 独具慧眼的, 敏锐的
perspicuous [ˌpɜːrˈspɪkjʊəs]	*adj.* 明晰的, 明了的(clearly expressed or presented)
perspire [pərˈspaɪər]	*v.* 出汗(to sweat) 记 词根记忆: per + spir(呼吸) + e → 全身都呼吸 → 出汗
persuasive [pərˈsweɪsɪv]	*adj.* 易使人信服的, 有说服力的(tending or having the power to persuade)
pertinent [ˈpɜːrtnənt]	*adj.* 有关的, 相关的(having a clear decisive relevance to the matter in hand) 记 词根记忆: per(始终) + tin(拿住) + ent → 始终拿着不放的 → 有关的 例 Those interested in learning more about how genetics applies to trees will have to resort to the excellent technical journals where most of the *pertinent* material is found. 同 germane
pervade [pərˈveɪd]	*v.* 弥漫, 遍及(to become diffused throughout) 记 词根记忆: per(贯穿) + vad(走) + e → 走遍 → 弥漫, 遍及
pervasive [pərˈveɪsɪv]	*adj.* 弥漫的, 遍布的(pervading or tending to pervade) 记 来自 pervade(*v.* 弥漫, 遍及) 例 The influence of the Timaeus among early philosophical thinkers was *pervasive*, if only because it was the sole dialogue available in Europe for almost 1,000 years.

pesticide [ˈpestɪsaɪd]	*n.* 杀虫剂（an agent used to kill pests） 记 词根记忆：pest(害虫) + i + cide(杀) → 杀虫剂
pestilential [ˌpestɪˈlenʃl]	*adj.* 引起瘟疫的（causing or tending to cause pestilence），致命的；〈口〉极讨厌的 同 deadly; irritating
petroleum [pəˈtrouliəm]	*n.* 石油
petulant [ˈpetʃələnt]	*adj.* 暴躁的，易怒的（insolent; peevish） 记 来自 pet(*n.* 不高兴，不悦)
pharmaceutical [ˌfɑːrməˈsuːtɪkl]	*adj.* 制药的，卖药的（of the manufacture and sale of medicines） 记 来自 pharmacy(*n.* 药房；药剂学)
phenomenal [fəˈnɑːmɪnl]	*adj.* 显著的，非凡的（extraordinary; remarkable） 记 来自 phenomenon(*n.* 现象；奇迹)；phen(出现) + omen(征兆) + on → 出现征兆 → 现象；奇迹
philanthropic [fɪˈlænθrəpɪk]	*adj.* 慈善(事业)的，博爱的（of, relating to, or characterized by philanthropy; humanitarian） 记 词根记忆：phil(爱) + anthrop(人) + ic → 爱人的 → 博爱的 例 The marketers' motivations in donating the new basketball backboards to the school system are not solely *philanthropic*; they plan to sell advertising space on the backboards.
philistine [ˈfɪlɪstiːn]	*n.* 庸俗的人，对文化艺术无知的人（a smug, ignorant, especially middle-class person who is regarded as being indifferent or antagonistic to artistic and cultural values） 记 来自腓力斯人(Philistia)，是庸俗的市侩阶层
philosophic [ˌfɪləˈsɑːfɪk]	*adj.* 哲学(家)的（of or relating to philosophers or philosophy） 记 来自 philosophy(*n.* 哲学)
phlegmatic [fleɡˈmætɪk]	*adj.* 冷淡的，不动感情的（of slow and stolid temperature; unemotional） 记 来自 phlegm(痰)，西方人认为痰多的人不易动感情 同 apathetic, impassive, stoic, stolid
phobia [ˈfoubiə]	*n.* 恐惧症（an exaggerated illogical fear） 记 词根记忆：phob(恐惧) + ia(表病) → 恐惧症
phonetic [fəˈnetɪk]	*adj.* 语音的（about the sounds of human speech） 记 词根记忆：phon(声音) + etic → 语音的
photosensitive [ˌfoutouˈsensətɪv]	*adj.* 感光性的（sensitive or sensitized to the action of radiant energy）
photosynthesis [ˌfoutouˈsɪnθəsɪs]	*n.* 光合作用（synthesis of chemical compounds with the aid of radiant energy and especially light） 记 联想记忆：photo(光) + synthesis(合成) → 光合作用
physical [ˈfɪzɪkl]	*adj.* 实质的，有形的（having material existence）；身体的，肉体的（of or relating to the body）

physiological [ˌfɪzɪə'lɑːdʒɪkl]	*adj.* 生理(技能)的(of, or concerning the bodily functions)；生理学的(of, or concerning physiology) 記 来自 physiology(*n.* 生理学)
picturesque [ˌpɪktʃə'resk]	*adj.* 如画的(resembling a picture)；独特的，别具风格的(charming or quaint in appearance)
piercing ['pɪrsɪŋ]	*adj.* 冷得刺骨的(penetratingly cold)；敏锐的(perceptive) 同 shrill
piety ['paɪəti]	*n.* 孝顺，孝敬(fidelity to natural obligations (as to parents))；虔诚(religious devotion and reverence to God; devoutness) 例 Their *piety* was expressed in quotidian behavior: they worshipped regularly, according all the regenerative processes of nature respect, and even awe.
pilgrim ['pɪlgrɪm]	*n.* 朝圣者(one who travels to a shrine as a devotee)；(在国外的)旅行者 同 wayfarer
pine [paɪn]	*n.* 松树 *v.* (因疾病等)憔悴(to lose vigor; anguish)；渴望(to yearn intensely and persistently especially for sth. unattainable) 記 联想记忆：松树(pine)的叶尖尖细细的，就像针(pin) 同 crave, dream, hanker, thirst pine
pinpoint ['pɪnpɔɪnt]	*v.* 准确地确定(to locate or aim with great precision or accuracy)；使突出，引起注意(to cause to stand out conspicuously) *adj.* 极精确的(very exact) 記 组合词：pin(针) + point(尖) → 像针尖一样精确 → 极精确的
pious ['paɪəs]	*adj.* 虔诚的(showing and feeling deep respect for God and religion) 同 devout, pietistic, prayerful, religious
piousness ['paɪəsnəs]	*n.* 虔诚 記 来自 pious(*adj.* 虔诚的)
pitcher ['pɪtʃər]	*n.* 有柄水罐(a container for liquids that usually has a handle) 同 jug
pitfall ['pɪtfɔːl]	*n.* 陷阱，隐患(a hidden or not easily recognized danger or difficulty) 記 组合词：pit(坑，洞) + fall(落下) → 让人下落的坑 → 陷阱
pithy ['pɪθi]	*adj.* (讲话或文章)简练有力的，言简意赅的(tersely cogent) 同 concise
pitiful ['pɪtɪfl]	*adj.* 值得同情的，可怜的(deserving pity) 記 来自 pity(*n.* 同情)
pivotal ['pɪvətl]	*adj.* 中枢的，枢轴的(of, relating to, or constituting a pivot)；极其重要的，关键的(vitally important)
placate ['pleɪkeɪt]	*v.* 抚慰，平息(to soothe or mollify) 記 词根记忆：plac(平静的) + ate → 使平静 → 抚慰，平息

□ physiological   □ picturesque   □ piercing   □ piety   □ pilgrim   □ pine
□ pinpoint   □ pious   □ piousness   □ pitcher   □ pitfall   □ pithy
□ pitiful   □ pivotal   □ placate
161

placebo [plə'siːbou]	*n.* 安慰剂(a substance containing no medication and prescribed or given to reinforce a patient's expectation to get well); 起安慰作用的东西(sth. tending to soothe) 记 词根记忆：plac(平静的) + ebo → 安慰剂
placid ['plæsɪd]	*adj.* 安静的，平和的(serenely free of interruption) 记 词根记忆：plac(平静的) + id → 平和的，安静的
plainspoken ['pleɪn'spoukən]	*adj.* 直言不讳的 同 candid, frank
plaintive ['pleɪntɪv]	*adj.* 哀伤的，悲伤的(expressive of woe; melancholy) 记 来自 plaint(*n.* 哀诉)
plastic ['plæstɪk]	*adj.* 创造性的，塑造的(formative; creative); 易受影响的(easily influenced); 可塑的(capable of being molded or modeled); 塑性的(capable of being deformed continuously and permanently in any direction without rupture) 同 adaptable, ductile, malleable, moldable, pliant, supple
platitude ['plætɪtuːd]	*n.* 陈词滥调(a banal, trite, or stale remark) 记 词根记忆：plat(平的) + itude → 平庸之词 → 陈词滥调
platitudinous [ˌplætɪ'tuːdənəs]	*adj.* 陈腐的(having the characteristics of a platitude) 搭 platitudinous remarks 陈腐的言论
plausible ['plɔːzəbl]	*adj.* 看似有理的，似是而非的(superficially fair, reasonable, or valuable but often specious); 有道理的，可信的(appearing worthy of belief) 记 词根记忆：plaus (鼓掌) + ible → 值得鼓掌的 → 看似有理的，似是而非的 例 Eric was frustrated because, although he was adept at making lies sound *plausible*, when telling the truth, he lacked the power to make himself believed. 同 believable, colorable, credible, creditable
plethora ['pleθərə]	*n.* 过多，过剩(excess; superfluity) 记 词根记忆：plet(满的) + hora → 满满的 → 过多，过剩 例 At the present time, we are suffering from a *plethora* of stories about the war. 同 overabundance, overflow, overmuch, overplus
pliable ['plaɪəbl]	*adj.* 易弯曲的，柔软的(supple enough to bend freely; ductile); 易受影响的(easily influenced) 记 词根记忆：pli(=ply 弯，折) + able → 易弯曲的
pliant ['plaɪənt]	*adj.* 易受影响的(easily influenced); 易弯的(pliable) 同 malleable
plot [plɑːt]	*n.* 情节(the plan or main story of a literary work); 阴谋(a secret plan; intrigue) *v.* 密谋，策划(to form a plot for; prearrange secretly or deviously)

plumb [plʌm]	*n.* 测深锤，铅锤 *adj.* 垂直的(exactly vertical) *adv.* 精确地(exactly) *v.* 深入了解(to examine minutely and critically)；测量深度(to measure the depth with a plumb)
plump [plʌmp]	*adj.* 丰满的(having a full rounded usually pleasing form) *v.* 使丰满，使变圆(to make well-rounded or full in form)
plunge [plʌndʒ]	*v.* 跳进，陷入(to thrust or cast oneself into or as if into water)；俯冲(to move suddenly forwards and downwards) 记 发音记忆："扑浪急" → 掉入水里，着急地扑打着浪花 → 跳进
poignant [ˈpɔɪnjənt]	*adj.* 令人痛苦的，伤心的(painfully affecting the feelings)；尖锐的，尖刻的(cutting) 记 词根记忆：poign(刺) + ant → 用针刺的 → 尖锐的
poise [pɔɪz]	*v.* 使平衡(to hold in equilibrium) *n.* 泰然自若，沉着自信(easy self-possessed assurance of manner)
polar [ˈpoʊlər]	*adj.* 极地的，两极的，近地极的(of or near the North or South Pole)；磁极的(connected with the poles of a magnet) 记 来自pole(*n.* 地极；磁极)
polarize [ˈpoʊləraɪz]	*v.* (使人、观点等)两极化，(使)截然对立(to divide into groups based on two completely opposite principles or political opinions) 记 来自polar(*adj.* 两极的)
polish [ˈpoʊlɪʃ]	*v.* 磨光，擦亮(to make smooth and glossy) *n.* 上光剂(a preparation that is used to polish sth.)；优雅(freedom from rudeness or coarseness) 记 联想记忆：波兰(Polish)产的擦光剂(polish) 同 burnish, furbish, gloss, refine
polite [pəˈlaɪt]	*adj.* 文雅的，有教养的(of, relating to, or having the characteristics of advanced culture) 同 courteous, genteel, mannerly
politically [pəˈlɪtɪkli]	*adv.* 政治上 记 来自political(*adj.* 政治的；政治性的)
pollen [ˈpɑːlən]	*n.* 花粉(a mass of microspores in a seed plant)
pollinate [ˈpɑːləneɪt]	*v.* 对…授粉(to carry out the transfer of pollen)
pomposity [pɑːmˈpɑːsəti]	*n.* 自大的行为或言论(pompous behavior, demeanor, or speech) 记 来自pomp(*n.* 炫耀；盛况)
pompous [ˈpɑːmpəs]	*adj.* 自大的(having or exhibiting self-importance) 同 arrogant
ponderous [ˈpɑːndərəs]	*adj.* 笨重的，(因太重太大而)不便搬运的(unwieldy or clumsy because of weight and size) 记 词根记忆：pond(重量) + er + ous(多…的) → 重的 → 笨重的

plunge

15

pop [pɑːp]	*v.* 发出"砰"的一声(to make or burst with a sharp sound); 突然出现(to go, come, or appear suddenly)
populous [ˈpɑːpjələs]	*adj.* 人口稠密的(densely populated) 记 词根记忆: popul(人) + ous(多…的) → 人口稠密的
porous [ˈpɔːrəs]	*adj.* 可渗透的(capable of being penetrated); 多孔的(full of pores) 记 来自pore(*n.* 孔)
portend [pɔːrˈtend]	*v.* 预兆, 预示(to give an omen) 记 联想记忆: port(港口) + end(尽头) → 港口到了尽头, 预示着临近海洋 → 预示
portray [pɔːrˈtreɪ]	*v.* 描述(to depict or describe in words); 描绘, 描画(to make a picture of) 记 联想记忆: por(看作pour, 倒) + tray(碟) → 将(颜料)倒在碟子上 → 描绘, 描画
positive [ˈpɑːzətɪv]	*adj.* 积极的(marked by optimism); 明确的(expressed clearly or peremptorily); 有信心的(confident); 无条件的(independent of changing circumstances; unconditioned) *n.* 正片(a photographic image in which the lights and darks appear as they do in nature); 积极的要素或特点(an affirmative element or characteristic) 记 联想记忆: posit(看作post, 邮件) + ive → 邮件上的地址要写清楚 → 明确的 例 Although most worthwhile criticism concentrates on the *positive*, one should not indiscriminately praise everything.
possess [pəˈzes]	*v.* 拥有(to have as an attribute, knowledge, or skill; own); 支配, 主宰(to gain or exert influence or control over; dominate); 受摆布, 缠住, 迷住(to bring or cause to fall under the influence, possession, or control of some emotional or intellectual response or reaction) 记 联想记忆: poss(看作boss, 老板) + ess → 老板拥有很多财产 → 拥有 例 The architects of New York's early skyscrapers, hinting here at a twelfth-century cathedral, there at a fifteenth-century palace, sought to legitimize the city's social strivings by evoking a history the city did not truly *possess*.
possessed [pəˈzest]	*adj.* 着迷的, 入迷的(influenced or controlled by sth.) 记 来自possess(*v.* 拥有; 迷住)
postdate [ˈpɑːstdeɪt]	*v.* 填迟…的日期(to put a date on (a check, for example) that is later than the actual date)
posthumous [ˈpɑːstʃəməs]	*adj.* 死后的, 身后的(following or occurring after death) 记 词根记忆: post(在…之后) + hum(地面) + ous → 埋到地下以后 → 死后的, 身后的

posthumously [ˈpɑːstʃəməsli]	*adv.* 死后地（after death） 例 Like many other pioneers, Dr. Elizabeth Blackwell, founder of the New York Infirmary, the first American hospital staffed entirely by women, faced ridicule from her contemporaries but has received great honor *posthumously*.
postoperative [ˌpɑːstˈɑːpərətɪv]	*adj.* 手术后的（following a surgical operation） 搭 postoperative care 术后护理
postulate [ˈpɑːstʃəleɪt]	*v.* 要求（to demand; claim）; 假定（to assume; presume） 记 词根记忆: post(放) + ul + ate → 放出观点 → 要求; 假定
postwar [ˈpɑːstwɔːr]	*adj.* 战后的（occurring or existing after a war） 记 组合词: post(在…之后) + war(战争) → 战后的
potable [ˈpoʊtəbl]	*adj.* 适于饮用的（suitable for drinking） 记 词根记忆: pot(喝) + able → 可以喝的 → 适于饮用的
potent [ˈpoʊtnt]	*adj.* 强有力的，有影响力的，有权力的（having or wielding force, authority, or influence）; 有效力的，有效能的（exerting or capable of exerting strong physiological or chemical effects）
potential [pəˈtenʃl]	*adj.* 潜在的，可能的（capable of development into actuality） 记 词根记忆: pot(有力的) + ent + ial → 潜在的，可能的 例 A major goal of law, to deter *potential* criminals by punishing wrongdoers, is not served when the penalty is so seldom invoked that it ceases to be a credible threat. 同 hidden, latent, lurking
potshot [ˈpɑːtʃɑːt]	*n.* 盲目射击（a shot taken from ambush or at a random or easy target）; 肆意抨击（a critical remark made in a random or sporadic manner）*v.* 肆意抨击
potted [ˈpɑːtɪd]	*adj.* 盆栽的（planted or grown in a pot）; 瓶装的，罐装的，壶装的（preserved in a pot, jar, or can）
pottery [ˈpɑːtəri]	*n.* 制陶（the manufacture of clayware）; 制陶工艺（the art or craft of the potter）; 陶器（earthenware）
pounce [paʊns]	*n.* (猛禽的)爪（the claw of a bird of prey）; 猛扑（the act of pouncing） *v.* 猛扑（to swoop upon and seize sth. with or as if with talons）; 突然袭击（to make a sudden assault or approach） 搭 pounce on 突然袭击
pragmatic [præɡˈmætɪk]	*adj.* 实际的（relating to matters of fact or practical affairs often to the exclusion of intellectual or artistic matters）; 务实的，注重实效的（practical as opposed to idealistic）; 实用主义的（of or relating to pragmatism） 记 词根记忆: prag(做) + matic → 付诸行动的 → 务实的，注重实效的 例 Although skeptics say financial problems will probably prevent our establishing a base on the Moon, supporters of the project remain enthusiastic, saying that human curiosity should overcome such *pragmatic* constraints.

15

□ posthumously　□ postoperative　□ postulate　　□ postwar　　□ potable　　□ potent
□ potential　　□ potshot　　□ potted　　□ pottery　　□ pounce　　□ pragmatic

165

precarious [prɪˈkerəriəs]	*adj.* 根据不足的，未证实的(dependent on uncertain premises)；不稳固的，危险的(characterized by a lack of security or stability that threatens with danger; unsafe) 记 联想记忆：pre(在前面) + car(汽车) + ious → 在汽车前面 → 危险的 例 Although his broker had told him that the stock was a *precarious* investment, he insisted on buying 100 shares.
precede [prɪˈsiːd]	*v.* 在…之前，早于(to be earlier than) 记 词根记忆：pre(在前面) + ced(走) + e → 走在…之前 → 早于
precedent [ˈpresɪdənt]	*adj.* 在先的，在前的(prior in time, order, arrangement, or significance) *n.* 先例(an earlier occurrence of sth. similar)；判例(a judicial decision that may be used as a standard in subsequent similar cases) 例 In failing to see that the justice's pronouncement merely qualified previous decisions rather than actually establishing a *precedent*, the novice law clerk overemphasized the scope of the justice's judgment.
precipitate	[prɪˈsɪpɪteɪt] *v.* 使突然降临，加速，促成(to bring about abruptly; hasten) [prɪˈsɪpɪtət] *adj.* 鲁莽的，轻率的(impetuous) 记 词根记忆：pre(预先) + cip(落下) + it + ate → 预先落下 → 使突然降临，加速 搭 precipitate sb./sth. into sth. 使…突然陷入(某种状态)
precipitous [prɪˈsɪpɪtəs]	*adj.* 陡峭的(very steep, perpendicular, or overhanging in rise or fall)
precise [prɪˈsaɪs]	*adj.* 精确的，准确的，确切的(exactly or sharply defined or stated) 记 词根记忆：pre(表加强) + cis(切) + e → 细心地切下 → 精确的 例 One of photography's most basic and powerful traits is its ability to give substance to history, to present *precise* visual details of a time gone by. 现在是北京时间 10点49分50秒25毫秒 39微秒6纳秒 52皮秒… 问询处 precise
preclude [prɪˈkluːd]	*v.* 预防，排除(to rule out in advance; prevent)；阻止(to exclude or prevent (sb.) from a given condition or activity) 记 词根记忆：pre(预先) + clud(关闭) + e → 预先关闭 → 预防，排除 同 deter, forestall, forfend, obviate, ward
preconception [ˌpriːkənˈsepʃn]	*n.* 先入之见(a preconceived idea)；偏见(prejudice) 记 联想记忆：pre(在前面) + conception(观念) → 先入之见
precursor [priːˈkɜːrsər]	*n.* 先驱，先兆(one that precedes and indicates the approach of another) 记 词根记忆：pre(在前面) + curs(跑) + or → 跑在前面的人 → 先驱 同 forerunner, harbinger, herald, outrider
predator [ˈpredətər]	*n.* 食肉动物(an animal that lives by killing and consuming other animals) 记 词根记忆：pred(掠夺) + at + or → 食肉动物

166

□ precarious   □ precede   □ precedent   □ precipitate   □ precipitous   □ precise
□ preclude   □ preconception   □ precursor   □ predator

predatory ['predətɔːri]	*adj.* 掠夺的 (of, relating to, or practicing plunder, pillage, or rapine); 食肉的 (predaceous) 例 Aimed at curbing European attempts to seize territory in the Americas, the Monroe Doctrine was a warning to *predatory* foreign powers. 同 predatorial, rapacious, raptorial
predecessor ['predəsesər]	*n.* 前任, 前辈 (the person who held an office or position before sb. else); 原有事物, 前身 (sth. that has been replaced by another) 记 词根记忆: pre (在前面) + de + cess (走) + or → 在前面走的人 → 前任, 前辈
predestine [ˌpriːˈdestɪn]	*v.* 预先注定 (to destine or determine beforehand) 记 联想记忆: pre(在前面) + destine(注定) → 预先注定 同 foreordain, predetermine, preordain
predetermine [ˌpriːdɪˈtɜːrmɪn]	*v.* 预先注定 (to foreordain; predestine); 预先决定 (to determine beforehand) 记 联想记忆: pre(在前面) + determine(决定) → 预先决定
predictable [prɪˈdɪktəbl]	*adj.* 可预知的 例 Though dealers insist that professional art dealers can make money in the art market, even an insider's knowledge is not enough: the art world is so fickle that stock-market prices are *predictable* by comparison.
predispose [ˌpriːdɪˈspoʊz]	*v.* 使预先有倾向 (to dispose in advance); (使)易受感染 (to make susceptible; bring about susceptibility)
predominant [prɪˈdɑːmɪnənt]	*adj.* 支配的, 占优势的, 主导的 (having superior strength, influence, or authority; prevailing) 记 联想记忆: pre(在前面) + dominant(统治的) → 在前面统治的 → 支配的, 占优势的
predominate [prɪˈdɑːmɪneɪt]	*v.* 统治 (to exert control over; dominate); (数量上)占优势, 以…为主 (to hold advantage in numbers or quantity) 例 The author argues for serious treatment of such arts as crochet and needlework, finding in too many art historians a cultural blindness traceable to their prejudice against textiles as a medium in which women artists *predominate*.
preeminent [priˈemɪnənt]	*adj.* 出类拔萃的, 杰出的 (supreme; outstanding) 记 联想记忆: pre(在前面) + eminent(著名的) → 比著名的人还著名 → 出类拔萃的 例 Industrialists seized economic power only after industry had supplanted agriculture as the *preeminent* form of production; previously such power had resided in land ownership.
preempt [priˈempt]	*v.* 以优先权获得 (to gain possession of by prior right or opportunity, especially to settle on (public land) so as to obtain the right to buy before others); 取代 (to replace with) 记 词根记忆: pre(预先) + empt(拿到) → 预先拿到 → 以优先权取得
prefabricated [ˌpriːˈfæbrɪkeɪtɪd]	*adj.* 预制构件的 记 来自 prefabricate (*v.* 预制)

15

preferably [ˈprefrəbli]	*adv.* 更可取地，更好地，宁可 记 来自 prefer(*v.* 宁可，更喜欢)
pregnant [ˈpregnənt]	*adj.* 怀孕的(gravid)；充满的(full; teeming) 记 词根记忆：pre(在前面) + gn(出生) + ant → 尚未出生的 → 怀孕的
prehistoric [ˌpriːhɪˈstɔːrɪk]	*adj.* 史前的(of a time before recorded history) 记 联想记忆：pre(在前面) + historic(历史的) → 史前的
prejudice [ˈpredʒudɪs]	*n.* 偏见，成见(an adverse judgment or opinion that is not founded on experience or reason) *v.* 使产生偏见(to cause to have prejudice) 记 词根记忆：pre(预先) + jud(判断) + ice → 预先判断 → 偏见，成见 搭 prejudice against... 对…有偏见、成见
preliminary [prɪˈlɪmɪneri]	*adj.* 预备的，初步的，开始的(coming before a more important action or event; preparatory) 记 词根记忆：pre(预先) + limin(门槛；起点) + ary → 预先跨入 → 预备的
premature [ˌpriːməˈtʃʊr]	*adj.* 早熟的，过早的(developing or happening before the natural or proper time) 记 联想记忆：pre(预先) + mature(成熟的) → 还没成熟的 → 早熟的，过早的
premeditate [ˌpriːˈmedɪteɪt]	*v.* 预谋，预先考虑或安排(to plan, arrange, or plot in advance) 记 词根记忆：pre(预先) + med(注意) + itate → 事先就加以注意 → 预谋
premise [ˈpremɪs]	*n.* 前提(a proposition antecedently supposed or proved as a basis of argument or inference) 记 词根记忆：pre(在前面) + mis(放) + e → 放在前面的东西 → 前提
premonition [ˌpriːməˈnɪʃn]	*n.* 预感，预兆(a feeling that sth. is going to happen) 记 词根记忆：pre(预先) + mon(警告) + it + ion → 预先给出的警告 → 预感，预兆 同 foreboding, prenotion, presage, presentiment
preoccupation [priˌɑːkjuˈpeɪʃn]	*n.* 全神贯注，专注(the state of being preoccupied)；使人专注的东西(sth. that takes up one's attention) 例 Certainly Murray's *preoccupation* with the task of editing the *Oxford English Dictionary* begot a kind of monomania, but it must be regarded as a beneficent or at least an innocuous one.
prerequisite [ˌpriːˈrekwəzɪt]	*n.* 先决条件(sth. that is necessary to an end) 记 词根记忆：pre(预先) + re(一再) + quis(要求) + ite → 预先一再要求 → 先决条件
prerogative [prɪˈrɑːgətɪv]	*n.* 特权(privilege; the discretionary power) 记 词根记忆：pre(预先) + rog(要求) + ative → 预先要求的权力 → 特权 例 Wearing the latest fashions was exclusively the *prerogative* of the wealthy until the 1850's, when mass production, aggressive entrepreneurs, and the availability of the sewing machine made them accessible to the middle class. 同 birthright, perquisite

168

□ preferably　　□ pregnant　　□ prehistoric　　□ prejudice　　□ preliminary　　□ premature
□ premeditate　　□ premise　　□ premonition　　□ preoccupation　　□ prerequisite　　□ prerogative

prescient [ˈpresiənt]	*adj.* 有先见的，预知的（knowing or appearing to know about things before they happen） 例 Famed athlete Bobby Orr was given his first pair of skates by a *prescient* Canadian woman who somehow "knew" he would use them to attain sporting greatness.
prescribe [prɪˈskraɪb]	*v.* 开处方（to say what treatment a sick person should have）；规定（to lay down a rule） 记 词根记忆：pre(预先) + scrib(写) + e → 预先写好 → 规定
preservative [prɪˈzɜːrvətɪv]	*adj.* 保护的；防腐的（having the power of preserving）*n.* 防腐剂（an additive used to protect against decay） 记 来自 preserve(*v.* 保护；保存)
preserve [prɪˈzɜːrv]	*v.* 保护（to keep safe from injury, harm, or destruction; protect）；保存（to keep alive, intact, or free from decay; maintain） 记 联想记忆：pre(在前面) + serve(服务) → 提前提供服务 → 保护；保存 例 The discovery by George Poinar and Roberta Hess that amber could *preserve* intact tissue from million-year-old insects raised the possibility, since proved correct, that it also could *preserve* intact DNA. 同 conserve, reserve
press [pres]	*v.* 挤压（to act upon through steady pushing） 同 squeeze
prestigious [preˈstɪdʒəs]	*adj.* 有名望的，有威望的（having prestige; honored） 记 来自 prestige(声望，威望)；pre(预先) + stig(捆绑) + e → 事先把人捆住 → 声望，威望 例 Many of the early Hollywood moguls sought to aggrandize themselves and enhance their celluloid empires by snaring *prestigious* writers and intellectuals as screenwriters. 同 distinguished, eminent, notable, prominent, renowned
presume [prɪˈzuːm]	*v.* 推测，假定（to take for granted as being true in the absence of proof to the contrary）；认定（to give reasonable evidence for assuming） 记 词根记忆：pre(预先) + sum(抓住) + e → 预先抓住 → 推测，假定
presumptuous [prɪˈzʌmptʃuəs]	*adj.* 放肆的，过分的（going beyond what is right or proper; excessively forward） 例 Not wishing to appear *presumptuous*, the junior member of the research group refrained from venturing any criticism of the senior members' plan for dividing up responsibility for the entire project. 同 overweening, presuming, uppity
presuppose [ˌpriːsəˈpouz]	*vt.* 预先假定（to suppose beforehand）；以…为先决条件（to require as an antecedent in logic or fact）

15

pretense	*n.* 妄称，自称(a claim made or implied)；假装，伪装，假象(a false show; an affectation；make-before)；借口，托词(a professed but feigned reason or excuse; a pretext)
[prɪ'tens]	
	例 An example of an illegitimate method of argument is to lump dissimilar cases together deliberately under the *pretense* that the same principles apply to each.
pretentious	*adj.* 夸耀的，炫耀的(making or marked by an extravagant outward show; ostentatious)；自命不凡的，狂妄的(making usually unjustified or excessive claims as of value or standing)
[prɪ'tenʃəs]	
preternatural	*adj.* 异常的(extraordinary)；超自然的(existing outside of nature)
[ˌpriːtər'nætʃrəl]	记 联想记忆：preter(超越) + natural(自然的) → 超自然的
prevail	*v.* 战胜(to gain ascendancy through strength or superiority)；流行，盛行(to be frequent)
[prɪ'veɪl]	
	记 词根记忆：pre(在前面) + vail(=val 力量) → 在力量上胜过他人 → 战胜
	同 conquer, master, predominate, triumph
prevalent	*adj.* 流行的，盛行的(widespread)
['prevələnt]	记 词根记忆：pre(在前面) + val(力量) + ent → 有走在前面的力量的 → 流行的
	同 prevailing, rampant, regnant, rife
previous	*adj.* 在先的，以前的(prior; preceding)
['priːviəs]	记 词根记忆：pre(在前面) + vi(道路) + ous → 走在前面的 → 在先的，以前的
prig	*n.* 自命清高者，道学先生(a person who demonstrates an exaggerated conformity or propriety, especially in an irritatingly arrogant or smug manner)
[prɪg]	
primal	*adj.* 原始的，最初的(original; primitive)；首要的(being first in importance)
['praɪml]	搭 primal chaos 原始的混沌状态
primitive	*adj.* 原始的，远古的(of or relating to an earliest or original stage or state)；基本的(assumed as a basis)
['prɪmətɪv]	记 词根记忆：prim(第一，首先) + itive(具…性质的) → 第一时间的 → 原始的
	例 Tacitus' descriptions of Germanic tribal customs were limited by the *primitive* state of communications in his day, but they match the accounts of other contemporary writers.
	同 original, prime, primeval
primordial	*adj.* 原始的，最初的(first created or developed)
[praɪ'mɔːrdiəl]	同 primeval, primitive
prior	*adj.* 在前的(previous)；优先的(taking precedence)
['praɪər]	记 词根记忆：pri(=prim 第一，首先) + or → 在前的；优先的
	例 Students of the Great Crash of 1929 have never understood why even the most informed observers did not recognize and heed the *prior* economic danger signals that in retrospect seem so apparent.
	同 antecedent, anterior, former, preceding

170

□ pretense □ pretentious □ preternatural □ prevail □ prevalent □ previous
□ prig □ primal □ primitive □ primordial □ prior

pristine [ˈprɪstiːn]	*adj.* 原始的(belonging to the earliest period or state); 质朴的，纯洁的(not spoiled or corrupted by civilization; pure); 新鲜的，干净的 (fresh and clean) 记 词根记忆：pri(=prim 第一，首先) + st(站) + ine → 站在首位的 → 原始的 例 Scientists' *pristine* reputation as devotees of the disinterested pursuit of truth has been compromised by recent evidence that some scientists have deliberately fabricated experimental results to further their own careers.
privacy [ˈpraɪvəsi]	*n.* 隐居，隐退(the quality or state of being apart from company or observation); 隐私(freedom from unauthorized intrusion); 秘密(secrecy) 例 Though extremely reticent about his own plans, the man allowed his associates no such *privacy* and was constantly soliciting information about what they intended to do next. 同 concealment, privateness
probity [ˈproʊbəti]	*n.* 刚直，正直(uprightness; honesty) 例 Such was Brandon's *probity* that he was at times described as being honest as the day was long.
problematic [ˌprɑːbləˈmætɪk]	*adj.* 成问题的(posing a problem); 有疑问的，值得怀疑的(open to doubt; debatable); 未知的，未解决的(not definite or settled) 例 As early as the seventeenth century, philosophers called attention to the *problematic* character of the issue, and their twentieth-century counterparts still approach it with uneasiness.
procedure [prəˈsiːdʒər]	*n.* 程序，手续(a particular way of accomplishing sth. or of acting) 记 来自 proceed(*v.* 前进) 例 Despite the apparently bewildering complexity of this *procedure*, the underlying principle is quite elementary.
proclamation [ˌprɑːkləˈmeɪʃn]	*n.* 宣布，公布(an official public statement) 记 词根记忆：pro(在前面) + clam(=claim 叫喊) + ation → 在前面喊 → 宣布，公布
proclivity [prəˈklɪvəti]	*n.* 倾向(an inclination or predisposition toward sth.) 同 leaning
procurement [prəˈkjʊrmənt]	*n.* 取得，获得(the obtaining by effort or careful attention); 采购 记 来自动词 procure(*v.* 取得，获得) 例 Remelting old metal cans rather than making primary aluminum from bauxite ore shipped from overseas saves producers millions of dollars in *procurement* and production costs.
prod [prɑːd]	*v.* 戳，刺(to poke); 刺激，激励(to stir up; urge) 搭 prod sb. into doing sth. 促使或推动某人做某事

15

Word List 16 🄜 MP3-16

prodigal [ˈprɑːdɪgl]	*adj.* 挥霍的（lavish）*n.* 挥霍者（one who spends lavishly） 记 词根记忆：prodig(巨大，浪费) + al(…的) → 挥霍的 例 Left to endure a penniless old age, the improvident man lived to regret his *prodigal* youth.
prodigious [prəˈdɪdʒəs]	*adj.* 巨大的（extraordinary in bulk, quantity, or degree）；惊人的，奇异的 记 来自 prodigy(*n.* 惊人的事物；奇观) 例 Although Barbara Tuchman never earned a graduate degree, she nonetheless pursued a scholarly career as a historian noted for her vivid style and *prodigious* erudition. 同 colossal, gigantic, immense, marvelous, stupendous
proficiency [prəˈfɪʃnsi]	*n.* 进步（advancement in knowledge or skill）；熟练，精通（the quality or state of being proficient）
proficient [prəˈfɪʃnt]	*adj.* 熟练的，精通的（skillful; expert） 记 词根记忆：pro(在前) + fic(做) + ient → 做在别人前面的 → 熟练的 例 Experienced and *proficient*, Susan is a good, reliable trumpeter; her music is often more satisfying than Carol's brilliant but erratic playing.
profile [ˈproʊfaɪl]	*n.* 轮廓，外形（outline）；（尤指人面部的）侧面（a human head or face represented or seen in a side view） 记 词根记忆：pro(前面) + fil(线条) + e → 外部的线条 → 轮廓，外形
profitable [ˈprɑːfɪtəbl]	*adj.* 有利可图的（affording profits） 例 There are simply no incentives for buying stock in certain industries since rapidly changing environmental restrictions will make a *profitable* return on any investment very unlikely. 同 advantageous, gainful, lucrative, remunerative
profligacy [ˈprɑːflɪgəsi]	*n.* 放荡；肆意挥霍（the quality or state of being profligate）

profile

profound [prəˈfaʊnd]	*adj.* 深的；深刻的，深远的（deep；very strongly felt）；渊博的；深奥的（difficult to fathom or understand） 记 联想记忆：pro（在…前）+ found（创立）→ 有超前创见性的 → 深刻的，深远的 例 No one is neutral about Stephens; he inspires either uncritical adulation or *profound* antipathy in those who work for him. 同 abstruse, esoteric, occult, recondite
profundity [prəˈfʌndəti]	*n.* 深奥的事物（something profound or abstruse）；深刻，深厚（the quality or state of being profound or deep）
profuse [prəˈfjuːs]	*adj.* 丰富的（bountiful）；浪费的（extravagant） 记 词根记忆：pro（许多）+ fus（流）+ e → 多得向外流 → 丰富的
prohibit [proʊˈhɪbɪt]	*v.* 禁止（to forbid by authority）；阻止（to prevent from doing sth.） 记 词根记忆：pro（提前）+ hibit（拿住）→ 提前拿住 → 禁止；阻止 同 inhibit, interdict
prohibitive [prəˈhɪbətɪv]	*adj.* 禁止的，抑制的（tending to prohibit or restrain）；贵得买不起的（so high or burdensome as to discourage purchase or use） 记 词根记忆：pro（提前）+ hibit（拿住）+ ive（…的）→ 提前拿住的 → 禁止的，抑制的
proliferate [prəˈlɪfəreɪt]	*v.* 激增（to increase rapidly；multiply）；（迅速）繁殖，增生（to grow by rapid production） 记 词根记忆：pro（许多）+ lifer（生命）+ ate → 产生许多生命 → 繁殖，增生
prolific [prəˈlɪfɪk]	*adj.* 多产的，多果实的（fruitful；fertile） 记 联想记忆：pro（许多）+ lif（看作 life，生命）+ ic（…的）→ 产生许多生命的 → 多产的 例 Having written 140 books to date, he may well be considered one of the most *prolific* novelists of the century. 同 fecund, productive
prolong [prəˈlɑːŋ]	*v.* 延长，拉长（lengthen） 记 词根记忆：pro（向前）+ long（长）→ 延长，拉长 例 In their determination to discover ways to *prolong* human life, doctors fail to take into account that longer lives are not always happier ones. 同 elongate, extend, prolongate, protract
prominence [ˈprɑːmɪnəns]	*n.* 突出物（something prominent）；突出，显著（the quality, state, or fact of being prominent or conspicuous） 例 Despite the growing *prominence* of Hispanic actors in the American theater, many Hispanic experts feel that the Spanish speaking population is underrepresented on the stage. 同 eminence, kudos, preeminence, prestige

16

promote [prə'moʊt]	v. 提升(to give sb. a higher position or rank); 促进(to help in the growth or development) 记 词根记忆: pro(向前) + mot(动) + e → 向前动 → 促进 例 Some activists believe that because the health-care system has become increasingly unresponsive to those it serves, individuals must circumvent bureaucratic impediments in order to develop and *promote* new therapies.
promotion [prə'moʊʃn]	n. 晋升(the act or fact of being raised in position or rank); 促进(the act of furthering the growth or development of sth.) 例 By idiosyncratically refusing to dismiss an insubordinate member of his staff, the manager not only contravened established policy, but he also jeopardized his heretofore good chances for *promotion*.
promptness ['prɑːmptnəs]	n. 敏捷, 迅速; 机敏
promulgate ['prɑːmlgeɪt]	v. 颁布(法令)(to put a law into action or force); 宣传, 传播(to spread the news) 记 词根记忆: pro(前面) + mulg(人民) + ate → 放到人民前面 → 宣传, 传播 同 announce, annunciate, declare, disseminate, proclaim
prone [proʊn]	adj. 俯卧的(lying flat or prostrate); 倾向于…的(being likely) 搭 prone to sth./do sth. 易于…; 有做…的倾向
pronounced [prə'naʊnst]	adj. 显著的, 明确的(strongly marked) 记 来自pronounce(v. 宣称, 宣布)
proofread ['pruːfriːd]	v. 校正, 校对(to read and mark corrections) 记 组合词: proof(校对) + read(读) → 校正, 校对
propaganda [ˌprɑːpə'gændə]	n. 宣传(the spreading of ideas, information)
propagate ['prɑːpəgeɪt]	v. 繁殖(to multiply); 传播(to cause to spread out; publicize) 记 词根记忆: pro + pag(砍, 切) + ate → 把树的旁枝剪掉使主干成长 → 繁殖
propel [prə'pel]	v. 推进, 促进(to drive forward or onward; push) 记 词根记忆: pro(向前) + pel(推) → 推进, 促进
propensity [prə'pensəti]	n. 嗜好, 习性(an often intense natural inclination or preference) 记 词根记忆: pro(提前) + pens(挂) + ity → 总是喜欢预先挂好 → 嗜好, 习性 例 The poet W. H. Auden believed that the greatest poets of his age were almost necessarily irresponsible, that the possession of great gifts engenders the *propensity* to abuse them. 同 bent, leaning, tendency, penchant, proclivity
prophesy ['prɑːfəsaɪ]	v. 预言(to predict with assurance or on the basis of mystic knowledge) 同 adumbrate, augur, portend, presage, prognosticate

prophetic [prə'fetɪk]	*adj.* 先知的，预言的，预示的（correctly telling of things that will happen in the future） 记 词根记忆：pro（提前）+ phe（说）+ tic → 提前说出来 → 先知的，预言的
propitiate [prə'pɪʃieɪt]	*v.* 讨好（to gain or regain the favor or goodwill of）；抚慰（to appease） 记 词根记忆：pro（向前）+ piti（=pet 寻求）+ ate → 主动寻求和解 → 讨好 例 At the height of the storm, the savages tried to *propitiate* the angry gods by offering sacrifices. 同 assuage, conciliate, mollify, pacify, placate
propitious [prə'pɪʃəs]	*adj.* 吉利的，顺利的（auspicious；favorable）；有利的（advantageous） 记 词根记忆：pro（向前）+ piti（=pet 寻求）+ ous → 寻求前进的 → 吉利的，顺利的 例 An experienced politician who knew better than to launch a campaign in troubled political waters, she intended to wait for a more *propitious* occasion before she announced her plans.
proposition [ˌprɑːpə'zɪʃn]	*n.* 看法，主张（statement that expresses a judgement or an opinion）；提议（proposal） 记 来自 propose（*v.* 建议，提议）
proprietary [prə'praɪəˌteri]	*adj.* 私有的（privately owned and managed）
propriety [prə'praɪəti]	*n.* 礼节（decorum）；适当，得体（appropriateness） 记 词根记忆：propr（拥有）+ iety → 拥有得体的行为 → 礼节；得体
prosaic [prə'zeɪɪk]	*adj.* 散文（体）的；单调的，无趣的（dull；unimaginative） 记 来自 prose（*n.* 散文） 例 He felt that the uninspiring routine of office work was too *prosaic* for someone of his talent and creativity.
proscribe [prou'skraɪb]	*v.* 禁止（to forbid as harmful or unlawful；prohibit） 记 词根记忆：pro（前面）+ scrib（写）+ e → 写在前面 → 禁止
prose [prouz]	*n.* 散文（written or spoken language that is not in verse form） 记 联想记忆：p + rose（玫瑰）→ 散文如玫瑰花瓣，形散而神聚 → 散文
prosecute ['prɑːsɪkjuːt]	*v.* 起诉（to carry on a legal suit）；告发（to carry on a prosecution） 记 词根记忆：pro（提前）+ secut（追踪）→ 事先追踪行进 → 告发
proselytize ['prɑːsələtaɪz]	*v.* （使）皈依（to recruit or convert to a new faith） 记 词根记忆：pros（靠近）+ elyt（来到）+ ize → 走到（佛祖）面前 → （使）皈依
prospect ['prɑːspekt]	*v.* 勘探（to explore）*n.* 期望（reasonable hope that sth. will happen）；前景（sth. which is possible or likely for the future）
prostrate ['prɑːstreɪt]	*adj.* 俯卧的（prone）；沮丧的（powerless；helpless）*v.* 使下跪鞠躬，使拜服（to make oneself bow or kneel down in humility or adoration）
protective [prə'tektɪv]	*adj.* 保护的，防护的 例 Why do some plant stems develop a *protective* bark that enables them to survive the winter, while others shrivel at the first frost?

16

protest	[prəˈtest] *v.* 抗议，反对
	[ˈproʊtest] *n.* 抗议，反对(organized public demonstration of disapproval)
	记 联想记忆：pro(很多) + test(测验) → 考试太多，遭到学生抗议 → 抗议，反对
	例 Black religion was in part a *protest* movement—a *protest* against a system and a society that was deliberately designed to demean the dignity of a segment of God's creation.
prototype [ˈproʊtətaɪp]	*n.* 原型(an original model; archetype)；典型(a standard or typical example)
	记 词根记忆：proto(起初) + type(形状) → 起初的形状 → 原型
	例 This project is the first step in a long-range plan of research whose ultimate goal, still many years off, is the creation of a new *prototype*.
protozoan [ˌproʊtəˈzoʊən]	*n.* 原生动物
	记 词根记忆：proto(起初) + zo(动物) + an → 原生动物
protract [prəˈtrækt]	*v.* 延长，拖长(prolong)
	记 词根记忆：pro(向前) + tract(拉) → 向前拉 → 延长，拖长
	同 elongate, extend, lengthen, prolongate
protrude [proʊˈtruːd]	*v.* 突出，伸出(to jut out)
	记 词根记忆：pro(向前) + trud(伸出) +e → 向前伸 → 伸出
proverb [ˈprɑːvɜːrb]	*n.* 谚语(a brief popular epigram or maxim)
	记 词根记忆：pro(起初) + verb(话) → 早期人们说的话 → 谚语
provident [ˈprɑːvɪdənt]	*adj.* 深谋远虑的(prudent)；节俭的(frugal; thrifty)
	记 词根记忆：pro(向前) + vid(看) + ent(…的) → 向前看的 → 深谋远虑的
provincial [prəˈvɪnʃl]	*adj.* 省的，地方的；偏狭的，粗俗的(limited in outlook)
	记 来自province(*n.* 省)
	例 This poetry is not *provincial*; it is more likely to appeal to an international audience than is poetry with strictly regional themes.
	同 agrestic, bucolic, countrified, rustic
provision [prəˈvɪʒn]	*n.* 供应(a stock of needed materials or supplies)；(法律等)条款(stipulation)
provisional [prəˈvɪʒənl]	*adj.* 暂时的，临时的(temporary)
	例 There is nothing tentative or *provisional* about Moore's early critical pronouncements; she deals confidently with what were then radical new developments in poetry.
provocation [ˌprɑːvəˈkeɪʃn]	*n.* 挑衅，激怒(the act of provoking; incitement)
	记 来自provoke(*v.* 激怒)
provocative [prəˈvɑːkətɪv]	*adj.* 挑衅的，煽动的(serving or tending to provoke, excite, or stimulate)
	例 The results of the experiments performed by Elizabeth Hazen and Rachel Brown were *provocative* not only because these results challenged old assumptions but also because they called the prevailing methodology into question.

176

☐ protest ☐ prototype ☐ protozoan ☐ protract ☐ protrude ☐ proverb
☐ provident ☐ provincial ☐ provision ☐ provisional ☐ provocation ☐ provocative

provoke [prəˈvoʊk]	*v.* 激怒 (to incite to anger)；引起 (evoke)；驱使 (to stir up purposely) 记 词根记忆：pro(在前) + vok(呼喊) + e → 在前面呼喊 → 激怒；引起 例 For many young people during the Roaring Twenties, a disgust with the excesses of American culture combined with a wanderlust to *provoke* an exodus abroad.
proximity [prɑːkˈsɪməti]	*n.* 接近，临近 (the quality or state of being proximate) 记 词根记忆：prox(接近) + imity → 接近，临近
prudent [ˈpruːdnt]	*adj.* 审慎的 (acting with or showing care and foresight)，精明的 (showing good judgement)；节俭的，精打细算的 (frugal) 记 词根记忆：prud(小心的) + ent → 审慎的 例 It was a war the queen and her more *prudent* counselors wished to avoid if they could and were determined in any event to postpone as long as possible. 同 judicious, sage, sane
prudish [ˈpruːdɪʃ]	*adj.* 过分守礼的，假道学的 (marked by prudery；priggish)
pseudonym [ˈsuːdənɪm]	*n.* 假名，笔名 (a fictitious name, especially penname) 记 词根记忆：pseudo(假) + nym(名字) → 假名
psyche [ˈsaɪki]	*n.* 心智，精神 (mind；soul)
psychological [ˌsaɪkəˈlɑːdʒɪkl]	*adj.* 心理学的 (of or relating to psychology)；心理的，精神的 (directed toward the will or the mind specifically in its conative function) 记 词根记忆：psycho(心灵，精神) + log(说) + ical(…的) → 心理的，精神的 例 In a nation where the economic reversals of the past few years have taken a *psychological* as well as a financial toll on many regions, what most distinguishes the South may be the degree of optimism throughout the region.
psychology [saɪˈkɑːlədʒi]	*n.* 心理学 (the study or science of the mind and the way it works and influences behavior) 记 词根记忆：psycho(心灵，精神) + logy(…学) → 心理学
publicize [ˈpʌblɪsaɪz]	*v.* (公开)宣传，宣扬；引人注意 记 联想记忆：public(公开的) + ize(使) → 使公开 → 宣传，宣扬 例 Though the ad writers had come up with a highly creative campaign to *publicize* the company's newest product, the head office rejected it for a more prosaic, down-to-earth approach.
pugnacious [pʌgˈneɪʃəs]	*adj.* 好斗的 (having a quarrelsome or combative nature) 记 词根记忆：pugn(打斗) + acious(…的) → 好斗的
puncture [ˈpʌŋktʃər]	*v.* 刺穿，戳破 (to pierce with a pointed instrument) *n.* 刺孔，穿孔 记 词根记忆：punct(点) + ure → 点破 → 刺穿，戳破

16

□ provoke   □ proximity   □ prudent   □ prudish   □ pseudonym   □ psyche
□ psychological   □ psychology   □ publicize   □ pugnacious   □ puncture

177

pungent [ˈpʌndʒənt]	*adj.* 辛辣的，刺激的(piquant)；尖锐的，尖刻的(being sharp and to the point) 记 词根记忆：pung(刺) + ent → 尖锐的，尖刻的 例 The *pungent* verbal give-and-take among the characters makes the novel tedious reading.
punishment [ˈpʌnɪʃmənt]	*n.* 惩罚，刑罚(suffering, pain, or loss that serves as retribution)；虐待(severe, rough, or disastrous treatment) 例 A sense of fairness dictates that the *punishment* should fit the crime; yet, in actual practice, judicial decisions vary greatly for the same type of criminal offense.
purchase [ˈpɜːtʃəs]	*n.* 支点(阻止东西下滑)(a mechanical hold) 记 purchase 作为"购买"之意大家都很熟悉
purified [ˈpjʊrɪfaɪd]	*adj.* 纯净的 记 来自purify(*v.* 使洁净；净化)
purport [ˈpɜːrpɔːrt]	*n.* 意义，涵义，主旨(meaning conveyed, implied; gist) 记 词根记忆：pur(附近) + port(带) → 带到主要意思附近，领会主旨 → 意义，主旨
purposiveness [ˈpɜːrpəsɪvnəs]	*n.* 目的性 记 来自purpose(*n.* 目的)
pursuit [pərˈsuːt]	*n.* 追赶(the act of pursuing)；职业(occupation) 记 联想记忆：钱包(purse)被小偷偷去，赶忙追赶(pursuit)
quagmire [ˈkwæɡmaɪər]	*n.* 沼泽地(soft miry land)；困境(predicament) 记 组合词：quag(沼泽) + mire(泥潭) → quagmire(沼泽地) 同 dilemma, plight, scrape
quaint [kweɪnt]	*adj.* 离奇有趣的(unusual and attractive)；古色古香的 记 联想记忆：和 paint(*n.* 油漆)一起记；paint to become quaint(漆上油漆变得离奇有趣)
qualified [ˈkwɑːlɪfaɪd]	*adj.* 合格的(having complied with the specific requirements or precedent conditions)；有限制的(limited) 记 来自动词 qualify(*v.* 具有资格；限制) 例 Even though the general's carefully *qualified* public statement could hardly be faulted, some people took exception to it.
qualm [kwɑːm]	*n.* 疑惧(a sudden access of disturbing emotion)；紧张不安(a feeling of uneasiness)
quantifiable [ˈkwɑːntɪfaɪəbl]	*adj.* 可以计量的；可量化的 记 词根记忆：quant(数量) + ifi + able(可…的) → 可以计量的
quantum [ˈkwɑːntəm]	*n.* 量子(any of the small subdivisions of a quantized physical magnitude)；定量 记 词根记忆：quant(数量) + um → 定量

刷卡 purchase

quarantine [ˈkwɔːrəntiːn]	n. 隔离检疫期，隔离（enforced isolation to prevent the spread of disease） 记 联想记忆：quarant（四十）+ ine → 隔开 40 天 → 隔离
quarrel [ˈkwɔːrəl]	n. 争吵（a usually verbal conflict between antagonists）v. 争吵（to contend or dispute actively） 例 Read's apology to Heflin was not exactly abject and did little to resolve their decades-long *quarrel*, which had been as acrimonious as the academic etiquette of scholarly journals permitted.
quash [kwɔːʃ]	v. 镇压（to suppress）;（依法）取消（to nullify by judicial action） 同 abrogate, repeal, rescind
querulous [ˈkwerələs]	adj. 抱怨的，爱发牢骚的（habitually complaining; fretful） 记 联想记忆：que（看作 question，质疑）+ rul（看作 rule，规则）+ ous（…的）→ 质疑规则 → 抱怨的 例 Safire as a political commentator is patently *querulous*; he writes biased editorials about every action the government takes.
quiescence [kwiˈesns]	n. 静止，沉寂（the quality or state of being quiescent） 同 quietness, stillness, tranquillity
quiescent [kwiˈesnt]	adj. 不动的，静止的（marked by inactivity or repose） 记 词根记忆：qui（=quiet 安静的）+ escent（状态）→ 静止的 例 The astronomer and feminist Maria Mitchell's own prodigious activity and the vigor of the Association for the Advancement of Women during the 1870s belie any assertion that feminism was *quiescent* in that period. 同 abeyant, dormant, latent
quixotic [kwɪkˈsɑːtɪk]	adj. 不切实际的，空想的（foolishly impractical） 记 来自 *Don Quixote*《堂·吉诃德》; 亦作 quixotical
quote [kwoʊt]	v. 引用，引述（to repeat in speech or writing the words of a person or a book）
raciness [ˈreɪsɪnəs]	n. 生动活泼
radiant [ˈreɪdiənt]	adj. 发光的（vividly bright and shining）; 容光焕发的（marked by or expressive of love, confidence, or happiness） 记 词根记忆：rad（光线）+ i + ant（的）→ 发光的
radicalism [ˈrædɪkəlɪzəm]	n. 激进主义（the quality or state of being radical） 记 来自 radical（adj. 激进的; 彻底的）
radically [ˈrædɪkli]	adv. 根本上（in origin or essence）; 以激进方式（in a radical or extreme manner） 例 When trees go dormant in winter, the procedure is anything but sleepy: it is an active metabolic process that changes the plant *radically*.

rag	n. 旧布，碎布(old cloth)；破旧衣服(an old worn-out garment)
[ræg]	搭 lose one's rag 发怒，生气
rage	n. 盛怒(violent and uncontrolled anger) v. 狂怒，
[reɪdʒ]	大发雷霆(to be in a rage)
	搭 be all the rage 十分流行，成为时尚
ragged	adj. 褴褛的，破烂的(torn or worn to tatters)
[ˈrægɪd]	
ragtime	n. 雷格泰姆音乐(a type of music of black US
[ˈrægtaɪm]	origin) adj. 使人发笑的，滑稽的(funny)
	记 联想记忆：rag(破衣服) + time(节拍) → 黑人穿破衣服打拍子 → 使人发笑的
raisin	n. 葡萄干(a grape that has been dried)
[ˈreɪzn]	
rampant	adj. 猖獗的，蔓生的(marked by a menacing wildness or absence of
[ˈræmpənt]	restraint)
	记 联想记忆：ram(羊) + pant(喘气) → 因为草生长猖獗，所以羊高兴得直喘气 → 猖獗的，蔓生的
ramshackle	adj. 摇摇欲坠的(rickety)
[ˈræmʃækl]	例 Most of the settlements that grew up near the logging camps were *ramshackle* affairs, thrown together in a hurry because people needed to live on the job.
ranching	n. 大牧场(a large farm for raising horses, beef cattle, or sheep)
[ˈræntʃɪŋ]	
rancid	adj. 不新鲜的，变味的(rank; stinking)
[ˈrænsɪd]	记 联想记忆：ran(跑)+cid(看作 acid，酸) → 变酸了 → 不新鲜的，变味的
rancor	n. 深仇，怨恨(bitter deep-seated ill will; enmity)
[ˈræŋkər]	例 For someone suffering from stress, a holiday can act as a tonic, dispelling *rancor*, transforming indecision, and renewing the spirit.
rarefy	v. 使稀少，使稀薄(to make rare, thin, porous, or less dense)
[ˈrerəfaɪ]	同 attenuate, dilute
ratify	v. 批准(to approve formally; confirm)
[ˈrætɪfaɪ]	记 词根记忆：rat(估算，清点) + ify → 一一地清点 → 批准
rationale	n. 基本原理(fundamental reasons; the basis)
[ˌræʃəˈnæl]	
raucous	adj. 刺耳的，沙哑的(disagreeably harsh; hoarse)；喧嚣的(boisterously
[ˈrɔːkəs]	disorderly)
	记 词根记忆：rauc(=hoarse 沙哑的)+ous → 沙哑的
ravage	v. 摧毁，使荒废(to ruin and destroy)
[ˈrævɪdʒ]	同 desolate, devastate, havoc
rave	n. 热切赞扬(an extravagantly favorable remark) v. 胡言乱语，说疯语(to
[reɪv]	talk irrationally in or as if in delirium)

rage

□ rag	□ rage	□ ragged	□ ragtime	□ raisin	□ rampant
□ ramshackle	□ ranching	□ rancid	□ rancor	□ rarefy	□ ratify
□ rationale	□ raucous	□ ravage	□ rave		

raze [reɪz]	*v.* 夷为平地(to destroy to the ground); 彻底破坏(to destroy completely)
reactionary [riˈækʃəneri]	*adj.* 极端保守的，反动的(ultraconservative in politics) 记 联想记忆: re(反)+action(动)+ary → 反动的
readable [ˈriːdəbl]	*adj.* 易读的(able to be read easily)
reaffirm [ˌriːəˈfɜːrm]	*v.* 再次确定(confirm again); 重申(to state again positively) 记 分析记忆: re(再次) + affirm(确定) → 再次确定
reaffirmation [ˌriːˌæfərˈmeɪʃn]	*n.* 再肯定(renewed affirmation)
realistic [ˌriːəˈlɪstɪk]	*adj.* 现实主义的(representing what is real) 例 The documentary film about high school life was so *realistic* and evocative that feelings of nostalgia flooded over the college-age audience.
realm [relm]	*n.* 王国(a country ruled over by a king or queen); 领域，范围(an area of activity, study, etc.)
reassure [ˌriːəˈʃʊr]	*v.* 使恢复信心(to restore to confidence); 使确信(to reinsure) 记 词根记忆: re(再次) + as + sure(确信) → 一再地确信 → 使恢复信心
rebellious [rɪˈbeljəs]	*adj.* 造反的，反叛的(given to or engaged in rebellion; refractory); 难控制的 记 词根记忆: re(反)+bell(打斗，战争)+ious → 打回去 → 造反的
rebroadcast [rɪˈbrɔːdkæst]	*v.* 重播(to broadcast again)
rebuke [rɪˈbjuːk]	*v.* 指责，谴责(to criticize sharply; reprimand) 记 词根记忆: re(再次)+buk(=beat 打)+e → 反复打 → 指责 同 admonish, chide, reproach
recalcitrant [rɪˈkælsɪtrənt]	*adj.* 顽抗的(obstinately defiant of authority or restraint; unruly) 记 词根记忆: re(反)+calcitr(=calc 石头)+ant → 像石头一样坚硬顽强地反抗 → 顽抗的
recapitulate [ˌriːkəˈpɪtʃuleɪt]	*v.* 扼要重述(to repeat the principal points; summarize) 记 词根记忆: re(重新) + capit(头) + ulate → 将核心(即"头")重新讲述一遍 → 扼要重述
recast [ˌriːˈkæst]	*v.* 重铸(to mold again); 更换演员(to change the cast of (a theatrical production)) 记 词根记忆: re(重新) + cast(铸) → 重铸
recede [rɪˈsiːd]	*v.* 后退，撤回(to move back; withdraw) 记 词根记忆: re(反)+ced(走) +e → 走回去 → 后退
receptive [rɪˈseptɪv]	*adj.* 善于接受的，能接纳的(able or inclined to receive) 例 The newborn human infant is not a passive figure, nor an active one, but what might be called an actively *receptive* one, eagerly attentive as it is to sights and sounds.

16

recessive	*adj.* 隐性遗传的; 后退的 (tending to recede; withdrawn)
[rɪˈsesɪv]	
recipient	*n.* 接受者, 收受者 (a person who receives)
[rɪˈsɪpiənt]	记 词根记忆: re + cip(拿) + ient → 拿东西的人 → 接受者, 收受者
reciprocally	*adv.* 相互地; 相反地
[rɪˈsɪprəkli]	同 mutually
reciprocate	*v.* 回报, 答谢 (to make a return for sth.)
[rɪˈsɪprəkeɪt]	记 词根记忆: re + cip(收下) + rocate → 再次收下 → 答谢
reciprocation	*n.* 互换 (a mutual exchange); 报答 (a return in kind or of like value); 往复运动 (an alternating motion)
[rɪˌsɪprəˈkeɪʃn]	搭 reciprocation of …的回报
reciprocity	*n.* 相互性 (the quality or state of being reciprocal); 互惠 (a mutual exchange of privileges)
[ˌresɪˈprɑːsəti]	例 The state is a network of exchanged benefits and beliefs, a *reciprocity* between rulers and citizens based on those laws and procedures that are conducive to the maintenance of community.
recital	*n.* 独奏会, 独唱会, 小型舞蹈表演会 (a concert given by an individual musician or dancer); 吟诵 (the act or process or an instance of reciting)
[rɪˈsaɪtl]	记 来自 recite(*v.* 背诵); re + cit(唤起) + e → 重新引出 → 背诵
	例 Halls and audiences for lieder *recitals* tend to be smaller than for opera and thus more conducive to the intimacy and sense of close involvement, which is the *recital's* particular charm.
recklessness	*n.* 鲁莽, 轻率
[ˈrekləsnəs]	记 来自 reckless(*adj.* 鲁莽的; 不计后果的)
reclaim	*v.* 纠正, 改造 (to rescue from an undesirable state); 开垦(土地) (to make available for human use by changing natural conditions)
[rɪˈkleɪm]	记 词根记忆: re + claim(喊) → 喊回来 → 纠正, 改造
recluse	*n.* 隐士 (a person who leads a secluded or solitary life) *adj.* 隐居的 (marked by withdrawal from society)
[ˈrekluːs]	记 词根记忆: re + clus (关闭) + e → 把门关上 → 隐居的
	同 cloistered, seclusive, sequestered
reclusive	*adj.* 隐遁的, 隐居的 (seeking or preferring seclusion or isolation)
[rɪˈkluːsɪv]	
recoil	*v.* 弹回, 反冲 (to fall back under pressure); 退却, 退缩 (to shrink back physically or emotionally)
[rɪˈkɔɪl]	记 词根记忆: re(反) + coil(卷, 盘绕) → 卷回去 → 退缩
recollect	*v.* 回忆 (to remember); 想起 (to remind oneself of sth. temporarily forgotten)
[ˌrekəˈlekt]	同 reminisce, retrospect
recommendation	*n.* 推荐 (the act of recommending); 推荐信 (sth. that recommends or expresses commendation)
[ˌrekəmenˈdeɪʃn]	

recompose [ˌriːkəmˈpoʊz]	*v.* 重写(to compose again)；重新安排
reconcile [ˈrekənsaɪl]	*v.* 和解，调和(to restore to friendship or harmony) 记 联想记忆：re(再次) + con(共同) + cile → 重新回到原来的关系 → 和解 例 In attempting to *reconcile* estranged spouses, counselors try to foster a spirit of compromise rather than one of stubborn implacability. 同 attune, harmonize, reconciliate
reconciliation [ˌrekənsɪliˈeɪʃn]	*n.* 和解(the action of reconciling)；调解 例 Their change of policy brought out a *reconciliation* with Britain.
recondite [ˈrekəndaɪt]	*adj.* 深奥的，晦涩的(difficult or impossible for understanding) 记 词根记忆：re(反) + con(共同) + dit(说) + e → 不是对所有人都能说明白 → 深奥的
reconnaissance [rɪˈkɑːnɪsns]	*n.* 侦察，预先勘测(a preliminary survey to gain information) 记 注意不要和 renaissance(*n.* 复兴；复活)相混
recount [rɪˈkaʊnt]	*v.* 叙述，描写(to relate in detail; narrate)
recourse [ˈriːkɔːrs]	*n.* 求助，依靠(a turning to sb. or sth. for help or protection) 例 Any population increase beyond a certain level necessitates greater *recourse* to vegetable foods; thus, the ability of a society to choose meat over cereals always arises, in part, from limiting the number of people.
recreational [ˌrekriˈeɪʃənl]	*adj.* 娱乐的，休闲的(of, relating to, or characteristic of recreation)
rectify [ˈrektɪfaɪ]	*v.* 改正，矫正(to correct by removing errors; adjust)；提纯(to purify by repeated distillation) 记 词根记忆：rect(直) + ify → 使…变直 → 改正，矫正
recuperate [rɪˈkuːpəreɪt]	*v.* 恢复(健康、体力)，复原(to regain; to recover) 记 词根记忆：re(再次) + cuper(=gain 获得) + ate → 再次获得原来的状态 → 复原
recur [rɪˈkɜːr]	*v.* 重现，再发生(to come up again)；复发(to occur again after an interval)
recurrent [rɪˈkɜːrənt]	*adj.* 循环的(running or turning back in a direction opposite to a former course)；一再发生的(returning or happening time after time)
recurring [rɪˈkɜːrɪŋ]	*adj.* 反复的；再次发生的 例 Because it has no distinct and recognizable typographical form and few *recurring* narrative conventions, the novel is, of all literary genres, the least susceptible to definition.
redeem [rɪˈdiːm]	*v.* 弥补，赎回，偿还(to atone for; expiate) 记 词根记忆：re(重新) + deem(买) → 重新买回 → 赎回

□ recompose	□ reconcile	□ reconciliation	□ recondite	□ reconnaissance	□ recount
□ recourse	□ recreational	□ rectify	□ recuperate	□ recur	□ recurrent
□ recurring	□ redeem				

Word List 17  MP3-17

redirect [ˌriːdə'rekt]	*v.* 改寄（信件）(to send in a new direction)；改变方向(to change the course or direction) 记 词根记忆：re(重新) + direct(指向) → 改变方向
redistribution [ˌriːdɪ'strɪbjuːʃn]	*n.* 重新分配(altering the distribution) 记 联想记忆：re(重新) + distribution(分配) → 重新分配
redundant [rɪ'dʌndənt]	*adj.* 累赘的，多余的(exceeding what is necessary or normal；superfluous) 记 词根记忆：red(=re) + und(波动) + ant → 反复波动 → 反复出现的 → 累赘的，多余的 同 diffuse, prolix, verbose, wordy
reenact [ˌriːɪ'nækt]	*v.* 再制定(to enact (as a law) again) 例 To have true disciples, a thinker must not be too idiosyncratic: any effective intellectual leader depends on the ability of other people to *reenact* thought processes that did not originate with them.
reexamination [ˌriːɪgˌzæmɪ'neɪʃn]	*n.* 重考；复试；再检查
referent ['refərənt]	*n.* 指示对象(one that refers or is referred to)
reflective [rɪ'flektɪv]	*adj.* 反射的，反照的(capable of reflecting light, images, or sound waves)；深思熟虑的(thoughtful) 搭 be reflective of 是…的反映或体现
refractory [rɪ'fræktəri]	*adj.* 倔强的，难管理的(stubborn；unmanageable)；(病)难治的(resistant to treatment or cure) 记 词根记忆：re + fract(断裂) + ory → 宁折不弯 → 倔强的
refrain [rɪ'freɪn]	*v.* 抑制(to curb；restrain) *n.* (歌曲或诗歌中的)叠句(a regular recurring phrase or verse) 记 词根记忆：re + frain(笼头) → 上笼头 → 抑制
refrigerate [rɪ'frɪdʒəreɪt]	*v.* 使冷却，冷藏(to make or keep cold or cool)

□ redirect □ redistribution □ redundant ■ reenact □ reexamination □ referent
□ reflective □ refractory □ refrain ■ refrigerate

regale [rɪˈgeɪl]	*v.* 款待，宴请(to feast with delicacies)；使…快乐(to give pleasure or amusement to) 记 词根记忆：re(使) + gale(高兴) → 使客人高兴 → 款待
regenerate [rɪˈdʒenəreɪt]	*v.* 改造，改进(to change radically and for the better)；使再生，新生(to generate or produce anew)
regimental [ˌredʒɪˈmentl]	*adj.* 团的，团队的(of or relating to a regiment) 记 来自 regiment(*n.* 团；大量)
regressive [rɪˈgresɪv]	*adj.* 退步的，退化的(moving backward to a primitive state or condition) 同 recessive, retrograde, retrogressive
regretfully [rɪˈgretfəli]	*adv.* 懊悔地(with regret) 记 来自 regret(*v.* 懊悔，惋惜)
regulatory [ˈregjələtɔːri]	*adj.* 按规矩来的，依照规章的；调整的
rehabilitate [ˌriːəˈbɪlɪteɪt]	*v.* 使恢复(健康、能力、地位等)(to restore to a former health, capacity, rank, etc.) 记 词根记忆：re + hab(拥有) + ilit + ate → 使重新拥有 → 使恢复
reigning [ˈreɪnɪŋ]	*adj.* 统治的，起支配作用的
reimburse [ˌriːɪmˈbɜːrs]	*v.* 偿还(to pay back to sb.; repay) 记 词根记忆：re + im(进入) + burse(钱包) → 重新进入钱包 → 偿还
reinstate [ˌriːɪnˈsteɪt]	*v.* (使)恢复(原来的地位或职位)(to restore to a previous effective state or position) 记 词根记忆：re(重新) + in(进入) + state(状态) → 重新进入原来的状态 → 恢复
reiterate [riˈɪtəreɪt]	*v.* 重申，反复地说(to state over again or repeatedly) 记 词根记忆：re(反复) + iter (重申) + ate → 重申，反复地说 同 ingeminate, iterate
rekindle [ˌriːˈkɪndl]	*v.* 再点火；使重新振作 搭 to rekindle hopes 重新点燃希望
relegate [ˈreləgeɪt]	*v.* 使降级，贬谪(to send to exile; assign to oblivion)；交付，托付(to refer or assign for decision or action) 记 词根记忆：re + leg(选择) + ate → 重新选择职位 → 使降级
relent [rɪˈlent]	*adj.* 变宽厚，变温和，怜悯(commiserate) 同 relax, slacken, soften
relentless [rɪˈlentləs]	*adj.* 无情的，残酷的(cruel) 同 merciless, pitiless, ruthless
relevance [ˈreləvəns]	*n.* 相关性(the quality of being connected with and important to sth. else) 记 来自 relevant(*adj.* 相关的) 例 Adam Smith's *Wealth of Nations* (1776) is still worth reading, more to appreciate the current **relevance** of Smith's valid contributions to

17

economics than to see those contributions as the precursors of present-day economics.

reliable [rɪ'laɪəbl]	*adj.* 可信赖的 (suitable or fit to be relied on) *n.* 可信赖的人 (one that is reliable) 例 Experienced and proficient, Susan is a good, *reliable* trumpeter; her music is often more satisfying than Carol's brilliant but erratic playing.
relieve [rɪ'liːv]	*v.* 减轻，解除 (to free from a burden; mitigate) 记 词根记忆：re + liev(=lev 轻) + e → 减轻，解除 同 allay, alleviate, assuage, mollify
relieved [rɪ'liːvd]	*adj.* 宽慰的，如释重负的 (experiencing or showing relief especially from anxiety or pent-up emotions) 例 Sponsors of the bill were *relieved* because there was no opposition to it within the legislature until after the measure had been signed into law.
religion [rɪ'lɪdʒən]	*n.* 宗教；宗教信仰 记 联想记忆：reli(=rely, 依赖)+gi(看作 giant, 巨大的) + on → 可以依赖的巨大的力量 → 宗教
relinquish [rɪ'lɪŋkwɪʃ]	*v.* 放弃，让出 (to give up; withdraw or retreat from) 记 词根记忆：re + linqu(=leave, 离开) + ish → 放弃，让出
relish ['relɪʃ]	*n.* 美味，风味 (pleasing flavor)；喜好，兴趣 (a strong liking) *v.* 喜好，享受 (to be gratified by) 记 联想记忆：rel(看作 real, 真正的) + ish(看作 fish, 鱼) → 真正的鱼 → 美味 例 Although I have always been confused by our transit system, I *relish* traveling on the subways occasionally.
reluctance [rɪ'lʌktəns]	*n.* 勉强，不情愿 (the quality or state of being reluctant)
remarkable [rɪ'mɑːrkəbl]	*adj.* 值得注意的，显著的 (worthy of being or likely to be noticed) 例 As delicate and fragile as insect bodies are, it is *remarkable* that over the ages enough of them have survived, preserved in amber, for scientists to trace insect evolution. 同 extraordinary, singular
reminiscent [ˌremɪ'nɪsnt]	*adj.* 回忆的 (marked by or given to reminiscence)；使人联想的 (tending to remind) 搭 reminiscent of sb./sth. 使回忆起某人或某事
remiss [rɪ'mɪs]	*adj.* 疏忽的，不留心的 (negligent in the performance of work or duty) 记 词根记忆：re(一再) + miss(放) → 一再放掉 → 疏忽的
remorse [rɪ'mɔːrs]	*n.* 懊悔，悔恨 (a gnawing distress; self-reproach) 记 词根记忆：re(反) + mors(咬) + e → 反过去咬自己 → 悔恨 例 Although *remorse* is usually thought to spring from regret for having done something wrong, it may be that its origin is the realization that one's own nature is irremediably flawed. 同 compunction, contriteness, contrition, penance, penitence

186

□ reliable   □ relieve   □ relieved   □ religion   □ relinquish   □ relish
□ reluctance   □ remarkable   □ reminiscent   □ remiss   □ remorse

remorselessly [rɪˈmɔːrsləsli]	*adv.* 冷酷地，无悔意地(mercilessly)
remote [rɪˈmoʊt]	*adj.* 遥远的(far removed in space, time, or relation)；偏僻的(secluded) 记 词根记忆：re(反) + mot(移动) + e → 向相反方向移动，越来越远的 → 遥远的
remoteness [rɪˈmoʊtnəs]	*n.* 遥远；偏僻
remunerative [rɪˈmjuːnərətɪv]	*adj.* 报酬高的，有利润的(providing payment; profitable) 同 gainful, lucrative
render [ˈrendər]	*v.* 呈递，提供(to present or send in)；给予，归还(to give sth. in return or exchange) 记 联想记忆：给予(render)后自然成为出借人(lender)
renegade [ˈrenɪɡeɪd]	*n.* 叛教者，叛徒(a deserter from a faith, cause, or allegiance) 记 词根记忆：re(反) + neg(否定)+ade → 回头否定的人 → 叛教者，叛徒 例 Because he had abandoned his post and joined forces with the Indians, his fellow officers considered the hero of *Dances with Wolves* a *renegade*. 同 apostate, defector
renewal [rɪˈnuːəl]	*n.* 更新(the act or process of renewing, the quality or state of being renewed)；复兴，振兴
renounce [rɪˈnaʊns]	*v.* 声明放弃(to give up or resign by formal declaration)；拒绝，否认(to refuse to follow, obey, or recognize any further) 记 词根记忆：re(重新) + nounc(讲话，通告) + e → 重新宣布 → 声明放弃
renown [rɪˈnaʊn]	*n.* 名望，声誉(fame) 记 词根记忆：re(反复) + nown(=nomen 名字) → 名字反复出现 → 名望 例 For many years an unheralded researcher, Barbara McClintock gained international *renown* when she won the Nobel Prize in Physiology and Medicine.
renowned [rɪˈnaʊnd]	*adj.* 有名的(having renown) 同 celebrated, famous
reparable [ˈrepərəbl]	*adj.* 能补救的，可挽回的(capable of being repaired) 记 来自 repair(*v.* 修补)
reparation [ˌrepəˈreɪʃn]	*n.* 赔偿，补偿(repairing; restoration; compensation)
repeal [rɪˈpiːl]	*v.* 废除(法律)(to annul by authoritative act) 记 词根记忆：re(反) + peal(=call 叫) → 叫回 → 废除
repel [rɪˈpel]	*v.* 击退(to fight against; resist)；使反感(to cause aversion) 记 词根记忆：re(反) + pel(推) → 反推 → 击退 例 Gaddis is a formidably talented writer whose work has been, unhappily, more likely to intimidate or *repel* his readers than to lure them into his fictional world.

17

□ remorselessly	□ remote	□ remoteness	□ remunerative	□ render	□ renegade
□ renewal	□ renounce	□ renown	□ renowned	□ reparable	□ reparation
□ repeal	□ repel				

187

repellent	*adj.* 令人厌恶的(arousing disgust; repulsive)
[rɪˈpelənt]	同 loathsome, odious, repugnant, revolting
repertoire	*n.* (剧团等)常备剧目(the complete list or supply of dramas, operas, or musical works)
[ˈrepərtwɑːr]	记 联想记忆：和 report(汇报)一起记，汇报演出需要常备节目
repetition	*n.* 重复(the act or an instance of repeating or being repeated)；背诵(recital)
[ˌrepəˈtɪʃn]	记 来自 repeat(*v.* 重复)
repetitious	*adj.* 重复的(characterized or marked by repetition)
[ˌrepəˈtɪʃəs]	
repetitive	*adj.* 重复的(repetitious)；反复性的(containing repetition)
[rɪˈpetətɪv]	记 词根记忆：re(再次) + pet(寻找) + itive → 再次寻找 → 重复的
replenish	*v.* 补充，把…再备足(to fill or build up again)
[rɪˈplenɪʃ]	记 词根记忆：re(重新) + plen(满) + ish → 重新填满 → 补充
replete	*adj.* 充满的，供应充足的(fully or abundantly provided or filled)
[rɪˈpliːt]	记 词根记忆：re + plet(满) + e → 充满的
replicate	*v.* 复制(to produce a replica of itself)
[ˈreplɪkeɪt]	记 词根记忆：re(再次) + plic(折叠) + ate → 再次折叠 → 复制
reportorial	*adj.* 记者的；报道的
[ˌrepərˈtɔːriəl]	
reprehensible	*adj.* 应受谴责的(deserving reprehension; culpable)
[ˌreprɪˈhensəbl]	例 When such *reprehensible* remarks are circulated, we can only blame and despise those who produce them.
	同 blameworthy, blamable, blameful, censurable
represent	*v.* 呈现(to present)；代表(to typify)；体现(to describe as having a specified character or quality)
[ˌreprɪˈzent]	记 联想记忆：re + present(出席) → 代表
	例 Although the discovery of antibiotics led to great advances in clinical practice, it did not *represent* a panacea for bacterial illness, for there are some bacteria that cannot be effectively treated with antibiotics.
repress	*v.* 抑制，压抑(to hold in by self-control)；镇压(to put down by force)
[rɪˈpres]	
repressive	*adj.* 抑制的(inhibitory)；镇压的，残暴的
[rɪˈpresɪv]	同 oppressive
reprimand	*n.* 训诫，谴责(a severe or formal reproof) *v.* 训诫，谴责(to reprove sharply or censure formally)
[ˈreprɪmænd]	记 联想记忆：re(重新) + prim(首要) + (m)and(命令) → 再次给以严厉的命令 → 谴责
reprisal	*n.* 报复，报复行动(practice in retaliation for damage or loss suffered)
[rɪˈpraɪzl]	记 词根记忆：re(回) + pris(=price 代价) + al → 还给对方代价 → 报复

reproach [rɪˈprəʊtʃ]	*n.* 谴责, 责骂(an expression of rebuke or disapproval) 记 联想记忆: re(反) + proach(靠近) → 以反对的方式靠近 → 谴责 同 admonish, chide, monish, reprimand, reprove
repudiate [rɪˈpjuːdieɪt]	*v.* 拒绝接受, 回绝, 抛弃(to refuse to accept) 记 词根记忆: re + pudi(=put 想) + ate → 重新思考 → 拒绝接受 例 Fashion is partly a search for a new language to discredit the old, a way in which each generation can *repudiate* its immediate predecessor and distinguish itself. 同 dismiss, reprobate, spurn
repudiation [rɪˌpjuːdiˈeɪʃn]	*n.* 拒绝接受, 否认(the act of repudiating) 例 The *repudiation* of Puritanism in seventeenth-century England expressed itself not only in retaliatory laws to restrict Puritans, but also in a general attitude of contempt for Puritans.
repugnance [rɪˈpʌɡnəns]	*n.* 嫌恶, 反感(strong dislike, distaste, or antagonism) 例 Few of us take the pains to study our cherished convictions; indeed, we almost have a natural *repugnance* to doing so.
repugnant [rɪˈpʌɡnənt]	*adj.* 令人厌恶的(strong distaste or aversion) 记 词根记忆: re + pugn(打斗) + ant → 总是打斗 → 令人厌恶的 搭 be repugnant to sb. 使某人嫌恶, 使某人反感
repulse [rɪˈpʌls]	*v.* 击退(to repel); (粗暴无礼地)回绝(to repel by discourtesy, coldness, or denial) *n.* 击退(the act of repulsing or the state of being repulsed); 回绝, 拒绝(rebuff; rejection) 记 词根记忆: re(反) + pulse(推) → 推回去 → 击退
repute [rɪˈpjuːt]	*v.* 认为, 以为 *n.* 名声, 名誉(reputation) 记 词根记忆: re + put(想) + e → 认为, 以为
requisite [ˈrekwɪzɪt]	*n.* 必需物(sth. that is needed or necessary) *adj.* 必要的, 必不可少的(required) 记 联想记忆: requi(看作 require, 要求) + site → 要求的 → 必要的 例 Biography is a literary genre whose primary *requisite* is an ability to reconstruct imaginatively the inner life of a subject on the basis of all the knowable external evidence.
rescind [rɪˈsɪnd]	*v.* 废除, 取消(to make void) 记 词根记忆: re + scind(=cut 砍) → 砍掉 → 废除
rescue [ˈreskjuː]	*v.* 解救(to save or set free from harm, danger, or loss); 把…从法律监管下强行夺回(to take from legal custody by force) *n.* 解救(the act of rescuing) 记 联想记忆: res(看作 rest, 休息) + cue(线索) → 放弃休息紧追线索, 进行营救 → 解救
resemble [rɪˈzembl]	*v.* 与…相似, 像(to be like or similar to) 记 词根记忆: re + sembl(类似) + e → 与…相似, 像

17

□ reproach　　□ repudiate　　□ repudiation　　□ repugnance　　□ repugnant　　□ repulse
□ repute　　□ requisite　　□ rescind　　□ rescue　　□ resemble

189

resent [rɪˈzent]	*v.* 憎恶，怨恨(to feel or express annoyance or ill will) 记 词根记忆：re(反) + sent(感情) → 反感 → 憎恶 例 Was he so thin-skinned, then, to *resent* any small jest at his expense?
resentful [rɪˈzentfl]	*adj.* 忿恨的，怨恨的(full of resentment) 同 indignant
reside [rɪˈzaɪd]	*v.* 居住(to dwell permanently or continuously) 搭 reside in sb./sth. 在于；由…造成
residential [ˌrezɪˈdenʃl]	*adj.* 住宅的，与居住有关的(of or relating to residence or residences)
residual [rɪˈzɪdʒuəl]	*n.* 剩余，残余 *adj.* 残余的，剩余的(of, relating to, or constituting a residue) 记 词根记忆：re + sid(坐) + ual → 坐下来收拾残余 → 剩余，残余
resign [rɪˈzaɪn]	*v.* 委托(to consign); 放弃(to give up deliberately); 辞职(to quit) 记 联想记忆：re(不) + sign(签名) → 不签名 → 放弃 同 abandon, cede, relinquish, surrender
resignation [ˌrezɪɡˈneɪʃn]	*n.* 听从，顺从(submissiveness); 辞职(a formal notification of resigning) 记 来自 resign(v. 放弃；辞职)
resilient [rɪˈzɪliənt]	*adj.* 有弹性的；能恢复活力的，适应力强的(tending to recover from or adjust easily to misfortune or change)
resonant [ˈrezənənt]	*adj.* (声音)洪亮的(enriched by resonance); 回响的，共鸣的(echoing) 记 词根记忆：re(反) + son(声音) + ant → 回声 → 回响的
resort [rɪˈzɔːrt]	*v.* 求助，诉诸(to have recourse) *n.* 度假胜地(a place providing recreation and entertainment) 记 联想记忆：向上级打报告(report)求助(resort)
respect [rɪˈspekt]	*v.* 尊敬(to consider worthy of high regard) *n.* 尊敬(high or special regard) 记 词根记忆：re + spect(看) → 一再地看望 → 尊敬
respiratory [ˈrespərətɔːri]	*adj.* 呼吸的 例 Artificial light enhances the *respiratory* activity of some microorganisms in the winter but not in the summer, in part because in the summer their respiration is already at its peak and thus cannot be increased.
respite [ˈrespɪt]	*n.* 休息(an interval of rest or relief); 暂缓(a period of temporary delay) 记 词根记忆：re + spit(=spect 看) + e → 再看一下 → 暂缓
responsive [rɪˈspɑːnsɪv]	*adj.* 响应的，做出反应的(giving response); 敏感的，反应快的 同 respondent; sensitive
restatement [ˌriːˈsteɪtmənt]	*n.* 再声明，重述

restitution [ˌrestɪˈtuːʃn]	*n.* 归还(a restoration to its rightful owner); 赔偿(giving an equivalent for some injury) 记 词根记忆：re + stitut(站立) + ion → 重新站过去 → 归还
restive [ˈrestɪv]	*adj.* 不安静的，不安宁的(marked by impatience) 记 注意不要看作"休息的"的意思；restive=restless 例 Waiting impatiently in line to see Santa Claus, even the best-behaved children grow *restive* and start to fidget.
restoration [ˌrestəˈreɪʃn]	*n.* 恢复，复原(an act of restoring or the condition of being restored) 例 Despite careful *restoration* and cleaning of the murals in the 1960s, the colors slowly but steadily deteriorated.
restore [rɪˈstɔːr]	*v.* 使回复，恢复(to bring sb./sth. back to a former position or condition); 修复，修补(to rebuild or repair sth. so that it is like the original) 记 联想记忆：re(重新) + store(储存) → 重新储存能量 → 恢复；修复
restrict [rɪˈstrɪkt]	*v.* 限制，约束(to confine within bounds) 记 联想记忆：re(一再) + strict(严格的) → 一再对其严格 → 限制，约束 例 Getting into street brawls is no minor matter for professional boxers, who are required by law to *restrict* their aggressive impulses to the ring. 同 circumscribe, confine, delimit, prelimit
resume [rɪˈzuːm]	*v.* 重新开始，继续(to begin again after interruption) 记 词根记忆：re + sum(拿起) + e → 重新拿起 → 重新开始
resurge [rɪˈsɜːrdʒ]	*v.* 复活(to rise again into life) 记 词根记忆：re(再) + surg(起来) → 再次站起来 → 复活
resurrect [ˌrezəˈrekt]	*v.* 使复活(to raise from the dead); 复兴(to bring to view) 记 词根记忆：re + sur(下面) + rect(直) → 再次从下面直立起来 → 使复活
resuscitate [rɪˈsʌsɪteɪt]	*v.* 使复活，使苏醒(to restore life or consciousness) 记 词根记忆：re + sus(在下面) + cit(引起) + ate → 再次从下面唤起来 → 使复活
retain [rɪˈteɪn]	*v.* 保留，保持(to keep possession of); 留住，止住(to hold in place) 记 词根记忆：re + tain(拿) → 拿住 → 保留，保持
retaliate [rɪˈtælieɪt]	*v.* 报复，反击(to get revenge) 记 词根记忆：re + tali(邪恶) + ate → 把邪恶还回去 → 报复
retentive [rɪˈtentɪv]	*adj.* 有记性的，记忆力强的(capable of keeping the memory of)
reticent [ˈretɪsnt]	*adj.* 沉默寡言的(inclined to be silent; reserved) 记 词根记忆：re + tic(=silent 安静) + ent → 安静的 → 沉默寡言的 例 Though extremely *reticent* about his own plans, the man allowed his associates no such privacy and was constantly soliciting information about what they intended to do next. 同 taciturn, uncommunicative

17

□ restitution	□ restive	□ restoration	□ restore	□ restrict	□ resume
□ resurge	□ resurrect	□ resuscitate	□ retain	□ retaliate	□ retentive
□ reticent					

retire [rɪˈtaɪər]	*v.* 撤退，后退(to withdraw; move back)；退休，退役 记 联想记忆：re + tire(劳累) → 不再劳累 → 退休，退役 搭 retire from 退出
retract [rɪˈtrækt]	*v.* 撤回，取消(to take back or withdraw)；缩回，拉回(to draw or pull back) 记 词根记忆：re(反) + tract(拉) → 拉回去 → 拉回
retribution [ˌretrɪˈbjuːʃn]	*n.* 报应，惩罚(sth. given as punishment) 记 词根记忆：re(反) + tribut(给予) + ion → 反过来给予 → 报应 搭 retribution for 因…而受到的报应
retrieve [rɪˈtriːv]	*v.* 寻回，取回(to regain)；挽回(错误)(to remedy the evil consequences) 记 词根记忆：re + triev (=find 找到) + e → 重新找到 → 寻回
retrospect [ˈretrəspekt]	*n.* 回顾(a review of or meditation on past events) *v.* 回顾(to refer back)；回想(to go back over in thought) 搭 in retrospect 回顾，回想 同 reconsideration, reexamination, retrospection
retrospective [ˌretrəˈspektɪv]	*adj.* 回顾的，追溯的(of, relating to, or given to retrospection) 例 Famous in her time and then forgotten, the 17th century Dutch painter Judith Leyster was rescued from obscurity when, in 1993, the Worcester Art Museum organized the first *retrospective* exhibition of her work.
return [rɪˈtɜːrn]	*v.* 回复(to revert)；归还；回答，反驳(to retort) *n.* 回报(sth. given in repayment or reciprocation) *adj.* 返回的；重现的(taking place for the second time)
reveal [rɪˈviːl]	*v.* (神)启示；揭露(to make sth. secret or hidden publicly or generally known)；显示 (to open up to view) 记 联想记忆：re (相反) + veal (看作 veil, 面纱) → 除去面纱 → 显示 例 Hampshire's assertions, far from showing that we can dismiss the ancient puzzles about objectivity, *reveal* the issue to be even more relevant than we had thought. 同 disclose, divulge
revelation [ˌrevəˈleɪʃn]	*n.* 显示(an act of making sth. known or seen)；揭露的事实(sth. revealed) 记 来自 reveal(*v.* 揭露；显示) 例 Although the *revelation* that one of the contestants was a friend left the judge open to charges of lack of disinterestedness, the judge remained adamant in her assertion that acquaintance did not necessarily imply partiality.
reverberate [rɪˈvɜːrbəreɪt]	*v.* 发出回声，回响(to resound, echo) 记 词根记忆：re + verber(打，振动) + ate → 振动回来 → 发出回声
revere [rɪˈvɪr]	*v.* 尊敬(to have deep respect) 记 联想记忆：我们都很敬畏(revere)这位严厉(severe)的老师

reveal

打死我也不说

□ retire	□ retract	□ retribution	□ retrieve	□ retrospect	□ retrospective
□ return	□ reveal	□ revelation	□ reverberate	□ revere	

reverential [ˌrevəˈrenʃl]	*adj.* 表示尊敬的，恭敬的（expressing or having a quality of reverence） 例 The columnist was almost *reverential* when he mentioned his friends, but he was unpleasant and even acrimonious when he discussed people who irritated him.
reverse [rɪˈvɜːrs]	*n.* 反面（the back part of sth.）；相反的事物（opposite）*v.* 倒车（to perform action in the opposite direction）；反转（to turn backward）；彻底转变（to change to the opposite） 记 词根记忆：re + vers(转) + e → 反转 同 invert, revert, transplace, transpose
reversible [rɪˈvɜːrsəbl]	*adj.* 可逆的，可反转的（capable of being reversed or of reversing）
revert [rɪˈvɜːrt]	*v.* 恢复，回复到（to go back to）；重新考虑（to talk about or consider again） 记 词根记忆：re(重新) + vert(转) → 转回去 → 恢复
revile [rɪˈvaɪl]	*v.* 辱骂，恶言相向（to use abusive language; rail） 记 词根记忆：re + vil(卑鄙的，邪恶的) + e → 辱骂
revise [rɪˈvaɪz]	*v.* 校订，修正（to change because of new information or more thought） 记 词根记忆：re(一再) + vis(看) + e → 反复看 → 校订，修正 同 redraft, redraw, revamp
revitalize [ˌriːˈvaɪtəlaɪz]	*v.* 使重新充满活力（to give new life or vigor to; rejuvenate） 记 词根记忆：re(反) + vital(有活力的) + ize(使) → 使重新有活力
revival [rɪˈvaɪvl]	*n.* 苏醒；恢复；复兴（renewed attention to or interest in sth.） 记 词根记忆：re(又) + viv(生命) + al → 生命重现 → 恢复 例 Crowther maintained that the current *revival* was the most fatuous and inane production of the entire theatrical season. 同 reanimation, renaissance, renascence, resuscitation, revivification 复活吧 revitalize
revoke [rɪˈvoʊk]	*v.* 撤销，废除（to rescind）；召回（to bring or call back）
reward [rɪˈwɔːrd]	*n.* 报酬，奖赏 *v.* 酬谢，奖赏（to give a reward to） 记 联想记忆：re + ward(看作 word, 话语) → 再次发话给予奖赏 → 奖赏 例 He was indifferent to success, painting not for the sake of fame or monetary *reward*, but for the sheer love of art.
rhapsodic [ræpˈsɑːdɪk]	*adj.* 狂热的，狂喜的（extravagantly emotional）；狂想曲的（resembling or characteristic of a rhapsody）
rhetoric [ˈretərɪk]	*n.* 修辞，修辞学；浮夸的言辞（insincere or grandiloquent language） 记 来自 Rhetor(古希腊的修辞学教师、演说家)

17

rhetorical [rɪˈtɔːrɪkl]	*adj.* 修辞的，修辞学的（of, relating to, or concerned with rhetoric）；虚夸的，辞藻华丽的（characterized by overelaborate or bombastic rhetoric）
rhythmic [ˈrɪðmɪk]	*adj.* 有节奏的（marked by pronounced rhythm） 记 来自 rhythm（*n.* 节奏）
ribaldry [ˈrɪbldri]	*n.* 下流的语言，粗鄙的幽默（ribald language or humor） 同 obscenity
ridge [rɪdʒ]	*n.* 脊（如屋脊、山脊等）；隆起物 同 crest
ridicule [ˈrɪdɪkjuːl]	*n.* 嘲笑，奚落（unkind expression of amusement） 记 词根记忆：rid（笑）+ icule → 嘲笑 例 Like many other pioneers, Dr. Elizabeth Blackwell, founder of the New York Infirmary, the first American hospital staffed entirely by women, faced *ridicule* from her contemporaries but has received great honor posthumously.
ridiculous [rɪˈdɪkjələs]	*adj.* 荒谬的，可笑的（absurd, preposterous） 记 词根记忆：rid（笑）+ icul + ous（…的）→ 被人嘲笑的 → 荒谬的，可笑的 同 comical, droll, farcical, laughable, ludicrous
rift [rɪft]	*n.* 裂口，断裂（fissure; crevasse）；矛盾（a separation between people） 例 With the *rift* between the two sides apparently widening, analysts said they considered the likelihood of a merger between the two corporations to be deteriorating.
righteousness [ˈraɪtʃəsnəs]	*n.* 正当，正义，正直
rigid [ˈrɪdʒɪd]	*adj.* 严格的；僵硬的，刚硬的（stiff; not flexible or pliant） 记 词根记忆：rig（=rog 要求）+ id → 不断要求 → 严格的 例 He was regarded by his followers, as something of a martinet, not only because of his insistence on strict discipline, but also because of his *rigid* adherence to formal details. 同 incompliant, inflexible, unpliable, unyielding
rigidity [rɪˈdʒɪdəti]	*n.* 严格；坚硬，僵硬（the quality or state of being rigid） 例 The child needed physical therapy to counteract the *rigidity* that had tragically immobilized his legs.
rigorous [ˈrɪɡərəs]	*adj.* 严格的，严峻的（manifesting, exercising, or favoring rigor） 同 austere, rigid, severe, stern
rip [rɪp]	*v.* 撕，撕裂（to tear or split apart or open） 搭 rip at sth. 猛烈撕扯；用力割
ritual [ˈrɪtʃuəl]	*n.* 仪式，惯例（ceremonial act or action） 记 来自 rite（*n.* 仪式）

194

☐ rhetorical ☐ rhythmic ☐ ribaldry ☐ ridge ☐ ridicule ☐ ridiculous
☐ rift ☐ righteousness ☐ rigid ☐ rigidity ☐ rigorous ☐ rip
☐ ritual

rival [ˈraɪvl]	*n.* 竞争者，对手（one striving for competitive advantage）*v.* 竞争，与…匹敌（to attempt to equal or surpass） 记 联想记忆：对手（rival）隔河（river）相望，分外眼红 同 compete, contend, vie
rivalry [ˈraɪvlri]	*n.* 竞争，对抗（the state of being a rival） 同 competition, contention, contest
rivet [ˈrɪvɪt]	*n.* 铆钉 *v.* 吸引（注意力）（to attract completely） 搭 be riveted to the spot/ground 呆若木鸡
roam [roʊm]	*v.* 漫游，漫步（to go from place to place without purpose or direction） 记 联想记忆：他的思绪漫游（roam）在广阔的空间（room）里
robust [roʊˈbʌst]	*adj.* 健壮的（having or exhibiting strength） 记 联想记忆：中国的矿泉水品牌"乐百氏"就来自这个单词
rocky [ˈrɑːki]	*adj.* 多岩石的（abounding in or consisting of rocks）；坚若磐石的（firmly held）
romance [ˈroʊmæns]	*n.* 传奇故事；虚构（something that lacks basis in fact）；浪漫氛围；风流韵事（love affair）*v.* 虚构（to exaggerate or invent detail or incident）
roseate [ˈroʊziət]	*adj.* 玫瑰色的（resembling a rose especially in color）；过分乐观的（overly optimistic）

17

Ordinary people merely think how they shall spend their time; a man of talent tries to use it.

普通人只想到如何度过时间，有才能的人设法利用时间。

——德国哲学家 叔本华（Arthur Schopenhauer, German philosopher）

☐ rival　　　☐ rivalry　　　☐ rivet　　　☐ roam　　　☐ robust　　　☐ rocky

☐ romance　　　☐ roseate

Word List 18  MP3 - 18

routine [ruːˈtiːn]	*n.* 常规(a reiterated speech or formula) *adj.* 平常的(ordinary); 常规的(of, relating to, or being in accordance with established procedure) 记 联想记忆：例行公事(routine)就是按常规路线(route)走 例 He felt that the uninspiring *routine* of office work was too prosaic for someone of his talent and creativity. 同 accustomed, customary, quotidian, unremarkable
rowdy [ˈraʊdi]	*adj.* 吵闹的; 粗暴的 记 联想记忆：row(吵闹) + dy → 吵闹的 例 In the light of Dickens's description of the lively, even *rowdy* dance parties of his time, Sharp's approach to country dancing may seem overly formal, suggesting more decorum than is necessary.
rubbery [ˈrʌbəri]	*adj.* 橡胶似的, 有弹性的(resembling rubber (as in elasticity, consistency, or texture))
rudimentary [ˌruːdɪˈmentri]	*adj.* 初步的(fundamental; elementary); 未充分发展的 记 词根记忆：rudi(无知的, 粗鲁的) + ment + ary → 无知状态 → 初步的
rueful [ˈruːfl]	*adj.* 抱憾的(feeling or showing pity or sympathy); 后悔的, 悔恨的(mournful; regretful)
rugged [ˈrʌɡɪd]	*adj.* 高低不平的; 崎岖的(having a rough uneven surface) 同 bumpy, craggy
ruin [ˈruːɪn]	*n.* 废墟; 祸根(a cause of destruction); 毁坏 *v.* 毁坏(to devastate); 毁灭(to damage irreparably); 使破产(to bankrupt) 记 联想记忆：大雨(rain)毁坏了(ruin)庄稼 例 According to poet John Berryman, there were so many ways to *ruin* a poem that it was quite amazing good ones ever got written. 同 demolish, dilapidate, wreck
ruminant [ˈruːmɪnənt]	*adj.* (动物)反刍的; 沉思的(meditative; thoughtful) 记 词根记忆：rumin(=rumen 反刍动物的第一胃, "瘤胃") + ant → 反刍的
rush [rʌʃ]	*v.* 急促; 匆忙行事(to perform in a short time or at a high speed) *n.* 冲, 奔(a violent forward motion) 例 Having just published his fourth novel in an almost 40-year career,

	Gaddis describes himself, with some understatement, as a writer who has never been in a *rush* to get into print.
rustic [ˈrʌstɪk]	*adj.* 乡村的，乡土气的(of, relating to, or suitable for the country) 记 词根记忆：rust(乡村) + ic → 乡村的
ruthless [ˈruːθləs]	*adj.* 无情的(merciless)；残忍的(cruel) 例 Wemmick, the soul of kindness in private, is obliged in public to be uncompassionate and even *ruthless* on behalf of his employer, the harsh lawyer Jaggers.
sabotage [ˈsæbətɑːʒ]	*n.* 阴谋破坏，颠覆活动(deliberate subversion) 搭 an act of military sabotage 军事破坏活动
sacred [ˈseɪkrɪd]	*adj.* 神圣的，庄严的(holy; inviolable) 同 divine
sagacious [səˈgeɪʃəs]	*adj.* 聪明的，睿智的(showing keen perception and foresight) 记 来自sage(*n.* 智者)
sage [seɪdʒ]	*adj.* 智慧的(wise; discerning) *n.* 智者(a very wise person) 例 The *sage*, by definition, possesses wisdom; the virtuoso, by definition, possesses expertise.
salient [ˈseɪliənt]	*adj.* 显著的，突出的(noticeable; conspicuous; prominent) 记 词根记忆：sal(跳) + ient → 跳起来 → 突出的 例 Ultimately, the book's credibility is strained; the slender, though far from nonexistent, web of evidence presented on one *salient* point is expected to support a vast superstructure of implications.
saline [ˈseɪliːn]	*adj.* 含盐的，咸的(consisting of or containing salt) 搭 saline water 盐水；海水
salubrious [səˈluːbriəs]	*adj.* 有益健康的(promoting health; healthful) 记 词根记忆：sal(健康) + ubrious → 健康的 → 有益健康的
salutary [ˈsæljəteri]	*adj.* 有益的，有益健康的(promoting or conducive to health) 记 词根记忆：sal(健康) + utary → 有益的，有益健康的
salvage [ˈsælvɪdʒ]	*v.* (从灾难中)抢救，海上救助(to save sth. from loss, fire, wreck, etc.) *n.* 海上救助 记 词根记忆：salv(救) + age → 抢救 例 Many industries are so beleaguered by the impact of government sanctions, equipment failure, and foreign competition that they are beginning to rely on industrial psychologists to *salvage* what remains of employee morale.
salvation [sælˈveɪʃn]	*n.* 拯救(deliverance from the power and effects of sin)；救助(deliverance from danger or difficulty)
sanctimonious [ˌsæŋktɪˈmoʊniəs]	*adj.* 假装虔诚的(hypocritically pious or devout) 搭 sanctimonious preaching 伪善的讲道

18

sanctuary	*n.* 圣地；庇护所，避难所；庇护
[ˈsæŋktʃueri]	搭 wildlife sanctuary 野生动物保护区
sanctum	*n.* (寺庙或教堂的)圣所(a sacred place)
[ˈsæŋktəm]	搭 inner sanctum 私室，密室
sane	*adj.* 神志清楚的(having a normal, healthy mind)；
[seɪn]	明智的(sensible)
	同 rational
sanguine	*adj.* 乐观的(cheerful and confident; optimistic)；
[ˈsæŋgwɪn]	红润的(of a healthy reddish color)
	记 词根记忆：sangui(血) + ne → 有血色的 → 红润的
sanitary	*adj.* (有关)卫生的，清洁的(of or relating to health)
[ˈsænəteri]	记 词根记忆：sanit(=sanat 健康) + ary → 卫生的，清洁的
sap	*n.* 树液(the watery fluid that circulates through a plant)；活力(vigor;
[sæp]	vitality) *v.* 削弱，耗尽(to weaken; exhaust)
	同 attenuate, cripple, debilitate, enfeeble, unbrace, undermine
sarcastic	*adj.* 讽刺的(sneering; caustic; ironic)
[sɑːrˈkæstɪk]	搭 sarcastic comments 讽刺的评论
satiated	*adj.* 厌倦的，生腻的(tired of)；充分满足的(fully satisfied)
[ˈseɪʃieɪtɪd]	记 联想记忆：sat(坐) + i + ate(吃) + d → 我可以坐下吃东西了 → 充分满足的
satirize	*v.* 讽刺(to use satire against)
[ˈsætəraɪz]	同 lampoon, mock, quip, scorch
saturate	*v.* 浸湿，浸透(to imbue or impregnate thoroughly)；使大量吸收或充满(to
[ˈsætʃəreɪt]	soak, fill, or load to capacity completely)
	记 词根记忆：sat(足够) + urate → 使足够 → 使大量吸收或充满
saturnine	*adj.* 忧郁的，阴沉的(sluggish; sullen)
[ˈsætərnaɪn]	记 来自 Saturn(*n.* 土星)
scale	*n.* 鱼鳞；音阶(a graduated series of musical tones)
[skeɪl]	
scant	*adj.* 不足的，缺乏的(barely or scarcely)
[skænt]	搭 scant attention/consideration 缺乏注意/考虑
scarcity	*n.* 不足，缺乏(a state of being scarce)
[ˈskersəti]	搭 scarcity of... …的短缺
scarlet	*adj.* 猩红的，鲜红的(bright red in colour)
[ˈskɑːrlət]	搭 scarlet fever 猩红热
scavenge	*v.* 清除(to cleanse)；从废物中提取有用物质(to salvage from discarded or
[ˈskævɪndʒ]	refuse material)
scenic	*adj.* 风景如画的(of or relating to natural scenery)
[ˈsiːnɪk]	搭 scenic lift 观光电梯

schematic [skiː'mætɪk]	*adj.* 纲要的，图解的(of, relating to, or in the form of a scheme or diagram) 记 来自 schema(*n.* 图表；纲要)
scheme [skiːm]	*n.* 阴谋(a crafty or secret plan)；(作品等)体系，结构(a systematic or organized framework; design) 记 注意不要和 schema(*n.* 图表)相混
schism ['skɪzəm]	*n.* 教会分裂(formal division in or separation from a church or religious body)；分裂(division; separation) 例 Unenlightened authoritarian managers rarely recognize a crucial reason for the low levels of serious conflict among members of democratically run work groups: a modicum of tolerance for dissent often prevents *schism*. 同 fissure, fracture, rift
scorn [skɔːrn]	*n.* 轻蔑(disrespect or derision mixed with indignation) *v.* 轻蔑，瞧不起(to show disdain or derision) 同 contemn, despise
scour ['skaʊər]	*v.* 冲刷(to clear, dig, or remove by or as if by a powerful current of water)；擦掉(to rub hard)；四处搜索(to go through or range over in a search)
scourge [skɜːrdʒ]	*n.* 鞭笞(whip)；磨难(a cause of great affliction) *v.* 鞭笞；磨难 记 和 courage(*n.* 勇气)一起记 例 One of the great killers until barely 50 years ago, tuberculosis ("consumption" as it was then named) seemed a *scourge* or plague rather than the long-term chronic illness it was.
scramble ['skræmbl]	*v.* 攀登(to move or climb hastily)；搅乱，使混杂(to toss or mix together)；争夺(to struggle eagerly for possession of sth.) 记 联想记忆: scr(看作 scale，攀登) + amble(行走) → 攀登
scrappy ['skræpi]	*adj.* 碎片的(made of disconnected pieces)；好斗的(liking to fight)；坚毅的(determined; gutsy)
scruple ['skruːpl]	*n.* 顾忌，迟疑(an ethical consideration or principle that inhibits action) *v.* 顾忌(to hesitate) 同 boggle, stickle
scrupulous ['skruːpjələs]	*adj.* 恪守道德规范的(having moral integrity)；一丝不苟的(punctiliously exact) 搭 be scrupulous in sth./doing sth. 审慎正直的；恪守道德规范的 同 conscientious, meticulous, punctilious
scrutinize ['skruːtənaɪz]	*v.* 仔细检查(to examine closely and minutely) 搭 scrutinize balloting 监票
sculpt [skʌlpt]	*v.* 雕刻(to carve; sculpture)；造型(to shape, mold, or fashion especially with artistry or precise)
sculptural ['skʌlptʃərəl]	*adj.* 雕刻的(of or relating to sculpture)；雕刻般的 搭 sculptural arts 雕塑艺术

要仔细检查合同

scrutinize

□ schematic	□ scheme	□ schism	□ scorn	□ scour	□ scourge
□ scramble	□ scrappy	□ scruple	□ scrupulous	□ scrutinize	□ sculpt
□ sculptural					

seclude [sɪˈkluːd]	*v.* 使隔离，使孤立(to isolate) 记 词根记忆：se(分开) + clude(关闭) → 分开关闭 → 使隔离，使孤立
seclusion [sɪˈkluːʒn]	*n.* 隔离（the act of secluding）；隔离地（a secluded or isolated place） 搭 be in seclusion 处于被隔离状态
sectarianism [sekˈterɪənɪzəm]	*n.* 宗派主义；教派意识
secular [ˈsekjələr]	*adj.* 世俗的，尘世的（worldly rather than spiritual） 例 For those Puritans who believed that *secular* obligations were imposed by divine will, the correct course of action was not withdrawal from the world but conscientious discharge of the duties of business.
security [səˈkjʊrəti]	*n.* 安全(safety)；保证(surety)；保护(protection) 例 Having sufficient income of her own constituted for Alice a material independence that made possible a degree of *security* in her emotional life as well.
sedate [sɪˈdeɪt]	*adj.* 镇静的(keeping a quiet steady attitude or pace; unruffled) 记 词根记忆：sed(=sid 坐下) + ate → 坐下来的 → 镇静的 同 sober, staid
sedative [ˈsedətɪv]	*adj.*（药物）镇静的(tending to calm excitement) *n.* 镇静剂 同 calming, relaxing, soothing; tranquillizer
sedentary [ˈsednteri]	*adj.* 久坐的(requiring much sitting) 记 词根记忆：sed(坐) + entary → 久坐的 例 Noting the murder victim's flaccid musculature and pearlike figure, she deduced that the unfortunate fellow had earned his living in some *sedentary* occupation.
sedimentary [ˌsedɪˈmentri]	*adj.* 沉积的，沉淀性的(of, relating to, or containing sediment) 搭 sedimentary rock 沉积岩
seductive [sɪˈdʌktɪv]	*adj.* 诱人的(tending to seduce) 同 attractive, captivating
sedulous [ˈsedʒələs]	*adj.* 聚精会神的；勤勉的(diligent in application or pursuit) 记 词根记忆：sed(坐) + ulous(多…的) → 坐得多的 → 勤勉的
segment [ˈsegmənt]	*n.* 部分(bit; fragment) 记 词根记忆：seg(=sect 部分) + ment → 部分

seclusion

□ seclude　　□ seclusion　　□ sectarianism　　□ secular　　□ security　　□ sedate
□ sedative　　□ sedentary　　□ sedimentary　　□ seductive　　□ sedulous　　□ segment

segregate [ˈsegrɪgeɪt]	*v.* 分离，隔离（to separate or set apart from others or from the general mass） 记 词根记忆：seg（切割）+ reg + ate → 隔离
seismic [ˈsaɪzmɪk]	*adj.* 地震的，由地震引起的（of or caused by an earthquake） 记 词根记忆：seism（地震）+ ic → 地震的
self-adulation [ˌselfædʒəˈleɪʃn]	*n.* 自我吹捧（the act of praising or flattering excessively by oneself） 例 It is ironic that a critic of such overwhelming vanity now suffers from a measure of the oblivion to which he was forever consigning others; in the end, all his *self-adulation* has only worked against him.
self-analysis [ˌselfəˈnæləsɪs]	*n.* 自我分析
self-assured [ˌselfəˈʃʊrd]	*adj.* 有自信的（sure of oneself） 同 confident
self-confident [ˌselfˈkɑːnfɪdənt]	*adj.* 自信的（confident in oneself and in one's powers and abilities）
self-conscious [ˌselfˈkɑːnʃəs]	*adj.* 自觉的；害羞的，不自然的 同 awkward, bashful, embarrassed
self-deprecating [ˌselfˈdeprəkeɪtɪŋ]	*adj.* 自贬的（conscious of one's own shortcomings） 例 Egocentric, at times vindictive when he believed his authority was being questioned, White could also be kind, gracious, and even *self-deprecating* when the circumstances seemed to require it.
self-deprecation [ˌselfdeprəˈkeɪʃn]	*n.* 自嘲（self-mockery） 例 Comparatively few rock musicians are willing to laugh at themselves, although a hint of *self-deprecation* can boost sales of video clips very nicely.
self-determination [ˌselfdɪˌtɜːrmɪˈneɪʃn]	*n.* 自主，自决（free choice of one's own acts or states without external compulsion）
self-doubt [ˌselfˈdaʊt]	*n.* 自我怀疑（a lack of faith or confidence in oneself）
self-effacement [ˌselfɪˈfesmənt]	*n.* 自谦 例 His submissiveness of manner and general air of *self-effacement* made it unlikely he would be selected to take command of the firm.
self-procession [ˌselfprəˈseʃn]	*n.* 自行列队
self-realization [ˌselfˌriːələˈzeɪʃn]	*n.* 自我实现，自我完成（fulfillment by oneself of the possibilities of one's character or personality）
self-righteousness [ˌselfˈraɪtʃəsnəs]	*n.* 自以为是 例 The action and characters in a melodrama can be so immediately classified that all observers can hiss the villain with an air of smug but enjoyable *self-righteousness*.

18

self-sacrifice	*n.* 自我牺牲(sacrifice of oneself or one's interest for others or for a cause or ideal)
[ˌself ˈsækrɪfaɪs]	
self-sufficient	*adj.* 自给自足的(able to maintain oneself or itself without outside aid)
[ˌselfsə ˈfɪʃnt]	同 independent
semimolten	*adj.* 半熔化的
[ˌsemi ˈmoʊltən]	
seminal	*adj.* 有创意的(creative)
[ˈsemɪnl]	记 词根记忆: semin(种) + al → 种子的 → 有创意的
sensitive	*adj.* 敏感的(highly responsive or susceptible)
[ˈsensətɪv]	记 词根记忆: sens(感觉) + itive → 敏感的
	搭 be sensitive to sth. 对某事敏感
	同 susceptive
sensitivity	*n.* 敏感, 敏感性(the quality or state of being sensitive)
[ˌsensə ˈtɪvəti]	例 The successful reconstruction of an archaeological site requires scientific knowledge as well as cultural *sensitivity*.
sensitize	*v.* 使某人或某事物敏感(to make sb./sth. sensitive)
[ˈsensətaɪz]	记 词根记忆: sens(感觉) + itize → 使某人或某事物敏感
sensory	*adj.* 感觉的, 感官的(of or relating to sensation or to the senses)
[ˈsensəri]	记 词根记忆: sens(感觉) + ory → 感觉的
sentient	*adj.* 有知觉的(responsive to or conscious of sense impressions); 知悉的 (aware)
[ˈsentiənt]	
sentimentalize	*v.* (使)感伤(to indulge in sentiment; to look upon or imbue with sentiment)
[ˌsentɪ ˈmentəlaɪz]	
separate	[ˈsepəreɪt] *v.* 使分开(to set or keep apart)
	[ˈseprət] *adj.* 不同的(not the same); 独自的(not shared with another)
septic	*adj.* 腐败的(of, relating to, or causing putrefaction); 脓毒性的(relating to, involving, caused by, or affected with sepsis)
[ˈseptɪk]	记 词根记忆: sept(细菌; 腐烂) + ic → 腐败的
sequential	*adj.* 连续的, 一连串的(serial)
[sɪ ˈkwenʃl]	记 词根记忆: sequ(跟随) + ent + ial → 连续的, 一连串的
sequester	*v.* (使)隐退(to seclude; withdraw); 使隔离(to set apart)
[sɪ ˈkwestər]	记 注意不要和 sequestrate(*v.* 扣押)相混
serendipity	*n.* 意外发现新奇事物的才能或现象(the faculty or phenomenon of finding valuable or agreeable things not sought for)
[ˌserən ˈdɪpəti]	记 出自18世纪英国作家 Horace(荷拉斯)的童话故事 *The Three Princes of Serendip*, 书中主人公具有随处发现珍宝的本领
	例 Many scientific discoveries are a matter of *serendipity*: Newton was not sitting there thinking about gravity when the apple dropped on his head.

serendipity

地下有珠宝!

serene [səˈriːn]	*adj.* 平静的，安详的（marked by or suggestive of utter calm and unruffled repose or quietude）；清澈的；晴朗的 例 The paradoxical aspect of the myths about Demeter, when we consider the predominant image of her as a tranquil and *serene* goddess, is her agitated search for her daughter.
serenity [səˈrenəti]	*n.* 平静（the quality or state of being serene） 例 As painted by Constable, the scene is not one of bucolic *serenity*; rather it shows a striking emotional and intellectual tension. 同 placidity, repose, tranquility
serial [ˈsɪriəl]	*adj.* 连续的，一系列的（arranged in a series of things） 搭 serial killings 系列杀人
seriousness [ˈsɪriəsnəs]	*n.* 认真，严肃；严重性，严峻 例 The *seriousness* of the drought could only be understood by those who had seen the wilted crops in the fields.
serrated [səˈreɪtɪd]	*adj.* 锯齿状的（saw-toothed） 搭 serrated knife/edge 锯齿状刀子/边缘
serviceable [ˈsɜːrvɪsəbl]	*adj.* 可用的，耐用的（fit for use） 记 来自 service（*n.* 服务）
servile [ˈsɜːrvl]	*adj.* 奴性的，百依百顺的（meanly or cravenly submissive; abject） 记 词根记忆：serv（服务）+ ile → 百依百顺的
settled [ˈsetld]	*adj.* 固定的（fixed） 搭 settled life 稳定的生活
shallowness [ˈʃæloʊnəs]	*n.* 浅；浅薄 同 superficiality
sharpen [ˈʃɑːrpən]	*v.* 削尖（to make sharp or sharper）；使敏锐，使敏捷 同 hone
shatter [ˈʃætər]	*v.* 使落下，使散开（to cause to drop or be dispersed）；砸碎，粉碎（to break at once into pieces）；破坏，毁坏（to cause the disruption or annihila-tion of sth.） 记 发音记忆："筛它" → 使落下，使散开
shed [ʃed]	*v.* 流出（眼泪等）（to pour forth in drops）；脱落，蜕，落（to lose by natural process） 搭 shed tears 流泪
shell [ʃel]	*n.* 贝壳；炮弹 *v.* 剥去…的壳（to take out of a natural enclosing cover） 搭 shell fish 水生贝壳类动物
sheltered [ˈʃeltərd]	*adj.* 遮蔽的 同 covered, shielded
shifting [ˈʃɪftɪŋ]	*adj.* 变动的；运动的 同 changing, moving

shiftless [ˈʃɪftləs]	*adj.* 没出息的，懒惰的（lacking in ambition or incentive; lazy）；无能的（inefficient）
shiny [ˈʃaɪni]	*adj.* 有光泽的（having a smooth glossy surface）；发光的（filled with light） 同 bright, gleaming, glistening
shoal [ʃoʊl]	*n.* 浅滩，浅水处（a sandbank where the water is shallow）；一群（鱼等） *adj.* 浅的，薄的（shallow） 记 联想记忆：形似拼音 shao，水少的地方 → 浅滩，浅水处
shopworn [ˈʃɑːpwɔːrn]	*adj.* 在商店中陈列久了的（ruined or damaged from being on display in a store）；陈旧的，磨损的
shortrange [ˌʃɔːrt ˈreɪndʒ]	*adj.* 近程的（relating to or fit for short distances） 搭 shortrange missles 短程导弹
shortsighted [ˌʃɔːrt ˈsaɪtɪd]	*adj.* 缺乏远见的（lacking foresight）；近视的 同 nearsighted
short-sightedness [ˌʃɔːrt ˈsaɪtɪdnəs]	*n.* 目光短浅，近视（the state of being able to see things clearly only if they are very close to you） 例 Many elderly people are capable of working, but they are kept from gainful employment by the *short-sightedness* of those employers who mistakenly believe that young people alone can give them adequate service.
shrivel [ˈʃrɪvl]	*v.* （使）枯萎（to draw into wrinkles especially with a loss of moisture） 同 mummify, wilt, wither
shrug [ʃrʌg]	*v.* 耸肩（表示怀疑等）（to raise in the shoulders to express aloofness, indifference, or uncertainty） 记 联想记忆：shru（看作拼音 shu，舒）+ g（音似：胳）→ 舒展舒展胳膊 → 耸肩 搭 shrug sth. off/aside 不把…当回事；对…满不在乎
shuffle [ˈʃʌfl]	*v.* 洗牌（to rearrange (as playing cards, dominoes, or tiles) to produce a random order）；拖步走，支吾（to act or speak in an evasive manner） 记 参考：reshuffle（*n./v.* 重新改组）
shun [ʃʌn]	*v.* 避免，闪避（to avoid deliberately） 同 bilk, duck, elude, eschew, evade
shunt [ʃʌnt]	*v.* 使（火车）转到另一轨道（to switch a train from one track to another）；改变（某物的）方向
sibling [ˈsɪblɪŋ]	*n.* 兄弟或姊妹 记 词根记忆：sib（同胞）+ ling → 兄弟或姊妹
sight [saɪt]	*n.* 景象（spectacle）；视力（the process, power, or function of seeing）；视野（the range of vision）*v.* 看到（to get or catch sight of） 同 eyesight, seeing

□ shiftless	□ shiny	□ shoal	□ shopworn	□ shortrange	□ shortsighted
□ short-sightedness	□ shrivel	□ shrug	□ shuffle	□ shun	□ shunt
□ sibling	□ sight				

significant [sɪɡˈnɪfɪkənt]	*adj.* 相当数量的（considerable）; 意义重大的（having an important meaning） 记 联想记忆: sign(标记)+i+fic(做)+ant → 做了很多标记的 → 相当数量的; 意义重大的 同 substantial; momentous
simplistic [sɪmˈplɪstɪk]	*adj.* 过分简单化的（of, relating to, or characterized by simplism; oversimple） 例 Our new tools of systems analysis, powerful though they may be, lead to *simplistic* theories, especially, and predictably, in economics and political science, where productive approaches have long been highly elusive.
simulation [ˌsɪmjuˈleɪʃn]	*n.* 模拟（the act or process of simulating） 搭 simulation training 模拟训练
sincere [sɪnˈsɪr]	*adj.* 诚实的，坦率的（honest; straightforward）; 诚挚的（not pretended; genuine） 记 联想记忆: sin(罪) + cere → 把自己的罪过告诉你 → 诚挚的 例 Einstein's humility was so profound that it might have seemed a pose affected by a great man had it not been so obviously *sincere*.
sincerity [sɪnˈserəti]	*n.* 诚挚（the quality or state of being sincere） 同 candour, frankness, genuineness, honesty
singularity [ˌsɪŋɡjuˈlærəti]	*n.* 独特（unusual or distinctive manner or behavior; peculiarity）; 奇点（天文学上密度无穷大、体积无穷小的点） 记 来自 singular(*adj.* 单数的; 非凡的) 例 The Gibsons were little given to conformism in any form; not one of them was afraid of *singularity*, of being and seeming unlike their neighbors.
sinuous [ˈsɪnjuəs]	*adj.* 蜿蜒，迂回的（characterized by many curves and twists; winding） 记 词根记忆: sinu(弯曲) + ous → 弯曲的 → 蜿蜒的
skeptical [ˈskeptɪkl]	*adj.* 怀疑的; 多疑的（marked by or given to doubt） 搭 be skeptical of 怀疑…
sketch [sketʃ]	*n.* 草图，概略（a brief description or outline）*v.* 画草图，写概略（to make a sketch, rough draft, or outline） 同 compendium, digest, syllabus
skew [skjuː]	*adj.* 不直的，歪斜的（running obliquely; slanting） 同 crooked
skimp [skɪmp]	*v.* 节省花费（to give barely sufficient funds for sth.） 搭 be skimp on... 对…吝惜
skinflint [ˈskɪnflɪnt]	*n.* 吝啬鬼（miser; niggard） 记 参考词组: skin a flint(爱财如命)
slanderous [ˈslændərəs]	*adj.* 诽谤的（false and defamatory） 同 abusive

□ significant □ simplistic □ simulation □ sincere □ sincerity □ singularity
□ sinuous □ skeptical □ sketch □ skew □ skimp □ skinflint
□ slanderous

205

slash	*v.* 大量削减(to reduce sharply)
[slæʃ]	同 cut

slavish	*adj.* 卑屈的；效仿的，无创造性的(copying obsequiously or without originality)
[ˈsleɪvɪʃ]	记 词根记忆：slav(e)(奴隶) + ish(形容词后缀，表属性) → 奴性的 → 卑屈的

slimy	*adj.* 黏滑的(of, relating to, or resembling slime)
[ˈslaɪmi]	同 glutinous, miry, muddy, viscous

slipperiness	*n.* 滑溜；防滑性
[ˈslɪpərinəs]	

slipshod	*adj.* 马虎的，草率的(not exact or thorough)
[ˈslɪpʃɑːd]	同 careless, slovenly

sloping	*adj.* 倾斜的，有坡度的
[ˈsloʊpɪŋ]	搭 sloping line 斜线

slothful	*adj.* 迟钝的，懒惰的(lazy)
[ˈsloʊθfl]	记 联想记忆：sloth(树獭，在树上生活，行动迟缓) + ful → 像树獭一样懒散的 → 懒惰的
	同 sluggish

slovenly	*adj.* 不整洁的，邋遢的(untidy especially in personal appearance)
[ˈslʌvnli]	同 dirty

sluggish	*adj.* 缓慢的，行动迟缓的 (markedly slow in movement, flow, or growth)；反应慢的(slow to respond)
[ˈslʌgɪʃ]	例 Species with relatively *sluggish* metabolic rates, including hibernators, generally live longer than those whose metabolic rates are more rapid.
	同 torpid

smother	*v.* 熄灭；覆盖(to cover thickly)；使窒息(to make sb. unable to breathe)
[ˈsmʌðər]	记 联想记忆：s(看作 she) + mother(母亲) → 母亲的爱使她快要窒息 → 使窒息

smug	*adj.* 自满的，自命不凡的(highly self-satisfied)
[smʌg]	记 联想记忆：s + mug(杯子) → 杯子满了 → 自满的
	例 The action and characters in a melodrama can be so immediately classified that all observers can hiss the villain with an air of *smug* but enjoyable self-righteousness.

snippet	*n.* 小片，片段(a small part, piece, or thing)
[ˈsnɪpɪt]	搭 snippet of information/news 简短的信息/新闻

snobbery	*n.* 势利(snobbish conduct or character)
[ˈsnɑːbəri]	

snub	*v.* 冷落，不理睬(to treat with contempt or neglect)
[snʌb]	同 cold-shoulder, rebuff

snug [snʌg]	*adj.* 温暖舒适的（warm and comfortable；cozy） 搭 snug harbor 避风港
sobriety [sə'braɪəti]	*n.* 节制（moderation）；庄重（gravity） 例 The sumptuous costumes of Renaissance Italy, with their gold and silver embroidery and figured brocades, were the antithesis of Spanish *sobriety*, with its dark muted colors, plain short capes, and high collars edged with small ruffs.
sociable ['souʃəbl]	*adj.* 好交际的，合群的（fond of the company of other people）；友善的（friendly） 记 词根记忆：soci(结交) + able → 好交际的
solder ['sɑːdər]	*v.* 焊接，焊在一起，焊合（to bring into firm union） 记 和 soldier(*n.* 战士)一起记
solemn ['sɑːləm]	*adj.* 严肃的，庄严的，隆重的（made with great seriousness）；黑色的 记 词根记忆：sol(太阳)+emn → 古代把太阳看作是神圣的 → 庄严的
solemnity [sə'lemnəti]	*n.* 庄严，肃穆（formal or ceremonious observance） 记 来自 solemn(*adj.* 严肃的) 同 sedateness, solemness, staidness
solicit [sə'lɪsɪt]	*v.* 恳求（to make petition to）；教唆（to entice into evil） 记 词根记忆：soli(=sole 唯一，全部)+cit(引出) → 引出大家做某事 → 恳求；教唆
solicitous [sə'lɪsɪtəs]	*adj.* 热切的（full of desire; eager）；挂念的（expressing care or concern） 搭 be solicitous of/for/about... 为…操心
solicitude [sə'lɪsɪtuːd]	*n.* 关怀，牵挂（anxious, kind, or eager care） 搭 solicitude for... 对…的关怀/牵挂
soliloquy [sə'lɪləkwi]	*n.* 自言自语（the act of talking to oneself）；戏剧独白（a dramatic monologue that represents a series of unspoken reflections）
solitary ['sɑːləteri]	*adj.* 孤独的（without companions）*n.* 隐士（recluse） 记 词根记忆：solit(单独) + ary → 孤独的 例 There are no *solitary*, free-living creatures; every form of life is dependent on other forms. 同 forsaken, lonesome, lorn

solo	*adj.* 单独的(without companion) *n.* 独唱
[ˈsoʊloʊ]	记 词根记忆：sol(独自) + o → 单独的
solvent	*adj.* 有偿债能力的(capable of meeting financial obligations) *n.* 溶剂
[ˈsɑːlvənt]	记 来自solve(*v.* 解决；溶化)
somber	*adj.* 忧郁的(melancholy)；阴暗的(dark and gloomy)
[ˈsɑːmbər]	同 dim, grave, shadowy, shady
sonorous	*adj.* (声音)洪亮的(full or loud in sound)
[ˈsɑːnərəs]	记 词根记忆：son(声音)+orous → (声音)洪亮的
soothe	*v.* 抚慰(to comfort or calm)；减轻(to make less painful)
[suːð]	记 来自sooth(*adj.* 抚慰的)
	同 allay, becalm, lull, tranquilize
sophisticated	*adj.* 老于世故的；(仪器)精密的(highly complicated)
[səˈfɪstɪkeɪtɪd]	记 联想记忆：sophist(诡辩家) + icated → 诡辩家都是老于世故的 → 老于世故的
	例 Totem craftsmanship reached its apex in the 19th century, when the introduction of metal tools enabled carvers to execute more *sophisticated* designs.
sophomoric	*adj.* 一知半解的(conceited and overconfident of knowledge but poorly informed and immature)
[ˌsɑːfəˈmɔːrɪk]	
soporific	*adj.* 催眠的(tending to cause sleep) *n.* 安眠药
[ˌsɑːpəˈrɪfɪk]	记 词根记忆：sopor(昏睡) + ific → 催眠的
sordid	*adj.* 卑鄙的；肮脏的(dirty, filthy)
[ˈsɔːrdɪd]	同 foul, mean, seedy
soundproof	*v.* 使隔音(to insulate so as to obstruct the passage of sound) *adj.* 隔音的
[ˈsaʊndpruːf]	搭 soundproof door 隔音门
span	*n.* 跨度；两个界限间的距离(a stretch between two limits)
[spæn]	同 extent, length, reach, spread
spanking	*adj.* 强烈的(strong)；疾行的(fast)
[ˈspæŋkɪŋ]	搭 at a spanking pace/rate 步伐/速度非常快地
sparing	*adj.* 节俭的(frugal, thrifty)
[ˈsperɪŋ]	记 来自spare(*v.* 节约)；注意不要和sparring(*n.* 拳击)相混
sparse	*adj.* 稀少的, 贫乏的(not thickly grown or settled)；稀疏的
[spɑːrs]	记 联想记忆：稀疏的(sparse)火花(spark)
spartan	*adj.* 简朴的(of simplicity or frugality)；刻苦的(strict self-discipline or self-denial)
[ˈspɑːrtn]	记 来自Sparta (斯巴达)，希腊城邦，该地区的人以简朴刻苦著称
spatial	*adj.* 有关空间的，在空间的(of, relating to, involving, or having the nature of space)
[ˈspeɪʃl]	

specialization [ˌspeʃələˈzeɪʃn]	*n.* 特殊化(making sth. become specialized) 例 The new *specialization* of knowledge has created barriers between people: everyone believes that his or her subject cannot and possibly should not be understood by others.
specialize [ˈspeʃəlaɪz]	*v.* 专门研究(to limit to a particular activity or subject) 记 来自 special(*adj.* 特殊的)
specified [ˈspesɪfaɪd]	*adj.* 特定的 同 designated, indicated
specimen [ˈspesɪmən]	*n.* 范例, 样品, 标本(a portion or quantity of material for use in testing, or study) 记 词根记忆：speci(种类) + men → 不同种类的东西 → 样品 例 It is possible to analyze a literary work to death, dissecting what should be a living experience as if it were a laboratory *specimen*.
specious [ˈspiːʃəs]	*adj.* 似是而非的(having a false look of truth or genuineness); 华而不实的(having deceptive attraction or allure) 记 词根记忆：spec(看) + ious → 用来看的 → 华而不实的
spectator [ˈspekteɪtər]	*n.* 目击者(an observer of an event); 观众, 观看者 记 词根记忆：spect (看) + ator → 旁观者 → 观众 同 beholder, bystander, eyewitness
specter [ˈspektər]	*n.* 鬼怪, 幽灵(a ghostly apparition); 缠绕心头的恐惧, 凶兆(sth. that haunts or perturbs the mind) 记 词根记忆：spect(看) + er → 看到而摸不着的东西 → 鬼怪 同 eidolon, phantasm, phantom, spirit
spectral [ˈspektrəl]	*adj.* 幽灵的(ghostly); 谱的, 光谱的(of, relating to, or produced by a spectrum) 搭 spectral analysis 光谱分析
spectrum [ˈspektrəm]	*n.* 光谱; 范围(a continuous sequence or range) 记 词根记忆：spectr(看) + um → 看到颜色的范围 → 光谱
speculate [ˈspekjuleɪt]	*v.* 沉思, 思索(to mediate on or ponder); 投机(to assume a business risk in hope of gain) 记 词根记忆：spec(看) + ulate(做) → 看得多想得也多 → 思索
speculative [ˈspekjələtɪv]	*adj.* 推理的, 思索的(based on speculation); 投机的(risky) 同 conjectured, guessed, supposed, surmised
spherical [ˈsferɪkl]	*adj.* 球的, 球状的(having the form of a sphere or of one of its segments) 同 globe-shaped, globular, rotund, round

spectator

19

spice [spaɪs]	*n.* 香料(any of various aromatic vegetable products) *v.* 给…调味(to add spice to food in order to give it more flavour)
spinal ['spaɪnl]	*adj.* 脊骨的, 脊髓的(of, relating to, or situated near the spinal column)
spined [spaɪnd]	*adj.* 有背骨的, 有脊柱的
spineless ['spaɪnləs]	*adj.* 没骨气的, 懦弱的(lacking courage or willpower) 记 联想记忆: spine(脊椎, 刺)+less → 无脊椎的 → 没骨气的 例 Are we to turn into *spineless* equivocators, afraid to take a forthright stand, unable to answer a question without pussyfooting?
spinning ['spɪnɪŋ]	*adj.* 旋转的 同 revolving, rotating, turning, twirling, wheeling, whirling
spiny ['spaɪni]	*adj.* 针状的(slender and pointed like a spine); 多刺的, 棘手的(thorny) 记 词根记忆: spin(刺) + y → 多刺的
spiral ['spaɪrəl]	*adj.* 螺旋形的; 上升的 *v.* 螺旋式上升或下降 记 来自 spire(*n.* 螺旋) 同 coil, curl, entwine, twist
spiritedness ['spɪrɪtɪdnəs]	*n.* 有精神, 活泼 同 liveliness, vivaciousness
spiritual ['spɪrɪtʃuəl]	*adj.* 精神的(of the spirit rather than the body) 例 Because medieval women's public participation in *spiritual* life was not welcomed by the male establishment, a compensating involvement with religious writings, inoffensive to the members of the establishment because of its privacy, became important for many women.
spongy ['spʌndʒi]	*adj.* 像海绵的(resembling a sponge); 不坚实的(not firm or solid) 搭 spongy topsoil 松软的表土
spontaneity [ˌspɑːntə'neɪəti]	*n.* 自然, 自发(the quality or state of being spontaneous) 例 Unfortunately, excessive care in choosing one's words often results in a loss of *spontaneity*.
sporadic [spə'rædɪk]	*adj.* 不定时发生的(occurring occasionally) 例 These *sporadic* raids seem to indicate that the enemy is waging a war of attrition rather than attacking us directly.
sprawl [sprɔːl]	*v.* 散乱地延伸; 四肢摊开着坐、卧或倒下(to lie or sit with arms and legs spread out)
sprawling ['sprɔːlɪŋ]	*adj.* 植物蔓生的, (城市)无计划地扩展的(spreading out ungracefully) 搭 sprawling handwriting 潦草的笔迹
sprout [spraʊt]	*v.* 长出, 萌芽(to grow; spring up) *n.* 嫩芽(a young shoot) 记 联想记忆: spr(看作 spring) + out(出) → 春天来了, 嫩芽长出来了 → 长出, 萌芽

spice

□ spice	□ spinal	□ spined	□ spineless	□ spinning	□ spiny
□ spiral	□ spiritedness	□ spiritual	□ spongy	□ spontaneity	□ sporadic
□ sprawl	□ sprawling	□ sprout			

spruce	*n.* 云杉 *adj.* 整洁的 (neat or smart; trim)
[spruːs]	
spurious	*adj.* 假的 (false); 伪造的 (falsified; forged)
[ˈspjʊriəs]	记 来自 spuria (*n.* 伪造的作品)
	例 Lovejoy, the hero of Jonathan Gash's mystery novels, is an antique dealer who gives the reader advice on how to tell *spurious* antiques from the real thing.
	同 artificial, counterfeit, dummy, ersatz, pseudo
spurn	*n.* 拒绝, 摈弃 (disdainful rejection)
[spɜːrn]	记 联想记忆: spur (刺激) + n (看作 no) → 不再刺激, 不再鼓励 → 拒绝, 摈弃
squalid	*adj.* 污秽的, 肮脏的 (filthy and degraded from neglect or poverty)
[ˈskwɑːlɪd]	同 dirty, seedy, slummy, sordid, unclean
squander	*v.* 浪费, 挥霍 (to spend extravagantly)
[ˈskwɑːndər]	记 源自方言, 因莎士比亚在《威尼斯商人》一剧中使用而广泛流传
squirt	*v.* 喷出, 溅进 (to spurt)
[skwɜːrt]	搭 squirt...with... 用…喷…
stabilize	*v.* 使稳定, 使坚固 (to make stable, steadfast, or firm)
[ˈsteɪbəlaɪz]	记 来自 stable (*adj.* 稳固的)
stagger	*v.* 蹒跚, 摇晃 (to move on unsteadily)
[ˈstæɡər]	同 lurch, reel, sway, waver, wobble
stagnant	*adj.* 停滞的 (not advancing or developing)
[ˈstæɡnənt]	记 词根记忆: stagn (=stand 站住) + ant → 停滞的
stagnate	*v.* 停滞 (to become or remain stagnant)
[ˈstæɡneɪt]	
stagnation	*n.* 停滞
[stæɡˈneɪʃn]	搭 blood stagnation 瘀血
stained	*adj.* 污染的, 玷污的
[steɪnd]	同 blemished, discolored, marked, spotted, tarnished
stalk	*v.* 隐伏跟踪(猎物) (to pursue quarry or prey stealthily)
[stɔːk]	记 stalk 作为 "茎, 秆" 之意大家都熟悉
stalwart	*adj.* 健壮的 (of outstanding strength); 坚定的
[ˈstɔːlwərt]	记 联想记忆: stal (=support) + wart (=worth) → 值得依靠的 → 坚定的
stark	*adj.* 光秃秃的; 荒凉的 (barren; desolate); (外表) 僵硬的 (rigid as if in death); 完全的 (utter; sheer)
[stɑːrk]	例 Melodramas, which presented *stark* oppositions between innocence and criminality, virtue and corruption, good and evil, were popular precisely because they offered the audience a world devoid of neutrality.
stash	*v.* 藏匿 (to store in a usually secret place for future use)
[stæʃ]	记 联想记忆: st (看作 stay, 待) +ash (灰) → 待在灰里 → 藏匿

19

stasis	*n.* 停滞（motionlessness）
['steɪsɪs]	例 Some paleontologists debate whether the diversity of species has increased since the Cambrian period, or whether imperfections in the fossil record only suggest greater diversity today, while in actuality there has been either *stasis* or decreased diversity.
stately	*adj.* 庄严的，堂皇的；宏伟的（marked by lofty or imposing dignity）
['steɪtli]	同 august, dignified, majestic
static	*adj.* 静态的（showing little change; stationary）；呆板的
['stætɪk]	记 联想记忆：stat（看作 state，处于某种状态）+ ic（…的）→ 静态的
	例 That the brain physically changes when stimulated, instead of remaining *static* from infancy to death, as previously thought, was Doctor Marian Diamond's first, and perhaps most far reaching discovery.
steadfast	*adj.* 忠实的（faithful）；不动的，不变的（fixed or unchanging）
['stedfæst]	记 联想记忆：stead（=stand 站）+ fast（稳固的）→ 不变的
steadiness	*n.* 稳健，坚定
['stedinəs]	同 firmness, stablilety
steady	*adj.* 稳定的（direct or sure in movement）；不变的（fixed）
['stedi]	记 联想记忆：st + eady（看作 ready，有准备的）→ 事先有准备，心里就有底 → 稳定的
	例 Although some consider forcefulness and persistence to be two traits desirable to the same degree, I think that making a violent effort is much less useful than maintaining a *steady* one.
	同 abiding, constant, equable, stabile, steadfast
stellar	*adj.* 星的，星球的（of or relating to the stars）
['stelər]	记 词根记忆：stell（星星）+ ar → 星的，星球的
	例 Although supernovas are among the most luminous of cosmic events, these *stellar* explosions are often hard to detect, either because they are enormously far away or because they are dimmed by intervening dust and gas clouds.
stem	*n.* （植物的）茎，叶柄 *v.* 阻止，遏制（水流等）（to stop or dam up）
[stem]	例 This new government is faced not only with managing its economy but also with implementing new rural development programs to *stem* the flow of farm workers to the city.
stereotype	*n.* 固定形式，老套（sth. conforming to a fixed or general pattern）
['steriətaɪp]	记 联想记忆：stereo（立体）+ type（形状）→ 固定形式
sterile	*adj.* 贫瘠且无植被的（producing little vegetation）；无细菌的（free from living organisms）
['sterəl]	
stiffen	*v.* 使硬，使僵硬（to make stiff or stiffer）
['stɪfn]	同 congeal, harden, solidify
stilted	*adj.* （文章、谈话）不自然的；夸张的（pompous）
['stɪltɪd]	记 来自 stilt（*n.* 高跷）

stimulate	*v.* 激励(to animate); 激发(to arouse)
[ˈstɪmjuleɪt]	记 词根记忆: stimul(刺，刺激) + ate → 激励；激发
	例 In retrospect, Gordon's students appreciated her enigmatic assignments, realizing that such assignments were specifically designed to *stimulate* original thought rather than to review the content of her course.
	同 excite, galvanize, motivate, provoke
stimulus	*n.* 刺激物，激励
[ˈstɪmjələs]	同 incentive
stingy	*adj.* 吝啬的，小气的(not generous or liberal)
[ˈstɪndʒi]	同 chinchy, miserly, niggard, parsimonious, penurious, pinchpenny
stint	*v.* 节制，限量，节省(to restrict or limit, as in amount or number)
[stɪnt]	搭 stint on sth. 吝惜…
stipulate	*v.* 要求以…为条件 (to demand an express term in an agreement); 约定，规定(to make an agreement)
[ˈstɪpjuleɪt]	记 词根记忆: stip(点) + ulate → 点明 → 要求以…为条件
stocky	*adj.* (人或动物)矮而结实的，粗壮的(compact, sturdy, and relatively thick in build)
[ˈstɑːki]	记 来自 stock(*n.* 树桩)
stodgy	*adj.* 乏味的(boring, dull)
[ˈstɑːdʒi]	例 For a young person, Winston seems remarkably *stodgy*; you'd expect someone his age to show a little more life.
stoic	*n.* 坚忍克己之人(a person firmly restraining response to pain or distress)
[ˈstoʊɪk]	记 来自希腊哲学流派 Stoic(斯多葛学派)，主张坚忍克己
storage	*n.* 仓库(space or a place for storing); 贮存(the act of storing)
[ˈstɔːrɪdʒ]	例 Created to serve as perfectly as possible their workaday function, the wooden *storage* boxes made in America's Shaker communities are now valued for their beauty.
stout	*adj.* 肥胖的(bulky in body); 强壮的(sturdy, vigorous)
[staʊt]	记 联想记忆: st + out(出来) → 肌肉都鼓出来了 → 强壮的
strait	*n.* 海峡 *adj.* 狭窄的(narrow)
[streɪt]	记 参考: isthmus(*n.* 地峡)
stratagem	*n.* 谋略，策略(a cleverly contrived trick or scheme)
[ˈstrætədʒəm]	记 词根记忆: strata(层次) + gem → 有层次的计划 → 谋略
	例 That the Third Battalion's fifty-percent casualty rate transformed its assault on Hill 306 from a brilliant *stratagem* into a debacle does not gainsay eyewitness reports of its commander's extraordinary cleverness in deploying his forces.
strategic	*adj.* 战略上的(of, relating to, or marked by strategy); 关键的，重要的(necessary to or important in the initiation, conduct, or completion of a strategic plan)
[strəˈtiːdʒɪk]	

19

stout

stratify [ˈstrætɪfaɪ]	*v.* (使)层化(to divide or arrange into classes, castes, or social strata) 记 词根记忆：strat(层次) + ify → (使)层化
streak [striːk]	*n.* 条纹(a line or mark of a different color or texture from the ground) *v.* 加线条(to have a streak) 例 People who don't outgrow their colleges often don't grow in other ways; there remained in Forster's life and imagination a *streak* of the undergraduate, clever but immature.
strength [streŋθ]	*n.* 体力(the quality or state of being strong); 强度(power of resisting attack); 力量(legal, logical, or moral force) 例 While Parker is very outspoken on issues she cares about, she is not fanatical; she concedes the *strength* of opposing arguments when they expose weaknesses inherent in her own.
strenuous [ˈstrenjuəs]	*adj.* 奋发的(vigorously active); 热烈的(fervent, zealous) 同 earnest, energetic, spirited
stride [straɪd]	*v.* 大步行走(to move with or as if with long steps) 记 联想记忆：st + ride(骑自行车) → 走得像骑自行车一样快 → 大步行走 *stride*
stringent [ˈstrɪndʒənt]	*adj.* (规定)严格的, 苛刻的(severe); 缺钱的(marked by scarcity of money, credit restrictions, or other financial strain) 记 联想记忆：string (线，绳) + ent → 像用绳限制住一样 → 严格的 例 These regulations are so *stringent* that we feel we have lost all our privileges. 同 draconian, rigorous
strip [strɪp]	*v.* 剥去(to remove clothing on covering from) *n.* 狭长的一片(a long narrow piece) 记 联想记忆：s(音似：死) + trip(旅行) → 死亡剥夺了人在世间的时间之旅 → 剥去 同 denude, disrobe
strive [straɪv]	*v.* 奋斗, 努力(to struggle hard; make a great effort) 记 联想记忆：st(看作 stress，压力) + rive(看作 drive，动力) → 奋斗的过程需要压力和动力 → 奋斗，努力
stronghold [ˈstrɔːŋhoʊld]	*n.* 要塞(a fortified place); 堡垒, 根据地(a place of security or survival) 同 fortress
structure [ˈstrʌktʃər]	*n.* 结构(makeup) *v.* 建造(to construct) 例 Even though the basic organization of the brain does not change after birth, details of its *structure* and function remain plastic for some time, particularly in the cerebral cortex.
stumble [ˈstʌmbl]	*v.* 绊倒(to strike one's foot against sth. and almost fall) 同 lurch, stagger, trip

□ stratify	□ streak	□ strength	□ strenuous	□ stride	□ stringent
□ strip	□ strive	□ stronghold	□ structure	□ stumbie	

stunning [ˈstʌnɪŋ]	*adj.* 极富魅力的 (strikingly impressive in beauty or excellence) 同 amazing, dazzling, marvellous
stylize [ˈstaɪlaɪz]	*v.* 使…风格化 (to conform to a conventional style)
stymie [ˈstaɪmi]	*v.* 妨碍, 阻挠 (to present an obstacle to) 记 原指高尔夫球中的妨碍球
subdue [səbˈduː]	*v.* 征服 (to conquer, vanquish); 压制 (to bring under control); 减轻 (to reduce the intensity or degree of) 记 词根记忆: sub (在下面) + due (=duce 引导) → 引到下面 → 征服 同 crush, overpower, subjugate
subdued [səbˈduːd]	*adj.* (光和声) 柔和的, 缓和的; (人) 温和的 (unnaturally or unusually quiet in behavior)
subjective [səbˈdʒektɪv]	*adj.* 主观的, 想象的 (influenced by personal feelings and therefore perhaps unfair) 记 来自 subject (*n.* 主题)
submerged [səbˈmɜːrdʒd]	*adj.* 在水中的, 淹没的 (covered with water) 同 dipped, immersed, sinked
submission [səbˈmɪʃn]	*n.* 从属, 服从 (an act of submitting to the authority or control of another) 记 词根记忆: sub (下面) + miss (放) + ion → 放在下面 → 从属, 服从 例 The losing animal in a struggle saves itself from destruction by an act of *submission*, an act usually recognized and accepted by the winner.
subordinate [səˈbɔːrdɪnət]	*adj.* 次要的 (inferior); 下级的 (submissive to or controlled by authority) *n.* 下级 (one that is subordinate) 记 sub (在下面) + ordin (顺序) + ate → 顺序在下的 → 次要的; 下级的
subservient [səbˈsɜːrviənt]	*adj.* 次要的, 从属的 (useful in an inferior capacity); 恭顺的 (obsequiously submissive)
subside [səbˈsaɪd]	*v.* (建筑物等) 下陷 (to tend downward, descend); 平息, 减退 (to become quiet or less) 记 词根记忆: sub (下面) + side (坐) → 坐下去 → 下陷 例 Because he had assumed that the child's first, fierce rush of grief would quickly *subside*, Murdstone was astonished to find him still disconsolate. 同 ebb, lull, moderate, slacken, wane
subsidize [ˈsʌbsɪdaɪz]	*v.* 津贴, 资助 (to furnish with a subsidy) 同 finance, fund, sponsor
subsist [səbˈsɪst]	*v.* 生存下去; 继续存在 (to exist); 维持生活 记 词根记忆: sub (下面) + sist (站) → 站下去, 活下去 → 生存下去

19

subordinate

substantiate [səbˈstænʃieɪt]	*v.* 证实、确证(to establish by proof or competent evidence, verify) 例 The value of Davis' sociological research is compromised by his unscrupulous tendency to use materials selectively in order to *substantiate* his own claims, while disregarding information that points to other possible conclusions. 同 embody, externalize, incarnate, materialize
substantive [səbˈstæntɪv]	*adj.* 根本的(dealing with essentials);独立存在的(being a totally independent entity)
substitute [ˈsʌbstɪtuːt]	*n.* 代替品(a person or thing that takes the place or function of another) *v.* 代替(to replace) 记 词根记忆:sub(下面)+ stit(站)+ ute → 站在下面的 → 代替品 例 Many welfare reformers would *substitute* a single, federally financed income support system for the existing welter of overlapping programs.
subterranean [ˌsʌbtəˈreɪniən]	*adj.* 地下的, 地表下的(being under the surface of the earth) 记 词根记忆:sub(下面)+ terr(地)+ anean → 地下的
subtle [ˈsʌtl]	*adj.* 微妙的, 精巧的(delicate; refined) 例 An obvious style, easily identified by some superficial quirk, is properly decried as a mere mannerism, whereas a complex and *subtle* style resists reduction to a formula.
subtly [ˈsʌtli]	*adv.* 敏锐地, 巧妙地 同 artfully, shrewdly
subtract [səbˈtrækt]	*v.* 减去, 减掉(to take away by or as if by deducting) 记 词根记忆:sub(下面)+ tract(拉)→ 拉下去 → 减去
subtractive [səbˈtræktɪv]	*adj.* 减法的(tending to subtract);负的
subversive [səbˈvɜːrsɪv]	*adj.* 颠覆性的, 破坏性的(intended to overthrow or undermine an established government) 记 词根记忆:sub(下面)+ vers(转)+ ive → 转到下面的 → 颠覆性的
subvert [səbˈvɜːrt]	*v.* 颠覆, 推翻(to overturn or overthrow from the foundation) 记 词根记忆:sub(下面)+ vert(转)→ 在下面转 → 推翻
successively [səkˈsesɪvli]	*adv.* 接连地, 继续地(in proper order or sequence) 例 Not all the indicators necessary to convey the effect of depth in a picture work simultaneously; the picture's illusion of uniform three-dimensional appearance must therefore result from the viewer's integration of various indicators perceived *successively*. 同 consecutively, continuously, uninterruptedly
succinct [səkˈsɪŋkt]	*adj.* 简明的, 简洁的(marked by compact, precise expression) 记 词根记忆:suc(下面)+ cinct(=gird 束起)→ 原指把下面的衣服束起来方便干活 → 简洁的

	例 You should delete this paragraph in order to make your essay more *succinct*.
	同 concise, compendiary, compendious, curt, laconic
succinctness [sək'sɪŋktnəs]	*n.* 简明, 简洁
	同 conciseness, concision
succor ['sʌkər]	*v.* 救助, 援助 (to go to the aid of)
	记 词根记忆: suc(下面)+cor(跑) → 跑到下面来 → 救助
succumb [sə'kʌm]	*v.* 屈从, 屈服 (to yield to superior strength); 因…死亡 (to die)
	记 词根记忆: suc(下面) + cumb(躺) → 躺下去 → 因…死亡
suffrage ['sʌfrɪdʒ]	*n.* 选举权, 投票权 (the right of voting)
	记 词根记忆: suf (=sub 下面) + frag(表示拥护的喧闹声) + e → 选举权
suffragist ['sʌfrədʒɪst]	*n.* 参政权扩大论者; 妇女政权论者 (one who advocates extension of suffrage especially for women)
	记 联想记忆: suff + rag (破布) + ist → 主张让穿破布的人也参政 → 参政权扩大论者
sully ['sʌli]	*v.* 玷污, 污染 (to make soiled or tarnished; defile)
	同 stain, tarnish
sultry ['sʌltri]	*adj.* 闷热的 (very hot and humid; sweltering); (人)风骚的 (capable of exciting strong sexual desires)
summary ['sʌməri]	*n.* 摘要, 概要 (an abstract; abridgment) *adj.* 摘要的, 简略的 (converting the main points succinctly)
	记 词根记忆: sum(总和) + mary → 摘要, 概要
	例 No *summary* of the behavior of animals toward reflected images is given, but not much else that is relevant seems missing from this comprehensive yet compact study of mirrors and mankind.
	同 epitome, recapitulation
sumptuous ['sʌmptʃuəs]	*adj.* 豪华的, 奢侈的 (extremely costly, luxurious, or magnificent)
	记 词根记忆: sumpt(拿, 取) + uous → (把钱)拿出去 → 奢侈的
	例 The *sumptuous* costumes of Renaissance Italy, with their gold and silver embroidery and figured brocades, were the antithesis of Spanish sobriety, with its dark muted colors, plain short capes, and high collars edged with small ruffs.
	同 deluxe, palatial
sun-bronzed ['sʌnbrɑːnzd]	*adj.* 被太阳晒成古铜色的
sunlit ['sʌnlɪt]	*adj.* 阳光照射的 (lighted by or as if by the sun)
	记 联想记忆: sun(太阳) + lit(light 的过去式, 照亮) → 阳光照射的
superannuate [ˌsuːpər'ænjueɪt]	*v.* 使退休领养老金 (to retire and pension because of age or infirmity)

19

superb [suː'pɜːrb]	*adj.* 上乘的，出色的(marked to the highest degree by excellence, brilliance, or competence) 记 词根记忆：super(超过) + b → 超群的 → 上乘的，出色的 同 lofty, sublime
supercilious [ˌsuːpər'sɪliəs]	*adj.* 目中无人的(coolly or patronizingly haughty) 记 词根记忆：super(超过) + cili(眉毛) + ous → 超过眉毛 → 目中无人的
superficial [ˌsuːpər'fɪʃl]	*adj.* 表面的，肤浅的(shallow) 记 词根记忆：super(在…上面) + fic(做) + ial → 在上面做 → 表面的 例 He continually describes what superhuman labor it has cost him to compose his poems and intimates that, in comparison with his own work, the poetry of other poets is *superficial*.
superficially [ˌsuːpər'fɪʃəli]	*adv.* 表面上地 同 shallowly
superfluous [suː'pɜːrfluəs]	*adj.* 多余的，累赘的(exceeding what is needed) 记 词根记忆：super(超过) + flu(流) + ous → 流得过多 → 多余的 例 Joe spoke of *superfluous* and vital matters with exactly the same degree of intensity, as though for him serious issues mattered neither more nor less than did trivialities.
supernova [ˌsuːpər'noʊvə]	*n.* 超新星 记 联想记忆：super(超级) + nova(新星) → 超新星
supersede [ˌsuːpər'siːd]	*v.* 淘汰(to force out of use as inferior)；取代(to take the place, room, or position of) 记 词根记忆：super(在…上面) + sede(坐) → 坐在别人上面 → 取代

superstructure [ˈsuːpərstrʌktʃər]	*n.* 上层建筑 (an entity, concept, or complex based on a more fundamental one); 上层构造 (a structure built as a vertical extension of sth. else) 例 Ultimately, the book's credibility is strained; the slender, though far from nonexistent, web of evidence presented on one salient point is expected to support a vast *superstructure* of implications.
supplant [səˈplænt]	*v.* 排挤, 取代 (to supersede by force or treachery) 记 词根记忆: sup(下面) + plant(种植) → 在下面种植 → 排挤, 取代 例 When railroads first began to *supplant* rivers and canals as highways of commerce, they were regarded as blessings and their promoters were looked upon as benefactors.
supple [ˈsʌpl]	*adj.* 柔软的, 灵活的 (readily adaptable or responsive to new situations); 柔顺的, 顺从的 同 flexible, limber, pliable
supplement [ˈsʌplɪmənt]	*n.* 增补, 补充 (sth. that completes or makes an addition) *v.* 增补 (to add or serve as a supplement to) 记 联想记忆: supple(=supply 提供) + ment → 提供补充 → 增补, 补充 例 Supporters of the proposed waterway argue that it will *supplement* rather than threaten railroad facilities, since the waterway will be icebound during the only months when the railroads can absorb much traffic. 同 appendix, addendum, codicil, complement
supplementary [ˌsʌplɪˈmentri]	*adj.* 增补的, 补充的 (added or serving as a supplement) 例 Because its average annual rainfall is only about four inches, one of the major tasks faced by the country has been to find *supplementary* sources of water.
suppliant [ˈsʌpliənt]	*adj.* 恳求的, 哀求的 (humbly imploring) *n.* 恳求者, 哀求者 (one who supplicates) 同 beggar, prayer, suitor, supplicant
supportive [səˈpɔːrtɪv]	*adj.* 支持的 (showing agreement and giving encouragement) 搭 be supportive of 支持…

suppress [sə'pres]	*v.* 镇压(to put down by authority or force); 抑制(to inhibit the growth or development of) 例 As serious as she is about the bullfight, she does not allow respect to *suppress* her sense of whimsy when painting it. 同 quell, quench, repress, squash
surly ['sɜːrli]	*adj.* 脾气暴躁的(bad tempered); 阴沉的(sullen) 记 联想记忆：sur(=sir 先生) + ly → 像高高在上的先生一般 → 脾气暴躁的
surmise	['sɜːrmaɪz] *n.* 推测，猜测(conjecture) [sər'maɪz] *v.* 推测，猜测(to infer on slight ground) 记 词根记忆：sur(在…下) + mise(放) → 放下想法 → 推测，猜测
surmount [sər'maʊnt]	*v.* 克服，战胜(to prevail over; overcome); 登上(to get to the top of) 记 词根记忆：sur(在…下) + mount(山) → 将山踩在脚下 → 克服，战胜
surpass [sər'pæs]	*v.* 超过(to go beyond in amount, quality, or degree) 记 词根记忆：sur(超过，在上面) + pass(通过) → 在上面通过 → 超过 例 No real life hero of ancient or modern days can *surpass* James Bond with his nonchalant disregard of death and the fortitude with which he bears torture. 同 exceed, excel, outshine, outstrip
surrender [sə'rendər]	*v.* 投降(to give in to the power); 放弃(to give up possession or control); 归还(to give back) 记 词根记忆：sur(在…下) + render(给予) → 把(枪)交出来，放在地上 → 投降
surreptitious [ˌsɜːrəp'tɪʃəs]	*adj.* 鬼鬼祟祟的(acting or doing sth. clandestinely) 记 词根记忆：sur(在…下) + rep (=rap 拿，抓住) + titious → 偷偷拿 → 鬼鬼祟祟的 例 The Turner Network's new production is an absorbing *Heart of Darkness*, watchful, *surreptitious*, almost predatory as it waits to pounce on our emotions.
surrogate ['sɜːrəɡət]	*n.* 代替品(one that serves as a substitute); 代理人(one appointed to act in place of another, deputy)
surveillance [sɜːr'veɪləns]	*n.* 监视，盯梢(close observation of a person) 同 inspection, supervision
survive [sər'vaɪv]	*v.* 幸存(to continue to exist or live after) 记 词根记忆：sur(在…下) + viv(存活) + e → 在(事故)下面活下来 → 幸存 例 If a species of parasite is to *survive*, the host organisms must live long enough for the parasite to reproduce; if the host species becomes extinct, so do its parasites.
survivor [sər'vaɪvər]	*n.* 幸存者(someone who continues to live after an accident, war, or illness)

□ suppress　　□ surly　　□ surmise　　□ surmount　　□ surpass　　□ surrender
□ surreptitious　　□ surrogate　　□ surveillance　　□ survive　　□ survivor

susceptible [səˈseptəbl]	*adj.* 易受影响的，敏感的 (unresistant to some stimulus, influence, or agency) 例 Because it has no distinct and recognizable typographical form and few recurring narrative conventions, the novel is, of all literary genres, the least *susceptible* to definition.
suspend [səˈspend]	*v.* 暂停，中止 (to stop to be inactive or ineffective for a period of time)；吊，悬 (to hang from above) 记 词根记忆：sus + pend(挂) → 挂在下面 → 吊，悬
suspense [səˈspens]	*n.* 悬念 (pleasant excitement as to a decision or outcome)；挂念 (anxiety) 同 apprehension, uncertainty
suspension [səˈspenʃn]	*n.* 暂停 (the state or period of being suspended)；悬浮 例 To avoid annihilation by parasites, some caterpillars are able to curtail periods of active growth by pre-maturely entering a dormant state, which is characterized by the *suspension* of feeding. 同 abeyance, quiescence
suspicious [səˈspɪʃəs]	*adj.* 怀疑的 (expressing or indicative of suspicion) 搭 be suspicious of/about... 对…怀疑的 同 doubtful, dubious, problematic
sustain [səˈsteɪn]	*v.* 承受(困难) (undergo)；支撑(重量或压力) (to carry or withstand a weight or pressure) 记 词根记忆：sus + tain (拿住) → 在下面支撑住 → 支撑 同 bolster, prop, underprop
swampy [swɑːmpɪ]	*adj.* 沼泽的，湿地的 (marshy) 搭 swampy lake 沼泽湖泊
sweep [swiːp]	*v.* 席卷，扫过 (to clean with or as if with a broom or brush) 搭 sweep the board (在比赛中)囊括所有奖项
swift [swɪft]	*adj.* 迅速的 (able to move at a great speed)；敏捷的 (ready or quick in action) 记 联想记忆：电梯(lift)飞快(swift)上升
sycophant [ˈsɪkəfænt]	*n.* 马屁精 (a servile self-seeking flatterer) 记 词根记忆：syco(无花果) + phan(显现) + t → 献上无花果 → 马屁精
syllable [ˈsɪləbl]	*n.* 音节 *v.* 分成音节 (to give a number or arrangement of syllables to (a word or verse)) 记 联想记忆：syll(音似：say) + able → 可以说出来的 → 音节
symbiosis [ˌsɪmbaɪˈoʊsɪs]	*n.* 共生(关系) (the living together in more or less intimate association or closer union of two dissimilar organisms) 记 词根记忆：sym(共同) + bio(生命) + sis → 共生(关系)

20

suspicious

美金

symbolic [sɪmˈbɑːlɪk]	*adj.* 符号的（using, employing, or exhibiting a symbol）；象征的（consisting of or proceeding by means of symbols） 例 Once Renaissance painters discovered how to render volume and depth, they were able to replace the medieval convention of *symbolic*, two-dimensional space with the more realistic illusion of actual space.
symbolize [ˈsɪmbəlaɪz]	*v.* 象征（to represent, express, or identify by a symbol） 同 denote, signify
symmetrical [sɪˈmetrɪkl]	*adj.* 对称的（having, involving, or exhibiting symmetry） 同 balanced, proportional, proportionate
symmetry [ˈsɪmətri]	*n.* 对称；匀称（balanced proportions） 记 词根记忆：sym（共同）+ metry（测量）→ 两边所测量的距离相同 → 对称
sympathetic [ˌsɪmpəˈθetɪk]	*adj.* 有同情心的（given to, marked by, or arising from sympathy） 同 commiserative, compassionate, condolatory, pitying
symptomatic [ˌsɪmptəˈmætɪk]	*adj.* 有症状的（being a symptom of a disease） 例 Many artists believe that successful imitation, far from being *symptomatic* of a lack of originality, is the first step in learning to be creative.
synchronization [ˌsɪŋkrənəˈzeɪʃn]	*n.* 同步（the act or result of synchronizing, the state of being synchronous）
synchronous [ˈsɪŋkrənəs]	*adj.* 同时发生的（happening at precisely the same time） 同 coexistent, concurrent
synergic [ˈsɪnərdʒɪk]	*adj.* 协同作用的（of combined action or cooperation） 记 来自 synergy（*n.* 协同作用）
synonymous [sɪˈnɑːnɪməs]	*adj.* 同义的（having the same connotations, implications, or reference） 记 来自 synonym（*n.* 同义词）
synoptic [sɪˈnɑːptɪk]	*adj.* 摘要的（affording a general view of a whole） 例 The sheer bulk of data from the mass media seems to overpower us and drive us to *synoptic* accounts for an easily and readily digestible portion of news.
synthesis [ˈsɪnθəsɪs]	*n.* 综合，合成（the combining of separate things or ideas into a complete whole） 例 Even though the survey was designated as an interdisciplinary course, it involved no real *synthesis* of subject matter.
synthesize [ˈsɪnθəsaɪz]	*v.* 综合；合成（to combine or produce by synthesis） 记 词根记忆：syn（共同，相同）+ thes（放）+ ize → 放到一起 → 合成
systematic [ˌsɪstəˈmætɪk]	*adj.* 系统的，体系的（relating to or consisting of a system） 例 It has been argued that politics as a practice, whatever its transcendental claims, has always been the *systematic* organization of common hatreds.

tacit [ˈtæsɪt]	*adj.* 心照不宣的（understood without being put into words） 记 注意和 taciturn（*adj.* 沉默寡言的）区分开，tacit 指"心里明白但嘴上不说" 例 Samuel Johnson gave more than *tacit* cooperation to his biographer, James Boswell; he made himself available to Boswell night after night, furnished Boswell with correspondence, and even read his biographer's notes.
tact [tækt]	*n.* 机智；圆滑（a keen sense of what to do or say） 例 She has sufficient *tact* to handle the ordinary crises of diplomatic life; however, even her diplomacy is insufficient to enable her to weather the current emergency.
tactile [ˈtæktl]	*adj.* 有触觉的（relating to the sense of touch） 记 词根记忆：tact（接触）+ ile → 有触觉的
talent [ˈtælənt]	*n.* 天赋（the natural endowments of a person）；天才（a special often creative or artistic aptitude） 记 联想记忆：tal(l)（高）+ ent（人）→ 高人 → 天才 同 aptness, faculty, flair, genius
talented [ˈtæləntɪd]	*adj.* 天才的（showing a natural aptitude for sth.） 例 Gaddis is a formidably *talented* writer whose work has been, unhappily, more likely to intimidate or repel his readers than to lure them into his fictional world.
tangential [tænˈdʒenʃl]	*adj.* 切线的（of the nature of a tangent）；离题的（divergent; digressive） 同 discursive, excursive, rambling
tangible [ˈtændʒəbl]	*adj.* 可触摸的（touchable; palpable） 例 Her remarkable speed, which first became apparent when she repeatedly defeated the older children at school, eventually earned for her some *tangible* rewards, including a full athletic scholarship and several first-place trophies.
tangle [ˈtæŋgl]	*v.* 缠结（to become a confused mass of disordered and twisted threads） *n.* 纷乱（a confused disordered state） 记 联想记忆：两人缠结（tangle）在一起跳探戈（tango）
tantalize [ˈtæntəlaɪz]	*v.* 挑惹，挑逗（to tease or torment by a sight of sth. that is desired but cannot be reached） 记 来自希腊神话人物 Tantalus（坦塔洛斯），他因泄露天机而被罚立在近下巴深的水中，口渴欲饮时水即流失；头上有果树，腹饥欲食时果子即消失
tantamount [ˈtæntəmaʊnt]	*adj.* 同等的，相当于（equivalent in value, significance, or effect） 记 词根记忆：tant（相等）+ a + mount（数量）→ 同等的，相当于
tapering [ˈteɪpərɪŋ]	*adj.* 尖端细的 记 来自 caper（*v.* 逐渐变细）
tardy [ˈtɑːrdi]	*adj.* 迟延，迟到的（delayed beyond the expected or proper time）；缓慢的，迟钝的（slow to act; sluggish） 记 词根记忆：tard（迟缓）+ y → 缓慢的，迟钝的

20

tangible

□ tacit　　　□ tact　　　□ tactile　　　□ talent　　　□ talented　　　□ tangential
□ tangible　　□ tangle　　□ tantalize　　□ tantamount　　□ tapering　　□ tardy

223

tarnish [ˈtɑːrnɪʃ]	*v.* 失去光泽，晦暗 (to dull or destroy the luster by air, dust, or dirt) *n.* 晦暗，无光泽 记 词根记忆：tarn (隐藏) + ish → 隐藏光泽 → 失去光泽，晦暗
tasteless [ˈteɪstləs]	*adj.* 没味道的 (having no taste) 同 bland, flat, flavorless, insipid, unsavory
taunt [tɔːnt]	*n.* 嘲笑，讥讽 (a sarcastic challenge or insult) *v.* 嘲弄，嘲讽 (to reproach or challenge in a mocking or insulting manner)
taut [tɔːt]	*adj.* 绷紧的，拉紧的 (having no slack; tightly drawn) 同 stiff, tense
tawdry [ˈtɔːdri]	*adj.* 华而不实的，俗丽的 (cheap but showy) 搭 tawdry clothing 廉价而花哨的衣服
taxing [ˈtæksɪŋ]	*adj.* 繁重的 (burdensome) 记 来自 tax (*v.* 向…征税；使负重担)
technique [tekˈniːk]	*n.* 技能，方法，手段 (the manner in which technical details are treated or basic physical movements are used) 记 词根记忆：techn (技艺) + ique (…术) → 技能 例 Dr. Charles Drew's *technique* for preserving and storing blood plasma for emergency use proved so effective that it became the model for the present blood bank system used by the American Red Cross.
tedious [ˈtiːdiəs]	*adj.* 冗长的，乏味的 (tiresome because of length or dullness) 例 The pungent verbal give-and-take among the characters makes the novel *tedious* reading, and this very inventiveness suggests to me that some of the opinions voiced may be the author's. 同 boresome, insipid, irksome, wearisome
tedium [ˈtiːdiəm]	*n.* 冗长乏味 (boredom) 记 联想记忆：媒体 (medium) 的节目都很乏味 (tedium)
teem [tiːm]	*v.* 充满 (to abound)；到处都是 (to be present in large quantity)；(雨、水等) 暴降，倾注
temperate [ˈtempərət]	*adj.* (气候等) 温和的 (marked by moderation)；(欲望、饮食等) 适度的，有节制的
temporal [ˈtempərəl]	*adj.* 时间的 (relating to time)；世俗的 (relating to earthly things) 记 词根记忆：tempor (时间) + al → 时间的
temporary [ˈtempəreri]	*adj.* 暂时的，临时的 (lasting for a limited time) 记 词根记忆：tempor (时间) + ary → 时间很短 → 暂时的 例 Only by ignoring decades of mismanagement and inefficiency could investors conclude that a fresh infusion of cash would provide anything more than a *temporary* solution to the company's financial woes.

224

□ tarnish	□ tasteless	□ taunt	□ taut	□ tawdry	□ taxing
□ technique	□ tedious	□ tedium	□ teem	□ temperate	□ temporal
□ temporary					

temptation	*n.* 诱惑，诱惑物（sth. tempting）
[temp'teɪʃn]	例 In discussing Rothko's art, Breslin is scrupulous in keeping to the facts and resisting the *temptation* of fanciful interpretation.
	同 allurement, decoy, enticement, inveiglement, lure
tempting	*adj.* 诱惑人的（having an appeal）
['temptɪŋ]	同 alluring, attractive, enticing, inviting, seductive
tenable	*adj.* 站得住脚的，合理的（defensible, reasonable）
['tenəbl]	记 词根记忆：ten（拿住）+ able（能…的）→ 能够拿住的 → 站得住脚的
tenacious	*adj.* 坚韧的，顽强的（persistent in maintaining or adhering to sth. valued or habitual）
[tə'neɪʃəs]	记 词根记忆：ten（拿住）+ acious（有…性质的）→ 拿住不放 → 坚韧的
tenacity	*n.* 坚持，固执（the quality or state of being tenacious）
[tə'næsəti]	同 doggedness, persistence, perverseness, stubbornness
tendentious	*adj.* 有偏见的（marked by a tendency in favor of a particular point of view）
[ten'denʃəs]	记 词根记忆：tend（倾向）+ ent（存在）+ ious → 有倾向的 → 有偏见的
tenet	*n.* 信条（a principle, belief, or doctrine generally held to be true）；教义
['tenɪt]	记 词根记忆：ten（握住）+ et → 紧抓不放的东西 → 信条
	例 "The show must go on" is the oldest *tenet* of show business; every true performer lives by that creed.
tension	*n.* 紧张，焦虑（anxiety）；张力（the amount of a force stretching sth.）
['tenʃn]	记 词根记忆：tens（伸展）+ ion → 伸展出的状态 → 张力
	例 As painted by Constable, the scene is not one of bucolic serenity; rather it shows a striking emotional and intellectual *tension*.
tentative	*adj.* 试探性的，尝试性的（not fully worked out or developed）
['tentətɪv]	记 词根记忆：tent（测试）+ ative → 尝试性的
	例 Science is always *tentative*, expecting that modifications of its present theories will sooner or later be found necessary.
tentatively	*adv.* 试验性地
['tentətɪvli]	同 experimentally
tenuous	*adj.* 纤细的；稀薄的（not dense; rare）；脆弱的，无力的（flimsy; weak）
['tenjuəs]	记 词根记忆：tenu（薄，细）+ ous → 纤细的；稀薄的
tepid	*adj.* 微温的（moderately warm）；不热情的（lacking in emotional warmth or enthusiasm）
['tepɪd]	例 Considering how long she had yearned to see Italy, her first reaction was curiously *tepid*.
	同 halfhearted, lukewarm, unenthusiastic
termite	*n.* 白蚁
['tɜːrmaɪt]	
terrestrial	*adj.* 地球的（of the earth）；陆地的（relating to land）
[tə'restriəl]	记 词根记忆：terr（地）+ estrial → 地球的
terrifying	*adj.* 恐怖的（causing terror or apprehension）
['terɪfaɪɪŋ]	同 frightening, intimidating, shocking

20

| **territorial** | *adj.* 领土的（of or relating to a territory）；地方的（nearby; local） |
| [ˌterəˈtɔːriəl] | 例 territorial economy 地方经济 |

| **terrorize** | *v.* 恐吓（to fill with terror or anxiety） |
| [ˈterəraɪz] | 同 intimidate, menace, threaten |

| **terse** | *adj.* 简洁的，简明的（concise） |
| [tɜːrs] | 记 联想记忆：诗歌（verse）力求简洁明了（terse） |

| **texture** | *n.* 质地（identifying quality）；结构（overall structure） |
| [ˈtekstʃər] | 记 词根记忆：text（编织）+ ure → 质地 |

| **textured** | *adj.* 手摸时有感觉的；有织纹的 |
| [ˈtekstʃərd] | 记 来自 texture（*n.* 质地；结构） |

| **thatch** | *v.* 以茅草覆盖（to cover with or as if with thatch）*n.* 茅草屋顶；茅草（a plant material used as a sheltering cover） |
| [θætʃ] | |

| **theatrical** | *adj.* 戏剧的，戏剧性的（of or relating to the theater or the presentation of plays; dramatic） |
| [θiˈætrɪkl] | 例 Crowther maintained that the current revival was the most fatuous and inane production of the entire *theatrical* season. |

| **thematic** | *adj.* 主题的（of, relating to, or constituting a theme） |
| [θiːˈmætɪk] | 记 来自 theme（*n.* 主题） |

| **theoretical** | *adj.* 假设的（existing only in theory）；理论（上）的（relating to or having the character of theory） |
| [ˌθiːəˈretɪkl] | 记 来自 theory（*n.* 理论） |

therapeutic	*adj.* 治疗的（of the treatment of diseases）
[ˌθerəˈpjuːtɪk]	记 词根记忆：therap（照看，治疗）+ eutic → 治疗的
	例 For centuries animals have been used as surrogates for people in experiments to assess the effects of *therapeutic* and other agents that might later be used in humans.

| **therapy** | *n.* 治疗（therapeutic treatment especially of bodily, mental, or behavioral disorder） |
| [ˈθerəpi] | 例 The child needed physical *therapy* to counteract the rigidity that had tragically immobilized his legs. |

| **thesis** | *n.* 论题，论文（statement of theory put forward and supported by arguments） |
| [ˈθiːsɪs] | |

| **thorny** | *adj.* 有刺的；多刺的（full of thorns）；多障碍的，引起争议的（full of difficulties or controversial points） |
| [ˈθɔːrni] | 记 来自 thorn（*n.* 刺） |

thoughtful	*adj.* 深思的（absorbed in thought）
[ˈθɔːtfl]	例 Even those who disagreed with Carmen's views rarely faulted her for expressing them, for the positions she took were as *thoughtful* as they were controversial.
	同 cogitative, contemplative, meditative, pensive

thousandfold	adj. 千倍的（a thousand times as much）adv. 千倍地
[ˈθaʊzndfoʊld]	记 组合词：thousand(一千) + fold(折叠) → 一千个叠起来 → 千倍的
threadlike	adj. 线状的
[ˈθredlaɪk]	记 组合词：thread(线) + like(像……一样) → 像线一样 → 线状的
threat	n. 威胁，恐吓（expression of intention to inflict evil, injury, or damage）；凶
[θret]	兆，征兆（indication of future danger）
threaten	v. 威胁（to utter threats against）
[ˈθretn]	同 browbeat, bully, intimidate, menace
thrifty	adj. 节俭的（marked by economy and good management）
[ˈθrɪfti]	记 来自 thrift（n. 节约）
thrive	v. 苗壮成长；繁荣，兴旺（to prosper; flourish）
[θraɪv]	记 联想记忆：th + rive（看作 river, 河）→ 清明上河图描绘了宋代市集的繁荣景象 → 繁荣，兴旺
thwart	v. 阻挠，使受挫折，挫败（to defeat the hopes or aspirations of）
[θwɔːrt]	同 baffle, balk, foil, frustrate
tidy	adj. 整齐的，整洁的（neat and orderly）；相当好的
[ˈtaɪdi]	记 发音记忆："泰迪" → 出售的泰迪熊是整洁漂亮的 → 整洁的
	例 Regardless of what *tidy* theories of politics may propound, there is nothing that requires daily politics to be clear, thorough, and consistent—nothing, that is, that requires reality to conform to theory.
	同 shipshape, trim, uncluttered
tie	n. 平局，不分胜负（an equality in number）v. 系，拴，绑（to fasten, attach, or close by means of a tie）
[taɪ]	
time-consuming	adj. 费时间的（using or taking up a great deal of time）
[ˈtaɪmkənsuːmɪŋ]	搭 a time-consuming job 一项费时的工作
timeliness	n. 及时，适时
[ˈtaɪmlinəs]	记 来自 timely（adj. 及时的，适时的）
timorous	adj. 胆小的，胆怯的（of timid disposition, fearful）
[ˈtɪmərəs]	记 词根记忆：tim(胆怯) + orous → 胆怯的
tined	adj. 尖端的（of a slender pointed projecting part）
[taɪnd]	记 来自 tine（n. 叉尖，尖端）
tint	n. 色泽（slight degree of a color）v. 给……淡淡地着色（to give a slight color to）；染
[tɪnt]	
tissue	n. （动植物的）组织（animal or plant cells）；薄纸，棉纸（light thin paper）
[ˈtɪʃuː]	
titanic	adj. 巨人的，力大无比的（colossal）
[taɪˈtænɪk]	记 来自希腊神话中的巨神 Titan；也可以联想电影 *Titanic*（《泰坦尼克号》）
titular	adj. 有名无实的，名义上的（existing in title only）
[ˈtɪtʃələr]	记 来自 title（n. 头衔）

20

toady	*n.* 谄媚者，马屁精（one who flatters）
[ˈtoʊdi]	记 联想记忆：toad(癞蛤蟆) + y → 像蛤蟆一样趴在地上的人 → 马屁精
	例 Just as sloth is the mark of the idler, obsequiousness is the mark of the *toady*.
	同 bootlicker, brownnoser, cringer, fawner
toed	*adj.* 有趾的（having a toe or toes）
[toʊd]	记 来自 toe(*n.* 脚趾)
topographical	*adj.* 地形学的（concerned with the artistic representation of a particular
[ˌtɑːpəˈɡræfɪkl]	locality）
topple	*v.* 倾覆，推倒（to overthrow）
[ˈtɑːpl]	记 联想记忆：top(顶) + ple → 使顶向下 → 倾覆，推倒
torpid	*adj.* 懒散的，迟钝的（lacking in energy or vigor; dull）
[ˈtɔːrpɪd]	同 lethargic, sluggish, stupid
torpor	*n.* 死气沉沉（extreme sluggishness of function）
[ˈtɔːrpər]	同 dullness, languor, lassitude, lethargy
tortuous	*adj.* 曲折的，拐弯抹角的（marked by devious or indirect tactics）；弯弯曲曲
[ˈtɔːrtʃuəs]	的（winding）
	记 词根记忆：tort(弯曲) + uous → 弯弯曲曲的
totalitarian	*adj.* 极权主义的（authoritarian; dictatorial）
[toʊˌtæləˈteriən]	同 autocratic, despotic, tyrannic
touch	*v.* 涉及（to relate to or have an influence on）；触动（to hurt the feelings
[tʌtʃ]	of）；接触（to be in contact）*n.* 触摸（a light stroke, tap, or push）
	例 Although Henry was not in general a sentimental man, occasionally he
	would feel a *touch* of nostalgia for the old days and would contemplate
	making a brief excursion to Boston to revisit his childhood friends.
	同 feel, finger
touched	*adj.* 被感动的（emotionally stirred）
[tʌtʃt]	同 affected, inspired, moved
touching	*adj.* 动人的，感人的（moving）；令人同情的（causing a feeling of pity or
[ˈtʌtʃɪŋ]	sympathy）
touchy	*adj.* 敏感的，易怒的（acutely sensitive or irritable）
[ˈtʌtʃi]	记 联想记忆：touch(触摸) + y → 一触即发的 → 敏感的，易怒的
tout	*v.* 招徕顾客；极力赞扬（to praise or publicize loudly）
[taʊt]	例 In recent decades the idea that Cezanne influenced Cubism has been
	caught in the crossfire between art historians who credit Braque with its
	invention and those who *tout* Picasso.
towering	*adj.* 高耸的（reaching a high point of intensity）；杰出的
[ˈtaʊərɪŋ]	记 联想记忆：tower(塔) + ing → 像塔一样的 → 高耸的

toxic	*adj.* 有毒的, 中毒的 (of a poison or toxin)
['tɑːksɪk]	记 词根记忆: tox(毒) + ic → 有毒的
	例 People who take megadoses of vitamins and minerals should take care: though beneficial in small quantities, in large amounts these substances may have *toxic* effects.
toxin	*n.* 毒素, 毒质 (a poisonous substance)
['tɑːksɪn]	同 poison, venom
trace	*n.* 痕迹 *v.* 追踪
[treɪs]	例 As delicate and fragile as insect bodies are, it is remarkable that over the ages enough of them have survived, preserved in amber, for scientists to *trace* insect evolution.
	同 engram, relic
traceable	*adj.* 可追踪的 (capable of being trailed)
['treɪsəbl]	记 来自 trace(*v.* 追踪)
tractable	*adj.* 易处理的, 驯良的 (capable of being easily taught or controlled; docile)
['træktəbl]	记 词根记忆: tract(拉) + able → 拉得动的 → 易处理的
trademark	*n.* 特征 (a distinguishing characteristic or feature firmly associated with a person or thing); 商标 *v.* 保证商标权 (to secure trademark rights)
['treɪdmɑːrk]	
tragic	*adj.* 悲惨的 (of, marked by, or expressive of tragedy)
['trædʒɪk]	例 Though set in a mythical South American country, Isabel Allende's novel is rooted in the *tragic* history of Chile.
trait	*n.* (人的)显著特性 (a distinguishing feature, as of a person's character)
[treɪt]	同 attribute, characteristic, peculiarity
trample	*v.* 踩坏, 践踏 (to tread heavily so as to bruise, crush, or injure); 蹂躏
['træmpl]	记 联想记忆: tr(看作 tree, 树) + ample(大量的) → 大量的树苗被踩坏 → 踩坏, 践踏
tranquil	*adj.* 平静的 (free from agitation of mind or spirit)
['træŋkwɪl]	例 Their married life was not *tranquil* since it was fraught with bitter fighting and arguments.
transcend	*v.* 超出, 超越, 胜过 (to rise above or go beyond the limit)
[træn'send]	记 词根记忆: trans(超过) + (s)cend(爬) → 爬过 → 超越
transcendent	*adj.* 超越的, 卓越的, 出众的 (extremely great; supreme)
[træn'sendənt]	同 ultimate, unsurpassable, utmost, uttermost
transcontinental	*adj.* 横贯大陆的 (extending or going across a continent)
[ˌtrænzˌkɑːntɪ'nentl]	
transcribe	*v.* 抄写, 转录 (to make a written copy)
[træn'skraɪb]	记 词根记忆: trans(交换) + (s)cribe(写) → 交换着写 → 抄写
transcription	*n.* 誊写, 抄写 (an act, process, or instance of transcribing); 抄本, 副本 (copy, transcript)
[træn'skrɪpʃn]	

20

□ toxic	□ toxin	□ trace	□ traceable	□ tractable	□ trademark
□ tragic	□ trait	□ trample	□ tranquil	□ transcend	□ transcendent
□ transcontinental	□ transcribe	□ transcription			

transferable [trænsˈfɜːrəbl]	*adj.* 可转移的(that can be moved from one place, person or use to another)
transform [trænsˈfɔːrm]	*v.* 改变，变化(to change in composition or structure)；变换，转换(to subject to mathematical transformation) 记 词根记忆：trans(改变) + form(形状) → 改变，变化 同 convert, mutate, transfer, transmogrify, transmute
transformation [ˌtrænsfərˈmeɪʃn]	*n.* 转化，转变(an act, process, or instance of transforming or being transformed) 例 Doreen justifiably felt she deserved recognition for the fact that the research institute had been returned to a position of preeminence, since it was she who had directed the *transformation*.
transgress [trænzˈgres]	*v.* 冒犯，违背(to go beyond limits prescribed by; violate) 记 词根记忆：trans(横向) + gress(走) → 横着走 → 冒犯
transient [ˈtrænʃnt]	*adj.* 短暂的，转瞬即逝的(passing quickly into and out of existence; transitory) 记 词根记忆：trans(穿过) + ient → 时光穿梭，转瞬即逝 → 短暂的 例 Lexy's joy at finding the perfect Christmas gift for John was *transient*, for she still had to find presents for the cousins and Uncle Bob. 同 ephemeral, evanescent, fleeting, fugacious, fugitive
transit [ˈtrænzɪt]	*n.* 通过(passage)；改变(change; transition)；运输(conveyance) *v.* 通过(to pass over or through) 记 词根记忆：trans(改变) + it → 改变它的地点 → 运输 例 Although I have always been confused by our *transit* system, I relish traveling on the subways occasionally.

transitional [træn'zɪʃənl]	*adj.* 转变的，变迁的（of, relating to, or characterized by transition） 例 Current data suggest that, although *transitional* states between fear and aggression exist, fear and aggression are as distinct physiologically as they are psychologically.
transitoriness ['trænsətɔːrinəs]	*n.* 暂时，短暂（the state of being not persistent） 例 Parts of seventeenth-century Chinese pleasure gardens were not necessarily intended to look cheerful; they were designed expressly to evoke the agreeable melancholy resulting from a sense of the *transitoriness* of natural beauty and human glory.
transitory ['trænsətɔːri]	*adj.* 短暂的（transient） 记 词根记忆：trans(改变) + (s)it(坐) + ory → 坐一下就改变了 → 短暂的
translucent [træns'luːsnt]	*adj.* （半）透明的（allowing light to pass through but not transparent） 记 词根记忆：trans(穿过) + luc(明亮) + ent → 光线能穿过 → （半）透明的
transmit [træns'mɪt]	*v.* 传送，传播（to send or convey from one person or place to another） 记 词根记忆：trans（横过）+ mit（送）→ 送过去 → 传送
transmute [trænz'mjuːt]	*v.* 变化（to change or alter） 记 词根记忆：trans(改变) + mute(变化) → 变化
trauma ['traʊmə]	*n.* 创伤，外伤（an injury to living tissue caused by an extrinsic agent） 例 Because of the *trauma* they have experienced, survivors of a major catastrophe are likely to exhibit aberrations of behavior and may require the aid of competent therapists.
treacherous ['tretʃərəs]	*adj.* 背叛的，叛逆的（showing great disloyalty and deceit） 记 词根记忆：treach(=trick 诡计)+erous → 背叛的
tread [tred]	*v.* 踏，践踏（to press beneath the feet; trample）；行走 *n.* 步态；车轮胎面 同 step
treatise ['triːtɪs]	*n.* 论文（a long written work dealing systematically with one subject） 记 联想记忆：treat(对待) + ise → 对待问题 → 论文

transmit

□ transitional	□ transitoriness	□ transitory	□ translucent	□ transmit	□ transmute
□ trauma	□ treacherous	□ tread	□ treatise		

trenchant	*adj.* 犀利的，尖锐的（sharply perceptive; penetrating）
[ˈtrentʃənt]	记 联想记忆：trench(沟) + ant → 说话像挖沟，入木三分 → 犀利的
trend	*v.* 趋向，倾向（to show a tendency）*n.* 趋势，倾向（a prevailing tendency or inclination）
[trend]	
trendsetter	*n.* 引领新潮的人（a person or institution that starts a new fashion or trend）
[ˈtrendsetər]	
trepidation	*n.* 恐惧，惶恐（timorousness; uncertainty; agitation）
[ˌtrepɪˈdeɪʃn]	记 词根记忆：trep（害怕）+ id + ation → 恐惧，惶恐
	例 Salazar's presence in the group was so reassuring to the others that they lost most of their earlier *trepidation*; failure, for them, became all but unthinkable.
trespass	*v.* 侵犯，闯入私人领地（to make an unwarranted or uninvited incursion）
[ˈtrespəs]	记 词根记忆：tres(横向) + pass(经过) → 横着经过某人的地盘 → 侵犯
tribal	*adj.* 部落的，部族的（of, relating to, or characteristic of a tribe）
[ˈtraɪbl]	
tribulation	*n.* 苦难，忧患（distress or suffering resulting from oppression or persecution）
[ˌtrɪbjuˈleɪʃn]	记 词根记忆：tribul(给予) + ation → 上天给予的(惩罚) → 苦难
tributary	*n.* 支流，进贡国 *adj.* 支流的；辅助的；进贡的（making additions or yielding supplies; contributory）
[ˈtrɪbjəteri]	
trickle	*v.* 细细地流（to flow in a thin gentle stream）*n.* 细流
[ˈtrɪkl]	同 dribble, drip, filter
tricky	*adj.* 狡猾的（inclined to or marked by trickery）
[ˈtrɪki]	同 crafty, cunning
trigger	*n.* 扳机 *v.* 引发，引起，触发（to initiate, actuate, or set off）
[ˈtrɪgər]	同 activate, spark, trip
trilogy	*n.* 三部曲（a group of three related books）
[ˈtrɪlədʒi]	记 词根记忆：tri(三) + logy(说话，作品) → 三部曲
trite	*adj.* 陈腐的，陈词滥调的（hackneyed or boring）
[traɪt]	例 The plot of this story is so *trite* that I can predict the outcome.
	同 bathetic, commonplace
triumph	*n.* 成功，胜利(的喜悦或满足) *v.* 成功，获胜（to obtain victory）
[ˈtraɪʌmf]	记 联想记忆：胜利(triumph)之后吹喇叭(trump)
	同 conquer, overcome, prevail
trivial	*adj.* 琐碎的；没有价值的（concerned with or involving trivia; of little worth）
[ˈtrɪviəl]	记 词根记忆：tri(三) + via(路) + l → 三条路的会合点 → 没有价值的；古罗马妇女喜欢停在十字路口同人闲聊些无关紧要或琐碎的事情，故 trivial 有 "琐碎的；没有价值的"意思
	同 paltry, picayune, picayunish, trifling

truce [truːs]	*n.* 停战，休战（协定）（agreement between enemies to stop fighting for a certain period）
truculence ['trʌkjələns]	*n.* 野蛮，残酷（the quality or state of being truculent） 同 truculency
truculent ['trʌkjələnt]	*adj.* 残暴的，凶狠的（feeling or displaying ferocity; cruel） 记 词根记忆：truc(凶猛) + ulent → 残暴的，凶狠的
truncate ['trʌŋkeɪt]	*v.* 截短，缩短（to shorten by cutting off） 记 联想记忆：trun(k)(树干) + cate → 截去树干 → 截短 例 Rather than allowing these dramatic exchanges between her characters to develop fully, Ms. Norman unfortunately tends to *truncate* the discussions involving the two women.
trustworthy ['trʌstwɜːði]	*adj.* 值得信赖的，可靠的（warranting trust; reliable） 记 组合词：trust(信赖) + worthy(值得的) → 值得信赖的 例 Since she believed him to be both candid and *trustworthy*, she refused to consider the possibility that his statement had been insincere.
turbulent ['tɜːrbjələnt]	*adj.* 混乱的（causing unrest, violence, or disturbance）；骚乱的（tempestuous） 记 词根记忆：turb(搅动) + ulent → 搅得厉害 → 骚乱的
turmoil ['tɜːrmɔɪl]	*n.* 混乱，骚乱（a state of extreme confusion or agitation） 记 词根记忆：tur(=turbulent 混乱的) + moil(喧闹) → 混乱，骚乱 例 Many of her followers remain loyal to her, and even those who have rejected her leadership are unconvinced of the wisdom of replacing her during the current *turmoil*. 同 tumult, turbulence
tussle ['tʌsl]	*n.* 扭打，争斗（a physical contest or struggle）；争辩（an intense argument; controversy）*v.* 扭打，争斗（to struggle roughly） 记 联想记忆：tuss（看作 fuss，忙乱）+ le → 为什么忙乱，因为有人扭打搏斗 → 扭打，争斗
typify ['tɪpɪfaɪ]	*v.* 代表，是…的典型（to represent in typical fashion） 同 epitomize, symbolize
typographical [taɪ'pɑːgrəfɪkl]	*adj.* 印刷上的（of typography） 记 来自 typography(*n.* 印刷术) 例 Because it has no distinct and recognizable *typographical* form and few recurring narrative conventions, the novel is, of all literary genres, the least susceptible to definition.
tyrannical [tɪ'rænɪkl]	*adj.* 暴虐的，残暴的（being or characteristic of a tyrant or tyranny） 同 despotic, oppressive, tyrannic
tyrant ['taɪrənt]	*n.* 暴君（a ruler who exercises absolute power oppressively or brutally） 同 autocrat, despot

21

ubiquitous [juː'bɪkwɪtəs]	*adj.* 无处不在的（existing or being everywhere at the same time） 记 联想记忆：ubi（=where）+ qu（=any）+ itous → anywhere → 无处不在的
ulterior [ʌl'tɪriər]	*adj.* 较远的，将来的（more distant; further）；隐秘的，别有用心的（going beyond what is openly said or shown and especially what is proper） 记 词根记忆：ult（高，远）+ erior → 较远的 例 He was so convinced that people were driven by *ulterior* motives that he believed there was no such thing as a purely unselfish act.
ultimate ['ʌltɪmət]	*adj.* 最后的（being or happening at the end of a process or course of action） 记 词根记忆：ultim（最后）+ ate（…的）→ 最后的 例 This project is the first step in a long-range plan of research whose *ultimate* goal, still many years off, is the creation of a new prototype.
ultimately ['ʌltɪmətli]	*adv.* 最后，终于（in the end, eventually） 例 Just as all roads once led to Rome, all blood vessels in the human body *ultimately* empty into the heart.
ultimatum [ˌʌltɪ'meɪtəm]	*n.* 最后通牒（a final proposition, condition, or demand） 记 联想记忆：ultim（最后的）+ a + tum（看作 term，期限）→ 最后的期限 → 最后通牒
ultrasonic [ˌʌltrə'sɑːnɪk]	*adj.* 超音速的，超声（波）的 同 supersonic
umbrage ['ʌmbrɪdʒ]	*n.* 不快，愤怒（a feeling of pique, resentment or insult） 记 词根记忆：umbra（影子）+ ge → 心里的影子 → 不快
unadorned [ˌʌnə'dɔːrnd]	*adj.* 未装饰的，朴素的 例 Rousseau's short discourse, a work that was generally consistent with the cautious, *unadorned* prose of the day, deviated from that prose style in its unrestrained discussion of the physical sciences.
unaesthetic [ˌʌnəs'θetɪk]	*adj.* 无美感的（deficient in tastefulness or beauty） 记 和 inaesthetic（*adj.* 不美的）一起记
unalterable [ʌn'ɔːltərəbl]	*adj.* 不能改变的（not capable of being altered or changed） 同 changeable, inalterable
unarticulated [ˌʌnɑːr'tɪkjələtɪd]	*adj.* 表达不清的（not articulated）
unavoidable [ˌʌnə'vɔɪdəbl]	*adj.* 不可避免的（not avoidable） 同 ineluctable, inescapable
unbecoming [ˌʌnbɪ'kʌmɪŋ]	*adj.* 不合身的（not suited to the wearer）；不得体的（improper） 记 联想记忆：un（不）+ becoming（合适的）→ 不合身的
unbiased [ʌn'baɪəst]	*adj.* 没有偏见的（free from all prejudice and favoritism） 例 The fact that a theory is plausible does not necessarily ensure its scientific truth, which must be established by *unbiased* controlled studies.

最后三天

ultimatum

unbridgeable [ʌnˈbrɪdʒəbl]	*adj.* 不能架桥的, 不能逾越的 (impossible to span)
unbridled [ʌnˈbraɪdld]	*adj.* 放纵的, 不受约束的 (unrestrained) 同 unchecked, uncurbed, ungoverned
unbroken [ʌnˈbroʊkən]	*adj.* 完整的; 连续的 (not interrupted or disturbed) 同 unplowed, unploughed
uncanny [ʌnˈkæni]	*adj.* 神秘的, 离奇的 (weird; supernatural) 记 联想记忆: un(不) + canny(安静的, 谨慎的) → 神秘的
uncharitable [ʌnˈtʃærɪtəbl]	*adj.* 无慈悲心的 (lacking in charity) 例 Being cynical, he was reluctant to credit the unselfishness of any kind act until he had ruled out all possible secret, *uncharitable* motives.
uncharted [ˌʌnˈtʃɑːrtɪd]	*adj.* 图上未标明的 (not marked on a map or chart) 同 chartless, unmapped
uncommitted [ˌʌnkəˈmɪtɪd]	*adj.* 不受约束的, 不承担责任的 (not pledged to a particular belief or allegiance) 记 联想记忆: un(不) + committed(有责任的) → 不承担责任的
uncommunicative [ˌʌnkəˈmjuːnɪkətɪv]	*adj.* 不爱说话的, 拘谨的 (not disposed to talk or impart information) 记 与 incommunicative(*adj.* 不爱交际的, 沉默寡言的)一起记
uncompromising [ʌnˈkɑːmprəmaɪzɪŋ]	*adj.* 不妥协的 (not making or accepting a compromise) 例 Despite her compassionate nature, the new nominee to the Supreme Court was single-minded and *uncompromising* in her strict adherence to the letter of the law.
unconfirmed [ˌʌnkənˈfɜːrmd]	*adj.* 未经证实的 (not proved to be true; not confirmed)
unconscious [ʌnˈkɑːnʃəs]	*adj.* 不省人事的 (having lost consciousness); 未发觉的, 无意识的 (not knowing about sth.)
uncontroversial [ˌʌnkɑːntrəˈvɜːrʃl]	*adj.* 未引起争论的 (not causing, or not likely to cause, any disagreement) 同 noncontroversial
unconvinced [ˌʌnkənˈvɪnst]	*adj.* 不信服的 (not certain that sth. is true or right) 例 Many of her followers remain loyal to her, and even those who have rejected her leadership are *unconvinced* of the wisdom of replacing her during the current turmoil.
unctuous [ˈʌŋktʃuəs]	*adj.* 油质的 (fatty); 油腔滑调的 (oily) 例 Far from being *unctuous*, Pat was always loath to appear acquiescent. 同 greasy, oleaginous
undecipherable [ˌʌndɪˈsaɪfrəbl]	*adj.* 难破译的 (not easily deciphered)
undemanding [ˌʌndɪˈmɑːndɪŋ]	*adj.* 不严格的 (not demanding); 要求不高的 (requiring little if any patience or effort or skill)

undemonstrable [ˌʌndɪˈmɑːnstrəbl]	*adj.* 无法证明的，难以证明的
undercut [ˌʌndərˈkʌt]	*v.* 削价(与竞争者)抢生意(to sell goods or services more cheaply than a competitor) 记 联想记忆：under(在…下面) + cut(砍) → 偷偷把价格砍掉 → 削价(与竞争者)抢生意
underdeveloped [ˌʌndərdɪˈveləpt]	*adj.* 不发达的(not fully grown or developed)
underestimate [ˌʌndərˈestɪmeɪt]	*v.* 低估(to estimate as being less than the actual size, quantity, or number)；看轻(to place too low a value on)
underestimated [ˌʌndərˈestɪmeɪtɪd]	*adj.* 低估的 记 来自 underestimate(*v.* 低估)
underground [ˌʌndəˈɡraʊnd]	*adv.* 在地下；秘密地(in or into hiding or secret operation) *adj.* 地下的；秘密的 例 Just as astrology was for centuries an *underground* faith, countering the strength of established churches, so today believing in astrology is an act of defiance against the professional sciences. 同 subterranean, subterrestrial, underearth, underfoot
underhanded [ˌʌndərˈhændɪd]	*adj.* 秘密的，狡诈的(marked by secrecy and deception; sly) 记 联想记忆：under(在…下面) + handed(有手的) → 在下面做手脚 → 秘密的
underlie [ˌʌndərˈlaɪ]	*v.* 位于…之下(to lie or be situated under)；构成…的基础(to be at the basis of)；【经】(权力、索赔等)优先于(to constitute a prior financial claim over)
undermine [ˌʌndərˈmaɪn]	*v.* 破坏，削弱(to subvert or weaken insidiously) 记 组合词：under(在…下面) + mine(挖) → 在下面挖 → 破坏 例 It is no accident that most people find Davis' book disturbing, for it is calculated to *undermine* a number of beliefs they have long cherished. 同 attenuate, cripple, debilitate, sap, unbrace
underplay [ˌʌndərˈpleɪ]	*v.* 弱化…的重要性(to make sth. appear less important than it really is)；表演不充分(to underact) 记 联想记忆：under(不足，少于) + play(玩) → 没玩够 → 表演不充分 例 Those who fear the influence of television deliberately *underplay* its persuasive power, hoping that they might keep knowledge of its potential to effect social change from being widely disseminated.
underrate [ˌʌndəˈreɪt]	*v.* 低估，轻视(to rate too low) 记 联想记忆：under(不足，少于) + rate(估价) → 低估 例 The discovery that, friction excluded, all bodies fall at the same rate is so simple to state and to grasp that there is a tendency to *underrate* its significance.

236

□ undemonstrable　□ undercut　□ underdeveloped　□ underestimate　□ underestimated　□ underground
□ underhanded　□ underlie　□ undermine　□ underplay　□ underrate

underrepresented [ˌʌndəˌreprɪˈzentɪd]	*adj.* 未被充分代表的 (inadequately represented) 例 Despite the growing prominence of Hispanic actors in the American theater, many Hispanic experts feel that the Spanish-speaking population is *underrepresented* on the stage.
underscore [ˌʌndərˈskɔːr]	*v.* 在…下面画线 (to draw a line under)；强调 (to make evident) 记 组合词：under (在…下面) + score (画线) → 在…下面画线
understate [ˌʌndərˈsteɪt]	*v.* 保守地说，轻描淡写地说 (to state with less completeness or truth than seems warranted by the facts) 记 联想记忆：under (在…下面) + state (说话) → 在衣服下面说 → 保守地说 例 Because of its inclination to *understate*, most Indian art is reminiscent of Japanese art, where symbols have been minimized and meaning has been conveyed by the merest suggestion.
understated [ˌʌndərˈsteɪtɪd]	*adj.* 轻描淡写的，低调的 (avoiding obvious emphasis or embellishment) 同 unostentatious, unpretentious
undertake [ˌʌndərˈteɪk]	*v.* 承担 (to take upon oneself)；担保，保证 (to guarantee, promise) 记 联想记忆：under (在…下面) + take (拿) → 在下面拿 → 承担
underutilized [ˌʌndərˈjuːtəlaɪzd]	*adj.* 未充分利用的 记 联想记忆：under (不足，少于) + utilize (利用) + d → 未充分利用的
underwater [ˌʌndərˈwɔːtər]	*adj.* 在水下的，在水中的 (lying or growing below the surface of the water)
undeserving [ˌʌndɪˈzɜːrvɪŋ]	*adj.* 不值得的 (not deserving to have or receive sth.) 同 unworthy
undesirable [ˌʌndɪˈzaɪərəbl]	*adj.* 不受欢迎的，讨厌的 (not desirable; unwanted) 记 联想记忆：un (不) + desirable (可取的) → 不可取的 → 不受欢迎的
undifferentiated [ˌʌndɪfəˈrenʃieɪtɪd]	*adj.* 无差别的，一致的 同 uniform
undirected [ˌʌndaɪˈrektɪd]	*adj.* 未受指导的 (not planned or guided) 记 联想记忆：un (不) + direct (指导) + ed → 未受指导的
undiscovered [ˌʌndɪsˈkʌvərd]	*adj.* 未被发现的 (not noticed or known about) 同 unexplored
undistorted [ˌʌndɪˈstɔːrtɪd]	*adj.* 未失真的
undisturbed [ˌʌndɪˈstɜːrbd]	*adj.* 未受干扰的，安静的 (not disturbed; calm) 同 unmolested
unearth [ʌnˈɜːrθ]	*v.* 挖出 (to dig up out of the earth; exhume)；发现 (to bring to light) 记 联想记忆：un (打开) + earth (地) → 挖出
unecological [ˌʌniːkəˈlɑːdʒɪkl]	*adj.* 非生态的

21

unedited [ʌnˈedɪtɪd]	*adj.* 未编辑的（not yet edited）
unencumbered [ˌʌnɪnˈkʌmbərd]	*adj.* 无阻碍的（free of encumbrance） 例 Isozaki's love for detail is apparent everywhere in the new museum, but fortunately the details are subordinated to the building's larger formal composition, which is *unencumbered* by the busyness of much recent architecture.
unenlightened [ˌʌnɪnˈlaɪtnd]	*adj.* 愚昧无知的（without knowledge or understanding）；不文明的（having wrong beliefs because of lack of knowledge） 记 联想记忆：un(不) + enlightened(有知识的，开明的) → 愚昧无知的
unequivocal [ˌʌnɪˈkwɪvəkl]	*adj.* 毫无疑问的（leaving no doubt; unquestionable） 例 Dr. Smith cautioned that the data so far are not sufficiently *unequivocal* to warrant dogmatic assertions by either side in the debate.
unerringly [ʌnˈɜːrɪŋlɪ]	*adv.* 无过失地
uneven [ʌnˈiːvn]	*adj.* 不平坦的（not even）；不一致的（not uniform）；不对等的（unequal） 例 All critics have agreed that the opera's score is *uneven*, but, curiously, no two critics have agreed which passages to praise and which to damn.
uneventful [ˌʌnɪˈventfl]	*adj.* 平凡的；平安无事的（marked by no noteworthy or untoward incidents） 例 The biographer of Tennyson is confronted with the problem, rarely solved, of how to make a basically *uneventful* life interesting.
unexceptionable [ˌʌnɪkˈsepʃənəbl]	*adj.* 无可挑剔的（incapable of being disapproved of） 记 联想记忆：un(不) + exceptionable(可反对的) → 无可挑剔的 例 Although some of her fellow scientists decried the unorthodox laboratory methodology that others found innovative, unanimous praise greeted her experimental results: at once pioneering and *unexceptionable*.
unfailing [ʌnˈfeɪlɪŋ]	*adj.* 无尽的，无穷的（everlasting; inexhaustible）
unfeigned [ʌnˈfeɪnd]	*adj.* 真实的，真诚的（genuine） 记 联想记忆：un(不) + feigned(假的) → 真实的
unfertilized [ʌnˈfɜːrtəlaɪzd]	*adj.* 未施肥的；未受精的 同 unimpregnated
unfettered [ʌnˈfetərd]	*adj.* 自由的，不受约束的（free, unrestrained） 例 Liberty is not easy, but far better to be an *unfettered* fox, hungry and threatened on its hill, than a well-fed canary, safe and secure in its cage.
unfounded [ʌnˈfaʊndɪd]	*adj.* 无事实根据的（groundless; unwarranted） 记 联想记忆：un(不) + founded(有根据的) → 无事实根据的 例 The true historian finds the facts about Marlowe and Shakespeare far more interesting than people's *unfounded* conjectures.

ungainly [ʌnˈgeɪnli]	*adj.* 笨拙的 (lacking in smooth or dexterity; clumsy) 记 联想记忆：un(不) + gainly(优雅的) → 笨拙的
ungrateful [ʌnˈgreɪtfl]	*adj.* 不感激的，不领情的 (showing no gratitude)
unheralded [ʌnˈherəldɪd]	*adj.* 未预先通知的，未预先警告过的 (not previously mentioned; happening without any warning) 例 For many years an *unheralded* researcher, Barbara McClintock gained international renown when she won the Nobel Prize in Physiology and Medicine.
unidimensional [ˌjuːnɪdaɪˈmenʃənl]	*adj.* 一维的 (one-dimensional) 记 词根记忆：uni(单一) + dimensional(空间的) → 一维的
uniform [ˈjuːnɪfɔːrm]	*n.* 制服 *adj.* 相同的，一致的 (consistent) 记 词根记忆：uni(单一) + form(形式) → 一致的 例 Not all the indicators necessary to convey the effect of depth in a picture work simultaneously; the picture's illusion of *uniform* three-dimensional appearance must therefore result from the viewer's integration of various indicators perceived successively.
unify [ˈjuːnɪfaɪ]	*v.* 统一，使成一体；使相同 (to make all the same) 记 词根记忆：uni(单一) + fy(动词后缀) → 统一 例 The text brims with details, but there are no overarching theses to *unify* them.
unimpassioned [ˌʌnɪmˈpæʃnd]	*adj.* 没有激情的 (without passion or zeal) 记 联想记忆：un(不) + impassioned(充满激情的) → 没有激情的
unimpeachable [ˌʌnɪmˈpiːtʃəbl]	*adj.* 无可指责的，无可怀疑的 (irreproachable; blameless) 记 联想记忆：un(不) + impeachable(可指责的) → 无可指责的
unimpressed [ˌʌnɪmˈprest]	*adj.* 没有印象的
uninitiated [ˌʌnɪˈnɪʃieɪtɪd]	*adj.* 外行的，缺乏经验的 (not knowledgeable or skilled; inexperienced) 记 联想记忆：un(不) + initiate(传授) + d → 没有被传授过相关知识的 → 外行的 例 The systems analyst hesitated to talk to strangers about her highly specialized work, fearing it was too esoteric for people *uninitiated* in the computer field to understand.
uninspired [ˌʌnɪnˈspaɪərd]	*adj.* 无灵感的，枯燥的 (having no intellectual, emotional, or spiritual excitement; dull) 例 Although Simpson was ingenious at contriving to appear innovative and spontaneous, beneath the ruse he remained *uninspired* and rigid in his approach to problem-solving.
unintelligible [ˌʌnɪnˈtelɪdʒəbl]	*adj.* 不可理解的，难懂的 (being such that understanding or comprehension is difficult or impossible; incomprehensible)

□ ungainly   □ ungrateful   □ unheralded   □ unidimensional   □ uniform   □ unify
□ unimpassioned □ unimpeachable   □ unimpressed   □ uninitiated   □ uninspired   □ unintelligible

239

unique [juˈniːk]	*adj.* 独一无二的，独特的（being the only one of this type）；无与伦比的（being without a like or equal） 记 词根记忆：uni(单一) + que → 独一无二的，独特的 例 The semantic opacity of ancient documents is not *unique*; even in our own time, many documents are difficult to decipher. 同 singular, sole
universal [ˌjuːnɪˈvɜːrsl]	*adj.* 全体的（including or covering all or a whole collectively or distributively without limit or exception）；普遍的（present or occurring every-where） 例 If Amelia Earhart's acceptance was by no means *universal*, her fame was unusually widespread and her popularity long-lived. 同 cosmic, cosmopolitan, omnipresent, ubiquitous
universality [ˌjuːnɪvɜːrˈsæləti]	*n.* 普遍性（the quality or state of being universal）；广泛性（universal comprehensiveness in range）
unjustifiable [ʌnˈdʒʌstɪfaɪəbl]	*adj.* 不合道理的（incapable of being justified or explained） 例 The commission of inquiry censured the senator for his lavish expenditure of public funds, which they found to be *unjustifiable*.
unleash [ʌnˈliːʃ]	*v.* 发泄，释放（to set feelings and forces free from control） 记 联想记忆：un(不) + leash(控制，约束) → 不去控制 → 发泄
unlikely [ʌnˈlaɪkli]	*adj.* 不太可能的（not likely）；没有希望的（unpromising） 同 improbable, unbelievable, unconvincing
unliterary [ʌnˈlɪtəreri]	*adj.* 不矫揉造作的，不咬文嚼字的 记 和 nonliterary(*adj.* 不咬文嚼字的)一起记
unmatched [ˌʌnˈmætʃt]	*adj.* 无可匹敌的（cannot be matched） 同 matchless, nonpareil, unmatchable, unrivaled
unmitigated [ʌnˈmɪtɪgeɪtɪd]	*adj.* 未缓和的，未减轻的（not lessened or excused in any way） 记 词根记忆：un(不) + mitigate(缓和的) + d → 未缓和的
unmoved [ˌʌnˈmuːvd]	*adj.* 无动于衷的，冷漠的（not affected by feelings of pity, sympathy） 记 联想记忆：un(不) + moved(感动的) → 无动于衷的
unnoteworthy [ˌʌnˈnoʊtwɜːrði]	*adj.* 不显著的，不值得注意的
unobstructed [ˌʌnəbˈstrʌktɪd]	*adj.* 没有阻碍的（free from obstructions）
unobtrusive [ˌʌnəbˈtruːsɪv]	*adj.* 不引人注目的（not very noticeable or easily seen） 记 联想记忆：un(不) + obtrusive(突出的) → 不引人注目的
unpack [ˌʌnˈpæk]	*v.* 打开包裹(或行李)，卸货（to take packed things out of）
unpalatable [ʌnˈpælətəbl]	*adj.* 味道差的，不好吃的（not palatable; unpleasant to taste）；令人不快的（unpleasant and difficult for the mind to accept） 记 联想记忆：un(不) + palatable(合意的) → 令人不快的

□ unique	□ universal	□ universality	□ unjustifiable	□ unleash	□ unlikely
□ unliterary	□ unmatched	□ unmitigated	□ unmoved	□ unnoteworthy	□ unobstructed
□ unobtrusive	□ unpack	□ unpalatable			

	例 Animals that have tasted *unpalatable* plants tend to recognize them afterward on the basis of their most conspicuous features, such as their flowers.
unparalleled [ʌnˈpærəleld]	*adj.* 无比的，空前的（having no parallel or equal） 同 unique, unequaled
unprecedented [ʌnˈpresidentid]	*adj.* 前所未有的（never having happened before） 记 联想记忆：un(不) + precedent(先例) + ed → 没有先例的 → 前所未有的
unpredictable [ˌʌnprɪˈdɪktəbl]	*adj.* 不可预知的
unpremeditated [ˌʌnpriːˈmedɪteɪtɪd]	*adj.* 无预谋的，非故意的 记 联想记忆：un(不) + premeditated(预谋的) → 无预谋的
unpretentious [ˌʌnprɪˈtenʃəs]	*adj.* 不炫耀的（not attempting to seem special, important or wealthy） 记 联想记忆：un(不) + pretentious(自命不凡的) → 不炫耀的
unpromising [ʌnˈprɑːmɪsɪŋ]	*adj.* 无前途的，没有希望的（not promising） 记 不要和 uncompromising(*adj.* 不妥协的)相混
unproven [ʌnˈpruːvn]	*adj.* 未经证实的（not proved or tested）
unqualified [ˌʌnˈkwɑːlɪfaɪd]	*adj.* 无资格的，不合格的（not having suitable qualifications）；无限制的，绝对的（not limited）
unquestionable [ʌnˈkwestʃənəbl]	*adj.* 毫无疑问的，无懈可击的（not questionable） 同 authentic, veritable
unquestioning [ʌnˈkwestʃənɪŋ]	*adj.* 无异议的，不犹豫的（not questioning） 同 implicit
unreasonable [ʌnˈriːznəbl]	*adj.* 不讲道理的（not governed by or acting according to reason）；非理智的，过分的（exceeding the bounds of reason or moderation） 例 Although Tom was aware that it would be impolitic to display annoyance publicly at the sales conference, he could not hide his irritation with the client's *unreasonable* demands.
unrecognized [ʌnˈrekəgnaɪzd]	*adj.* 未被承认的，未被认出的
unregulated [ˌʌnˈregjuleɪtɪd]	*adj.* 未受控制的，未受约束的（not controlled by a government or law） 记 联想记忆：un(不) + regulat(e)(管制) + ed → 未受控制的，未受约束的
unreliable [ˌʌnrɪˈlaɪəbl]	*adj.* 不可靠的（that cannot be trusted or depended on） 例 The testimony of eyewitnesses is notoriously *unreliable*; emotion and excitement all too often cause our minds to distort what we see.

21

unremitting [ˌʌnrɪˈmɪtɪŋ]	*adj.* 不间断的，持续的（never stopping） **记** 联想记忆：un（不）+ remitting（间断的）→ 不间断的，持续的 **例** In the nineteenth century, novelists and unsympathetic travelers portrayed the American West as a land of *unremitting* adversity, whereas promoters and idealists created a compelling image of a land of infinite promise.
unrepresentative [ˌʌnˌreprɪˈzentətɪv]	*adj.* 没有代表性的（not exemplifying a class） **例** It would be misleading to use a published play to generalize about fifteenth-century drama: the very fact of publication should serve as a warning of the play's *unrepresentative* character.

The man who has made up his mind to win will never say "impossible".
凡是决心取得胜利的人是从来不说"不可能的"。
——法国皇帝 拿破仑（Bonaparte Napoleon, French emperor）

unreserved [ˌʌnrɪˈzɜːrvd]	*adj.* 无限制的(without limited)；未被预订的(not reserved) 记 联想记忆：un(不) + reserved(预订的) → 未被预订的
unrestricted [ˌʌnrɪˈstrɪktɪd]	*adj.* 无限制的，自由的(not limited by anyone or anything)
unscathed [ʌnˈskeɪðd]	*adj.* 未受损伤的，未受伤害的(wholly unharmed) 记 联想记忆：un(不) + scathed(损伤的) → 未受损伤的
unscented [ʌnˈsentɪd]	*adj.* 无气味的(without scent) 记 联想记忆：un(不) + scented(有气味的) → 无气味的
unscrupulous [ʌnˈskruːpjələs]	*adj.* 肆无忌惮的(unprincipled) 记 联想记忆：un(不) + scrupulous(小心的) → 肆无忌惮的 例 The value of Davis' sociological research is compromised by his *unscrupulous* tendency to use materials selectively in order to substantiate his own claims, while disregarding information that points to other possible conclusions.
unseemly [ʌnˈsiːmli]	*adj.* 不适宜的，不得体的(not according with established standards of good form or taste) 记 联想记忆：un(不) + seemly(适宜的) → 不适宜的
unskilled [ˌʌnˈskɪld]	*adj.* 不熟练的(lacking skill or technical training)；无需技能的(not requiring skill)
unsound [ˌʌnˈsaʊnd]	*adj.* 不健康的，不健全的(not healthy or whole)；不结实的，不坚固的(not firmly made, placed, or fixed)；无根据的(not valid or true) 记 联想记忆：un(不) + sound(健康的) → 不健康的
unspoiled [ˌʌnˈspɔɪld]	*adj.* 未损坏的，未宠坏的 记 联想记忆：un(不) + spoil(损坏) + ed → 未损坏的
unspotted [ˌʌnˈspɑːtɪd]	*adj.* 清白的，无污点的(without spot; flawless) 记 联想记忆：un(不) + spot(污点) + ted → 无污点的
unstable [ʌnˈsteɪbl]	*adj.* 不稳定的(not stable) 记 联想记忆：un(不) + stable(稳定的) → 不稳定的

22

unstinting [ʌnˈstɪntɪŋ]	*adj.* 慷慨的，大方的（very generous） 记 联想记忆：un(不) + stint(吝惜，限制) + ing → 慷慨的
unsubstantiated [ˌʌnsəbˈstænʃieɪtɪd]	*adj.* 未经证实的，无事实根据的（not proved to be true by evidence） 同 uncorroborated
unsure [ˌʌnˈʃʊr]	*adj.* 缺乏自信的（having little self-confidence）；不确定的（not having certain knowledge）
unsurpassed [ˌʌnsərˈpæst]	*adj.* 未被超越的（unrivalled） 同 unexceeded, unexcelled
unsuspecting [ˌʌnsəˈspektɪŋ]	*adj.* 不怀疑的，无猜疑的，可信任的（feeling no suspicion; trusting）
untainted [ʌnˈteɪntɪd]	*adj.* 无污点的（not damaged or spoiled） 同 stainless, unstained, unsullied, untarnished
untalented [ʌnˈtæləntɪd]	*adj.* 没有天赋的（without a natural ability to do sth. well）
untamed [ˌʌnˈteɪmd]	*adj.* 未驯服的（not controlled by anyone）
untapped [ˌʌnˈtæpt]	*adj.* 未开发的，未利用的（not yet put to use） 记 来自 tap(*v.* 开发，利用)
untarnished [ˌʌnˈtɑːrnɪʃt]	*adj.* 未失去光泽的（unblemished） 同 stainless, unstained, unsullied, untained
untasted [ˌʌnˈteɪstɪd]	*adj.* 未尝过的，未体验过的 例 Either the Polynesian banquets at Waikiki are *untasted*, or the one I visited was a poor example.
untenable [ʌnˈtenəbl]	*adj.* 难以防守的（not able to be defended）；不能租赁的（not able to be occupied） 例 Upon realizing that his position was *untenable*, the general ordered his men to retreat to a neighboring hill.
untimely [ʌnˈtaɪmli]	*adj.* 过早的（occurring or done before the due, natural, or proper time）；不合时宜的（inopportune, unseasonable） 记 联想记忆：un(不) + timely(及时的，适时的) → 不合时宜的
untold [ˌʌnˈtoʊld]	*adj.* 无数的，数不清的（too great or numerous to count）
untouched [ʌnˈtʌtʃt]	*adj.* 未触动过的，未改变的（not changed in any way） 同 uninfluenced, unswayed
untreated [ˌʌnˈtriːtɪd]	*adj.* 未治疗的（not receiving medical treatment）；未经处理的（in a natural state）
untrustworthy [ʌnˈtrʌstwɜːrði]	*adj.* 不能信赖的，靠不住的（not capable of being trusted or depended on） 记 和 untrusty(*adj.* 不可靠的)一起记

untutored [ˌʌnˈtuːtərd]	*adj.* 未受教育的(having no formal learning or training)
unwarranted [ʌnˈwɑːrəntɪd]	*adj.* 没有根据的(unwelcome and done without good reason) 记 联想记忆：un(不) + warranted(有根据的) → 没有根据的
unwieldy [ʌnˈwiːldi]	*adj.* 难控制的；笨重的(not easily managed or used; cumbersome) 记 联想记忆：un(不) + wieldy(支配的，控制的) → 不可控制的 → 难控制的
unwitting [ʌnˈwɪtɪŋ]	*adj.* 无意的，不知不觉的(not intended; inadvertent; unaware) 记 联想记忆：un(不) + witting(知道的，有意的) → 无意的，不知不觉的
unwonted [ʌnˈwoʊntɪd]	*adj.* 不寻常的，不习惯的(unusual; unaccustomed)
unworldly [ʌnˈwɜːrldli]	*adj.* 非世俗的(not swayed by mundane considerations)；精神上的(spiritual) 记 联想记忆：un(不) + world(世界，尘世) + ly → 非世俗的 例 Without seeming *unworldly*, William James appeared wholly removed from the commonplaces of society, the conventionality of academe.
unyielding [ʌnˈjiːldɪŋ]	*adj.* 坚定的，不屈的(characterized by firmness or obduracy)；坚硬的，不能弯曲的(characterized by lack of softness or flexibility)
uphold [ʌpˈhoʊld]	*v.* 维护，支持(to give support to) 记 联想记忆：up(向上) + hold(举) → 举起来 → 支持
upscale [ˌʌpˈskeɪl]	*v.* 升高级，升档(to raise to a higher level)
upstage [ˌʌpˈsteɪdʒ]	*adj.* 高傲的(haughty) 记 联想记忆：up(向上) + stage(舞台) → 在舞台上 → 高高在上的 → 高傲的
upstart [ˈʌpstɑːrt]	*n.* 突然升官的人，暴发户(one that has risen suddenly; parvenu) 记 联想记忆：up(向上) + start(开始) → 开始向上 → 暴发户
urbane [ɜːrˈbeɪn]	*adj.* 温文尔雅的(notably polite or polished in manner) 同 refined, svelte
urbanize [ˈɜːrbənaɪz]	*v.* 使都市化，使文雅(to cause to take on urban characteristics)
urgency [ˈɜːrdʒənsi]	*n.* 紧急(的事)(the quality or state of being urgent) 同 importunity, urging
usable [ˈjuːzəbl]	*adj.* 可用的(capable of being used)；好用的(convenient and practicable for use)
utilitarian [ˌjuːtɪlɪˈteriən]	*adj.* 功利的，实利的(exhibiting or preferring mere utility)
utility [juːˈtɪləti]	*n.* 实用(fitness for some purpose or worth to some end)；有用(something useful or designed for use) 记 词根记忆：util(使用) + ity → 实用；有用

22

□ untutored	□ unwarranted	□ unwieldy	□ unwitting	□ unwonted	□ unworldly
□ unyielding	□ uphold	□ upscale	□ upstage	□ upstart	□ urbane
□ urbanize	□ urgency	□ usable	□ utilitarian	□ utility	

245

例 We look with pride at our new bridges and dams, for they are works of art as well as of *utility*.

utilize [ˈjuːtəlaɪz]	*v.* 利用，使用(to make use of) 记 词根记忆：ut(用) + ilize → 利用 utilize 例 The failure of many psychotherapists to *utilize* the results of pioneering research could be due in part to the specialized nature of such findings: even momentous findings may not be useful. 同 apply, exercise, exploit, handle
utopian [juːˈtoupiən]	*adj.* 乌托邦的，空想的(impossibly ideal; visionary) 例 The impracticability of such *utopian* notions is reflected by the quick disintegration of the idealistic community at Brooke Farm.
vacillate [ˈvæsəleɪt]	*v.* 游移不定，踌躇(to waver in mind, will or feeling) 记 词根记忆：vacill(摇摆) + ate → 游移不定
vagueness [ˈveɪɡnəs]	*n.* 含糊(unclearness by virtue of being vague) 例 Wincing at the *vagueness* of the interviewer's wording, the scholar was as sensitive to words and phrases as a sectarian is to creeds.
vainglorious [ˌveɪnˈɡlɔːriəs]	*adj.* 自负的(marked by vainglory; boastful)
vainglory [ˌveɪnˈɡlɔːri]	*n.* 自负(excessive or ostentatious pride especially in one's achievements)；虚荣(vanity) 同 egoism, egotism, swellheadedness
valiant [ˈvæliənt]	*adj.* 勇敢的，英勇的(courageous) 同 valorous
validate [ˈvælɪdeɪt]	*v.* 使生效(to make legally valid) 记 联想记忆：valid(有效) + ate → 使生效
valorous [ˈvælərəs]	*adj.* 勇敢的(brave) 记 联想记忆：val(强大) + orous → 勇敢使人强大 → 勇敢的
valve [vælv]	*n.* 活门，阀门
vanity [ˈvænəti]	*n.* 虚荣，自负(inflated pride in oneself; conceit) 记 词根记忆：van(空) + ity → 空虚 → 虚荣 例 It is ironic that a critic of such overwhelming *vanity* now suffers from a measure of the oblivion to which he was forever consigning others; in the end, all his self-adulation has only worked against him.
variability [ˌveriəˈbɪləti]	*n.* 变化性(the quality, state, or degree of being variable or changeable) 同 unevenness, variableness, variance
variety [vəˈraɪəti]	*n.* 多样性(the quality or state of having different forms or types)；种类(assortment)；变种(subspecies) 记 词根记忆：vari(改变) + ety → 多样性

	例 The theory of cosmic evolution states that the universe, having begun in a state of simplicity and homogeneity, has differentiated into great *variety*.
	同 diversity, multeity, multiformity, multiplicity
vaulted ['vɔːltɪd]	*adj.* 拱形的
veer [vɪr]	*v.* 转向，改变(话题等)(to change direction or course)
	同 curve, sheer, slew, slue, swerve
vehement ['viːəmənt]	*adj.* 猛烈的，热烈的(marked by forceful energy)
	同 exquisite, fierce, furious, intense, violent
vehicle ['viːəkl]	*n.* 交通工具；传播媒介(an agent of transmission)
	记 词根记忆：veh(带来) + icle(东西) → 带人的东西 → 交通工具
veil [veɪl]	*n.* 面纱；遮蔽物 *v.* 以面纱掩盖(to cover, obscure, or conceal with a veil)
venal ['viːnl]	*adj.* 腐败的，贪赃枉法的(characterized by or associated with corrupt bribery)
venerable ['venərəbl]	*adj.* 值得尊敬的，庄严的(deserving to be venerated)
	同 august, revered
venerate ['venəreɪt]	*v.* 崇敬，敬仰(to regard with reverential respect)
	记 词根记忆：vener(尊敬) + ate → 崇敬
	同 adore, revere, worship
venial ['viːniəl]	*adj.* (错误等)轻微的，可原谅的(forgivable; pardonable)
	记 联想记忆：ven(=venus 维纳斯) + ial → 出于爱而原谅的 → 可原谅的
	例 In view of the fact that there are mitigating circumstances, we must consider this a *venial* offense.
	同 excusable, remittable
venomous ['venəməs]	*adj.* 有毒的(full of venom; poisonous)
	同 deadly, vicious, virulent
vent [vent]	*v.* 发泄(感情，尤指愤怒)(to discharge; expel)；开孔(to provide with a vent) *n.* 孔，口(an opening)
venture ['ventʃər]	*v.* 敢于(to expose to hazard)；冒险(to undertake the risks and dangers of) *n.* 冒险(an undertaking involving chance, risk, or danger)
	记 发音记忆："玩车" → 玩车一族追求的就是冒险 → 冒险
	同 adventure
venturesome ['ventʃərsəm]	*adj.* 好冒险的(inclined to court or incur risk or danger)；(行为)冒险的(involving risk)
veracious [vəˈreɪʃəs]	*adj.* 诚实的，说真话的(truthful; honest)
	例 I can vouch for his honesty, because I have always found him *veracious* and carefully observant of the truth.
	同 faithful, veridical

22

veracity [vəˈræsəti]	n. 真实 (devotion to the truth); 诚实 (truthfulness)
	记 词根记忆: ver(真实的) + acity → 真实
	例 Trying to prove Hill a liar, Senator Specter repeatedly questioned her *veracity*.
verbose [vɜːrˈboʊs]	adj. 冗长的, 啰嗦的 (containing more words than necessary)
	记 词根记忆: verb(词语) + ose(多…的) → 多词的 → 冗长的
	例 He is much too *verbose* in his writings: he writes a page when a sentence should suffice.
	同 prolix, redundant, wordy
verbosity [vɜːrˈbɑːsəti]	n. 冗长 (an expressive style that uses excessive words)
	例 Her *verbosity* is always a source of irritation: she never uses a single word when she can substitute a long clause or phrase in its place.
verdant [ˈvɜːrdnt]	adj. 葱郁的, 翠绿的 (green in tint or color)
	记 词根记忆: verd(绿色) + ant → 翠绿的
verifiable [ˈverɪfaɪəbl]	adj. 能作证的 (capable of being verified)
	同 confirmable, falsifiable
verification [ˌverɪfɪˈkeɪʃn]	n. 确认, 查证 (the act or process of verifying)
verified [ˈverɪfaɪd]	adj. 已查清的, 已证实的
	例 A hypothesis must not only account for what we already know, but it must also be *verified* by continued observation.
verify [ˈverɪfaɪ]	v. 证明, 证实 (to establish the accuracy of)
	记 词根记忆: ver(真实的) + ify(使…) → 使…真实 → 证明, 证实
	同 confirm, corroborate, justify, substantiate, validate
verse [vɜːrs]	n. 诗歌 (a line of metrical writing, poems)
	记 词根记忆: vers(转) + e → 诗歌的音节百转千回 → 诗歌
vertebrate [ˈvɜːrtɪbrət]	n./adj. 脊椎动物(的) (an animal that has a spine)
	记 来自 vertebra(n. 脊椎骨)
	例 Just as the authors' book on eels is often a key text for courses in marine *vertebrate* zoology, their ideas on animal development and phylogeny inform teaching in this area.
vessel [ˈvesl]	n. 血管; 容器 (a container); 船只 (a watercraft)
	记 注意不要和 vassal(n. 陪臣, 诸侯)相混
vestige [ˈvestɪdʒ]	n. 痕迹, 遗迹 (the very small slight remains of sth.)
	同 relic, trace
vestigial [veˈstɪdʒiəl]	adj. 退化的 (degraded)
	同 rudimentary
vex [veks]	v. 使烦恼, 使恼怒 (to bring agitation to)
	同 annoy, bother, fret, irk
vexation [vekˈseɪʃn]	n. 恼怒, 苦恼 (the act of harassing; irritation)
	记 联想记忆: vex(烦恼, 恼怒) + ation → 恼怒, 苦恼

vessel

viable [ˈvaɪəbl]	*adj.* 切实可行的(capable of working, functioning, or developing adequately); 能活下去的(capable of living) 记 词根记忆：via(道路) + able → 有路可走 → 切实可行的 例 It is true that the seeds of some plants have germinated after two hundred years of dormancy, but reports that *viable* seeds have been found in ancient tombs such as the pyramids are entirely unfounded.
vibrant [ˈvaɪbrənt]	*adj.* 振动的；响亮的；明快的(bright)；充满生气的，精力充沛的(pulsating with life) 记 词根记忆：vibr(振动) + ant → 振动的 例 The attorney's *vibrant* voice and outstanding sense of timing were as useful to him as his prodigious preparation, attention to detail, and mastery of the law.
vicious [ˈvɪʃəs]	*adj.* 邪恶的，堕落的(having the nature or quality of vice or immorality)；恶意的，恶毒的(spiteful; malicious)；凶猛的，危险的(dangerously aggressive) 记 联想记忆：vice(邪恶) + ious → 邪恶的；恶毒的
vicissitude [vɪˈsɪsɪtuːd]	*n.* 变迁，兴衰(natural change or mutation visible in nature or in human affairs)
vigilance [ˈvɪdʒɪləns]	*n.* 警惕，警觉(the quality or state of being vigilant) 同 alertness, watchfulness
vigilant [ˈvɪdʒɪlənt]	*adj.* 机警的，警惕的(alertly watchful to avoid danger)
vigorous [ˈvɪɡərəs]	*adj.* 精力充沛的，有力的(strong, healthy, and full of energy) 记 联想记忆：vigor(活力) + ous → 精力充沛的 例 One of Detroit's great success stories tells of Lee Lacocca's revitalization of the moribund Chrysler Corporation, turning it into a *vigorous* competitor. 同 energetic, lusty, strenuous
vilify [ˈvɪlɪfaɪ]	*v.* 诽谤，中伤(to lower in estimation or importance)
vindicate [ˈvɪndɪkeɪt]	*v.* 辩白(to free from allegation or blame)；证明…正确(to provide justification or defense for) 记 词根记忆：vin(=force 力量) + dic(说) + ate → 使有力地说 → 证明…正确
vindictive [vɪnˈdɪktɪv]	*adj.* 报复的(vengeful) 例 The Muses are *vindictive* deities: they avenge themselves without mercy on those who weary of their charms.
violate [ˈvaɪəleɪt]	*v.* 违反，侵犯(to disregard or act against) 记 发音记忆："why late" → 违反制度迟到了 → 违反，侵犯 例 Scientists who are on the cutting edge of research must often *violate* common sense and make seemingly absurd assumptions because existing theories simply do not explain newly observed phenomena. 同 breach, contravene, infract, infringe, transgress

□ viable	□ vibrant	□ vicious	□ vicissitude	□ vigilance	□ vigilant
□ vigorous	□ vilify	□ vindicate	□ vindictive	□ violate	

viral	*adj.* 病毒性的（caused by a virus）
[ˈvaɪrəl]	记 来自 virus（*n.* 病毒）
virtue	*n.* 美德（conformity to a standard of right）；优点（merit）；潜能（potency）
[ˈvɜːrtʃuː]	例 People should not be praised for their *virtue* if they lack the energy to be wicked; in such cases, goodness is merely the effect of indolence.
	同 morality, probity, rectitude, righteousness
virtuoso	*n.* 艺术大师（a person who has great skill at some endeavor）
[ˌvɜːrtʃuˈoʊsoʊ]	例 The sage, by definition, possesses wisdom; the *virtuoso*, by definition, possesses expertise.
virtuous	*adj.* 有美德的（showing virtue）
[ˈvɜːrtʃuəs]	记 来自 virtue（*n.* 美德）
virulence	*n.* 恶意，毒性（the quality or state of being virulent）
[ˈvɪrələns]	
viscous	*adj.* 黏滞的，黏性的，黏的（glutinous）
[ˈvɪskəs]	
visible	*adj.* 可见的，看得见的（capable of being seen）；能注意到的（exposed to view）；明显的，可察觉到的（capable of being discovered or perceived）
[ˈvɪzəbl]	记 词根记忆：vis（看）+ ible（可…的）→ 看得见的；明显的
visionary	*adj.* 有远见的；幻想的 *n.* 空想家（one who is given to impractical or speculative ideas）
[ˈvɪʒəneri]	例 Although the architect's concept at first sounded too *visionary* to be practicable, his careful analysis of every aspect of the project convinced the panel that the proposed building was indeed, structurally feasible.
	同 dreamy, idealistic, utopian
vital	*adj.* 极其重要的；充满活力的（full of life and force）
[ˈvaɪtl]	记 词根记忆：vit（生命）+ al → 事关生命的 → 极其重要的
	例 The president was noncommittal about farm subsidies, nor did he say much about the even more *vital* topic of unemployment.
vitality	*n.* 活力，精力（capacity to live and develop）；生命力（power of enduring）
[vaɪˈtæləti]	
vitiate	*v.* 削弱，损害（to make faulty or defective; impair）
[ˈvɪʃieɪt]	记 联想记忆：viti（=vice 恶的）+ ate → 损害
vitriolic	*adj.* 刻薄的（virulent of feeling or of speech）
[ˌvɪtriˈɑːlɪk]	记 词根记忆：vitri（玻璃，引申为"刻薄"）+ olic → 刻薄的
	例 Although a few delegates gave the opposition's suggestions a *vitriolic* response, most greeted the statement of a counterposition with civility.

visible

invisible

vivid	*adj.* 鲜艳的；生动的；逼真的
[ˈvɪvɪd]	记 词根记忆：viv(生命) + id → 有生命力的 → 生动的
	例 She writes across generational lines, making the past so *vivid* that our belief that the present is the true locus of experience is undermined.
vogue	*n.* 时尚，流行(popular acceptation or favor)
[voʊg]	
volatile	*adj.* 反复无常的(subject to rapid or unexpected change)；易挥发的 (readily vaporizable)
[ˈvɑːlətl]	记 词根记忆：volat(飞) + ile → 飞走的 → 易挥发的
	例 Despite the mixture's *volatile* nature, we found that by lowering its temperature in the laboratory we could dramatically reduce its tendency to vaporize.
	同 capricious, fickle, inconstant, mercurial
volcanic	*adj.* 火山的(of, relating to, or produced by a volcano)
[vɑːlˈkænɪk]	
voluble	*adj.* 健谈的(talkative)；易旋转的(rotating)
[ˈvɑːljəbl]	
voluminous	*adj.* 长篇的(filling or capable of filling a large volume or several volumes)；大量的(having or marked by great volume or bulk)
[vəˈluːmɪnəs]	记 联想记忆：volum(=volume 容量) + in + ous → 大量的
voluntary	*adj.* 自愿的，志愿的(of, relating to, subject to, or regulated by the will)
[ˈvɑːlənteri]	记 词根记忆：volunt(自动) + ary(…的) → 自己选择的 → 自愿的
voluptuous	*adj.* 撩人的(suggesting sensual pleasure)；沉溺酒色的(abandoned to enjoyments of luxury, pleasure, or sensual gratification)
[vəˈlʌptʃuəs]	记 词根记忆：volupt(享乐，快感) + uous → 沉溺酒色的
voyeur	*n.* 窥淫癖者(one who habitually seeks sexual stimulation by visual means)
[vwaɪˈɜːr]	
vulgar	*adj.* 无教养的，庸俗的(morally crude, undeveloped)
[ˈvʌlgər]	记 词根记忆：vulg(庸俗) + ar → 庸俗的
vulnerable	*adj.* 易受伤的，脆弱的(capable of being physically wounded; assailable)
[ˈvʌlnərəbl]	记 词根记忆：vulner(伤) + able → 总是受伤 → 易受伤的
walrus	*n.* 海象(a large gregarious marine mammal)
[ˈwɔːlrəs]	
wanderlust	*n.* 漫游癖，旅游癖(strong longing for or impulse toward wandering)
[ˈwɑːndərlʌst]	记 组合词：wander(漫游) + lust(欲望) → 漫游癖
	例 For many young people during the Roaring Twenties, a disgust with the excesses of American culture combined with a *wanderlust* to provoke an exodus abroad.
wane	*v.* 减少，衰落(to decrease in size, extent, or degree; dwindle)
[weɪn]	记 联想记忆：天鹅(swan)的数量在减少(wane)
	同 abate, ebb, shrink, slacken, subside

22

□ vivid	□ vogue	□ volatile	□ volcanic	□ voluble	□ voluminous
□ voluntary	□ voluptuous	□ voyeur	□ vulgar	□ vulnerable	□ walrus
□ wanderlust	□ wane				

warp	*v.* 弯曲，变歪（to turn or twist out of or as if out of shape）*n.* 弯曲，歪斜
[wɔ:rp]	（a twist or curve that has developed in something flat or straight）
	记 发音记忆："卧铺" → 卧铺太窄，只有弯曲身体才能睡下 → 弯曲
warrant	*n.* 正当理由（justification）；许可证（a commission or document giving
['wɔ:rənt]	authority）*v.* 保证；批准
	例 Dr. Smith cautioned that the data so far are not sufficiently unequivocal
	to *warrant* dogmatic assertions by either side in the debate.
	同 certify, guarantee, vindicate
warrantable	*adj.* 可保证的，可承认的（capable of being warranted）
['wɔ:rəntəbl]	
warranted	*adj.* 保证的；担保的
['wɔ:rəntɪd]	例 Despite many decades of research on the gasification of coal, the
	data accumulated are not directly applicable to environmental questions;
	thus a new program of research specifically addressing such questions is
	warranted.
wary	*adj.* 谨慎的，小心翼翼的（marked by keen caution, cunning, and watchfulness
['weri]	especially in detecting and escaping danger）
wavy	*adj.* 波状的，多浪的（rising or swelling in waves）；波动起伏的（marked by
['weɪvi]	undulation）
waxy	*adj.* 像蜡的，苍白的，光滑的（looking or feeling like wax）
['wæksi]	
wearisome	*adj.* 使人感到疲倦或厌倦的（causing one to feel tired or bored）
['wɪrɪsəm]	记 来自 weary（*v.* 疲倦，厌倦）
weather	*v.* 风化，侵蚀；经受住风雨；平安度过危难（to come through (sth.) safely;
['weðər]	survive）
weightless	*adj.* 无重力的，失重的（having little weight; lacking apparent gravitational
['weɪtləs]	pull）
well-deserved	*adj.* 当之无愧的；罪有应得的
[ˌweldɪ'zɜ:rvd]	
well-intentioned	*adj.* 出于善意的
[ˌwelɪn'tenʃnd]	
welter	*n.* 混乱，杂乱无章（a disordered mixture）
['weltər]	记 联想记忆：像一个大熔炉（melter）一样一片混乱（welter）
whimsical	*adj.* 古怪的，异想天开的（exhibiting whims）
['wɪmzɪkl]	同 capricious, impulsive
whimsy	*n.* 古怪，异想天开（whim; a fanciful creation）
['wɪmzi]	例 It is to the novelist's credit that all of the episodes in her novel are
	presented realistically, without any *whimsy* or playful supernatural tricks.
	同 boutade, caprice, crotchet, freak

whittle [ˈwɪtl]	*v.* 削(木头)(to pare or cut off chips)；削减(to reduce; pare) 记 联想记忆：wh(看作 whet, 磨刀) + ittle(看作 little, 小) → 磨刀把木头削小 → 削(木头)
wholesale [ˈhoʊlseɪl]	*adj.* 批发的(of, relating to, or engaged in the sale of commodities in quantity for resale)；大规模的(performed or existing on a large scale)
willful [ˈwɪlfl]	*adj.* 任性的(perversely self-willed)；故意的(intentional) 同 deliberate, knowing, wilful
wilt [wɪlt]	*v.* 凋谢，枯萎(to lose vigor from lack of water) 同 mummify, shrivel, wither
wistful [ˈwɪstfl]	*adj.* 惆怅的，渴望的(thoughtful and rather sad) 同 pensive, yearning
withhold [wɪðˈhoʊld]	*v.* 抑制(to hold back from action)；扣留，保留(to keep on purpose) 记 联想记忆：with(附带着) + hold(拿住) → 保留 同 bridle, constrain, inhibit, restrain
withstand [wɪðˈstænd]	*v.* 反抗(to oppose with force or resolution)；经受(to endure successfully) 记 词根记忆：with(反) + st(站) + and → 反着站 → 反抗 例 Having billed himself as "Mr. Clean", Hosokawa could not *withstand* the notoriety of a major financial scandal.
witty [ˈwɪti]	*adj.* 机智的(having good intellectual capacity)；风趣的(marked by or full of wit)
woolly [ˈwʊli]	*adj.* 羊毛的；模糊的(lacking sharp detail or clarity)
wordy [ˈwɜːrdi]	*adj.* 冗长的，多言的(using or containing many and usually too many words)
world-beater [ˈwɜːrldbiːtər]	*n.* 举世无双的人(a person or thing that is better than all others)
worthwhile [ˌwɜːrθˈwaɪl]	*adj.* 值得做的(being worth the time or effort spent) 记 组合词：worth(值得) + while(时间) → 值得花时间的 → 值得做的 例 Although most *worthwhile* criticism concentrates on the positive, one should not indiscriminately praise everything.
worthy [ˈwɜːrði]	*adj.* 值得的(having worth or value)；有价值的(having sufficient worth or importance) *n.* 知名人士(a worthy or prominent person)
wring [rɪŋ]	*v.* 绞，拧，扭(to squeeze or twist) 同 contort, deform, distort
wrongheaded [ˌrɔːŋˈhedɪd]	*adj.* 坚持错误的，固执的(stubborn in adherence to wrong opinions or principles)
xenophobic [ˌzenəˈfoʊbik]	*adj.* 恐外的，恐惧外国人的(having abnormal fear or hatred of the strange or foreign)

22

□ whittle	□ wholesale	□ willful	□ wilt	□ wistful	□ withhold
□ withstand	□ witty	□ woolly	□ wordy	□ world-beater	□ worthwhile
□ worthy	□ wring	□ wrongheaded	□ xenophobic		

253

yearn [jɜːrn]	*v.* 盼望，渴望（to long persistently）
	记 联想记忆：year（年）+ n → 一年到头盼望 → 盼望，渴望
	同 crave, hanker, lust, pine
zealot [ˈzelət]	*n.* 狂热者（a zealous person）
	同 bigot, enthusiast, fanatic
zenith [ˈzenɪθ]	*n.* 天顶（the highest point of the celestial sphere）；极点（the highest point）
	例 Her novel published to universal acclaim, her literary gifts acknowledged by the chief figures of the Harlem Renaissance, her reputation as yet untarnished by envious slights, Hurston clearly was at the *zenith* of her career.
	同 acme, apex, culmination, meridian, pinnacle

Few things are impossible in themselves; and it is often for want of will, rather than of means, that man fails to succeed.

事情很少有根本做不成的；其所以做不成，与其说是条件不够，不如说是由于决心不够。

——法国作家 罗切福考尔德（La Rocheforcauld, French writer）

拓展词汇

abase [ə'beɪs]	*v.* 降低…的地位，贬抑，使卑下（to lower oneself/sb. in dignity; degrade oneself/sb.） 🔲 词根记忆：a(到) + base(降低) → 降低…的地位
abash [ə'bæʃ]	*v.* 使羞愧，使尴尬(to make embarrassed) 🔲 联想记忆：ab + ash(灰) → 中间有灰，灰头灰脸 → 使尴尬
abate [ə'beɪt]	*v.* 减轻，减少(to make less in amount; wane) 🔲 词根记忆：a(加强) + bate(减弱，减少) → 减轻
abdicate ['æbdɪkeɪt]	*v.* 退位(to give up a throne or authority)；放弃(to cast off) 🔲 词根记忆：ab(脱离) + dic(说话，命令) + ate → 不再命令 → 退位；放弃
abhorrent [əb'hɔːrənt]	*adj.* 可恨的，讨厌的(causing disgust or hatred; detestable; hateful) 🔲 obscene, repugnant, repulsive
abject ['æbdʒekt]	*adj.* 极可怜的(miserable; wretched)；卑下的(degraded; base) 🔲 词根记忆：ab(脱离) + ject(抛，扔) → 被人抛弃的 → 极可怜的
abjure [əb'dʒʊr]	*v.* 发誓放弃(to give up on oath; renounce) 🔲 词根记忆：ab(脱离) + jur(发誓) + e → 发誓去掉 → 发誓放弃
abnegate ['æbnɪgeɪt]	*v.* 否认，放弃(to deny; renounce) 🔲 词根记忆：ab(脱离) + neg(否认) + ate → 否认，放弃
abnegation [ˌæbnɪ'geɪʃn]	*n.* 放弃(renunciation)；自我牺牲(self-sacrifice)
abolish [ə'bɑːlɪʃ]	*v.* 废止，废除(法律、制度、习俗等)(to end the observance or effect of) 🔲 联想记忆：ab(脱离) + (p)olish(抛光，优雅) → 不优雅的东西就应该废除 → 废除
abominate [ə'bɑːmɪneɪt]	*v.* 痛恨；厌恶(to feel hatred and disgust for; loathe) 🔲 词根记忆：ab(脱离) + om (=hom=man, 人) + in + ate → 脱离人的模样 → 痛恨；厌恶
abortive [ə'bɔːrtɪv]	*adj.* 无结果的，失败的(fruitless; unsuccessful) 🔲 词根记忆：ab(脱落) + or(=ori 产生) + tive → 从产生的地方脱落 → 无结果的，失败的

☐ abase	☐ abash	☐ abate	☐ abdicate	☐ abhorrent	☐ abject
☐ abjure	☐ abnegate	☐ abnegation	☐ abolish	☐ abominate	☐ abortive

255

abound [ə'baʊnd]	*v.* 大量存在(to be great in number or amount); 充满, 富于(to be fully supplied or filled of; teem with) 记 联想记忆: a + bound(边界) → 没有边界 → 充满
aboveboard [ə,bʌv'bɔːrd]	*adj./adv.* 光明正大的(地)(honest(ly) and open(ly)) 记 联想记忆: above (在…上) + board (会议桌) → 可以放到桌面上谈 → 光明正大的(地)
abrade [ə'breɪd]	*v.* 擦伤, 磨损(to scrape or rub off) 记 词根记忆: ab(脱离) + rade(磨擦) → 摩擦掉 → 磨损
abrogate ['æbrəgeɪt]	*v.* 废止, 废除(to repeal by authority; abolish) 记 词根记忆: ab(脱离) + rog(要求) + ate → 要求离开 → 废除
abrupt [ə'brʌpt]	*adj.* 突然的, 意外的; 唐突的(sudden and unexpected) 记 词根记忆: ab(脱离) + rupt(断) → 突然断掉了 → 突然的, 意外的
abscond [əb'skɑːnd]	*v.* 潜逃, 逃亡(to run away and hide in order to escape the law) 记 词根记忆: abs(脱离) + cond(藏起来) → 潜逃
absolve [əb'zɑːlv]	*v.* 赦免, 免除(to set free from guilt or obligation; forgive) 记 词根记忆: ab(脱离) + solv(放开) + e → 放开使脱离罪责 → 赦免, 免除
abstemious [əb'stiːmiəs]	*adj.* 有节制的, 节俭的(moderate in eating and drinking; temperate) 记 词根记忆: abs(脱离) + tem(酒) + ious → 不喝酒 → 有节制的
abstention [əb'stenʃn]	*n.* 戒除; 弃权(the act or practice of abstaining) 记 来自abstain(*v.* 禁绝, 放弃)
abstentious [əb'stenʃəs]	*adj.* 有节制的(temperate)
abstinent ['æbstɪnənt]	*adj.* 饮食有度的, 有节制的, 禁欲的(constraining from indulgence of an appetite or craving or from eating some foods) 记 词根记忆: abs(脱离) + tin(拿住) + ent → 抓住自己脱离某物 → 禁欲的
abuse	[ə'bjuːz] *v.* 辱骂(to use insulting language; revile); 滥用(to use wrongly; misuse) [ə'bjuːs] *n.* 辱骂; 滥用 记 词根记忆: ab(脱离) + us(用) + e → 用到不能再用 → 滥用
abusive [ə'bjuːsɪv]	*adj.* 谩骂的, 毁谤的(using harsh insulting language); 虐待的(physically injurious)
acarpous [eɪ'kɑːpəs]	*adj.* 不结果实的(impotent to bear fruit)
accessory [ək'sesəri]	*adj.* 附属的, 次要的(additional; supplementary; subsidiary)
acclaim [ə'kleɪm]	*v.* 欢呼, 称赞(to greet with loud applause; hail) 记 词根记忆: ac(向) + claim(叫喊) → 向某人大声叫喊 → 欢呼, 称赞 搭 universal acclaim 普遍赞誉; 广受好评

acclimate [ˈækləmeɪt]	*v.* (使)服水土(to adjust to climate); (使)适应(to adapt) 记 词根记忆：ac(向) + clim(倾斜) + ate → (使)向某物倾斜 → (使)服水土
accolade [ˈækəleɪd]	*n.* 推崇(approval; appreciation); 赞扬(words of praise) 记 词根记忆：ac(附近) + col(脖子) + ade → 挂在脖子附近 → 赞扬
accomplished [əˈkɑːmplɪʃt]	*adj.* 完成了的(being achieved); 有技巧的(skilled) 搭 accomplished performer 有技巧的表演者
accost [əˈkɔːst]	*v.* 搭话(to approach and speak first to a person boldly) 记 联想记忆：ac(靠近) + cost(花费) → 和人认识后要花钱 → 搭话
accountability [əˌkaʊntəˈbɪləti]	*n.* 有责任(responsibility) 记 联想记忆：account(解释) + ability → 对事情应做解释 → 有责任
accrete [əˈkriːt]	*v.* 逐渐增长(to grow or increase by means of gradual additions); 添加生长; 连生(to grow together) 记 词根记忆：ac(加强) + cre(增长)+te → 逐渐增长
accrue [əˈkruː]	*v.* (利息等)增加(to increase the interest on money); 积累(to accumulate) 记 词根记忆：ac(加强) + cru(增长)+te → 更加增长 → 增加; 积累
accumulate [əˈkjuːmjəleɪt]	*v.* 积聚, 积累(to pile up; collect) 记 词根记忆：ac(加强) + cumul(堆积) + ate → 不断堆积 → 积累 搭 accumulate power to... 为…积攒能量
accurate [ˈækjərət]	*adj.* 精确的, 准确的(free from error) 记 词根记忆：ac(加强) + cur(关心) + ate → 不断关心使之正确无误 → 精确的
acedia [əˈsiːdiə]	*n.* 无精打采的样子(apathy; boredom); 懒惰
acerbity [əˈsɜːrbəti]	*n.* 涩, 酸, 刻薄(sourness of taste, character, or tone) 记 词根记忆：acerb(酸涩的, 刻薄的)+ity → 涩, 酸, 刻薄
acquiesce [ˌækwiˈes]	*v.* 勉强同意, 默许(to agree or consent quietly without protest; consent) 记 词根记忆：ac(加强) + qui(安静)+esce → 面对某事变得安静 → 默许
acquisitive [əˈkwɪzətɪv]	*adj.* 渴望得到的, 贪婪的(eager to acquire; greedy) 记 词根记忆：ac(加强) + quisit(要求) + ive → 一再想得到 → 贪婪的
acquit [əˈkwɪt]	*v.* 宣告无罪 (to declare sb. to be not guilty); 脱卸义务和责任(to free or clear sb. of blame, responsibility, etc.); 还清(债务)(to pay off) 记 词根记忆：ac(向) + qui(安静) + t → 让某人心境平和 → 宣告无罪
acrid [ˈækrɪd]	*adj.* 辛辣的, 刻薄的(bitterly pungent; bitter; sharp)
acrobat [ˈækrəbæt]	*n.* 特技演员, 杂技演员(one that performs gymnastic feats requiring skillful control of the body) 记 词根记忆：acro(高) + bat(走) → 高空走的人 → 杂技演员

accumulate

23

acuity [əˈkjuːəti]	*n.*（尤指思想或感官）敏锐（sharpness; acuteness） 记 词根记忆：acu(尖，酸，锐利) + ity(表性质) → 锐利 → 敏锐
acumen [ˈækjəmən]	*n.* 敏锐，精明（keenness and depth of perception） 记 词根记忆：acu(尖，酸，锐利) + men(表名词) → 敏锐，精明
adapt [əˈdæpt]	*v.* 使适应（to make fit）；修改（to modify） 记 词根记忆：ad(向) + apt(适应) → 使适应
additive [ˈædətɪv]	*n.* 添加剂（substance added in small amounts to sth. especially to food or medicine）
addle [ˈædl]	*v.* 使腐坏（to make rotten）；使昏乱（to become muddled or confused） 记 联想记忆：add(增加) + le → 事情增加容易混乱 → 使昏乱
adduce [əˈduːs]	*v.* 给予（理由）（to give as reason or proof）；举出（例证）（to cite as an example） 记 词根记忆：ad(向) + duc(引导) + e → 引导出 → 举出
adherent [ədˈhɪrənt]	*n.* 拥护者，信徒（one that adheres as a follower or a believer） 记 词根记忆：ad(一再) + her(粘连) + ent → 粘在身后的人 → 拥护者
adjourn [əˈdʒɜːrn]	*v.*（使）延期，（使）推迟（to suspend indefinitely）；（使）休会（to suspend a session indefinitely or to another time or place） 记 词根记忆：ad(附近) + journ(日期) → 改到近日 → 推迟
adjudicate [əˈdʒuːdɪkeɪt]	*v.* 充当裁判（to serve as a judge in a dispute）；判决（to settle judicially） 记 词根记忆：ad(来) + jud(判断) + icate → 进行判断 → 充当裁判
adjunct [ˈædʒʌŋkt]	*n.* 附加物，附件（sth. joined or added to another thing but not essentially a part of it） 记 词根记忆：ad(附近) + junct(结合，连接) → 连在上面的东西 → 附加物
adolescent [ˌædəˈlesnt]	*adj.* 青春期的（of or typical of adolescence）*n.* 青少年（young person between childhood and adulthood） 记 联想记忆：ado(看作 adult, 成人) + lescent(看作 licence, 许可证) → 青少年即将拿到成年的许可证 → 青春期的
adroit [əˈdrɔɪt]	*adj.* 熟练的，灵巧的（skillful; expert; dexterous） 记 词根记忆：a(…的) + droit(灵巧) → 灵巧的
adulate [ˈædjuleɪt]	*v.* 谄媚，奉承（to praise or flatter excessively）
adulterate [əˈdʌltəreɪt]	*v.* 掺杂，掺假（to make food or drink less pure by adding another substance to it）*adj.* 掺杂的，掺假的
advent [ˈædvent]	*n.* 到来，来临（coming or arrival） 记 词根记忆：ad(来) + vent(到来) → 到来
adventitious [ˌædvenˈtɪʃəs]	*adj.* 偶然的（accidental; casual） 记 联想记忆：advent(到来) + itious → （突然）到来的 → 偶然的
advert [ˈædvɜːrt]	*v.* 注意，留意；提及（to call attention; refer） 记 词根记忆：ad(向) + vert(转) → 一再转到这个话题 → 注意，留意

advisable	*adj.* 适当的，可取的（proper to be advised or recommended）
[əd'vaɪzəbl]	记 来自 advise（*v.* 建议）
advocate	['ædvəkeɪt] *v.* 提倡，主张，拥护（to speak publicly in favor）
	['ædvəkət] *n.* 支持者，拥护者（person who supports）
	记 词根记忆：ad（向）+ voc（叫喊，声音）+ ate → 为其摇旗呐喊 → 拥护
aerate	*v.* 充气，让空气进入（to cause air to circulate through）
['ereɪt]	记 词根记忆：aer（空气）+ ate（表动作）→ 充气
aerial	*adj.* 空中的，空气的（of, relating to, or occurring in the air or atmosphere）
['eriəl]	记 词根记忆：aer（空气）+ ial（…的）→ 空中的
affected	*adj.* 不自然的（behaving in an artificial way）；假装的（assumed）
[ə'fektɪd]	记 factitious, fictitious, unnatural
affiliate	[ə'fɪlieɪt] *v.* 使隶属于（to bring or receive into close connection as a member or branch）；追溯…的来源（to trace the origin of）；联合（to connect or associate）
	[ə'fɪliət] *n.* 成员，附属机构
	记 词根记忆：af（=ad 附近）+ fil（儿子）+ iate → 形成近乎和儿子一样的关系 → 使隶属于
affiliation	*n.* 联系，联合（link or connection made by affiliating）
[əˌfɪli'eɪʃn]	
affix	[ə'fɪks] *v.* 黏上，贴上（to stick; attach）；（尤指在末尾）添上（to add sth. in writing）
	['æfɪks] *n.* 词缀（prefix or suffix）
	记 词根记忆：af + fix（固定）→ 固定上去 → 黏上，贴上
affliction	*n.* 折磨，痛苦；痛苦的原因；灾害
[ə'flɪkʃn]	
aftermath	*n.* 后果，余波（an unpleasant result or consequence）
['æftərmæθ]	记 联想记忆：after（在…之后）+ math（数学）→ 做完数学后一塌糊涂的结果 → 后果
agape	*adj./adv.* （嘴）大张着的（地）（open-mouthed）
[ə'geɪp]	记 词根记忆：a（…的）+ gape（张开，张大）→ 大张着的（地）
agenda	*n.* 议程（program of things to be done）
[ə'dʒendə]	记 词根记忆：ag（做）+ enda（表示名词）→ 要做的事情 → 议程
aggregate	*v.* 集合（to gather into a whole）；合计（to total; sum）
['ægrɪɡeɪt]	记 词根记忆：ag（做）+ greg（团体）+ ate → 成为团体 → 集合
aggrieve	*v.* 使受委屈，使痛苦（to give pain or trouble to）
[ə'griːv]	记 词根记忆：ag（做）+ griev（悲伤）+ e → 使受委屈，使痛苦
agile	*adj.* 敏捷的，灵活的（able to move quickly and easily）
['ædʒl]	记 词根记忆：ag（做）+ ile（易…的）→ 动作容易的 → 敏捷的

23

agitated [ˈædʒɪteɪtɪd]	*adj.* 激动的 (excited); 不安的 (perturbed)
agnostic [æɡˈnɑːstɪk]	*adj.* 不可知论的 (of, relating to, or being an agnostic or the beliefs of agnostics) *n.* 不可知论者 记 词根记忆: a(不) + gno(知道) + stic → 认为无法了解神是否存在的人 → 不可知论者
agog [əˈɡɑːɡ]	*adj.* 兴奋的, 有强烈兴趣的 (in a state of eager anticipation or excitement) 记 agog 可以作词根, 意为 "引导", 如: demagog(*n.* 煽动者)
agreeable [əˈɡriːəbl]	*adj.* 令人愉快的 (pleasing); 欣然同意的 (ready to agree) 记 来自 agree(*v.* 同意)
ague [ˈeɪɡjuː]	*n.* 冷颤, 发冷 (a fit of shivering)
ail [eɪl]	*v.* 生病 (to have physical or emotional pain, discomfort, or trouble, especially to suffer ill health) 记 联想记忆: 和 air(*n.* 空气)一起记, 多呼吸空气(air)就会少生病(ail)
airtight [ˈeərtaɪt]	*adj.* 密闭的, 不透气的 (too tight for air or gas to enter or escape) 记 组合词: air(空气)+tight(紧的, 不透气的) → 密闭的, 不透气的
albeit [ˌɔːlˈbiːɪt]	*conj.* 虽然, 尽管 (although)
aleatory [ˈeɪliətɔːri]	*adj.* 侥幸的, 偶然的 (depending on an uncertain event or contingency as to both profit and loss)
alert [əˈlɜːrt]	*adj.* 警惕的, 机警的 (watchful and prompt to meet danger or emergency) *n.* 警报 (warning) 记 Red Alert "红色警戒", 20 世纪 90 年代风靡全球的电脑游戏
allay [əˈleɪ]	*v.* 减轻, 缓和 (to relieve; reduce the intensity) 同 assuage, ease, quench
allergic [əˈlɜːrdʒɪk]	*adj.* 过敏的 (of allergy); 对…讨厌的 (averse or disinclined)
alleviate [əˈliːvieɪt]	*v.* 减轻, 缓和 (to lighten or relieve) 记 词根记忆: al(加强) + lev(轻) + iate(使…) → 使…轻 → 减轻, 缓和
allocate [ˈæləkeɪt]	*v.* 配给, 分配 (to assign sth. for a special purpose; distribute) 记 词根记忆: al + loc (地方) + ate → 不断送给地方 , 配给, 分配
allowance [əˈlaʊəns]	*n.* 津贴, 补助 (amount of money allowed or given regularly); 承认, 允许 (permission) 记 联想记忆: allow(允许) + ance → 允许自由支配的钱 → 津贴
alluring [əˈlʊrɪŋ]	*adj.* 吸引人的, 迷人的 (attractive; charming) 记 来自 allure(*v.* 引诱)

allergic

260

□ agitated	□ agnostic	□ agog	□ agreeable	□ ague	□ ail
□ airtight	□ albeit	□ aleatory	□ alert	□ allay	□ allergic
□ alleviate	□ allocate	□ allowance	□ alluring		

alter	*v.* 改变，更改（to change）
[ˈɔːltər]	记 alter 本身就是词根，意为"改变"
amalgamate	*v.* 合并（to unite; combine）；混合（to mix）
[əˈmælgəmeɪt]	
amass	*v.* 积聚（to collect; gather; accumulate）
[əˈmæs]	记 联想记忆：a + mass（一团）→ 变成一团 → 积聚
ambience	*n.* 环境，气氛（environment; atmosphere）
[ˈæmbiəns]	记 词根记忆：ambi（在…周围）+ ence → 环境，气氛
ambush	*n.* 埋伏（the act of lying in wait to attack by surprise）；伏击（a sudden attack made from a concealed position）*v.* 埋伏
[ˈæmbʊʃ]	记 联想记忆：am + bush（矮树丛）→ 埋伏在矮树丛里 → 埋伏
amiable	*adj.* 和蔼的，亲切的（good natured; affable; genial）
[ˈeɪmiəbl]	记 联想记忆：am（爱，友爱）+ i + able → 和蔼的，亲切的
amity	*n.* （人们或国家之间的）友好关系（friendly relationship between people or countries）
[ˈæməti]	记 词根记忆：am（爱，友爱）+ ity → 友好关系
amnesia	*n.* 健忘症（loss of memory due usually to brain injury, illness, etc.）
[æmˈniːʒə]	记 词根记忆：a（无）+ mnes（记忆）+ ia（病）→ 没有记忆的病 → 健忘症
amnesty	*n.* 大赦，特赦（the act of an authority by which pardon is granted to a large group of individuals）
[ˈæmnəsti]	记 词根记忆：a（无）+ mnes（记忆）+ ty → 不再记仇 → 大赦，特赦
ample	*adj.* 富足的（abundant）；充足的（enough; adequate）
[ˈæmpl]	记 联想记忆：apple（苹果）很 ample（充足）
amplify	*v.* 放大（to make larger; extend）；详述（to develop with details）
[ˈæmplɪfaɪ]	记 词根记忆：ampl（大）+ ify → 放大
amuse	*v.* 使愉快，逗某人笑（to make sb. smile）
[əˈmjuːz]	记 联想记忆：a + muse（缪斯，古希腊文艺女神）→ 使愉快
analgesia	*n.* 无痛觉，痛觉丧失（insensibility to pain without loss of consciousness）
[ˌænəlˈdʒiːʒə]	记 词根记忆：an（没有）+ alg（痛）+ esia → 无痛觉
analogy	*n.* 相似（partial resemblance）；类比（the likening of one thing to another）
[əˈnælədʒi]	记 词根记忆：ana（并列）+ log（说话）+ y → 放在一起说 → 类比
ancillary	*adj.* 辅助的（subordinate; auxiliary）*n.* 助手（aid）
[ˈænsəleri]	
anesthetic	*adj.* 麻醉的；麻木的（lacking awareness or sensitivity）*n.* 麻醉剂（a drug that makes people feel unconscious）
[ˌænəsˈθetɪk]	记 词根记忆：an（无）+ esthet（感觉）+ ic 无感觉 → 麻醉的
anguish	*n.* 极大的痛苦（great suffering; distress）
[ˈæŋgwɪʃ]	记 词根记忆：angu（痛苦）+ ish → 极大的痛苦

alter

23

animadvert [ˌænəmædˈvət]	v. 苛责, 非难(to remark or comment critically, usually with strong disapproval or censure)
animate [ˈænɪmət]	[ˈænɪmət] adj. 活的, 有生命的(alive; having life) [ˈænɪmeɪt] v. 赋予生命(to give life to) 记 词根记忆: anim(生命, 精神) + ate → 有生命的; 赋予生命
animation [ˌænɪˈmeɪʃn]	n. 兴奋, 活跃 同 brio, invigoration, spiritedness, vivification
animus [ˈænɪməs]	n. 敌意, 憎恨(animosity) 同 enmity, hatred, hostility, rancour
anneal [əˈniːl]	v. 使(金属、玻璃等)退火; 使加强, 使变硬(to strengthen or harden)
annihilate [əˈnaɪəleɪt]	v. 消灭(to destroy completely; demolish) 记 词根记忆: an(接近) + nihil(无) + ate → 使接近没有 → 消灭
announce [əˈnaʊns]	v. 宣布, 发表(to proclaim); 通报…的到来(to give notice of the arrival) 记 词根记忆: an(来) + nounc(讲话, 说出) + e → 讲出来 → 宣布
annoy [əˈnɔɪ]	v. 惹恼(to cause slight anger); 打搅, 骚扰(to cause trouble to sb.) 同 bother, chafe, irritate, nettle, rile, vex
annul [əˈnʌl]	v. 宣告无效(to invalidate); 取消(to cancel; abolish) 记 词根记忆: an(来) + nul(消除) → 取消
anonymity [ˌænəˈnɪməti]	n. 无名, 匿名(the quality or state of being anonymous) 记 词根记忆: an(没有) + onym(名称) + ity → 无名, 匿名
antecedence [ˌæntɪˈsiːdns]	n. 居先, 先行(priority; precedence) 记 词根记忆: ante(前面) + ced(走) + ence → 走在前面 → 居先, 先行
anthem [ˈænθəm]	n. 圣歌(a religious choral song); 赞美诗(a song of praise); 国歌 记 联想记忆: an + them → 一首他们一起唱的歌 → 圣歌
antic [ˈæntɪk]	adj. 古怪的(fantastic and queer) 记 和 antique(n. 古董)来自同一词源
anticipate [ænˈtɪsɪpeɪt]	v. 预先处理(to foresee and deal with in advance); 预期, 期望(to look forward to; expect) 记 词根记忆: anti(前) + cip(落下) + ate → 提前落下 → 预期, 期望
anvil [ˈænvɪl]	n. 铁砧(a steel block)
aplomb [əˈplɑːm]	n. 沉着, 镇静(complete and confident composure) 记 联想记忆: apl(看作 apple) + omb(看作 tomb) → 坟墓中的苹果, 很静 → 镇静
apocryphal [əˈpɑːkrɪfl]	adj. 假冒的, 虚假的(of doubtful authenticity) 同 inveracious, mendacious, ostensible

apologize [əˈpɒlədʒaɪz]	v. 道歉(to say one is sorry); 辩解(to make a formal defence) 记 词根记忆：apo(远) + log(说话) + ize → 离(别人)远一点说话，不面对面骂 → 道歉
apostate [əˈpɒsteɪt]	n. 背教者; 变节者(a person guilty of apostasy) 同 flopper, renegade, turnabout, turncoat
appeal [əˈpiːl]	v. 恳求(to supplicate); 有吸引力(to be attractive or interesting); 上诉(to take a lower court's decision to a higher court for review) 记 词根记忆：ap + peal(=pull 拉) → 拉过去 → 有吸引力 搭 appeal to 吸引; 呼吁, 恳求
applicant [ˈæplɪkənt]	n. 申请人(person who applies, especially for a job) 同 applier, proposer
appoint [əˈpɔɪnt]	v. 任命, 指定(to name for an office or position); 约定 记 联想记忆：ap(加强) + point(指向, 指出) → 指定某人做某事 → 任命, 指定
appraise [əˈpreɪz]	v. 评价, 鉴定(to assess the value or quality) 记 联想记忆：ap(加强) + praise(价值, 赞扬) → 给以价值 → 评价
apprentice [əˈprentɪs]	n. 学徒(one who is learning by practical experience under skilled workers) 记 词根记忆：ap(接近) + prent(=prehend 抓住) + ice → 为了抓住技术的人 → 学徒
apron [ˈeɪprən]	n. 围裙(a protective skirt worn over one's clothing) 记 联想记忆：在四月(April)穿上围裙(apron)去干活
apt [æpt]	adj. 易于…的; 恰当的 搭 be apt to... 容易…的; 很可能…
aquiline [ˈækwɪlaɪn]	adj. 鹰的, 似鹰的(of, relating to, or resembling an eagle) 记 词根记忆：aquil(鹰) + ine → 鹰的
arbitrate [ˈɑːrbɪtreɪt]	v. 仲裁, 公断(to decide (a dispute) as an arbitrator) 同 intercede, intermediate, liaise, mediate
archer [ˈɑːrtʃər]	n. (运动或战争中的)弓箭手, 射手(a person who shoots with a bow and arrows) 记 词根记忆：arch(弓) + er → 弓箭手; arch 本身是一个单词, 意为"使…弯成弓形"
archetype [ˈɑːkitaɪp]	n. 原型(the original pattern; prototype); 典型(a perfect example) 记 词根记忆：arch(旧的) + e + typ(模型, 印象) + e → 原型
ardent [ˈɑːrdnt]	adj. 热心的, 热烈的(intensely enthusiastic or devoted; passionate) 记 词根记忆：ard(热) + ent → 热心的, 热烈的

实在抱歉！ apologize

23

aristocracy	*n.* 贵族（the people of the highest social class especially from noble families）；贵族政府，贵族统治（government in which power is held by the nobility）
[ˌærɪˈstɑːkrəsi]	记 词根记忆：aristo（最好的）+ cracy（统治）→ 贵族统治
aroma	*n.* 芳香，香气（a pleasant, often spicy odor; fragrance）
[əˈroʊmə]	记 发音记忆："爱了吗" → 爱了就有芳香 → 芳香，香气
arouse	*v.* 唤醒（to wake up）；激发（to cause to become active）
[əˈraʊz]	同 brace, energize, stimulate, stir
arraign	*v.* 传讯（to charge in court; indict）；指责（to accuse）
[əˈreɪn]	记 联想记忆：安排（arrange）对犯人传讯（arraign）
arrant	*adj.* 完全的，彻底的（thoroughgoing）；极坏的，臭名昭著的（being notoriously without moderation）
[ˈærənt]	
array	*v.* 部署（to place armed forces in battle order）*n.* 陈列（impressive display）；大批
[əˈreɪ]	
arrest	*v.* 逮捕；阻止，制止（to stop or check）
[əˈrest]	记 联想记忆：ar（加强）+ rest（休息）→ 强制休息 → 逮捕
arson	*n.* 纵火（罪），放火（罪）（the crime of purposely setting fire）
[ˈɑːrsn]	记 词根记忆：ars（=ard 热）+ on → 火在燃烧 → 纵火（罪）
artifact	*n.* 人工制品（object made by human beings）
[ˈɑːrtɪfækt]	记 词根记忆：arti（技巧）+ fact（制作）→ 用技巧制作出来的东西 → 人工制品
artifice	*n.* 巧妙办法（skill or ingenuity）；诡计（a sly trick）
[ˈɑːrtɪfɪs]	记 词根记忆：arti（技巧）+ fice（做）→ 做的技巧 → 巧妙办法
artificial	*adj.* 人造的，假的（unnatural）
[ˌɑːrtɪˈfɪʃl]	记 词根记忆：arti（=skill 技巧）+ fic（面）+ ial（…的）→ 在表面使技术的 → 人造的，假的
ashen	*adj.* 灰色的，苍白的（resembling ashes（as in color），especially deadly pale）
[ˈæʃn]	
asinine	*adj.* 愚笨的（of asses; stupid; silly）
[ˈæsɪnaɪn]	记 联想记忆：as（看作 ass，驴子）+ in + in + e → 笨得像驴 → 愚笨的
askance	*adv.* 斜视地（with a sideways or indirect look）
[əˈskæns]	记 联想记忆：ask + ance（看作 ounce，盎司，黄金的计量单位）→ 问黄金价恪，斜着眼问 → 斜视地
askew	*adj./adv.* 歪斜的（地）（to one side; awry）
[əˈskjuː]	记 联想记忆：a + skew（歪斜的）→ 歪斜的（地）
aspersion	*n.* 诽谤，中伤（disparaging remark; slander）
[əˈspɜːrʒn]	记 词根记忆：a + spers（散开）+ ion → 散布坏东西 → 诽谤

arrest

□ aristocracy	□ aroma	□ arouse	□ arraign	□ arrant	□ array
□ arrest	□ arson	□ artifact	□ artifice	□ artificial	□ ashen
□ asinine	□ askance	□ askew	□ aspersion		

aspirant [əˈspaɪərənt]	*n.* 有抱负者（a person who aspires after honors or high positions） 同 aspirer
aspire [əˈspaɪə]	*v.* 渴望，追求，向往（to direct one's hopes and efforts to some important aims） 记 词根记忆：a + spir（呼吸）+ e → 因为太渴望得到，所以不停地呼吸 → 向往
assault [əˈsɔːlt]	*n.* 突袭（a sudden attack）；猛袭（a violent attack） 记 联想记忆：ass(驴子) + ault(看作 aunt, 姑妈) → 驴子袭击姑妈 → 突袭 搭 victims of assault 袭击事件牺牲者
assemble [əˈsembl]	*v.* 集合，聚集（to collect）；装配，组装（to fit together the parts） 记 联想记忆：as(加强) + semble(类似) → 物以类聚 → 集合

My fellow Americans, ask not what your country can do for you, ask what you can do for your country. My fellow citizens of the world: ask not what American will do for you, but what together we can do for the freedom of man.

美国同胞们，不要问国家能为你们做些什么，而要问你们能为国家做些什么。全世界的公民们，不要问美国将为你们做些什么，而要问我们共同能为人类的自由做些什么。

——美国总统 肯尼迪（John Kennedy, American president）

23

Word List 24  MP3-24

assent [ə'sent]	*v.* 同意，赞成(to express acceptance; concur; consent) 记 词根记忆：as(接近) + sent(感觉) → 感觉一致 → 同意
assert [ə'sɜːrt]	*v.* 断言，主张(to state positively; declare; affirm) 记 词根记忆：as (加强) + sert (提出) → 强烈地提出、表达自己的主张 → 主张
assess [ə'ses]	*v.* 评定，核定(to evaluate)；估计，估价(to estimate the quality)
associate 	[ə'souʃiət] *adj.* 联合的(joined) *n.* 合伙人(partner; colleague) [ə'souʃieɪt] *v.* 使发生联系，使联合(to join people or things together) 记 词根记忆：as(加强) + soci(同伴，引申为"社会") + ate → 成为社团 → 联合的
assoil [ə'sɔɪl]	*v.* 赦免，释放，补偿(to absolve; acquit; expiate) 同 clear, discharge, exculpate, exonerate
assuage [ə'sweɪdʒ]	*v.* 缓和，减轻(to lessen; relieve) 记 词根记忆：as + suage(甜) → 变甜 → 缓和
asterisk ['æstərɪsk]	*n.* 星号(a mark like a star used to draw attention) 记 词根记忆：aster(星星) + isk → 星号
asteroid ['æstərɔɪd]	*n.* 小行星(a small planet) 记 词根记忆：aster(星星) + oid(像…一样) → 小行星
astrology [ə'strɑːlədʒi]	*n.* 占星术；占星学(primitive astronomy) 记 词根记忆：astro(星) + (o)logy(学) → 占星学
atheism ['eɪθiɪzəm]	*n.* 无神论，不信神(the belief that there is no god) 记 词根记忆：a(无) + the(神) + ism → 无神论
atonal [eɪ'toʊnl]	*adj.* (音乐)无调的(marked by avoidance of traditional musical tonality) 记 词根记忆：a + ton(声音) + al → 无声的 → 无调的
atone [ə'toʊn]	*v.* 赎罪，补偿(to make amends for a wrongdoing) 记 联想记忆：a + tone(看作 stone, 石头) → 女娲用石头补天 → 补偿
atrocious [ə'troʊʃəs]	*adj.* 残忍的，凶恶的(very cruel, brutal; outrageous) 记 词根记忆：atroc(阴沉，凶残) + ious → 残忍的

□ assent	□ assert	□ assess	□ associate	□ assoil	□ assuage
□ asterisk	□ asteroid	□ astrology	□ atheism	□ atonal	□ atone
□ atrocious					

| **attach** | v. 系上，贴上，附上（to fasten sth. to sth.） |
| [əˈtætʃ] | 记 词根记忆：at(向) + tach(接触) → 将某物系在(另一物)上 → 系上，贴上，附上 |

| **attenuate** | v. 变薄（to make slender）；变弱（to lessen; weaken）adj. 减弱的 |
| [əˈtenjueɪt] | 记 词根记忆：at(加强) + ten(薄) + uate → 变薄 |

| **attire** | v. 使穿衣；打扮（to dress in fine garments）n. 盛装，服装（rich apparel; finery） |
| [əˈtaɪər] | 记 词根记忆：at(加强) + tire(梳理) → 梳洗打扮 → 使穿衣；打扮 |

收件人: 123@123.com
抄送:
主题: Hello
附件: file.doc

attach

| **augmentation** | n. 增加（increase） |
| [ˌɔːgmenˈteɪʃn] | 记 来自 augment(v. 增加，增大) |

| **augury** | n. 占卜术；预兆 |
| [ˈɔːgjʊri] | 记 来自 augur(v. 占卜，预言) |

| **august** | adj. 威严的，令人敬畏的（impressive; majestic） |
| [ɔːˈgʌst] | 记 联想记忆：八月(August)丰收大地金黄，金黄色是威严的帝王的象征 → 威严的 |

| **austerity** | n. 朴素，艰苦 |
| [ɔːˈsterəti] | 同 asceticism, nonindulgence |

| **authorization** | n. 授权，认可（action of authorizing） |
| [ˌɔːθərəˈzeɪʃn] | 记 来自 authorize(v. 授权，认可) |

| **autocracy** | n. 独裁政府（government by one person that with unlimited power） |
| [ɔːˈtɑːkrəsi] | 记 词根记忆：auto(自己) + cracy(统治) → 自己一个人统治 → 独裁政府 |

| **autocrat** | n. 独裁者（a ruler with absolute power; dictator） |
| [ˈɔːtəkræt] | 记 词根记忆：auto(自己) + crat(统治者) → 独裁者 |

| **automation** | n. 自动装置（mechanism that imitates actions of humans） |
| [ˌɔːtəˈmeɪʃn] | 记 词根记忆：auto(自己) + mat(动) + ion → 自动 → 自动装置 |

| **auxiliary** | adj. 辅助的，附加的，补充的（subordinate; additional; supplementary） |
| [ɔːgˈzɪliəri] | 记 词根记忆：aux(=aug 提高) + iliary(形容词后缀) → 提高的 → 辅助的 |

| **aver** | v. 极力声明；断言；证实（to state positively; affirm） |
| [əˈvɜːr] | 记 词根记忆：a(向) + ver(真实的) → 向人们说出真相 → 证实 |

| **aversion** | n. 厌恶，反感（an intense dislike; loathing） |
| [əˈvɜːrʒn] | 搭 aversion toward sb./sth. 对…的厌恶 |

| **avert** | v. 避免，防止（to ward off; prevent）；转移（to turn away） |
| [əˈvɜːrt] | 记 词根记忆：a(向) + vert(转) → 转开 → 避免 |

| **avocation** | n. 副业，嗜好（hobby; distraction） |
| [ˌævoʊˈkeɪʃn] | 记 a (不) + vocation (职业) → 非正规职业 → 副业；注意不要把 vocation (职业)和 vacation(度假)相混 |

| **avow** | v. 承认（to acknowledge or claim）；公开宣称（to declare openly） |
| [əˈvaʊ] | 记 词根记忆：a(来) + vow(誓言) → 发誓 → 承认 |

24

awry [əˈraɪ]	*adj.* 扭曲的，走样的(not straight; askew)
	记 词根记忆: a(加强) + wry(歪的) → 扭曲的
azure [ˈæʒər]	*n.* 天蓝色(sky blue) *adj.* 蔚蓝的
	同 cerulean, lazuline, sapphire
backdrop [ˈbækdrɑːp]	*n.* (事情的)背景；背景幕布(printed cloth hung at the back of a theatre)
	记 组合词: back + drop(后面挂下的幕布) → 背景幕布
backset [ˈbækset]	*n.* 倒退，逆流(reversal; countercurrent)
	同 countermatch, regradation, retrogress, retroversion
backslide [ˈbækslaɪd]	*v.* 故态复萌(to revert to bad habits)
	记 组合词: back(向后) + slide(滑动) → 往后滑 → 故态复萌
badge [bædʒ]	*n.* 徽章 (a distinctive token, emblem, or sign)
badger [ˈbædʒər]	*n.* 獾 *v.* 烦扰，纠缠不休(to torment; nag)
	同 beleaguer, bug, pester, tease
badinage [ˌbædənˈɑːʒ]	*n.* 玩笑，打趣(playful teasing)
	记 联想记忆: bad + inage(看作 image, 形象) → 破坏形象 → 打趣
bait [beɪt]	*n.* 诱饵(lure; enticement) *v.* 逗弄(to tease)；激怒(to provoke a reaction)
	同 decoy, hook, sweetener
balderdash [ˈbɔːldərdæʃ]	*n.* 胡言乱语，废话(nonsense)
	同 fiddle-faddle, piffle
bale [beɪl]	*n.* 大包，大捆(a large bundle)；灾祸，不幸(disaster)
	记 来自 ball(*n.* 球)
ballot [ˈbælət]	*n./v.* 投票
	记 联想记忆: ball(球) + (l)ot(签) → 用球抽签 → 投票
ballyhoo [ˈbælihuː]	*n.* 喧闹，呐喊(noisy shouting or uproar) *v.* 大肆宣传，大吹大擂(to publicize by sensational methods)
bamboozle [bæmˈbuːzl]	*v.* 欺骗，隐瞒(to deceive by underhanded methods)
	记 联想记忆: bamboo(竹子)+zle → 把东西装在竹筒里 → 欺骗，隐瞒
ban [bæn]	*n.* 禁令(an order banning sth.) *v.* 禁止，取缔(to officially forbid)
	记 发音记忆: "颁" → (颁布)禁令 → 禁止
bar [bɑːr]	*v.* 禁止，阻挡(to prevent, forbid) *n.* 条，棒(a straight piece of material that is longer than it is wide)
bare [ber]	*v.* 暴露(to make or lay bare; uncover) *adj.* 赤裸的(without clothing)
	记 和 bear(*n.* 熊)一起记
barefaced [ˈberfeɪst]	*adj.* 厚颜无耻的，公然的(shameless; blatant)
	记 联想记忆: bare(空的，没有的) + face(脸) + d → 不要脸的 → 厚颜无耻的

bait

bargain	*n.* 交易（an agreement made between two people or groups to do sth. in return for sth. else）；特价商品 *v.* 讨价还价（to negotiate the terms and conditions of a transaction）
[ˈbɑːrgən]	记 联想记忆：bar(看作 barter, 交易) + gain(获得) → 交易获得好价钱 → 讨价还价
barn	*n.* 谷仓（a farm building for sheltering harvested crops）
[bɑːrn]	记 酒吧(bar)加了个门(n)，就变成了谷仓(barn)
barrister	*n.* 出庭律师；律师（counselor at law or lawyer）
[ˈbærɪstər]	记 词根记忆：barr(阻挡) + ister(人) → 阻挡法官判罪的人 → 律师
barter	*v.* 易货贸易（to give goods in return for other goods）
[ˈbɑːrtər]	记 和 banter(*v.* 打趣)一起记
bawl	*v.* 大叫，大喊（to shout or call out noisily）
[bɔːl]	记 联想记忆：b + awl(尖钻) → 被尖钻戳到而大喊 → 大叫，人喊
bazaar	*n.* 集市，市场（a market or street of shops）
[bəˈzɑːr]	记 外来词，原指"东方国家的大集市"，今天的中国新疆一带仍把集市叫"巴扎"
beacon	*n.* 烽火；灯塔（a signal light for warning or guiding）
[ˈbiːkən]	记 联想记忆：beac(=beach 海岸) + on → 在海岸上的灯塔 → 灯塔
beam	*n.* (房屋等的)大梁；光线（a shaft or stream of light）
[biːm]	记 联想记忆：be + am → 做我自己，成为国家的栋梁 → 大梁
bearing	*n.* 关系，意义（connection with or influence on sth.）；方位（the situation or horizontal direction of one point with respect to another）
[ˈberɪŋ]	
beatific	*adj.* 幸福的，快乐的（blissful or blessed; delightful）
[ˌbiːəˈtɪfɪk]	记 词根记忆：beat(幸福) + ific → 幸福的
beckon	*v.* 召唤，示意（to make a gesture to sb. to come nearer or follow）
[ˈbekən]	记 联想记忆：beck(听人命令) + on → 召唤，示意
bedraggled	*adj.* (衣服、头发等)弄湿的；凌乱不堪的（made wet and dirty）
[bɪˈdrægld]	记 联想记忆：be + draggled(拖湿的；凌乱的) → 弄湿的；凌乱不堪的
befoul	*v.* 弄脏，诽谤（to make foul as with dirt or waste）
[bɪˈfaʊl]	同 defile, maculate
befuddle	*v.* 使迷惑不解；使酒醉昏迷（to confuse; muddle or stupefy with or as if with drink）
[bɪˈfʌdl]	记 联想记忆：be + fuddle(迷糊) → 使迷惑不解
beget	*v.* 产生，引起（to bring into being; produce）
[bɪˈget]	记 联想记忆：be + get(得到) → 确实得到了 → 产生
begrudge	*v.* 吝啬，勉强给（to give with ill-will or reluctance）
[bɪˈɡrʌdʒ]	记 联想记忆：be + grudge(吝啬) → 吝啬
behold	*v.* 注视，看见（to hold in view; look at）
[bɪˈhoʊld]	记 联想记忆：be + hold(拿住) → 被拿住 → 注视，看见

24

□ bargain	□ barn	□ barrister	□ barter	□ bawl	□ bazaar
□ beacon	□ beam	□ bearing	□ beatific	□ beckon	□ bedraggled
□ befoul	□ befuddle	□ beget	□ begrudge	□ behold	

269

beholden [bɪ'houldən]	*adj.* 因受恩惠而心存感激，感谢；欠人情（owing sth. such as gratitude or appreciation, to another） 同 grateful, owing
behoove [bɪ'huːv]	*v.* 理应，有必要（to be right or necessary to）
belabor [bɪ'leɪbər]	*v.* 过分冗长地做或说（to spend too much time or effort on）；痛打（to beat severely） 记 联想记忆：be + labor(劳动) → 不断劳动 → 过分冗长地做或说
belligerence [bə'lɪdʒərəns]	*n.* 交战（the state of being at war）；好战性，斗争性（an aggressive attitude, atmosphere, etc.） 记 词根记忆：bell(战斗) + iger + ence → 交战；好战性
bellow ['belou]	*v.* 咆哮；吼叫 同 bawl, roar
belongings [bɪ'lɔːŋɪŋz]	*n.* 所有物，财产（possessions; property） 同 estate, holding
bemused [bɪ'mjuːzd]	*adj.* 茫然的，困惑的（confused） 记 联想记忆：be + muse(沉思) + d → 进入沉思 → 困惑的
berate [bɪ'reɪt]	*v.* 猛烈责骂（to scold or rebuke severely） 记 联想记忆：be + rate(责骂) → 猛烈责骂
berserk [bər'zɜːrk]	*adj.* 狂怒的，狂暴的（frenzied, crazed） 同 amok, demoniac, demoniacal
beseech [bɪ'siːtʃ]	*v.* 恳求 记 词根记忆：be + seech(=seek 寻求) → 寻求 → 恳求
besmirch [bɪ'smɜːrtʃ]	*v.* 诽谤（to defile; make dirty） 记 联想记忆：be + smirch(污点，弄脏) → 诽谤
besot [bɪ'sɑːt]	*v.* 使沉醉，使糊涂（to make dull or stupid, especially to muddle with drunkness）
betoken [bɪ'toukən]	*v.* 预示，表示（to signify; indicate） 记 联想记忆：be(使…成为) + token(记号，标志) → 使…成为标志 → 预示
bewildering [bɪ'wɪldərɪŋ]	*adj.* 令人困惑的；令人费解的（puzzling） 搭 the bewildering complexity 令人费解的复杂性
bicker ['bɪkər]	*v.* 争吵，口角（to quarrel about unimportant things） 同 brabble, niggle, pettifog, quibble, squabble
bid [bɪd]	*v.* 命令（to command）；出价，投标（to make a bid） 记 发音记忆："必得" → 出价时抱着必得的态度 → 出价，投标
bide [baɪd]	*v.* 等待，逗留（to wait for; continue in a place） 同 abide, stay
bifurcate ['baɪfərkeɪt]	*v.* 分为两支，分叉（to divide into two parts or branches） 记 联想记忆：bi(两个) + furc(看作 fork, 叉) + ate → 分为两支

□ beholden	□ behoove	□ belabor	□ belligerence	□ bellow	□ belongings
□ bemused	□ berate	□ berserk	□ beseech	□ besmirch	□ besot
□ betoken	□ bewildering	□ bicker	□ bid	□ bide	□ bifurcate

bigot [ˈbɪgət]	*n.* (宗教、政治等的)顽固盲从者(a person who holds blindly to a particular creed);偏执者(a narrow-minded person) 记 联想记忆:big + (g)ot → 得到大东西不放的人 → 偏执者
bile [baɪl]	*n.* 胆汁(gall);愤怒(bitterness of temper)
bilk [bɪlk]	*v.* 躲债(to avoid paying money borrowed from others);骗取(to cheat sb. out of sth.)
bin [bɪn]	*n.* 大箱子(a large container)
blackball [ˈblækbɔːl]	*v.* 投票反对(to vote against);排斥(to ostracize) 记 组合词:black(黑) + ball(投票) → 投票反对
blade [bleɪd]	*n.* 刀刃,刀口(the cutting part of a tool)
blanch [blæntʃ]	*v.* 使变白(to make white);使(脸色)变苍白(to turn pale) 记 词根记忆:blanc(白) + h → 使变白
blandishment [ˈblændɪʃmənt]	*n.* 奉承,讨好 记 来自 blandish(*v.* 讨好)
blare [bler]	*v.* 高声发出(to sound or utter raucously) 记 联想记忆:和 bleat(*n.* 羊的叫声)来自同一词源
blasé [blɑːˈzeɪ]	*adj.* 厌倦享乐的,玩厌了的(bored with pleasure or dissipation) 记 联想记忆:对责骂(blame)已经厌倦(blasé)
blasphemy [ˈblæsfəmi]	*n.* 亵渎(神明)(profane or contemptuous speech; cursing) 记 词根记忆:blas(=blame 责备) + phem(出现) + y → 受责备的事出现 → 亵渎
blather [ˈblæðər]	*v.* 喋喋不休地胡说,唠叨(to talk foolishly at length) 同 babble, blether, blither, smatter
bleak [bliːk]	*adj.* 寒冷的;阴沉的(cold; frigid);阴郁的,暗淡的(depressing) 同 black, cutting, dim, raw
blear [blɪr]	*v.* 使模糊(to dim, blur) *adj.* 模糊的(obscure to the view or imagination) 同 bleary, blear-eyed, bleary-eyed
bleary [ˈblɪri]	*adj.* 视线模糊的,朦胧的(dull or dimmed especially from fatigue or sleep; poorly outlined or defined);精疲力尽的(tired to the point of exhaustion)
blemish [ˈblemɪʃ]	*v.* 损害;玷污(to mar; spoil the perfection of) *n.* 瑕疵,缺点(defect) 记 词根记忆:blem(弄伤) + ish → 把…弄伤 → 损害;玷污
bliss [blɪs]	*n.* 狂喜,极乐(great joy);福气,天赐的福(complete happiness) 记 联想记忆:得到祝福(bless)是有福气(bliss)的
bloated [ˈbloʊtɪd]	*adj.* 肿胀的(swelled, as with water or air);傲慢的(arrogant) 记 联想记忆:bloat(膨胀) + ed → 肿胀的

24

□ bigot	□ bile	□ bilk	□ bin	□ blackball	□ blade
□ blanch	□ blandishment	□ blare	□ blasé	□ blasphemy	□ blather
□ bleak	□ blear	□ bleary	□ blemish	□ bliss	□ bloated

271

blockade	*v./n.* 封锁
[blɑːˈkeɪd]	记 联想记忆：block(阻碍) + ade → 阻碍物 → 封锁
blockage	*n.* 障碍物(thing that blocks)
[ˈblɑːkɪdʒ]	同 closure, occlusion, stop, stoppage
blooming	*adj.* 开着花的(having flowers)；旺盛的
[ˈbluːmɪŋ]	记 来自 bloom(*v.* 花；开花)
blossom	*n.* 花(flower) *v.* (植物)开花(to produce blossom)
[ˈblɑːsəm]	记 联想记忆：bloom 中间开出两个 s 形的花
blunt	*adj.* 钝的(without a sharp edge)；直率的(frank and straightforward) *v.* 使迟钝
[blʌnt]	
boast	*v.* 自夸(to speak of or assert with excessive pride) *n.* 自夸
[boust]	记 和 roast(*v.* 烤，烘)一起记
bob	*v.* 轻拍，轻扣(to strike with a quick light blow)；使上下快速摆动(to move up and down in a short quick movement)
[bɑːb]	
bode	*v.* 预示(to be an omen of; presage)
[boud]	同 auspicate, portend
boding	*n.* 凶兆，前兆，预感(an omen, prediction, etc., especially of coming evil)
[ˈboudɪŋ]	*adj.* 凶兆的，先兆的
boggle	*v.* 犹豫(to hesitate)；退缩(to overwhelm with wonder or bewilderment)
[ˈbɑːgl]	记 联想记忆：bog(使…陷入泥沼) + gle → 陷入泥沼，会使人退缩 → 退缩
bogus	*adj.* 伪造的，假的(not genuine; spurious)
[ˈbougəs]	记 联想记忆：来自一种叫"Bogus"的机器，用于制造伪钞
bombast	*n.* 高调，夸大之辞(pompous language)
[ˈbɑːmbæst]	记 联想记忆：bomb(空洞的声音；炸弹) + ast → 像炮弹声 → 高调
bondage	*n.* 奴役，束缚(slavery, captivity)
[ˈbɑːndɪdʒ]	记 词根记忆：bond(使黏合) + age → 束缚
bonhomie	*n.* 好性情，和蔼(good-natured easy friendliness)
[ˌbɑːnəˈmiː]	记 联想记忆：bon (好)+homie (看作 home，家) → 好好待在家里 → 好性情，和蔼
bonny	*adj.* 健美的，漂亮的(attractive, fair)
[ˈbɑːni]	同 bonnie, comely
boo	*v.* 发出嘘声 *int.* (表示不满，轻蔑等)嘘
[buː]	记 发音记忆："不" → 发出嘘声
boom	*n.* 繁荣(prosperity) *v.* 发出隆隆声(to make a deep hollow sound)
[buːm]	记 联想记忆：原来是象声词；"嘣"的一声
boor	*n.* 粗野的人(a rude, awkward person)；农民(a peasant)
[bʊr]	记 联想记忆：粗野的人(boor)的人通常比较穷(poor)

boast

王婆卖瓜
自卖自夸

☐ blockade	☐ blockage	☐ blooming	☐ blossom	☐ blunt	☐ boast
☐ bob	☐ bode	☐ boding	☐ boggle	☐ bogus	☐ bombast
☐ bondage	☐ bonhomie	☐ bonny	☐ boo	☐ boom	☐ boor

boreal	*adj.* 北方的，北风的（of, relating to, or located in northern regions）
[ˈbɔːrɪəl]	
boring	*adj.* 无趣的，乏味的（uninteresting; dull）
[ˈbɔːrɪŋ]	记 来自 bore（*v.* 使厌烦）
bouffant	*adj.* 蓬松的，鼓胀的（puffed out）
[buːˈfɑːnt]	同 puffy
bough	*n.* 大树枝（a tree branch, especially a large or main branch）
[baʊ]	
boulder	*n.* 巨砾（large rock worn by water or the weather）
[ˈboʊldər]	记 联想记忆：用肩膀（shoulder）扛着巨砾（boulder）
bouncing	*adj.* 活泼的；健康的（lively, animated; enjoying good health）
[ˈbaʊnsɪŋ]	
bounteous	*adj.* 慷慨的（giving freely and generously, without restraint）；丰富的（provided in abundance; plentiful）
[ˈbaʊntɪəs]	记 词根记忆：bount(=bon 好) + eous → 好的 → 慷慨的
bouquet	*n.* 花束（a bunch of cut flowers）；芳香（fragrance）
[buˈkeɪ]	同 redolence, sweetness
bovine	*adj.* (似)牛的（of an ox）；迟钝的（slow; stolid）
[ˈboʊvaɪn]	记 词根记忆：bov(牛) + ine → 牛的
bowdlerize	*v.* 删除，删改（to expurgate）
[ˈbaʊdləraɪz]	记 来自人名 Thomas Bowdler，他删改出版了莎士比亚的戏剧
brace	*v.* 支撑，加固（to strengthen; prop up）*n.* 支撑物（fastener）
[breɪs]	记 联想记忆：brac(手臂) + e → 用手臂支撑使稳固 → 支撑，加固
bracelet	*n.* 手镯，臂镯（an ornamental band or chain worn around the wrist）
[ˈbreɪslət]	记 词根记忆：brac（手臂）+ e + let（小东西）→ 戴在手上的小东西 → 手镯
bracing	*adj.* 令人振奋的（invigorating）
[ˈbreɪsɪŋ]	同 brisk, energizing, fresh, refreshful, refreshing, tonic
brackish	*adj.* 微咸的（somewhat saline）；难吃的（distasteful）
[ˈbrækɪʃ]	记 联想记忆：brack(看作 black) + ish(看作 fish) → 黑色的咸鱼 → 微咸的
brag	*v.* 吹嘘（to boast）
[bræg]	记 联想记忆：bag(口袋)中间加个 r，"r"像一个嘴巴在吹
braise	*v.* 炖，蒸（to cook slowly in fat and little moisture in a closed pot）
[breɪz]	
brake	*n.* 刹车；阻碍 *v.* 刹车（to slow down or stop with a brake）；阻止（to retard as if by a brake）
[breɪk]	记 是 break（*v.* 打破，违反）的古典形式

boulder

brat [bræt]	*n.* 孩子；顽童（a badly behaved child） 记 联想记忆：b + rat(耗子) → 像耗子般的小孩 → 顽童
brattish ['brætɪʃ]	*adj.* （指小孩）讨厌的，被宠坏的，无礼的（(of a child) ill-mannered; annoying） 记 联想记忆：brat(小孩)+tish → 小孩有时候有点讨厌 → 讨厌的
bray [breɪ]	*v.* 大声而刺耳地发出（叫唤或声音）(to emit (an utterance or a sound) loudly and harshly) 记 联想记忆：在海湾(bay)能听到波浪发出很大的声音(bray)
brew [bruː]	*v.* 酿酒（to brew beer or ale）；沏(茶)，煮(咖啡) (to make a hot drink of tea or coffee)；酝酿，即 将发生（to be in the process of forming）
bribe [braɪb]	*v.* 贿赂（to induce or influence by bribery）
bricklayer ['brɪkleɪər]	*n.* 砖匠（a person who lays brick） 记 联想记忆：brick(砖) + lay(铺设) + er → 铺砖的人 → 砖匠
bridle ['braɪdl]	*n.* 马笼头（a head harness）*v.* 抑制，控制（to curb or control） 记 和bride(*n.* 新娘)一起记
brisk [brɪsk]	*adj.* 敏捷的，活泼的（quick, lively）；清新健康的（giving a healthy feeling） 记 联想记忆：b + risk(冒险) → 喜欢冒险的人 → 敏捷的，活泼的
bristling ['brɪslɪŋ]	*adj.* 竖立的（be stiffly erect）
brittle ['brɪtl]	*adj.* 易碎的，脆弱的（hard but easily broken） 记 联想记忆：br(看作break) + ittle(看作little) → 易碎的，脆弱的
brochure [brəʊ'ʃʊr]	*n.* 小册子，说明书（a small thin book with a paper cover）
bromide ['brəʊmaɪd]	*n.* 庸俗的人；陈词滥调（a commonplace or tiresome person; a trite saying）；镇静剂，安眠药（medicine as a sedative）
browbeat ['braʊbiːt]	*v.* 欺辱；吓唬（to bully） 记 组合词：brow(眉毛) + beat(打) → 用眉毛来打人 → 吓唬
browse [braʊz]	*v.* 吃草（to nibble at leaves or twigs）；浏览（to look through a book casually）*n.* 嫩叶；嫩芽 记 联想记忆：brow(眉毛) + se → 吃像眉毛一样的草 → 吃草
bruise [bruːz]	*v.* 受伤，擦伤（to injure the skin） 记 联想记忆：和cruise(*v.* 乘船巡游)一起记
bruit [bruːt]	*v.* 散布(谣言)（to spread a rumor） 记 联想记忆：br(看作bring) + u(看作you) + it → 把它带给你 → 散布(谣言)
brusque [brʌsk]	*adj.* 唐突的，鲁莽的（rough or abrupt; blunt） 记 发音记忆："不如屎壳(郎)" → 鲁莽的

brew

brutal ['bruːtl]	*adj.* 残忍的，野蛮的（savage; violent）；冷酷的（very harsh and rigorous） 记 来自 brute（*n.* 人面兽心的人；残暴的人）
buck [bʌk]	*v.* 反抗，抵制（to oppose; resist）*n.* 雄鹿；雄兔（male deer or rabbit）； <美俚>元，钱
bucolic [bjuː'kɑːlɪk]	*adj.* 乡村的（of country life; rural）；牧羊的（pastoral） 记 词根记忆：buc（牛）+ olic（养…的）→ 养牛的 → 乡村的 搭 bucolic serenity 乡村的宁静
budget ['bʌdʒɪt]	*n.* 预算（plan of how money will be spent over a period of time）*v.* 做预算，安排开支（to plan in advance the expenditure of） 记 联想记忆：bud（花蕾）+ get（得到）→ 得到花蕾 → 用钱卖花 → 做预算 搭 on a（tight）budget 拮据
buffer ['bʌfər]	*v.* 缓冲，减轻（to lessen the effect of a blow or collision） 记 联想记忆：buff（软皮）+er → 缓冲
buffet ['bʌfɪt]	*v.* 反复敲打；连续打击（to strike sharply especially with the hand; to strike repeatedly）
buffoon [bə'fuːn]	*n.* 丑角（clown）；愚蠢的人（fool） 记 联想记忆：buf（看作 but）+ foon（看作 fool）→ but a fool → 只是个笨蛋 → 愚蠢的人

24

You never know what you can do till you try.

除非你亲自尝试一下，否则你永远不知道你能够做什么。

——英国小说家 马里亚特（Frederick Marryat, British novelist）

Word List 25

MP3-25

bulge [bʌldʒ]	*n.* 凸起，膨胀（a protruding part; an outward curve or swelling）*v.* 膨胀，鼓起（to（cause to）curve outward）
bullion ['buliən]	*n.* 金条，银条（gold or silver in the form of ingots） 记 联想记忆：bull（公牛）+（l）ion（狮子）→ 卖公牛，狮子得金银 → 金条，银条
bully ['buli]	*v.* 威胁，以强欺弱（to frighten or tyrannize）*n.* 欺凌弱小者 记 联想记忆：bully 古意为 "情人"，因为在争夺情人的斗争中总是强的打败弱的，所以演化为"以强欺弱"之意
bumble ['bʌmbl]	*v.* 说话含糊（to stumble）；拙劣地做（to proceed clumsily） 同 burr, buzz, hum
bump [bʌmp]	*v.* 碰撞（to hit or knock against）*n.* 碰撞声（dull sound of a blow） 同 collision, crash, impact, jolt, smash
bumptious ['bʌmpʃəs]	*adj.* 傲慢的，自夸的（crudely or loudly assertive） 记 联想记忆：bump（碰撞）+ tious → 顶撞人 → 傲慢的
bungle ['bʌŋgl]	*v.* 笨拙地做（to act or work clumsily and awkwardly） 同 botch, bumble, fumble, muff, stumble
buoy ['buːi]	*n.* 浮标（a floating object）；救生圈 *v.* 支持，鼓励（to encourage） 同 animate, elate, exhilarate, flush, inspirit
burial ['beriəl]	*n.* 埋葬，埋藏（the act or ceremony of putting a dead body into a grave） 记 来自 bury（*v.* 埋葬，掩埋）
burlesque [bɜːr'lesk]	*n.* 讽刺或滑稽的戏剧，滑稽剧（derisive caricature; parody） 记 发音记忆："不如乐死去" → 玩笑话 → 滑稽剧
burnish ['bɜːrnɪʃ]	*v.* 擦亮，磨光（to become shining by rubbing; polish） 记 联想记忆：burn（烧）+ ish → 烧得发亮 → 擦亮，磨光
burrow ['bɜːroʊ]	*v.* 挖掘，钻进，翻寻（to dig a hole; penetrate by means of a burrow） *n.* 地洞 记 联想记忆：用犁（furrow）来翻寻（burrow）
bust [bʌst]	*n.* 半身（雕）像 记 联想记忆：灌木丛（bush）中发现了一尊佛的半身像（bust）

bustle [ˈbʌsl]	*v.* 奔忙，忙乱(to be busily astir) *n.* 喧闹，熙熙攘攘(noisy, energetic, and often obtrusive activity)
butt [bʌt]	*v.* 用头抵撞，顶撞(to strike with the head) *n.* 粗大的一端；烟蒂 搭 butt in 插嘴；插手
buxom [ˈbʌksəm]	*adj.* 体态丰满的(having a shapely, full-bosomed figure) 同 curvaceous, curvy
byline [ˈbaɪlaɪn]	*n.* (报刊等的文章开头或结尾)标出作者名字的一行(a line identifying the writer) 记 联想记忆：by + line (字行) → 第二行 → 大标题下面写着作家姓名的一行 → 标出作者名字的一行
cacophony [kəˈkɑːfəni]	*n.* 刺耳的声音(harsh, jarring sound) 记 词根记忆：caco(坏) + phony(声音) → 声音不好 → 刺耳的声音
cadence [ˈkeɪdns]	*n.* 抑扬顿挫(rhythmic rise and fall)；节奏，韵律(rhythm) 记 词根记忆：cad(落下) + ence → 声音的落下上升 → 抑扬顿挫
cadet [kəˈdet]	*n.* 军校或警官学校的学生(a student at a military school) 搭 army cadets 军校学员
cadge [kædʒ]	*v.* 乞讨(to get sth. from sb. by asking)；占便宜 搭 cadge from/off 乞讨
cajole [kəˈdʒoʊl]	*v.* (以甜言蜜语)哄骗(to coax with flattery; wheedle) 记 联想记忆：caj(=cage 笼子) + ole → 把(鸟)诱入笼子 → 哄骗
calibrate [ˈkælɪbreɪt]	*v.* 量…口径(to determine the calibre of)；校准(to adjust precisely) 记 来自 calibre(*n.* 口径)
callow [ˈkæloʊ]	*adj.* (鸟)未生羽毛的(unfledged)；(人)未成熟的(immature) 记 联想记忆：call + (l)ow → 叫做低的东西 → 未成熟的
calorie [ˈkæləri]	*n.* 卡路里；卡(热量单位) 记 发音记忆："卡路里" → 卡
calumniate [kəˈlʌmnieɪt]	*v.* 诽谤，中伤(to make maliciously false statements) 同 defame, malign, slander, slur, vilify
cameo [ˈkæmioʊ]	*n.* 刻有浮雕的宝石(jewel carved in relief)；生动刻画；(演员)出演 记 联想记忆：came(来) + o → 来哦 → 演员来哦 → 出演
camouflage [ˈkæməflɑːʒ]	*v.* 掩饰，伪装(to disguise in order to conceal) *n.* 伪装 记 联想记忆：cam(看作 came) + ou(看作 out) + flag(旗帜) + e → 扛着旗帜出来 → 伪装成革命战士 → 伪装
canard [kəˈnɑːrd]	*n.* 谣言，假新闻(a false malicious report) 记 联想记忆：金丝雀(canary)在造谣(canard)
canary [kəˈneri]	*n.* 金丝雀；女歌星 记 联想记忆：can(能够) + ary → 有能耐，能歌善舞的人 → 女歌星
candidacy [ˈkændɪdəsi]	*n.* 候选人资格(the state of being a candidate) 记 联想记忆：经过公正的(candid)选拔，他获得了候选人资格(candidacy)

25

□ bustle	□ butt	□ buxom	□ byline	□ cacophony	□ cadence
□ cadet	□ cadge	□ cajole	□ calibrate	□ callow	□ calorie
□ calumniate	□ cameo	□ camouflage	□ canard	□ canary	□ candidacy

277

canon [ˈkænən]	*n.* 经典，真作(the works that are genuine) 记 联想记忆：can（能）+ on（在…上）→ 能放在桌面上的真家伙 → 经典，真作
canonical [kəˈnɑːnɪkl]	*adj.* 符合规定的(according to, or ordered by church canon)；经典的 同 orthodox
canopy [ˈkænəpi]	*n.* 蚊帐(a cloth covering suspended over a bed)；华盖(a drapery, awning, or other rooflike covering)
canorous [kəˈnɔːrəs]	*adj.* 音调优美的，有旋律的(pleasant sounding; melodious)
canvass [ˈkænvəs]	*v.* 细查(to scrutinize)；拉选票(to go around an area asking people for political support) 记 联想记忆：can(能) + v(胜利的标志) + ass(驴子) → 能让驴子得胜 → 拉选票
canyon [ˈkænjən]	*n.* 峡谷(a long, narrow valley between cliffs) 记 联想记忆：can(能) + y(像峡谷的形状) + on(在…上) → 能站在峡谷上 → 峡谷 参 gorge(*n.* 山谷，峡谷); gully(*n.* 溪谷，冲沟); ravine(*n.* 峡谷，溪谷); valley(*n.* 山谷)
capacious [kəˈpeɪʃəs]	*adj.* 容量大的，宽敞的(containing a great deal; spacious) 记 词根记忆：cap(抓) + acious → 能抓住东西 → 宽敞的
caper [ˈkeɪpər]	*n.* 雀跃，跳跃(a gay, playful jump or leap) *v.* 雀跃 记 联想记忆：cape(披风) + r → 第一次穿披风走路的人 → 雀跃
caprice [kəˈpriːs]	*n.* 奇思怪想，反复无常，任性(sudden change in attitude or behavior) 记 联想记忆：cap(帽子) + rice(米饭) → 戴上帽子才吃米饭 → 任性
capsule [ˈkæpsjuːl]	*n.* 荚膜，蒴果(seed case of a plant)；胶囊(small soluble case containing a dose of medicine)
caption [ˈkæpʃn]	*n.* 标题(short title of an article) 记 词根记忆：capt(拿，抓) + ion → 抓住主要内容 → 标题
captivate [ˈkæptɪveɪt]	*v.* 迷惑，迷住(to fascinate, attract) 记 联想记忆：captiv(e)(俘房) + ate → 使成为漂亮的俘虏来迷惑敌人 → 迷惑
carbohydrate [ˌkɑːrbouˈhaɪdreɪt]	*n.* 碳水化合物(a natural class of food that provides energy to the body) 记 词根记忆：carbo(碳) + hydr(水) + ate → 碳水化合物
cardiologist [ˌkɑːrdiˈɑːlədʒɪst]	*n.* 心脏病专家(an expert of the heart disease) 记 词根记忆：cardi(=card 心) + olog(=ology 学科) + ist(人) → 研究心脏的人 → 心脏病专家
careen [kəˈriːn]	*v.* (船)倾斜(to lean sideways)；使倾斜(to cause a ship to lean) 记 联想记忆：船倾斜(careen)了，但船家并不在意(care)
caress [kəˈres]	*n.* 爱抚，抚摸(loving touch) *v.* 爱抚或抚摸(to touch or stroke lightly in a loving or endearing manner)

careworn [ˈkerwɔːrn]	*adj.* 忧心忡忡的，饱经忧患的 (showing the effects of worry, anxiety, or burdensome responsibility)
cargo [ˈkɑːrɡoʊ]	*n.* (船、飞机等装载的)货物 (load of goods carried in a ship or aircraft) 记 联想记忆：car(汽车) + go(走) → 汽车运走的东西 → 货物
carouse [kəˈraʊz]	*n.* 狂饮寻乐 (a noisy, merry drinking party) 记 联想记忆：car + (r)ouse(唤起) → 开着汽车欢闹 → 狂饮寻乐
carp [kɑːrp]	*n.* 鲤鱼 *v.* 吹毛求疵 (to complain continually) 记 联想记忆：结婚这么多年还买不起车（car），妻子对丈夫总是吹毛求疵（carp）
carpenter [ˈkɑːrpəntər]	*n.* 木匠 (worker who builds or repairs wooden structures) 记 联想记忆：美国六七十年代风靡一时的乐队 Carpenters
carrion [ˈkæriən]	*n.* 腐肉 (the decaying flesh of a dead body) 记 词根记忆：carr(=carn 肉) + ion → 腐肉
cartoon [kɑːrˈtuːn]	*n.* 漫画 (amusing drawing that comments satirically on current events) 记 发音记忆："卡通" → 漫画
casual [ˈkæʒuəl]	*adj.* 偶然的 (occurring by chance)；非正式的，随便的 记 联想记忆：平常的(usual)时候可以穿非正式的(casual)服装 搭 casual conversations 闲谈
catalog [ˈkætəlɔːɡ]	*n.* 目录 (complete list of items of a book)；系列 (series) 记 词根记忆：cata(下面) + log(说话) → 概括在下面要说的话 → 目录
catharsis [kəˈθɑːrsɪs]	*n.* 宣泄，净化 (the purifying of the emotions) 记 词根记忆：cathar(清洁) + sis → 净化
catholic [ˈkæθlɪk]	*adj.* 普遍的；广泛的 (all inclusive; universal)；宽容的 (broad in understanding; liberal) 记 联想记忆：和天主教"Catholic"的拼写一致，但第一个字母不大写
caucus [ˈkɔːkəs]	*n.* 政党高层会议 (a private meeting of leaders of a political party)
caudal [ˈkɔːdl]	*adj.* 尾部的，像尾部的 (of, relating to, or being a tail; situated in or directed toward the hind part of the body)
caulk [kɔːk]	*v.* 填塞(缝隙)使不漏水 (to stop up the cracks, seams, etc.)
cauterize [ˈkɔːtəraɪz]	*v.* (用腐蚀性物质或烙铁)烧灼(表皮组织)以消毒或止血 (to sear with a cautery or caustic)
cavalry [ˈkævlri]	*n.* 骑兵部队，装甲部队 记 联想记忆：骑兵(cavalier)组成了骑兵部队(cavalry)
cavort [kəˈvɔːrt]	*v.* 腾跃，欢跃 (to prance; gambol) 记 发音记忆："渴望他" → 兴奋得跳跃 → 欢跃
cede [siːd]	*v.* 割让(领土)，放弃 (to transfer the title or ownership of) 同 abandon, abdicate, demit, relinquish, surrender

25

celebrated [ˈselɪbreɪtɪd]	*adj.* 有名的，知名的(famous; renowned) 记 来自 celebrate(*v.* 庆祝，赞扬) 搭 be widely celebrated 广泛知名的
celebrity [səˈlebrəti]	*n.* 名声(wide recognition)；名人(a famous or well-publicized person) 记 词根记忆：celebr(著名) + ity → 名人
celerity [sɪˈlerəti]	*n.* 快速，迅速(swiftness in acting or moving; speed) 记 词根记忆：celer(速度) + ity → 快速，迅速
cello [ˈtʃeloʊ]	*n.* 大提琴 记 联想记忆：violin(*n.* 小提琴)；viola(*n.* 中提琴)
cement [sɪˈment]	*n.* 水泥；黏合剂 *v.* 黏合，巩固(to unite or make firm by or as if by cement) 记 联想记忆：ce + ment(看作 mend, 修补) → 修补材料 → 水泥；黏合剂
centrifugal [ˌsentrɪˈfjuːɡl]	*adj.* 离心的(moving or tending to move away from a center) 记 词根记忆：centri(中心) + fug(逃跑) + al → 逃离中心的 → 离心的
centripetal [senˈtrɪpɪtl]	*adj.* 向心的(moving or tending to move toward a center) 记 词根记忆：centri(中心) + pet(追求) + al → 追求中心 → 向心的
cephalic [sɪˈfælɪk]	*adj.* 头的，头部的(of the head or skull) 记 词根记忆：cephal(头) + ic → 头的
ceremony [ˈserəmoʊni]	*n.* 典礼，仪式(formal acts performed on a religious or public occasion) 记 联想记忆：cere(蜡) + mony(看作 money, 钱) → 古代做典礼时，蜡烛和钱是少不了的 → 典礼
certification [ˌsɜːrtɪfɪˈkeɪʃn]	*n.* 证明(action of certifying) 记 词根记忆：cert(搞清) + ify(…化) → 搞清楚 → 证明
cession [ˈseʃn]	*n.* 割让，转让 记 来自 cede(*v.* 割让)
chaffing [ˈtʃæfɪŋ]	*adj.* 玩笑的，嘲弄的(of, relating to jest, banter) 记 来自 chaff(*v.* 开玩笑)
chameleon [kəˈmiːliən]	*n.* 变色龙，蜥蜴；善变之人(someone who is very changeable)
chandelier [ˌʃændəˈlɪr]	*n.* 枝形吊灯(烛台)(a lighting fixture)
chant [tʃænt]	*n.* 圣歌 *v.* 歌唱，吟诵(to sing or recite) 记 发音记忆："唱" → 歌唱
chaos [ˈkeɪɑːs]	*n.* 混乱(extreme confusion or disorder) 记 发音记忆："吵死" → 混乱
char [tʃɑːr]	*v.* 烧焦(to make or become black by burning)；把…烧成炭 记 联想记忆：椅子(chair)的一个腿(i)儿被烧焦(char)了
characterization [ˌkærəktəraɪˈzeɪʃn]	*n.* 描绘，刻画(the delineation of character) 记 来自 character(*n.* 性格，角色)

charade	*n.* 猜字谜游戏 *v.* 凭动作猜字谜
[ʃəˈreɪd]	
charisma	*n.* (大众爱戴的)领袖气质(a special quality of leadership); 魅力(a special charm or allure that inspires devotion)
[kəˈrɪzmə]	记 联想记忆: cha(看作 China) + ris(看作 rise) + ma(看作 mao, 引申为毛泽东) → 中国升起毛(泽东) → 领袖气质
charity	*n.* 慈善(benevolence); 施舍(a voluntary giving of money)
[ˈtʃærəti]	记 联想记忆: cha(音似: 茶) + rity → 请喝茶 → 施舍
charm	*n.* 魅力(a physical grace or attraction); 咒语, 咒符(incantation; amulet)
[tʃɑːrm]	*v.* 吸引, 迷住(to delight, attract or influence by charm)
	记 联想记忆: char(音似: 茶) + m(看作 man) → 被男士约出去喝茶, 因为很有魅力 → 魅力
	搭 particular charm 独特的魅力
chase	*v.* 雕镂(to make a groove in); 追逐(to follow rapidly); 追捕
[tʃeɪs]	记 联想记忆: 谁动了我的奶酪(cheese), 我就去追赶(chase)谁
chaste	*adj.* 贞洁的(virtuous); 朴实的(restrained and simple)
[tʃeɪst]	记 联想记忆: 贞洁的(chaste)姑娘被追逐(chase)
chasten	*v.* (通过惩罚而使坏习惯等)改正(to punish in order to correct or make better); 磨炼
[ˈtʃeɪsn]	记 联想记忆: chaste(纯洁的) + n → 变纯洁 → 改正
chastise	*v.* 严惩(to punish by beating); 谴责(to scold or condemn)
[tʃæˈstaɪz]	记 联想记忆: 追赶(chase)上小偷进行严惩(chastise)
chauvinistic	*adj.* 沙文主义的, 盲目爱国的(excessive or blind patriotism)
[ˌʃoʊvɪˈnɪstɪk]	记 来自人名 Chauvin, 因其过分的爱国主义和对拿破仑的忠诚而闻名
checkered	*adj.* 多变的(with many changes of fortune)
[ˈtʃekərd]	记 来自 checker(*n.* 棋盘花格或棋子)
cheeky	*adj.* 无礼的, 厚颜无耻的(insolently bold; impudent)
[ˈtʃiːki]	同 audacious, brash, brazen, impertinent
cherubic	*adj.* 天使的, 无邪的, 可爱的(angelic; innocent looking)
[tʃəˈruːbɪk]	记 来自 cherub(*n.* 小天使)
chic	*adj.* 漂亮的, 时髦的(cleverly stylish; currently fashionable)
[ʃiːk]	同 modish, posh, swanky
chicanery	*n.* 欺骗, 欺诈(deception by artful sophistry; trickery)
[ʃɪˈkeɪnəri]	记 词根记忆: chic(聪明) + anery → 耍聪明 → 欺诈
chide	*v.* 斥责, 责骂(to scold; reprove mildly)
[tʃaɪd]	记 联想记忆: 斥责(chide)孩子(child)
chimera	*n.* 神话怪物(fabulous monster); 梦幻(an impossible or foolish fancy)
[kaɪˈmɪrə]	记 联想记忆: 原指"希腊神话中一种狮头羊身蛇尾的会喷火的女妖怪" → 神话怪物

25

□ charade	□ charisma	□ charity	□ charm	□ chase	□ chaste
□ chasten	□ chastise	□ chauvinistic	□ checkered	□ cheeky	□ cherubic
□ chic	□ chicanery	□ chide	□ chimera		

281

chipmunk	*n.* 花栗鼠(像松鼠的美洲小动物)
['tʃɪpmʌŋk]	
chipper	*adj.* 爽朗的, 活泼的(sprightly)
['tʃɪpər]	记 联想记忆: 她很爽朗(chipper), 将新研发的芯片(chip)拿出来给大家看
chirp	*v.* (鸟或虫)唧唧叫(to utter in a sharp, shrill tone)
[tʃɜːrp]	记 动物的不同叫声: 狗–bark(吠); 狼–howl(嚎); 牛、羊–blat(叫); 狮、虎–roar(吼)
chisel	*n.* 凿子 *v.* 凿
['tʃɪzl]	
choice	*adj.* 上等的(of high quality); 精选的(selected with care)
[tʃɔɪs]	同 dainty, delicate, elegant, exquisite, superior
choke	*v.* (使)窒息, 阻塞(to have great difficulty in breathing)
[tʃoʊk]	记 联想记忆: 喝可乐(coke)给呛着(choke)了
choleric	*adj.* 易怒的, 暴躁的(having irascible nature; irritable)
['kɑːlərɪk]	记 词根记忆: choler(胆汁) + ic → 胆汁质的 → 易怒的, 暴躁的
choosy	*adj.* 挑三拣四的, 挑剔的(fastidiously selective; particular)
['tʃuːzi]	同 finical, fussy, meticulous
chortle	*v.* 开心地笑, 咯咯地笑(to utter with a gleeful chuckling sound) *n.* 得意的笑
['tʃɔːrtl]	记 各种笑: chuckle(*v./n.*轻声笑); giggle(*v./n.* 咯咯笑); grin(*v./n.* 咧嘴笑); guffaw(*v./n.* 哄笑); simper(*v./n.* 傻笑); smirk(*v./n.* 假笑)
chronic	*adj.* 慢性的, 长期的(marked by long duration or frequent recurrence)
['krɑːnɪk]	记 词根记忆: chron(时间) + ic(…的) → 长时间的 → 慢性的
	搭 chronic illness 慢性病
chuck	*v.* 丢弃, 抛弃(to discard), 解雇(to dismiss); 辞职(to give up one's job)
[tʃʌk]	同 oust, throw
chuckle	*v.* 轻声地笑, 咯咯地笑(to laugh softly in a low tone)
['tʃʌkl]	同 chortle
churl	*n.* 粗鄙之人(a surly, illbred person)
[tʃɜːrl]	记 联想记忆: 粗鄙之人(churl)不宜进教堂(church)
ciliate	*adj.* 有纤毛的(having minute hairs); 有睫毛的
['sɪliɪt]	记 词根记忆: cili(毛) + ate → 有纤毛的
cinder	*n.* 余烬, 煤渣(slag from the reduction of metallicores)
['sɪndər]	记 联想记忆: 灰姑娘(cinderella)每天必须掏煤渣(cinder)
circular	*adj.* 圆形的; 循环的(shaped like a circle)
['sɜːrkjələr]	记 词根记忆: circ(圆) + ular → 圆形的; 循环的
citation	*n.* 引证; 引文; 传票(an official summons to appear, as before a court)
[saɪ'teɪʃn]	记 来自 cite(*v.* 引证, 引用)

□ chipmunk	□ chipper	□ chirp	□ chisel	□ choice	□ choke
□ choleric	□ choosy	□ chortle	□ chronic	□ chuck	□ chuckle
□ churl	□ ciliate	□ cinder	□ circular	□ citation	

282

civilian	*n.* 百姓，平民(any person not an active member of the armed forces or
[sə'vɪliən]	police)
	记 词根记忆：civil(市民的) + ian → 百姓，平民

clairvoyance	*n.* 超人的洞察力(keen perception or insight)
[kler'vɔɪəns]	记 联想记忆：clair(看作 clear，清楚) + voy(看) + ance → 看得很清楚 → 超人的洞察力

clairvoyant	*adj.* 透视的，有洞察力的(having power that can see in the mind either
[kler'vɔɪənt]	future events or things that exist or are happening out of sight)
	记 联想记忆：clair(看作 clear，清楚的) + voy(看) + ant → 看得清楚的 → 有洞察力的

clammy	*adj.* 湿冷的，发粘的(being damp, soft, sticky, and usually cool)
['klæmi]	记 联想记忆：clam(蛤蜊) + my → 像蛤蜊一样又冷又湿 → 湿冷的，发粘的

clandestine	*adj.* 秘密的，偷偷摸摸的(surreptitious; furtive; secret)
[klæn'destɪn]	记 联想记忆：clan(宗派) + destine(命中注定) → "宗派"和"命中注定"都有一些"秘密"色彩 → 秘密的

clarity	*n.* 清楚，明晰(condition of being clear; clearness)
['klærəti]	记 词根记忆：clar(清楚，明白) + ity → 清楚，明晰

clash	*v.* 冲突，撞击(to collide or strike together with aloud, harsh and metallic
[klæʃ]	noise)
	同 bump

clasp	*n.* 钩子，扣子(device for fastening things)；紧握(firm hold)
[klæsp]	同 clench, clutch, grasp, grip

cleft	*n.* 裂缝(an opening; crack; crevice) *adj.* 劈开的(partially split or divided)
[kleft]	记 联想记忆：c + left(左) → 左边的裂缝像 c 的形状 → 裂缝

clement	*adj.* 仁慈的(merciful)；温和的(mild)
['klemənt]	搭 clement weather 温和的气候

clench	*v.* 握紧(to grip tightly)；咬紧(牙关等)(to close the teeth firmly)
[klentʃ]	同 clasp, clutch, grab, grapple, grasp, seize

cliché	*adj.* 陈腐的((of phrase or idea) used so often that it has become stale or
[kliː'ʃeɪ]	meaningless) *n.* 陈词滥调

clinch	*v.* 钉牢(to secure a nail, bolt, etc.)；彻底解决(to settle an argument
[klɪntʃ]	definitely)
	记 联想记忆：cl + inch(英寸) → 一英寸一英寸地钉 → 钉牢

cling	*v.* 紧紧抓住(to hold on tightly)；坚持(to be unwilling to abandon)
[klɪŋ]	搭 cling to 紧握不放；坚持

clot	*n.* 凝块(a thickened lump formed within a liquid) *v.* 使凝结成块(to thicken
[klɑːt]	into a clot)

cloudburst	*n.* 大暴雨(a sudden, very heavy rain)
['klaʊdbɜːrst]	记 组合词：cloud(云) + burst(爆裂) → 乌云爆裂，要下暴雨 → 大暴雨

25

cloy	v. (吃甜食)生腻，吃腻 (to surfeit by too much of sth. sweet)
[klɔɪ]	同 satiate
cluster	n. 串，簇，群 v. 群集，丛生 (to gather or grow in a cluster or clusters)
[ˈklʌstər]	记 词根记忆：clust (=clot, 凝成块) + er → 凝块 → 群集
coagulate	v. 使凝结 (to curdle; clot)
[koʊˈægjuleɪt]	记 词根记忆：co(一起) + ag(做) + ulate → 做 到一起 → 使凝结
coagulation	n. 凝结
[koʊˌægjuˈleɪʃn]	记 来自 coagulate(v. 使凝结)
coarsen	v. (使)变粗糙 (to cause sth. to become coarse)
[ˈkɔːrsn]	记 来自 coarse(adj. 粗糙的)
coda	n. 乐曲结尾部 (final passage of a piece of music)
[ˈkoʊdə]	
coddle	v. 溺爱；悉心照料 (to treat with great care and tenderness)
[ˈkɑːdl]	同 cater, cosset, pamper, spoil
coeval	adj. 同时代的 (existing at the same time)
[koʊˈiːvl]	记 词根记忆：co(共同) + ev(时代) + al → 同时代的
coffer	n. 保险柜，保险箱 (a strongbox)
[ˈkɔːfər]	记 联想记忆：保险柜(coffer)里珍藏了一种颇有价值的咖啡(coffee)
cogitate	v. 慎重思考，思索 (to think seriously and deeply; ponder)
[ˈkɑːdʒɪteɪt]	记 联想记忆：有说服力的(cogent)东西总是经过慎重思考(cogitate)的
cohesion	n. 内聚力；凝聚力 (tendency to stick together)
[koʊˈhiːʒn]	搭 group cohesion 团体凝聚力
collage	n. 拼贴画 (an artistic composition made of various materials)
[kəˈlɑːʒ]	记 和 college(n. 学院)一起记
collapse	v. 坍塌，塌陷 (to break into pieces and fall down suddenly)；虚脱，晕倒 (to become unconscious)
[kəˈlæps]	记 词根记忆：col(共同) + lapse(滑倒) → 全部滑倒 → 坍塌
collate	v. 对照，核对 (to compare critically in order to consolidate)
[kəˈleɪt]	记 词根记忆：col(共同) + late(放) → 放到一起 → 核对
collision	n. 碰撞，冲突 (an act or instance of colliding)
[kəˈlɪʒn]	记 来自 collide(v. 冲撞)
colloquy	n. (非正式的)交谈，会谈 (informal discussion; conversation)
[ˈkɑːləkwi]	同 chat, dialogue, discourse
collude	v. 串通，共谋 (to act in conspire)
[kəˈluːd]	记 词根记忆：col(共同) + lud(玩弄) + e → 共同玩弄 → 串通

cluster

colt [koʊlt]	*n.* 小雄马（a young male horse）；新手（a youthful or inexperienced person）
coma ['koʊmə]	*n.* 昏迷（deep, prolonged unconsciousness） 搭 go into/be in a coma 陷入/处于昏迷状态
comatose ['koʊmətoʊs]	*adj.* 昏迷的（unconscious; torpid） 记 来自 coma（*n.* 昏迷）
combat ['kɑːmbæt]	*n./v.* 搏斗，战斗（(to) fight between two people, armies） 记 词根记忆：com（共同）+ bat（打，击）→ 共同打 → 战斗
comedienne [kəˌmiːdi'en]	*n.* 喜剧女演员（a woman who is a comedian）；滑稽人物 记 来自 comedy（*n.* 喜剧）
comely ['kʌmli]	*adj.* 动人的，美丽的（pleasant to look at） 记 联想记忆：come（来）+ ly，吸引别人过来 → 动人的
comestible [kə'mestɪbl]	*n.* 食物，食品（sth. fit to be eaten）*adj.* 可吃的（edible） 记 联想记忆：come（来）+ s + tible（看作 table，桌子）→ 来到桌上 → 食品
comeuppance [kʌm'ʌpəns]	*n.* 应得的惩罚，因果报应（a deserved rebuke or penalty） 记 联想记忆：come up（发生）+ p + ance（表名词）→ 某些信念认为世上发生（come up）的所有坏事都是有因果报应的 → 因果报应
comma ['kɑːmə]	*n.* 逗号（punctuation mark to indicate a light pause） 记 和 coma（*n.* 昏迷）一起记
commemorate [kə'meməreɪt]	*v.* 纪念(伟人、大事件等)（to call to remembrance）；庆祝 记 词根记忆：com（共同）+ memor（记住）+ ate → 大家一起记住 → 纪念
commence [kə'mens]	*v.* 开始，着手（to begin; start; originate） 记 词根记忆：com（共同）+ mence（说，做）→ 一起说，做 → 开始，着手
commencement [kə'mensmənt]	*n.* 开始；毕业典礼（the ceremony at which degrees or diplomas are conferred at a school or college）

25

□ colt □ coma □ comatose □ combat □ comedienne □ comely
□ comestible □ comeuppance □ comma □ commemorate □ commence □ commencement

285

Word List 26

commit [kəˈmɪt]	*v.* 托付(to consign); 承诺(to bind or obligate); 犯罪(to perpetrate) 记 词根记忆: com(共同) + mit(送) → 一起送给 → 托付
commonplace [ˈkɑːmənpleɪs]	*adj.* 普通的, 平庸的(ordinary) 记 组合词: common(普通的) + place(地方) → 普通的地方 → 普通的
commonsense [ˈkɑːmənsens]	*adj.* 有常识的(having practical judgment gained from experience of life, not by special study) 记 组合词: common(普通的) + sense(认识) → 具有常识的
compact [ˈkɑːmpækt]	*adj.* 坚实的(dense; solid); 简洁的(not diffuse or wordy) *n.* 合同, 协议(an agreement or covenant between two or more parties) 记 词根记忆: com(一起) + pact(打包, 压紧) → 一起压紧 → 坚实的
compatible [kəmˈpætəbl]	*adj.* 能和谐共处的, 相容的(capable of living together harmoniously) 记 词根记忆: com(一起) + pat(=path 感情) + ible → 有共同感情的 → 相容的 搭 be compatible with 与…和谐相处
compensate [ˈkɑːmpenseɪt]	*v.* 补偿, 赔偿(to make equivalent return to; recompense) 记 词根记忆: com(一起) + pens(挂; 花费) + ate → 全部给予花费 → 赔偿 搭 compensate for 补偿, 弥补
compile [kəmˈpaɪl]	*v.* 汇集(to gather and put together); 编辑(to compose of materials gathered from various sources) 记 词根记忆: com(一起) + pile(堆) → 堆在一起 → 汇集
complaisance [kəmˈpleɪzəns]	*n.* 彬彬有礼; 殷勤; 柔顺(willingness to do what pleases others) 记 联想记忆: com(共同) + plais(看作 please, 使喜欢) + ance → 彬彬有礼才能使大家喜欢 → 彬彬有礼
complaisant [kəmˈpleɪzənt]	*adj.* 顺从的; 讨好的(affably agreeable; obliging) 同 accommodating, indulgent

这是公司的赔偿!

compensate

complicity [kəmˈplɪsəti]	*n.* 合谋, 串通(participation; involvement in a crime) 记 词根记忆: com(共同) + plic(重叠) + ity → 共同重叠 → 同谋关系 → 合谋
compress [kəmˈpres]	*v.* 压缩; 压紧(to press together; contract) 记 词根记忆: com(全部) + press(挤压) → 全部挤压 → 压缩
compulsion [kəmˈpʌlʃn]	*n.* 强迫(that which compels); (难以抗拒的)冲动(an irresistible, irrational impulse to perform some act) 记 词根记忆: com(一起) + puls(推, 冲) + ion → 一起推 → 强迫
compulsory [kəmˈpʌlsəri]	*adj.* 强制性的, 必须做的(compelling; coercive) 搭 compulsory education 义务教育
compunction [kəmˈpʌŋkʃn]	*n.* 懊悔; 良心不安(a sense of guilt; remorse; penitence) 记 词根记忆: com+punct(刺, 点)+ion → (心)不断被刺 → 良心不安
con [kɑːn]	*n.* 反对论(an argument or evidence in opposition) *v.* 欺骗(to swindle) 搭 pros and cons 有利有弊, 正反两方面
concatenate [kənˈkætəneɪt]	*v.* 连结; 连锁(to link together) 记 词根记忆: con(共同) + caten(铁链) + ate → 在同一根铁链中 → 连锁
concave [kɑːnˈkeɪv]	*adj.* 凹的(hollow and curved like the inside of a bowl) 记 词根记忆: con + cave(洞) → 洞是凹进去的 → 凹的
conceit [kənˈsiːt]	*n.* 自负, 自大(an exaggerated opinion of oneself; vanity) 记 词根记忆: con + ceit(=ceive 拿) → 拿架子 → 自负
concession [kənˈseʃn]	*n.* 让步(the act of conceding) 记 来自 concede(*v.* 让步)
conciliate [kənˈsɪlieɪt]	*v.* 安抚; 安慰(to soothe the anger of; placate); 调和(to reconcile; pacify) 记 词根记忆: concil(=council 协商) + iate → 协商(解决) → 调和
concinnity [kənˈsɪnɪti]	*n.* 优美; 雅致; 协调(harmony or elegance of design)
concise [kənˈsaɪs]	*adj.* 简洁的(brief) 记 词根记忆: con + cis(切掉) + e → 把(多余的)全部切掉 → 简洁的
concord [ˈkɑːŋkɔːrd]	*n.* 一致(agreement); 和睦(friendly and peaceful relations) 记 词根记忆: con(一起) + cord(心) → 心在一起 → 一致; 和睦
condemn [kənˈdem]	*v.* 谴责(to disapprove of strongly); 判刑(to inflict a penalty upon) 记 词根记忆: con + demn(=damn 诅咒) → 一再诅咒 → 谴责
condescend [ˌkɑːndɪˈsend]	*v.* 屈尊, 俯就(to deal with people in a patronizingly superior manner) 记 词根记忆: con + de + scend(爬) → 向下爬 → 俯就
condign [kənˈdaɪn]	*adj.* 罪有应得的((of punishment) severe and well deserved); 适宜的 记 词根记忆: con + dign(高贵) → 惩罚罪行, 弘扬高贵 → 罪有应得的
condole [kənˈdoʊl]	*v.* 同情, 哀悼(to express sympathy; commiserate) 记 词根记忆: con(一起) + dole(痛苦) → 一起痛苦 → 哀悼

□ complicity	□ compress	□ compulsion	□ compulsory	□ compunction	□ con
□ concatenate	□ concave	□ conceit	□ concession	□ conciliate	□ concinnity
□ concise	□ concord	□ condemn	□ condescend	□ condign	□ condole

conducive [kənˈduːsɪv]	*adj.* 有助于…的，有益的（that contributes or leading to） 搭 be conducive to 对…有帮助
confederacy [kənˈfedərəsi]	*n.* 联盟，同盟（alliance） 记 词根记忆：con（加强）+ feder（联盟）+ acy → 联盟
confer [kənˈfɜːr]	*v.* 商议，商谈（to have discussions）；授予，赋予（to reward to） 记 词根记忆：con（共同）+ fer（带来，拿来）→ 共同带来观点 → 商谈
confess [kənˈfes]	*v.* 承认，供认（to admit that one has done wrong） 记 词根记忆：con（全部）+ fess（说）→ 全部说出 → 供认
confidant [ˈkɑːnfɪdænt]	*n.* 心腹朋友，知己，密友（one to whom secrets are entrusted） 记 词根记忆：con（加强）+ fid（相信）+ ant → 非常信任的人 → 知己，密友
confidential [ˌkɑːnfɪˈdenʃl]	*adj.* 机密的（kept secret） 记 联想记忆：confident（相信）+ ial → 亲信才知道 → 机密的
confiscate [ˈkɑːnfɪskeɪt]	*v.* 没收；充公（to seize private property for the public treasury） 记 词根记忆：con（共同）+ fisc（钱财）+ ate → 钱财归大家 → 充公
congeal [kənˈdʒiːl]	*v.* 凝结，凝固（to solidify or thicken by cooling or freezing） 记 词根记忆：con（一起）+ geal（冻结）→ 冻结到一起 → 凝结
congregate [ˈkɑːnɡrɪɡeɪt]	*v.* 聚集，集合（to gather into a crowd；assemble） 记 词根记忆：con + greg（群体）+ ate → 聚成群体 → 集合
conjoin [kənˈdʒɔɪn]	*v.* 使结合（to cause people or things to join together） 记 词根记忆：con + join（结合，连接）→ 使结合
conscience [ˈkɑːnʃəns]	*n.* 良心，是非感（a person's awareness of right and wrong） 记 词根记忆：con（全部）+ sci（知道）+ ence → 全部知道 → 有良知 → 是非感 搭 the reproaches of conscience 良心上的谴责
conscript [kənˈskrɪpt]	*v.* 征兵，征召（某人）入伍（to enroll for compulsory service in the armed forces） 记 词根记忆：con + script（写）→ 把（名字）写入名单 → 征召（某人）入伍
consecrate [ˈkɑːnsɪkreɪt]	*v.* 奉献，使神圣（to dedicate；sanctify） 记 词根记忆：con + secr（神圣）+ ate → 献给神 → 奉献
consensus [kənˈsensəs]	*n.* 意见一致（agreement in opinion） 记 词根记忆：con（共同）+ sens（感觉）+ us → 感觉相同 → 意见一致 搭 develop a consensus on 在…上达成一致
consent [kənˈsent]	*v.* 同意，允许（to give agreement） 记 词根记忆：con（共同）+ sent（感觉）→ 有共同的感觉 → 同意
consequential [ˌkɑːnsəˈkwenʃl]	*adj.* 傲慢的，自尊自大的（thinking oneself very important；self-important） 同 arrogant

consecrate

慈善事业

console [kənˈsoʊl]	*v.* 安慰，抚慰（to make feel less sad; comfort） 记 词根记忆：con（共同）+ sole（孤单）→ 大家孤单 → 同病相怜 → 安慰
consolidate [kənˈsɑːlɪdeɪt]	*v.* 巩固（to make stable and firmly established）；加强（to strengthen）；合并（to merge; unite; join） 记 词根记忆：con（加强）+ solid（结实）+ ate → 巩固
consonance [ˈkɑːnsənəns]	*n.* 一致，调和（harmony or agreement among components）；和音 记 con（共同）+ son（声音）+ ance → 共同的声音 → 一致，调和
consonant [ˈkɑːnsənənt]	*adj.* 协调的，一致的（being in agreement or accord） 记 词根记忆：con（共同）+ son（声音）+ ant → 同声的 → 一致的
conspicuous [kənˈspɪkjuəs]	*adj.* 显著的，显而易见的（obvious; easy to perceive） 记 词根记忆：con（全部）+ spic（看）+ uous → 全部人都能看到的 → 显而易见的 搭 conspicuous feature 显著的特征
conspire [kənˈspaɪər]	*v.* 密谋，共谋（to act together secretly in order to commit a crime） 记 词根记忆：con（共同）+ spir（呼吸）+ e → 一个鼻孔出气 → 搞阴谋 → 密谋
constellation [ˌkɑːnstəˈleɪʃn]	*n.* 星座，星群（an arbitrary configuration of stars） 记 词根记忆：con（一起）+ stell（星星）+ ation → 星星在一起 → 星群
construct [kənˈstrʌkt]	*v.* 建造，构造（to build sth.） 记 词根记忆：con（加强）+ struct（建立）→ 建造，构造
consul [ˈkɑːnsl]	*n.* 领事（an official appointed by a state to live in a foreign country） 记 联想记忆：领事（consul）常常收到来自各方的咨询（consult）
contain [kənˈteɪn]	*v.* 包含，含有（to hold sth. within itself）；控制（to keep sth. under control）；阻止，遏制（to restrain, check） 记 词根记忆：con + tain（拿住）→ 全部拿住 → 包含，含有
contaminate [kənˈtæmɪneɪt]	*v.* 弄脏，污染（to make impure; pollute; smudge） 记 词根记忆：con + tamin（接触）+ ate → 接触脏东西 → 弄脏，污染
contend [kənˈtend]	*v.* 竞争，争夺（to struggle in order to overcome a rival）；争论，争辩（to strive in controversy） 记 词根记忆：con + tend（伸展）→ 你拉我夺 → 竞争，争夺 搭 contend with 与…竞争
contented [kənˈtentɪd]	*adj.* 心满意足的（showing content and satisfied） 记 来自 content（*v.* 满意，满足）
contest [ˈkɑːntest]	*v.* 竞争（to compete）；质疑（to claim that sth. is not proper） 记 词根记忆：con（共同）+ test（测试）→ 共同测试 → 竞争
contiguous [kənˈtɪgjuəs]	*adj.* 接壤的，接近的（near, adjacent） 记 词根记忆：con（共同）+ tig（接触）+ uous → 共同接触 → 接近的 搭 be contiguous with 与…接壤

26

contort [kən'tɔːrt]	*v.* 歪曲(to deform); 扭曲(to twist or wrench into grotesque form) 记 词根记忆：con + tort(弯曲) → 歪曲；扭曲
controvert ['kɑːntrəvɜːrt]	*v.* 反驳，驳斥(to argue or reason against; contradict; disprove) 记 词根记忆：contro(反) + vert(转) → 反转 → 反驳，驳斥
contumacious [ˌkɑːntuˈmeɪʃəs]	*adj.* 违抗的，不服从的(unreasonably disobedient, esp. to an order made by a court) 记 词根记忆：con + tum(肿胀；骄傲) + acious(…的) → 坚持自己的骄傲，不受欺压 → 违抗的，不服从的
contumacy ['kɑːntuməsi]	*n.* 抗命，不服从(insubordination; disobedience) 记 词根记忆：oon + tum(肿胀；骄傲) + acy(表名词) → 坚持自己的骄傲，不受欺压 → 抗命，不服从
contumely ['kɑːntumili]	*n.* 无礼，傲慢(haughty and contemptuous rudeness) 记 词根记忆：con + tume(骄傲) + ly → 傲慢
conundrum [kəˈnʌndrəm]	*n.* 谜语(a riddle whose answer is or involves a pun); 难题 记 联想记忆：con + un(d)(看作 under) + drum(鼓) → 全部蒙在鼓里 → 谜语
convalescent [ˌkɑːnvəˈlesnt]	*adj./n.* 康复中的(病人)((a person who is) recovering from illness) 记 来自 convalesce(*v.* 康复，复原)
convene [kənˈviːn]	*v.* 集合(to come together; assemble); 召集(to call to meet) 记 词根记忆：con(共同) + ven(来) + e → 共同来 → 集合
convergent [kənˈvɜːrdʒənt]	*adj.* 会聚的(tending to move toward one point or to approach each other) 记 来自 converge(*v.* 汇集，聚集)
convict	[kənˈvɪkt] *v.* 定罪(to find guilty of an offence) ['kɑːnvɪkt] *n.* 罪犯(a person found guilty of a crime and sentenced by a court) 记 词根记忆：con + vict(征服，胜利) → 征服罪犯 → 定罪
convoke [kənˈvoʊk]	*v.* 召集；召开(会议)(to summon to assemble; convene) 记 词根记忆：con(一起) + vok(喊) + e → 喊到一起 → 召集
convoy ['kɑːnvɔɪ]	*v.* 护航，护送(to escort; accompany) 记 词根记忆：con + voy(路；看) → 一路(照看) → 护送
convulse [kənˈvʌls]	*v.* 使剧烈震动；震撼(to shake or disturb violently; agitate) 记 词根记忆：con + vuls(拉) + e → 一再拉 → 使剧烈震动
cordial ['kɔːrdʒəl]	*adj.* 热诚的(warmly friendly; gracious; heartfelt) *n.* 兴奋剂(a stimulating medicine or drink) 记 词根记忆：cord(心脏；一致) + ial → 发自内心的 → 热诚的
coronation [ˌkɔːrəˈneɪʃn]	*n.* 加冕礼(a ceremony at which a person is made king or queen) 记 词根记忆：corona(王冠) + tion → 加冕礼

corporeal [kɔːˈpɔːriəl]	*adj.* 肉体的，身体的(of the body)；物质的(material, rather than spiritual) 记 词根记忆：corpor(身体) + eal(看作real，真的) → 真身 → 肉体的
correspondent [ˌkɔːrəˈspɑːndənt]	*adj.* 符合的，一致的(agreeing；matching) *n.* 记者，通讯员(a person who writes for a magazine or newspaper) 记 联想记忆：cor + respond(反应) + ent(…的) → 有共同反应的 → 符合的，一致的
corrode [kəˈroʊd]	*v.* 腐蚀，侵蚀(to destroy slowly by chemical action) 记 词根记忆：cor(全部) + rod(咬) + e → 全部咬掉 → 腐蚀，侵蚀
corrugate [ˈkɔːrəgeɪt]	*v.* 起波纹，起皱纹 (to shape into folds or parallel and alternating ridges and grooves) 记 词根记忆：cor + rug(=wrinkle 皱) + ate → 起波纹，起皱纹
corrugated [ˈkɔːrəgeɪtɪd]	*adj.* 起皱纹的(folded, wrinkled or furrowed) 记 来自corrugate(*v.* 起皱纹)
corrupt [kəˈrʌpt]	*adj.* 腐败的，堕落的(venal；immoral)；(语言、版本等)讹误的，走样的((of language, text, etc.) containing errors or changes) *v.* 使腐败，使堕落 记 词根记忆：cor(全部) + rupt(断) → 全断了 → 腐败的 搭 corrupt the morals of 败坏…的道德
coruscate [ˈkɔːrəskeɪt]	*v.* 闪亮(to give off flashes of light；glitter；sparkle) 记 来自拉丁文coruscate(*v.* 闪亮)
cosmopolitanism [ˌkɑːzməˈpɑːlɪtənɪzəm]	*n.* 世界性，世界主义 记 来自cosmopolis(*n.* 国际都市)
cosmos [ˈkɑːzmoʊs]	*n.* 宇宙(the universe considered as a harmonious and orderly system) 记 词根记忆：cosm(宇宙) + os → 宇宙
cosset [ˈkɑːsɪt]	*v.* 宠爱，溺爱(to protect too carefully) 记 联想记忆：cos(看作cost，花费) + set(固定) → 固定将一笔花费给孩子 → 宠爱，溺爱
costume [ˈkɑːstuːm]	*n.* 服装(dress including accessories)；戏装(a set of clothes worn in a play or at a masquerade) 记 联想记忆：cost(花费) + u(你)+me(我) → 你我都免不了花钱买服装 → 服装
cosy(cozy) [ˈkoʊzi]	*adj.* 温暖而舒适的(warm and comfortable；snug) 搭 a cosy feeling 惬意的感觉
coterminous [koʊˈtɜːrmɪnəs]	*adj.* 毗连的，有共同边界的(contiguous；having a boundary in common) 记 词根记忆：co(n)(共同) + termin(边界，结束) + ous → 有共同边界的
countrified [ˈkʌntrɪfaɪd]	*adj.* 乡村的(rural)；粗俗的 记 词根记忆：countri(=country 乡下) + fied → 来自乡下的 → 乡村的
coup [kuː]	*n.* 妙计，成功之举(surprising and successful action) 记 发音记忆："酷" → 一夜暴富真得挺酷 → 成功之举

26

covenant [ˈkʌvənənt]	*n.* 契约（a binding and solemn agreement）*v.* 立书保证（to promise by a covenant） 记 词根记忆：co + ven(来) + ant → 来到一起立约 → 契约
covert [ˈkoʊvɜːrt]	*adj.* 秘密的，隐蔽的（concealed；hidden） 记 联想记忆：cover(遮盖) + t → 盖住的 → 秘密的
cow [kaʊ]	*n.* 母牛 *v.* 威胁（to threat）
coward [ˈkaʊərd]	*n.* 胆小鬼（a person who lacks courage） 记 联想记忆：cow(威胁) + ward(未成年人) → 从很小的时候就开始经常被威胁，长大后一直像个胆小鬼 → 胆小鬼
cower [ˈkaʊər]	*v.* 畏缩，蜷缩（to crouch or huddle up from fear or cold） 记 联想记忆：cow(威胁) + er → 受到威胁 → 畏缩，蜷缩
coy [kɔɪ]	*adj.* 腼腆的，忸怩作态的（shy；shrinking from contact with others） 记 和 boy 及 toy 一起记；a coy boy plays toys(害羞男孩玩玩具)
cozen [ˈkʌzən]	*v.* 欺骗，哄骗（to coax；deceive） 记 联想记忆：编了一打(dozen)的谎话来欺骗(cozen)她
crab [kræb]	*n.* 蟹，螃蟹（ten-legged shellfish）*v.* 抱怨，发牢骚（to complain；grumble） 记 联想记忆：总是抱怨(crab)的生活是单调无趣的(drab)
crabbed [ˈkræbɪd]	*adj.* 暴躁的（peevish；ill-tempered；cross）
crack [kræk]	*n.* 爆裂声；裂缝（line along which sth. has broken）*v.* 裂开，破解 同 bang, clap, explosion, snap
crackpot [ˈkrækpɑːt]	*n.* 怪人，疯子；狂想家（one given to eccentric or lunatic notions） 记 组合词：crack(砸) + pot(罐子) → 疯狂砸开罐子的人 → 疯子
crafty [ˈkræfti]	*adj.* 狡诈的（subtly deceitful；sly）；灵巧的（proficient） 记 来自 craft(*n.* 手腕，技巧)
cramp [kræmp]	*n.* 铁箍，夹子 *v.* 把…箍紧（to fasten or hold with a cramp） 搭 cramp one's style 束缚…的手脚，限制…的才华
cranky [ˈkræŋki]	*adj.* 怪癖的（queer；eccentric）；不稳的（unsteady） 记 来自 crank(*n.* 怪人)
crass [kræs]	*adj.* 愚钝的；粗糙的（crude and unrefined） 记 和 class(*n.* 班级；课)一起记
craven [ˈkreɪvn]	*adj.* 懦弱的，畏缩的（lacking the least bit of courage；cowardly） 记 联想记忆：c + raven(乌鸦) → 像乌鸦一样胆小 → 畏缩的
credence [ˈkriːdns]	*n.* 相信，信任（belief in the reports or testimony of another） 记 词根记忆：cred(相信) + ence → 相信

credo [ˈkriːdoʊ]	n. 信条(creed) 记 词根记忆：cred(相信，信任) + o → 信条
creep [kriːp]	v. 匍匐前进(to move with body close to the ground)；悄悄地移动，蹑手蹑脚地走(to move stealthily or slowly) 记 联想记忆：兔子偷懒睡觉(sleep)时乌龟缓慢地行进(creep)
crepuscular [krɪˈpʌskjələr]	adj. 朦胧的，微明的(of or like twilight; dim) 记 来自 crepuscle(n. 黄昏；黎明)
crescendo [krəˈʃendoʊ]	n. (音乐)渐强(a gradual increase in loudness)；高潮 记 词根记忆：crescend(成长；上升) + o → (音乐)渐强
crib [krɪb]	v. 抄袭，剽窃(to steal, plagiarize) 记 和 crab(v. 发牢骚)一起记
crimp [krɪmp]	v. 使起皱，使(头发)卷曲(to cause to become wavy, bent, or pinched)；抵制，束缚(to be an inhibiting or restraining influence on)
cringing [ˈkrɪndʒɪŋ]	n./adj. 谄媚(的)，奉承(的) 记 联想记忆：cring(= cringe 畏缩) + ing → 一直向后退缩 → 谄媚的
croak [kroʊk]	n. 蛙鸣声(a croaking sound) v. 发牢骚，抱怨(to grumble) 记 联想记忆：童话故事里，披着斗篷(cloak)的一群青蛙发出一阵蛙鸣声(croak)
cronyism [ˈkroʊniɪzəm]	n. 任人唯亲；对好朋友的偏袒(favoritism shown to cronies as in political appointments to office) 记 来自 crony(n. 密友，亲密的伙伴)
crook [krʊk]	v. 使弯曲(to bend or curve) n. 钩状物 记 注意不要和 creek(n. 小河)相混
croon [kruːn]	v. 低声歌唱(to sing in a soft manner) 记 联想记忆：cr(看作 cry，哭泣) + oon(看作 moon，月亮) → 对着月亮哭泣 → 低声歌唱
crouch [kraʊtʃ]	v. 蹲伏，弯腰(to stoop or bend low) 记 注意不要和 couch(n. 长沙发)相混
crucial [ˈkruːʃl]	adj. 决定性的(very important; decisive) 记 词根记忆：cruc(十字形) + ial → 十字路口 → 决定性的 搭 the crucial stage 关键的阶段；the crucial reason 决定性原因
crudity [ˈkruːdəti]	n. 粗糙，生硬(the quality or state of being crude) 记 来自 crude(adj. 粗糙的)
crumb [krʌm]	n. 糕饼屑，面包屑(small particles of bread or cake)；少许，点滴(any bit or scrap) 记 和 crumble(v. 弄碎)一起记；crumble the bread into crumbs(把面包弄碎)
crumble [ˈkrʌmbl]	v. 弄碎(to break into crumbs or small pieces)；崩溃(to fall to pieces; disintegrate)

26

crusade [kruːˈseɪd]	*n.* 为维护理想、原则而进行的运动或斗争（vigorous, concerted action for some cause or idea, or against some abuse） 记 词根记忆：crus（十字）+ ade → 十字军东征 → 为维护理想、原则而进行的运动或斗争
cub [kʌb]	*n.* 幼兽（one of the young of certain animals）；笨手笨脚的年轻人（an inexperienced and awkward youth） 记 和 cube（*n.* 立方体）一起记
cuddle [ˈkʌdl]	*v.* 搂抱，拥抱（to hold lovingly and gently; embrace and fondle）*n.* 搂抱，拥抱 记 注意不要和 puddle（*n.* 水坑）相混
cue [kjuː]	*v.* 暗示，提示（to give a sign to sb.）*n.* 暗示，提示（thing said or done to signal sb.'s turn to say or do sth.） 记 联想记忆：线索（clue）有提示（cue）作用
cull [kʌl]	*v.* 挑选，精选（to select from a group）*n.* 剔除的东西（sth. rejected especially as being inferior or worthless）
culmination [ˌkʌlmɪˈneɪʃn]	*n.* 顶点；高潮（eventual conclusion or result） 记 来自 culminate（*v.* 达到顶点）
culprit [ˈkʌlprɪt]	*n.* 罪犯（one who is guilty of a crime） 记 联想记忆：犯罪（sin）的人被称为罪犯（culprit）
cult [kʌlt]	*n.* 异教，教派（a system of religious beliefs and ritual）；狂热的崇拜（worship） 记 联想记忆：culture（文化）去掉 ure → 没文化，搞崇拜 → 狂热的崇拜
cultivate [ˈkʌltɪveɪt]	*v.* 种植（to grow from seeds）；培养（友谊）（to seek to develop familiarity with） 记 词根记忆：cult（培养，种植）+ iv + ate（表示动作）→ 种植
cultivated [ˈkʌltɪveɪtɪd]	*adj.* 耕种的，栽培的（planted）；有教养的（(of people, manner, etc.) having or showing good taste and refinement） 搭 a cultivated environment 有修养的环境
cumber [ˈkʌmbər]	*v.* 拖累，妨碍（to hinder by obstruction or interference; hamper） 记 词根记忆：cumb（睡）+ er → 睡在（路上）→ 拖累，妨碍
cunning [ˈkʌnɪŋ]	*adj.* 狡猾的，奸诈的（clever at deceiving people）；灵巧的，精巧的（ingenious）*n.* 狡猾，奸诈（cunning behavior or quality）
cupidity [kjuːˈpɪdəti]	*n.* 贪婪（strong desire for wealth; avarice; greed） 记 联想记忆：Cupid（丘比特）是罗马神话中的爱神，爱神引起人们对爱情的"贪婪" → 贪婪
curator [kjʊˈreɪtər]	*n.* （博物馆等）馆长（a person in charge of a museum, library, etc.） 记 联想记忆：这个地区的副牧师（curato）和博物馆馆长（curator）是至交好友
curdle [ˈkɜːrdl]	*v.* 使凝结，变稠（to form into curd; coagulate; congeal） 记 来自 curd（*n.* 凝乳）

curfew	*n.* 宵禁（regulation requiring all people to leave the streets at stated times）
[ˈkɜːrfjuː]	记 发音记忆："可否" → 可否上街 → 不可上街，因为有宵禁 → 宵禁
cutlery	*n.*（刀、叉、匙等）餐具（knives, forks and spoons used for eating and serving food）
[ˈkʌtləri]	记 联想记忆：cut(割) + lery(看作 celery，芹菜) → 割芹菜的东西 → 刀具 → (刀、叉、匙等)餐具
cyclone	*n.* 气旋，飓风（a windstorm with violent, whirling movement；tornado or hurricane）
[ˈsaɪkloʊn]	记 词根记忆：cycl(圆；转) + one → 转的东西 → 气旋
cynic	*n.* 犬儒主义者，愤世嫉俗者（one who believes that human conduct is motivated wholly by self-interest）
[ˈsɪnɪk]	记 词根记忆：cyn(狗) + ic → 犬儒主义者
cynosure	*n.* 注意的焦点（any person or thing that is a center of attention or interest）
[ˈsɪnəʃʊr]	记 来自 Cynosure（*n.* 小熊星，北极星）
dabble	*v.* 涉足，浅尝（to do sth. superficially, not seriously）
[ˈdæbl]	记 注意不要和 babble(*v.* 说蠢话)相混
daft	*adj.* 傻的，愚蠢的（silly；foolish）
[dæft]	
dainty	*n.* [常 pl.] 美味；精美的食品（small tasty piece of food, especially a small cake） *adj.* 娇美的（delicately pretty）；挑剔的（fastidious；particular）
[ˈdeɪnti]	记 词根记忆：dain(=dign 高贵) + ty → 高级食品 → 精美的食品
dalliance	*n.* 虚度光阴；调情（an act of dallying）
[ˈdæliəns]	记 来自 dally(*v.* 闲荡，嬉戏)
dally	*v.* 闲荡，嬉戏（to waste time；loiter；trifle）
[ˈdæli]	记 和 daily(*adj.* 每日的)一起记
damn	*v.*（严厉地）批评，谴责（to criticize severely） *adj.* 该死的（expressing disapproval, anger, impatience, etc.）
[dæm]	记 发音记忆："打母" → 殴打母亲应该受到严厉的批评 → 谴责
damp	*v.* 减弱，抑制（to make sth. less strong） *adj.* 潮湿的（moist）
[dæmp]	记 联想记忆：dam(水坝) + p → 水坝上很潮湿 → 潮湿的
dangle	*v.* 悬荡，悬摆（to hang loosely so as to swing back and forth）；吊胃口
[ˈdæŋgl]	记 发音记忆："荡够" → 悬荡，悬摆
dank	*adj.* 阴湿的，透水的（damp；unpleasantly wet）
[dæŋk]	记 联想记忆：河岸(bank)边一定是阴湿的(dank)
dapper	*adj.* 整洁漂亮的（neat and trim）；动作敏捷的（quick in movements）
[ˈdæpər]	记 联想记忆：那只花斑(dapple)猫动作敏捷(dapper)
daredevil	*adj.* 胆大的，冒失的（bold and reckless） *n.* 胆大的人，冒失的人
[ˈderdevl]	记 组合词：dare(大胆) + devil(鬼) → 比鬼还大胆 → 胆大的

26

dash [dæʃ]	*v.* 猛撞，猛砸，击碎(to ruin)；使受挫，挫败(to depress)；使羞愧，使窘迫(to make ashamed) 搭 dash one's hopes 使某人的希望化为泡影
daub [dɔːb]	*v.* 涂抹(to cover or smear with sticky, soft matter)；乱画(to paint coarsely or unskillfully)
dawdle ['dɔːdl]	*v.* 闲荡，虚度光阴(to waste time in trifling；idle；loiter) 记 联想记忆：daw(n)(黎明) + dle → 漫无目的地游荡到黎明 → 闲荡
daze [deɪz]	*n.* 迷乱，恍惚 *v.* 使茫然，使眩晕(tso stun as with a blow or shock；bcnumb) 搭 in a daze 迷茫
deaden ['dedn]	*v.* 减弱，缓和(to lessen the power or intensity of sth.) 记 词根记忆：dead(死) + en → 死掉 → 减弱
deadlock ['dedlɑːk]	*n.* 相持不下，僵局(standstill；stalemate) 记 组合词：dead(死) + lock(锁) → 僵局
debar [dɪ'bɑːr]	*v.* 阻止(to bar；forbid；exclude) 记 词根记忆：de(加强) + bar(阻拦) → 阻止
debark [dɪ'bɑːrk]	*v.* 下船，下飞机，下车；卸载(客、货) 记 词根记忆：de(下) + bark(船) → 下船

Victory won't come to me unless I go to it.
胜利是不会向我走来的，我必须自己走向胜利。
——美国女诗人 穆尔(M. Moore, American poetess)

debility [dɪˈbɪləti]	*n.* 衰弱，虚弱（weakness or feebleness） 记 词根记忆：de(去掉) + bility(=ability 能力) → 失去能力 → 衰弱
debonair [ˌdebəˈner]	*adj.* 美丽的（charming）；温雅的（friendly） 记 联想记忆：deb(看作 debutante，初进社交界的女孩) + on + air → 在空气中的女孩 → 美丽的
debrief [ˌdiːˈbriːf]	*v.* 盘问，听取报告（to question someone who has returned from a mission） 记 词根记忆：de + brief(简述) → 听取报告
debris [dəˈbriː]	*n.* 碎片，残骸（the remains of sth. broken down or destroyed） 记 发音记忆："堆玻璃" → 一堆碎玻璃 → 碎片，残骸
debunk [ˌdiːˈbʌŋk]	*v.* 揭穿真相，暴露（to expose the false or exaggerated claims） 记 联想记忆：de + bunk(看作 bank，岸) → 去掉河岸 → 暴露
decamp [dɪˈkæmp]	*v.* (士兵)离营（to leave camp）；匆忙秘密地离开（to go away suddenly and secretly） 记 词根记忆：de(离开) + camp(营地) → 离营
decant [dɪˈkænt]	*v.* 轻轻倒出（to pour off gently） 记 词根记忆：de(离开) + cant(瓶口) → 轻轻倒出
deceit [dɪˈsiːt]	*n.* 欺骗，欺诈，诡计（a dishonest action or trick; fraud or lie） 记 词根记忆：de + ceit(拿) → 在(底下)拿 → 欺骗
decency [ˈdiːsnsi]	*n.* 正派，端庄体面（the quality or state of being decent） 记 来自 decent(*adj.* 得体的)
decentralize [ˌdiːˈsentrəlaɪz]	*v.* 分散，权力下放（to transfer (power, authority) from central government to regional government） 记 词根记忆：de(离开) + centr(中心) + alize → 离开中心 → 分散
deception [dɪˈsepʃn]	*n.* 欺骗，诡计（a ruse; trick） 记 词根记忆：de(坏) + cept(拿，抓) + ion → 拿坏的东西来 → 欺骗

decant

□ debility	□ debonair	□ debrief	□ debris	□ debunk	□ decamp
□ decant	□ deceit	□ decency	□ decentralize	□ deception	

297

declaim [dɪˈkleɪm]	*v.* 高谈阔论(to speak in a pompous way) 记 词根记忆：de(向下) + claim(喊) → 向下喊 → 高谈阔论
decomposition [ˌdiːkɑːmpəˈzɪʃn]	*n.* 分解, 腐烂；崩溃 同 breakdown, decay, deterioration, disintegration, rot
decoy [ˈdiːkɔɪ]	*v.* 诱骗(to lure or bait)
decree [dɪˈkriː]	*n.* 命令, 法令(an official order, edict, or decision) *v.* 颁布命令 记 发音记忆："敌克令" → 克服敌人的命令 → 命令
dedication [ˌdedɪˈkeɪʃn]	*n.* 奉献, 献身(devotion to a cause or an aim) 记 来自dedicate(*v.* 奉献)
deduce [dɪˈduːs]	*v.* 演绎, 推断(to arrive at a conclusion by reasoning) 记 词根记忆：de(向下) + duce(引导) → 向下引导 → 推断
deduct [dɪˈdʌkt]	*v.* 减去, 扣除(to take away an amount or a part)；演绎(to deduce) 同 abate, discount, rebate, subtract
deductive [dɪˈdʌktɪv]	*adj.* 推论的, 演绎的(reasoning by deduction) 记 来自deduce(*v.* 演绎, 推断)
deed [diːd]	*n.* 行动, 行动(action)；(土地或建筑物的)转让契约、证书(a document which transfers a present interest in property)
deface [dɪˈfeɪs]	*v.* 损坏(to mar the appearance of; destroy) 记 词根记忆：de(变坏) + face(脸面) → 把脸面弄坏 → 损坏
defame [dɪˈfeɪm]	*v.* 诽谤, 中伤(to malign, slander, or libel) 记 词根记忆：de(变坏) + fame(名声) → 使名声变坏 → 诽谤
deficit [ˈdefɪsɪt]	*n.* 不足额(insufficiency; shortage)；赤字 搭 a trade deficit 贸易逆差
defile [dɪˈfaɪl]	*v.* 弄污, 弄脏(to make filthy or dirty; pollute) *n.* (山间)峡谷, 隘路(any narrow valley or mountain pass) 记 词根记忆：de + file(=vile 卑鄙的) → 使…卑下 → 弄污
deflect [dɪˈflekt]	*v.* 偏离, 转向(to turn to aside; deviate) 记 词根记忆：de + flect(弯曲) → 弯到旁边 → 偏离
defraud [dɪˈfrɔːd]	*v.* 欺骗, 诈骗(to cheat) 记 词根记忆：de(变坏) + fraud(欺骗) → 欺骗, 诈骗
defray [dɪˈfreɪ]	*v.* 支付, 支出(to provide for the payment of) 记 联想记忆：def(看作deaf, 聋) + ray(光线) → 聋人得到光线 → 有人帮助付款 → 支付
defuse [ˌdiːˈfjuːz]	*v.* 拆除(爆破物的)引信, 使除去危险性(to remove the fuse from a mine)；平息(to remove the tension from a potentially dangerous situation) 记 词根记忆：de + fuse(导火线) → 拆除(爆破物的)引信
dejected [dɪˈdʒektɪd]	*adj.* 沮丧的, 失望的, 灰心的(in low spirits; depressed; disheartened) 记 词根记忆：de + ject(扔) + ed → 被扔掉的 → 沮丧的, 失望的, 灰心的

delectation [ˌdiːlekˈteɪʃn]	*n.* 享受，愉快（delight; enjoyment; entertainment） 同 joy, pleasure
delegate	[ˈdelɪɡət] *n.* 代表（representative） [ˈdelɪɡeɪt] *v.* 委派…为代表，授权（to appoint as sb's representative） 记 词根记忆：de + legate(使者) → 出去的使者 → 代表
delicate [ˈdelɪkət]	*adj.* 娇弱的（tender when touched）；雅致的，精美的（very carefully made） 搭 delicate and fragile 娇嫩而脆弱的
delinquent [dɪˈlɪŋkwənt]	*adj.* 怠忽职守的（failing or neglecting to do what duty or law requires） 记 词根记忆：de + linqu(=linger 闲荡) + ent → 闲荡过去 → 怠忽职守的
delirium [dɪˈlɪriəm]	*n.* 精神错乱（a temporary state of extreme mental disorder；insanity；mania）
delusion [dɪˈluːʒn]	*n.* 欺骗；幻想（illusion; hallucination） 记 来自delude(*v.* 欺骗)
deluxe [dəˈlʌks]	*adj.* 豪华的，华丽的（notably luxurious, elegant, or expensive） 搭 a deluxe hotel 豪华宾馆
delve [delv]	*v.* 深入探究，钻研（to investigate for information；search） 搭 delve into 探索，探究
demagogue [ˈdeməɡɑːɡ]	*n.* 蛊惑民心的政客（political leader who tries to win people's support by using emotional and often unreasonable arguments） 记 来自demagogy(*n.* 煽动，蛊惑民心)
demarcate [ˈdiːmɑːrkeɪt]	*v.* 划分，划界（to mark the limits；to mark the difference between） 记 词根记忆：de + marc(=mark 标记) + ate → 做标记 → 划分，划界
demeanour [dɪˈmiːnər]	*n.* 举止，行为（outward behavior, conduct, deportment） 记 来自demean，古义等于conduct(*n.* 行为)
demented [dɪˈmentɪd]	*adj.* 疯狂的（insane） 记 词根记忆：de(去掉) + ment(神智) + ed → 没有理智 → 疯狂的
demolition [ˌdeməˈlɪʃn]	*n.* 破坏，毁坏（destruction by explosives） 记 来自demolish(*v.* 拆毁)
demonstrative [dɪˈmɑːnstrətɪv]	*adj.* 证明的，论证的（demonstrating as real or true）；感情流露的（showing the feelings readily）
demoralize [dɪˈmɔːrəlaɪz]	*v.* 使士气低落（to dispirit） 记 词根记忆：de(去掉) + moral(e)(士气) + ize → 去掉士气 → 使士气低落
demote [ˌdiːˈmoʊt]	*v.* 降级，降职（to reduce to a lower grade） 记 词根记忆：de + mote(动) → 动下去 → 降级
demure [dɪˈmjʊr]	*adj.* 严肃的，矜持的（reserved；affectedly modest or shy） 记 词根记忆：de + mure(墙) → 脸板得像墙一样 → 严肃的

den	n. 兽穴，窝(animal's hidden home)
[den]	同 burrow, hole, lair
dentures	n. 假牙(artificial teeth)
['dentʃərz]	记 词根记忆：dent(牙) + ure + s → 假牙
denude	v. 脱去(to make bare or naked)；剥蚀(to lay bare by erosion)；剥夺(to
[dɪ'nuːd]	deprive of sth. important)
	记 词根记忆：de + nude(赤裸的) → 完全赤裸 → 脱去
denunciate	v. 公开指责，公然抨击，谴责(to pronounce especially publicly to be
[dɪ'nʌnsi'eɪt]	blameworthy or evil)
	记 词根记忆：de(变坏) + nunci(讲话，说出)+ate → 公开指责，公然抨击
depose	v. 免职(to remove from office or a position of power)；宣誓作证(to state
[dɪ'pouz]	by affidavit)
	记 词根记忆：de + pose(放) → 放下去 → 免职
deposit	v. 存放；使沉积(to let fall (as sediment))
[dɪ'pɑːzɪt]	记 词根记忆：de+posit(放) → 存放
depraved	adj. 堕落的，腐化的(morally bad; corrupt)
[dɪ'preɪvd]	记 来自 deprave(v. 使堕落)
depravity	n. 堕落，恶习(a morally bad condition; corruption;
[dɪ'prævəti]	wickedness)
	记 词根记忆：de + prav(坏) + ity → 变坏 → 堕落
depredation	n. 劫掠，蹂躏(act of robbing, plundering)
[ˌdeprə'deɪʃn]	记 词根记忆：de + pred(=plunder 掠夺) + ation → 劫掠
depressed	adj. 消沉的(sad and without enthusiasm)；凹陷的(flattened downward)
[dɪ'prest]	记 来自 depress(v. 消沉，沮丧)
depression	n. 抑郁，消沉(low spirits)
[dɪ'preʃn]	搭 clinical depression 临床抑郁症
deprivation	n. 剥夺(removal from an office, dignity, or benefice)；丧失(the state of
[ˌdepri'veɪʃn]	being deprived)
	记 来自 deprive(v. 剥夺)
depute	v. 派…为代表或代理(to give authority to someone else as deputy)
[dɪ'pjuːt]	记 词根记忆：de + pute(放) → 放某人出去 → 派…为代表或代理
deputize	v. 代理，代表(to work or appoint as a deputy)
['depjutaɪz]	记 来自 depute(v. 派…为代表或代理)
deputy	n. 代表(a person appointed to act for another)；副手
['depjuti]	记 联想记忆：de + puly(看作 duty, 责任) → 代理人应负责 → 代表
deracinate	v. 根除，灭绝(to pull up by the roots; eradicate)
[diː'ræsɪneɪt]	记 词根记忆：de + rac(=race 种族) + inate → 消灭种族 → 根除
dereliction	n. 遗弃(state of being deserted)；玩忽职守的
[ˌderə'lɪkʃn]	记 来自 derelict(adj. 遗弃的)

deposit

derivation [ˌderɪˈveɪʃn]	*n.* 发展，起源(development or origin)；词源(first form and meaning of a word) 记 来自 derive(*v.* 派生，导出)
derogate [ˈderəgeɪt]	*v.* 贬低，诽谤(to lower in esteem；disparage) 记 词根记忆：de(坏) + rog(问，说) + ate → 说坏话 → 贬低
desert [dɪˈzɜːrt]	*v.* 遗弃，离弃(to abandon) 记 词根记忆：de(分开) + sert(加入) → 不再加入 → 离弃
deserter [dɪˈzɜːrtər]	*n.* 背弃者；逃兵 记 来自 desert(*v.* 遗弃，离弃)
desiccate [ˈdesɪkeɪt]	*v.* (使)完全干涸，脱水(to dry completely；preserve by drying) 记 词根记忆：de + sicc(干) + ate → 弄干 → 脱水
desideratum [dɪˌzɪdəˈreɪtəm]	*n.* 必需品(sth. needed and wanted) 记 词根记忆：desider(=desire 渴望) + atum → 渴望的东西 → 必需品
desist [dɪˈzɪst]	*v.* 停止，中止(to cease to proceed or act) 同 abandon, discontinue, quit, relinquish, remit
desolate [ˈdesələt]	*adj.* 荒凉的，被遗弃的(left alone；solitary；deserted) 记 词根记忆：de + sol(孤独) + ate → 变得孤独 → 被遗弃的
despise [dɪˈspaɪz]	*v.* 鄙视，蔑视(to look down on with contempt or aversion) 同 contemn, disdain, scorn, scout
despoil [dɪˈspɔɪl]	*v.* 夺取，抢夺(to rob；plunder；ravage) 记 词根记忆：de + spoil(夺取，宠坏) → 夺取，抢夺
despotic [dɪˈspɑːtɪk]	*adj.* 专横的，暴虐的(autocratic；tyrannical) 记 来自 despot(*n.* 暴君)
despotism [ˈdespətɪzəm]	*n.* 专政；暴政
destitute [ˈdestɪtuːt]	*adj.* 缺乏的(being without；lacking)；穷困的(living in complete poverty) 记 词根记忆：de + stitute(建立) → 没有建立 → 穷困的
destitution [ˌdestɪˈtuːʃn]	*n.* 缺乏，穷困(the state of being destitute) 记 来自 destitute(*adj.* 贫困的)
destructible [dɪˈstrʌktəbl]	*adj.* 可破坏的(capable of being destroyed) 记 词根记忆：de(坏) + struct(建立) + ible → 把建造的东西弄坏 → 可破坏的
desuetude [dɪˈsjuːɪtjuːd]	*n.* 废止，不用(discontinuance from use or exercise) 记 词根记忆：de + suet(=suit 适合) + ude → 不再适合 → 废止
detach [dɪˈtætʃ]	*v.* 使分离，使分开，拆卸(to separate without violence or damage) 记 词根记忆：de(去掉) + tach(接触) → 去掉接触 → 使分离
detergent [dɪˈtɜːrdʒənt]	*n.* 清洁剂 记 词根记忆：de + terg(擦) + ent → 擦掉的东西 → 清洁剂

27

detonate [ˈdetəneɪt]	*v.* (使)爆炸，引爆(to cause a bomb or dynamite to explode) 记 词根记忆：de + ton(声音，雷声) + ate → 雷声四散 → (使)爆炸
detonation [ˌdetəˈneɪʃn]	*n.* 爆炸，爆炸声(explosion) 记 来自 detonate(*v.* 引爆)
detraction [dɪˈtrækʃn]	*n.* 贬低，诽谤(unfair criticism) 记 词根记忆：de(向下) + tract(拉，拖) + ion → 向下拉 → 贬低
deviate [ˈdiːvieɪt]	*v.* 越轨，偏离(to diverge；digress) 记 词根记忆：de(偏离) + vi(道路) + ate → 偏离道路的 → 偏离 搭 deviate from 偏离…
devise [dɪˈvaɪz]	*v.* 发明，设计(to invent)；图谋(to plan to obtain or bring about)；遗赠给 (to give estate by will) 记 联想记忆：发明(devise)设备(device)
devotee [ˌdevəˈtiː]	*n.* 爱好者，献身者(people who devote to sth.) 同 fanatic, sectary, votary, zealot
devotional [dɪˈvoʊʃənl]	*adj.* 献身的，虔诚的(used in religious worship) 记 来自 devotion(*n.* 献身)
dexterity [dekˈsterəti]	*n.* 纯熟，灵巧(skill in using one's hands or body；adroitness) 记 词根记忆：dexter(右) + ity → 像右手一样 → 纯熟，灵巧
diagnose [ˌdaɪəɡˈnoʊs]	*v.* 判断，诊断(to find out the nature of an illness by observing its symptoms) 记 词根记忆：dia(穿过) + gnose(知道) → 穿过 (皮肤)知道 → 诊断
diagram [ˈdaɪəɡræm]	*n.* 图解，图表(drawing that uses simple lines to illustrate a machine, structure, or process) 记 词根记忆：dia(穿过，二者之间) + gram(写，图) → 交叉对着画 → 图表
diaphanous [daɪˈæfənəs]	*adj.* (布)精致的；半透明的(characterized by such fineness of texture as to permit seeing through) 记 词根记忆：dia + phan(呈现) + ous → 对面显现 → 半透明的
diatribe [ˈdaɪətraɪb]	*n.* (口头或书面猛烈的)抨击(a bitter, abusive criticism or denunciation) 记 词根记忆：dia(两者之间) + tribe(摩擦) → 两方摩擦 → 抨击
dicker [ˈdɪkər]	*v.* 讨价还价(to bargain) 同 haggle, higgle, huckster, negotiate, palter
dictator [ˈdɪkteɪtər]	*n.* 独裁者(a ruler with absolute power and authority) 同 autocrat, despot, totalitarian, tyrant
dictum [ˈdɪktəm]	*n.* 格言，声明(a formal statement of fact, principle or judgement)
differentiate [ˌdɪfəˈrenʃieɪt]	*v.* 辨别，区别(to mark or show a difference in) 记 词根记忆：different(不同的) + iate → 辨别，区别

diffuse [dɪˈfjuːs]	*v.* 散布，(光等)漫射(to disperse in every direction) *adj.* 漫射的，散漫的(spreading out or dispersed) 记 词根记忆: dif(不同) + fuse(流) → 向不同方向流动 → 漫射
digestion [daɪˈdʒestʃən]	*n.* 消化，吸收(the action, process, or power of digesting) 记 来自 digest(*v.* 消化)
dignity [ˈdɪgnəti]	*n.* 尊严，尊贵(quality that deserves respect) 记 词根记忆: dign(高贵) + ity → 尊贵 搭 insult/demean to one's dignity 伤害/贬低…的尊严
digress [daɪˈgres]	*v.* 离题(to depart temporarily from the main subject) 记 词根记忆: di(离开) + gress(走) → 走离 → 离题
digression [daɪˈgreʃn]	*n.* 离题，题外话(an act of turning aside from the main subject or talk about sth. else)
dilapidate [dɪˈlæpɪdeɪt]	*v.* (使)荒废，(使)毁坏(to bring into a condition of decay or partial ruin) 记 词根记忆: di(二)+lapid(石头)+ate → 石基倒塌成为两半 → (使)荒废，(使)毁坏
dilemma [dɪˈlemə]	*n.* 困境，左右为难(predicament; any situation between unpleasant alternatives) 记 发音记忆: "地雷嘛" → 陷入雷区 → 进退两难的局面 → 困境
diligence [ˈdɪlɪdʒəns]	*n.* 勤勉，勤奋(steady effort) 记 联想记忆: dili(音似: 地里)+gence → 每天在地里劳作 → 勤勉
dillydally [ˈdɪlidæli]	*v.* 磨蹭，浪费时间(to waste time by loitering or delaying)
dim [dɪm]	*v.* 使暗淡，使模糊(to make or become not bright) *adj.* 昏暗的，暗淡的 记 联想记忆: 没有目标(aim)的生活很昏暗(dim)
dimple [ˈdɪmpl]	*n.* 酒窝，笑靥(a small dent or pucker, especially in the skin of sb.'s cheeks or chin) 记 联想记忆: d + imp(小精灵) + le → 像小精灵一样可爱 → 笑靥
dingy [ˈdɪndʒi]	*adj.* 肮脏的，昏暗的(dirty colored; grimy; shabby)
dint [dɪnt]	*v.* 击出凹痕(to make a dent in) 搭 by dint of 凭借…
dire [ˈdaɪər]	*adj.* 可怕的(dreadful; miserable) 同 appalling, fearful, formidable, frightful, ghastly, tremendous
disaffect [ˌdɪsəˈfekt]	*v.* 使不满；使疏远(to make disloyal) 记 词根记忆: dis(不) + affect(感动) → 不再感动 → 使不满
disaster [dɪˈzæstər]	*n.* 灾难，灾祸，不幸(calamity; catastrophe; cataclysm) 记 词根记忆: dis(离开) + aster(星星) → 离开星星，星位不正 → 灾难
disavow [ˌdɪsəˈvaʊ]	*v.* 否认，否定，抵赖(to say one does not know of, is not responsible for, or does not approve of) 记 词根记忆: dis + avow(承认) → 不承认 → 否认，否定

27

□ diffuse	□ digestion	□ dignity	□ digress	□ digression	□ dilapidate
□ dilemma	□ diligence	□ dillydally	□ dim	□ dimple	□ dingy
□ dint	□ dire	□ disaffect	□ disaster	□ disavow	

disburse [dɪs'bɜːrs]	v. 支付，支出(to pay out; expend) 记 词根记忆：dis(除去) + burse(=purse 钱包) → 从钱包里拿(钱) → 支出
discern [dɪ'sɜːrn]	v. 识别，看出(to recognize as separate or different; distinguish) 记 词根记忆：dis(除去) + cern(=sift 筛) → 筛出来 → 识别
disclaim [dɪs'kleɪm]	v. 放弃权利(to give up or renounce)；拒绝承认(to refuse to acknowledge; deny) 记 词根记忆：dis(不) + claim(要求) → 不再要求 → 放弃权利
disclose [dɪs'kloʊz]	v. 揭露(to allow sth. to be seen; reveal) 记 词根记忆：dis(不) + close(关闭) → 不再关闭 → 揭露
discombobulated [ˌdɪskəm'bɑːbjuleɪtɪd]	adj. 扰乱的，打乱的(in a state of confusion)
discord ['dɪskɔːrd]	n. 不和，纷争(disagreement; dissension) 记 词根记忆：dis(不) + cord(一致) → 不一致 → 不和，纷争
discrepancy [dɪs'krepənsi]	n. 差异，矛盾(lack of agreement; inconsistency) 记 联想记忆：dis(分开) + crop(破裂) + ancy → 裂开 → 矛盾
discretionary [dɪ'skreʃəneri]	adj. 自由决定的(left to one's own discretion or judgement) 记 词根记忆：discret (互不相连的) + ion + ary → 互不相连的决定 → 自由决定的
discriminate [dɪ'skrɪmɪneɪt]	v. 区别，歧视(to make a clear distinction) 记 联想记忆：dis + crimin (=crime 罪行) + ate → 区别对待有罪的人 → 区别，歧视
disembodied [ˌdɪsɪm'bɑːdid]	adj. 无实体的，空洞的(free from bodily existence; incorporeal) 记 词根记忆：dis(不) + embodied(实体的) → 无实体的
disenchant [ˌdɪsɪn'tʃænt]	v. 使不抱幻想，使清醒(to free from illusion) 记 词根记忆：dis(不) + enchant(使陶醉) → 使不再陶醉在(幻想中) → 使清醒
disengage [ˌdɪsɪn'geɪdʒ]	v. 脱离，解开(to release from sth. engaged) 记 词根记忆：dis(不) + engage(与…建立密切关系) → 不与…建立密切关系 → 脱离
disentangle [ˌdɪsɪn'tæŋgl]	v. 解决；解脱，解开(to make straight and free of knots) 记 词根记忆：dis(不) + entangle(纠缠) → 摆脱纠缠 → 解脱
disfigure [dɪs'fɪɡjər]	v. 损毁…的外形；使变丑(to mar the appearance of; spoil) 记 词根记忆：dis(除去) + figure(形体) → 去掉形体 → 损毁…的外形
disfranchise [ˌdɪs'fræntʃaɪz]	v. 剥夺…的权利，剥夺…公民权(to deprive of the rights of citizenship) 记 词根记忆：dis(剥夺) + franchise(选举权，赋予权利) → 剥夺…的权利
disgruntle [dɪs'ɡrʌntl]	v. 使不高兴(to make discontented) 同 disappoint, dissatisfy

discriminate

disguise [dɪs'gaɪz]	*v.* 假扮(to furnish with a false appearance or an assumed identity); 掩饰(to obscure real nature of) 记 词根记忆：dis + guise(姿态，伪装)→ 假扮；掩饰
disgust [dɪs'gʌst]	*n.* 反感，厌恶(strong dislike) 记 词根记忆：dis(不) + gust(胃口)→ 没有胃口 → 反感 例 For many young people during the Roaring Twenties, a *disgust* with the excesses of American culture combined with a wanderlust to provoke an exodus abroad.
dishevel [dɪ'ʃevl]	*v.* 使蓬乱，使(头发)凌乱(to throw into disorder or disarray) 记 联想记忆：dish(盘子)+eve(夏娃)+l → 夏娃吃完饭，盘子脏乱 → 使蓬乱
disheveled [dɪ'ʃevld]	*adj.* (头发、服装等)不整的，凌乱的(untidy of hair or clothing) 记 来自 dishevel(*v.* 使蓬乱)
disinter [ˌdɪsɪn'tɜːr]	*v.* 挖出，掘出(to unearth; remove from a grave, tomb) 记 词根记忆：dis(除去) + inter(埋葬)→ 把埋葬的(东西)掘出 → 挖出
disjunction [dɪs'dʒʌŋkʃn]	*n.* 分离，分裂(a sharp cleavage) 记 词根记忆：dis(不) + junction(连接)→ 不再连接 → 分离 例 The *disjunction* between educational objectives that stress independence and individuality and those that emphasize obedience to rules and cooperation with others reflects a conflict that arises from the values on which these objectives are based.
dislocate ['dɪsloʊkeɪt]	*v.* 使脱臼(to displace a bone from its proper position at a joint); 把…弄乱(to disarrange; disrupt) 记 dis(不) + locate(安置)→ 不安置 → 使脱臼；把…弄乱
dismantle [dɪs'mæntl]	*v.* 拆除(to take a part; disassemble) 记 词根记忆：dis(除去) + mantle(覆盖物)→ 拆掉覆盖物 → 拆除
dismay [dɪs'meɪ]	*n.* 沮丧，气馁(feeling of shock and discouragement) *v.* 使气馁 记 词根记忆：dis(不) + may(可能)→ 不可能做 → 沮丧 搭 to one's dismay 令…沮丧
disparity [dɪ'spærəti]	*n.* 不同，差异(inequality or difference) 搭 the wide disparity between rich and poor 贫富悬殊
dispatch [dɪ'spætʃ]	*v.* 派遣(to send off or out promptly); 迅速处理(to dispose of rapidly or efficiently); 匆匆吃完(to eat up quickly) *n.* 迅速(promptness; haste) 记 词根记忆：dis(除去) + patch(妨碍)→ 去掉妨碍，迅速完成 → 迅速处理
dispense [dɪ'spens]	*v.* 分配，分发(to distribute in portions) 记 词根记忆：dis(分开) + pens(花费) + e → 分开花费 → 分配，分发
disport [dɪ'spɔːrt]	*v.* 玩耍，嬉戏(to indulge in amusement) 记 词根记忆：dis(加强) + port(带)→ 带走(时间)→ 玩耍

27

dispose [dɪ'spəʊz]	*v.* 使倾向于；处理（to give a tendency to; to settle a matter finally） 搭 dispose of 去掉，清除
disposed [dɪ'spəʊzd]	*adj.* 愿意的，想干的（inclined） 记 来自 dispose（*v.* 使倾向于；处理） 例 It is said that the custom of shaking hands originated when primitive men held out empty hands to indicate that they had no concealed weapons and were thus amicably *disposed*.
disproof [ˌdɪs'pruːf]	*n.* 反证，反驳（the act of refuting or disproving） 记 词根记忆：dis（相反的）+ proof（看作 prov，证明）→ 相反的证明 → 反证
disruptive [dɪs'rʌptɪv]	*adj.* 制造混乱的（causing disruption） 记 来自 disrupt（*v.* 打乱，扰乱）
dissemble [dɪ'sembl]	*v.* 假装，掩饰（感情、意图等）（to conceal; disguise） 记 词根记忆：dis（不）+ semble（相同）→ 不和（本来面目）相同 → 掩饰
dissertation [ˌdɪsər'teɪʃn]	*n.* 专题论文（long essay on a particular subject） 记 词根记忆：dis（加强）+ sert（断言）+ ation → 加强言论，说明言论的东西 → 专题论文
dissimulate [dɪ'sɪmjuleɪt]	*v.* 隐藏，掩饰（感情、动机等）（to hide one's feelings or motives by pretense; dissemble） 记 词根记忆：dis（不）+ simul（相同）+ ate → 不和（本来面目）相同 → 掩饰
dissociate [dɪ'səʊʃieɪt]	*v.* 分离，游离，分裂（to separate from association or union with another） 记 词根记忆：dis（不）+soci（社会）+ate → 不能进入社会的 → 分离，游离
dissociation [dɪˌsəʊʃi'eɪʃn]	*n.* 分离，脱离关系 记 词根记忆：dis（分开）+ soci（社会）+ ation → 和社会分开 → 分离
dissolute ['dɪsəluːt]	*adj.* 放荡的，无节制的（dissipated and immoral; profligate） 记 词根记忆：dis（分开）+ solute（溶解）→（精力）溶解掉 → 放荡的
dissuade [dɪ'sweɪd]	*v.* 劝阻，阻止（to advise against an action） 记 词根记忆：dis（不）+ suade（敦促）→ 敦促某人不做 → 劝阻
distain [dɪs'teɪn]	*v.* 贬损，伤害名誉（to dispraise; derogate） 记 词根记忆：dis（不）+tain（拿住）→ 不再拿住好好珍惜 → 贬损，伤害名誉
distaste [dɪs'teɪst]	*v.* 厌恶 *n.* 厌恶，不喜欢 记 词根记忆：dis（不）+ taste（爱好）→ 不爱好 → 厌恶
distrait [dɪ'streɪ]	*adj.* 心不在焉的（absent-minded; distracted）
distress [dɪ'stres]	*n.* 痛苦，悲痛（pain; suffering; agony; anguish） 记 词根记忆：di(s)（加强）+ stress（压力，紧张）→ 压倒 → 悲痛
district ['dɪstrɪkt]	*n.* 地区；行政区；区域（a fixed division of a country, a city made for various official purposes）
dither ['dɪðər]	*v.* 慌张；犹豫不决（to act nervously or indecisively）*n.* 紧张；慌乱 搭 to be in a dither about 对某事犹豫不决

divagate [ˈdaɪvəgeɪt]	*v.* 离题(to stray from the subject); 飘泊(to wander about) 记 词根记忆: di(离开) + vag(走) + ate → 走开 → 离题; 漂泊
diversity [daɪˈvɜːrsəti]	*n.* 多样, 千变万化(the condition of being diverse) 例 The sheer *diversity* of tropical plants represents a seemingly inexhaustible source of raw materials, of which only a few have been utilized.
divine [dɪˈvaɪn]	*v.* 推测, 预言(to discover or guess by or as if by magic) 例 For those Puritans who believed that secular obligations were imposed by *divine* will, the correct course of action was not withdrawal from the world but conscientious discharge of the duties of business.
dock [dɑːk]	*v.* 剪短(尾巴等)(to shorten the tail by cutting); 扣去(薪水, 津贴等)(to deduct apart from wages) 记 和 lock(*v.* 锁上, 锁住)一起记
dodge [dɑːdʒ]	*v.* 闪开, 躲避(to shift suddenly to avoid a blow) 记 联想记忆: do + dge(看作 edge, 边缘) → 在边上躲避 → 躲避
doff [dɑːf]	*v.* 脱掉(外衣、帽子)(to take off) 记 联想记忆: d + off(脱掉) → 把衣服脱掉 → 脱掉(外衣、帽子)
dogmatism [ˈdɔːgmətɪzəm]	*n.* 教条主义, 武断((quality of) being dogmatic) 记 词根记忆: dogma(教条) + t + ism(表主义) → 教条主义
doleful [ˈdoʊlfl]	*adj.* 悲哀的, 忧郁的(full of sorrow or sadness) 记 词根记忆: dole(悲哀) + ful → 悲哀的
dolorous [ˈdoʊlərəs]	*adj.* 悲哀的, 忧伤的(very sorrowful or sad; mournful) 记 词根记忆: dol(悲哀) + orous → 悲哀的
domesticate [dəˈmestɪkeɪt]	*v.* 驯养, 驯化(to tame wild animals and breed for human use) 记 来自 domestic(*adj.* 家庭的)
dominant [ˈdɑːmɪnənt]	*adj.* 支配的; 占优势的(exercising the most influence or control) 记 词根记忆: domin(=dom 支配) + ant → 支配的
donate [ˈdoʊneɪt]	*v.* 捐赠, 赠送(to give money, goods to a charity) 记 词根记忆: don(给予) + ate → 捐赠, 赠送

doodle [ˈduːdl]	*v.* 涂鸦(to make meaningless drawings)；混时间(to kill time) 记 和 noodle(*n.* 面条)一起记；吃着面条(noodle)混时间(doodle)
dormancy [ˈdɔːrmənsi]	*n.* 休眠状态(state of being temporarily inactive) 记 词根记忆：dorm(睡眠) + ancy → 在睡眠状态 → 休眠状态 例 It is true that the seeds of some plants have germinated after two hundred years of *dormancy*, but reports that viable seeds have been found in ancient tombs such as the pyramids are entirely unfounded. **dormancy**
dote [doʊt]	*v.* 溺爱(to be excessively or foolishly fond)；昏聩(to be foolish or weak minded)
double-cross [ˌdʌbl ˈkrɔːs]	*v.* 欺骗，出卖(to betray or swindle by an action contrary to an agreed upon course)
dour [ˈdaʊər]	*adj.* 严厉的，阴郁的，倔强的(sullen; gloomy; stubborn) 同 glum, moody, morose, saturnine, sour, sulky
douse [daʊs]	*v.* 把…浸入水中(to plunge into water)；熄灭(to extinguish) 记 联想记忆：do + use → 又做又用 → 在水中做 → 把…浸入水中
dowdy [ˈdaʊdi]	*adj.* 不整洁的，过旧的(not neat or stylish; shabby) 同 antique, archaic, fusty, vintage
downpour [ˈdaʊnpɔːr]	*n.* 倾盆大雨(a heavy fall of rain) 记 组合词：down(向下) + pour(倾倒) → 向下倾倒 → 倾盆大雨
draconian [drəˈkoʊniən]	*adj.* 严厉的，严酷的(extremely severe) 记 来自 Draco(德拉古)，Draco 是雅典政治家，制定了雅典的法典，该法典因其公平受到赞扬，但因其严酷而不受欢迎
draggy [ˈdrægi]	*adj.* 拖拉的，极为讨厌的 记 联想记忆：drag(乏味无聊的事) + gy → 做乏味无聊的事 → 极为讨厌的
drain [dreɪn]	*v.* 排水(to flow off gradually or completely)；喝光(to drink the entire contents of) 记 联想记忆：d + rain(雨水) → 排去雨水 → 排水
drainage [ˈdreɪnɪdʒ]	*n.* 排水，排水系统(the act or method of drawing off)；污水 记 来自 drain(*v.* 排水)
drawl [drɔːl]	*v.* 慢吞吞地说(to speak slowly) *n.* 慢吞吞的说话方式 记 联想记忆：draw(抽) + l → 一点点抽出来 → 慢吞吞地说
drawn [drɔːn]	*adj.* 憔悴的(showing the effects of tension, pain, or illness) 同 careworn, gaunt, haggard, wan, worn
dreary [ˈdrɪri]	*adj.* 沉闷的，乏味的(cheerless; dull) 记 和 dream(*n.* 梦想)一起记；A dream is not dreary. (梦想不会乏味。)
drench [drentʃ]	*v.* 使湿透(to wet through; soak) 记 词根记忆：drench(=drink 喝) → 喝饱 → 使湿透；注意不要和 trench (*v.* 挖战壕)相混

drenched [drent∫d]	*adj.* 湿透的 (soaked or saturated in liquid)
drip [drɪp]	*v.* (使)滴下 (to let fall in drops) 记 和 drop(*v.* 落下)一起记
drivel ['drɪvl]	*v.* 胡说 (to talk nonsense) *n.* 糊涂话 (nonsense) 记 联想记忆：drive(开车) + l → 一边开车一边胡说 → 胡说
droll [droʊl]	*adj.* 古怪的，好笑的 (amusing in an odd or wry way; funny) 记 发音记忆："倔老儿" → 倔老头又古怪又好笑 → 古怪的，好笑的
drool [druːl]	*v.* 流口水；胡说 (to drivel) 同 dribble, salivate, slaver, slobber
droop [druːp]	*v.* 低垂 (to bend or hang downward)；萎靡 (to become weakened) 记 由 drop(*v.* 落下)变化而来
drought [draʊt]	*n.* 干旱，旱灾；干旱期 (period of continuous dry weather) 记 联想记忆：dr(看作 dry, 干的) + ought(应该) → 应该干 → 干旱 例 The seriousness of the *drought* could only be understood by those who had seen the wilted crops in the fields.
drub [drʌb]	*v.* 重击 (to beat severely)；打败 (to defeat decisively)
dulcet ['dʌlsɪt]	*adj.* 美妙的，悦耳的 (soothing or pleasant to hear; melodious) 记 词根记忆：dulc(=sweet 甜) + et → 声音甜的 → 美妙的，悦耳的
duplicitous [duː'plɪsɪtəs]	*adj.* 两面派的，奸诈的 (marked by duplicity)；双重的 记 词根记忆：dup(双的) + licit + ous → 双重的
duress [du'res]	*n.* 胁迫 (the use of force or threats; compulsion) 记 和 dress(*v.* 穿衣)一起记
dyspeptic [dɪs'peptɪk]	*adj.* 消化不良的 (indigestible)；不高兴的 (morose; grouchy)
eaglet ['iːglət]	*n.* 小鹰 (a young eagle) 记 来自 eagle(*n.* 鹰)
earring ['ɪrɪŋ]	*n.* 耳环，耳饰 记 组合词：ear(耳朵) + ring(环) → 耳朵上戴的环 → 耳环，耳饰
earthshaking ['ɜːrθˌ∫eɪkɪŋ]	*adj.* 极其重大或重要的 (very important) 记 组合词：earth(地球) + shaking(震动) → 使地球震动的 → 极其重大或重要的
earthy ['ɜːrθi]	*adj.* 粗俗的，土气的 (rough, plain in taste) 记 词根记忆：earth(土地) + y → 土气的
easel ['iːzl]	*n.* 黑板架，画架 (wooden frame for holding a blackboard or a picture) 记 联想记忆：ease(轻松) + l → 有了画架，画起画来轻松多了 → 画架
ebullience [ɪ'bʌliəns]	*n.* (感情等的)奔放，兴高采烈 (high spirits; exuberance)；沸腾 记 联想记忆：e + bull(公牛) + ience → 像公牛一样出来 → 兴高采烈

28

□ drenched	□ drip	□ drivel	□ droll	□ drool	□ droop
□ drought	□ drub	□ dulcet	□ duplicitous	□ duress	□ dyspeptic
□ eaglet	□ earring	□ earthshaking	□ earthy	□ easel	□ ebullience

309

ecstasy	*n.* 狂喜（great delight; rapture）；出神，入迷
[ˈekstəsi]	记 词根记忆：ec（出）+ stasy（站住）→（高兴得）出群 → 狂喜
ecstatic	*adj.* 狂喜的，心花怒放的（enraptured）
[ɪkˈstætɪk]	记 来自 ecstasy（*n.* 狂喜）
ecumenical	*adj.* 世界范围的，普遍的（of worldwide scope or applicability; universal）
[ˌiːkjuːˈmenɪkl]	记 发音记忆：“一口闷” → 把世界一口闷下 → 世界范围的
edgy	*adj.* 急躁的，易怒的（irritable）；尖利的，（刀口）锐利的（sharp）
[ˈedʒi]	
eerie	*adj.* 可怕的，怪异的（causing fear; weird）
[ˈɪri]	同 uncanny, unearthly
effeminate	*adj.* 缺乏勇气的，柔弱的（having the qualities generally attributed to women）
[ɪˈfemɪnət]	记 词根记忆：ef + femin（女）+ ate → 露出女人气 → 柔弱的
effervesce	*v.* 冒泡（to bubble; foam）；热情洋溢（to show liveliness or exhilaration）
[ˌefərˈves]	记 词根记忆：ef（出）+ ferv（热）+ esce → 释放出热力 → 热情洋溢
effrontery	*n.* 厚颜无耻，放肆（unashamed boldness; impudence）
[ɪˈfrʌntəri]	记 词根记忆：ef + front（脸，面）+ ery → 不要脸面 → 厚颜无耻
effulgent	*adj.* 灿烂的，光辉的（of great brightness）
[ɪˈfʌldʒənt]	记 词根记忆：ef + fulg（闪亮）+ ent → 闪亮的 → 灿烂的
egoism	*n.* 利己主义（a doctrine that self-interest is the valid end）
[ˈeɡoʊɪzəm]	记 词根记忆：ego（自我）+ ism → 自私自利 → 利己主义
egotist	*n.* 自私自利者（selfish person）；自我主义者
[ˈeɡətɪst]	记 词根记忆：ego（我，自己）+ t + ist → 以自我为中心的人 → 自私自利者
eidetic	*adj.*（印象）异常清晰的；极为逼真的（marked by or involving extraordinarily accurate）
[aɪˈdetɪk]	
ejaculate	*v.* 突然叫出或说出（to utter suddenly and vehemently）；射出（to eject from a living body; discharge）
[ɪˈdʒækjuleɪt]	记 词根记忆：e + jacul（喷射）+ ate → 喷发 → 突然叫出或说出
elated	*adj.* 得意洋洋的，振奋的（marked by high spirits; exultant）
[iˈleɪtɪd]	记 词根记忆：e + lat（放）+ ed → 放出（高兴神态）→ 得意洋洋的
	搭 be elated by 因…而欢欣的
elegy	*n.* 哀歌，挽歌（a song or poem expressing sorrow or lamentation）
[ˈelədʒi]	记 联想记忆：e（出）+ leg（腿）+ y → 悲伤得迈不动步 → 哀歌
elephantine	*adj.* 笨拙的（clumsy）；巨大的（having enormous size; massive）
[ˌelɪˈfæntiːn]	记 来自 elephant（*n.* 大象）
elevate	*v.* 举起；提升
[ˈelɪveɪt]	记 词根记忆：e（出）+ lev（举起）+ ate（使…）→ 举起
elixir	*n.* 万能药，长生不老药（cure-all; panacea）
[ɪˈlɪksər]	记 源自阿拉伯人卖药时的叫来：“阿里可舍”，意思是：这个药好啊

elliptical [ɪˈlɪptɪkl]	*adj.* 椭圆的(of, relating to, or shaped like an ellipse); 晦涩的(ambiguous); 省略的 记 来自 ellipse(*n.* 椭圆(形))
elocution [ˌeləˈkjuːʃn]	*n.* 演说术(the art of effective public speaking) 记 词根记忆: e + locu(说) + tion → 说出去 → 演说术
eloquence [ˈeləkwəns]	*n.* 雄辩, 口才(the ability to express ideas and opinions readily and well) 记 词根记忆: e + loqu(说) + ence → 能说 → 雄辩
emaciate [ɪˈmeɪʃieɪt]	*v.* 使瘦弱(to become very thin) 记 词根记忆: e + maci(瘦) + ate → 使瘦弱
emaciation [ɪˌmeɪsiˈeɪʃn]	*n.* 消瘦, 憔悴, 衰弱(the state of being weaker) 同 boniness, gauntness, maceration
emanate [ˈeməneɪt]	*v.* 散发, 发出; 发源(to come out from a source) 记 词根记忆: e(出) + man(手) + ate → 用手发出(指令) → 发出
emasculate [ɪˈmæskjuleɪt]	*v.* 使柔弱(to weaken); 阉割(to castrate) *adj.* 柔弱的 记 词根记忆: e(不) + mascul(男人) + ate → 不让做男人 → 阉割
embargo [ɪmˈbɑːrɡoʊ]	*n.* 禁港令, 封运令(a legal prohibition on commerce) 记 联想记忆: em(进入) + bar(阻挡) + go(去) → 阻拦(船等)进入 → 禁港令, 封运令
embarrass [ɪmˈbærəs]	*v.* 使局促不安, 使窘迫(to cause sb. to feel self-conscious or ashamed) 记 词根记忆: em(进入) + barrass(套子) → 进入套子 → 使窘迫
embitter [ɪmˈbɪtər]	*v.* 使痛苦, 使难受(to make bitter) 记 词根记忆: em + bitter(苦) → 使痛苦
embody [ɪmˈbɑːdi]	*v.* 使具体化, 体现(to make concrete and perceptible; incorporate) 记 词根记忆: em(进入) + body(身体) → (思想)进入身体 → 体现
embolden [ɪmˈboʊldən]	*v.* 鼓励(to give confidence to sb.) 记 词根记忆: em + bold(大胆) + en → 使人大胆 → 鼓励
embroil [ɪmˈbrɔɪl]	*v.* 使混乱, 使卷入纠纷(to involve in conflict or difficulties) 记 词根记忆: em(进入) + broil(争吵) → 进入争吵 → 使混乱, 使卷入纠纷
emerald [ˈemərəld]	*n.* 翡翠(green gemstones) *adj.* 翠绿色的(brightly or richly green)
emergency [iˈmɜːrdʒənsi]	*n.* 紧急情况, 不测事件, 非常时刻(exigency) 记 注意不要和 emergence(*n.* 出现)相混 例 Dr. Charles Drew's technique for preserving and storing blood plasma for *emergency* use proved so effective that it became the model for the present blood bank system used by the American Red Cross.
emigrate [ˈemɪɡreɪt]	*v.* 移居国外(或外地)(to leave one's place of residence or country to live elsewhere) 记 注意: emigrate 表示"移出", immigrate 表示"移入", migrate 指"动物或人来回迁移", 它们都来自词根 migr(移动)

embarrass

28

emissary	*n.* 密使(a secret agent)，特使(representative sent on a specific mission)
['emɪseri]	记 词根记忆：e(出去) + miss(送) + ary(人) → 送出去的人 → 特使

emit	*v.* 发出(光、热、声音等)(to send out; eject)
[i'mɪt]	记 词根记忆：e(出) + mit(送) → 送出 → 发出(光、热、声音等)

龟派气功

emit

emolument	*n.* 报酬，薪水(remuneration)
[ɪ'mɑːljumənt]	记 词根记忆：e + molu(碾碎) + ment → 磨坊主加工粮食后所得的钱 → 报酬

emote	*v.* 激动地表达感情(to act in an emotional or theatrical manner)
[ɪ'mout]	记 词根记忆：e(出) + mote(动) → 感动地说出来 → 激动地表达感情

empirical	*adj.* 经验的，实证的(based on observation or experience)
[ɪm'pɪrɪkl]	记 来自 empiric(*n.* 经济主义者)

empower	*v.* 授权，准许(to give lawful power or authority to)
[ɪm'pauər]	记 联想记忆：em(进入) + power(权力) → 进入权力的状态 → 授权

empyreal	*adj.* 天空的(celestial; sublime)
[ˌempaɪ'riːəl]	

enchant	*v.* 使陶醉(to rouse to ecstatic admiration)；施魔法于(to bewitch)
[ɪn'tʃænt]	记 词根记忆：en + chant(唱歌) → (巫婆)唱歌以施魔法 → 施魔法于

encipher	*v.* 译成密码(to convert a message into cipher)
[ɪn'saɪfər]	记 词根记忆：en(进入) + cipher(密码) → 译成密码

enclosure	*n.* 圈地，围场(the act or action of enclosing)
[ɪn'klouʒər]	记 词根记忆：en + clos(=close) + ure → 进入围绕状态 → 圈地
	例 From the outset, the concept of freedom of the seas from the proprietary claims of nations was challenged by a contrary notion—that of the *enclosure* of the oceans for reasons of national security and profit.

encomiast	*n.* 赞美者(a person who delivers or writes an encomium; a eulogist)
[en'koumɪæst]	记 联想记忆：en + com(看作 come) + iast → 有目的而来的人 → 赞美者

encompass	*v.* 包围，围绕(to enclose; envelop)
[ɪn'kʌmpəs]	记 词根记忆：en(进入) + compass(罗盘，范围) → 进入范围 → 包围

出去

进去

encompass

encyclopedia	*n.* 百科全书(books dealing with every branch of knowledge or with one particular branch)
[ɪnˌsaɪklə'piːdiə]	记 联想记忆：en + cyclo(看作 cycle，全套) + ped(儿童) + ia → 为儿童提供全套教育 → 百科全书

encyclopedic	*adj.* 广博的，知识渊博的
[ɪnˌsaɪklə'piːdɪk]	记 词根记忆：en + cyclo(圆圈) + ped(儿童教育) + ic → 受遍教育 → 广博，知识渊博的

endearing	*adj.* 讨人喜欢的(resulting in affection)
[ɪn'dɪrɪŋ]	记 词根记忆：en(进入) + dear(喜爱) + ing → 进入被喜爱的状态 → 讨人喜欢的

□ emissary	□ emit	□ emolument	□ emote	□ empirical	□ empower
□ empyreal	□ enchant	□ encipher	□ enclosure	□ encomiast	□ encompass
□ encyclopedia	□ encyclopedic	□ endearing			

endue	*v.* 赋予，授予 (to provide；endow)
[ɪnˈdjuː]	
enfeeble	*v.* 使衰弱 (to deprive of strength)
[ɪnˈfiːbl]	记 词根记忆：en (使) + feeble (虚弱的) → 使衰弱
enfetter	*v.* 给…上脚镣 (to bind in fetters)；束缚，使受制于 (to enchain)
[ɪnˈfetər]	记 词根记忆：en (进入) + fetter (镣铐) → 给…上脚镣
enflame	*v.* 燃烧
[ɪnˈfleɪm]	记 联想记忆：en (进入) + flame (燃烧) → 进入燃烧 → 燃烧
engaging	*adj.* 迷人的，美丽动人的 (tending to draw favorable attention)
[ɪnˈɡeɪdʒɪŋ]	记 来自 engage (*v.* 吸引)
engross	*v.* 全神贯注于 (to occupy completely)
[ɪnˈɡrəʊs]	记 联想记忆：en (进入) + gross (总的) → 全部进入状态 → 全神贯注于
engulf	*v.* 吞噬 (to flow over and enclose；overwhelm)
[ɪnˈɡʌlf]	记 联想记忆：en (进入) + gulf (大沟) → 吞噬
enjoin	*v.* 命令，吩咐 (to direct or impose by authoritative order；command)
[ɪnˈdʒɔɪn]	记 联想记忆：en (使) + join (参加) → 使 (别人)参加 → 命令
enlightening	*adj.* 有启迪作用的 (giving spiritual and intellectual insight)；使人领悟的
[ɪnˈlaɪtnɪŋ]	例 A family physician is unlikely to be an *enlightening* source of general information about diet.
enliven	*v.* 使…更活跃或更愉快 (to make sb./sth. more lively or cheerful)
[ɪnˈlaɪvn]	记 联想记忆：en + live (充满活动的，令人愉快的) + n → 使…更活跃或更愉快
ennoble	*v.* 授予爵位，使高贵 (to make noble)
[ɪˈnəʊbl]	记 词根记忆：en (使) + noble (贵族；高贵的) → 使高贵
ennui	*n.* 倦怠 (weariness of mind)；无聊 *v.* 使无聊
[ɑːnˈwiː]	同 boredom
enormity	*n.* 极恶 (great wickedness)；暴行 (an outrageous, improper, or immoral act)；巨大 (immensity)
[ɪˈnɔːrməti]	记 词根记忆：e (出) + norm (正常) + ity → 出了正常状态 → 极恶；暴行；巨大
enrapture	*v.* 使狂喜，使高兴 (to fill with delight；elate)
[ɪnˈræptʃər]	记 词根记忆：en + rapture (狂喜) → 使狂喜
ensconce	*v.* 安置，安坐 (to shelter；establish；settle)
[ɪnˈskɑːns]	记 联想记忆：en (进入) + sconce (小堡垒，遮蔽) → 进入遮盖 → 安置
enshrine	*v.* 奉为神圣，珍藏 (to preserve or cherish as sacred)
[ɪnˈʃraɪn]	记 词根记忆：en (进入) + shrine (圣地) → 奉为神圣

engulf

欲望

28

ensign	n. 舰旗(船上表示所属国家的旗帜)
[ˈensən]	记 联想记忆：en + sign(标志) → 表示所属国家标志的旗帜 → 舰旗
ensnare	v. 诱入陷阱，进入罗网(to take in a snare; catch; trap)
[ɪnˈsner]	记 词根记忆：en(进入) + snare(罗网，陷阱) → 诱入陷阱，进入罗网
ensue	v. 接着发生(to happen afterwards)
[ɪnˈsuː]	记 词根记忆：en(进入) + sue(跟从；起诉) → 接着发生
enthrall	v. 迷惑，迷住(to hold spellbound; charm)
[ɪnˈθrɔːl]	记 联想记忆：en(使) + thrall(奴隶) → 成为(爱的)奴隶 → 迷住
enthralling	adj. 迷人的，吸引人的(holding the complete attention and interest of as if by magic)
[ɪnˈθrɔːlɪŋ]	记 联想记忆：en(使) + thrall(奴隶) + ing → 成为(爱的)奴隶的 → 迷人的
entirety	n. 整体，全面(completeness)
[ɪnˈtaɪərəti]	记 来自entire(v. 完整的)
entourage	n. 随从(group of attendants; retinue); 环境(surroundings)
[ˈɑːntʊrɑːʒ]	记 联想记忆：en + tour（旅行）+ age（年龄）→ 上了年龄旅行必须有随从 → 随从
entrance	v. 使出神，使入迷(to fill with great wonder and delight as if by magic)
[ˈentrəns]	记 来自enter(v. 进入)
entreat	v. 恳求(to make an earnest request; plead)
[ɪnˈtriːt]	记 联想记忆：en(进入) + treat(处理) → 要求进入处理 → 恳求
entreaty	n. 恳求，哀求(an act of entreating; plea)
[ɪnˈtriːti]	记 来自entreat(v. 恳求)
entrust	v. 委托(to invest with a trust or duty); 托付(to assign the care of)
[ɪnˈtrʌst]	记 联想记忆：en(使) + trust(相信) → 给予信任 → 委托
entwine	v. 使缠绕，交织(to twine, weave, or twist together)
[ɪnˈtwaɪn]	记 词根记忆：en(使) + twine(缠绕) → 使缠绕
enunciate	v. 发音(to pronounce clearly and distinctly; utter); (清楚地)表达(to state definitely; express in a systematic way)
[ɪˈnʌnsieɪt]	记 词根记忆：e(出) + nunci(=nounce 报告，说) + ate → 说出来 → 发音，表达
environ	v. 包围，围绕(to encircle, surround)
[ɪnˈvaɪrən]	记 词根记忆：en(进入) + viron(圆) → 进入圆 → 包围，围绕
envisage	v. 正视(to face; confront); 想象(to visualize; imagine)
[ɪnˈvɪzɪdʒ]	记 词根记忆：en(进入) + vis(看) + age → 进入看的状态 → 正视
epideictic	adj. 夸耀的(pretentious)
[ˌepɪˈdaɪktɪk]	
epidermis	n. 表皮，外皮(the outmost layer of the skin)
[ˌepɪˈdɜːrmɪs]	记 词根记忆：epi(在…外) + derm(皮肤) + is → 外皮

epigram [ˈepɪɡræm]	*n.* 讽刺短诗，警句(terse, witty statement) 记 词根记忆：epi(在…旁边) + gram(写) → 旁敲侧击写的东西 → 讽刺短诗
epilogue [ˈepɪlɔːɡ]	*n.* 收场白；尾声(a closing section) 记 词根记忆：epi(在…后) + logue(说话) → 在后面说话 → 尾声
episode [ˈepɪsoʊd]	*n.* 一段情节(one event in a chain of events)；插曲，片断 同 circumstance, development, happening, incident
epithet [ˈepɪθet]	*n.* (贬低人的)短语或形容词(an adjective or phrase used to characterize a person or thing in a derogative sense)；绰号，称号 记 词根记忆：epi(在…下) + thet(=put 放) → (人)放到下面的话 → (贬低人的)短语或形容词
epitomize [ɪˈpɪtəmaɪz]	*v.* 概括，摘要(to be typical of; to be an epitome of) 记 词根记忆：epi(在…后) + tom(看作 tome，一卷书) + ize → 写在一卷书后面的话 → 概括
equable [ˈekwəbl]	*adj.* 稳定的，不变的(not varying or fluctuating; steady)；(脾气)温和的 (tranquil; serene) 记 词根记忆：equ(平等) + able → 能够平等的 → 稳定的
equine [ˈiːkwaɪn]	*adj.* 马的，似马的(characteristic of a horse) 参 equitation(*n.* 骑马术)
equity [ˈekwəti]	*n.* 公平，公正(fairness; impartiality; justice) 记 词根记忆：equ(=equal 相同的) + ity → 公平，公正
equivocate [ɪˈkwɪvəkeɪt]	*v.* 模棱两可地说，支吾其词，推诿(to use equivocal terms in order to deceive, mislead or hedge)
erase [ɪˈreɪs]	*v.* 擦掉，抹去(to rub, scrape, or wipe out) 记 词根记忆：e + rase(擦) → 擦掉
erect [ɪˈrekt]	*adj.* 竖立的，笔直的(vertical in position) 记 词根记忆：e + rect(竖，直) → 竖立的，笔直的
errand [ˈerənd]	*n.* 差使(a trip to do a definite thing)；差事(a mission) 记 词根记忆：err(漫游) + and → 跑来跑去的事情 → 差使
ersatz [ˈersɑːts]	*adj.* 代用的，假的(substitute or synthetic; artificial)
erupt [ɪˈrʌpt]	*v.* 爆发(to burst out)；喷出(to force out or release suddenly) 记 词根记忆：e(出) + rupt(断) → 断裂后喷出 → 爆发
escalation [ˌeskəˈleɪʃn]	*n.* 逐步上升，逐步扩大(state of being more intense) 记 来自 escalate(*v.* 使逐步扩大)
escort	[ɪˈskɔːrt] *v.* 护送(to accompany to protect or show honor or courtesy) [ˈeskɔːrt] *n.* 护送者 记 联想记忆：e + scor (看作 score，得分) + t → 得到好分数，一路护送你 上大学 → 护送

28

espionage	*n.* 间谍活动(the act of spying)
[ˈespiənɑːʒ]	记 来自法语：e + spion(=spy 看) + age → 出去看 → 间谍活动
espy	*v.* 突然看到；望见(to catch sight of；descry)
[eˈspaɪ]	记 联想记忆：e + spy(间谍，发现) → 突然看到
etch	*v.* 蚀刻(to make a drawing on metal or glass by the action of an acid);
[etʃ]	铭记
	[记]不要和 itch(*n.* 痒)相混
eternal	*adj.* 永久的，永恒的(without beginning or end)
[ɪˈtɜːrnl]	记 联想记忆：外部(external)世界是永恒的(eternal)诱惑
	例 In sharp contrast to the intense idealism of the young republic, with its utopian faith in democracy and hopes for *eternal* human progress, recent developments suggest a mood of almost unrelieved cynicism.
ethics	*n.* 伦理学(science that deals with morals); 道德规范(moral correctness)
[ˈeθɪks]	记 联想记忆：e(看作 east, 东方) + thics(看作 thick, 厚的) → 东方有深厚的道德规范 → 伦理学
	搭 code of ethics 道德准则
etymology	*n.* 语源学 (the branch of linguistics dealing with word origin and development)
[ˌetɪˈmɑːlədʒi]	记 来自 etymon(*n.* 词源，字根)
eugenic	*adj.* 优生(学)的(relating to, or improved by eugenics)
[juˈdʒenɪk]	记 词根记忆：eu(优，好) + gen(产生) + ic → 优生的
eulogy	*n.* 颂词，颂文(high speech or commendation)
[ˈjuːlədʒi]	同 acclaim, applause, celebration, compliment
euphoria	*n.* 愉快的心情(a feeling of well-being or elation)
[juːˈfɔːriə]	记 词根记忆：eu(好) + phor(带来) + ia(病) → 带来好处的病 → 幸福感 → 愉快的心情
evacuate	*v.* 撤离(to withdraw from); 疏散(to remove inhabitants from a place for protective purposes)
[ɪˈvækjueɪt]	记 词根记忆：e + vacu(空) + ate → 空出去 → 撤离
evasion	*n.* 躲避，借口(a means of evading)
[ɪˈveɪʒn]	记 词根记忆：e(出) + vas(走) + ion → 走出去 → 躲避
even-tempered	*adj.* 性情平和的(placid；calm); 不易生气的(not easily angered or excited)
[ˌiːvnˈtempərd]	
everlasting	*adj.* 永恒的，永久的(lasting a long time); 无休止的
[ˌevərˈlæstɪŋ]	记 组合词．ever(永远)+lasting(持续) → 永久的
evict	*v.* (依法)驱逐(to force out, expel)
[ɪˈvɪkt]	记 词根记忆：e + vict(征服) → 把…征服出去 → 驱逐
exactitude	*n.* 正确，精确，严格(over-correctness)
[ɪɡˈzæktɪtuːd]	同 accuracy, accurateness, exactness, precision
exalt	*v.* 赞扬，歌颂(to praise；glorify；extol)
[ɪɡˈzɔːlt]	记 词根记忆：ex + alt(高) → 评价高 → 赞扬

☐ espionage	☐ espy	☐ etch	☐ eternal	☐ ethics	☐ etymology
☐ eugenic	☐ eulogy	☐ euphoria	☐ evacuate	☐ evasion	☐ even-tempered
☐ everlasting	☐ evict	☐ exactitude	☐ exalt		

exaltation [ˌegzɔːlˈteɪʃn]	*n.* (成功带来的)得意，高兴（elation；rapture） 记 联想记忆：exalt(提拔) + ation → 得到提拔后的心情 → 得意、高兴
exceptionable [ɪkˈsepʃənəbl]	*adj.* 引起反感的（open to objection） 记 联想记忆：except(把…除去) + ion + able → 因为反感而把…除去 → 引起反感的
exceptional [ɪkˈsepʃənl]	*adj.* 特别(好)的（not ordinary or average） 例 Perhaps predictably, since an ability to communicate effectively is an important trait of any great leader, it has been the *exceptional* Presidents who have delivered the most notable inaugural addresses.
excerpt [ˈeksɜːrpt]	*n.* 摘录，选录，节录（passage, extract from a book, film, piece of music, etc.） 参 except(*prep.* 除…之外)；expert(*n.* 专家)
excitability [ɪkˌsaɪtəˈbɪləti]	*n.* 易兴奋，易激动（quality of being excitable） 记 来自 excite(*v.* 使兴奋，使激动)
exclaim [ɪkˈskleɪm]	*v.* 惊叫，呼喊（to cry out suddenly and loudly） 记 词根记忆：ex(出) + claim(叫喊) → 惊叫， 呼喊 搭 exclaim over 对…感叹
exclamation [ˌekskləˈmeɪʃn]	*n.* 惊叹词；惊呼（a sharp or sudden utterance） 记 词根记忆：ex(出) + clam(叫，喊) + ation → 大声喊出来 → 惊呼
excogitate [eksˈkɑːdʒiteɪt]	*v.* 认真想出（to think out carefully and fully） 记 词根记忆：ex + co（共同）+ g（=ag 开动）+ itate → 共同开动脑子 → 认真想出
excoriate [ˌeksˈkɔːrieɪt]	*v.* 剥皮（to strip, scratch, or rub off the skin）；严厉批评（to denounce harshly） 记 词根记忆：ex + cor(皮) + iate → 把皮弄掉 → 剥皮
excrete [ɪkˈskriːt]	*v.* 排泄，分泌（to pass out waste matter） 记 词根记忆：ex + cret(分离) + e → 分离出来 → 排泄

exclaim

安红！
我想你！

□ exaltation　□ exceptionable　□ exceptional　□ excerpt　□ excitability　□ exclaim
□ exclamation　□ excogitate　□ excoriate　□ excrete

317

excruciate [ɪkˈskruːʃieɪt]	*v.* 施酷刑；折磨（to subject to intense mental distress） 记 联想记忆：ex + cruci(看作 crude, 残忍的) + ate → 给人施酷刑是很残忍的 → 施酷刑
exculpate [ˈekskʌlpeɪt]	*v.* 开脱（to free from blame）；申明无罪，证明无罪(to declare or prove guiltless) 记 词根记忆：ex(出) + culp(指责) + ate → 使不受指责 → 开脱
excursive [ɪksˈkɜːrsɪv]	*adj.* 离题的(digressive) 记 词根记忆：ex(出) + curs(跑) + ive → 跑出去 → 离题的
execrable [ˈeksɪkrəbl]	*adj.* 可憎的，讨厌的(deserving to be execrated; abominable; detestable) 搭 execrable poetry 拙劣的诗
execrate [ˈeksɪkreɪt]	*v.* 憎恶(to loathe; detest; abhor)；咒骂(to call down evil upon; curse) 记 词根记忆：ex(出) + ecr(=secr 神圣的) + ate → 走出了神圣 → 咒骂
exhaustive [ɪgˈzɔːstɪv]	*adj.* 彻底的，无遗漏的(covering every possible detail; thorough) 搭 an exhaustive report 详尽的报告
exhume [ɪgˈzuːm]	*v.* 掘出，发掘(to dig out of the earth) 记 词根记忆：ex + hum(地) + e → 从地下挖出 → 发掘
exigent [ˈeksɪdʒənt]	*adj.* 迫切的，紧急的(requiring immediate action) 记 词根记忆：ex(出) + ig(赶) + ent → 赶到外面 → 迫切的
exiguous [egˈzɪgjuəs]	*adj.* 太少的，不足的(scanty; meager) 同 scarce, skimpy, sparse
expatiate [ɪkˈspeɪʃieɪt]	*v.* 细说，详述(to speak or write in detail) 记 词根记忆：ex(出) + pat(走) + iate → 走出去 → 细说，详述
expatriate [ˌeksˈpeɪtriət]	*v.* 驱逐，流放(to banish; exile)；移居国外(to withdraw from residence in one's native country) 记 词根记忆：ex(出) + patri(国家) + ate → 驱逐；移居国外
expeditious [ˌekspəˈdɪʃəs]	*adj.* 迅速的，敏捷的(prompt; quick) 记 来自 expedite(*v.* 使加速，促进)
expel [ɪkˈspel]	*v.* 排出(to discharge; eject)；开除(to cut off from membership) 记 词根记忆：ex(出) + pel(推) → 向外推 → 排出；开除
expend [ɪkˈspend]	*v.* 花费(to pay out; spend)；用光(to use up) 记 词根记忆：ex(出) + pend(支付) → 花费
expenditure [ɪkˈspendɪtʃər]	*n.* 花费，支出；支出额(amount expended) 搭 lavish expenditure 过多的开支
expiate [ˈekspieɪt]	*v.* 补偿(to make amends or reparation for) 记 词根记忆：ex(加强) + pi(神圣的) + ate → 使变得非常神圣 → 补偿
expire [ɪkˈspaɪər]	*v.* 期满，断气，去世(to breathe one's last breath; die) 记 词根记忆：ex + pir(呼吸) + e → 没有了呼吸 → 去世
explicable [ɪkˈsplɪkəbl]	*adj.* 可解释的(capable of being explained; explainable) 记 词根记忆：ex + plic(重叠) + able → 能从多重状态中出来 → 可解释的

excruciate

说不说！

expostulate	v. (对人或行为的) 抗议 (to object to a person's actions or intentions); 告诫
[ɪkˈspɑːstʃuleɪt]	记 词根记忆: ex(出) + post(放) + ulate → 放出意见 → 抗议
expound	v. 解释 (to explain or interpret); 阐述 (to state in detail)
[ɪkˈspaʊnd]	记 词根记忆: ex + pound(放) → 把(道理)放出来 → 解释
expropriate	v. 充公, 没收 (to deprive of ownership; dispossess)
[eksˈprouprieɪt]	记 词根记忆: ex + propr(拥有) + iate → 不再拥有 → 没收
expulsion	n. 驱逐, 逐出 (the act of expelling)
[ɪkˈspʌlʃn]	记 词根记忆: ex + puls(推) + ion → 推出去 → 驱逐, 逐出
expunge	v. 删除 (to erase or remove completely; delete; cancel)
[ɪkˈspʌndʒ]	记 词根记忆: ex + pung(刺) + e → 把刺挑出 → 删除
expurgate	v. 删除, 删节 (to remove passages considered obscene or objectionable)
[ˈekspɜːrgeɪt]	记 词根记忆: ex + purg(清洗) + ate → 清洗掉不好的东西 → 删除
extemporize	v. 即兴演说 (to speak extemporaneously)
[ɪkˈstempəraɪz]	记 词根记忆: ex + tempor(时间) + ize → 不在(安排的)时间之内 → 即兴演说
extenuate	v. 掩饰(罪行), 减轻(罪行等) (to lessen the seriousness of an offense or guilt by giving excuses)
[ɪkˈstenjueɪt]	记 词根记忆: ex + tenu(细的) + ate → 使…微不足道 → 掩饰(罪行)
externalize	v. 使…表面化 (to make sth. external)
[ɪkˈstɜːrnəlaɪz]	记 来自 external(adj. 外来的, 在外的)
extinguish	v. 使…熄灭 (to cause to cease burning); 使…不复存在 (to end the existence of)
[ɪkˈstɪŋɡwɪʃ]	记 词根记忆: ex(出) + ting(=sting 刺) + uish → 用针刺使没有 → 使…熄灭
extirpation	n. 消灭, 根除 (extermination)
[ˌekstərˈpeɪʃn]	记 来自 extirpate(v. 消灭, 根除)
extort	v. 勒索, 敲诈 (to get money from sb. by violence or threats; extract)
[ɪkˈstɔːrt]	记 词根记忆: ex + tort(扭曲) → 扭出来 → 勒索
extradite	v. 引渡
[ˈekstrədaɪt]	记 词根记忆: ex + trad(递交) + ite → 把…递交出去 → 引渡
extremist	n. 极端主义者 (a person who holds extreme views)
[ɪkˈstriːmɪst]	记 来自 extreme(n. 极端, 极度)
extricate	v. 摆脱, 脱离; 拯救, 救出 (to set free; release)
[ˈekstrɪkeɪt]	记 词根记忆: ex + tric(小障碍物) + ate → 从小障碍物中出来 → 救出
extrovert	n. 性格外向者 (a person who is active and unreserved)
[ˈekstrəvɜːrt]	记 词根记忆: extro(外) + vert(转) → 向外转的人 → 性格外向者
extrude	v. 挤出, 推出, 逐出 (to force or push out; thrust out); 伸出, 突出 (to protrude)
[ɪkˈstruːd]	记 词根记忆: ex + trud(刺) + e → 向外刺 → 挤出

29

exuberance [ɪɡˈzuːbərəns]	*n.* 愉快(the quality of being cheerful); 茁壮(the quality or state of being exuberant) 记 来自 exuberant(*adj.* 茁壮的，繁茂的)
exude [ɪɡˈzuːd]	*v.* 渗出，慢慢流出(to pass out in drops through pores; ooze); 洋溢(to diffuse or seem to radiate) 记 词根记忆：ex + ud(=sud 汗) + e → 出汗 → 渗出，慢慢流出
exult [ɪɡˈzʌlt]	*v.* 欢腾，喜悦(to rejoice greatly; be jubilant) 记 词根记忆：ex + ult(=sult 跳) → 欢腾
exultant [ɪɡˈzʌltənt]	*adj.* 非常高兴的，欢跃的，狂喜的(filled with or expressing great joy or triumph) 记 来自 exult(*v.* 欢腾，喜悦)
fabric [ˈfæbrɪk]	*n.* 纺织品; 结构(framework of basic structure) 记 联想记忆：fab(音似：帆布) + ric → 纺织品
fabulous [ˈfæbjələs]	*adj.* 难以置信的(incredible; astounding); 寓言的(imaginary; fictitious) 记 词根记忆：fab(说) + ulous → 传说中的 → 难以置信的
factitious [fækˈtɪʃəs]	*adj.* 人为的，不真实的(not natural; artificial) 记 词根记忆：fact(做) + itious → 做出来的 → 人为的
faculty [ˈfæklti]	*n.* 全体教员(all the lecturers in a department or group of related departments in a university); 能力，技能(any of the powers of the body or mind)
fad [fæd]	*n.* 时尚(a custom, style in a short time; fashion) 记 和 fade(*v.* 褪色)一起记
fake [feɪk]	*v.* 伪造(to make seem real by any sort of deception or tampering); 佯装(to practice deception by simulating) *adj.* 假的 记 联想记忆：严惩造(make)假(fake)
fallacy [ˈfæləsi]	*n.* 错误，谬论(a false or mistaken idea) 记 词根记忆：fall(犯错) + acy → 错误
fallibility [ˌfæləˈbɪləti]	*n.* 易出错，不可靠(liability to err) 记 来自 fall(*n.* 失败)
falsehood [ˈfɔːlshʊd]	*n.* 谎言(an untrue statement) 记 联想记忆：false(虚伪的) + hood(名词后缀) → 谎言
familiarity [fəˌmɪliˈærəti]	*n.* 熟悉(close acquaintance); 亲近，亲密(intimacy); 不拘礼仪(an excessively informal act) 记 来自 familiar(*adj.* 熟悉的)
famine [ˈfæmɪn]	*n.* 饥荒(instance of extreme scarcity of food in a region) 记 联想记忆：fa(看作 far, 远的) + mine(我的) → 粮食离我很远 → 饥荒 例 The technical know-how, if not the political commitment, appears already at hand to feed the world's exploding population and so to eradicate at last the ancient scourges of malnutrition and *famine*.

famish	*v.* 使饥饿(to make or be very hungry)
[ˈfæmɪʃ]	记 词根记忆：fam(饿的) + sh → 使饥饿
fancied	*adj.* 空想的，虚构的(of or relating to fancy)
[ˈfænsɪd]	记 来自 fancy(*n.* 想象的事物)
fang	*n.* (蛇的)毒牙
[fæŋ]	记 联想记忆：和 tang(*n.* 强烈的气味)一起记
farewell	*interj.* 再会，再见 *n.* 辞行，告别(saying goodbye)
[ˌferˈwel]	记 联想记忆：fare(看作 far, 远的) + well(好) → 朋友去远方，说些好听的话 → 告别
fasten	*v.* 使固定(to fix sth. firmly)
[ˈfæsn]	记 来自 fast(*adj.* 紧的，牢固的)
fatal	*adj.* 致命的(causing death)；灾难性的(causing disaster)
[ˈfeɪtl]	记 来自 fate(*n.* 命运)
fathom	*n.* 英寻 *v.* 彻底了解，弄清真相(to understand thoroughly)
[ˈfæðəm]	
fatidic	*adj.* 预言的(of or relating to prophecy)
[fæˈtɪdɪk]	同 prophetic
fatigue	*n.* 疲乏，劳累(physical or mental exhaustion; weariness)
[fəˈtiːɡ]	记 联想记忆：fat(胖的) + igue → 胖人容易劳累 → 疲乏
fatten	*v.* 长胖，变肥(to become fat)；使…肥沃(to make fertile)；装满
[ˈfætn]	记 来自 fat(*adj.* 胖的)
fatuity	*n.* 愚蠢，愚昧(stupidity; foolishness)
[fəˈtjuiti]	记 词根记忆：fatu(愚蠢的) + ity → 愚蠢
faze	*v.* 打扰，扰乱(to disconcert; dismay; embarrass)
[feɪz]	记 和 laze(*v.* 懒散)一起记
fealty	*n.* 效忠，忠诚(duty and loyalty; allegiance)
[ˈfiːəlti]	记 发音记忆："肺而铁" → 掏心掏肺的铁哥们 → 忠诚
feasible	*adj.* 可行的，可能的(capable of being done or carried out; practicable)
[ˈfiːzəbl]	记 词根记忆：feas(=fac 做) + ible → 能做的 → 可行的
	例 Although the architect's concept at first sounded too visionary to be practicable, his careful analysis of every aspect of the project convinced the panel that the proposed building was indeed, structurally *feasible*.
feat	*n.* 功绩，壮举(remarkable deed)
[fiːt]	记 联想记忆：f + eat(吃) → 取得功绩，要大吃一顿，犒劳自己 → 功绩
	例 The art critic Vasari saw the painting entitled the *Mona Lisa* as an original and wonderful technical *feat*.
febrile	*adj.* 发烧的，热病的(of fever; feverish)
[ˈfiːbraɪl]	记 词根记忆：febr(热) + ile → 发热的 → 发烧的

29

fecundity [fɪˈkʌndəti]	*n.* 多产，丰饶(fruitfulness in offspring or vegetation)；繁殖力，生殖力 例 The Neoplatonists' conception of a deity, in which perfection was measured by abundant *fecundity*, was contradicted by that of the Aristotelians, in which perfection was displayed in the economy of creation.
feeble [ˈfiːbl]	*adj.* 虚弱的(weak；faint) 同 fragile, frail, powerless
feint [feɪnt]	*n.* 佯攻，佯击(a pretended attack or blow) *v.* 佯攻；伪装 记 注意不要和 faint(*adj.* 虚弱的)相混
feisty [ˈfaɪsti]	*adj.* 活跃的(being frisky and exuberant)；易怒的(being touchy and quarrelsome)
felicitate [fəˈlɪsɪteɪt]	*v.* 祝贺，庆祝(to wish happiness to；congratulate) 记 词根记忆：felic(幸福的) + itate → 使…幸福 → 祝贺
felicitous [fəˈlɪsɪtəs]	*adj.* (话语等)适当的，得体的(used or expressed in a way suitable to the occasion；appropriate) 记 词根记忆：felic(幸福的) + itous → (讲话)使人幸福的 → 得体的
feline [ˈfiːlaɪn]	*adj.* 猫的，猫科的(of, relating to, or affecting cats or the cat family) 记 词根记忆：fel(猫) + ine → 猫的，猫科的
felon [ˈfelən]	*n.* 重罪犯(a person guilty of a major crime) 记 联想记忆：fel(=fell 倒下) + on → 倒在罪恶之上 → 重罪犯
feral [ˈferəl]	*adj.* 凶猛的，野性的(wild or savage) 同 fierce, inhumane, untamed
fermentation [ˌfɜːrmenˈteɪʃn]	*n.* 发酵(a chemical change with effervescence；ferment) 记 来自 ferment(*v.* 使发酵)
ferocious [fəˈroʊʃəs]	*adj.* 凶猛的，残暴的(fierce；savage；violently cruel) 记 词根记忆：fer(野的) + oc(看上去的) → ious → 凶猛的
fertile [ˈfɜːrtl]	*adj.* 多产的(productive；fecund)；肥沃的 记 词根记忆：fert(=fer 带来) + ile → 带来果实的 → 多产的
fiat [ˈfiːæt]	*n.* 法令，政令(an order issued by legal authority；decree) 记 联想记忆：fi(看作 fire) + at → 对…开火 → 政令
figurine [ˌfɪɡjəˈriːn]	*n.* 小塑像，小雕像(a small sculptured or molded figure；statuette) 记 联想记忆：figur(雕像) + ine(小的) → 小雕像
file [faɪl]	*n.* 锉刀 *v.* 锉平(to smooth with a file) 记 file"文件"之意众所周知
filial [ˈfɪliəl]	*adj.* 子女的(of a son or daughter) 记 词根记忆：fil(儿子) + ial → 子的 → 子女的
filibuster [ˈfɪlɪbʌstər]	*v.* 妨碍议事，阻挠议案通过(to obstruct the passage of) *n.* 阻挠议事的人或行动 记 发音记忆："费力拍死它" → 阻碍法案或议事的通过 → 阻挠议案通过

filter [ˈfɪltər]	*n.* 过滤材料，（尤指）滤纸（a porous article（as of paper）through which a gas or liquid is passed to separate out matter in suspension）*v.* 过滤（to remove by means of a filter）
filth [fɪlθ]	*n.* 污物（foul or putrid matter）；猥亵的东西（anything viewed as grossly indecent or obscene） 记 和 filch（*v.* 偷）一起记
finable [ˈfaɪnəbl]	*adj.* 应罚款的（liable to a fine） 记 来自 fine（*v.* 罚款）
finagle [fɪˈneɪgl]	*v.* 骗取，骗得（to obtain by trickery） 同 cheat, defraud, swindle
finale [fɪˈnæli]	*n.* 最后，最终（end）；终曲（the concluding part of a musical composition） 记 来自 final（*adj.* 最后的）
finite [ˈfaɪnaɪt]	*adj.* 有限的（having an end or limit） 记 词根记忆：fin（范围）+ ite → 有限的
firearm [ˈfaɪərɑːrm]	*n.* （便携式）枪支（portable gun of any sort） 记 组合词：fire（火）+ arm（武器）→ 枪支
fiscal [ˈfɪskl]	*adj.* 国库的（relating to public treasury or revenues）；财政的（financial） 记 词根记忆：fisc（金库）+ al → 国库的；财政的
fissile [ˈfɪsl]	*adj.* 易分裂的（capable of being split; fissionable） 记 词根记忆：fiss（裂开）+ ile（易…的）→ 易分裂的
fissure [ˈfɪʃər]	*n.* 裂缝，裂隙（a long, narrow and deep cleft or crack） 记 词根记忆：fiss（裂开）+ ure → 裂缝
fitful [ˈfɪtfl]	*adj.* 间歇的，不规则的 记 联想记忆：fit（一阵）+ ful（充满…的）→ 一阵阵的 → 间歇的
flaccid [ˈflæsɪd]	*adj.* 松弛的（soft and limply flabby）；软弱的（weak; feeble） 记 词根记忆：flac（=flab 松的）+ cid → 松弛的
flagellate [ˈflædʒəleɪt]	*v.* 鞭打，鞭笞（to whip; flog） 记 词根记忆：flagel（鞭）+ late → 鞭打
flair [fler]	*n.* 天赋，本领，天资（a natural talent or ability） 记 和 fair（*adj.* 公正的；美丽的）一起记
flak [flæk]	*n.* 高射炮（antiaircraft guns）；抨击（strong and clamorous criticism） 记 和 flake（*n.* 薄片；雪片）一起记
flammable [ˈflæməbl]	*adj.* 易燃的（easily set on fire） 记 词根记忆：flamm（=flam 火）+ able → 易燃的
flatten [ˈflætn]	*v.* （使）变平（to become or make sth. flat）；彻底打败，击倒（to defeat sb. completely）
flatulent [ˈflætʃələnt]	*adj.* 自负的，浮夸的（pompously overblow; bloated） 记 词根记忆：fla（吹）+ tul + ent → 吹嘘的 → 自负的

29

flay [fleɪ]	*v.* 剥皮（to strip off the skin or hide）；抢夺，掠夺（to rob；pillage）；严厉指责（to criticize or scold mercilessly） 记 和 fray（*v.* 吵架，冲突）一起记
fleece [fliːs]	*n.* 生羊皮，羊毛（the wool covering a sheep；wool）*v.* 骗取，欺诈（to strip of money or property by fraud or extortion） 记 联想记忆：flee（逃跑）+ ce → 骗完钱就跑 → 骗取
fleet [fliːt]	*adj.* 快速的（fast）*v.* 消磨，疾驰（to pass or run light and quickly）；飞逝，掠过（to fly swiftly） 记 和 flee（*v.* 逃跑）一起记
flicker ['flɪkər]	*v.* 闪烁，摇曳（to burn or shine unsteadily） 记 和 flick（*v.* 轻弹）一起记
flighty ['flaɪti]	*adj.* 轻浮的（skittish）；反复无常的（capricious） 记 联想记忆：f + light（轻的）+ y → 因为轻而飘浮着 → 轻浮的
flimflam ['flɪmflæm]	*n.* 欺骗（deception）；胡言乱语（deceptive nonsense） 同 poppycock, swindle
flinch [flɪntʃ]	*v.* 畏缩，退缩（to draw back；wince；cower） 记 联想记忆：fl（看作 fly，飞）+ inch（寸）→ 一寸一寸向后飞 → 退缩
flit [flɪt]	*v.* 掠过，迅速飞过（to fly lightly and quickly） 记 联想记忆：fl（看作 fly，飞）+ it → 飞过它 → 掠过，迅速飞过
floppy ['flɑːpi]	*adj.* 松软的（soft and flexible）；软弱的（flabby；flaccid） 记 联想记忆：f + loppy（下垂的）→ 松软的
flossy ['flɑːsi]	*adj.* 华丽的，时髦的（stylish or glamorous especially at first impression）；丝棉般的，柔软的（of, relating to, or having the characteristics of floss）
fluke [fluːk]	*n.* 侥幸（thing that is accidentally successful）；意想不到的事（a result brought about by accident） 记 和 flake（*n.* 雪片）一起记
flunk [flʌŋk]	*v.* （考试）不及格（to fail in schoolwork） 搭 flunk out（of sth.）（因不及格而）退学
flush [flʌʃ]	*v.* 脸红（to become red in the face；blush）；奔流（to flow and spread suddenly and rapidly）；冲洗（to pour liquid over or through）*n.* 激动；脸红 记 和 blush（*v.* 脸红）一起记
flutter ['flʌtər]	*v.* 拍翅（(of the wings) to move lightly and quickly） 同 flap
fluvial ['fluːviəl]	*adj.* 河流的，生长在河中的（of, or living in a stream or river） 记 词根记忆：fluv（=flu 流）+ ial → 河流的
flux [flʌks]	*n.* 不断的变动，变迁，动荡不安（continual change；condition of not being settled） 记 词根记忆：flu（流动）+ x → 不断的变动
foist [fɔɪst]	*v.* 偷偷插入（to introduce or insert surreptitiously or without warrant）；（以欺骗的方式）强加（to force another to accept especially by stealth or deceit）

fold [fould]	*n.* 羊栏(a pen in which to keep sheep) *v.* 折叠(to lay one part over another part of) 记 联想记忆：f + old(旧) → 旧东西有许多褶 → 折叠
folksy ['fouksi]	*adj.* 亲切的，友好的(friendly) 记 来自folks(*n.* 亲属)
foment [fou'ment]	*v.* 煽动(to incite) 记 注意不要和ferment(*v.* 使发酵；酝酿)相混
fondle ['fɑːndl]	*v.* 抚弄，抚摸(to stroke or handle in a tender and loving way; caress) 记 来自fond(*adj.* 喜爱的)
foolproof ['fuːlpruːf]	*adj.* 极易懂的，十分简单的(so simple, well designed as not to be mishandled) 记 组合词：fool(笨蛋) + proof(防…的) → 以防受限于人的无能而做得尤其简单好用 → 人人都会操作的 → 极易懂的
footle ['fuːtl]	*v.* 说胡话，做傻事(to act or talk foolishly)；浪费(时间)(to waste (time)) 记 联想记忆：foot(脚) + le → 走来走去 → 浪费(时间)
foppish ['fɑːpɪʃ]	*adj.* (似)纨绔子弟的(of or like a fop)；浮华的，俗丽的 记 来自fop(*n.* 纨绔子弟)
foray ['fɔːreɪ]	*v.* 突袭，偷袭；劫掠，掠夺(to raid for spoils; plunder; pillage) *n.* 突袭 记 联想记忆：fo(看作for，为了) + ray(光线) → 为了光明，偷袭敌人 → 突袭，偷袭
forbidding [fər'bɪdɪŋ]	*adj.* 令人生畏的；(形势)险恶的(looking dangerous, threatening)；令人反感的，讨厌的(disagreeable) 记 来自forbid(*v.* 禁止)
forecast ['fɔːrkæst]	*v.* 预报，预测(to tell in advance) *n.* 预测(statement that predicts) 记 词根记忆：fore(预先) + cast(扔) → 预先扔下 → 预测
foreclose [fɔːr'kloʊz]	*v.* 排除(to shut out; exclude)；取消(抵押品的)赎回权(to extinguish the right to redeem a mortgage) 记 词根记忆：fore(预先) + clos(关闭) + e → 预先关闭 → 排除
forensic [fə'rensɪk]	*adj.* 公开辩论的，争论的(of public debate or formal argumentation) 记 来自forum(*n.* 讨论会)
foreword ['fɔːrwɜːrd]	*n.* 前言，序(prefatory comments) 记 联想记忆：fore(前面的) + word(话) → 写在前面的话 → 前言
forfeiture ['fɔːrfətʃər]	*n.* (名誉等)丧失(the act of forfeiting) 记 来自forfeit(*v.* 被没收)
forge [fɔːrdʒ]	*n.* 铁匠铺(smithy) *v.* 使形成，达成(to form or shape)；伪造(to counterfeit)；锻制，打铁 记 发音记忆："仿制" → 伪造
forger ['fɔːrdʒər]	*n.* 伪造者(one who commits forgery)；打铁匠(one who forges metal) 记 来自forge(*v.* 伪造；打铁)

29

| **forgery** | *n.* 伪造(物)(something forged) |
| ['fɔːrdʒəri] | 记 来自 forge(*v.* 伪造) |

| **forgo** | *v.* 放弃，抛弃(to abstain from; give up; relinquish) |
| [fɔːr'gou] | 记 联想记忆：for(为了) + go(走) → 为了寻求新事物而出去 → 放弃 |

forgo
减肥中…

| **formative** | *adj.* 形成的；影响发展的(helping to shape, develop, or mold) |
| ['fɔːrmətɪv] | 记 来自 form(*v.* 形成) |

| **forswear** | *v.* 誓绝，发誓放弃(to renounce on oath) |
| [fɔːr'swer] | 记 联想记忆：for(出去) + swear(发誓) → 为了改过自新而发誓 → 誓绝 |

| **forum** | *n.* 辩论的场所，论坛(a public meeting place for open discussion) |
| ['fɔːrəm] | 记 词根记忆：for(门) + um → 门外 → 广场 → 论坛 |

| **forward** | *adj.* 过激的(extreme)；莽撞的(bold)，冒失的，无礼的 |
| ['fɔːrwərd] | 记 词根记忆：for(=fore 前面) + ward(向…的) → 向前的 → 莽撞的 |

| **fossilize** | *v.* 使成为化石(to cause sth. to become a fossil)；使过时(to make sth. out of date) |
| ['fɑːsəlaɪz] | 记 来自 fossil(*n.* 化石) |

| **foyer** | *n.* 门厅，休息室(an entrance hall or lobby) |
| ['fɔɪər] | 记 和 foy(*n.* 临别礼物)一起记 |

| **fractional** | *adj.* 微小的，极少的，微不足道的(very small; unimportant) |
| ['frækʃənl] | 记 来自 fraction(*n.* 少量，一点儿) |

| **fracture** | *n.* 骨折(a break in the body part)；折断，裂口(a break; crack) |
| ['fræktʃər] | 记 词根记忆：fract(碎裂) + ure → 骨头碎了 → 骨折 |

| **fragrance** | *n.* 香料；香味(pleasant or sweet smell) |
| ['freɪɡrəns] | 记 来自 fragrant(*adj.* 芳香的) |

| **fragrant** | *adj.* 芳香的(having a pleasant odor) |
| ['freɪɡrənt] | 记 和 flagrant(*adj.* 恶名昭著的)一起记 |

| **fraternal** | *adj.* 兄弟的，兄弟般的(brotherly) |
| [frə'tɜːrnl] | 记 词根记忆：frater(兄弟) + nal → 兄弟的 |

| **frenzy** | *n.* 狂乱，狂暴(the state of extreme excitement)；暂时性疯狂(temporary madness) |
| ['frenzi] | 记 词根记忆：fren(=phren 心灵) + zy → 有关心灵状态的 → 狂暴 |

| **friable** | *adj.* 脆的，易碎的(easily broken up or crumbled) |
| ['fraɪəbl] | 搭 friable soil 松散的土壤 |

| **friction** | *n.* 摩擦(the rubbing of one body against another)；矛盾，冲突(disagreement between people with different views) |
| ['frɪkʃn] | 记 联想记忆：润滑油的功能(function)是减小摩擦(friction) |

frigidity [frɪˈdʒɪdəti]	*n.* 寒冷；冷淡（the quality or state of being frigid） 记 来自 frigid（*adj.* 寒冷的）
fringe [frɪndʒ]	*n.* （窗帘等）须边；边缘（an outer edge; border; margin） 记 联想记忆：f + ring（一圈）+ e → 周围一圈 → 边缘；和 flange（*n.* 凸出的轮缘）一起记
frisk [frɪsk]	*n.* 欢跃，蹦跳（a lively, playful movement）*v.* 欢跃，嬉戏 记 联想记忆：f（看作 for）+ risk（冒险）→ 欢跃不是冒险 → 欢跃
frolic [ˈfrɑːlɪk]	*n.* 嬉戏（a lively party or game）；雀跃（gaiety; fun）*v.* 嬉戏 例 The young lambs were *frolicing* in the field.
frothy [ˈfrɔːθi]	*adj.* 起泡的（foamy）；空洞的（frivolous in character and content） 搭 frothy coffee 泡沫咖啡
frowzy [ˈfraʊzi]	*adj.* 不整洁的，污秽的（dirty and untidy; slovenly; unkempt） 记 联想记忆：和 frown（*v.* 皱眉）一起记：看到 frowzy 就 frown
fructify [ˈfrʌktɪfaɪ]	*v.* （使）结果实（to bear fruit）；（使）成功（to cause to be or become fruitful） 记 词根记忆：fruct（=fruit 果实）+ ify（使）→（使）结果实
fruition [fruˈɪʃn]	*n.* 实现，完成（fulfillment of hopes, plans, etc.） 记 联想记忆：fruit（水果）+ ion → 有果实，有成果 → 实现，完成
frumpy [ˈfrʌmpi]	*adj.* 邋遢的（dowdy）；老式的，过时的（outdated） 记 来自 frump（*n.* 衣着邋遢或老式的女子）
full-blown [ˌfʊlˈbloʊn]	*adj.* 成熟的；（花）盛开的；全面的，完善的 记 组合词：full（完全的）+ blown（开花的）→ 盛开的
full-bodied [ˌfʊlˈbɑːdid]	*adj.* 魁梧的；（味道）浓烈的；重要的 记 联想记忆：full（完全的）+ bodi（=body 身体）+ ed（…的）→ 全身都有的 →（味道）浓烈的
fulminate [ˈfʊlmɪneɪt]	*v.* 猛烈抨击，严厉谴责（to shout forth denunciations） 记 词根记忆：fulmin（闪电，雷声）+ ate → 像雷电一样 → 严厉谴责
fumble [ˈfʌmbl]	*v.* 摸索，笨拙地搜寻（to search by feeling about awkwardly; grope clumsily）；弄乱，搞糟

□ frigidity	fringe	□ frisk	□ frolic	□ frothy	□ frowzy
□ fructify	□ fruition	□ frumpy	□ full-blown	□ full-bodied	□ fulminate
□ fumble					

327

fume [fjuːm]	*v.* 发怒，愤怒 (to show anger, annoyance, etc.)；冒烟 (to give off smoke) *n.* 烟；愤怒，恼怒 记 联想记忆：有声望 (fame) 的人不会因为小事发怒 (fume)
funk [fʌŋk]	*n.* 怯懦，恐惧 (a state of paralyzing fear)；懦夫 (one that funks) 记 联想记忆：懦夫 (funk) 也要真诚坦率 (frank)
funky [fʌŋki]	*adj.* 有霉臭味的，有恶臭的 (having an offensive odor) 记 联想记忆：身上有恶臭的 (funky) 懦夫 (funk) 同 foul
furbish ['fɜːrbɪʃ]	*v.* 磨光，刷新 (to brighten by rubbing or scouring; polish) 记 注意不要和 furnish (*v.* 装饰；提供) 相混 同 renovate
furor ['fjʊrɔːr]	*n.* 喧闹，轰动 (a fashionable craze)；盛怒 (frenzy; great anger) 记 来自 fury (*n.* 狂怒) 同 rage, uproar
fury ['fjɜːri]	*n.* 狂怒，狂暴 (intense, disordered rage)；激烈，猛烈；狂怒的人 (one who resembles an avenging spirit)；（希腊神话中的）复仇女神 (the Furies goddesses in Greek mythology)
fuss ['fʌs]	*n.* 大惊小怪 (a flurry of nervous, needless bustle or excitement) 记 发音记忆："发丝" → 男朋友的外套上有别的女孩子的发丝，于是禁不住发怒，但被男朋友认为是大惊小怪 → 大惊小怪
fusty ['fʌsti]	*adj.* 霉臭的 (smelling of mildew or decay)；陈腐的，过时的 (old-fashioned; musty) 搭 a dark fusty room 阴暗霉湿的房间
futility [fjuːˈtɪləti]	*n.* 无用，无益 (the quality of being futile) 例 The legislators of 1563 realized the *futility* of trying to regulate the flow of labor without securing its reasonable remuneration, and so the second part of the statute dealt with establishing wages.
gab [gæb]	*n.* 饶舌，爱说话 (idle talk) *v.* 空谈，瞎扯 (to chatter)；闲逛，游荡 记 联想记忆：坐在大门 (gate) 口瞎扯 (gab)
gabble ['gæbl]	*v.* 急促而不清楚地说 (to talk rapidly and incoherently) 记 来自 gab (*v.* 空谈，瞎扯)；不要和 gobble (*v.* 贪婪地大口吃) 相混
gabby ['gæbi]	*adj.* 饶舌的，多嘴的 (talkative) 记 来自 gab (*n.* 饶舌，多嘴)
gadget ['gædʒɪt]	*n.* 小工具，小机械 (any small mechanical contrivance or device) 记 联想记忆：gad (尖头棒) + get → 尖头棒是小工具的一种 → 小工具；还可以和 fidget (*n./v.* 坐立不安) 一起记，丢了心爱的小工具 (gadget)，他坐立不安 (fidget)
gaff [gæf]	*n.* 大鱼钩，鱼叉；【海】斜桁 (rough treatment) 例 A stay for racing or cruising vessels is used to steady the mast against the strain of the *gaff*.
gaffe [gæf]	*n.* （社交上令人不快的）失礼，失态 (a social or diplomatic blunder) 记 联想记忆：gaff (鱼叉) + e → 像用鱼叉刺人 → 失言，失态

gaiety [ˈɡeɪəti]	*n.* 欢乐，快活(cheerfulness) 记 来自 gay (*adj.* 欢乐的)
gambol [ˈɡæmbl]	*n.* 雀跃，嬉戏(a jumping and skipping about in play; frolic) *v.* 雀跃；耍闹 记 来自 gamb（腿，胫）+ ol → 用腿跳跃 → 雀跃；注意不要和 gamble (*n./ v.* 赌博)相混
gander [ˈɡændər]	*n.* 雄鹅，笨人，傻瓜 *v.* 闲逛 记 和 gender (*n.* 性别)一起记：连性别(gender)都分不清的笨人(gander)
gangling [ˈɡæŋlɪŋ]	*adj.* 瘦长得难看的(tall, thin and awkward-looking) 记 发音记忆："杠铃" → 像杠铃一样瘦而难看 → 瘦长得难看的
gangly [ˈɡæŋli]	*adj.* 身材瘦长难看的(tall, thin and awkward-looking) 同 gangling
gangway [ˈɡæŋweɪ]	*n.* （上下船的）跳板(gangplank)；样板；舷梯 记 词根记忆：gang(路) + way(路) → 通向路的路 → 跳板
gape [ɡeɪp]	*v.* 裂开 (to come apart)；目瞪口呆地凝视 (to look hard in surprise or wonder) 记 联想记忆：地面上裂开(gape)一个大裂口(gap)
garbled [ˈɡɑːrbld]	*adj.* 引起误解的(misleading)；窜改的(falsifying) 例 He gave a *garbled* account of what had happened.
gargantuan [ɡɑːrˈɡæntʃuən]	*adj.* 巨大的，庞大的(of tremendous size or volume) 记 来自法国作家拉伯雷的著作《巨人传》中的巨人 Gargantua 同 colossal, enormous, gigantic
gargoyle [ˈɡɑːrɡɔɪl]	*n.* （雕刻成怪兽状的）滴水嘴(a waterspout usually in the form of a grotesquely carved animal or fantastic creature)；面貌丑恶的人(a person with grotesque features) 记 来自 gargle (*n./v.* 漱口)
garment [ˈɡɑːrmənt]	*n.* 衣服(any article of clothing) 搭 wollen garments 毛衣
garner [ˈɡɑːrnər]	*v.* 把…储入谷仓；收藏，积累(to collect or gather)；获得 记 发音记忆："家纳" → 家里收纳下来 → 收藏 同 accumulate, earn, reap
garnish [ˈɡɑːrnɪʃ]	*v.* 装饰(to decorate; embellish) 记 词根记忆：gar(花) + nish → 布满花 → 装饰
garrulity [ɡəˈruːləti]	*n.* 唠叨，饶舌(the quality or state of being garrulous) 记 来自 garrulous (*adj.* 唠叨的，饶舌的)
gaseous [ˈɡæsiəs]	*adj.* 气体的，气态的(like, containing or being gas) 记 来自 gas (*n.* 气体)
gauche [ɡoʊʃ]	*adj.* 笨拙的，不会社交的(lacking social polish; tactless) 同 awkward
gaunt [ɡɔːnt]	*adj.* 憔悴的，瘦削的(thin and bony; hollowed-eyed and haggard) 记 联想记忆：和 taunt (*n./v.* 嘲弄)一起记：因被嘲弄 (taunt)，所以憔悴 (gaunt)

30

□ gaiety	□ gambol	□ gander	□ gangling	□ gangly	□ gangway
□ gape	□ garbled	□ gargantuan	□ gargoyle	□ garment	□ garner
□ garnish	□ garrulity	□ gaseous	□ gauche	□ gaunt	

| **gavel** | *n.* (法官所用的) 槌，小木槌 |
| [ˈgævl] | 记 联想记忆：gave(给) + l → 敲小木槌，给以注意 → 槌，小木槌 |

| **gawky** | *adj.* 迟钝的，笨拙的 (awkward) |
| [ˈgɔːki] | 记 来自 gawk (*v.* 呆头呆脑地盯着) |

| **gaze** | *v.* 凝视，注视 (to look intently and steadily; stare) *n.* 凝视，注视 |
| [geɪz] | 记 发音记忆："盖茨" → 比尔·盖茨令世人瞩目 → 凝视，注视 |

| **genesis** | *n.* 创始，起源 (beginning; origin) |
| [ˈdʒenəsɪs] | 记 词根记忆：gene(产生，基因) + sis → 创始；大写 Genesis 专指《圣经》中的《创世纪》 |

| **genteel** | *adj.* 有教养的，彬彬有礼的 (well bred; elegant)；冒充上流的，附庸风雅的 (striving to convey an appearance of refinement) |
| [dʒenˈtiːl] | 记 来自 gentle (*adj.* 文雅的) |

genuine	*adj.* 真的 (real)；真诚的 (sincere)
[ˈdʒenjuɪn]	记 词根记忆：genu(出生，产生) + ine → 产生的来源清楚 → 真的
	例 Paradoxically, while it is relatively easy to prove a fraudulent work of art is a fraud, it is often virtually impossible to prove that an authentic one is *genuine*.

| **germicide** | *n.* 杀菌剂 (substance used for killing germs) |
| [ˈdʒɜːrmɪsaɪd] | 记 词根记忆：germ(细菌) + i + cid(切) + e → 杀菌剂 |

| **gerontocracy** | *n.* 老人统治的政府 (a government in which a group of old men dominates) |
| [ˌdʒerənˈtɑːkrəsi] | 记 词根记忆：geront(老人) + o + cracy(统治) → 老人统治的政府 |

| **gestate** | *v.* 怀孕，孕育 (to carry in the uterus during pregnancy)；构思 |
| [ˈdʒesteɪt] | 记 词根记忆：gest(=carry 带有) + ate → 有了 → 怀孕 |

| **gesticulate** | *v.* 做手势表达 (to make or use gestures) |
| [dʒeˈstɪkjuleɪt] | 记 来自 gesture (*n.* 手势，姿势) |

| **gesture** | *n.* 姿势，手势 (the movement of the body to express a certain meaning)；姿态，表示 |
| [ˈdʒestʃər] | 例 As a *gesture* of good will, we have decided to waive the charges on this occasion. |

| **giggle** | *v.* 咯咯笑 (to laugh with repeated short catches of the breath) |
| [ˈgɪgl] | 记 发音记忆："叽咯" → 发出叽咯咯的笑声 → 咯咯笑 |

| **gild** | *v.* 镀金 (to overlay with a thin covering of gold)；虚饰 (to give an attractive but often deceptive appearance to) |
| [gɪld] | 搭 a gilded frame 镀金框架 |

| **gimmick** | *n.* 吸引人的花招，噱头 (a trick or device used to attract business or attention) |
| [ˈgɪmɪk] | 例 The pretty girl on the cover of the pictorial is just a sales *gimmick*. |

gingerly	*adj./adv.* 小心的(地)；谨慎的(地) (very careful or very carefully)
[ˈdʒɪndʒərli]	记 联想记忆：切生姜(ginger)的时候要小心(gingerly)，别让生姜汁溅到眼睛里
	例 He opened the box *gingerly* and looked inside.

gist	*n.* 要点，要旨 (the essence or main point)
[dʒɪst]	记 联想记忆：和 list(*v.* 列出)一起记：list(列出)the gists(要点)
	例 Peter has a bad habit of making digressive remarks that cause us to forget the *gist* of what he is saying.

gladiator	*n.* 角斗士，与野兽搏斗者 (a person engaged in a fight to the death as
[ˈɡlædieɪtər]	public entertainment for ancient Romans)
	记 来自 gladius(*n.* 古罗马军队之短剑)

| **glamor** | *v.* 迷惑 (to attract and confuse) *n.* 魔法，魔力 (a magic spell)；迷人的美，|
| [ˈɡlæmər] | 魅力 (an exciting and often illusory and romantic attractiveness) |

glare	*v.* 发炫光 (to shine with dazzling light)；怒目而视 (to stare fiercely or
[ɡler]	angrily)
	记 联想记忆：和 flare(*n./v.* 闪光) 起记

| **gleam** | *n.* 微光，闪光 (a flash or beam of light) *v.* 发微光，闪烁 (to flash) |
| [ɡliːm] | 记 联想记忆：拾起(glean)的金色落穗闪闪发光(gleam) |

glean	*v.* 拾 (落穗) (to gather grains left by reapers)；收集 (材料等)(to gather
[ɡliːn]	information or material bit by bit)
	同 reap

| **glee** | *n.* 欢喜，高兴 (lively joy; gaiety; merriment) |
| [ɡliː] | 记 联想记忆：和 flee(*v.* 逃跑)一起记：因 flee(逃跑)而 glee(欢喜，高兴) |

| **glib** | *adj.* 圆滑的，能言善道的，善辩的 (speaking or spoken in a smooth, fluent, |
| [ɡlɪb] | easy manner) |

| **glide** | *v.* 滑行，滑动 (to flow or move smoothly and easily)；消消地溜走；渐变 |
| [ɡlaɪd] | 例 Youth *glided* past without our awareness. |

| **glimmer** | *v.* 发微光 (to give faint, flickering light) *n.* 摇曳的微光 |
| [ˈɡlɪmər] | 记 联想记忆：glim(*n.* 灯，灯光) + mer → 灯光摇曳 → 发微光 |

| **glimpse** | *v.* 瞥见，看一眼 (to look quickly; glance) *n.* 一瞥，一看 |
| [ɡlɪmps] | 记 联想记忆：glim(灯光) + pse → 像灯光一闪 → 瞥见 |

| **glisten** | *v.* 闪烁，闪耀 (to shine or sparkle with reflected light) |
| [ˈɡlɪsn] | 记 来自 glist(*n.* 闪光)；联想记忆：g + listen(听) → 因为善于倾听，所以智慧闪耀 → 闪烁，闪耀 |

glitter	*v.* 闪烁，闪耀 (to shine brightly) *n.* 灿烂的光华 (sparkling light)；诱惑力，
[ˈɡlɪtər]	魅力 (attractiveness)
	同 flash

gloomy	*adj.* 阴暗的 (dismally and depressingly dark)；没
[ˈɡluːmi]	有希望的 (lacking in promise or hopefulness)；
	阴郁的，忧郁的 (low in spirits)
	记 来自 gloom(*n.* 黑暗，阴暗)
	同 pessimistic, sullen

glorify	*v.* 吹捧，美化 (to make ordinary or bad appear
[ˈɡlɔːrɪfaɪ]	better)
	记 词根记忆：glor(光荣) + ify(使) → 使光荣 → 美化

gloomy

glow [gloʊ]	*v.* 发光，发热 (to give out heat or light) ; (脸) 发红 (to show redness) *n.* 发光；兴高采烈 同 blush, flush; incandescence
glower ['glaʊər]	*v.* 怒目而视 (to stare with sullen anger; scowl) 记 联想记忆：glow (发光) + er → 眼睛发亮看对方 → 怒目而视
glowing ['gloʊɪŋ]	*adj.* 热情赞扬的 (giving enthusiastic praise) 例 The critics were distressed that an essayist of such *glowing* promise could descend to writing such dull, uninteresting prose.
gnaw [nɔː]	*v.* 啃，咬 (to bite bit by bit with the teeth) ; 腐蚀，侵蚀 例 The dog was *gnawing* a bone. // The waves are *gnawing* the rocky shore.
gnawing ['nɔːɪŋ]	*n.* 啃，咬 *adj.* 痛苦的，折磨人的 (excruciating) 记 来自 gnaw (*v.* 啃，咬) 搭 gnawing doubts 令人痛苦的疑虑
goad [goʊd]	*n.* 赶牛棒；刺激，激励 (any driving impulse; spur) *v.* 刺激，激励 搭 goad sb. toward a goal 激励某人走向目标
gobble ['gɑːbl]	*v.* 贪婪地吃，狼吞虎咽 (to eat quickly and greedily) ; 吞没 记 来自 gob (*n.* 一块，大量) 同 gulp, swallow
goblet ['gɑːblət]	*n.* 高脚酒杯 (a drinking glass with a base and stem) 同 wineglass
goggle ['gɑːgl]	*n.* 护目镜 (goggles) *v.* 瞪大眼睛看 (to stare with wide and bulging eyes) 例 They were *goggling* at us as if we were freaks.
goldbrick ['goʊldbrɪk]	*v.* 逃避责任，偷懒 (to shirk one's assigned duties or responsibility) 记 联想记忆：gold (金) + brick (砖) → 一边偷懒一边梦想金砖 → 偷懒
goof [guːf]	*v.* 犯错误 (to make a usually foolish or careless mistake) ; 闲逛，消磨时间 (to spend time idly or foolishly) 记 联想记忆：经过仔细调查，找到了他犯错 (goof) 的证据 (proof)
gorge [gɔːrdʒ]	*n.* 峡谷 (a narrow steep-walled canyon or part of a canyon) 搭 the Rhine Gorge 莱茵峡谷
gourmand ['gʊrmɑːnd]	*n.* 嗜食者 (a person who indulges in food and drink, glutton) 记 联想记忆：g (看作 go，去) + our + man + d → 我们的人都爱去吃各种美食 → 嗜食者
gourmet ['gʊrmeɪ]	*n.* 美食家 (a person who is an excellent judge of fine foods and drinks) 记 注意与 gourmand 的不同：gourmand 指贪吃的人，而 gourmet 指品尝食品是否美味的人
governance ['gʌvərnəns]	*n.* 统治，支配 (power of government) 记 来自 govern (*v.* 统治)
gracile ['græsaɪl]	*adj.* 细弱的，纤细优美的 (slender, graceful) 例 这位女子虽然纤弱 (gracile) 但却十分优雅 (graceful) 同 slight

□ glow	□ glower	□ glowing	□ gnaw	□ gnawing	□ goad
□ gobble	□ goblet	□ goggle	□ goldbrick	□ goof	□ gorge
□ gourmand	□ gourmet	□ governance	□ gracile		

gracious	*adj.* 大方的，和善的（kind, polite and generous）；奢华的（marked by
[ˈɡreɪʃəs]	luxury）；优美的，雅致的
	例 Egocentric, at times vindictive when he believed his authority was being questioned, while could also be kind, *gracious*, and even self-deprecating when the circumstances seemed to require it.
grant	*v.* 同意给予（to agree to give what is asked for）；授予
[ɡrænt]	记 联想记忆：授予（grant）显赫的（grand）贵族爵位
	同 award, grant, vouchsafe
granule	*n.* 小粒，微粒（a small grain）
[ˈɡrænjuːl]	记 词根记忆：gran(=grain 颗粒)+ule → 小粒，微粒
	同 particle
grasping	*adj.* 贪心的，贪婪的（eager for gain; greedy）
[ˈɡræspɪŋ]	记 联想记忆：grasp(*v.* 抓取) + ing → 不停地抓取自己喜爱的东西 → 贪婪的
	同 avaricious, covetous
grate	*v.* 吱嘎磨碎（to grind into small particles）；使人烦躁，刺激（to irritate; annoy; fret）
[ɡreɪt]	记 联想记忆：g + rat(耗子) + e → 耗子发出吱嘎声 → 使人烦躁
gratification	*n.* 满足，喜悦（the state of being gratified）
[ˌɡrætɪfɪˈkeɪʃn]	记 来自 gratify(*v.* 使高兴，使满意)
gratuity	*n.* 赏钱，小费（sth. given voluntarily or beyond obligation usually for some service; tip）
[ɡrəˈtuːəti]	记 词根记忆：grat(感激) + uity → 表示感激的小费 → 小费
gravel	*n.* 碎石，砂砾（a loose mixture of pebbles and rock fragments）
[ˈɡrævl]	记 联想记忆：和 gavel(*n.* 小木槌)一起记；词根记忆：grav(重) + el → 堆在一起很重的东西 → 碎石
gravitate	*v.* 被强烈地吸引（to be drawn or attracted especially by natural inclination）；受引力作用而运动
[ˈɡrævɪteɪt]	记 词根记忆：grav(重) + it(走) + ate → 受重力作用走 → 受引力作用而运动
greenhorn	*n.* 初学者（beginner; novice）；容易受骗的人（dupe）
[ˈɡriːnhɔːrn]	记 组合词：green(绿色) + horn(角) → 原指初生牛犊等动物 → 初学者
gregariousness	*n.* （动物）群居；合群，爱交友
[ɡrɪˈɡeriəsnəs]	记 来自 gregarious(*adj.* 交际的，合群的)
grievance	*n.* 委屈，抱怨，牢骚（complaint or resentment）
[ˈɡriːvəns]	记 词根记忆：griev(悲痛) + ance(表名词) → 委屈
grievous	*adj.* 痛苦的，悲伤的（causing suffering or sorrow）；极严重的
[ˈɡriːvəs]	记 词根记忆：griev(悲痛) + ous → 痛苦的，悲伤的
grill	*v.* 烤（to broil）；拷问（to question relentlessly）*n.* 烤架
[ɡrɪl]	记 联想记忆：gr + ill(生病) → 严刑拷打会打出病的 → 拷问
grimace	*n.* 鬼脸，面部扭曲（a twisting or distortion of the face）*v.* 扮鬼脸
[ɡrɪˈmeɪs]	记 联想记忆：grim(可怕的) + ace(看作 face) → 可怕的脸 → 鬼脸

30

grin	*v.* 露齿而笑(to smile broadly); (因痛苦, 愤恨等)龇牙咧嘴
[grɪn]	记 联想记忆: 老人看着收获的谷物(grain)欣慰地露齿而笑(grin)
gripe	*v.* 抱怨(to complain naggingly); 惹恼, 激怒
[graɪp]	记 联想记忆: g(看作 go) + ripe(成熟的) → 成年人容易抱怨 → 抱怨
	同 irritate, vex
grisly	*adj.* 恐怖的, 可怕的(inspiring horror or greatly frightened)
[ˈgrɪzli]	同 frightening, ghastly, horrible
grit	*n.* 沙粒 (rough, hard particles of sand); 决心, 勇气 (stubborn courage;
[grɪt]	pluck) *v.* 下定决心, 咬紧牙关 (to clench or grind the teeth in anger or
	determination)
groan	*v.* 呻吟, 叹息(to make a deep sad sound) *n.* 呻吟, 叹息
[groʊn]	记 联想记忆: 长大后(grown)比小孩更爱叹息(groan)
groom	*n.* 马夫; 新郎(bridegroom)
[gruːm]	记 联想记忆: g(谐音"哥") + room(房间) → 哥进房间接自己的新娘 → 新郎
groove	*n.* 沟, 槽, 辙(a long, narrow furrow); (刻出的)字沟; 习惯(habitual way; rut)
[gruːv]	记 联想记忆: 戴手套 (glove) 是一种习惯(groove); 注意不要和 grove(*n.* 树丛)相混
gross	*adj.* 总的(total; entire); 粗野的(vulgar; coarse) *n.* 全部, 总额
[groʊs]	记 联想记忆: 青草(grass)地占了这个公园总的(gross)面积的三分之一
grotesque	*adj.* (外形或方式)怪诞的, 古怪的(bizarre; fantastic); (艺术等)风格怪异的
[groʊˈtesk]	记 来自 grotto(岩洞) + picturesque(图画的), 原意为"岩洞里的图画" → (绘画, 雕刻等)怪诞的 → (艺术等)风格怪异的
grouch	*n.* 牢骚, 不满(a complaint); 好抱怨的人
[graʊtʃ]	同 grudge, grumble
grove	*n.* 小树林, 树丛(a small wood or group of trees)
[groʊv]	记 联想记忆: gro(看作 grow) + ve(看作 five) → 五棵树长在一起 → 小树林
grovel	*v.* 摇尾乞怜, 奴颜婢膝(to behave humbly or abjectly; stoop); 匍匐
[ˈgrɑːvl]	记 联想记忆: 在小树林(grove)中匍匐(grovel)前进
growl	*v.* (动物)咆哮, 吼叫(to make a low, rumbling, menacing sound); (雷电等)轰鸣
[graʊl]	记 联想记忆: gr + owl(猫头鹰) → 猫头鹰叫 → 咆哮, 吼叫
gruesome	*adj.* 令人毛骨悚然的, 阴森的(causing horror or disgust; grisly)
[ˈgruːsəm]	记 联想记忆: grue(发抖) + some(…的) → 发抖的 → 令人毛骨悚然的
	同 ghastly
gruff	*adj.* 粗鲁的, 板着脸孔的(rough); (声音)粗哑的(hoarse)
[grʌf]	例 Though she tried to be happy living with Clara in the city, Heidi pined for the mountains and for her *gruff* but loving grandfather.

groom

grumpy [ˈɡrʌmpi]	*adj.* 脾气暴躁的（grouchy; peevish） 记 来自 grump（*v.* 发脾气，生气） 例 The *grumpy* man found fault with everything.
guarantee [ˌɡærənˈtiː]	*v.* 保证，担保（to undertake to do or secure） 记 联想记忆：guar（看作 guard，保卫）+ antee → 保证，担保
guffaw [ɡəˈfɔː]	*n.* 哄笑，粗声大笑（a loud, coarse burst of laughter）*v.* 哄笑 记 联想记忆：guff（胡言，废话）+ aw → 听了他的一番胡言，大家一阵哄笑 → 哄笑
guileless [ˈɡaɪlləs]	*adj.* 厚道的，老实的（innocent, naive） 记 组合词：guile（奸诈，诡计）+ less（没有）→ 没有诡计 → 老实的
guise [ɡaɪz]	*n.* 外观，装束（outward manner or appearance）；伪装，假装 记 发音记忆："盖子" → 外观，装束
gulch [ɡʌltʃ]	*n.* 深谷，峡谷（a steep walled valley; narrow ravine） 记 联想记忆：峡谷（gulch）是大地上的深沟，海湾（gulf）是海中的深沟
gulp [ɡʌlp]	*v.* 吞食，咽下（to swallow hastily or greedily）；抵制，忍住 同 gobble
gum [ɡʌm]	*n.* 树胶，树脂；橡皮糖，口香糖 记 chewing gum 口香糖
gumption [ˈɡʌmpʃn]	*n.* 进取心，魄力（boldness of enterprise; initiative）；精明强干 例 He didn't have the *gumption* to quit such a good paying job.
gusher [ˈɡʌʃər]	*n.* 滔滔不绝的说话者（a person who gushes）；喷油井（an oil well） 记 来自 gush（*v.* 喷出，涌出；滔滔不绝地说话）
gustation [ɡʌˈsteɪʃn]	*n.* 品尝（the act of tasting）；味觉（the sensation of tasting） 记 联想记忆：一阵强风（gust）吹来，他们没办法在露天茶座惬意地进行美食品尝（gustation）了
gustatory [ˈɡʌstətəri]	*adj.* 味觉的，品尝的（relating to or associated with eating or the sense of taste） 记 来自 gustation（*n.* 味觉；品尝）
gutless [ˈɡʌtləs]	*adj.* 没有勇气的，怯懦的（lacking courage） 记 联想记忆：gut（勇气）+ less（无）→ 没有勇气的 同 cowardly, spineless
gutter [ˈɡʌtər]	*n.* 水槽；街沟（a channel at the edge of a street） 记 词根记忆：gut（肠胃，引申为"沟"）+ ter → 街沟
guttle [ˈɡʌtl]	*v.* 狼吞虎咽（to eat quickly and greedily） 记 联想记忆：gut（肠子）+ tle → 肠子容量很大，消化快 → 狼吞虎咽 同 gobble, gulp, swallow
guzzle [ˈɡʌzl]	*v.* 大吃大喝（to drink greedily or immoderately）；大量消耗 搭 guzzle beer（狂饮啤酒）

他可以做
担保人！

guufaw → guarantee

30

☐ grumpy	☐ guarantee	☐ guffaw	☐ guileless	☐ guise	☐ gulch
☐ gulp	☐ gum	☐ gumption	☐ gusher	☐ gustation	☐ gustatory
☐ gutless	☐ gutter	☐ guttle	☐ guzzle		

gyrate [ˈdʒaɪreɪt]	*adj.* 旋转的(spiral; convoluted) *v.* 旋转，回旋(to move in a circular or spiral motion) 记 词根记忆：gyr(转) + ate → 旋转的 同 revolve, swirl
habitable [ˈhæbɪtəbl]	*adj.* 可居住的 (capable of being lived in; suitable for habitation) 记 词根记忆：habit(居) + able(可…的) → 可居住的
habitat [ˈhæbɪtæt]	*n.* 自然环境，栖息地(native environment) 记 词根记忆：habit(住) + at → 住的地方 → 栖息地 例 The moth's *habitat* is being destroyed and it has nearly died out.
haggard [ˈhægərd]	*adj.* 憔悴的，消瘦的(gaunt; drawn) 记 联想记忆：hag(巫婆) + gard → 像巫婆一样 → 形容枯槁的 → 消瘦的
halcyon [ˈhælsiən]	*adj.* 平静的(tranquil; calm)；愉快的(happy; idyllic)；繁荣的(prosperous) 记 原指传说中一种能平息风浪的"神翠鸟(halcyon)"
hallowed [ˈhæloʊd]	*adj.* 神圣的(holy) 记 来自hallow(*vt.* 使神圣，把…视作神圣) 搭 to be buried in hallowed ground 被安葬在神圣的土地上
hallucination [həˌluːsɪˈneɪʃn]	*n.* 幻觉(illusion of seeing or hearing) 记 联想记忆：hall(大厅) + uci(发音相当于 you see 你看) + nation(国家) → 在大厅里你看到了一个国家 → 产生了幻觉 → 幻觉
hammer [ˈhæmər]	*n.* 锤子，槌(tool used for breaking things, etc.) *v.* 锤击，锤打(to pound) 例 She *hammered* the nail into the wall.
hangdog [ˈhæŋdɔːg]	*adj.* 忧愁的(downcast)；低贱的(shamefaced) 记 组合词：hang(吊) + dog(狗) → 吊起来的狗 → 低贱的 同 dejected, despicable
hanker [ˈhæŋkər]	*v.* 渴望，追求(to have a strong or persistent desire) 记 hanger(绞刑执行者)渴望(hanker)心灵的平静
hankering [ˈhæŋkərɪŋ]	*n.* 渴望，向往(craving; yearning) 记 来自hanker(*v.* 渴望，追求)
haphazard [hæpˈhæzərd]	*adj.* 任意的，偶然的，无秩序的(without plan or order) 记 联想记忆：hap(机会，运气) + hazard(冒险) → 运气 + 冒险 → 偶然的 同 casual, random
harangue [həˈræŋ]	*n.* 长篇攻击性演说(a long, scolding speech; tirade) 记 联想记忆：har(看作 hard) + angue(看作 argue) → 强硬的辩论 → 长篇攻击性演说
harbinger [ˈhɑːrbɪndʒər]	*n.* 先驱，先兆(herald) 同 forerunner, precursor
hardbitten [ˌhɑːrdˈbɪtn]	*adj.* 不屈的，顽强的(stubborn; tough; dogged) 记 组合词：hard(硬) + bitten(咬) → 硬得咬不动 → 顽强的

hardihood [ˈhɑːrdihʊd]	*n.* 大胆，刚毅(boldness; fortitude)；厚颜 记 来自 hardy(*adj.* 强壮的；大胆的，勇敢的)
hardy [ˈhɑːrdi]	*adj.* 耐寒的（able to endure cold）；强壮的 (robust; vigorous)；大胆的，勇敢的 记 联想记忆：hard(硬的) + y(…的) → 强壮的； 耐寒的 例 Quick-breeding and immune to most pesticides, cockroaches are so *hardy* that even a professional exterminator may fail to eliminate them. hardy
harness [ˈhɑːrnɪs]	*n.* 马具，挽具 *v.* 束以马具；利用，控制(to control so as to use the power) 记 联想记忆：har(看作 hard，结实的) + ness(表名词) → 马具通常都很 结实 → 马具
harp [hɑːrp]	*n.* 竖琴 *v.* 弹竖琴；喋喋不休地说或写（to talk or write about to an excessive and tedious degree） 记 联想记忆：要学会弹竖琴(harp)就需要不懈刻苦努力(hard)
harpsichord [ˈhɑːrpsɪkɔːrd]	*n.* 键琴(钢琴的前身) 记 组合词：harp(竖琴) + si + chord(琴弦) → 键琴
harrow [ˈhærəʊ]	*n.* 耙 *v.* 耙地；使痛苦(to inflict great distress or torment on) 记 联想记忆：农民把土地视作神圣(hallow) 的，勤勤恳恳地进行耙地 (harrow)
harrowing [ˈhærəʊɪŋ]	*adj.* 悲痛的，难受的(mentally distressful) 记 来自 harrow(*v.* 使痛苦) 搭 a harrowing experience 痛苦的经历
harry [ˈhæri]	*v.* 掠夺；袭扰；折磨(to harass; annoy; torment) 记 联想记忆：掠夺(harry)时要搬运(carry)；和人名 Harry 一样拼写

30

Word List 31

harshly [ˈhɑːrʃli]	*adv.* 严酷地，无情地 同 severely, toughly
hash [hæʃ]	*n.* 杂乱，混乱(a jumble; a hodgopodge)；杂烩菜(chopped food, specifically: chopped meat mixed with potatoes and browned)
hasten [ˈheɪsn]	*v.* 加速，加快，促进(to speed up; accelerate) 同 hurry, quicken
hasty [ˈheɪsti]	*adj.* 急急忙忙的(said, made or done too quickly) 记 来自 haste(*n.* 急速)
hauteur [hɔːˈtɜːr]	*n.* 傲慢(haughtiness; snobbery) 记 来自 haut(*adj.* 高级的；上流社会的)
havoc [ˈhævək]	*n.* 大破坏，混乱(great destruction and devastation) 记 联想记忆：hav(看作 have, 有) + oc(看作 occur, 发生) → 有事发生 → 混乱
hawk [hɔːk]	*n.* 隼，鹰(a kind of eagle)
hazy [ˈheɪzi]	*adj.* 朦胧的，不清楚的(made dim or cloudy by or as if by haze) 同 foggy, misty, smoky
headlong [ˈhedlɔːŋ]	*adj./adv.* 轻率的/地，迅猛的/地 记 组合词：head + long → 头很长 → 做事长驱直入不假思索 → 轻率的/地
headway [ˈhedweɪ]	*n.* 进步，进展(progress) 搭 make headway 取得进展
heady [ˈhedi]	*adj.* 任性的(willful)；鲁莽的(impetuous) 同 unruly, rash
heal [hiːl]	*v.* 治愈(to restore to health or soundness) 同 cure, remedy
hearken [ˈhɑːrkən]	*v.* 倾听(to listen attentively) 记 来自 hear(*v.* 听)

| **hearsay** | *n.* 谣传，道听途说 (rumor; gossip) |
| [ˈhɪrseɪ] | 记 组合词：hear (听到) + say (说) → 道听途说 |

| **heartrending** | *adj.* 令人心碎的 (heartbreaking) |
| [ˈhɑːrtrendɪŋ] | 记 组合词：heart (心) + rending (撕碎) → 令人心碎的 |

| **heave** | *v.* 用力举 (to raise or lift with an effort) |
| [hiːv] | 记 联想记忆：heaven (天堂) 去掉 n → 想把天堂举起，却掉了个 n → 用力举 |

| **heckle** | *v.* 诘问，责问 (to annoy or harass by interrupting with questions or taunts) |
| [ˈhekl] | 记 联想记忆：he (他) + ckle (看作 buckle，扣上) → 他因无故把人扣住不放受到诘问 → 诘问 |

| **hectic** | *adj.* 兴奋的，繁忙的，忙乱的 (characterized by confusion, rush or excitement) |
| [ˈhektɪk] | 同 busy, exciting |

| **hector** | *v.* 欺凌，威吓 (to browbeat; bully) |
| [ˈhektər] | 同 intimidate, threaten |

| **hedge** | *n.* 树篱；保护手段 (a means of defense)；障碍 (barrier; limit) |
| [hedʒ] | 记 联想记忆：边缘 (edge) 被 h 围成了树篱 |

| **herbivorous** | *adj.* 食草的 (feeding on plants) |
| [ɜːrˈbɪvərəs] | 记 词根记忆：herb (草) + i + vor (吃) + ous → 食草的 |

| **heresy** | *n.* 异端邪说 (a religious belief opposed to the orthodox doctrines) |
| [ˈherəsi] | 记 联想记忆：here (这里) + sy (看作 say，说) → 非熟悉的本地人所说的 → 异端邪说 |

| **hermetic** | *adj.* 密封的 (completely sealed by fusion; airtight)；神秘的，深奥的 (relating to or characterized by occultism or abstruseness) |
| [hɜːrˈmetɪk] | 记 来自 Hermes (古希腊具有发明才能的神) |

| **hew** | *v.* 砍伐 (to chop or cut with an ax)；遵守 (to conform; adhere) |
| [hjuː] | 记 联想记忆：早上去砍伐 (hew) 树木，露珠 (dew) 被震下来 |

| **hidebound** | *adj.* 思想偏狭且顽固的 (obstinately conservative and narrow minded) |
| [ˈhaɪdbaʊnd] | 记 组合词：hide (兽皮) + bound (包裹) → 被皮包裹起来 → 思想偏狭且顽固的 |

| **hie** | *v.* 疾走，快速 (to go quickly; hasten) |
| [haɪ] | 同 hurry, speed |

| **hieroglyphic** | *n.* 象形文字 (a system of writing which uses hieroglyphs) |
| [ˌhaɪərəˈɡlɪfɪk] | |

| **highbrow** | *n.* 自以为文化修养很高的人 (a person pretending highly cultivated, or having intellectual tastes) |
| [ˈhaɪbraʊ] | 记 组合词：high (高) + brow (额头，眉毛) → 眉毛挑得很高的人 → 自以为文化修养很高的人 |

| **hike** | *v.* 抬高，提高 (to increase or raise in amount) *n.* 徒步旅行 |
| [haɪk] | 搭 hike...up 拉起，提起 |

31

hilarious [hɪˈleriəs]	*adj.* 欢闹的(noisily merry)；引起大笑的(producing great merriment) 记 词根记忆：hilar(高兴) + ious → 高兴的 → 欢闹的；引起大笑的
hinder [ˈhɪndər]	*v.* 阻碍，妨碍(to thwart; impede; frustrate) 记 词根记忆：hind(后面) + er → 落在后面 → 阻碍，妨碍
hinge [hɪndʒ]	*n.* 铰链(a joint)；关键(a determining factor)
hoarse [hɔːrs]	*adj.* 嘶哑的，粗哑的(rough and husky in sound) 记 联想记忆：horse(马)中间加一个 a → 马的叫声很嘶哑 → 嘶哑的
hoary [ˈhɔːri]	*adj.* (头发)灰白的(gray)；古老的(very old) 记 发音记忆："好理" → 头发灰白，该好好整理了 → 灰白的
hoax [hoʊks]	*n.* 骗局，恶作剧(a trick or fraud) *v.* 欺骗(to deceive; cheat) 记 联想记忆：不要和 coax(*v.* 哄骗)混淆
hobble [ˈhɑːbl]	*v.* 蹒跚(to go unsteadily)；跛行(to walk lamely; limp) 记 联想记忆：和 hobby(*n.* 癖好)一起记
hoe [hoʊ]	*n.* 锄头(any of various implements for tilling, mixing or raking) 记 联想记忆：用锄头(hoe)挖洞(hole)
hoist [hɔɪst]	*v.* 提起，升起(to raise or haul up) *n.* 起重机 同 elevate, lift
homage [ˈhɑːmɪdʒ]	*n.* 效忠(allegiance)；敬意(honor) 记 词根记忆：hom(=hum 人) + age → 对别人表示敬意 → 敬意
homely [ˈhoʊmli]	*adj.* 朴素的(simple and unpretentious)；不漂亮的(plain or unattractive) 记 联想记忆：home(家) + ly → 家庭用的 → 朴素的
hone [hoʊn]	*n.* 磨刀石 *v.* 磨刀(to sharpen with a hone) 记 注意不要和 horn(*n.* 号角)相混
hoodoo [ˈhuːduː]	*n.* 厄运；招来不幸的人(sb. that brings bad luck)
hoodwink [ˈhʊdwɪŋk]	*v.* 蒙混，欺骗(to mislead or confuse by trickery; dupe) 记 联想记忆：hood(帽兜) + wink(眨眼) → 眨眼之间从帽兜中变出(像变魔术一样) → 蒙混，欺骗
hoop [huːp]	*n.* (桶的)箍，铁环(a circular band or ring for holding together the staves of a barrel)
horizontal [ˌhɔːrəˈzɑːntl]	*adj.* 水平的(level) 记 来自 horizon(*n.* 地平线)
horn [hɔːrn]	*n.* 角(bony outgrowth usually pointed on head of some animals)；喇叭(an apparatus which makes a loud warning sound)
horrendous [hɔːˈrendəs]	*adj.* 可怕的，令人恐惧的(horrible; frightful) 记 词根记忆：horr(发抖) + endous → 令人发抖的 → 可怕的

hortative	*adj.* 劝告的；激励的（serving to encourage or urge）
[ˈhɔːrtətɪv]	记 词根记忆：hort(敦促) + ative → 激励的
horticulture	*n.* 园艺学
[ˈhɔːrtɪkʌltʃər]	记 词根记忆：horti(花园) + cult(种植；培养) + ure → 园艺学
howler	*n.* 嚎叫的人或动物；滑稽可笑的错误（a ludicrous blunder）
[ˈhaʊlər]	记 来自 howl(*v.* 嚎叫)
hubris	*n.* 傲慢，目中无人（overbearing pride or presumption; arrogance）
[ˈhjuːbrɪs]	记 联想记忆：hub(中心) + ris(看作 rise, 升起) → 中心升起 → 以(自我)为中心 → 目中无人
hue	*n.* 色彩，色泽（color）；信仰
[hjuː]	搭 hue and cry 公众的强烈抗议
huffish	*adj.* 不高兴的，发怒的（peevish; sulky）；傲慢的
[ˈhʌfɪʃ]	记 来自 huff(*v./n.* 生气)
huffy	*adj.* 愤怒的，恼怒的（irritated or annoyed; indignant）
[ˈhʌfi]	同 angry, irate
hull	*n.* 外壳（the outer covering）；船身 *v.* 剥去外壳（to remove the hulls of）
[hʌl]	记 联想记忆：空有外壳(hull)的东西是没有价值的(null)
humid	*adj.* 湿润的（damp）
[ˈhjuːmɪd]	记 联想记忆：hum(嗡嗡声) + id → 蚊虫总有嗡嗡的声音，而潮湿的地方多蚊虫 → 湿润的
	例 Even as the local climate changed from *humid* to arid and back—a change that caused other animals to become almost extinct—our human ancestors survived by learning how to use the new flora.
humor	*v.* 纵容，迁就（to comply with the mood or whim; indulge）
[ˈhjuːmər]	记 humor 最常见的是作"幽默"讲
hunker	*v.* 蹲下（to squat close to the ground）；顽固地坚持（to hold stubbornly to a position）
[ˈhʌŋkər]	
hurdle	*n.* 跨栏；障碍（obstacle） *v.* 克服(障碍)（to overcome; surmount）
[ˈhɜːrdl]	同 barrier, block, obstruction, snag
hurtle	*v.* 呼啸而过，快速通过（to move rapidly or forcefully）；猛投，用力投掷（to hurl; fling）
[ˈhɜːrtl]	记 和 turtle(*n.* 海龟)一起记
husband	*v.* 节省，节约（to manage prudently and economically）
[ˈhʌzbənd]	记 联想记忆：丈夫(husband)省钱(husband)，老婆花钱
husbandry	*n.* (广义上的)农业（the cultivation or production of plants or animals）
[ˈhʌzbəndri]	记 联想记忆：husband(丈夫) + ry → 丈夫所干的活 → 农业
hush	*n.* 肃静，安静（absence of noise; silence） *v.* (使)安静下来
[hʌʃ]	记 联想记忆：不要和 husk(*n.* 种子等的外壳)混淆
hymn	*n.* 赞美诗（any song of praise）
[hɪm]	同 psalm

31

□ hortative	□ horticulture	□ howler	□ hubris	□ hue	□ huffish
□ huffy	□ hull	□ humid	□ humor	□ hunker	□ hurdle
□ hurtle	□ husband	□ husbandry	□ hush	□ hymn	

341

hype [haɪp]	*n.* 夸大的广告宣传(promotional publicity of an extravagant or contrived kind)
hyperactivity [ˌhaɪpərækˈtɪvəti]	*n.* 活动过度，极度活跃(the state or condition of being excessively or pathologically active)
	记 词根记忆: hyper(过分) + activity(活动) → 活动过度
hypocrite [ˈhɪpəkrɪt]	*n.* 伪善者，伪君子(a person who pretends to have opinions or to be what he is not)
	记 词根记忆: hypo(在下面) + crit(判断) + e → 在背后下判断 → 伪君子
	例 The *hypocrite* simulates feelings which he does not possess but which he feels he should display
icicle [ˈaɪsɪkl]	*n.* 冰柱，冰垂(a tapering, pointed, hanging piece of ice)
	记 词根记忆: ic(=ice 冰) + icle(小东西) → 冰柱
icon [ˈaɪkɑːn]	*n.* 圣像(an image or picture of Jesus, Mary, a saint, etc); 偶像
	记 icon 本身可作构词成分，如: iconize(*v.* 盲目崇拜)，iconoclasm(*n.* 打破圣像的行动)
iconoclast [aɪˈkɑːnəklæst]	*n.* 攻击传统观念或风俗的人(one who attacks and seeks to destroy widely accepted ideas, beliefs)
	记 词根记忆: icon(圣像) + o + clas(打破) + t → 打破圣像的人 → 攻击传统观念或风俗的人
idiom [ˈɪdiəm]	*n.* 方言，土语; 术语，特有用语(the language peculiar to a people or to a district, community, or class); 风格，特色(manner, style)
idle [ˈaɪdl]	*adj.* (指人)无所事事的(avoiding work); 无效的(useless) *v.* 懒散，无所事事(to do nothing)
	记 发音记忆: "爱斗" → 无所事事的人才爱斗 → 无所事事
idolatrize [aɪˈdɒlətraɪz]	*v.* 奉为偶像，盲目崇拜(to admire intensely and often blindly)
	记 来自 idol(*n.* 偶像)
idolize [ˈaɪdəlaɪz]	*v.* 将…当作偶像崇拜(to treat as an idol); 极度仰慕，崇拜(to admire very much)
ignite [ɪɡˈnaɪt]	*v.* 发光(to make glow with heat); 点燃，燃烧(to set fire to)
	记 词根记忆: ign(点火) + ite → 点燃
ignorant [ˈɪɡnərənt]	*adj.* 无知的，愚昧的(knowing little or nothing)
	记 词根记忆: ig(不) + nor(=gnor 知道) + ant → 不知道的 → 无知的
	搭 be ignorant of 对…无知
ilk [ɪlk]	*n.* 类型，种类(sort, kind)
	记 联想记忆: 和 ink(*n.* 墨水)一起记
illiberal [ɪˈlɪbərəl]	*adj.* 偏执的，思想狭隘的(intolerant; bigoted)
	记 联想记忆: il(不) + liberal(开明的) → 不开明的 → 偏执的

idle

illuminate	v. 阐明, 解释 (to make understandable); 照亮 (to brighten with lights)
[ɪˈluːmɪneɪt]	记 词根记忆: il(向内) + lumin(光) + ate → 投入光 → 照亮
	例 Since most if not all learning occurs through comparisons, relating one observation to another, it would be strange indeed if the study of other cultures did not also *illuminate* the study of our own.

| **illuminati** | n. 先觉者, 先知 (persons who are or who claim to be unusually enlightened) |
| [ɪˌluːmɪˈnɑːti] | 记 词根记忆: il + lumin(光) + ati → 给人带来光明的人 → 先知 |

| **illusive** | adj. 迷惑人的, 迷幻的 (deceiving and unreal) |
| [ɪˈluːsɪv] | 记 词根记忆: il + lus(玩耍) + ive → 头脑对某事闹着玩的 → 迷幻的 |

illustrate	v. 举例说明, 用图表等说明 (to explain by examples, diagrams, pictures); 阐明 (to make clear)
[ˈɪləstreɪt]	记 词根记忆: il(向内) + lus(照亮, 光) + trate → 向内给光明 → 阐明
	用图来表示··· illustrate
	例 Numerous historical examples *illustrate* both the overriding influence that scientists' prejudices have on their interpretation of data and the consequent impairment of their intellectual objectivity.

| **illustrious** | adj. 著名的, 显赫的 (very distinguished; outstanding) |
| [ɪˈlʌstriəs] | 记 词根记忆: il(进入) + lus(光) + tr + ious → 进入光中 → 著名的 |

| **imbecile** | n. 低能者, 弱智者, 极愚蠢的 (a very foolish or stupid person) |
| [ˈɪmbəsl] | 记 dolt, fool, idiot |

| **imbibe** | v. 喝 (to drink); 吸入 (to absorb) |
| [ɪmˈbaɪb] | 记 词根记忆: im(进入) + bib(喝) + e → 喝入 → 吸入 |

| **imbroglio** | n. 纠纷, 纠葛, 纠缠不清 (confused misunderstanding or disagreement) |
| [ɪmˈbrəʊliəʊ] | 记 词根记忆: im(进入) + bro(混乱) + glio → 纠纷 |

| **immanent** | adj. 内在的, 固有的 (inherent); 普遍存在的, 无所不在的 (present through the universe) |
| [ˈɪmənənt] | 记 词根记忆: im(进入) + man(停留) + ent → 停留在内部的 → 内在的 |

| **immemorial** | adj. 太古的, 极古的 (extending beyond memory or record; ancient) |
| [ˌɪməˈmɔːriəl] | 记 词根记忆: im(不) + memor(记住) + ial → 在记忆之外的 → 太古的 |

| **immensity** | n. 巨大的事物 (sth. immense); 巨大, 广大, 无限 (the quality or state of being immense) |
| [ɪˈmensəti] | |

| **immerse** | v. 浸入 (to plunge, drop, or dip into liquid); 沉浸于 (to engross) |
| [ɪˈmɜːrs] | 记 词根记忆: im(进入) + mers(浸入) + e → 浸入 |

| **immolate** | v. 牺牲, 献祭 (to offer or kill as a sacrifice) |
| [ˈɪməleɪt] | 记 词根记忆: im(在···之上) + mola(用作祭品的肉) + te → 放上祭品 → 牺牲 |

| **immortal** | adj. 不朽的, 流芳百世的 (deathless) |
| [ɪˈmɔːrtl] | 记 词根记忆: im(不) + mort(死) + al → 不死的 → 不朽的 |

31

immune	*adj.* 免疫的 (not susceptible to some specified disease) ; 免除的，豁免的
[ɪˈmjuːn]	记 词根记忆：im (没有) + mun (服务) + e → 不提供服务的 → 免疫的
	例 No computer system is *immune* to a virus, a particularly malicious program that is designed to infect and electronically damage the disks on which data are stored.
immunity	*n.* 免疫力；豁免 (exemption)
[ɪˈmjuːnəti]	搭 immunity to/against 对…的免疫力
immunize	*v.* (通过接种) 使免疫 (to give immunity by inoculation)
[ˈɪmjunaɪz]	记 来自 immune (*adj.* 免疫的)
immure	*v.* 监禁 (to imprison; confine; seclude)
[ɪˈmjʊr]	记 词根记忆：im (进入) + mur (墙) + e → 进入墙 → 监禁
impact	*n.* 冲击，影响 (the effect and impression of one thing on another)
[ˈɪmpækt]	记 词根记忆：im (进入) + pact (系紧) → 用力系紧 → 影响
	例 The *impact* of a recently published collection of essays, written during and about the last presidential campaign, is lessened by its timing; it comes too late to affect us with its immediacy and too soon for us to read it out of historical curiosity.
impale	*v.* 刺入，刺穿 (to pierce with a sharp-pointed object)
[ɪmˈpeɪl]	记 联想记忆：im + pale (苍白的) → 被针刺到，脸色苍白 → 刺入
impalpable	*adj.* 无法触及的；不易理解的 (too slight or subtle to be grasped)
[ɪmˈpælpəbl]	记 联想记忆：im (不) + palpable (可触摸的) → 无法触及的
impasse	*n.* 僵局 (deadlock) ；死路 (blind alley)
[ˈɪmpæs]	记 联想记忆：im (不) + pass (通过) + e → 通不过 → 僵局；死路
impeach	*v.* 控告 (to accuse) ；怀疑 (to challenge or discredit; accuse) ；弹劾 (to charge with a crime or misdemeanor)
[ɪmˈpiːtʃ]	记 联想记忆：im (进入) + peach (告发) → 控告；弹劾
impel	*v.* 推进 (to push; propel) ；驱使 (to force, compel, or urge)
[ɪmˈpel]	记 词根记忆：im (在…里面) + pel (推) → 推进
impend	*v.* 威胁 (to menace) ；即将发生 (to be about to occur)
[ɪmˈpend]	记 词根记忆：im + pend (悬挂) → 事情挂在眼前 → 即将发生
impenitent	*adj.* 不知悔悟的 (without regret; unrepentant)
[ɪmˈpenɪtənt]	记 联想记忆：im (不) + penitent (悔过的) → 死不悔改的 → 不知悔悟的
imperil	*v.* 使陷于危险，危及 (to put in peril; endanger)
[ɪmˈperəl]	记 联想记忆：im (进入) + peril (危险) → 使陷于危险
impermeability	*n.* 不渗透性
[ɪmˌpɜːrmiəˈbɪləti]	记 联想记忆：im (不) + permeability (可渗透性) → 不渗透性
impertinence	*n.* 无礼，粗鲁 (rudeness)
[ɪmˈpɜːrtnəns]	记 联想记忆：im (不) + pertinence (恰当，适当) → 行为不恰当 → 无礼
impetus	*n.* 推动力；刺激 (incentive; impulse)
[ˈɪmpɪtəs]	记 词根记忆：im (在内) + pet (追求) + us → 内心的追求 → 刺激

□ immune	□ immunity	□ immunize	□ immure	□ impact	□ impale
□ impalpable	□ impasse	□ impeach	□ impel	□ impend	□ impenitent
□ imperil	□ impermeability	□ impertinence	□ impetus		

impinge [ɪmˈpɪndʒ]	*v.* 侵犯(to infringe; encroach); 撞击(to collide with) 记 词根记忆: im(进入) + ping(系紧; 强加于) + e → 强行进入 → 侵犯
implant [ɪmˈplænt]	*v.* 植入, 插入(to plant firmly or deeply); 灌输(to instill; inculcate) 记 联想记忆: im(进入) + plant(种植) → 植入; 灌输
implicate [ˈɪmplɪkeɪt]	*v.* 牵连(于罪行中)(to involve in a crime); 暗示(to imply) 记 词根记忆: im(进入) + plic(重叠) + ate → 重叠进去 → 牵连
implicit [ɪmˈplɪsɪt]	*adj.* 含蓄的, 暗示的(not directly expressed) 记 词根记忆: im(进入) + plic(重叠) + it → (意义)叠在里面 → 含蓄的
implode [ɪmˈploʊd]	*v.* 内爆(to burst inward); 剧减(to undergo violent compression) 记 词根记忆: im(向内) + plod(打击; 撞击) + e → 在内部横冲直撞 → 内爆
implore [ɪmˈplɔːr]	*v.* 哀求, 恳求(to beg) 记 词根记忆: im(进入) + plor(哭泣) + e → 哭泣 → 哀求
importune [ˌɪmpɔːrˈtuːn]	*v.* 强求, 胡搅蛮缠(to entreat persistently or repeatedly) 记 词根记忆: im(进入) + port(搬运) + une → 向内搬 → 强求
impose [ɪmˈpoʊz]	*v.* 征收(to establish or apply by authority); 强加 记 词根记忆: im(进入) + pos(放) + e → 放进去 → 强加
impoverish [ɪmˈpɑːvərɪʃ]	*v.* 使贫穷(to make poor; reduce to poverty) 记 词根记忆: im(进入) + pover(贫困) + ish → 进入贫困 → 使贫穷
imprecation [ˌɪmprɪˈkeɪʃn]	*n.* 诅咒(oath or curse) 记 来自 imprecate(*v.* 诅咒)
impregnable [ɪmˈpregnəbl]	*adj.* 固若金汤的, 无法攻破的(not capable of being captured or entered by force) 记 词根记忆: im(不) + pregn(拿住) + able(能…的) → 拿不住的 → 无法攻破的
imprint [ɪmˈprɪnt]	*v.* 盖印, 刻印(to mark by pressing or stamping) 记 联想记忆: im(不) + print(印记) → 留下印记 → 盖印
impuissance [ɪmˈpjuːɪsəns]	*n.* 无力, 虚弱(weakness) 记 联想记忆: im(不) + puissance(力量) → 无力
imputation [ˌɪmpjuˈteɪʃn]	*n.* 归咎, 归罪(an attribution of fault or crime; accusation) 记 词根记忆: im(进入) + put(计算) + ation → 算计别人 → 归罪
inadvertence [ˌɪnədˈvɜːrtəns]	*n.* 粗心, 疏忽, 漫不经心(the fact or action of being inadvertent) 记 词根记忆: in(不) + ad(往) + vert(转) + ence → 不转向某物 → 不加以注意 → 漫不经心
inadvertently [ˌɪnədˈvɜːrtəntli]	*adv.* 不小心地, 疏忽地(by accident) 记 来自 inadvertent(*adj.* 疏忽的)
inanimate [ɪnˈænɪmət]	*adj.* 无生命的(not animate; lifeless) 记 词根记忆: in(无) + anim(生命) + ate → 无生命的

inappreciable [ˌɪnəˈpriːʃəbl]	*adj.* 微不足道的（too small to be perceived） 记 词根记忆：in(不) + ap + preci(价值) + able(能…的) → 没有价值的 → 微不足道的
incarcerate [ɪnˈkɑːrsəreɪt]	*v.* 把…关进监狱，监禁，禁闭（to imprison; confine） 记 词根记忆：in(进入) + carcer(监狱) + ate → 把…关进监狱，监禁，禁闭
incertitude [ɪnˈsɜːrtɪtjuːd]	*n.* 不确定(性)（uncertainty）；无把握，怀疑 记 词根记忆：in(不) + cert(确定的) + itude(表状态) → 不确定(性)
inch [ɪntʃ]	*v.* 慢慢前进，慢慢移动（to move by small degrees） 记 联想记忆：一寸一寸(inch)地移动，引申为"慢慢前进"
inchoate [ɪnˈkoʊət]	*adj.* 刚开始的（just begun; incipient）；未充分发展的，不成熟的（not yet completed or fully developed） 记 联想记忆：inch(英寸) + oat(燕麦) + e → 燕麦刚长了一英寸 → 未充分 发展的，不成熟的
incinerate [ɪnˈsɪnəreɪt]	*v.* 焚化，焚毁（to burn to ashes; cremate） 记 词根记忆：in(进入) + ciner(灰) + ate → 变成灰 → 焚化
incision [ɪnˈsɪʒn]	*n.* 切口（a cut; gash）；切割 记 词根记忆：in(向内) + cis(切) + ion → 切割
incite [ɪnˈsaɪt]	*v.* 激发，刺激（to stimulate to action; foment） 记 词根记忆：in(进入) + cit(唤起) + e → 唤起情绪 → 激发
inclement [ɪnˈklemənt]	*adj.* (天气)严酷的（severe; stormy）；严厉的（rough; severe） 记 联想记忆：in(不) + clement(仁慈的) → 不仁慈的 → 严酷的；严厉的
incogitant [ɪnˈkɑːdʒɪtənt]	*adj.* 未经思考的，考虑不周的（thoughtless; inconsiderate） 记 词根记忆：in(不) + co(共同) + g(=ag 开动) + it + ant → 不开动脑筋 的 → 未经思考的
incongruent [ɪnˈkɑːŋgruənt]	*adj.* 不协调的，不和谐的，不合适的（not congruent） 记 联想记忆：in(不) + congruent(协调的，合适的) → 不协调的，不合适的
inconstancy [ɪnˈkɑːnstənsi]	*n.* (指人)反复无常（the state or quality of being eccentrically variable or fickle） 记 联想记忆：in(不) + constancy(恒久不变) → 反复无常
incorrigibility [ɪnˌkɔrɪdʒəˈbɪləti]	*n.* 无可救药（incapability of being corrected or amended） 记 词根记忆：in(不) + cor(=com 一起) + rig(直的) + ibility → 无法一起 拉直 → 无可救药
increment [ˈɪŋkrəmənt]	*n.* 增加（increase; gain; growth） 记 词根记忆：in(进入) + cre(生长) + ment → 使生长 → 增加
incriminate [ɪnˈkrɪmɪneɪt]	*v.* 连累，牵连（to involve in） 记 词根记忆：in(进入) + crimin(罪行) + ate → 被牵连在罪行中 → 连累
incubation [ˌɪŋkjuˈbeɪʃn]	*n.* 孵卵期；潜伏期（the phase of development of a disease between the infection and the first appearance of symptoms）
incubus [ˈɪŋkjʊbəs]	*n.* 梦魇（a nightmare）；沉重的负担（an oppressive burden） 记 词根记忆：in + cub(躺) + us → 躺在某物内 → 梦魇

inculcate [ɪnˈkʌlkeɪt]	v. 谆谆教诲，反复灌输（to impress upon the mind by persistent urging; implant） 记 词根记忆：in(进入) + culc(=cult 培养；种植) + ate → 种进去 → 反复灌输
inculpate [ˈɪnkʌlpeɪt]	v. 控告；归咎于（to incriminate） 记 词根记忆：in(使) + culp(错，罪) + ate → 使(别人)有罪 → 控告
incur [ɪnˈkɜːr]	v. 招惹（to bring upon oneself） 记 词根记忆：in(进入) + cur(跑) → 跑进来 → 招惹 例 Lizzie was a brave woman who could dare to *incur* a great danger for an adequate object.
indelible [ɪnˈdeləbl]	adj. 擦拭不掉的，不可磨灭的（incapable of being erased） 记 词根记忆：in(不) + de(消失) + li(=liv 石灰) + ble → 用石灰无法去掉的 → 擦拭不掉的
indemnify [ɪnˈdemnɪfaɪ]	v. 赔偿，偿付（to compensate for a loss; reimburse） 记 词根记忆：in(不) + demn(损坏) + ify → 使损坏消除 → 赔偿
indifferent [ɪnˈdɪfrənt]	adj. 不感兴趣的，漠不关心的（having or showing no particular interest in or concern for; disinterested） 记 联想记忆：in(不) + different(不同的) → 对任何事的态度都没什么不同 → 漠不关心的 搭 be indifferent to 对…冷漠
indignant [ɪnˈdɪgnənt]	adj. 愤慨的，愤愤不平的（feeling or expressing anger） 同 angry
indignity [ɪnˈdɪgnəti]	n. 侮辱，轻蔑（insult）；侮辱性的行为（an act that offends against a person's dignity or self-respect） 记 联想记忆：in(不) + dignity(高贵) → 不高贵的行为 → 侮辱性的行为
induce [ɪnˈduːs]	v. 诱导（to lead into some action）；引起（to bring out） 记 词根记忆：in(进入) + duc(拉) + e → 拉进去 → 诱导
induct [ɪnˈdʌkt]	v. 使就职（to install）；使入伍（to enroll in the armed forces） 记 词根记忆：in(进去) + duct(拉) → 拉进 → 使入伍
induction [ɪnˈdʌkʃn]	n. 就职（installation）；归纳（inference of a generalized conclusion from particular instances）
industrious [ɪnˈdʌstriəs]	adj. 勤劳的，勤勉的（hard-working; diligent） 记 词根记忆：in (在里面) + du + str (=struct 建造) + ious → 在里面建造 → 勤劳的
inebriate [ɪˈniːbrieɪt]	v. 使…醉（to intoxicate）n. 酒鬼，酒徒（a drunkard） 记 词根记忆：in(进入) + ebri(醉的) + ate → 使…醉
ineffable [ɪnˈefəbl]	adj. 不可言喻的，难以表达的（inexpressible）；避讳的 记 词根记忆：in(不) + ef(出) + fa(说) + ble → 不能说出的 → 不可言喻的
inelasticity [ˌɪnɪlæˈstɪsəti]	n. 无弹性，无伸缩性 记 联想记忆：in(无) + elastic(有弹性的) + ity(表性质) → 无弹性，无伸缩性

31

□ inculcate	□ inculpate	□ incur	□ indelible	□ indemnify	□ indifferent
□ indignant	□ indignity	□ induce	□ induct	□ induction	□ industrious
□ inebriate	□ ineffable	□ inelasticity			

347

ineluctable [ˌɪnɪˈlʌktəbl]	*adj.* 不能逃避的(certain; inevitable) 记 词根记忆：in(不) + e(出) + luct(挣扎) + able → 无法挣脱的 → 不能逃避的
inexpedient [ˌɪnɪkˈspiːdiənt]	*adj.* 不适当的，不明智的(inadvisable; unwise) 记 联想记忆：in(不) + expedient(有利的) → 不利的 → 不明智的
inexpiable [ˌɪnɪkˈspɪəbl]	*adj.* 不能补偿的(incapable of being expiated or atoned) 记 联想记忆：in(不) + expiable(可抵偿的) → 不能补偿的；来自 expiate(*v.* 补偿)

You have to believe in yourself. That's the secret of success.
人必须相信自己，这是成功的秘诀。

——美国演员 卓别林(Charles Chaplin, American actor)

infantry [ˈɪnfəntri]	*n.* 步兵(soldiers who fight on foot)
	记 联想记忆：infant(婴儿) + (t)ry(尝试) → 婴儿在尝试走路时很慢，相对其他兵种而言，步兵的行军速度也较慢 → 步兵
infatuate [ɪnˈfætʃueɪt]	*v.* 使迷恋(to inspire with a foolish or extravagant love or admiration)；使糊涂(to cause to deprive of sound judgment)
	记 词根记忆：in(进入) + fatu(愚蠢的) + ate → 因迷恋而变得愚蠢 → 使迷恋
infelicitous [ˌɪnfɪˈlɪsɪtəs]	*adj.* 不幸的(unfortunate)；不妥当的(unsuitable)
	记 词根记忆：in(不) + felic(幸运的) + it + ous → 不幸的
infelicity [ˌɪnfɪˈlɪsɪti]	*n.* 不幸(the quality or state of being infelicitous)；不恰当的事物(sth. that is infelicitous)
infernal [ɪnˈfɜːrnl]	*adj.* 地狱的(of hell)；可恶的(hateful; outrageous)
	记 词根记忆：infern(更低的) + al → 更低的地方 → 地狱的
inflame [ɪnˈfleɪm]	*v.* 使燃烧(to set on fire)；激怒(某人)(to excite intensely with anger)
	记 词根记忆：in(进入) + flam(火焰) + e → 进入火焰 → 使燃烧
inflammation [ˌɪnfləˈmeɪʃn]	*n.* 发炎；炎症
	记 词根记忆：in(进入) + flam(燃烧) + mation → 仿似开始燃烧 → 发炎
influx [ˈɪnflʌks]	*n.* 注入，涌入(arrival of people or things in large numbers or quantities)
	记 词根记忆：in(进入) + flux(流动) → 注入，涌入
informed [ɪnˈfɔːrmd]	*adj.* 有学识的(having or showing knowledge)；见多识广的，消息灵通的(having or displaying reliable information)
	例 There is some irony in the fact that the author of a book as sensitive and *informed* as Indian Artisans did not develop her interest in Native American art until adulthood, for she grew up in a region rich in American Indian culture.
informer [ɪnˈfɔːrmər]	*n.* 告发者，告密者(a person who secretly accuses)
	记 联想记忆：inform(通知) + er(人) → 通知的人 → 告发者，告密者
infraction [ɪnˈfrækʃn]	*n.* 违反，违犯(violation; infringement)
	记 词根记忆：in(使) + fract(破裂) + ion → 使(法律)破裂 → 违反

infringe [ɪnˈfrɪndʒ]	*v.* 违反，侵害(to break a law; violate; trespass) 记 词根记忆：in + fring(破坏) + e → 违反
ingestion [ɪnˈdʒestʃən]	*n.* 摄取，吸收(the act of taking food or drink into the body) 记 词根记忆：in(进入) + gest(搬运) + ion → 运入体内 → 摄取
ingratiate [ɪnˈɡreɪʃieɪt]	*v.* 逢迎，讨好(to bring oneself into another's favor or good graces by conscious effort) 记 词根记忆：in(使) + grat(感激) + iate → 使别人感激自己 → 讨别人 欢心 → 讨好
ingress [ˈɪnɡres]	*n.* 进入(the act of entering) 记 词根记忆：in(进去) + gress(走) → 走进去 → 进入
inhale [ɪnˈheɪl]	*v.* 吸入，吸气(to breathe air, smoke, or gas into lungs) 记 词根记忆：in(进) + hale(呼吸) → 吸入
inherit [ɪnˈherɪt]	*v.* 继承(to receive property) 记 词根记忆：in + her(继承人) + it → 继承
iniquity [ɪˈnɪkwəti]	*n.* 邪恶，不公正，不道德(lack of righteousness or justice; wickedness) 记 联想记忆：in(不) + iqu(相同的) + ity → 不相 同 → 不公正
inkling [ˈɪŋklɪŋ]	*n.* 暗示(hint)；略知，模糊概念(a slight knowledge or vague notion) 记 联想记忆：ink(墨水) + ling(小东西) → 小墨迹 → 暗示
inmate [ˈɪnmeɪt]	*n.* 同住者，同居者(any of a group occupying a single place of residence) 记 联想记忆：in + mate(配偶) → 配偶住在一起 → 同住者
innuendo [ˌɪnjuˈendoʊ]	*n.* 含沙射影，暗讽(an indirect remark, gesture, or reference, usually implying sth. derogatory; insinuation) 记 词根记忆：in(向) + nuen(摇头) + do → 向某人摇头 → 暗讽 例 Demonstrating a mastery of *innuendo*, he issued several veiled insults in the course of the evening's conversation.
inoculate [ɪˈnɑːkjuleɪt]	*v.* 注射预防针(to inject a serum, vaccine to create immunity) 记 词根记忆：in(进入) + ocul(萌芽) + ate → 在萌芽时进入 → 注射 预防针
inroad [ˈɪnroʊd]	*n.* 袭击(a hostile invasion)；(以牺牲他者为代价而取得的)进展(advance often at the expense of sb. or sth.) 记 联想记忆：in(进) + road(路) → 进了别人的路 → 袭击
insane [ɪnˈseɪn]	*adj.* 疯狂的(deranged; demented; mad) 记 联想记忆：in(不) + sane(清醒的) → 头脑不清醒的 → 疯狂的
insanity [ɪnˈsænəti]	*n.* 疯狂(derangement)；愚昧(great folly) 同 madness
inscribe [ɪnˈskraɪb]	*v.* (在某物上)写、题写(to write words on sth. as a formal or permanent record) 记 词根记忆：in(进入) + scrib(写) + e → 刻写进去 → 题写

inherit
财产继承人：
小咪

□ infringe	□ ingestion	□ ingratiate	□ ingress	□ inhale	□ inherit
□ iniquity	□ inkling	□ inmate	□ innuendo	□ inoculate	□ inroad
□ insane	□ insanity	□ inscribe			

inscrutable [ɪnˈskruːtəbl]	*adj.* 高深莫测的，神秘的（unfathomable；enigmatic；mysterious） 记 词根记忆：in(不) + scrut(调查) + able → 不能调查的 → 高深莫测的
insignia [ɪnˈsɪɡniə]	*n.* 徽章（badge；emblem） 记 词根记忆：in + sign(标志，记号) + ia → 作为标志的东西 → 徽章
insolence [ˈɪnsələns]	*n.* 傲慢，无礼（the quality or condition of being rude and not showing respect） 记 词根记忆：in(不) + sol(习惯了的) + ence → 不寻常 → 傲慢，无礼
insolvency [ɪnˈsɑːlvənsi]	*n.* 无力偿还（inability to pay debts）；破产（bankruptcy） 记 词根记忆：in(无) + solvency(还债能力) → 无还债能力 → 无力偿还
insouciance [ɪnˈsuːsiəns]	*n.* 漠不关心，漫不经心（lighthearted unconcern） 记 词根记忆：in(不) + souc(担心) + iance → 不担心 → 漠不关心
insouciant [ɪnˈsuːsiənt]	*adj.* 漫不经心的（unconcerned） 同 indifferent, nonchalant
inspiration [ˌɪnspəˈreɪʃn]	*n.* 启示，灵感（thought or emotion inspired by sth.） 记 词根记忆：in(进入) + spir(呼吸) + ation → 吸入(灵气) → 灵感
inspired [ɪnˈspaɪərd]	*adj.* 有创见的，有灵感的（outstanding or brilliant in a way or to a degree suggestive of divine inspiration） 记 词根记忆：in(进入) + spir(呼吸) + ed → 吸入(灵气) → 有灵感的 例 Her first concert appearance was disappointingly perfunctory and derivative, rather than the *inspired* performance in the innovative style we had anticipated.
inspissate [ɪnˈspɪseɪt]	*v.* (使)浓缩（to make thick or thicker） 记 词根记忆：in + spiss(厚的；密集的) + ate → 使变密集 → (使)浓缩
install [ɪnˈstɔːl]	*v.* 安装，装置（to fix equipment, etc.）；使就职（to induct into an office） 记 词根记忆：in(进) + stall(放) → 放进去 → 安装
instate [ɪnˈsteɪt]	*v.* 任命（to put sb. in office） 同 inaugurate, install, place
instill [ɪnˈstɪl]	*v.* 滴注（to put in drop by drop）；逐渐灌输（to impart gradually） 记 词根记忆：in(进入) + still(水滴) → 像水滴一样进入 → 滴注
insufficient [ˌɪnsəˈfɪʃnt]	*adj.* 不足的（not enough；inadequate） 记 联想记忆：in(不) + sufficient(足够的) → 不足的 例 She has sufficient tact to survive the ordinary crises of diplomatic life; however, even her diplomacy is *insufficient* to enable her to exaggerate the current emergency.
insuperable [ɪnˈsuːpərəbl]	*adj.* 难以克服的（impossible to overcome） 记 词根记忆：in(不) + super(在…之上) + able → 不可超越的 → 难以克服的
insurrection [ˌɪnsəˈrekʃn]	*n.* 造反，叛乱（rebellion；revolt） 记 词根记忆：in(反) + surrect(升起) + ion → 反对活动出现 → 造反

32

□ inscrutable	□ insignia	□ insolence	□ insolvency	□ insouciance	□ insouciant
□ inspiration	□ inspired	□ inspissate	□ install	□ instate	□ instill
□ insufficient	□ insuperable	□ insurrection			

intangibility	*n.* 无形
[ɪnˌtændʒəˈbɪləti]	记 词根记忆：in(不) + tang(触摸) + ibility → 触摸不到的 → 无形
integral	*adj.* 构成整体所必需的(necessary for completeness)；完整的(whole)
[ˈɪntɪɡrəl]	记 词根记忆：in(不) + tegr(触摸) + al → 未被触摸的 → 完整的
integrlty	*n.* 正直，诚实(honesty and sincerity)；完整(entirety)
[ɪnˈteɡrəti]	记 词根记忆：in(不) + tegr(触摸) + ity → 未被触摸 → 正直；完整
	例 In some cultures the essence of magic is its traditional *integrity*; it can be efficient only if it has been transmitted without loss from primeval times to the present practitioners.
intensify	*v.* 使加剧(to cause to become more intense)
[ɪnˈtensɪfaɪ]	记 来自 intense(*adj.* 强烈的)
inter	*v.* 埋葬(to put into a grave or tomb; bury)
[ɪnˈtɜːr]	记 词根记忆：in(进入) + ter(=terr 泥土) → 埋进泥土 → 埋葬
intercede	*v.* 说好话，代为求情(to plead or make a request on behalf of another)
[ˌɪntərˈsiːd]	记 词根记忆：inter(在…中间) + ced(走) + e → 走到中间 → 代为求情
intercept	*v.* 拦截，阻止(to seize or stop on the way)
[ˌɪntərˈsept]	记 词根记忆：inter(在…中间) + cept(拿) → 从中间拿 → 拦截
interdisciplinary	*adj.* 跨学科的(covering more than one area of study)
[ˌɪntərˈdɪsəplɪneri]	记 联想记忆：inter(在…中间) + disciplinary(学科的) → 跨学科的
	搭 interdisciplinary course 跨学科课程
interference	*n.* 干涉，妨碍(interfering)
[ˌɪntərˈfɪrəns]	搭 interference with 干扰
interjection	*n.* 插入语(sth. that is interjected)；感叹词(words used as an exclamation)
[ˌɪntərˈdʒekʃn]	记 来自 interject(*v.* 插入)
interlace	*v.* 编织(to weave together)；交错(to connect intricately)
[ˌɪntərˈleɪs]	记 词根记忆：inter(在…中间) + lac(线) + e → 使线在中间交叉 → 编织
interlard	*v.* 使混杂，混入(to vary by intermixture; intersperse)
[ˌɪntərˈlɑːrd]	同 interlace, intertwine
interlock	*v.* 互锁，连结(to lock together)
[ˌɪntərˈlɑːk]	记 联想记忆：inter + lock(锁) → 互相锁 → 互锁
interloper	*n.* 闯入者(intruder; one who interferes)
[ˈɪntərloʊpər]	记 联想记忆：inter(在…中间) + lope(大步跑) + (e)r → 人步跑进某地的人 → 闯入者
interlude	*n.* 间歇(time between two events)
[ˈɪntərluːd]	记 词根记忆：inter + lud(玩耍) + e → 在活动与活动中间的玩闹时间 → 间歇

intercede

他不是故意的

□ intangibility	□ integral	□ integrity	□ intensify	□ inter	□ intercede
□ intercept	□ interdisciplinary	□ interference	□ interjection	□ interlace	□ interlard
□ interlock	□ interloper	□ interlude			

intermingle [ˌɪntərˈmɪŋgl]	*v.* 混合，掺杂（to mix together） 记 联想记忆：inter + mingle(混合) → 混合
intermission [ˌɪntərˈmɪʃn]	*n.* 暂停，间歇（an interval of time） 记 联想记忆：inter + mission(发送) → 在发送之间 → 间歇
intermittent [ˌɪntərˈmɪtənt]	*adj.* 断断续续的（periodic；recurrent）；间歇的（alternate） 记 来自 intermit（*v.* 暂停，中断）
interpose [ˌɪntərˈpouz]	*v.* 置于…之间（to place or put between）；使介入（to introduce by way of intervention） 记 词根记忆：inter + pos(放) + e → 放入中间 → 置于…之间 例 Literature is inevitably a distorting rather than a neutral medium for the simple reason that writers *interpose* their own vision between the reader and reality.
interrogate [ɪnˈterəgeɪt]	*v.* 审问，审讯（to question formally and systematically） 记 词根记忆：inter + rog(问) + ate → 在中间问 → 审问
interrogative [ˌɪntəˈrɑːgətɪv]	*adj.* 疑问的（having the form or force of a question）；质疑的 搭 an interrogative gesture 疑问的手势
interrupt [ˌɪntəˈrʌpt]	*v.* 暂时中止（to break the continuity of sth. temporarily）；打断，打扰（to stop sb. speaking or causing some other sort of disturbance） 记 词根记忆：inter（在…之间）+ rupt（断裂）→ 在中间断裂 → 暂时中止；打断
intersperse [ˌɪntərˈspɜːrs]	*v.* 散布，点缀（to place sth. at intervals in or among） 记 词根记忆：inter + spers(撒播) + e → 在中间撒播 → 点缀
interstice [ɪnˈtɜːrstɪs]	*n.* 裂缝，空隙（a small or narrow space；crevice） 记 词根记忆：inter(在…中间) + sti(站) + ice → 站在二者之间 → 空隙
intertwine [ˌɪntərˈtwaɪn]	*v.* 纠缠，缠绕（to twine together） 记 联想记忆：inter + twine(细绳) → 多股绳交织在一起 → 纠缠
intervene [ˌɪntərˈviːn]	*v.* 干涉，介入（to interfere with the outcome or course） 记 词根记忆：inter + ven(来) + e → 来到中间 → 干涉，介入
interweave [ˌɪntərˈwiːv]	*v.* 交织（to weave together；interlace） 记 联想记忆：inter(在…中间) + weave(编织) → 交织
intestate [ɪnˈtesteɪt]	*adj.* 未留遗嘱的（having made no legal will） 记 词根记忆：in(无) + test(看到) + ate → 没有留下可以看的东西 → 未留遗嘱的
intoxicate [ɪnˈtɑːksɪkeɪt]	*v.* (使)沉醉，(使)欣喜若狂（to excite sb. greatly）；(使)喝醉（to cause sb. to lose self-control as a result of the effects of the alcohol） 记 联想记忆：in(进入) + toxic(有毒的) + ate → 中毒了 → (使)沉醉
intrude [ɪnˈtruːd]	*v.* 把(思想等)强加于；闯入（to thrust or force in or upon someone or sth. especially without permission or fitness） 记 词根记忆：in(进入) + trud(推；刺) + e → 推进去 → 闯入

32

inundate [ˈɪnʌndeɪt]	*v.* 淹没，泛滥（to cover or engulf with a flood）；压倒（to overwhelm with a great amount）
invective [ɪnˈvektɪv]	*n.* 谩骂，痛骂（a violent verbal attack；diatribe） 记 词根记忆：in(进入) + vect(搬运) + ive → 把不好的东西往人心里运 → 谩骂
inveigh [ɪnˈveɪ]	*v.* 痛骂，猛烈抨击（to utter censure or invective） 记 联想记忆：in(进入) + veigh(看作 weigh，重量) → 重重地骂 → 痛骂
inveigle [ɪnˈveɪgl]	*v.* 诱骗，诱使（to win with deception；lure） 记 联想记忆：in + veigle(看作 veil，面纱) → 盖上面纱 → 诱骗
inventory [ˈɪnvəntɔːri]	*n.* 详细目录（a detailed, itemized list）；存货清单（a list of goods on hand） 记 词根记忆：in + vent(来) + ory → 对进来的东西进行清查 → 存货清单
inveterate [ɪnˈvetərət]	*adj.* 积习已深的，根深蒂固的（habitual；chronic） 记 词根记忆：in(进入) + vet(老的) + erate → 长时间占据于内的 → 积习已深的
invidious [ɪnˈvɪdiəs]	*adj.* 惹人反感的，导致伤害和仇恨的，招人嫉妒的（tending to cause discontent, harm, animosity, or envy） 记 词根记忆：in(不) + vid(看) + ious → 不看的 → 惹人反感的
invoice [ˈɪnvɔɪs]	*n.* 发票，发货清单（bill）*v.* 给开发票（to send an invoice for or to） 记 联想记忆：in + voice(声音) → 大声把人叫进来开发票 → 发票
invoke [ɪnˈvoʊk]	*v.* 祈求，恳求（to implore；entreat）；使生效（to put into effect or operation use） 记 词根记忆：in(进入) + vok(叫喊) + e → 叫起来 → 祈求
iota [aɪˈoʊtə]	*n.* 极少量，极少（a very small quantity） 记 来自希腊语第九个字母，相当于英语中的字母 i，因其位置靠后而引申为"极少量"
ire [ˈaɪər]	*n.* 愤怒（anger）*v.* 激怒（to make angry） 记 联想记忆：愤怒(ire)之火(fire)
iridescence [ˌɪrɪˈdesns]	*n.* 彩虹色（colors of rainbow） 记 词根记忆：irid(=iris 虹光) + escence → 彩虹色
irk [ɜːrk]	*v.* 使苦恼，使厌烦（to annoy；disgust） 记 发音记忆："饿渴" → 又饿又渴，当然很苦恼 → 使苦恼
irksome [ˈɜːrksəm]	*adj.* 令人苦恼的，讨厌的（tending to irk） 记 来自 irk(*v.* 使苦恼)
irremediable [ˌɪrɪˈmiːdiəbl]	*adj.* 无法治愈的，无法纠正的（incurable；not remediable） 记 联想记忆：ir(不) + remediable(可治疗的) → 无法治愈的
irritation [ˌɪrɪˈteɪʃn]	*n.* 愤怒，恼怒（the state of being irritated） 例 Her verbosity is always a source of *irritation*: she never uses a single word when she can substitute a long clause or phrase in its place.
itinerary [aɪˈtɪnəreri]	*n.* 旅行路线（proposed route of a journey） 记 词根记忆：it(走) + in + er + ary → 旅行路线

jab [dʒæb]	*v.* 猛刺 (to make quick or abrupt thrusts with a sharp object) 记 联想记忆：和 job (*n.* 工作) 一起记
jabber ['dʒæbər]	*v.* 快而含糊地说 (to talk or say quickly and not clearly) 记 发音记忆："结巴" → 快而含糊地说
jagged ['dʒægɪd]	*adj.* 锯齿状的，参差不齐的 (notched or ragged) 记 来自 jag (*v.* 使成锯齿状)
jamb [dʒæm]	*n.* 侧柱 (an upright piece or surface forming the sides of a door, window frame) 记 联想记忆：jam (果酱) + b → 果酱抹在了门框上 → 侧柱
jamboree [,dʒæmbə'riː]	*n.* 喧闹的集会 (a boisterous party or noisy revel)
jape [dʒeɪp]	*v.* 开玩笑，戏弄 (to joke or quip) 记 联想记忆：j + ape (猿) → 把人当猴耍 → 戏弄
jar [dʒɑːr]	*v.* 震动，摇晃，冲突，抵触 (to clash)；震惊 (to give a sudden shock)；发出刺耳声 (to make a harsh or discordant sound) *n.* 广口坛子 记 联想记忆：酒吧 (bar) 里摆满了酒坛子 (jar) 例 Instead of taking exaggerated precautions against touching or tipping or *jarring* the bottle of wine, the waitress handled it quite nonchalantly, being careful only to use a napkin to keep her hands from the cool bottle itself.
jargon ['dʒɑːrgən]	*n.* 胡言乱语 (confused language)；行话 (the technical terminology) 例 The First World War began in a context of *jargon* and verbal delicacy and continued in a cloud of euphemism as impenetrable as language and literature, skillfully used, could make it.
jarring ['dʒɑːrɪŋ]	*adj.* 声音刺耳的 (of sounds that have a harsh or an unpleasant effect) 记 来自 jar (*v.* 发出刺耳声)
jaundice ['dʒɔːndɪs]	*n.* 偏见 (the state of mind in which one is jealous or suspicious)；黄疸 同 bias, prejudgment, prejudice
jaundiced ['dʒɔːndɪst]	*adj.* 有偏见的 (prejudiced) 记 来自 jaundice (*n.* 偏见)
jaunt [dʒɔːnt]	*v.* 短途旅游 (to take a short trip for pleasure) *n.* 短途旅行 同 excursion, outing, tour
jaunty ['dʒɔːnti]	*adj.* 轻松活泼的 (gay and carefree；sprightly) 记 来自 jaunt (*n.* 短途旅行)
jealousy ['dʒeləsi]	*n.* 嫉妒 (the state of being jealous) 记 来自 jealous (*adj.* 嫉妒的)
jeer [dʒɪr]	*v.* 嘲笑 (to mock；taunt；scoff at) 搭 jeer at 嘲笑
jejune [dʒɪ'dʒuːn]	*adj.* 空洞的 (devoid of significance)；不成熟的 (not mature) 记 词根记忆：jejun (空肠) + e → 空洞的

32

jeopardy ['dʒepərdi]	*n.* 危险(great danger; peril) 搭 in jeopardy 处于危险境地，受到威胁
jerk [dʒɜːrk]	*v.* 猛拉(to pull with a sudden, sharp movement) *n.* 猛拉 搭 jerk off (紧张得)结结巴巴地说
jesting ['dʒestɪŋ]	*adj.* 滑稽的(ridiculous)；爱开玩笑的 同 jocose, jocular
jettison ['dʒetɪsn]	*v.* (船等)向外抛弃货物(to cast overboard off) *n.* 抛弃的货物(jetsam) *n.* 抛弃(action of throwing) 记 来自 jet(*v.* 喷出)
jibe [dʒaɪb]	*v.* 与…一致，符合(to be in harmony, agreement, or accord) 注 jibe 作为"嘲笑"一义大家较为熟悉，但"符合"一义在 GRE 考试中更重要
jingoism ['dʒɪŋgoʊɪzəm]	*n.* 沙文主义，侵略主义(extreme chauvinism or nationalism marked especially by a belligerent foreign policy) 记 来自 jingo(*n.* 沙文主义者)
jockey ['dʒɑːki]	*n.* 骑师 *v.* 谋取(to maneuver to gain an advantage) 搭 jockey for 耍手腕获取
jocund ['dʒɑːkənd]	*adj.* 快乐的，高兴的(cheerful; genial; gay) 记 词根记忆：joc(=joke 玩笑) + und → 充满玩笑的 → 快乐的
jog [dʒɑːg]	*v.* 慢跑(to run in a slow, steady manner) 记 联想记忆：一边慢跑(jog)一边遛狗(dog) 例 Fitness experts claim that jogging is addictive; once you begin to *jog* regularly, you may be unable to stop, because you are sure to love it more and more all the time.
jolly ['dʒɑːli]	*adj.* 欢乐的，快乐的(merry; gay; convivial) 记 词根记忆：jol(冬季节日) + ly → 有关节日的 → 快乐的
jolt [dʒoʊlt]	*v.* (使)颠簸(to cause jerky movements) *n.* 震动，摇晃(jerk) 记 联想记忆：防止颠簸(jolt)用门闩(bolt)固定
josh [dʒɑːʃ]	*v.* (无恶意地)戏弄，戏耍(to tease good-naturedly) 同 banter, jest
jostle ['dʒɑːsl]	*v.* 推挤(to push and shove)；挤开通路(to make one's way by pushing) 搭 jostle for 争夺，争抢
jot [dʒɑːt]	*v.* 草草记下(to write briefly or hurriedly) 记 联想记忆：与 lot(*n.* 一堆，许多)一起记
jounce [dʒaʊns]	*v.* 颠簸地移动(to move in an up-and-down manner) 同 bounce, bump, jolt
jovial ['dʒoʊviəl]	*adj.* 愉快的(very cheerful and good-humored) 同 gleeful, jolly, merry
jubilation [ˌdʒuːbɪ'leɪʃn]	*n.* 欢腾，欢庆(great joy) 记 词根记忆：jubil(大叫) + ation → 高兴得大叫 → 欢腾，欢庆

□ jeopardy	□ jerk	□ jesting	□ jettison	□ jibe	□ jingoism
□ jockey	□ jocund	□ jog	□ jolly	□ jolt	□ josh
□ jostle	□ jot	□ jounce	□ jovial	□ jubilation	

356

judicial [dʒuˈdɪʃl]	*adj.* 法庭的，法官的(of law, courts, judges; judiciary) 记 词根记忆：jud(判断) + icial → 判案的 → 法庭的 搭 judicial decisions 司法判决
judiciousness [dʒuˈdɪʃəsnəs]	*n.* 明智 记 来自 judicious(*adj.* 明智的)
jug [dʒʌg]	*v.* 用陶罐等炖(to stew in an earthenware vessel)；关押(to jail; imprison)
jumpy [ˈdʒʌmpi]	*adj.* 紧张不安的，心惊肉跳的(on edge; nervous) 记 来自 jump(*v.* 跳；惊跳)
junction [ˈdʒʌŋkʃn]	*n.* 交叉路口(an intersection of roads)；连接(an act of joining) 记 词根记忆：junct(连接) + ion → 连接；交叉路口
jurisdiction [ˌdʒʊrɪsˈdɪkʃn]	*n.* 司法权，审判权，裁判权(right to exercise legal authority) 记 词根记忆：jur(法律) + is + dict(说话) + ion → 在法律上说话 → 司法权，审判权
justification [ˌdʒʌstɪfɪˈkeɪʃn]	*n.* 正当的理由(an acceptable reason)；辩护(the act of justifying) 记 来自 justify(*v.* 证明⋯是正当的)
juxtapose [ˌdʒʌkstəˈpəʊz]	*v.* 并列，并置(to put side by side or close together) 记 词根记忆：juxta(接近) + pos(放) + e → 挨着放 → 并列，并置
kaleidoscopic [kəˌlaɪdəˈskɑːpɪk]	*adj.* 千变万化的(changing constantly) 记 来自 kaleidoscope(万花筒)
kangaroo [ˌkæŋɡəˈruː]	*n.* 袋鼠 记 发音记忆："看加入" → 看着袋鼠宝宝进入妈妈的口袋 → 袋鼠
ken [ken]	*n.* 视野(perception)；知识范围 搭 beyond one's ken 为某人所不理解，在某人的知识范围外
kennel [ˈkenl]	*n.* 狗舍，狗窝(a doghouse) 记 词根记忆：ken (=can 犬) + nel → 狗窝；注意：不要和 kernel(*n.* 核心)相混
kernel [ˈkɜːrnl]	*n.* 果仁；核心(the central; most important part; essence) 记 词根记忆：kern(=corn 种子) + el → 核心
kidnap [ˈkɪdnæp]	*v.* 绑架(to seize and detain unlawfully and usually for ransom) 记 联想记忆：kid(小孩) + nap(打盹) → 趁着大人打盹将小孩诱拐走 → 绑架
killjoy [ˈkɪldʒɔɪ]	*n.* 令人扫兴的人(a person who intentionally spoils the pleasure of other people) 记 组合词：kill(杀) + joy(欢乐) → 杀欢乐的人 → 令人扫兴的人
kin [kɪn]	*n.* 亲属(the members of one's family) 例 Their hierarchy of loyalties is first to oneself, next to *kin*, then to fellow tribe members, and finally to compatriots.
kindle [ˈkɪndl]	*v.* 着火，点燃(to set on fire; ignite) 记 联想记忆：和 candle(*n.* 蜡烛)一起记

32

kipper [ˈkɪpər]	*v.* 腌制，熏制 (to cure (split dressed fish) by salting and smoking) 🗒 联想记忆：和 copper (*n.* 铜) 一起记
knack [næk]	*n.* 特殊能力；窍门 (a clever, expedient way of doing sth.) 🗒 联想记忆：敲开 (knock) 脑袋，得到窍门 (knack)
knead [niːd]	*v.* 揉成，捏制 (to mix and work into a uniform mass) 🗒 联想记忆：捏制 (knead) 面包 (bread)
knit [nɪt]	*v.* 编织 (to make by joining woolen threads into a close network with needles)；密接，紧密相联 (to connect closely)
knotty [ˈnɑːti]	*adj.* 多节的，多瘤的 (having or full of knots)；困难的，棘手的 (hard to solve or explain; puzzling) 🗒 来自 knot (*n.* 节疤)
kudos [ˈkuːdɑːs]	*n.* 声誉，名声 (fame and renown) 🗒 reputation, prestige
labile [ˈleɪbaɪl]	*adj.* 易变化的，不稳定的 (open to change; unstable) 🗒 fickle, unsteady
lace [leɪs]	*n.* 带子 (a cord or leather strip)；网眼织物 (a netlike decorative cloth made of fine thread) 🗒 发音记忆："蕾丝" → 网眼织物
lacerate [ˈlæsəreɪt]	*v.* 撕裂 (to tear jaggedly)；深深伤害 (to cause sharp mental or emotional pain to) 🗒 词根记忆：lac (撕破) + er + ate → 撕裂
lachrymose [ˈlækrɪmoʊs]	*adj.* 爱哭的 (inclined to shed a lot of tears)；引人落泪的 (causing tears) 🗒 词根记忆：lachrym (眼泪) + ose → 爱哭的
lackluster [ˈlæklʌstər]	*adj.* 无光泽的 (lacking brightness)；呆滞的 (dull) 🗒 组合词：lack (缺少) + luster (光泽) → 缺少光泽的 → 无光泽的
lactic [ˈlæktɪk]	*adj.* 乳汁的 (of or relating to milk) 🗒 词根记忆：lact (乳) + ic → 乳汁的
lair [ler]	*n.* 窝，巢穴 (a resting place of a wild animal)；躲藏处 🗒 联想记忆：有些动物用毛发 (hair) 做窝 (lair)
lambaste [læmˈbeɪst]	*v.* 痛打 (to beat soundly)；痛骂 (to scold or denounce severely) 🗒 组合词：lam (鞭打) + baste (棒打) → 痛打
lamentable [ləˈmentəbl]	*adj.* 令人惋惜的，悔恨的 (expressing grief) 🗒 来自 lament (*n./v.* 悔恨；悲叹)
lampoon [læmˈpuːn]	*n.* 讽刺文章 (a broad satirical piece of writing) *v.* 讽刺 (to ridicule or satirize) 🗒 联想记忆：lamp (灯) + oon → 用灯照别人的缺点 → 讽刺
lancet [ˈlænsɪt]	*n.* 柳叶刀 (a sharp-pointed surgical instrument used to make small incisions)

landslide [ˈlændslaɪd]	*n.* 山崩(a slide of a large mass of dirt and rock down a mountain or cliff); 压倒性的胜利(an overwhelming victory) 记 组合词：land(地) + slide(滑行) → 地向下滑 → 山崩
languid [ˈlæŋgwɪd]	*adj.* 没精打采的，倦怠的(listless; without vigor) 记 词根记忆：lang(松弛) + uid → 精神懈怠的 → 没精打采的
languish [ˈlæŋgwɪʃ]	*v.* 衰弱，憔悴(to lose vigor or vitality) 记 词根记忆：lang(松弛) + uish → 衰弱
languor [ˈlæŋgər]	*n.* 无精打采，衰弱无力(lack of vigor or vitality; weakness) 记 词根记忆：lang(松弛) + uor → 无精打采
lank [læŋk]	*adj.* 细长的(long and thin; slender); 长、直且柔软的(long, straight and limp)

Trouble is only opportunity in work clothes.
困难只是穿上工作服的机遇。
——美国实业家 凯泽(H.J. Kaiser, American businessman)

32

| **lap** | *v.* 舔食(to take in food or drink with the tongue) |
| [læp] | 记 联想记忆：和 tap(*n.* 水龙头)一起记 |

lapse	*n.* 失误(small error；fault)；(时间等)流逝(a gliding or passing away of
[læps]	time)
	搭 lapse of time 时间流逝

| **lard** | *v.* 使丰富，使充满(to enrich or lace heavily with extra material) |
| [lɑːrd] | 搭 lard...with 大量穿插 |

largess	*n.* 赠送，赏赐(generous giving of money or gifts)；赠款，赏赐物(money
[lɑːr'dʒes]	or gifts given in this way)
	记 联想记忆：large(大的)+ ss → 大方 → 赠送；赠款

| **lark** | *v.* 玩乐，嬉耍(to play or frolic；have a merry time)*n.* 玩乐 |
| [lɑːrk] | 记 联想记忆：在公园(park)玩乐(lark) |

| **lassitude** | *n.* 疲惫无力，没精打采(listlessness；weariness) |
| ['læsɪtuːd] | 记 词根记忆：lass(疲倦的)+ itude → 没精打采 |

| **lasso** | *n.* (捕捉牛、马用的)套索(a long rope used to catch cattle or wild horses) |
| ['læsoʊ] | 记 谐音记忆：“拉索” → 套索 |

| **lasting** | *adj.* 持久的，永久的(continuing for a long time) |
| ['læstɪŋ] | 同 enduring |

| **latch** | *n.* 门闩 *v.* 用门闩闩牢 |
| [lætʃ] | 记 和 catch(*v.* 抓住)一起记 |

| **latent** | *adj.* 潜在的，潜伏的(present but invisible；dormant；quiescent) |
| ['leɪtnt] | 记 联想记忆：late(晚)+ nt → 晚到的 → 潜在的，潜伏的 |

| **lateral** | *adj.* 侧面的(of, at, from, or towards the side) |
| ['lætərəl] | 记 词根记忆：later(侧面)+ al → 侧面的 |

| **lathe** | *n.* 车床 *v.* 用车床加工 |
| [leɪð] | 记 联想记忆：用车床加工(lathe)板条(lath) |

lattice	*n.* (用木片或金属片叠成的)格子架(a frame of crossed strips of wood or
['lætɪs]	iron)
	记 联想记忆：l + attic(阁楼)+ e → 阁楼边上搭着一个格子架 → 格子架

□ lap   □ lapse   □ lard   □ largess   □ lark   □ lassitude
□ lasso   □ lasting   □ latch   □ latent   □ lateral   □ lathe
□ lattice

| **lavender** | *n.* 薰衣草 *adj.* 淡紫色的 |
| [ˈlævəndər] | 搭 lavender oil 薰衣草油 |

| **laxative** | *adj.* (药)通便的 *n.* 轻泻药(any laxative medicine) |
| [ˈlæksətɪv] | 记 词根记忆：lax(松的) + ative → 放松的 → 轻泻药 |

| **leach** | *v.* 过滤(to draw out or remove as if by percolation) |
| [liːtʃ] | 记 和 beach(*n.* 海滩)一起记 |

| **leak** | *v.* 泄漏(to enter or escape through an opening usually by a fault or mistake) *n.* 泄漏；漏出量；裂缝，漏洞(hole, crack, etc. through which liquid or gas may wrongly get in or out) |
| [liːk] | 记 联想记忆：航行于湖(lake)面上的小舟因船底有漏洞(leak)沉没了 |

| **leakage** | *n.* 渗漏，漏出(leaking) |
| [ˈliːkɪdʒ] | 记 来自 leak(*v.* 泄漏) |

| **lean** | *v.* 倾斜(to incline)；斜靠 *adj.* 瘦的(thin) |
| [liːn] | 搭 lean on 依靠，依赖 |

| **lease** | *n.* 租约(a rental contract)；租期 *v.* 出租(to rent a property to sb.) |
| [liːs] | 记 联想记忆：l + ease(安心) → 签了租约终于安心了 → 租约 |

| **leer** | *v.* 斜视，送秋波(to have a sly, sidelong look) |
| [lɪr] | 搭 leer at sb. 色迷迷地看某人，斜视某人 |

| **leery** | *adj.* 谨防的，怀疑的(wary; cautious; suspicious) |
| [ˈlɪri] | 记 联想记忆：你送秋波(leer)，我怀疑(leery)你的动机 |

| **leeward** | *adj.* 背风的(in the direction toward which the wind blows) |
| [ˈliːwərd] | 记 联想记忆：lee(背风处) + ward(向…的) → 向着背风走 → 背风的 |

leeward

legislature	*n.* 立法机关，立法团体(body of people with the power to make and change laws)
[ˈledʒɪsleɪtʃər]	记 词根记忆：leg (法律) + is + lature → 立法机关，立法团体
	例 Sponsors of the bill were relieved because there was no opposition to it within the *legislature* until after the measure had been signed into law.

| **leisureliness** | *n.* 悠然，从容 |
| [ˈliːʒərlinəs] | 记 来自 leisurely(*adj.* 悠然的) |

| **leniency** | *n.* 宽厚，仁慈 |
| [ˈliːniənsi] | 记 词根记忆：len(软的) + i + ency → 宽厚 |

| **lesion** | *n.* 损害，损伤(a wound or an injury) |
| [ˈliːʒn] | 记 联想记忆：大脑受到损伤(lesion)，精神时刻处于紧张(tension)状态 |

| **lethargy** | *n.* 昏睡(abnormal drowsiness)；呆滞，懒散(the state of being lazy, sluggish) |
| [ˈleθərdʒi] | 记 词根记忆：leth(死) + a(不) + rg(=erg 工作) + y → 像死了一样不动的状态 → 昏睡 |

33

□ lavender	□ laxative	□ leach	□ leak	□ leakage	□ lean
□ lease	□ leer	□ leery	□ leeward	□ legislature	□ leisureliness
□ leniency	□ lesion	□ lethargy			

361

levee [ˈlevi]	*n.* 堤岸，防洪堤（an embankment） 记 注意不要和 lever（*n.* 杠杆）相混
levelheaded [ˌlevlˈhedɪd]	*adj.* 头脑冷静的，清醒的（self-composed and sensible） 记 组合词：level（平坦的）+ head（头脑）+ ed → 大脑平坦的 → 头脑冷静的
levy [ˈlevi]	*v.* 征税（to impose a tax）；征兵（to draft into military service） 记 词根记忆：lev（升起）+ y → 把税收等起来 → 征税；征兵
lexical [ˈleksɪkl]	*adj.* 词汇的（of a vocabulary）；词典的 记 词根记忆：lex（词汇）+ ical → 词汇的
lexicographer [ˌleksɪˈkɑːɡrəfər]	*n.* 词典编纂者（a person who writes or compiles a dictionary） 记 词根记忆：lex（词汇）+ ico + graph（写）+ er → 写词典的人 → 词典编纂者 例 Although the meanings of words may necessarily be liable to change, it does not follow that the *lexicographer* is therefore unable to render spelling, in a great measure, constant.
lexicon [ˈleksɪkən]	*n.* 词典（a dictionary, especially of an ancient language） 记 词根记忆：lex（词汇）+ icon → 词典
liability [ˌlaɪəˈbɪləti]	*n.* 责任（the state of being liable）；债务（obligation; debt） 记 词根记忆：li（=lig 捆）+ ability → 将人捆住 → 责任
liaison [liˈeɪzɑːn]	*n.* 密切的联系（a close bond or connection）；暧昧的关系（an illicit love affair） 记 词根记忆：lia（捆）+ ison → 捆在一起 → 密切的联系
libel [ˈlaɪbl]	*n.* （文字）诽谤，中伤（a false and demanding statement）*v.* 诽谤，中伤（to make or publish a libel against） 记 词根记忆：lib（文字）+ el →（文字）诽谤；注意不要和 label（*n.* 标签）相混 例 Satisfied that her name had been cleared, she dropped her *libel* suit after the newspaper finally published a retraction of its original defamatory statement.
libelous [ˈlaɪbələs]	*adj.* 诽谤的（publishing libels） 同 defamatory
liberality [ˌlɪbəˈræləti]	*n.* 慷慨（generosity）；心胸开阔（the quality of being tolerant and open-minded） 记 来自 liberal（*adj.* 慷慨的；开明的）
liberty [ˈlɪbərti]	*n.* 随意（too much freedom in speech or behavior）；自由 记 词根记忆：liber（自由的）+ ty → 随意；自由 例 A war, even if fought for individual *liberty* and democratic rights, usually requires that these principles be suspended, for they are incompatible with the regimentation and discipline necessary for military efficiency.

licentious	*adj.* 放荡的，纵欲的(lascivious)；放肆的(marked by disregard for strict
[laɪ'senʃəs]	rules of correctness)
	记 词根记忆：lic(允许) + ent + ious → 过度允许的 → 纵欲的
licit	*adj.* 合法的(permitted by law; lawful; legal)
['lɪsɪt]	记 参考：illicit(*adj.* 违法的)
ligneous	*adj.* 木质的，木头般的(having the nature of wood; woody)
['lɪgnɪəs]	记 词根记忆：lign(木头) + eous → 木质的
liken	*v.* 把…比作(to compare to)
['laɪkən]	记 来自like(*prep.* 像)
limb	*n.* 肢，翼(an arm, leg, or wing)
[lɪm]	记 联想记忆：攀爬(climb)时，四肢(limb)要灵活
limbo	*n.* 不稳定的状态，中间状态(any intermediate, indeterminate state or
['lɪmbou]	condition)
	记 原指"地狱的边境"
limn	*v.* 描写(to describe)；画(to paint or draw)
[lɪm]	同 depict, picture, portray, represent
limnetic	*adj.* 淡水的，湖泊的(of, relating to, or inhabiting the open water of a body
[lɪm'netɪk]	of freshwater)
limousine	*n.* 大型轿车，(常指)大型豪华轿车(a large and usually luxurious car)
['lɪməziːn]	记 常简写为 limo
limp	*v.* 跛行(to walk lamely) *adj.* 软弱的，无力的(flaccid; drooping)；柔软的
[lɪmp]	同 floppy, loose
lineal	*adj.* 直系的，嫡系的(in the direct line of descent from an ancestor)
['lɪnɪəl]	记 词根记忆：lim(线) + eal → 直系的
linger	*v.* 逗留，继续存留(to continue to stay)；徘徊
['lɪŋgər]	记 联想记忆：那位歌手(singer)徘徊(linger)于
	曾经的舞台
lingual	*adj.* 舌的(of the tongue)；语言的(of language)
['lɪŋgwəl]	记 参考：linguist(*n.* 语言学家)
linguistics	*n.* 语言学(the science of language)
[lɪŋ'gwɪstɪks]	例 Gould claimed no technical knowledge of
	linguistics, but only a hobbyist's interest in
	language.
lionize	*v.* 崇拜，看重(to treat as an object of great interest or importance)
['laɪənaɪz]	记 联想记忆：lion(狮子；名流) + ize → 视为名流 → 崇拜
liquefy	*v.* (使)液化，(使)溶解(to make or become liquid; melt)
['lɪkwɪfaɪ]	记 词根记忆：liqu(液体) + efy → (使)液化
liquidate	*v.* 清算(to settle the affairs of a business by disposing of its assets and
['lɪkwɪdeɪt]	liabilities)；清偿(to pay or settle a debt)
	记 联想记忆：liquid(清澈的) + ate → 弄清 → 清算；清偿

linger

从白天到黑夜
我不愿离开

33

lissome [ˈlɪsəm]	*adj.* 柔软的(lithe; supple; limber) 记 词根记忆：liss(可弯曲的) + ome → 柔软的
list [lɪst]	*v.* 倾斜(to tilt to one side) *n.* 倾斜 记 list 意义很多，常见的有"名单，列表"
lithe [laɪð]	*adj.* 柔软的，易弯曲的(easily bent)；自然优雅的(characterized by easy flexibility and grace) 记 词根记忆：lith(可弯曲的)+e → 柔软的，易弯曲的
loaf [loʊf]	*n.* 一条(面包) *v.* 虚度光阴(to idle; dawdle) 同 dillydally, loiter, lounge
locus [ˈloʊkəs]	*n.* 地点，所在地(site; location) 记 词根记忆：loc(地方) + us → 地点，所在地 例 She writes across generational lines, making the past so vivid that our belief that the present is the true *locus* of experience is undermined.
locution [ləˈkjuːʃn]	*n.* 语言风格(a particular style of speech)；惯用语 记 词根记忆：locu(说话) + tion → 语言风格
log [lɔːg]	*n.* 日志，记录；一段木头 *v.* 记录 搭 log in/on 登录，注册
logistics [ləˈdʒɪstɪks]	*n.* 后勤学；后勤(the management of the details of an operation) 记 词根记忆：log(树阴，遮蔽处) + istics → 提供庇护 → 后勤
loiter [ˈlɔɪtər]	*v.* 闲逛，游荡(to linger)；慢慢前行(to travel or move slowly and indolently)；消磨时光，虚度光阴
long-winded [ˌlɔːŋˈwɪndɪd]	*adj.* 冗长的 记 组合词：long(长) + wind(空谈，废话) + ed → 冗长的
loosen [ˈluːsn]	*v.* 变松，松开(to become less firmed or fixed) 记 来自loose(*adj.* 宽松的)
lope [loʊp]	*n.* 轻快的步伐(an easy, swinging stride) *v.* 大步跑(to run with a steady, easy gait) 记 注意不要和lobe(*n.* 耳垂)相混
lopsided [ˌlɑːpˈsaɪdɪd]	*adj.* 倾向一方的，不平衡的(lacking in symmetry or balance or proportion) 记 组合词：lop(低重) + side(侧面，边) + (e)d → 垂向一边的 → 倾向一方的
lore [lɔːr]	*n.* 知识(knowledge)；特定的知识或传说(a particular body of knowledge or tradition) 记 参考：folklore(*n.* 民间传说)
lot [lɑːt]	*n.* 签(an object used as a counter)；命运(a person's destiny) *v.* 抽签；划分(to divide into lots)
lottery [ˈlɑːtəri]	*n.* 抽彩给奖法 记 来自lot(*n.* 签)
lout [laʊt]	*n.* 蠢人，笨蛋(a clumsy, stupid fellow; boor) 记 联想记忆：把那个笨蛋(lout)赶出去(out)

364

□ lissome   □ list   □ lithe   □ loaf   □ locus   □ locution
□ log   □ logistics   □ loiter   □ long-winded   □ loosen   □ lope
□ lopsided   □ lore   □ lot   □ lottery   □ lout

loutish [ˈlaʊtɪʃ]	*adj.* 粗鲁的(rough and rude) 记 来自lout(*n.* 蠢人，笨蛋)
lowbred [ˈloʊbred]	*adj.* 粗野的，粗俗的(ill-mannered; vulgar; crude) 记 组合词：low(低下) + bred(=breed 养育) → 教养不好 → 粗野的
lubricant [ˈluːbrɪkənt]	*n.* 润滑剂(a substance for reducing friction) 记 词根记忆：lubric(光滑) + ant → 润滑剂
lucre [ˈluːkər]	*n.* 〈贬〉钱，利益(money or profits) 记 词根记忆：lucr(获利) + e → 利益
lucubrate [ˈluːkjuːbreɪt]	*v.* 刻苦攻读，埋头苦干，专心著作(to work, study, or write laboriously) 记 词根记忆：luc(灯光) + ubrate → 在灯光下工作 → 刻苦攻读
lug [lʌg]	*v.* 拖，费力拉(to drag or carry with great effort) *n.* 拖，拉 同 haul, tow, tug
lukewarm [ˌluːk ˈwɔːrm]	*adj.* 微温的，不冷不热的(not very warm or enthusiastic) 记 词根记忆：luke(微温的) + warm(温暖的) → 微温的
lumber [ˈlʌmbər]	*v.* 跌跌撞撞地走，笨拙地走(to move with heavy clumsiness) *n.* 杂物 (miscellaneous discarded household articles)；木材(timber)
lumen [ˈluːmen]	*n.* 流明(光通量单位) 记 词根记忆：lum(光) + en → 流明
luminary [ˈluːmɪneri]	*n.* 杰出人物，名人(a person of prominence or brilliant achievement) 记 词根记忆：lumin(光) + ary → 发光的人 → 名人
lump [lʌmp]	*n.* 块；肿块 *v.* 形成块状(to become lumpy) 搭 lump...together 将…合在一起
lunatic [ˈluːnətɪk]	*n.* 疯子(an insane person) *adj.* 极蠢的(utterly foolish) 记 词根记忆：lun(月亮) + atic → 人们认为精神病与月亮的盈亏有关 → 疯子；Luna 原指罗马神话中的月亮女神
lunge [lʌndʒ]	*n.* 冲，扑(a sudden forward movement or plunge) 记 联想记忆：向长沙发(lounge)直扑(lunge)过去
lurch [lɜːrtʃ]	*n.* 突然的倾斜 *v.* 蹒跚而行(to stagger) 记 联想记忆：和lunch(*n.* 午餐)一起记
lurk [lɜːrk]	*v.* 潜伏，埋伏(to stay hidden; lie in wait) 记 联想记忆：为捉一只云雀(lark)埋伏(lurk)在小树林里
luscious [ˈlʌʃəs]	*adj.* 美味的(delicious)；肉感的(voluptuous)
lust [lʌst]	*n.* 强烈的欲望(overmastering desire) 记 参考：wanderlust(*n.* 旅行癖)
luster [ˈlʌstər]	*n.* 光辉；光泽 *v.* 使有光泽；使有光彩，给…增光；发光 记 词根记忆：lus(光) + ter → 光辉

33

| **lustrous** | *adj.* 有光泽的(having luster；bright) |
| [ˈlʌstrəs] | 记 来自 luster(*n.* 光辉；光泽) |

| **lusty** | *adj.* 流满活力的，精力充沛的(full of vigor) |
| [ˈlʌsti] | 记 词根记忆：lus(光) + ty → 充满活力的 |

| **luxurious** | *adj.* 奢侈的，豪华的(very fine and expensive) |
| [lʌɡˈʒʊriəs] | 记 词根记忆：lux(光) + ur + ious → 光彩四溢的 → 奢侈的，豪华的 |

| **lymphatic** | *adj.* 无力的(lacking in physical or mental energy)；迟缓的；淋巴的 |
| [limˈfætik] | 记 来自 lymph(*n.* 淋巴) |

| **macerate** | *v.* 浸软(to soften by soaking in liquid)；使消瘦(to cause to grow thin) |
| [ˈmæsəreit] | 记 形近词：lacerate(*v.* 划破，割裂；伤害) |

| **machination** | *n.* 阴谋(an artful or secret plot or scheme) |
| [ˌmæʃiˈneiʃn] | 记 词根记忆：machin(机械；制造) + ation → 阴谋 |

骗子↓ machination
把钱交给着 就等着发财啦

| **madrigal** | *n.* 抒情短诗(a short poem, often about love, suitable for being set to music)；合唱曲(a part-song) |
| [ˈmædriɡl] | 记 联想记忆：madri(看作 Madrid, 马德里) + gal → 马德里是个浪漫的城市 → 抒情短诗 |

| **magenta** | *adj.* 紫红色的(of deep purple red) *n.* 紫红色(purplish red) |
| [məˈdʒentə] | 记 源自意大利城市 Magenta |

| **magniloquent** | *adj.* 夸张的(characterized by a high-flown often bombastic style or manner) |
| [mæɡˈniloʊkwənt] | 记 词根记忆：magn(i)(大的) + loqu(话) + ent → 说大话 → 夸张的 |

| **magnitude** | *n.* 重要性(greatness)；星球的亮度(the degree of brightness of a celestial body) |
| [ˈmæɡnituːd] | 记 词根记忆：magn(大的) + itude(表状态) → 大的状态 → 重要性 |

majestic	*adj.* 雄伟的，庄严的(showing majesty)
[məˈdʒestik]	记 词根记忆：maj(大的) + estic → 雄伟的
	例 The eradication of pollution is not merely a matter of aesthetics, though the *majestic* beauty of nature is indeed an important consideration.

| **malaise** | *n.* 不适，不舒服(a feeling of illness) |
| [məˈleiz] | 记 发音记忆："没累死" → 差点没累死 → 不适 |

| **malediction** | *n.* 诅咒(curse; execration) |
| [ˌmæliˈdikʃn] | 记 词根记忆：male(坏的) + dict(说) + ion → 说坏话 → 诅咒 |

| **malefactor** | *n.* 罪犯，作恶者(criminal; evildoer) |
| [ˈmælifæktər] | 记 词根记忆：male(坏的) + fact(做) + or → 做坏事的人 → 作恶者 |

| **maleficent** | *adj.* 有害的；作恶的，犯罪的(doing evil) |
| [məˈlefisənt] | 记 词根记忆：male(坏的) + fic(做) + ent → 做坏事的 → 作恶的 |

| **malfeasance** | *n.* 不法行为，渎职(misconduct by a public official) |
| [ˌmælˈfiːzəns] | 记 词根记忆：mal(坏的) + feas(做，行为) + ance → 坏的行为 → 不法行为 |

malfunction [ˌmælˈfʌŋkʃn]	*v.* 发生故障，失灵（to fail to function）*n.* 故障（failure of this sort） 记 联想记忆：mal(坏的) + function(功能) → 功能不好 → 故障
malice [ˈmælɪs]	*n.* 恶意，怨恨（desire to do mischief；spite） 记 词根记忆：mal(坏的) + ice → 恶意
mandate [ˈmændeɪt]	*n.* 命令，训令（an authoritative order or command） 记 词根记忆：mand(命令) + ate → 命令
mangle [ˈmæŋgl]	*v.* 毁坏，毁损（to ruin or spoil）；（通过切、压等）损坏（to mutilate or disfigure by hacking or crushing；maim）
mania [ˈmeɪniə]	*n.* 癫狂（wild or violent mental disorder）；狂热（an excessive, persistent enthusiasm） 记 参考：kleptomania(*n.* 盗窃狂)；bibliomania(*n.* 藏书癖)
manifesto [ˌmænɪˈfestoʊ]	*n.* 宣言，声明（a public declaration） 记 来自manifest(*vt.* 表明)
manipulate [məˈnɪpjuleɪt]	*v.* （熟练地）操作，处理（to operate or control；handle） 记 词根记忆：mani(手) + pul(拉) + ate → 用手拉 → （熟练地）操作，处理 例 By dint of much practice in the laboratory, the anatomy student became ambidextrous and was able to *manipulate* her dissecting tools with either hand.
mansion [ˈmænʃn]	*n.* 公寓；大厦（a large imposing house） 记 词根记忆：man(逗留) + sion → 逗留之处 → 居住的地方 → 公寓
manure [məˈnʊr]	*n.* 粪肥（waste matter from animals）*v.* 给…施肥（to put manure on） 记 词根记忆：man(手) + ure → 用手施肥 → 给…施肥
maple [ˈmeɪpl]	*n.* 枫树 记 联想记忆：和apple(*n.* 苹果)一起记
mar [mɑːr]	*v.* 损坏，毁坏；损害…的健全 例 This final essay, its prevailing kindliness *marred* by occasional flashes of savage irony, bespeaks the dichotomous character of the author.
maraud [məˈrɔːd]	*v.* 抢劫，掠夺（to rove in search of plunder；pillage） 同 loot, rob
marine [məˈriːn]	*adj.* 海的（of the sea）；海生的（inhabiting in the sea） 记 词根记忆：mar(海) + ine → 海的 搭 marine vertebrate zoology 海洋脊椎动物学
mariner [ˈmærɪnər]	*n.* 水手，海员（sailor；seaman） 记 词根记忆：mar(海) + in + er(表人) → 海员
marrow [ˈmæroʊ]	*n.* 骨髓；精华，精髓（the innermost and choicest part；pith） 记 联想记忆：和narrow(*adj.* 狭窄的)一起记

33

□ malfunction	□ malice	□ mandate	□ mangle	□ mania	□ manifesto
□ manipulate	□ mansion	□ manure	□ maple	□ mar	□ maraud
□ marine	□ mariner	□ marrow			

marshal [ˈmɑːrʃl]	*v.* 整理，安排，排列（to arrange in good or effective order） 记 联想记忆：为行军（march）而作安排（marshal）
marsupial [mɑːrˈsuːpiəl]	*n./adj.* 有袋动物（的） 搭 marsupial mammal 有袋类哺乳动物
martial [ˈmɑːrʃl]	*adj.* 战争的，军事的（of or suitable to war and soldiers） 记 联想记忆：mar（毁坏）+ tial → 战争常常意味着毁灭 → 战争的 搭 martial law 戒严令
martyr [ˈmɑːrtər]	*n.* 烈士，殉道者（any of those persons who choose to suffer or die rather than give up their faith or principles） 记 词根记忆：本身为词根，指"目击者"
marvel [ˈmɑːrvl]	*v.* 对…感到惊异（to be very surprised）*n.* 奇迹（one that is wonderful or miraculous） 记 联想记忆：mar（毁坏）+ vel（音似：well 好）→ 遭到毁坏再重建好，真是奇迹 → 奇迹
mash [mæʃ]	*v.* 捣成糊状（to convert into a soft pulpy mixture） 记 联想记忆：m + ash（灰）→ 弄成灰 → 捣成糊状
masquerade [ˌmæskəˈreɪd]	*n.* 化装舞会（a gathering of persons wearing masks and fantastic costumes）；*v.* 伪装（to live or act as if in disguise） 记 来自 masque（=mask *n.* 面具）
massacre [ˈmæsəkər]	*n.* 大屠杀（the indiscriminate, merciless killing of a number of human beings） 记 联想记忆：mass（大批）+ acre（英亩）→ 把一大批人赶到一英亩宽的地方杀掉 → 大屠杀
massive [ˈmæsɪv]	*adj.* 巨大的，厚重的（very big and heavy） 记 来自 mass（*n.* 大量，大多数） 例 Unlike other creatures, who are shaped largely by their immediate environment, human beings are products of a culture accumulated over centuries, yet one that is constantly being transformed by *massive* infusions of new information from everywhere.
mast [mæst]	*n.* 船桅，桅杆（a vertical spar for supporting sails） 记 联想记忆：与 mat（*n.* 垫子）一起记
masticate [ˈmæstɪkeɪt]	*v.* 咀嚼（to chew food）；把…磨成浆（to grind to a pulp） 记 词根记忆：mast（乳房）+ icate → 原指小孩吃奶 → 咀嚼
mat [mæt]	*n.* 垫子，席子 *v.* （使）缠结；铺席于…上 记 联想记忆：猫（cat）在垫子（mat）上睡觉
materialize [məˈtɪriəlaɪz]	*v.* 赋予形体，使具体化（to represent in material form）；出现（to come into existence） 记 来自 material（*n.* 物质 *adj.* 物质的；具体的）
matriculate [məˈtrɪkjuleɪt]	*v.* 录取（to enroll in college or graduate school） 记 词根记忆：matr（母亲）+ iculate → 成为母校 → 录取

| **matte** | *adj.* 无光泽的(lacking or deprived of luster or gloss) |
| [mæt] | 记 为 mat 的变体 |

| **mattress** | *n.* 床垫(a large rectangular pad that is used to sleep on) |
| ['mætrəs] | |

mature	*adj.* 成熟的(fully developed); 深思熟虑的(carefully decided)
[mə'tʃʊr]	记 联想记忆: 当自然(nature)中的 n 变成 m, 万物变得成熟(mature)
	例 In television programming, a later viewing time often implies a more *mature* audience and, therefore, more challenging subjects and themes.

| **maul** | *v.* 打伤, 伤害(to injure by or as if by beating; lacerate) |
| [mɔːl] | 记 联想记忆: 和 haul(*n./v.* 用力拖)一起记 |

| **maunder** | *v.* 胡扯(to speak indistinctly or disconnectedly); 游荡(to wander slowly and idly) |
| ['mɔːndər] | |

| **mawkish** | *adj.* 自作多情的, 过度伤感的(sickly or puerilely sentimental); 淡而无味的, (味道上)令人作呕的(insipid or nauseating) |
| ['mɔːkɪʃ] | |

| **maze** | *n.* 迷宫(a confusing, intricate network of winding pathways; labyrinth) |
| [meɪz] | 记 联想记忆: 这个迷宫(maze)让人吃惊(amaze) |

| **mean** | *adj.* 吝啬的(selfish in a petty way; stingy) |
| [miːn] | 同 close-fisted, niggardly, miserly, ungenerous |

| **meander** | *v.* 蜿蜒而流(to take a winding or tortuous course); 漫步(to wander aimlessly; ramble) |
| [mi'ændər] | 记 来自 the Meander, 一条以蜿蜒曲折而著名的河流 |

| **measly** | *adj.* 患麻疹的; 少得可怜的, 微不足道的(contemptibly small; meager) |
| ['miːzli] | 记 来自 measles(*n.* 麻疹) |

| **measured** | *adj.* 量过的, 精确的(determined by measurement); 慎重的, 恰如其分的(careful, restrained) |
| ['meʒərd] | 记 来自 measure(*v.* 测量) |

| **mechanism** | *n.* 结构, 机制 |
| ['mekənɪzəm] | 搭 mechanism for resolving the conflict 解决冲突的机制 |

| **medal** | *n.* 奖牌, 勋章(an award for winning a championship or commemorating some other event) |
| ['medl] | 记 联想记忆: 奖牌(medal)是金属(metal)做的 |

| **meddle** | *v.* 干涉, 干预(to interfere) |
| ['medl] | 记 词根记忆: med(混杂) + dle → 混杂其中 → 干涉 |

| **medicate** | *v.* 用药物医治(to treat with medicine); 加药于 |
| ['medɪkeɪt] | 记 词根记忆: med(治疗) + ic + ate → 用药物医治 |

medieval	*adj.* 中世纪的, 中古的(of the Middle Ages)
[ˌmedi'iːvl]	记 词根记忆: medi(中间) + ev(时间) + al → 中世纪的
	搭 the medieval period 中世纪时期

| **meditation** | *n.* 沉思, 冥想 |
| [ˌmedɪ'teɪʃn] | 记 词根记忆: med(注意) + it + ation → 加以注意 → 沉思 |

33

□ matte	□ mattress	□ mature	□ maul	□ maunder	□ mawkish
□ maze	□ mean	□ meander	□ measly	□ measured	□ mechanism
□ medal	□ meddle	□ medicate	□ medieval	□ meditation	

meek [miːk]	*adj.* 温顺的，顺从的（gentle and uncomplaining） 同 mild, patient, subdued, tame
meld [meld]	*v.* (使)混合，(使)合并（to blend；mix） 同 fuse, merge, mingle
mellifluous [me'lɪfluəs]	*adj.* (音乐等)柔美流畅的（sweetly or smoothly flowing） 记 词根记忆：melli(蜂蜜) + flu(流) + ous → 像蜂蜜一样流出来的 → 柔美流畅的 例 The combination of elegance and earthiness in Edmund's speech can be startling, especially when he slyly slips in some juicy vulgarity amid the *mellifluous* circumlocutions of a gentleman of the old school.
melon ['melən]	*n.* 甜瓜（a large rounded fruit with a hard rind and juicy flesh） 记 词根记忆：mel(甜的) + on → 甜的东西 → 甜瓜
membrane ['membreɪn]	*n.* 薄膜（a thin sheet of synthetic material used as a filter, separator）；膜（a thin soft pliable sheet or layer especially of animal or plant origin） 记 词根记忆：membr(=member 成员) + ane → 身体的一部分 → 膜
menace ['menəs]	*n./v.* 威胁，恐吓（to threat） 记 联想记忆：men(人) + ace(看作 face，面临，面对) → 将在比赛中面对的人 → 威胁

The supreme happiness of life is the conviction that we are loved.

生活中最大的幸福是坚信有人爱我们。

——法国小说家 雨果（Victor Hugo, French novelist）

mend [mend]	*v.* 修改，改进（to put into good shape or working order） 同 amend, correct, improve
mendacious [men'deɪʃəs]	*adj.* 不真实的，虚假的（false or untrue）；习惯性说谎的（telling lies habitually） 记 联想记忆：mend（修改）+ acious → 过度修改 → 不真实的
mendacity [men'dæsəti]	*n.* 不诚实（untruthfulness） 记 来自 mendacious（*adj.* 习惯性说谎的）
mendicant ['mendɪkənt]	*adj.* 行乞的（practicing beggary）*n.* 乞丐（beggar） 记 联想记忆：mend（修补，改善）+ icant → 生活需要改善的人 → 乞丐
menthol ['menθɔːl]	*n.* 薄荷醇（a white substance which smells and tastes of mint）
mentor ['mentɔːr]	*n.* 导师（a wise and trusted counselor or teacher） 记 词根记忆：ment（精神）+ or → 精神上的指导人 → 导师
merit ['merɪt]	*v.* 值得（to be worthy of）*n.* 价值；长处 记 本身为词根，意为"值得" 例 In the midst of so many evasive comments, this forthright statement, whatever its intrinsic *merit*, plainly stands out as an anomaly.
merited ['merɪtɪd]	*adj.* 该得的，理所当然的（deserving, worthy of） 记 联想记忆：merit（价值）+ ed → 值得的 → 该得的
mesmerism ['mezmərɪzəm]	*n.* 催眠术，催眠引导法（hypnotic induction held to involve animal magnetism） 记 来自奥地利医生 Mesmer，其始创了催眠术
mete [miːt]	*v.* 给予，分配（to give out by measure）；测量（to measure）*n.* 边界 记 和 meet（*v.* 会面）一起记
metrical ['metrɪkl]	*adj.* 测量的（metric）；韵律的（written in poetic meter） 记 来自 meter（*n.* 米；韵律）
mettle ['metl]	*n.* 勇气，斗志（courage and fortitude）

□ mend	□ mendacious	□ mendacity	□ mendicant	□ menthol	□ mentor
□ merit	□ merited	□ mesmerism	□ mète	□ metrical	□ mettle

371

microbe	*n.* 微生物(tiny living creature)
[ˈmaɪkroʊb]	记 词根记忆: micro(小的) + be(=bio 生命) → 微生物
mien	*n.* 风采, 态度(air; bearing; demeanor)
[miːn]	记 发音记忆: "迷你" → 迷人的风采 → 风采
miff	*n.* 小争吵(a trivial quarrel)
[mɪf]	记 联想记忆: 爱人在一起时常有小争吵(miff), 分开时又彼此想念(miss)
mighty	*adj.* 强有力的, 强大的(very great in power, strength); 巨大的
[ˈmaɪti]	例 Telling gripping tales about a central character engaged in a *mighty* struggle with events, modern biographies satisfy the American appetite for epic narratives.
militia	*n.* 民兵(an army composed of ordinary citizens)
[məˈlɪʃə]	记 词根记忆: milit(军事, 战斗) + ia → 参与战争的人民 → 民兵
milk	*v.* 榨取(to coerce profit or advantage to an extreme degree)
[mɪlk]	
mince	*v.* 切碎(to chop into very small pieces); 装腔作势地小步走(to move with short, affected steps)
[mɪns]	记 参考: minute(*adj.* 微小的); minutia(*n.* 细节)
mingle	*v.* (使)混合(to bring or mix together)
[ˈmɪŋgl]	同 blend, merge
minnow	*n.* 鲤科, 小鱼
[ˈmɪnoʊ]	记 注意不要和 winnow(*v.* 簸; 筛选)相混
mint	*n.* 大量(an abundant amount); 造币厂
[mɪnt]	记 mint 作"薄荷(糖)"讲大家都较熟悉
minuet	*n.* 小步舞(a slow, stately dance in 3/4 time characterized by forward balancing, bowing, and toe pointing)
[ˌmɪnjuˈet]	记 词根记忆: min(小的) + uet → 小步舞
	例 Although the *minuet* appeared simple, its intricate steps had to be studied very carefully before they could be gracefully executed in public.
minutes	*n.* 会议记录
[ˈmɪnɪts]	搭 take the minutes 做会议记录
minutia	*n.* 细枝末节, 琐事(small or trifling matters)
[mɪˈnuːʃiə]	记 词根记忆: min(小的) + utia → 细小之处 → 细枝末节
mirage	*n.* 海市蜃楼; 幻想, 幻影(sth. illusory and unattainable)
[məˈrɑːʒ]	记 词根记忆: mir(惊奇) + age → 使人惊奇之物 → 海市蜃楼
mirth	*n.* 欢乐, 欢笑(gaiety or jollity)
[mɜːrθ]	记 发音记忆: "没事" → 没事当然很欢乐 → 欢乐
miscellany	*n.* 混合物(a collection of various items or parts)
[ˈmɪsəleɪni]	记 词根记忆: misc(混合) + ellany → 混合物

miscreant	*n.* 恶棍，歹徒（a vicious or depraved person）
['mɪskriənt]	记 词根记忆：mis（坏的）+ cre(=cred 相信）+ ant → 相信坏事物的人 → 恶棍
miserly	*adj.* 吝啬的（penurious）
['maɪzərli]	记 来自 miser（*n.* 吝啬鬼）
misgiving	*n.* 疑虑（doubt, distrust, or suspicion）
[mɪs 'gɪvɪŋ]	记 联想记忆：mis（错的）+ giving（给）→ 给出错误的解释 → 疑虑
misperceive	*v.* 误解（to misunderstand）
[mɪspər 'siːv]	记 联想记忆：mis（错的）+ perceive（理解，领会）→ 误解
misrepresentation	*n.* 误传，不实的陈述
[mɪsˌreprɪzen 'teɪʃn]	记 联想记忆：mis（错的）+ represent（表达）+ ation → 错误的表达 → 误传
misshapen	*adj.* 畸形的，奇形怪状的（badly shaped）
[mɪs 'ʃeɪpən]	记 联想记忆：mis（坏的）+ shapen（形状的）→ 畸形的
missive	*n.* 信件，（尤指）公函（letter especially written statement）
['mɪsɪv]	记 词根记忆：miss（发送）+ ive → 由他处送出的 → 信件
mistral	*n.* 寒冷且干燥的强风（a cold, dry wind）
['mɪstrəl]	记 联想记忆：mist（雾）+ ral → 风起雾散 → 寒冷且干燥的强风
mnemonics	*n.* 记忆法，记忆术（the technique of developing the memory）
[nɪ 'mɑːnɪks]	记 词根记忆：mne（记忆）+ mon + ics → 记忆法
moan	*n.* 呻吟（a low prolonged sound of pain or of grief）；抱怨（a complaint）
[moʊn]	*v.* 呻吟；抱怨（to complain）
moat	*n.* 壕沟，护城河（a deep, wide trench around the rampart of a fortified place that is usually filled with water）
[moʊt]	
mobile	*adj.* 易于移动的（easy to move）
['moʊbl]	记 词根记忆：mob（动）+ ile（易…的）→ 易于移动的
	搭 mobile home 活动房屋
mobility	*n.* 可动性，流动性（the quality of being mobile）
[moʊ 'bɪləti]	例 The hierarchy of medical occupations is in many ways a caste system; its strata remain intact and the practitioners in them have very little vertical *mobility*.
mock	*v.* 嘲笑（to treat with ridicule; deride）；（为嘲笑而）模仿（to mimic in derision）
[mɑːk]	记 联想记忆：和尚（monk）没头发常受到嘲笑（mock）
mode	*n.* 样式（style or fashion in clothes, art, etc.）；模式；方式，形式；时尚，风尚
[moʊd]	例 Irony can, after a fashion, become a *mode* of escape: to laugh at the terrors of life is in some sense to evade them.
modicum	*n.* 少量（a moderate or small amount）
['mɔːdɪkəm]	搭 a modicum of 一点，少数
modish	*adj.* 时髦的（fashionable; stylish）
['moʊdɪʃ]	记 来自 mode（*n.* 时尚）

34

moldy	*adj.* 发霉的 (covered with mold)
['moʊldi]	记 来自mold (*n.* 真菌)
molest	*v.* 骚扰, 困扰 (to bother or annoy)
[mə'lest]	记 词根记忆: mol(磨) + est → 摩擦 → 骚扰
mollify	*v.* 安慰, 安抚 (to soften in feeling or temper; appease)
['mɑːlɪfaɪ]	记 词根记忆: moll(柔软的) + ify → 使柔软 → 安抚
mollycoddle	*v.* 过分爱惜, 娇惯 (to overly coddle; pamper) *n.* 娇生惯养的人
['mɑːlikɑːdl]	记 联想记忆: moll(软的) + y + coddle(纵容) → 娇惯
moment	*n.* 瞬间; 重要 (importance)
['moʊmənt]	搭 the moment of truth (决策的)关键时刻
momentum	*n.* 推进力, 势头 (impetus; force or speed of movement)
[moʊ'mentəm]	记 来自 moment (*n.* 瞬间)
monarch	*n.* 君主, 帝王 (a hereditary sovereign)
['mɑːnərk]	记 词根记忆: mon(单个的) + arch(统治者) → 最高统治者 → 君主
monocle	*n.* 单片眼镜 (an eye glass for one eye only)
['mɑːnəkl]	记 词根记忆: mon(单个的) + oc(眼睛) + le → 单片眼镜
monograph	*n.* 专题论文 (a learned treatise on a particular subject)
['mɑːnəgræf]	记 词根记忆: mono(单个的) + graph(写) → 为一个主题而写 → 专题论文
monolithic	*adj.* 坚若磐石的; 巨大的 (huge; massive)
[ˌmɑːnə'lɪθɪk]	记 词根记忆: mono(单个的) + lith(石头) + ic → 单块大石头的 → 巨大的
monologue	*n.* 独白 (soliloquy); 长篇演说, 长篇大论 (a prolonged discourse)
['mɑːnəlɔːg]	记 词根记忆: mono(单个) + log(说话) + ue → 一个人说话 → 独白
monopoly	*n.* 垄断 (exclusive possession or control); 专利权
[mə'nɑːpəli]	记 词根记忆: mono(单个) + poly(出售) → 独享出售权 → 垄断
monsoon	*n.* 季风 (a wind system that influences large climatic regions and reverses direction seasonally); 雨季
[ˌmɑːn'suːn]	
monstrous	*adj.* 巨大的 (huge; immense); 丑陋的, 外表可怕 (frightful or hideous in appearance)
['mɑːnstrəs]	记 来自 monster (*n.* 妖怪)
moody	*adj.* 喜怒无常的 (given to changeable moods); 抑郁的 (gloomy)
['muːdi]	记 来自 mood (*n.* 情绪)
mope	*v.* 抑郁, 闷闷不乐 (to be gloomy and dispirited) *n.* 情绪低落
[moʊp]	记 联想记忆: 她天天拖地(map), 很抑郁(mope)
morale	*n.* 士气, 民心 (a sense of common purpose with respect to a group)
[mə'ræl]	记 联想记忆: 和 moral (*adj.* 道德的) 一起记
	例 Many industries are so beleaguered by the impact of government sanctions, equipment failure, and foreign competition that they are beginning to rely on industrial psychologists to salvage what remains of employee *morale*.

mores	*n.* 习俗，惯例（the fixed morally binding customs of a particular group）
['mɔːreɪz]	记 词根记忆：mor(风俗) + es → 习俗，惯例
moribund	*adj.* 即将结束的（coming to end）；垂死的（dying）
['mɔːrɪbʌnd]	记 词根记忆：mori(=mort 死) + bund(接近的) → 垂死的
	例 One of Detroit's great success stories tells of Lee Iacocca's revitalization of the *moribund* Chrysler Corporation, turning it into a vigorous competitor.
morsel	*n.* （食物的）一小口，一小块（a small bite or portion of food）；小量，一点（a small piece or amount）
['mɔːrsl]	记 词根记忆：mors(咬) + el → 咬一口 → 一小口
mortgage	*n.* 抵押；抵押证书 *v.* 用…作抵押
['mɔːrgɪdʒ]	记 词根记忆：mort(死亡) + gage(抵押品) → 用抵押品使债务死亡 → 抵押
mortification	*n.* 耻辱，屈辱（shame; humiliation）
[ˌmɔːrtɪfɪ'keɪʃn]	记 来自 mortify(*v.* 使难堪)
mote	*n.* 尘埃，微尘（a speck of dust）
[moʊt]	记 词根记忆：mot(微尘) + e → 微尘
motile	*adj.* 能动的（exhibiting or capable of movement）
['moʊtaɪl]	记 词根记忆：mot(动) + ile → 能动的
motility	*n.* 运动性
[moʊ'tɪləti]	记 词根记忆：mot(动) + ility → 运动性
motto	*n.* 座右铭；格言，箴言（a maxim）
['mɑːtoʊ]	同 adage, proverb, saying
mourn	*v.* 悲痛，哀伤（to feel or express sorrow or grief）；哀悼
[mɔːrn]	同 bemoan, bewail, grieve, lament
muck	*n.* 堆肥，粪肥（soft moist farmyard manure）*v.* 施肥（to dress (as soil) with muck）；捣乱（to interfere; meddle）
[mʌk]	
muddy	*adj.* 多泥的，泥泞的（full of or covered with mud）；浑浊的，不清的（lacking in clarity or brightness）
['mʌdi]	记 来自 mud(*n.* 泥)
muffle	*v.* 消音（to deaden the sound of）；裹住（to envelop）
['mʌfl]	记 来自 muff(*n.* 手笼)
muggy	*adj.* （天气）闷热而潮湿的（oppressively humid and damp）
['mʌgi]	搭 a muggy August day 八月里闷热的一天
mulish	*adj.* 骡一样的，执拗的（stubborn as a mule）
['mjuːlɪʃ]	同 adamant, headstrong, obstinate
mull	*v.* 思考，思索（to consider at length）*n.* 混乱（disorder）
[mʌl]	搭 mull sth. over 认真琢磨，反复思考
multifarious	*adj.* 多种的，各式各样的（numerous and varied）
[ˌmʌltɪ'feriəs]	记 词根记忆：multi(多) + fari(部分) + ous → 含有许多部分的 → 多种多样的

34

| **multiplicity** | *n.* 多样性（a large number or great variety） |
| [ˌmʌltɪˈplɪsəti] | 记 来自 multiple（*adj.* 多种多样的） |

| **mumble** | *v.* 咕哝，含糊不清地说（to speak or say unclearly） |
| [ˈmʌmbl] | 同 grumble, murmur, mutter |

| **munch** | *v.* 用力咀嚼，出声咀嚼（to eat with a chewing action） |
| [mʌntʃ] | 记 和 lunch（*n.* 午餐）一起记 |

| **municipality** | *n.* 自治市；市政当局（指城市行政区及管理者） |
| [mjuːˌnɪsɪˈpæləti] | 记 来自 municipal（*adj.* 市政的） |

| **muniments** | *n.* 契据 |
| [ˈmjuːnɪmənts] | 记 词根记忆：mun(保护，加强) + Iments → 加强买卖关系的东西 → 契据 |

| **munition** | *n.* 军火，军需品（weapons and ammunltion） |
| [mjuːˈnɪʃn] | 记 词根记忆：mun(保护，加强) + ition → 用于保家卫国的东西 → 军火 |

| **murmur** | *v.* 柔声地说；抱怨（to complain; grumble） |
| [ˈmɜːrmər] | 搭 murmur against（私下）发牢骚 |

| **muse** | *v.* 沉思，冥想（to think or meditate in silence） |
| [mjuːz] | 记 来自 Muse（希腊神话中的缪斯女神） |

| **mushy** | *adj.* 糊状的（having the consistency of mush）；感伤的，多情的（excessively |
| [ˈmʌʃi] | tender or emotional） |

| **musket** | *n.* 旧式步枪，毛瑟枪（a type of gun used in former times） |
| [ˈmʌskɪt] | 记 联想记忆：想把毛瑟枪(musket)藏在篮筐(basket)里 |

| **muster** | *v.* 召集，聚集（to gather or summon） |
| [ˈmʌstər] | 记 联想记忆：主人(master)有权召集(muster)家丁们 |

| **mutate** | *v.* 变异（to undergo mutation） |
| [ˈmjuːteɪt] | 记 词根记忆：mut(变化) + ate → 变异 |

mute	*adj.* 沉默的（silent）*v.* 减弱…的声音（to muffle the sound of）*n.* 弱音器（a
[mjuːt]	device to soften or alter the tone of a musical instrument）
	例 One theory about intelligence sees language as the logical structure underlying thinking and insists that since animals are *mute*, they must be mindless as well.

| **muted** | *adj.* （声音)减弱的，变得轻柔的 |
| [ˈmjuːtɪd] | 记 来自 mute（*v.* 减弱…的声音） |

| **mutineer** | *n.* 反叛者，背叛者（a person who mutinies） |
| [ˌmjuːtəˈnɪr] | 记 来自 mutiny（*n./v.* 叛变） |

| **mutinous** | *adj.* 叛变的（engaged in revolt）；反抗的（rebellious） |
| [ˈmjuːtənəs] | 搭 a mutinous expression 反抗的神色 |

| **mutter** | *v.* 咕哝，嘀咕（to speak in a low and indistinct voice） |
| [ˈmʌtər] | 记 联想记忆：m + utter(发出声音) → 只会发出 m 音 → 咕哝 |

| **muzzy** | *adj.* 头脑糊涂的（muddled；mentally hazy） |
| [ˈmʌzi] | 搭 a muzzy head 稀里糊涂的大脑 |

myopia	*n.* 近视；缺乏远见（lack of foresight or discernment）
[maɪˈoʊpiə]	记 词根记忆：my(闭上) + op(眼睛) + ia(表病) → 近视
myopic	*adj.* 近视眼的；目光短浅的，缺乏远见的（lacking of foresight or
[maɪˈoʊpɪk]	discernment）
	搭 a myopic child 近视的孩子
nadir	*n.* 最低点（the lowest point）
[ˈneɪdɪr]	搭 the nadir of one's career 某人事业上的低谷
nag	*v.* 不断叨扰，指责，抱怨（to find fault incessantly；complain）
[næg]	
naive	*adj.* 天真的，纯朴的（marked by unaffected simplicity）
[naɪˈiːv]	记 联想记忆：native(原始的，土著的)减去 t → 比土著人懂得还要少 → 天真的，纯朴的
namby-pamby	*adj.* 乏味的（insipid）；懦弱的（infirm）*n.* 懦弱的人
[ˌnæmbɪ ˈpæmbɪ]	
narcissism	*n.* 自恋，自爱（inordinate fascination with oneself）
[ˈnɑːrsɪsɪzəm]	记 来自 Narcissus，希腊神话中的美少年，因过于爱恋自己水中的影子而溺水身亡，化为水仙花（narcissus）
narcissist	*n.* 自恋狂，自恋者（a person who has abnormal and excessive love or
[nɑːrˈsɪsɪst]	admiration for oneself）
nasal	*adj.* 鼻的（pertaining to the nose）；有鼻音的
[ˈneɪzl]	记 词根记忆：nas(鼻) + al → 鼻的
nascent	*adj.* 初生的，萌芽的（beginning to exist or develop）
[ˈnæsnt]	记 词根记忆：nasc(出生) + ent → 刚出生的 → 初生的
natal	*adj.* 出生的，诞生时的（of, relating to, or present at birth）
[ˈneɪtl]	记 词根记忆：nat(出生) + al → 出生的，诞生时的
nausea	*n.* 作呕，恶心（a feeling of sickness in the stomach）
[ˈnɔːziə]	记 词根记忆：naus(=naut 船) + ea(病) → 在船上会犯的病 → 晕船 → 恶心
nauseate	*v.* (使)作呕，(使)厌恶（to feel or cause to feel disgust）
[ˈnɔːzieɪt]	同 sicken
nautical	*adj.* 船员的，船舶的，航海的（pertaining to sailors, ships or navigation）
[ˈnɔːtɪkl]	记 词根记忆：naut(船) + ical → 船舶的，航海的
naysay	*v.* 拒绝，否认，反对（to say no）
[ˈneɪseɪ]	记 联想记忆：nay(=no 不) + say(说) → 不说 → 拒绝
naysayer	*n.* 怀疑者，否定者（one who denies or is skeptical or cynical about sth.）
[ˈneɪseɪər]	记 来自 naysay(v. 拒绝，否认)+er → 怀疑者，否定者
necessitous	*adj.* 贫困的（needy；indigent）；紧迫的（urgent）
[nɪˈsesɪtəs]	记 来自 necessity(n. 必要，必然性；必需品)
needle	*n.* 针；针叶（a narrow stiff leaf of conifers）
[ˈniːdl]	搭 a needle in a haystack 几乎不可能找到的东西

34

□ myopia	□ myopic	□ nadir	□ nag	□ naive	□ namby-pamby
□ narcissism	□ narcissist	□ nasal	□ nascent	□ natal	□ nausea
□ nauseate	□ nautical	□ naysay	□ naysayer	□ necessitous	□ needle

nefarious [nɪˈfeəriəs]	*adj.* 极恶毒的, 邪恶的(extremely wicked; evil) 记 词根记忆: ne(=not) + far(公正) + ious → 不公正的 → 邪恶的
negation [nɪˈɡeɪʃn]	*n.* 否定, 否认(action of denying) 记 词根记忆: neg(否认) + ation → 否定, 否认
negligence [ˈneɡlɪdʒəns]	*n.* 粗心, 疏忽(disregard of duty; neglect) 记 词根记忆: neg(不) + lig(选择) + ence → 不加选择 → 粗心, 疏忽
nemesis [ˈneməsɪs]	*n.* 报应(an agent or act of retribution) 记 来自希腊神话中的复仇女神 Nemesis
neologism [niˈɑːlədʒɪzəm]	*n.* 新字, 新词(a new word or phrase) 记 词根记忆: neo(新的) + log(说话) + ism → 新的话语 → 新字, 新词
neonate [ˈniːoʊneɪt]	*n.* 新生儿(a new born child) 记 词根记忆: neo(新的) + nat(出生) + e → 新生儿
neophyte [ˈniːəfaɪt]	*n.* 初学者, 新手(a beginner or a novice) 记 词根记忆: neo(新的) + phyt(植物) + e → 新植物 → 新手
nerve [nɜːrv]	*n.* 勇气 *v.* 给予力量(to give strength to) 记 联想记忆: 军人为人民服务(serve)首先要有勇气(nerve)
nethermost [ˈneðəmoʊst]	*adj.* 最低的, 最下面的(lowest; the farthest down) 记 组合词: nether(下面的) + most(最) → 最下面的
nettle [ˈnetl]	*n.* 荨麻 *v.* 烦忧, 激怒(to irritate; provoke) 记 联想记忆: 用 nettle(荨麻)织网(net)
neurology [nʊˈrɑːlədʒi]	*n.* 神经学(the scientific study of the nervous system) 记 词根记忆: neur(神经) + ology(学科) → 神经学
neurosis [nʊˈroʊsɪs]	*n.* 神经官能症 记 词根记忆: neur(神经) + osis(表病) → 神经官能症
neutralize [ˈnuːtrəlaɪz]	*v.* 使无效(to make ineffective; nullify); 中和, 使中性(to make neutral) 记 词根记忆: ne(不) + utr(= uter 二者中的任一) + alize → 不偏向任何一方 → 中和
nifty [ˈnɪfti]	*adj.* 极好的, 极妙的(very good; very attractive) 同 great
niggle [ˈnɪɡl]	*v.* 拘泥小节(to spend too much effort on minor details); 小气地给(to give stingily or in tiny portions)
niggling [ˈnɪɡlɪŋ]	*adj.* 琐碎的(petty; trivial) 记 词根记忆: nig(小气的) + gling → 琐碎的
nil [nɪl]	*n.* 无, 零(nothing; zero) 记 词根记忆: ni(=ne 无, 没有) + l → 无, 零
nimble [ˈnɪmbl]	*adj.* 敏捷的, 灵活的(moving quickly and lightly) 记 联想记忆: 偷窃(nim)需要手脚灵活(nimble)

| **nip** | *v.* 小口啜饮 (to sip in a small amount) |
| [nɪp] | 记 和 lip(*n.* 嘴唇)一起记 |

| **nomad** | *n.* 流浪者 (any wanderer); 游牧部落的人 |
| ['noʊmæd] | 记 联想记忆：no + mad → 流浪者不疯也狂 → 流浪者 |

| **nominal** | *adj.* 名义上的，有名无实的 (in name only) |
| ['nɑːmɪnl] | 记 词根记忆：nomin(名字) + al → 名义上的 |

| **nominate** | *v.* 提名；任命，指定 (to appoint sb. to a position) |
| ['nɑːmɪneɪt] | 记 词根记忆：nomin(名字) + ate → 提名 |

任命你为经理！
nominate

| **nonplus** | *v.* 使困惑 (to put in perplexity, bewilder) *n.* 迷惑，困惑 |
| [ˌnɑːn'plʌs] | 记 联想记忆：non + plus (有利的因素) → 不利 → 迷惑 |

| **noose** | *n.* 绳圈，套索 (a loop formed in a rope) |
| [nuːs] | 记 和 loose(*adj.* 松的)一起记 |

| **nostrum** | *n.* 家传秘方，江湖药 (quack medicine); 万灵丹；妙策 (a usually questionable remedy or scheme) |
| ['nɑːstrəm] | 记 词根记忆：nost(家) + rum → 家传秘方 |

| **noxious** | *adj.* 有害的，有毒的 (injurious; pernicious) |
| ['nɑːkʃəs] | 记 词根记忆：nox(伤害) + ious → 有毒的 |

| **nucleate** | *v.* (使)成核 (to form a nucleus) *adj.* 有核的 |
| ['nuːklɪeɪt] | 记 词根记忆：nucle(核) + ate → (使)成核 |

| **nugatory** | *adj.* 无价值的，琐碎的 (trifling; worthless) |
| ['nuːgətɔːri] | 记 词根记忆：nug(玩笑) + atory → 让人一笑而过的 → 无价值的 |

| **nullify** | *v.* 使无效 (to invalidate); 抵消 (to cancel out) |
| ['nʌlɪfaɪ] | 记 联想记忆：null(无) + ify → 使无效 |

| **numinous** | *adj.* 超自然的，神的 (supernatural; divine) |
| ['nuːmɪnəs] | 记 联想记忆：numin(看作 numen，守护神) + ous → 守护神的 → 神的 |

| **numismatist** | *n.* 钱币学家，钱币收藏家 (a person who studies or collects coins, tokens, and paper money) |
| [nuː'mɪzmətɪst] | |

| **oasis** | *n.* 绿洲 (a fertile place in desert) |
| [oʊ'eɪsɪs] | 揽 a green oasis in the heart of the city 都市中心的绿茵 |

| **oath** | *n.* 誓言 (a formal promise to fulfill a pledge, especially one made in a court of law); 咒骂，诅咒 (swearword) |
| [oʊθ] | |

| **obedient** | *adj.* 服从的，顺从的 (submissive; docile) |
| [ə'biːdiənt] | 记 来自 obey(*v.* 服从) |

| **obeisance** | *n.* 鞠躬，敬礼 (a gesture of respect or reverence) |
| [oʊ'biːsns] | 记 词根记忆：ob(加强) + eis(=aud 听话) + ance → 表示听话 → 鞠躬 |

34

□ nip	□ nomad	□ nominal	□ nominate	□ nonplus	□ noose
□ nostrum	□ noxious	□ nucleate	□ nugatory	□ nullify	□ numinous
□ numismatist	□ oasis	□ oath	□ obedient	□ obeisance	

objection [əbˈdʒekʃn]	*n.* 厌恶，反对(dislike or disapproval)
	记 词根记忆：ob(反) + ject(扔) + ion → 反过来扔 → 厌恶，反对
	例 Since the author frequently attacks other scholars, his *objection* to disputes is not only irrelevant but also surprising.
objective [əbˈdʒektɪv]	*adj.* 客观的(not influenced by personal opinions) *n.* 目标(an aim)
	记 来自object(*n.* 物体；目标)
	例 The articles that he wrote ran the gamut from the serious to the lighthearted, from *objective* to the argumentative, from the innocuous to the hostile.
oblige [əˈblaɪdʒ]	*v.* 强迫，强制(to constrain)；施恩惠于…(to do sth. as a favor)
	记 词根记忆：ob(加强) + lig(绑住) + e → 用力绑住 → 强迫
oblique [əˈbliːk]	*adj.* 不直接的，不坦率的(not straightforward)；斜的(inclined)
	记 词根记忆：ob(反) + liqu(向上弯) + e → 不向上弯的 → 斜的
obloquy [ˈɑːbləkwi]	*n.* 辱骂，斥责(censure or vituperation)
	记 词根记忆：ob(反) + loqu(说话) + y → 说坏话 → 辱骂
obnoxious [əbˈnɑːkʃəs]	*adj.* 令人极不愉快的，可憎的(disgustingly objectionable)
	记 词根记忆：ob(to) + nox(伤害) + ious → 给人带来伤害的 → 令人极不愉快的
observance [əbˈzɜːrvəns]	*n.* (对法律、习俗等的)遵守，奉行
	记 词根记忆：ob(加强) + serv(保持) + ance → 遵守
obsess [əbˈses]	*v.* 迷住；使…困扰，使…烦扰(to haunt or excessively preoccupy the mind of)
	记 词根记忆：ob(反) + sess(=sit 坐) → 坐着不动，妨碍前进 → 迷住；使…困扰
obsession [əbˈseʃn]	*n.* 入迷，着迷(excessive preoccupation with an often unreasonable idea or feeling)；固执的念头(a persistent idea, desire or emotion)
	记 来自obsess(*v.* 迷住)
obsessive [əbˈsesɪv]	*adj.* 强迫性的，急迫的(excessive often to an unreasonable degree)；使人着迷的(tending to cause obsession)

obsolete [ˌɑːbsəˈliːt]	*adj.* 废弃的（no longer in use）；过时的（out of date；old） 同 old-fashioned
obstinate [ˈɑːbstɪnət]	*adj.* 固执的，倔强的（unreasonably determined；stubborn；dogged） 记 词根记忆：ob(向) + st(站) + inate → 就站在那里 → 固执的
obstreperous [əbˈstrepərəs]	*adj.* 吵闹的（noisy；boisterous）；难管束的（unruly） 同 clamorous, vociferous
obstruction [əbˈstrʌkʃn]	*n.* 阻碍(物)，妨碍（action of obstructing） 记 联想记忆：obstruct(阻隔，阻碍)+ion → 阻碍(物)，妨碍
obtrude [əbˈtruːd]	*v.* 突出（to thrust out）；强加（to force or impose） 记 词根记忆：ob(向外) + trud(伸出) + e → 向外伸 → 突出
obtuse [əbˈtuːs]	*adj.* 愚笨的（dull or insensitive）；钝的（blunt） 记 词根记忆：ob(向) + tus(敲击) + e → 用钝器敲击 → 钝的
obverse [ˈɑːbvɜːrs]	*n./adj.* 正面(的)（the front or main surface） 记 词根记忆：ob(外) + vers(转) + e → 转向外的 → 正面的
occlude [əˈkluːd]	*v.* 使闭塞（to prevent the passage of） 记 词根记忆：oc + clud(关闭) + e → 一再关起来 → 使闭塞
occult [əˈkʌlt]	*adj.* 秘密的，不公开的（hidden；concealed） 记 联想记忆：oc(外) + cult(教派) → 不在教派外公开的 → 秘密的
ocular [ˈɑːkjələr]	*adj.* 眼睛的（of the eye）；视觉的（based on what has been seen） 记 词根记忆：ocul(眼) + ar → 眼睛的
ode [oʊd]	*n.* 长诗，颂歌（a lyric poem usually marked by exaltation of feeling and style, varying length of line, and complexity of stanza forms）
odium [ˈoʊdiəm]	*n.* 憎恶，反感（hatred） 同 detestation
odometer [oʊˈdɑːmɪtər]	*n.* (汽车)里程表（an instrument for measuring the distance traveled (as by a vehicle)） 记 词根记忆：od(路) + o + meter(测量) → 测量路程的东西 → 里程表

obsolete

□ obsolete	□ obstinate	□ obstreperous	□ obstruction	□ obtrude	□ obtuse
□ obverse	□ occlude	□ occult	□ ocular	□ ode	□ odium
□ odometer					

odoriferous	*adj.* 有气味的（giving off an odor）
[ˌoʊdəˈrɪfərəs]	记 词根记忆：odor(气味) + i + fer(带有) + ous → 有气味的
offbeat	*adj.* 不规则的，不平常的（unconventional）
[ˌɑːfˈbiːt]	记 组合词：off(离开) + beat(节奏) → 无节奏 → 不规则的
offend	*v.* 得罪，冒犯（to be displeasing; violate）
[əˈfend]	搭 offend against sb. 触犯、冒犯或得罪某人
offensive	*adj.* 令人不快的，得罪人的（causing anger or displeasure）
[əˈfensɪv]	记 来自 offend(v. 得罪，冒犯)
offish	*adj.* 冷淡的（distant and reserved）
[ˈɔːfɪʃ]	记 联想记忆：off(离开) + (f)ish(鱼) → 鱼离开了，池塘冷清 → 冷淡的
offset	*v.* 补偿，抵消（to make up for）
[ˈɑːfset]	同 balance, compensate
ogle	*v.* 送秋波（to eye amorously or provocatively） *n.* 媚眼（an amorous or
[ˈoʊgl]	coquettish glance）
ointment	*n.* 油膏，软膏（salve; unguent）
[ˈɔɪntmənt]	记 词根记忆：oint(=oil 油) + ment → 油膏
oleaginous	*adj.* 油腻的（of or relating to oil）；圆滑的，满口恭维的（falsely or smugly
[ˌoʊliˈædʒɪnəs]	earnest; unctuous）
olfactory	*adj.* 嗅觉的（of the sense of smell）
[ɑːlˈfæktəri]	记 词根记忆：ol(=smell 味) + fact(做) + ory → 做出味道来的 → 嗅觉的
	搭 olfactory sense 嗅觉
omelet	*n.* 煎蛋卷（eggs beaten together and cooked in hot fat）
[ˈɑːmlət]	记 联想记忆：o(看作一个蛋) + me(我) + let(让) → 让我吃煎蛋 → 煎蛋卷
omnipresent	*adj.* 无处不在的（present in all places at all times）
[ˌɑːmnɪˈpreznt]	记 词根记忆：omni(全) + present(存在) → 无处不在的
omniscient	*adj.* 无所不知的，博识的（knowing all things）
[ɑːmˈnɪsiənt]	记 词根记忆：omni(全) + sci(知道) + ent → 全知道的 → 无所不知的
omnivorous	*adj.* 杂食的（eating both meat and vegetables or plants）；兴趣杂的（having
[ɑːmˈnɪvərəs]	wide interests in a particular area or activity）
	记 词根记忆：omni(全) + vor(吃) + ous → 全部吃的 → 杂食的
onset	*n.* 开始，发作（beginning; commencement）；攻击，袭击（attack; assault）
[ˈɑːnset]	例 Although adolescent maturational and developmental states occur in
	an orderly sequence, their timing varies with regard to *onset* and
	duration.
onslaught	*n.* 猛攻，猛袭（a fierce attack）
[ˈɑːnslɔːt]	记 联想记忆：on + slaught(打击) → 猛攻，猛袭
onus	*n.* 义务，负担（a difficult or disagreeable responsibility or necessity）
[ˈoʊnəs]	记 联想记忆：on + us → 在我们身上的"责任" → 义务，负担

ooze [uːz]	*v.* 慢慢地流，渗出(to leak out slowly)；(勇气)逐渐消失 记 联想记忆：oo(像水渗出来时冒的泡泡) + ze → 渗出
opalescence [ˌoʊpəˈlesns]	*n.* 乳白光(reflecting on iridescent light)
opaque [oʊˈpeɪk]	*adj.* 不透明的(not transparent)；难懂的(hard to understand; obscure) 记 联想记忆：opa(cus)(蔽光的) + que → 不透明的
opine [oʊˈpaɪn]	*v.* 想，以为(to hold or express an opinion) 记 通过 opinion(*n.* 看法)反推 opine(*v.* 想)
oppose [əˈpoʊz]	*v.* 反对(to be or act against) 记 词根记忆：op(反) + pos(放) + e → 反着放 → 反对 例 Candidates who *oppose* the present state income tax must be able to propose alternate ways to continue the financing of state operations.
oppress [əˈpres]	*v.* 压迫，压制(to rule in a hard and cruel way) 记 词根记忆：op(向) + press(压) → 压下去 → 压迫
opulence [ˈɑːpjələns]	*n.* 富裕(wealth; affluence)；丰富(great abundance; profusion)
oracle [ˈɔːrəkl]	*n.* 代神发布神谕的人(a person through whom a deity is believed to speak) 记 词根记忆：ora(说话) + cle → 代神发布神谕的人
oracular [əˈrækjələr]	*adj.* 神谕的(of an oracle)；玄妙难懂的(obscure; enigmatic)
oratory [ˈɔːrətɔːri]	*n.* 演讲术(the art of making good speeches) 记 来自 orate(*v.* 演讲)
orchard [ˈɔːrtʃərd]	*n.* 果园(an area of land devoted to the cultivation of fruit or nut trees) 搭 cherry orchard 樱桃园
ordain [ɔːrˈdeɪn]	*v.* 任命(神职)(to make sb. a priest or minister)；颁发命令(to decree; order)
ordinance [ˈɔːrdɪnəns]	*n.* 法令，条例(a governmental statute of regulation) 记 词根记忆：ordin(命令) + ance → 法令，条例
orient [ˈɔːrient]	*adj.* 上升的(rising) *v.* 确定方向(to ascertain the bearings of)；使熟悉情况(to acquaint with a particular situation) 记 词根记忆：ori(升起) + ent → 上升的
ornate [ɔːrˈneɪt]	*adj.* 华美的(showy or flowery)；充满装饰的(heavily ornamented or adorned) 记 词根记忆：orn(装饰) + ate → 装饰过的 → 华美的
ornery [ˈɔːrnəri]	*adj.* 顽固的，爱争吵的(having an irritable disposition) 同 cantankerous

35

orotund	*adj.* (声音)洪亮的((of sound) strong and deep; resonant); 夸张的 (bombastic or pompous)
['ɔːrətʌnd]	记 联想记忆: oro + tund(=round, 圆的)→ 把嘴张圆了(说)→ 洪亮的
orthodox	*adj.* 正统的(conforming to the usual beliefs of established doctrines)
['ɔːrθədɑːks]	记 词根记忆: ortho(正的, 直的)+ dox(观点)→ 正统观点 → 正统的
oscillate	*v.* 摆动(to swing regularly); 犹豫(to vacillate)
['ɑːsɪleɪt]	记 词根记忆: oscill(摆动)+ ate → 摆动
osmosis	*n.* 渗透(the diffusion of fluids); 潜移默化(gradual, and often hardly noticeable acceptance of ideas, etc.)
[ɑːz'moʊsɪs]	
osseous	*adj.* 骨的, 多骨的(composed of bone; bony)
['ɑːsiəs]	记 词根记忆: oss(骨)+ e + ous → 骨的
ostensible	*adj.* 表面上的(apparent; seeming; professed)
[ɑː'stensəbl]	记 词根记忆: os(向上)+ tens(拉)+ ible → 向上拉长的 → 表面上的
ostracism	*n.* 放逐, 排斥(act of stopping accepting someone as a member of the group)
['ɑːstrəsɪzəm]	记 词根记忆: ostrac(贝壳)+ ism → 古希腊人用贝壳投票决定是否应该放逐某人 → 放逐
other-directed	*adj.* 受人支配的(directed in thought and action by others)
[ˌʌðədɪ'rektɪd]	记 组合词: other(别人)+ direct(指挥)+ ed → 受人支配的
otiose	*adj.* 不必要的, 多余的(useless; superfluous)
['oʊʃioʊs]	同 unnecessary
outfox	*v.* 以机智胜过(to outwit; outsmart)
[ˌaʊt'fɑːks]	记 组合词: out(出)+ fox(狐狸)→ 胜过狐狸 → 以机智胜过
outlandish	*adj.* 古怪的(very odd, fantastic; bizarre)
[aʊt'lændɪʃ]	记 联想记忆: out(出)+ land(国家)+ ish → 从外国来的 → 古怪的
outlet	*n.* 出口(a way through which sth. may go out)
['aʊtlet]	记 组合词: out(出来)+ let(让)→ 让出来 → 出口
outmaneuver	*v.* 以策略制胜(to overcome an opponent by artful, clever maneuvering)
[ˌaʊtmə'nuːvər]	记 组合词: out(超出)+ maneuver(策略)→ 以策略制胜
outset	*n.* 开始, 开头(start; beginning)
['aʊtset]	记 来自词组 set out(出发)
	搭 from the outset 从一开始
outshine	*v.* 比…光亮(to shine brighter than); 出色, 优异(to excel in splendor or showiness)
[ˌaʊt'ʃaɪn]	记 联想记忆: out(超越)+ shine(闪耀)→ 比…光亮; 出色, 优异
outwit	*v.* 以机智胜过(to overcome by cleverness)
[ˌaʊt'wɪt]	记 组合词: out(出)+ wit(机智)→ 机智超过别人 → 以机智胜过
oven	*n.* 烤箱, 烤炉, 灶(a chamber used for baking, heating, or drying)
['ʌvn]	记 发音记忆: "爱闻" → 爱闻烤箱里的香味 → 烤箱, 烤炉

overbearing [ˌoʊvərˈberɪŋ]	*adj.* 专横的，独断的（arrogant; domineering） 📝 组合词：over（过分）+ bearing（忍受）→ 使别人过分忍受 → 专横的
overflow [ˌoʊvərˈfloʊ]	*v.* 溢出（to flow over the edges）；充满（to be very full） 📝 组合词：over（出）+ flow（流）→ 溢出
overhaul [ˈoʊvərhɔːl]	*v.* 彻底检查（to check thoroughly）；大修（to repair thoroughly） 📝 组合词：over（全部）+ haul（拉，拖）→ 全部拉上来修理 → 大修
overreach [ˌoʊvərˈriːtʃ]	*v.* 做事过头（to go to excess） 📝 组合词：over（过分）+ reach（伸出）→ 做过了 → 做事过头
overriding [ˌoʊvərˈraɪdɪŋ]	*adj.* 最主要的，优先的（chief; principal） 📕 Numerous historical examples illustrate both the *overriding* influence that scientists' prejudices have on their interpretation of data and the consequent impairment of their intellectual objectivity.
oversee [ˌoʊvərˈsiː]	*v.* 监督（to watch; supervise） 📝 组合词：over（全部）+ see（看）→ 监督
oversight [ˈoʊvərsaɪt]	*n.* 疏忽，失察，勘漏（unintentional failure to notice sth.） 📝 组合词：over（在…上）+ sight（视线）→ 错误在视线之上 → 疏忽
overthrow [ˌoʊvərˈθroʊ]	*v.* 推翻；终止（to throw over; overturn）*n.* 推翻；终止（an instance of overthrowing）
overture [ˈoʊvərtʃər]	*n.* 前奏曲，序曲（a musical introduction to an opera） 📝 词根记忆：o（出）+ ver（覆盖）+ ture → 去掉覆盖物，打开 → 序曲
overweening [ˌoʊvərˈwiːnɪŋ]	*adj.* 自负的，过于自信的（arrogant; excessively proud） 📝 组合词：over（过分）+ ween（想）+ ing → 把自己想得过分伟大 → 自负的
oxidize [ˈɑːksɪdaɪz]	*v.* 氧化，生锈（to combine with oxygen） 📝 联想记忆：oxid(e)（氧化物）+ ize → 氧化
pacify [ˈpæsɪfaɪ]	*v.* 使安静，抚慰（to make calm, quiet, and satisfied） 📝 词根记忆：pac（和平，平静）+ ify → 使变得平和 → 使安静，抚慰
pact [pækt]	*n.* 协定，条约（an agreement; covenant） 📘 treaty
pagan [ˈpeɪɡən]	*n.* 没有宗教信仰的人（a person who has little or no religion）；异教徒 📘 heathen
painstaking [ˈpeɪnzteɪkɪŋ]	*adj.* 煞费苦心的（involving diligent care and effort） 📝 联想记忆：pains（痛苦）+ taking（花费…的）→ 煞费苦心的
palate [ˈpælət]	*n.* 上腭；口味（sense of taste）；爱好（a usually intellectual taste or liking） 📝 联想记忆：pal + ate（eat 的过去式）→ 与吃有关的 → 口味
palatial [pəˈleɪʃl]	*adj.* 宫殿般的（like a palace）；宏伟的（magnificent; stately） 📝 来自 palace（*n.* 宫殿），注意不要和 palatable（*adj.* 美味的）相混
palaver [pəˈlɑːvər]	*n.* 空谈（idle chatter）*v.* 空谈（to chatter idly）；奉承（to flatter or cajole） 📝 联想记忆：pala(ce)（宫殿）+ aver（承认，说话）→ 宫殿里的话 → 奉承

35

palette	n. 调色板，颜料配置
[ˈpælət]	

pall	v. 令人发腻，失去吸引力（to become boring）
[pɔːl]	

palliate	v. 减轻（痛苦）（to reduce；abate）；掩饰（罪行）（to extenuate）
[ˈpælieɪt]	记 词根记忆：pall（罩子）+ itate → 盖上（罪行）→ 掩饰（罪行）

palliative	n. 缓释剂 adj. 减轻的，缓和的（serving to palliate）
[ˈpæliətɪv]	搭 a palliative measure 消极措施

pallid	adj. 苍白的，没血色的（wan, lacking sparkle or liveliness）
[ˈpælɪd]	记 词根记忆：pall（=pale 苍白的）+ id → 苍白的

palpitate	v.（心脏）急速跳动（to beat rapidly；throb）
[ˈpælpɪteɪt]	记 词根记忆：palp（摸）+ it + ate → 摸得着的心跳 →（心脏）急速跳动

pamper	v. 纵容，过分关怀（to treat with excess or extreme care）
[ˈpæmpər]	同 indulge

pan	v.〈口〉严厉批评（to criticize severely）
[pæn]	

pandemonium	n. 喧嚣，大混乱（a wild uproar；tumult）
[ˌpændəˈmoʊniəm]	记 联想记忆：pan（全部）+ demon（魔鬼）+ ium → 全是魔鬼 → 大混乱；来自弥尔顿的著作《失乐园》中的地狱之都（Pandemonium）

pander	v. 怂恿，迎合（不良欲望）（to cater to the low desires of others）
[ˈpændər]	记 联想记忆：pa（音似：拍）+ nder（看作 under，下面）→ 拍低级马屁 → 迎合

pane	n. 窗格玻璃（a single sheet of glass in a frame of a window）
[peɪn]	搭 a window pane 窗玻璃

pang	n. 一阵剧痛（a sudden sharp feeling of pain）
[pæŋ]	搭 pangs of remorse 悔恨的痛苦

panic	adj. 恐慌的 n. 恐慌，惊惶（a sudden unreasoning terror）
[ˈpænɪk]	记 来自希腊神话中的畜牧神潘（Pan），panic 是指潘的出现所引起的恐惧
	例 During the Battle of Trafalgar, Admiral Nelson remained imperturbable and in full command of the situation in spite of the hysteria and *panic* all around him.

panorama	n. 概观，全景（a comprehensive presentation；cyclorama）
[ˌpænəˈræmə]	记 词根记忆：pan（全部）+ orama（看）→ 全部看得到 → 全景

panoramic	adj. 全景的，全貌的，概论的（of or relating to a panorama）
[ˌpænəˈræmɪk]	记 来自 panorama（n. 概观，全景）

parallelism	n. 平行，类似（the state or quality of being parallel）
[ˈpærəlelɪzəm]	记 联想记忆：parallel（平行的）+ ism → 平行，类似

paralyze	v. 使瘫痪（to affect with paralysis）；使无效（to make ineffective）
[ˈpærəlaɪz]	记 词根记忆：para（一边）+ lyz（松开）+ e → 身体的一边松了 → 使瘫痪

| **parch** | *v.* 烘烤（to toast）; 烤焦（to become scorched） |
| [pɑːrtʃ] | 记 联想记忆：用火把（torch）来烘烤（parch） |

| **pare** | *v.* 削（to peel）; 修剪（to trim）; 削减，缩减（to diminish or reduce by or as |
| [per] | if by paring） |

| **parity** | *n.* （水平、地位、数量等的）同等，相等（equality） |
| [ˈpærəti] | 记 词根记忆：par（相等）+ ity → 同等，相等 |

parley	*n.* 和谈（a conference with an enemy）; 会谈（a conference for discussion
[ˈpɑːrli]	of points in dispute） *v.* 和谈，会谈（to speak with another）
	记 词根记忆：parl（讲话）+ ey → 会谈

| **parlous** | *adj.* 靠不住的，危险的（full of danger; hazardous） |
| [ˈpɑːrləs] | 记 和perilous（*adj.* 危险的）一起记 |

| **parochial** | *adj.* 教区的（of or relating to a church parish）; 地方性的，狭小的（restricted |
| [pəˈroʊkiəl] | to a small area or scope; narrow） |

| **parry** | *v.* 挡开，避开（武器、问题等）（to ward off; evade） |
| [ˈpæri] | 搭 parry a question 回避问题 |

| **particularize** | *v.* 详述，列举（to give the details of sth. one by one） |
| [pərˈtɪkjələraɪz] | 记 来自particular（*adj.* 详细的） |

| **partition** | *n.* 隔开（division）; 隔墙（an interior dividing wall） |
| [pɑːrˈtɪʃn] | 记 词根记忆：part（部分）+ i + tion → 分成部分 → 隔开 |

| **parturition** | *n.* 生产，分娩（the action or process of giving birth to offspring） |
| [ˌpɑːrtjʊˈrɪʃn] | 记 词根记忆：par（生产）+ turi + tion → 分娩 |

| **passe** | *adj.* 已过盛年的（past one's prime）; 过时的（behind the times） |
| [pæˈseɪ] | 同 outmoded |

passive	*adj.* 被动的，缺乏活力的（not active; submissive）
[ˈpæsɪv]	记 词根记忆：pass（感情）+ ive（…的）→ 感情用事的 → 被动的
	例 The amusements of modern urban people tend more and more to be *passive* and to consist of the observation of the skilled activities of others.

| **pastiche** | *n.* 混合拼凑的作品（a musical, literary, or artistic composition made up of |
| [pæˈstiːʃ] | selections from different works） |

| **pastoral** | *adj.* 田园生活的（idyllic; rural）; 宁静的（pleasingly peaceful and innocent） |
| [ˈpæstərəl] | 记 联想记忆：pastor（牧人）+ al → 田园生活的 |

| **pastry** | *n.* 糕点，点心（sweet baked goods） |
| [ˈpeɪstri] | 记 联想记忆：past（看作paste，面团）+ ry → 面团做成的糕点 → 糕点 |

patch

35

| **patch** | *n.* 补丁（a piece of material used to mend or |
| [pætʃ] | cover a hole）; 一小片（土地）（a small piece of land） |

patent	*adj.* 显而易见的（readily visible；obvious）*n.* 专利权（证书）
[ˈpeɪtnt]	例 Copyright and *patent* laws attempt to encourage innovation by ensuring that inventors are paid for creative work, so it would be ironic if expanded protection under these laws discouraged entrepreneurial innovation by increasing fears of lawsuits.
pathetic	*adj.* 引起怜悯的，令人难过的（marked by sorrow or melancholy）
[pəˈθetɪk]	记 词根记忆：path（感情）+ etic → 有感情的 → 引起怜悯的
pathology	*n.* 病理学（the study of the essential nature of diseases）
[pəˈθɑɪlədʒi]	记 词根记忆：path（病）+ ology（学科）→ 病理学
patriot	*n.* 爱国者，爱国主义者（one who loves his/her country and supports its authority and interests）
[ˈpeɪtriət]	记 词根记忆：patri（父亲）+ ot → 把祖国当父亲看待的人 → 爱国者

誓死不降

patriot

patriotism	*n.* 爱国主义，爱国心（love for or devotion to one's country）
[ˈpeɪtriətɪzəm]	记 来自 patriot（*n.* 爱国者）
pauper	*n.* 贫民（a very poor person）；乞丐
[ˈpɔːpər]	记 词根记忆：paup（少）+ er → 财富少的人 → 贫民
pavid	*adj.* 害怕的，胆小的（exhibiting or experiencing fear；timid）
[ˈpævɪd]	
pawn	*v.* 典当，抵押（to deposit in pledge）*n.* 典当，抵押；被利用的小人物
[pɔːn]	记 和 pawnbroker（*n.* 典当商，当铺老板）一起记
peachy	*adj.* 极好的，漂亮的（unusually fine）
[ˈpiːtʃi]	同 splendid
peak	*v.* 变得憔悴，消瘦（to become thin or sick；emaciate）
[piːk]	揣 peak and pine 憔悴
peaky	*adj.* 消瘦的，虚弱的（thin；weak）
[ˈpiːki]	记 来自 peak（*v.* 变得憔悴）
pecan	*n.* 山核桃（a nut with a long thin reddish shell）
[pɪˈkɑːn]	记 发音记忆："皮啃" → 皮很难啃动的坚果 → 山核桃
peck	*v.* 啄食，轻啄（to strike with a beak）
[pek]	揣 peck sth. out 啄出某物
peckish	*adj.* 饿的（hungry）；急躁的（crotchety）
[ˈpekɪʃ]	同 ill-tempered, irritable
peculate	*v.* 挪用（公款）（to embezzle）
[ˈpekjuleɪt]	记 词根记忆：pecu（原义为"牛"，引申为"钱财"）+ lat（搬运）+ e → 把公有钱财搬回家里 → 挪用（公款）
pedagogy	*n.* 教学学，教学法（the art, science of teaching）
[ˈpedəgɑːdʒi]	记 词根记忆：ped（儿童）+ agog（引导）+ y → 引导儿童之学 → 教育学
pedal	*n.* 踏板，脚蹬 *v.* 骑自行车（to ride a bicycle）
[ˈpedl]	记 词根记忆：ped（脚）+ al（东西）→ 踏板

□ patent	□ pathetic	□ pathology	□ patriot	□ patriotism	□ pauper
□ pavid	□ pawn	□ peachy	□ peak	□ peaky	□ pecan
□ peck	□ peckish	□ peculate	□ pedagogy	□ pedal	

peddle ['pedl]	*v.* 兜售 (to travel about selling wares) 同 sell
pedestal ['pedɪstl]	*n.* (柱石或雕像的)基座 (base; foundation) 记 词根记忆：ped(脚) + estal → 做脚的东西 → 基座
peek [piːk]	*v.* 偷看 (to look furtively; glance)
peel [piːl]	*v.* 削去…的皮 (to strip off an outer layer of)；剥落 (to come off in sheets or scales, as bark, skin, or paint) *n.* 外皮
peep [piːp]	*n./v.* 瞥见，偷看 (to look cautiously or slyly)；初现 (to show slightly) 记 联想记忆：偷看颠倒过来(peep → peep)还是偷看
peer [pɪr]	*n.* 同等之人，同辈 (one belonging to the same societal group especially based on age, grade, or status)
peery ['pɪrɪ]	*adj.* 窥视的；好奇的 (curious)；怀疑的 (suspicious) 记 联想记忆：peer(窥视) + y → 窥视的；好奇的
peeve [piːv]	*v.* 使气恼，怨恨 (to cause to be annoyed or resentful) 同 irritate
pell-mell [ˌpel 'mel]	*adv.* 混乱地 (in mingled confusion or disorder) 记 组合词：pell(羊皮纸) + mell(使混和) → 羊皮纸搀和在一起 → 混乱地
pellucid [pə 'luːsɪd]	*adj.* 清晰的，清澈的 (transparent; clear) 记 词根记忆：pel(=per 全部) + luc(光) + id → 光线充足的 → 清晰的
pelt [pelt]	*v.* 扔 (to hurl; throw) *n.* 毛皮 搭 pelt sth. at sb. 朝某人扔某物
penalty ['penəlti]	*n.* 刑罚，处罚 (punishment for breaking a law or contract) 例 A major goal of law, to deter potential criminals by punishing wrongdoers, is not served when the *penalty* is so seldom invoked that it ceases to be a credible threat.
penance ['penəns]	*n.* 自我惩罚 (an act of self-abatement) 记 词根记忆：pen(惩罚) + ance → 惩罚 → 自我惩罚
pendent ['pendənt]	*adj.* 吊着的，悬挂的 (overhanging) 记 词根记忆：pend(挂) + ent → 挂着的 → 吊着的，悬挂的
pendulous ['pendʒələs]	*adj.* 下垂的 (inclined or hanging downward)
pendulum ['pendʒələm]	*n.* 摆，钟摆 记 词根记忆：pend(挂) + ulum(东西) → 挂的东西 → 钟摆
penetrate ['penətreɪt]	*v.* 刺穿 (to pierce)；渗入 (to pass in)；了解 (to discover the meaning of) 记 联想记忆：pen(全部) + etr(=enter 进入) + ate → 全部进入 → 刺穿

penalty
迟到五次
奖金全扣

35

penicillin [ˌpenɪˈsɪlɪn]	*n.* 青霉素 记 发音记忆："盘尼西林"
penury [ˈpenjəri]	*n.* 贫穷(severe poverty)；吝啬(extreme and often niggardly frugality) 同 destitution
perambulate [pəˈræmbjuleɪt]	*v.* 巡视(to make an official inspection on foot)；漫步(to stroll) 记 词根记忆：per(贯穿) + ambul(行走) + ate → 到处走 → 巡视
perch [pɜːrtʃ]	*v.* (鸟等)栖息(to alight, settle, or rest on a roost or a height) 记 注意不要和 parch(*v.* 烘，烤)相混
percolate [ˈpɜːrkəleɪt]	*v.* 过滤出(to cause to pass through a permeable substance)；渗透(to penetrate; seep) 记 词根记忆：per(贯穿) + col(过滤) + ate → 过滤出
peremptory [pəˈremptəri]	*adj.* 不容反抗的；专横的(masterful) 记 词根记忆：per(加强) + empt(抓) + ory → 采取强硬态度的 → 专横的
perfidy [ˈpɜːrfədi]	*n.* 不忠，背叛(the quality of being faithless) 同 disloyalty, treachery
perforate [ˈpɜːrfəreɪt]	*v.* 打洞(to make a hole through) 记 词根记忆：per(贯穿) + for(门，开口) + ate → 打穿 → 打洞
peril [ˈperəl]	*n.* 危险(exposure to the risk; danger) 记 词根记忆：per(冒险) + il → 危险
periphrastic [ˌperiˈfræstɪk]	*adj.* 迂回的，冗赘的(of, relating to, or characterized by periphrasis) 记 联想记忆：peri(周围) + phras(=phrase 句子，词语) + tic → 绕圈子说话 → 迂回的
perish [ˈperɪʃ]	*v.* 死，暴卒(to become destroyed or ruined; die) 记 联想记忆：珍惜(cherish)生命，不应随意毁灭(perish)
perishing [ˈperɪʃɪŋ]	*adj.* 严寒的(very cold)

perjure [ˈpɜːrdʒər]	*v.* 使作伪证，发假誓(to tell a lie under oath) 记 词根记忆：per(假地，错地) + jur(发誓) + e → 虚假地发誓 → 使作伪证，发假誓
perjury [ˈpɜːrdʒəri]	*n.* 伪证，假誓(false swearing) 搭 commit perjury 犯伪证罪
perk [pɜːrk]	*v.* 恢复，振作(to gain vigor or cheerfulness especially after a period of weakness or depression)；打扮(to make smart or spruce in appearance)；竖起(to stick up)
perky [ˈpɜːrki]	*adj.* 得意洋洋的；活泼的(jaunty; lively) 同 sprightly
perpetual [pərˈpetʃuəl]	*adj.* 持续的，不间断的(continuing without interruption; uninterrupted)；永久的(lasting forever) 记 词根记忆：per(始终) + pet(追求) + ual → 自始至终的追求 → 永久的 例 Micawber's habit of spending more than he earned left him in a state of *perpetual* indigence, but he persevered in hoping to see a more affluent day.
persecute [ˈpɜːrsɪkjuːt]	*v.* 迫害(to oppress or harass with ill treatment) 记 词根记忆：per(始终) + secut(跟随) + e → 坏事一直跟着 → 迫害
persiflage [ˈpɜːrsɪflɑːʒ]	*n.* 挖苦，嘲弄(frivolous bantering talk; raillery) 记 词根记忆：per(始终) + sifl(吹哨) + age → 一直吹哨 → 嘲弄
persistence [pərˈsɪstəns]	*n.* 坚持不懈，执意，持续(the quality or state of being persistent) 记 来自 persist (*v.* 坚持，持续，固执) 例 Contrary to the popular conception that it is powered by conscious objectivity, science often operates through error, happy accidents, hunches and *persistence* in spite of mistakes.
persnickety [pərˈsnɪkəti]	*adj.* 势利的(of a snob)；爱挑剔的(fussy; fastidious) 搭 a persnickety job 难以应付的工作
pertain [pərˈteɪn]	*v.* 属于(to belong as a part)；关于(to have reference) 记 词根记忆：per(始终) + tain(拿住) → 始终都拿在手里 → 属于

pertinacious [ˌpɜːrtn'eɪʃəs]	*adj.* 固执的，坚决的（stubbornly or perversely persistent）；坚持的（holding tenaciously to a purpose belief, opinion, or course of action） 记 词根记忆：per(始终) + tin(拿住) + acious → 始终拿住不放 → 固执的
peruse [pə'ruːz]	*v.* 细读，精读（to read sth. in a careful way） 记 词根记忆：per(始终) + us(用) + e → 反复用 → 细读，精读
perverse [pər'vɜːrs]	*adj.* 刚愎自用的，固执的（obstinate in opposing；wrongheaded） 记 词根记忆：per(始终) + vers(转) + e → 始终和别人反着转 → 固执的
pervert [pər'vɜːrt]	*v.* 使堕落（to corrupt；debase）；滥用（to divert to a wrong purpose；misuse）；歪曲（to interpret incorrectly） 记 词根记忆：per(远离) + vert(转) → 越转越远离正途 → 使堕落
pervious ['pɜːrviəs]	*adj.* 可渗透的，可通过的（permeable；accessible） 记 词根记忆：per(始终) + vi(路) + ous → 始终都有路走的 → 可通过的
pester ['pestər]	*v.* 纠缠，烦扰（to harass with petty irritations） 记 联想记忆：pest(害虫) + er → 像害虫一样骚扰 → 纠缠
pestilent ['pestɪlənt]	*adj.* 致命的（deadly）；有害的（pernicious） 记 联想记忆：pest(害虫) + il + ent → 有害的
pestle ['pesl]	*n.* 杵，碾槌（a club shaped implementation for pounding or grinding substances in a mortar）
petal ['petl]	*n.* 花瓣（a leaf-like division of the corolla of a flower）
petitioner [pə'tɪʃənər]	*n.* 请愿人（the person who makes a request） 记 来自 petition（*v./n.* 请愿）
petrify ['petrɪfaɪ]	*v.* (使)石化（to convert into stone）；(使)吓呆（to confound with fear or awe） 记 词根记忆：petr(石头) + ify → (使)石化
pettish ['petɪʃ]	*adj.* 易怒的，闹情绪的（fretful；peevish） 同 petulant
petty ['peti]	*adj.* 琐碎的，次要的（trivial；unimportant）；小气的（marked by or reflective of narrow interests and sympathies） 同 minor, subordinate；small-minded
petulance ['petʃələns]	*n.* 易怒，性急，暴躁（the quality or state of being petulant） 同 peevishness
phantom ['fæntəm]	*n.* 鬼怪，幽灵（a ghost）；幻影，幻象（sth. elusive or visionary） 记 词根记忆：phan(显现) + tom → 显现的东西 → 幽灵
pharisaic [ˌfæri'seɪɪk]	*adj.* 伪善的，伪装虔诚的 记 来自公元前后犹太教的法利赛人（Pharisee），以形式上遵守教义的伪善作风闻名
pharmacology [ˌfɑːrmə'kɑːlədʒi]	*n.* 药理学，药物学；药理
philately [fɪ'lætəli]	*n.* 集邮（stamp-collecting） 记 词根记忆：phil(爱) + ately(邮票) → 集邮

philology [fɪˈlɑːlədʒi]	*n.* 语文学，语文研究 记 词根记忆：phil(爱) + o + log(说话) + y → 语文学
phoenix [ˈfiːnɪks]	*n.* 凤凰，长生鸟(an imaginary bird believed to live for 500 years and then burn itself and be born again from the ashes)
phony [ˈfəʊni]	*adj.* 假的，欺骗的(not genuine or real) 同 false, sham
picayunish [ˌpɪkəˈjuːnɪʃ]	*adj.* 微不足道的，不值钱的(of little value) 同 petty, small-minded
pictorial [pɪkˈtɔːriəl]	*adj.* 绘画的(of or relating to the painting or drawing of pictures)；用图片的(having or expressed in pictures) 记 词根记忆：pict(描绘) + orial → 起描绘作用的 → 用图片的 例 Although Irish literature continued to flourish after the sixteenth century, a comparable tradition is absent in the visual arts: we think about Irish culture in terms of the word, not in terms of *pictorial* images.
piddle [ˈpɪdl]	*v.* 鬼混，浪费(to spend time aimlessly; diddle) 同 dawdle, putter
piddling [ˈpɪdlɪŋ]	*adj.* 琐碎的，微不足道的(so trifling or trivial as to be beneath one's consideration)
piebald [ˈpaɪbɔːld]	*adj.* 花斑的，黑白两色的(of different colors, especially spotted or blotched with black and white)
piecemeal [ˈpiːsmiːl]	*adj.* 一件一件的，零碎的(done, or made piece by piece or in a fragmentary way)
pied [paɪd]	*adj.* 杂色的(of two or more colors in blotches) 记 联想记忆：pie(馅饼) + d → 馅饼中放各种颜色的菜 → 杂色的
pierce [pɪrs]	*v.* 刺穿(to run into or through; stab)；穿透(to force through) 记 联想记忆：r 从一片(piece)中穿过 → 刺穿
pigment [ˈpɪgmənt]	*n.* 天然色素(a coloring matter in animals and plants)；粉状颜料(a powdered substance that imparts colors to other materials)
pilfer [ˈpɪlfər]	*v.* 偷窃(to steal in small quantities) 同 filch, pinch
pillage [ˈpɪlɪdʒ]	*n.* 抢劫，掠夺(looting; plundering; ravage) *v.* 抢夺(to plunder ruthlessly) 记 来自 pill(v. 抢劫)
pilot [ˈpaɪlət]	*n.* 飞行员(one who operates the controls of an aircraft)；领航员(the person who is licensed to guide ships through a canal, the entrance to a harbour, etc.)
pinch [pɪntʃ]	*v.* 捏，掐(to compress; squeeze) *n.* 一撮，少量(a very small amount) 记 联想记忆：p + inch(英寸) → 以英寸计量的 → 一撮
piquant [ˈpiːkənt]	*adj.* 辛辣的，开胃的(agreeably stimulating to the palate; spicy)；刺激的(engagingly provocative)

36

pique	*n.* (因自尊心受伤害而导致的)不悦，愤怒 (resentment) *v.* 激怒 (to arouse
[piːk]	anger or resentment；irritate)
	记 词根记忆：piqu(刺激) + e → 因受刺激而不悦 → 不悦，愤怒
pirate	*n.* 海盗；剽窃者 (one who commits piracy) *v.* 盗印 (to reproduce without
['paɪrət]	authorization in infringement of copyright)；掠夺 (to take or appropriate by
	piracy)
	记 词根记忆：pir(=per 试验；冒险) + ate → 冒险去拿他人的东西 → 掠夺
pirouette	*n.* (舞蹈)脚尖着地的旋转 (a full turn on the toe in ballet)
[ˌpɪru'et]	记 词根记忆：pirou(转) + ette(小动作) → 小转 → 脚尖着地的旋转
piscatorial	*adj.* 捕鱼的，渔业的 (dependent on fishing；piscatory)
[ˌpɪskə'tɔːriəl]	记 来自 piscator(*n.* 捕鱼人)
piteous	*adj.* 可怜的 (of a kind to move to pity or compassion)
['pɪtiəs]	同 pathetic
pith	*n.* 精髓，要点 (the essential part；core)
[pɪθ]	
pithiness	*n.* 简洁 (state of being precisely brief)
['pɪθinəs]	记 来自 pithy(*adj.* 精练的)
pitiless	*adj.* 无情的，冷酷的，无同情心的 (devoid of pity)
['pɪtiləs]	同 cruel, harsh
pittance	*n.* 微薄的薪俸，少量的收入 (a meager monetary allowance, wage, or
['pɪtns]	remuneration)；少量 (a very small amount)
pivot	*n.* 枢轴，中心 *v.* 旋转 (to turn on as if on a pivot)
['pɪvət]	
placard	*n.* 招贴，布告 *v.* 张贴布告
['plækɑːrd]	同 poster
plagiarize	*v.* 剽窃，抄袭 (to take(sb. else's ideas, words. etc) and use them as if they
['pleɪdʒəraɪz]	were one's own)
	记 词根记忆：plagi(斜的) ar + ize → 做歪事 → 剽窃，抄袭
plague	*n.* 瘟疫 (fatal epidemic disease)；讨厌的人 (nuisance) *v.* 烦扰 (to disturb
[pleɪg]	or annoy persistently)
	例 One of the great killers until barely 50 years ago, tuberculosis
	("consumption" as it was then named) seemed a scourge or *plague*
	rather than the long-term chronic illness it was.
plain	*adj.* 简单的 (simple)；清楚的 (clear)；不漂亮的，不好看的 (lacking beauty
[pleɪn]	or distinction) *n.* 平原 (a large stretch of flat land)
	例 According to the Senator, it was not hypocrisy for a politician in search
	of votes to compliment a mother on the beauty of her *plain* child; it was
	merely sound political common sense.
plait	*n.* 发辫 (a braid of hair) *v.* 编成辫
[plæt]	同 pigtail

394

□ pique	□ pirate	□ pirouette	□ piscatorial	□ piteous	□ pith
□ pithiness	□ pitiless	□ pittance	□ pivot	□ placard	□ plagiarize
□ plague	□ plain	□ plait			

plangent [ˈplændʒənt]	*adj.* 轰鸣的；凄凉的（having a plaintive quality） 记 来自拉丁文 plangere，意为"拍打胸脯以示哀痛"
plank [plæŋk]	*n.* 厚木板（a heavy thick board）；要点（a principal item of a policy or program） *v.* 铺板（to cover, build, or floor with planks）
plaster [ˈplæstər]	*n.* 灰泥，石膏（a pasty composition）*v.* 抹灰泥 记 词根记忆：plas（形式）+ ter → 塑造成墙的东西 → 灰泥
plateau [plæˈtoʊ]	*n.* 高原（tableland）；平稳时期（a relatively stable period） 记 词根记忆：plat（平的）+ eau → 平稳时期
platonic [pləˈtɑːnɪk]	*adj.* 理论的（theoretical）；精神上的，纯友谊的（(of love or a friendship between two people) close and deep but not sexual） 记 来自哲学家柏拉图（Plato）
plaudit [ˈplɔːdɪt]	*v.* 喝彩，赞扬（to praise; approve enthusiastically） 记 词根记忆：plaud（鼓掌）+ it → 喝彩，赞扬
plaza [ˈplæzə]	*n.* 广场（a public square）；集市（shopping center） 记 来自拉丁语 platea，意为"庭院；宽敞的大街"
plead [pliːd]	*v.* 辩护（to offer as a plea in defense）；恳求（to appeal） 记 来自 plea（*n.* 恳求；辩护） 例 In their preface, the collection's editors *plead* that certain of the important articles they omitted were published too recently for inclusion, but in the case of many such articles, this excuse is not valid.
pleat [pliːt]	*n.* （衣服上的）褶（a fold in cloth） 记 来自 plait（*v.* 打褶；编辫子）
plebeian [pləˈbiːən]	*n.* 平民 *adj.* 平民的（of the common people）；平庸的，粗俗的（common or vulgar） 搭 plebeian tastes 庸俗的趣味
pledge [pledʒ]	*n.* 誓言，保证（a solemn promise）*v.* 发誓（to vow to do sth.） 同 commitment, swear
plenary [ˈpliːnəri]	*adj.* 全体出席的；完全的，绝对的，无限的 记 词根记忆：plen（满）+ ary → 满的 → 完全的
plenitude [ˈplenɪtuːd]	*n.* 完全（completeness）；大量（a great sufficiency） 记 词根记忆：plen（满）+ itude → 大量
plentitude [ˈplentɪtuːd]	*n.* 充分（the quality or state of being full） 记 词根记忆：plen（满）+ titude → 充分
pleonastic [ˌpliːəˈnæstɪk]	*adj.* 冗言的（using more words than necessary） 记 词根记忆：pleon（太多）+ astic → 太多的话 → 冗言的
plod [plɑːd]	*v.* 沉重地走（to walk heavily; trudge）；辛勤工作（to drudge）*n.* 艰难行进（the act of moving or walking heavily and slowly）
plough [plaʊ]	(= plow) *n.* 犁 *v.* 犁地 搭 snow plough 铲雪机

ploy [plɔɪ]	*n.* 花招，策略（a tactic；stratagem）
plumber [ˈplʌmər]	*n.* 管子工，铅管工（a person whose job is to fit and repair water pipes or bathroom apparatus）
plummet [ˈplʌmɪt]	*v.* 垂直或突然落下（to fall perpendicularly or abruptly） 记 plummet 原意为"测深锤"
plunder [ˈplʌndər]	*v.* 抢劫，掠夺（to take the goods by force；pillage） 记 联想记忆：pl(看作 place，放) + under(在…下面) → 放在自己下面 → 抢劫
pluralist [ˈplʊrəlɪst]	*n.* 兼任数个宗教职位者，兼职者（a person who holds two or more offices, especially two or more benefices, at the same time）
plush [plʌʃ]	*adj.* 豪华的（notably luxurious）
poach [poʊtʃ]	*v.* 偷猎，窃取（to catch without permission on sb. else's property） 搭 poach ideas from sb. 将某人的思想窃为已有
pod [pɑːd]	*n.* 豆荚 *v.* 剥掉(豆荚)（to take peas out of pods） 搭 like as peas in a pod 一模一样，酷似
podiatrist [pəˈdaɪətrɪst]	*n.* 足病医生（chiropodist） 记 词根记忆：pod(足，脚) + iatr(治疗) + ist → 足病医生
podium [ˈpoʊdiəm]	*n.* 讲坛，(乐队的)指挥台（a base especially for an orchestral conductor） 记 词根记忆：pod(脚) + ium → 站脚的地方 → 讲坛
poignancy [ˈpɔɪnjənsi]	*n.* 辛辣，尖锐（the quality or state of being poignant）
poisonous [ˈpɔɪzənəs]	*adj.* 有毒的（containing poison）；有害的（harmful） 同 venomous
poke [poʊk]	*v.* 刺，戳（to prod；stab；thrust） 搭 poke fun at 嘲弄，戏弄
polemic [pəˈlemɪk]	*n.* 争论，论战（an aggressive attack or refutation） 记 词根记忆：polem(战争) + ic → 争论，论战
polemical [pəˈlemɪkl]	*adj.* 引起争论的，好辩的（controversial；disputatious）
poll [poʊl]	*n.* 民意调查（a survey of the public opinion）；投票选举（voting in an election）
pollster [ˈpoʊlstər]	*n.* 民意调查员（one that conducts a poll） 记 联想记忆：poll(民意调查) + st + er(人) → 民意调查员
polymath [ˈpɑːlimæθ]	*n.* 博学者（a person of encyclopedic learning） 记 词根记忆：poly(多) + math(学习) → 学得多 → 博学者

poncho [ˈpɑːntʃoʊ]	*n.* 斗篷（a blanket worn as a sleeveless garment）；雨披（a waterproof garment）
ponder [ˈpɑːndər]	*v.* 仔细考虑，衡量（to weigh in the mind；reflect on） 记 词根记忆：pond(重量) + er → 掂重量 → 仔细考虑，衡量
ponderable [ˈpɔndərəbl]	*adj.* 可估量的（able to be assessed；appreciable）
pontifical [pɑːnˈtɪfɪkl]	*adj.* 教皇的（of or relating to a pontiff or pontifex）；自负的（pretentious；pompous）；武断的（dogmatic）
poohed [puːd]	*adj.* 疲倦的（worn；tired）
pool [puːl]	*n.* 资源的集合（a grouping of resources for the common advantage of the participants）；可共享的物资（a readily available supply）
portentous [pɔːrˈtentəs]	*adj.* 凶兆的（ominous） 记 来自 portent（*n.* 预兆，凶兆）
posit [ˈpɑːzɪt]	*v.* 断定，认定（to assume or affirm the existence of；postulate） 记 通过 position（*n.* 位置，立场）来反推 posit
positiveness [ˈpɑːzətɪvnəs]	*n.* 肯定，确信 记 来自 positive（*adj.* 肯定的）
poster [ˈpoʊstər]	*n.* 海报，招贴画（a large placard displayed in a public place） 记 联想记忆：post(邮寄；张贴)+er → 海报，招贴画
postiche [pɔˈstiːʃ]	*adj.* 伪造的，假的（false；sham）*n.* 伪造品（sth. false；a sham）；假发（a small hairpiece；a toupee）
potation [pəʊˈteɪʃn]	*n.* 喝，饮（the act of drinking or inhaling）；饮料，酒（an alcoholic drink）
potboiler [ˈpɑːtbɔɪlər]	*n.* 粗制滥造的文艺作品（a literary or artistic work of poor quality, produced quickly for profit） 记 来自 potboil（*v.* 为混饭吃而粗制滥造）
potentate [ˈpoʊtnteɪt]	*n.* 统治者，君主（ruler；sovereign） 记 词根记忆：pot(有力的) + ent + ate(人) → 有力量的人 → 统治者
potentiate [pəʊˈtenʃieɪt]	*v.* 加强，强化（to make effective or active）
pother [ˈpɔðə]	*n.* 喧扰，骚动（confused or fidgety flurry or activity）*v.* 烦恼（to put into a pother）
potpourri [ˌpoʊpʊˈriː]	*n.* 混杂物，杂烩（a miscellaneous collection；medley） 记 联想记忆：pot(锅) + pour(倾倒)+ri → 倒在一个锅里 → 混杂物
pouch [paʊtʃ]	*n.* 小袋 *v.* 使成袋状；将(某物)装入袋内

36

□ poncho	□ ponder	□ ponderable	□ pontifical	□ poohed	□ pool
□ portentous	□ posit	□ positiveness	□ poster	□ postiche	□ potation
□ potboiler	□ potentate	□ potentiate	□ pother	□ potpourri	□ pouch

pound [paʊnd]	*v.* 猛击，连续重击(to strike heavily or repeatedly)；(心脏)狂跳，怦怦地跳(to pulsate rapidly and heavily)
prance [præns]	*v.* 昂首阔步(to move about proudly and confidently) 记 联想记忆：那个法国(France)人昂首阔步(prance)地走在大街上
prank [præŋk]	*n.* 恶作剧，玩笑(a trick) 记 注意不要和 plank(*n.* 厚木板)相混
prate [preɪt]	*v.* 瞎扯，唠叨(to talk long and idly；chatter) 记 和 prattle(*v.* 闲聊)一起记
preach [priːtʃ]	*v.* 布道，讲道(to deliver a sermon) 记 联想记忆：p(看作 priest，牧师) + reach(到达) → 牧师到达 → 布道，讲道
preamble [priˈæmbl]	*n.* 前言，序言(an introductory statement)；先兆(an introductory factor or circumstance indicating what is to follow) 记 联想记忆：pre(在…之前) + amble(缓行，漫步) → 走在前面 → 前言
precept [ˈpriːsept]	*n.* 箴言，格言；规则(moral instruction；rule or principle that teaches correct behavior) 记 词根记忆：pre(预先) + cept(拿住) → 预先接受的话 → 格言
precocious [prɪˈkoʊʃəs]	*adj.* 早熟的(premature) 记 词根记忆：pre(预先) + coc(煮) + ious → 提前煮好的 → 早熟的
predilection [ˌpredlˈekʃn]	*n.* 偏爱，嗜好(a special liking that has become a habit) 记 联想记忆：pre + dilection(看作 direction，趋向) → 兴趣的趋向 → 偏爱，嗜好
preen [priːn]	*v.* (鸟用嘴)整理羽毛((of a bird) to clean or smooth its feathers (with its beak))；(人)打扮修饰(to dress up；primp) 记 和 green(*n.* 绿色)一起记
prefigure [ˌpriːˈfɪɡjər]	*v.* 预示(to show, suggest, or announce by an antecedent type)；预想(to foresee) 记 联想记忆：pre(提前) + figure(形象) → 提前想好形象 → 预想
prehensile [prɪˈhensl]	*adj.* 能抓住东西的，缠绕的(capable of grasping or holding) 记 词根记忆：prehens(=prehend 抓住) + ile(能…的) → 能抓住东西的
prelude [ˈpreljuːd]	*n.* 序幕，前奏(an introductory performance, action, or event) 记 词根记忆：pre(在…之前) + lud(表演) + e → 表演之前 → 序幕，前奏
premiere [prɪˈmɪr]	*n.* (电影、戏剧等)首次公演(a first performance or exhibition) 记 来自 premier(*adj.* 首要的；最早的)
premium [ˈpriːmiəm]	*n.* 保险费(the consideration paid for a contract of insurance)；奖金(a reward or recompense) 记 词根记忆：pre(在…之前) + m(=empt 拿；买) + ium → 提前买下的东西 → 保险费
preponderant [prɪˈpɑːndərənt]	*adj.* 占优势的，突出的，压倒性的(having superior weight, force, or influence) 记 词根记忆：pre(在…之前) + pond(重量) + er + ant → 重量超过前面 → 压倒性的
preponderate [prɪˈpɑːndəreɪt]	*v.* 超过，胜过(to exceed) 记 词根记忆：pre(在…之前) + pond(重量) + er + ate → 重量超过前面 → 超过，胜过

☐ pound	☐ prance	☐ prank	☐ prate	☐ preach	☐ preamble
☐ precept	☐ precocious	☐ predilection	☐ preen	☐ prefigure	☐ prehensile
☐ prelude	☐ premiere	☐ premium	☐ preponderant	☐ preponderate	

prepossessing [ˌpriːpə'zesɪŋ]	*adj.* 给人好感的(tending to create a favorable impression; attractive) 记 联想记忆: pre(预先) + possess(拥有) + ing → 预先就拥有了情感 → 给人好感的
preposterous [prɪ'pɑːstərəs]	*adj.* 荒谬的(contradictory to nature or common sense; absurd) 记 联想记忆: pre(前) + post(后) + erous → "前、后"两个前缀放在一起了 → 荒谬的
presage 	['presɪdʒ] *n.* 预感(an intuition or feeling of the future) [prɪ'seɪdʒ] *v.* 预示(to foreshadow; foretell) 记 联想记忆: pre(预先) + sage(智者; 智慧) → 预感
prescience ['presɪəns]	*n.* 预知, 先见(foreknowledge of events) 记 词根记忆: pre(预先) + sci(知道) + ence → 预知, 先见
presentation [ˌpriːzen'teɪʃn]	*n.* 介绍, 描述(the way in which sth. is shown to others) 记 来自 present(*v.* 介绍; 提出; 显示)
presentiment [prɪ'zentɪmənt]	*n.* 预感(a feeling that sth. will or is about to happen) 记 词根记忆: pre(预先) + sent(感觉) + iment → 预感
preside [prɪ'zaɪd]	*v.* 担任主席(to act as president or chairman); 负责(to be in charge of); 指挥(to exercise control) 记 词根记忆: pre(在…之前) + sid(坐) + e → 坐在前面 → 指挥
pressing ['presɪŋ]	*adj.* 紧迫的, 迫切的(urgently important); 恳切要求的(asking for sth. strongly)
prestige [pre'stiːʒ]	*n.* 威信, 威望(respect based on good reputation, past achievements, etc); 影响力 记 联想记忆: pres(看作 president, 总统) + tige(看作 tiger, 老虎) → 总统和老虎两者都是有威信、威望的 → 威信, 威望
presumption [prɪ'zʌmpʃn]	*n.* 放肆, 傲慢(presumptuous attitude or conduct); 假定(assumption) 记 来自 presume(*v.* 推测, 认定)
presupposition [ˌpriːsʌpə'zɪʃn]	*n.* 预想, 臆测(the act of supposing beforehand) 记 联想记忆: pre(预先) + supposition(假定, 推测) → 预先推测 → 预想, 臆测
pretence ['priːtens]	*n.* 假装(mere ostentation); 借口(pretext) 记 词根记忆: pre(预先) + tenc(=tens 伸展) + e → 预先伸展开来 → 假装
pretension [prɪ'tenʃn]	*n.* 自负, 骄傲(pretentiousness); 要求, 主张 记 联想记忆: pre(预先) + tension(紧张, 压力) → 预先感到了压力 → 要求, 主张
pretext ['priːtekst]	*n.* 借口(a purpose or motive assumed in order to cloak the real intention) 记 联想记忆: pre(预先) + text(课文) → 预先想好的文章 → 借口
prevaricate [prɪ'værɪkeɪt]	*v.* 支吾其词, 搪塞(to deviate from the truth; equivocate) 记 词根记忆: pre(预先) + varic(观望) + ate → 预先观望 → 搪塞
preview ['priːvjuː]	*n.* 预演, 预展(a private showing before shown to the general public) *v.* 预演, 预先查看 记 联想记忆: pre(预先) + view(观看) → 预先看到的演出 → 预演

36

| **prevision** [priˈviʒən] | *n.* 预知，先见(foresight; prescience) |
| | 记 词根记忆：pre(预先) + vis(看) + ion → 预先看到的 → 先见 |

prey [preɪ]	*n.* 被捕食的动物(an animal taken by a predator as food)；受害者
	记 联想记忆：心中暗自祈祷(pray)不要成为受害者(prey)
	例 The natural balance between *prey* and predator has been increasingly disturbed, most frequently by human intervention.

prey

prime [praɪm]	*n.* 全盛时期(the most active, thriving, or satisfying state or period) *adj.* 首先的(original)；主要的；最好的(first in rank, authority, or significance)
	记 词根记忆：prim(最早的) + e → 主要的
	例 The *Prime* Minister tried to act but the plans were frustrated by her cabinet.

| **privation** [praɪˈveɪʃn] | *n.* 匮乏，贫困(lack of what is needed for existence) |
| | 记 词根记忆：priv(分开) + ation → 人财两分 → 贫困 |

| **privilege** [ˈprɪvəlɪdʒ] | *n.* 特权，特殊利益(a right granted as a peculiar benefit, advantage, or favor) |
| | 记 词根记忆：priv(分开；个人) + i + leg(法律) + e → 在法律上将人分等级 → 特权 |

| **probe** [proʊb] | *v.* 调查，探测(to search into and explore) |
| | 记 词根记忆：prob(检查，试验) + e → 调查，探测 |

| **proceeds** [ˈproʊsiːdz] | *n.* 收入(the total amount brought in)；实收款项(the net amount received after deduction of any discount or charges) |

| **procession** [prəˈseʃn] | *n.* 行列(a group of individuals moving along in an orderly way)；列队行进(continuous forward movement) |
| | 记 词根记忆：pro(向前) + cess(走) + ion → 列队行进 |

| **proclaim** [prəˈkleɪm] | *v.* 宣告，公布(to declare officially)；显示，表明(to show clearly) |
| | 记 词根记忆：pro(在前) + claim(叫，喊) → 在前面喊 → 宣告，公布 |

| **procrastinate** [proʊˈkræstɪneɪt] | *v.* 耽搁，拖延(to put off intentionally and habitually) |
| | 记 词根记忆：pro(向前) + crastin(明天) + ate → 直到明天再干 → 拖延 |

| **procrustean** [ˌproʊˈkrʌstɪən] | *adj.* 强求一致的(marked by arbitrary often ruthless disregard of individual differences or special circumstances) |
| | 记 源自 Procrustes(希腊神话中的巨人)，抓到人后，缚之床榻，体长者截下肢，体短者拔之使与床齐长 |

| **profane** [prəˈfeɪn] | *v.* 亵渎，玷污(to treat with abuse; desecrate) |
| | 记 联想记忆：pro(在前) + fane(神庙) → 在神庙前(做坏事) → 亵渎 |

| **proffer** [ˈprɑːfər] | *v.* 奉献，贡献(to present for acceptance; offer)；提议，建议(to offer suggestion) *n.* 赠送，献出 |
| | 记 联想记忆：pr(o)(向前) + offer(提供) → 向前提供 → 奉献 |

| **profiteer** [ˌprɑːfəˈtɪr] | *n.* 奸商，牟取暴利者(one who makes an unreasonable profit) |
| | 记 联想记忆：profit(利润) + eer(人) → 只顾利益之人 → 奸商 |

profligate [ˈprɑːflɪgət]	*adj.* 挥霍的，浪费的（wildly extravagant）*n.* 恣意挥霍者 记 词根记忆：pro（向前）+ flig（拉）+ ate → 使向前拉了许多 → 挥霍的
progenitor [prouˈdʒenɪtər]	*n.* 祖先（an ancestor in the direct line；forefather） 记 词根记忆：pro（前）+ gen（产生）+ itor → 生在前面的人 → 祖先
progeny [ˈprɑːdʒəni]	*n.* 后代，子孙（descendants） 记 词根记忆：pro（前）+ gen（产生）+ y → 前人所生下的 → 后代
prognosis [prɑːgˈnousɪs]	*n.* 【医】（对病情的）预断，预后（forecast of the likely course of a disease or an illness） 记 词根记忆：pro（前）+ gno（知道）+ sis → 先知道 → 预后
prognosticate [prəgˈnɑːstɪkeɪt]	*v.* 预言，预示（to foretell from signs or symptoms；predict） 记 词根记忆：pro（提前）+ gno（知道）+ stic + ate → 预示
projectile [prəˈdʒektl]	*n.* 抛射体（a body projected by external force） 记 词根记忆：pro（向前）+ ject（扔）+ ile → 扔向前的东西 → 抛射体
projection [prəˈdʒekʃn]	*n.* 突起物，隆起物；设计，规划（the forming of a plan）；发射，投射 同 scheming
projector [prəˈdʒektər]	*n.* 电影放映机，幻灯机（an apparatus for projecting films or pictures onto a surface）
prolix [ˈproulɪks]	*adj.* 说话啰嗦的，冗长的（unduly prolonged） 同 wordy
prologue [ˈproulɔːg]	*n.* 开场白；序言；序幕 记 词根记忆：pro（在前）+ log（话语）+ ue → 前面说的话 → 开场白
promenade [ˌprɑːməˈneɪd]	*n.* 散步，开车兜风（a leisurely walk or ride for pleasure or display）*v.* 散步，开车兜风 记 词根记忆：pro（向前）+ men（to lead）+ ade → 引着自己向前 → 散步，开车兜风
prominent [ˈprɑːmɪnənt]	*adj.* 显著的（noticeable）；著名的（widely and popularly known） 记 词根记忆：pro（向前）+ min（伸出）+ ent → 向前伸出 → 显著的；著名的
promissory [ˈprɑːmɪsəri]	*adj.* 允诺的，约定的（containing or conveying a promise or assurance） 搭 promissory note 本票，期票

□ profligate □ progenitor □ progeny □ prognosis □ prognosticate □ projectile
□ projection □ projector □ prolix □ prologue □ promenade □ prominent
□ promissory

401

prompt [prɑ:mpt]	*v.* 促进，激起(to move to action; incite) *adj.* 敏捷的，迅速的(quick) 记 词根记忆：pro(向前) + mpt(=empt 拿，抓) → 提前拿 → 促进，激起
prong [prɔ:ŋ]	*v.* 刺，贯穿(to stab, pierce, or break up with a pronged device) *n.* 叉子，尖齿；齿状物
prop [prɑ:p]	*n.* 支撑物，支柱(support) *v.* 支持(to support) 同 strengthen, sustain
prophecy ['prɑ:fəsi]	*n.* 预言(a statement telling sth. that will happen in the future)
prophet ['prɑ:fit]	*n.* 先知，预言者(a person who claims to be able to tell the course of future events)
propulsion [prə'pʌlʃn]	*n.* 推进力(power or force to propel) 记 词根记忆：pro(向前) + puls(跳动，推动) + ion → 向前推 → 推进力
prorogue [prəu'rəug]	*v.* 休会(to suspend a legislative session)；延期(to postpone; adjourn) 记 词根记忆：pro(前面) + rog(问) + ue → 在前面通知下次开会(的日期) → 休会
prosecution [ˌprɑ:sɪ'kju:ʃn]	*n.* 起诉，检举(the act or process of prosecuting)；进行，经营(carrying out or being occupied with sth.) 记 来自 prosecute(*v.* 起诉，检举)
prosperity [prɑ:'sperəti]	*n.* 繁荣(state of being successful)；幸运(state of good fortune) 记 词根记忆：pro(前面) + sper(希望) + ity → 希望就在前方 → 繁荣 例 Paradoxically, England's colonization of North America was undermined by its success: the increasing *prosperity* of the colonies diminished their dependence upon, and hence their loyalty to, their home country.
prosperous ['prɑ:spərəs]	*adj.* 繁荣的，兴旺的(marked by success or economic well-being)
protagonist [prə'tægənist]	*n.* 倡导者，拥护者(proponent) 记 词根记忆：prot(首先) + agon(打，行动) + ist → 首先行动者 → 倡导者
protean ['proutiən]	*adj.* 变化多端的，多变的(continually changing) 同 versatile
protocol ['proutəkɔ:l]	*n.* 外交礼节(official etiquette)；协议，草案(an original draft of a document or transaction) 记 词根记忆：proto(首要的) + col(胶水) → 礼节很重要，把人凝聚到一起 → 外交礼节
protuberance [prou'tu:bərəns]	*n.* 突起，突出 记 词根记忆：pro(向前) + tuber(块茎) + ance → 像块茎一样突出 → 突起，突出
protuberant [prou'tu:bərənt]	*adj.* 突出的，隆起的(thrusting out; prominent) 记 词根记忆：pro(向前) + tuber(块茎) + ant → 像块茎一样突出的 → 突出的
provenance ['prɑ:vənəns]	*n.* 出处，起源(origin; source) 记 词根记忆：pro(前面) + ven(来) + ance → 前面来的东西 → 起源

☐ prompt ☐ prong ☐ prop ☐ prophecy ☐ prophet ☐ propulsion
☐ prorogue ☐ prosecution ☐ prosperity ☐ prosperous ☐ protagonist ☐ protean
☐ protocol ☐ protuberance ☐ protuberant ☐ provenance

proverbially [prə'vɜːrbiəli]	*adv.* 人皆尽知地 记 来自 proverb(*n.* 谚语)
providential [ˌprɑːvɪ'denʃl]	*adj.* 幸运的(fortunate); 适时的(happening as if through divine intervention; opportune)
prowess ['praʊəs]	*n.* 勇敢(distinguished bravery); 非凡的才能(extraordinary ability) 记 来自 prow(*adj.* 〈古〉英勇的)
prowl [praʊl]	*v.* 潜行, 悄悄踱步(to roam through stealthily) *n.* 四处觅食, 徘徊 搭 on the prowl 徘徊; 寻找
prude [pruːd]	*n.* 拘守礼仪的人(a person who is excessively attentive to propriety or decorum) 记 词根记忆: pr(=pro 向前) + ud(=vid 看) + e → 事先看 → 拘守礼仪的人
prune [pruːn]	*n.* 西梅干(a plum dried without fermentation) *v.* 修剪（树木等)(to cut away what is unwanted)
pry [praɪ]	*v.* 刺探(to make inquiry curiously); 撬开(to pull apart with a lever) *n.* 撬杠, 杠杆 同 leverage
puerile ['pjʊrəl]	*adj.* 幼稚的(immature); 孩子气的(juvenile) 记 词根记忆: puer(=boy 男孩) + ile → 孩子气的
puffery ['pʌfəri]	*n.* 极力称赞, 夸大广告, 吹捧(exaggerated commendation especially for promotional purposes) 记 联想记忆: puff(吹嘘) + ery → 极力称赞
puissant ['pjuːsənt]	*adj.* 强大的, 有权力的(having strength; powerful) 同 influential
pulchritude ['pʌlkrɪtjuːd]	*n.* 美丽, 标致(physical comeliness) 记 词根记忆: pulchr(美丽的) + itude(状态) → 美丽, 标致
pullet ['pʊlɪt]	*n.* 小母鸡(a young hen during its first year of laying eggs) 记 联想记忆: 子弹(bullet)打中了小母鸡(pullet)
pullulate ['pʌljʊleɪt]	*v.* 繁殖(to breed or produce freely); 充满(to teem) 记 词根记忆: pullul(小动物) + ate → 生小动物 → 繁殖
pulp [pʌlp]	*n.* 果肉(a soft mass of vegetable matter); 纸浆(a material prepared in making paper)
pulpit ['pʌlpɪt]	*n.* 讲道坛(a raised platform used in preaching)
pulverize ['pʌlvəraɪz]	*v.* 使成粉末, 粉碎(to reduce to very small particles); 彻底击败(to annihilate) 记 词根记忆: pulver(粉) + ize → 使成粉末
punch [pʌntʃ]	*v.* 以拳猛击(to strike with the fist); 打孔(to make a hole; pierce) 记 发音记忆: "乓哧"(重击的声音) → 以拳猛击
punctilious [pʌŋk'tɪliəs]	*adj.* 一丝不苟的(careful) 记 词根记忆: punct(刺) + ilious → 针刺般准确 → 一丝不苟的

37

| **pundit** | *n.* 权威人士，专家(one who gives opinions in an authoritative manner) |
| [ˈpʌndɪt] | 记 pandit(*n.* 学者，专家)变体 |

| **puny** | *adj.* 弱小的，孱弱的(slight or inferior in power) |
| [ˈpjuːni] | 同 feeble |

| **purgatory** | *n.* 炼狱(a place of great suffering) |
| [ˈpɜːrɡətɔːri] | 记 联想记忆：purg(清洁的) + at + ory → 使灵魂清洁的地方 → 炼狱 |

| **purge** | *v.* 清洗，洗涤(to make free of sth. unwanted) |
| [pɜːrdʒ] | 记 词根记忆：purg(清洁的) + e → 清洗，洗涤 |

| **purify** | *v.* 使纯净，净化(to make pure) |
| [ˈpjʊrɪfaɪ] | 记 词根记忆：pur(纯洁的) + ify → 使纯净，净化 |

| **purloin** | *v.* 偷窃(to appropriate wrongfully; steal) |
| [pɜːrˈlɔɪn] | 记 词根记忆：pur(向前，向外) + loin(=long 远) → 把别人的东西带到远方 → 偷窃；注意不要和 purlieu(*n.* 附近)相混 |

| **purported** | *adj.* 传言的，据称的(reputed; alleged) |
| [pərˈpɔːrtɪd] | 记 词根记忆：pur(向前，向外) + port(带) + ed → 带到外面的 → 传言的 |

| **purse** | *v.* 缩拢，皱起(to pucker; contract) *n.* 钱包(wallet) |
| [pɜːrs] | 搭 a deplenished purse 囊空如洗 |

| **purvey** | *v.* (大量)供给，供应(to supply as provisions) |
| [pərˈveɪ] | 记 和 survey(*v.* 测量，调查)一起记 |

| **pushy** | *adj.* 有进取心的，爱出风头的，固执己见的 (aggressive often to an objection-able degree) |
| [ˈpʊʃi] | |

| **pusillanimous** | *adj.* 胆小的(lacking courage; cowardly) |
| [ˌpjuːsɪˈlænɪməs] | 记 词根记忆：pusill(虚弱的) + anim(生命，精神) + ous → 胆小的 |

| **putative** | *adj.* 公认的，推定的(commonly accepted or supposed) |
| [ˈpjuːtətɪv] | 记 词根记忆：put(认为) + ative → 公认的 |

| **putrefy** | *v.* 使腐烂(to make putrid) |
| [ˈpjuːtrɪfaɪ] | 记 词根记忆：putr(腐烂的) + efy → 使腐烂；注意不要和 petrify(*v.* 石化)相混 |

| **putrid** | *adj.* 腐臭的(rotten) |
| [ˈpjuːtrɪd] | 同 malodorous |

quack	*n.* 冒牌医生，庸医(a pretender to medical skill) *adj.* 庸医的
[kwæk]	记 和 quick(*adj.* 快的)一起记：庸医骗完钱就很快消失
	例 The popularity of pseudoscience and *quack* medicines in the nineteenth century suggests that people were very credulous, but the gullibility of the public today makes citizens of yesterday look like hard-nosed skeptics.

| **quaff** | *v.* 痛饮，畅饮(to drink deeply) |
| [kwɑːf] | 记 发音记忆："夸父" → 夸父追日，渴急痛饮 → 痛饮，畅饮 |

404

□ pundit	□ puny	□ purgatory	□ purge	□ purify	□ purloin
□ purported	□ purse	□ purvey	□ pushy	□ pusillanimous	□ putative
□ putrefy	□ putrid	□ quack	□ quaff		

quail [kweɪl]	*v.* 畏缩，发抖，恐惧(to coil in dread or fear; cower)
	记 原意为"鹌鹑"，鹌鹑胆子较小，所以就有了"恐惧"的意思
qualm [kwɑːm]	*n.* 不安，良心的谴责(an uncomfortable feeling of uncertainty)
	记 联想记忆：捧在手掌(palms)怕丢了 → 不安(qualm)
quandary [ˈkwɑːndəri]	*n.* 困惑，进退两难，窘境(a state of perplexity or doubt; predicament)
	记 发音记忆："渴望得力" → 处于进退两难的境地，渴望得到力量 → 进退两难
queer [kwɪr]	*adj.* 奇怪的，反常的(eccentric; unconventional)
	记 和 queen(*n.* 女王)一起记
quell [kwel]	*v.* 制止，镇压(to thoroughly overwhelm)
	同 suppress
quench [kwentʃ]	*v.* 扑灭，熄灭(to put out; extinguish)；解(渴)，止(渴)
	同 slake
query [ˈkwɪri]	*v.* 质疑，疑问，询问(to question; inquiry; doubt) *n.* 问题，疑问
	记 词根记忆：que(追求) + ry → 追求答案 → 疑问
queue [kjuː]	*v.* 排队(to arrange or form in a queue) *n.* 长队(a line of persons waiting to be processed)
	记 联想记忆：q 站在前面，后面跟着 ue + ue → 长队
quibble [ˈkwɪbl]	*n.* 遁词(an evasion of the point)；吹毛求疵的反对意见或批评(a minor objection or criticism)
	记 quip(*n.* 妙语；借口)的变体
quirk [kwɜːrk]	*n.* 奇事(accident; vagary)；怪癖(a strange habit)
	例 An obvious style, easily identified by some superficial *quirk*, is properly decried as a mere mannerism, whereas a complex and subtle style resists reduction to a formula.
quondam [ˈkwɔndæm]	*adj.* 原来的，以前的(former)
quota [ˈkwoʊtə]	*n.* 定额，配额(a number or amount that has been officially fixed as someone's share)
quotidian [kwoʊˈtɪdiən]	*adj.* 每日的(occurring everyday)；平凡的(commonplace)
	记 词根记忆：quoti(每) + di(日子) + an → 每日的
	搭 quotidian behavior 日常行为
rabid [ˈræbɪd]	*adj.* 患狂犬病的(affected with rabies)；疯狂的，狂暴的(going to extreme lengths in expressing or pursuing a feeling, interest or opinion)
	记 来自 rabies(*n.* 狂犬病)
rack [ræk]	*v.* 使痛苦不堪，使受折磨(to cause great physical or mental suffering to)
	记 长距离赛跑(race)让他痛苦不堪(rack)
raff [ræf]	*n.* 大量，许多(a great deal, many)

37

☐ quail	☐ qualm	☐ quandary	☐ queer	☐ quell	☐ quench
☐ query	☐ queue	☐ quibble	☐ quirk	☐ quondam	☐ quota
☐ quotidian	☐ rabid	☐ rack	☐ raff		

rakish ['reɪkɪʃ]	*adj.* 潇洒的 (jaunty)；放荡的 (dissolute) 搭 rakish in manner 不拘小节的风格
ramble ['ræmbl]	*n.* 漫步 (a leisurely excursion for pleasure) *v.* 漫步 (to move aimlessly from place to place) 记 联想记忆：r + amble(缓行，漫步) → 漫步
rambunctious [ræm'bʌŋkʃəs]	*adj.* 骚乱的，喧闹的 (marked by uncontrollable exuberance) 记 联想记忆：ram(羊) + bunctious(看作 bumptious，傲慢的) → 像傲慢的羊一样乱叫 → 骚乱的，喧闹的
rampage 	[ræm'peɪdʒ] *v.* 乱冲乱跑 (to rush wildly about) ['ræmpeɪdʒ] *n.* 狂暴行为 (violent action or behavior) 记 联想记忆：ram(羊) + page(书页) → 羊翻书，使人怒 → 狂暴行为
rankle ['ræŋkl]	*v.* 怨恨 (to cause resentment)；激怒 (to cause anger and irritation) 记 联想记忆：ran(跑) + kle(看作 ankle，脚踝) → 跑路扭伤了脚踝 → 怒了 → 激怒
ransom ['rænsəm]	*n.* 赎金；赎身 *v.* 赎回 (to free from captivity or punishment by paying a price)
rant [rænt]	*v.* 大声责骂 (to scold vehemently)；咆哮 (to talk in a loud excited way) 搭 rant and rave (at sb./sth.) 大声地、狠狠地责备或训斥
rapacious [rə'peɪʃəs]	*adj.* 掠夺的；贪婪的 (excessively grasping or covetous) 记 词根记忆：rap(抓取) + acious → 抓得多 → 贪婪的
rapids ['ræpɪdz]	*n.* 急流，湍流 (a part of a river where the current is fast and the surface is broken by obstructions) 记 联想记忆：rapid(快速) + s → 急流，湍流
rapport [ræ'pɔːr]	*n.* 融洽，和谐 (relation marked by harmony, conformity) 记 和 support(*n.* 支持) 一起记
rapprochement [ˌræprɑːʃ'mɑːn]	*n.* 友好，友善关系的建立 (establishment of cordial relations) 记 联想记忆：r + approche(看作 approach，靠近) + ment → 靠在一起 → 友好
rapt [ræpt]	*adj.* 入迷的，全神贯注的 (engrossed; absorbed; enchanted) 记 词根记忆：rap(抓取) + t → 夺去了所有注意力 → 入迷的
rarefaction [ˌreri'fækʃn]	*n.* 稀薄 (the quality or state of being rarefied) 记 来自 rarefy (*v.* 稀薄)
rasp [ræsp]	*v.* 发出刺耳的声音 (to make a harsh noise)；锉，刮削 搭 rasp sth. away/off 锉掉某物
raspy ['ræspi]	*adj.* 刺耳的 (grating; harsh)；易怒的 (irritable)
ratification [ˌrætɪfɪ'keɪʃn]	*n.* 正式批准 (formal confirmation) 记 来自 ratify (*v.* 正式批准)
ratiocination [ˌreɪʃiousɪ'neɪʃn]	*n.* 推理，推论 (reasoning) 记 词根记忆：rat(清点) + iocination → 推理

ration [ˈræʃn]	*n.* 配给(a share of food allowed to one person for a period) *v.* 定量配给 (to limit sb. to a fixed ration) 记 词根记忆: rat(清点) + ion → 对现有物资进行清点 → 定量配给
rattle [ˈrætl]	*v.* 使发出咯咯声(to make a rapid succession of short sharp noises); 使慌乱(to make anxious and cause to lose confidence) 记 参考 rattlesnake(*n.* 响尾蛇)
ravel [ˈrævl]	*v.* 使纠缠, 纠结(to become twisted and knotted); 拆开, 拆散(to unravel) 同 entangle
ravening [ˈrævənɪŋ]	*adj.* 狼吞虎咽的(to devour greedily); 贪婪的 同 rapacious
ravenous [ˈrævənəs]	*adj.* 饥饿的(hungry); 贪婪的(rapacious) 记 来自 raven(*n.* 大乌鸦, 掠夺)
ravish [ˈrævɪʃ]	*v.* 使着迷(to overcome with emotion); 强夺(to take away by force) 记 词根记忆: rav(抓, 抢夺) + ish → 夺去注意力 → 使着迷; 注意不要和 lavish(*v.* 浪费)相混
ravishing [ˈrævɪʃɪŋ]	*adj.* 令人陶醉的(unusually attractive or striking) 记 来自 ravish(*v.* 使着迷)
razor [ˈreɪzər]	*n.* 剃刀, 刮胡刀(a keen cutting instrument for shaving) 记 来自 raze(*v.* 夷平; 抹掉)
readily [ˈredɪli]	*adv.* 乐意地(without hesitation; willingly); 容易地(without difficulty; easily) 记 来自 ready(*adj.* 乐意的, 情愿的) 例 The sheer bulk of data from the mass media seems to overpower us and drive us to synoptic accounts for an easily and *readily* digestible portion of news.
ready [ˈredi]	*adj.* 敏捷的, 迅速的(promp in reacting) 例 Broadway audiences have become inured to mediocrity and so desperate to be pleased as to make their *ready* ovations meaningless as an indicator of the quality of the production before them.
realign [ˌriːəˈlaɪn]	*v.* 重新排列(to form into new types of organization, etc.) 记 联想记忆: re(重新) + align(排列) → 重新排列
reap [riːp]	*v.* 收割, 收获(to cut and gather) 同 harvest
rebarbative [rɪˈbɑːrbətɪv]	*adj.* 令人讨厌的, 冒犯人的(repellent; irritating) 记 词根记忆: re(相对) + barb(钩子) + ative → 钩子对着别人 → 冒犯人的
rebuff [rɪˈbʌf]	*v.* 断然拒绝(to reject or criticize sharply; snub) 记 词根记忆: re(反) + buff(=puff 喷, 吹) → 反过喷气 → 断然拒绝

37

rebuttal	*n.* 反驳，反证(argument or proof that rebuts)
[rɪˈbʌtl]	记 联想记忆：re(反) + butt(顶撞) + al → 反过来顶撞 → 反驳
recall	*v.* 回想，回忆起(to bring back to the mind)；收回(to take back) *n.* 唤回
[rɪˈkɔːl]	(call to return)
	记 词根记忆：re(反) + call(喊，叫) → 唤回
recant	*v.* 撤回(声明)，放弃(信仰)(to withdraw or repudiate (a statement or
[rɪˈkænt]	belief))
	记 词根记忆：re(反) + cant(唱) → 唱反调 → 放弃(信仰)
receipt	*n.* 收到，接到(act of receiving or being received)；发票，收据(a writing
[rɪˈsiːt]	acknowledging the receiving of goods or money)
	记 来自receive(*v.* 收到)
recess	*n.* 壁凹(alcove; cleft)；休假(a suspension of business for rest and relax-
[ˈriːses]	ation)
	记 词根记忆：re(反) + cess(走) → 向内反着走 → 壁凹
recherche	*adj.* 精心挑选的；异国风味的(exotic, rare)
[ˌrəʃerˈʃeɪ]	
recipe	*n.* 食谱(a set of instructions for cooking)
[ˈresəpi]	记 词根记忆：re + cip(抓) + e → 为做饭提供抓的要点 → 食谱
reciprocal	*adj.* 相互的，互惠的(mutual; shared by both sides)
[rɪˈsɪprəkl]	搭 reciprocal banquet 答谢宴会
reckon	*v.* 推断，估计(to count; calculate)；猜想，设想(to think; suppose)
[ˈrekən]	同 estimate
recline	*v.* 斜倚，躺卧(to lie down)
[rɪˈklaɪn]	记 词根记忆：re(回) + clin(倾斜) + e → 斜回去 → 斜倚，躺卧
recollection	*n.* 记忆力(the power or action of remembering the past)；往事(sth. in one's
[ˌrekəˈlekʃn]	memory of the past)
	记 来自recollect(*v.* 回想)；re + col(一起) + lect(收集) → 回想
recombine	*v.* 重组，再结合(to combine again or anew)
[ˌriːkəmˈbaɪn]	记 联想记忆：re(重新) + combine(组合) → 重组
recompense	*v.* 报酬，赔偿(to give by way of compensation)
[ˈrekəmpens]	记 联想记忆：re(重新) + compense(补偿) → 重新补偿 → 赔偿
reconnoiter	*v.* 侦察，勘察(to make reconnaissance of)
[ˌrekəˈnɔɪtər]	记 联想记忆：re + connoiter(观察，源自法语) → 侦察，勘察
recruit	*n.* 新兵(a newly enlisted or drafted soldier)；新成
[rɪˈkruːt]	员(a newcomer) *v.* 征募，招募(to seek to enroll)
	记 词根记忆：re(重新) + cruit(=cres 成长) → 重
	新成长 → 新成员
rectitude	*n.* 诚实，正直，公正(moral integrity; righteousness)
[ˈrektɪtuːd]	记 词根记忆：rect(直的) + itude → 正直

下一个　小不点

征兵处

recruit

recumbent [rɪˈkʌmbənt]	*adj.* 斜靠的(lying down; prone); 休息的(resting) 记 词根记忆: re + cumb(躺) + ent → 斜靠的
recusant [rəˈkjuːzənt]	*n.* 拒绝服从的人(one who refuses to accept or obey established authority)
redemptive [rɪˈdemptɪv]	*adj.* 赎回的, 救赎的, 挽回的(acting to save someone from error or evil) 同 redeeming
redolent [ˈredələnt]	*adj.* 芬芳的, 芳香的(scented; aromatic) 记 词根记忆: red(=re 加强) + ol(气味) + ent → 散发出浓郁的气味 → 芳香的
redoubtable [rɪˈdaʊtəbl]	*adj.* 令人敬畏的, 可怕的(causing fear or alarm; formidable) 记 联想记忆: re(反复) + doubt(怀疑, 疑虑) + able → 行动时产生疑虑, 说明对手是可怕的, 可敬畏的 → 令人敬畏的, 可怕的
redress [rɪˈdres]	*n.* 矫正, 修正(correction; remedy) 记 联想记忆: re(重新) + dress(穿衣; 整理) → 重新整理 → 矫正, 修正
redundancy [rɪˈdʌndənsi]	*n.* 多余, 累赘; (因劳动力过剩而造成的)裁员; 人浮于事 记 本单词亦作 redundance 例 The chances that a species will persist are reduced if any vital function is restricted to a single kind of organ; *redundancy* by itself possesses an enormous survival advantage.
reek [riːk]	*v.* 发臭味(to give off an unpleasant odor); 冒烟(to give out smoke) 同 emit
reel [riːl]	*n.* 卷轴; 旋转 *v.* 卷…于轴上(to wind on a reel) 搭 a reel of film 一盘影片
refectory [rɪˈfektri]	*n.* (学院等的)餐厅, 食堂(a large room in a school or college in which meals are served) 记 来自 refection(*n.* 食品, 小吃)
refraction [rɪˈfrækʃn]	*n.* 折射(bending of a ray of light) 搭 atmosphere refraction 大气折射
refresh [rɪˈfreʃ]	*v.* 消除…的疲劳, 使精神振作(to bring back strength and freshness to) 记 联想记忆: re(重新) + fresh(新鲜的) → 使精神振作
refulgent [rɪˈfʌldʒənt]	*adj.* 辉煌的, 灿烂的(shining radiantly) 记 词根记忆: re + fulg(发光) + ent → 辉煌的, 灿烂的
refurbish [ˌriːˈfɜːrbɪʃ]	*v.* 刷新, 擦亮(to brighten or freshen up; renovate) 记 联想记忆: re + furbish(磨光, 磨亮) → 刷新, 擦亮
refute [rɪˈfjuːt]	*v.* 反驳, 驳斥(to prove wrong by argument or evidence; disprove) 记 词根记忆: re(向后) + fut(倾泻) + e → (观点等)向后倒 → 反驳, 驳斥
regime [reɪˈʒiːm]	*n.* 政权, 政治制度(government in power) 记 词根记忆: reg(统治) + ime → 政权 例 Even though political editorializing was not forbidden under the new *regime*, journalists still experienced discreet, though perceptible, governmental pressure to limit dissent.

37

□ recumbent	□ recusant	□ redemptive	□ redolent	□ redoubtable	□ redress
□ redundancy	□ reek	□ reel	□ refectory	□ refraction	□ refresh
□ refulgent	□ refurbish	□ refute	□ regime		

regress [rɪ'gres]	v. 倒退，复归，逆行 (to return to a former or a less developed state) 记 词根记忆：re(向后) + gress(行走) → 向后走 → 倒退，复归，逆行
regurgitate [rɪ'gɜːrdʒɪteɪt]	v. 涌回，流回 (to become thrown or poured back)；反胃，反刍 (to cause to pour back, especially to cast up)
rehearse [rɪ'hɜːrs]	v. 排练，预演 (to practice in order to prepare for a public performance)；详述 (to tell fully)
reincarnate [ˌriːɪn'kɑːrneɪt]	v. 使转世 (to incarnate again) 记 联想记忆：re(重新) + incarnate(化身) → 精神重新进入肉体 → 使转世
rejoice [rɪ'dʒɔɪs]	v. 欣喜，高兴 (to feel joy or great delight) 记 词根记忆：re+joic(=joy 高兴) + e → 欣喜，高兴
rejoin [ˌriː'dʒɔɪn]	v. 回答，答辩 (to say sharply or critically in response) 记 词根记忆：re(重新) + join(加入) → 重新加入讨论 → 答辩
rejoinder [rɪ'dʒɔɪndər]	n. 回答 (an answer to a reply) 同 retort
rejuvenate [rɪ'dʒuːvəneɪt]	v. 使变得年轻 (to make young or youthful again) 记 词根记忆：re + juven(年轻的) + ate → 使变得年轻
relapse [rɪ'læps]	n. 旧病复发 (a recurrence of symptoms of a disease)；再度恶化 (the act or an instance of backsliding, worsening) v. 旧病复发；再度恶化 (to slip or fall into a former worse state) 记 词根记忆：re + laps(滑) + e → (身体状况)再次下滑 → 再度恶化
relent [rɪ'lent]	v. 变温和，变宽厚 (to become compassionate or forgiving)；减弱 (to soften; mollify) 记 词根记忆：re + lent(柔软的) → 心肠软了下来 → 变温和，变宽厚
reliance [rɪ'laɪəns]	n. 信赖，信任 (the state of being dependent on or having confidence in) 记 来自 rely(v. 依赖) 例 The success of science is due in great part to its emphasis on objectivity: the *reliance* on evidence rather than preconceptions and the willingness to draw conclusions even when they conflict with traditional beliefs.
relic ['relɪk]	n. 遗物，遗迹，遗风 (a survivor or remnant left after decay, disintegration, or disappearance)
remainder [rɪ'meɪndər]	n. 剩余物 (the part of sth. that is left over) 记 来自 remain(v. 保留) 例 Because we have completed our analysis of the major components of the proposed project, we are free to devote the *remainder* of this session to a study of the project's incidental details.
remains [rɪ'meɪnz]	n. 残余，遗迹 (a remaining part or trace) 记 来自 remain(v. 保持)
remand [rɪ'mænd]	v. 遣回 (to send back)；召回 (to order back) 记 词根记忆：re(重新，又) + mand(命令) → 命令回来 → 遣回

reminder [rɪˈmaɪndər]	*n.* 提醒物，纪念品（sth. that makes one remember） 记 来自动词 remind(*v.* 提醒）；注意不要与 remainder(*n.* 剩余物）相混 例 Charlotte Salomon's biography is a ***reminder*** that the currents of private life, however diverted, dislodged, or twisted by overpowering public events, retain their hold on the individual recording them.
reminisce [ˌremɪˈnɪs]	*v.* 追忆，回想（to indulge in reminiscence） 记 词根记忆：re(重新) + min(=mind 思维) + isce → 重新回到思维中 → 追忆
remission [rɪˈmɪʃn]	*n.* 宽恕，豁免（the act or process of remitting） 记 词根记忆：re(向后) + miss(送) + ion → 送回去 → 宽恕

And gladly would learn, and gladly teach.
勤于学习的人才能乐于施教。

——英国诗人 乔叟（Chaucer, British poet）

37

Word List 38  MP3-38

remit [rɪˈmɪt]	*v.* 免除(to refrain from inflicting); 宽恕(to release from the guilt or penalty of); 汇款(to send money)
remittance [rɪˈmɪtns]	*n.* 汇款(transmittal of money as to a distant place)
remonstrance [rɪˈmɑːnstrəns]	*n.* 抗议, 抱怨(an earnest presentation of reasons for opposition or grievance) 记 词根记忆：re(重新) + monstr(显现) + ance → 一再表示对别人的不满 → 抗议, 抱怨
remonstrate [rɪˈmɑːnstreɪt]	*v.* 抗议(to earnestly present and urge reasons in opposition); 告诫(to expostulate) 记 词根记忆：re(重新) + monstr(显现) + ate → 一再表示对别人的不满 → 抗议
remunerate [rɪˈmjuːnəreɪt]	*v.* 酬劳, 赔偿(to pay or compensate a person for; reward) 记 词根记忆：re(重新) + muner(礼物) + ate → 回报人礼物 → 酬劳
renal [ˈriːnl]	*n.* 肾脏的, 肾的(relating to, involving, or located in the region of the kidneys)
renascent [rɪˈnæsnt]	*adj.* 再生的, 复活的, 新生的(reborn after being forgotten) 搭 renascent herbs 多年生草本植物
rend [rend]	*v.* 撕碎, 分裂(to split or tear apart); 抢夺 (to remove from place by violence) 记 联想记忆：因为被撕碎(rend)了, 所以要修补(mend)
rendering [ˈrendərɪŋ]	*n.* 表演(performance); 翻译(translation) 记 来自 render(*v.* 表演; 翻译)
rendition [renˈdɪʃn]	*n.* 表演, 演唱(the act or result of rendering) 同 execution, interpretation, performance
renege [rɪˈniːg]	*v.* 食言, 违约(to go back on a promise or commitment) 记 词根记忆：re(反) + neg(否认) + e → 反过来不承认 → 食言, 违约
renovate [ˈrenəveɪt]	*v.* 翻新, 修复, 整修(to put back into good condition) 同 furbish, refresh, rejuvenate, renew, restore

rent [rent]	*n.* 裂缝(an opening made by rending); (意见)分歧(a split in a party; schism) 记 rent 的"租金"之意众所周知
renunciate [rɪˈnʌnsieɪt]	*v.* 放弃(to give up; abandon) 记 词根记忆: re(相反) + nunci(讲话,说出) + ate → 表达相反的意见 → 放弃
repartee [ˌrepɑːrˈtiː]	*n.* 机敏的应答(a quick and witty reply) 记 词根记忆: re(反) + part(部分) + ee → 拿出部分作为回答 → 机敏的应答
repent [rɪˈpent]	*v.* 懊悔,后悔(to feel regret or contrition) 记 词根记忆: re(重新) + pent(惩罚) + → 心灵再次受到惩罚 → 懊悔
repercussion [ˌriːpərˈkʌʃn]	*n.* 反响(a reciprocal action); 反应,影响(a widespread, indirect effect of an act or event); 回声(reflection; resonance) 记 联想记忆: re(反复) + percussion(震动) → 反复震动 → 回声
repine [rɪˈpaɪn]	*v.* 不满,抱怨(to feel or express discontent) 记 联想记忆: re(重新) + pine(憔悴) → 因苦恼、不满而憔悴 → 不满
repose [rɪˈpoʊz]	*n./v.* 休息,安眠(to lie at rest) 记 词根记忆: re(重新) + pos(放) + e → 重新(将身体)放下去 → 躺下去(睡觉) → 休息
reprehend [ˌreprɪˈhend]	*v.* 谴责,责难(to voice disapproval of; censure) 记 词根记忆: re(反) + prehend(抓住) → 反过来抓住(缺点) → 谴责
repressed [rɪˈprest]	*adj.* 被抑制的,被压抑的(suffering from suppression of the emotions)
reprieve [rɪˈpriːv]	*v.* 缓期执行(to delay the punishment of); 暂时解救(to give relief for a time) *n.* 缓刑,暂缓 记 词根记忆: re(后)+priev(=prehend 抓住) → 抓住放在后面 → 暂不执行死刑 → 缓刑
reprobate [ˈreprəbeɪt]	*v.* 非难,斥责(to condemn strongly) *adj./n.* 堕落的(人)(a person morally corrupt) 记 词根记忆: re(反)+prob(赞扬)+ate → 不赞扬 → 斥责
reproof [rɪˈpruːf]	*n.* 责备,斥责(criticism for a fault; rebuke) 同 admonishment, reprimand, reproach, scolding
repulsion [rɪˈpʌlʃn]	*n.* 厌恶,反感(very strong dislike); 排斥力(the force by which one object drives another away from it)
reputation [ˌrepjuˈteɪʃn]	*n.* 名声(good name) 例 Although he had the numerous films to his credit and a *reputation* for technical expertise, the moviemaker lacked originality; all his films were sadly derivative of the work of others.
requite [rɪˈkwaɪt]	*v.* 报答(to repay); 报复(to make retaliation) 同 avenge, redress, vindicate

38

rescission	*n.* 撤销，废除(an act of rescinding)
[rɪ'sɪʒn]	记 词根记忆：re + sciss(切) + ion → 切除 → 废除
resentment	*n.* 愤恨，怨恨(the feeling of resenting sth.)
[rɪ'zentmənt]	例 Despite the team members' *resentment* of the new coach's training rules, they tolerated them as long as he did not apply them too strictly.
resident	*n.* 居民(one who lives or has a home in a place) *adj.* 定居的，常驻的(living in a place for some length of time)
['rezɪdənt]	记 来自reside(*v.* 居住，定居)
residue	*n* 剩余(remainder; what is left behind)
['rezɪduː]	
resigned	*adj.* 顺从的，听从的(acquiescent)
[rɪ'zaɪnd]	搭 be resigned to 对…顺从的
resilience	*n.* 恢复力，弹力(the capability of a strained body to recover its size and shape after deformation caused by compressive stress)
[rɪ'zɪliəns]	记 来自resile(*v.* 弹回；恢复活力)；re(向后) + sil(跳) +e → 向后跳起 → 弹回
resound	*v.* 回响(to produce a sonorous or echoing sound)；鸣响(to be loudly and clearly heard)
[rɪ'zaʊnd]	
resourceful	*adj.* 机智的(good at finding ways to deal with difficult situations)
[rɪ'sɔːrsfl]	记 和resource(*n.* 资源)一起记
resplendent	*adj.* 华丽的，光辉的(shining brilliantly)
[rɪ'splendənt]	记 词根记忆：re(反复) + splend(发光) + ent → 不断发光的 → 光辉的
restiveness	*n.* 倔强，难以驾驭
['restɪvnəs]	记 来自restive(*adj.* 不安静的，不安宁的)
restless	*adj.* 焦躁不安的，静不下来的(unable to relax)
['restləs]	
restorative	*adj.* 恢复健康的(having power to restore)
[rɪ'stɔːrətɪv]	记 词根记忆：re(重新) + stor(储存) + ative → 重新储存能量 → 恢复健康的
restored	*adj.* 恢复的(returned to an original or regular condition)
[rɪ'stɔːrd]	
restrain	*v.* 克制，抑制(to keep under control)
[rɪ'streɪn]	记 词根记忆：re(重新) + strain(拉紧) → 重新拉紧 → 克制，抑制
resurgence	*n.* 再起，复活，再现(the return of ideas, beliefs to a state of being active)
[rɪ'sɜːrdʒəns]	记 词根记忆：re(重新) + surg(升起) + ence → 再起
retaliation	*n.* 报复(the action of returning a bad deed to someone who has done a bad deed to oneself)
[rɪˌtæli'eɪʃn]	
retard	*v.* 妨碍(to impede)；使减速(to slow down)
[rɪ'tɑːrd]	记 词根记忆：re + tard(慢的) → 使迟缓 → 妨碍
retch	*v.* 作呕，恶心(to vomit)
[retʃ]	

retention [rɪˈtenʃn]	*n.* 保留, 保持 (the act of keeping in possession or use) 记 词根记忆：re (重新) + tent (拿住) + ion → 重新拿住 → 保留
retiring [rɪˈtaɪərɪŋ]	*adj.* 过隐居生活的, 不善社交的 (reserved; shy) 记 来自 retire (*v.* 退休; 隐居); re (后) + tir (拉) + e → 向后拉 → 隐居 例 Although *retiring*, almost self-effacing in his private life, he displays in his plays and essays a strong penchant for publicity and controversy.
retort [rɪˈtɔːrt]	*v.* 反驳 (to answer by a counter argument) 记 词根记忆：re (反) + tort (扭) → 反着扭 → 反驳
retouch [ˌriːˈtʌtʃ]	*v.* 修描 (照片) (to improve a picture or photograph by adding small strokes); 润色 记 联想记忆：re + touch (用画笔轻画) → 修描 (照片); 润色
retrace [rɪˈtreɪs]	*v.* 回顾, 追溯 (to go over sth. again) 记 联想记忆：re + trace (踪迹) → 找回踪迹 → 回顾, 追溯
retreat [rɪˈtriːt]	*n.* 撤退 (withdrawal of troops); 隐居处 (a place of privacy or safety; refuge) *v.* 撤退 记 词根记忆：re (后) + treat (=tract 拉) → 向后拉 → 撤退 例 Upon realizing that his position was untenable, the general ordered his men to *retreat* to a neighboring hill.
retrench [rɪˈtrentʃ]	*v.* 节省, 紧缩开支 (to economize; cut down expenses) 记 词根记忆：re (回) + trench (切掉) → 把开支再切掉 → 节省, 紧缩开支
revenge [rɪˈvendʒ]	*n.* 报复, 报仇 (retaliation) 记 词根记忆：re (反) + veng (惩罚) + e → 反惩罚 → 报复
revenue [ˈrevənuː]	*n.* 收入, 收益 (the total income); 税收 记 词根记忆：re (回) + ven (来) + ue → 回来的东西 → 收入
reversion [rɪˈvɜːrʒn]	*n.* 恢复, 复原 (an act of returning); 逆转 (an act of turning the opposite way) 记 词根记忆：re (回) + vers (转) + ion → 转回去, 返回 → 逆转
revive [rɪˈvaɪv]	*v.* 使苏醒 (to become conscious again); 使再流行 (to come or bring back into use) 例 The corporation expects only modest increases in sales next year despite a yearlong effort to *revive* its retailing business.
revolt [rɪˈvoʊlt]	*v.* 反叛, 造反 (to renounce allegiance or subjection; rebel); 反感, 厌恶 (to turn away with disgust) 记 词根记忆：re (反) + volt (转) → 反过来转 → 反叛
revulsion [rɪˈvʌlʃn]	*n.* 厌恶, 憎恶 (a sense of utter distaste); 剧变 (a sudden or strong reaction)
rewarding [rɪˈwɔːrdɪŋ]	*adj.* 有益的, 值得的 (worth doing or having) 同 advantageous, lucrative, profitable, remunerative
rhubarb [ˈruːbɑːrb]	*n.* 【植物】大黄; 热烈的讨论, 激烈的争论 (a heated dispute or controversy)

38

ribald [ˈrɪbld]	*adj.* 下流的, 粗俗的(crude; using coarse indecent humor) 记 联想记忆: ri(拼音: 日) + bald(光秃的) → 白天光着身子 → 下流的
rife [raɪf]	*adj.* 流行的, 普遍的(prevalent to an increasing degree) 记 和life(*n.* 生命)一起记
rifle [raɪfl]	*n.* 步枪 *v.* 抢夺, 偷走(to ransack with the intent to steal) 记 发音记忆: "来福" → 来福步枪 → 步枪
rig [rɪɡ]	*v.* (用不正当手段)操纵, 垄断(to manipulate by deceptive or dishonest means)
rigor [ˈrɪɡər]	*n.* 严厉, 严格, 苛刻(severity, strictness); 严密, 精确(strict precision) 例 By identifying scientific *rigor* with a quantitative approach, researchers in the social sciences may often have limited their scope to those narrowly circumscribed topics that are well suited to quantitative methods.
rile [raɪl]	*v.* 惹恼, 激怒(to irritate; vex) 同 aggravate, annoy, exasperate, provoke
rind [raɪnd]	*n.* (瓜、果等的)外皮(hard or tough outer layer) 记 和find(*v.* 找到)一起记
rinse [rɪns]	*v.* 冲洗掉, 漂净(to cleanse by clear water)
riot [ˈraɪət]	*v.* 暴动, 闹事(to create or engage in a riot) 同 carouse, frolic, revel
riotous [ˈraɪətəs]	*adj.* 暴乱的, 狂乱的(turbulent) 同 disorderly, tumultuous, unruly, uproarious
ripen [ˈraɪpən]	*v.* 使成熟(to become or make ripe) 记 来自ripe(*adj.* 成熟的)
ripple [ˈrɪpl]	*v.* (使)泛起涟漪(to move in small waves) *n.* 波痕, 涟漪 搭 a ripple of applause/laughter 一阵阵的掌声/笑声
ritzy [ˈrɪtsi]	*adj.* 高雅的(elegant); 势利的(snobbish) 同 exclusive, refined, polished
rive [raɪv]	*v.* 撕开, 分裂(to rend or tear apart) 同 break, fracture, rift, shatter, splinter
riven [ˈrɪvn]	*adj.* 撕开的, 分裂的(split violently apart)
riveting [ˈrɪvɪtɪŋ]	*adj.* 非常精彩的, 引人入胜的(engrossing; fascinating) 例 The English novelist William Thackeray considered the cult of the criminal so dangerous that he criticized Dickens' *Oliver Twist* for making the characters in the thieves' kitchen so *riveting*.
roe [roʊ]	*n.* 鱼卵(the eggs of fish)

416

□ ribald □ rife □ rifle □ rig □ rigor □ rile
□ rind □ rinse □ riot □ riotous □ ripen □ ripple
□ ritzy □ rive □ riven □ riveting □ roe

rollicking [ˈrɑːlɪkɪŋ]	*adj.* 欢乐的，喧闹的 (noisy and jolly)
	记 联想记忆：rol(卷) + lick(舔) + ing → 把好吃的东西卷起来舔，气氛很欢乐 → 欢乐的
rotate [ˈroʊteɪt]	*v.* (使)旋转，(使)转动 (to turn round a fixed point or axis)；轮流，循环
	记 词根记忆：rot(旋转) + ate(使…) → (使)旋转，(使)转动
rote [roʊt]	*n.* 死记硬背 (a memorizing process using routine or repetition, often without full attention or comprehension)
	记 词根记忆：rot(转) + e → 摇头晃脑地转着背 → 死记硬背
rotten [ˈrɑːtn]	*adj.* 腐烂的 (having rotted)；极坏的 (very bad, wretched)
	记 来自 rot(*n./v.* 腐烂)
roughen [ˈrʌfn]	*v.* (使)变粗糙 (to make or become rough)
	记 来自 rough(*adj.* 粗糙的)
roundabout [ˈraʊndəbaʊt]	*adj.* 绕道的，迂回的 (indirect; circuitous)
	记 组合词：round(迂回地，围绕地) + about(各处，附近) → 迂回的
rout [raʊt]	*n.* 溃败 (an overwhelming defeat)
	记 联想记忆：route(道路)去掉 e → 成功的道路上一失误就会溃败 → 溃败
rove [roʊv]	*v.* 流浪，漂泊 (to wander about; roam)
	同 drift, gallivant, meander, ramble
ruckus [ˈrʌkəs]	*n.* 喧闹，骚动 (row; disturbance)
	同 commotion
rudder [ˈrʌdər]	*n.* 船舵；领导者
	记 联想记忆：最前面的奔跑者(runner)是领导者(rudder)
ruddy [ˈrʌdi]	*adj.* (脸色)红润的，红的 (having a healthy red color)
	搭 a ruddy complexion 红润的脸色
rue [ruː]	*n.* 后悔，懊悔 (repent or regret)
	同 compunction, contrition, penitence, remorse
ruffle [ˈrʌfl]	*v.* 弄皱 (to become uneven or wrinkled)；激怒 (to become disturbed or irritated) *n.* 褶皱
rumble [ˈrʌmbl]	*v.* 发出低沉的隆隆声 (to make a low heavy rolling sound)
ruminate [ˈruːmɪneɪt]	*v.* 反刍；深思 (to turn sth. over in the mind; meditate)
	同 congitate, contemplate, deliberate, ponder
rumple [ˈrʌmpl]	*v.* 弄皱，弄乱 (to make or become disheveled or tousled)
	记 联想记忆：rum(看作 room，房间)+ple(看作 people，人) → 房间里面来了好多人，把房间弄乱了 → 弄乱
rumpus [ˈrʌmpəs]	*n.* 喧闹，骚乱 (a usually noisy commotion)
	同 clamor, tumult, uproar
runic [ˈruːnik]	*adj.* 古北欧文字的；神秘的
	记 联想记忆：run(追逐) + ic(…的) → 吸引人不断追逐的 → 神秘的

ruffle

38

rupture	*n./v.* 破裂, 断裂 (to break apart or burst)
[ˈrʌptʃər]	记 词根记忆: rupt(断) + ure → 断裂
rural	*adj.* 乡村的 (characteristic of the country)
[ˈrʊrəl]	记 词根记忆: rur(乡村) + al(…的) → 乡村的
	例 This new government is faced not only with managing its economy but also with implementing new *rural* development programs to stem the flow of farm workers to the city.
ruse	*n.* 骗术, 计策 (trick to deceive; stratagem)
[ruːz]	记 联想记忆: 送玫瑰(rose)是捕获姑娘的芳心的好计策(ruse) → 骗术, 计策
	例 Although Simpson was ingenious at contriving to appear innovative and spontaneous, beneath the *ruse* he remained uninspired and rigid in his approach to problem-solving.
rustle	*v.* 发出沙沙声 (to make slight sounds like silk moving or being rubbed together)
[ˈrʌsl]	记 联想记忆: 可能来自 rush(*n.* 匆促)
ruthlessness	*n.* 无情, 冷酷, 残忍 (cruelty)
[ˈruːθləsnəs]	记 来自 ruthless(*adj.* 残忍的, 无情的)
sacrament	*n.* 圣礼, 圣事 (any of certain rites instituted by Jesus)
[ˈsækrəmənt]	记 词根记忆: sacra(神圣) + ment → 圣事
sacrilege	*n.* 亵渎, 冒犯神灵 (outrageous violation of what is sacred)
[ˈsækrəlɪdʒ]	同 blasphemy, desecration, profanation
sadden	*v.* 使悲伤, 使难过 (to make sad)
[ˈsædn]	同 deject, depress, dispirit, oppress
saddle	*n.* 鞍, 马鞍 (a seat of a rider on a horse)
[ˈsædl]	记 联想记忆: sad(非常糟糕的) + dle → 骑马没鞍可就糟了 → 马鞍
sag	*v.* 松弛, 下垂 (to lose firmness, resiliency, or vigor)
[sæg]	
salmon	*n.* 大马哈鱼; 鲜肉色 (yellowish-pink)
[ˈsæmən]	
salutation	*n.* 招呼, 致意, 致敬 (expression of greeting by words or action)
[ˌsæljuˈteɪʃn]	同 salute, welcome
salute	*v.* 行礼致敬 (to make a salute); 致意 (to greet with polite words or with a sign) *n.* 行军礼 (a military sign of recognition)
[səˈluːt]	
salve	*n.* 药膏 (oily substance used on wounds) *v.* 减轻, 缓和 (to soothe; assuage)
[sælv]	记 词根记忆: salv(救) + e → 解救的东西 → 药膏
sampler	*n.* 刺绣样品 (decorative piece of needlework typically used as an example of skill); 样品检查员 (a person who prepares or selects samples for inspection)
[ˈsæmplər]	

418

□ rupture □ rural □ ruse □ rustle □ ruthlessness □ sacrament
□ sacrilege □ sadden □ saddle □ sag □ salmon □ salutation
□ salute □ salve □ sampler

sangfroid [sɑːŋˈfrwɑː]	*n.* 沉着，冷静（cool self-possession or composure） 记 来自法语，原意为"冷血的"；sang(血) + froid(冷的) → 冷血的
sanitize [ˈsænɪtaɪz]	*v.* 使清洁（to make clean） 同 decontaminate, disinfect, sterilize
sanity [ˈsænəti]	*n.* 头脑清楚，精神健全（soundness of mind and judgement）
sardonic [sɑːrˈdɑnɪk]	*adj.* 讽刺的，嘲笑的（disdainfully sneering, ironic, or sarcastic） 记 来自 sardinian plant(撒丁岛植物)，据说人食用后会狂笑而死
sartorial [sɑːrˈtɔːriəl]	*adj.* 裁缝的，缝制的（of or relating to a tailor or tailored clothes） 记 联想记忆：sartor(裁缝) + ial → 裁缝的
sash [sæʃ]	*n.* 肩带（an ornamental band, ribbon, or scarf worn over the shoulder）
satanic [səˈtænɪk]	*adj.* 似撒旦的，魔鬼的，邪恶的（like Satan; devilish; infernal） 记 来自 Satan(撒旦，与上帝作对的魔鬼)
sate [seɪt]	*v.* 使心满意足，使厌腻（to gratify completely; glut） 记 词根记忆：sat(满的) + e → 使心满意足
satiny [ˈsætni]	*adj.* 光滑的，柔软的（smooth, soft, and glossy） 记 联想记忆：satin(缎子) + y → 像缎子一样光滑的 → 光滑的
satire [ˈsætaɪər]	*n.* 讽刺（the use of irony to expose vices） 记 源自拉丁语，意为"讽刺杂咏"，现在在英语中多指"讽刺"或"讽刺文学"
saturated [ˈsætʃəreɪtɪd]	*adj.* 渗透的，饱和的（having high saturation）；深颜色的 同 soaked
saucy [ˈsɔːsi]	*adj.* 粗鲁的（rude and impudent）；俏皮的（impertinent in an entertaining way）；漂亮的（pretty）
saunter [ˈsɔːntər]	*n./v.* 闲逛，漫步（to walk about idly; stroll） 记 联想记忆：s(看作 see) + aunt(姑姑) + er → 看姑姑去 → 闲逛而去 → 闲逛，漫步
savvy [ˈsævi]	*adj.* 有见识的，精明的（well informed and perceptive; shrewd） 同 astute, canny, perspicacious, slick
scabrous [ˈskeɪbrəs]	*adj.* 粗糙的（rough with small points or knobs; scabby） 记 联想记忆：scab(疤) + rous → 多疤的 → 粗糙的
scads [skædz]	*n.* 许多，巨额（large numbers or amounts） 搭 scads of 大量，许多
scald [skɔːld]	*v.* 烫伤，烫洗（to burn with hot liquid or steam）*n.* 烫伤（an injury caused by scalding）
scalding [ˈskɔːldɪŋ]	*adj./adv.* 滚烫的（hot enough to scald） 搭 scalding hot 灼热

38

scamp [skæmp]	*v.* 草率地做 (to perform or deal with in a hasty manner) *n.* 流氓 (rascal; rogue); 顽皮的家伙
scamper [ˈskæmpər]	*v.* 奔跑，蹦蹦跳跳 (to run nimbly and playfully about) 记 联想记忆：s(音似：死) + camper(露营者) → 露营者死(跑) → 奔跑
scan [skæn]	*v.* 审视，细看 (to examine by point-by-point observation or checking); 浏览，扫描 (to glance from point to point, often hastily); 标出格律 (to read or mark so as to show metrical structure) 记 发音记忆："死看" → 四处看 → 扫描
scandal [ˈskændl]	*n.* 丑闻；流言飞语，诽谤 (malicious or defamatory gossip) 记 联想记忆：scan(扫描) + dal → 扫描时事，揭露丑闻 → 丑闻 例 She was accused of plagiarism in a disputo over a short story, and, though exonerated, she never recovered from the accusation and the *scandal*.
scar [skɑːr]	*n.* 伤痕，伤疤 (a mark remaining on the skin from a wound) 记 联想记忆：s + car (汽车) → 被汽车撞了一下 → 留下伤痕 → 伤痕，伤疤
scare [sker]	*n./v.* 惊吓，受惊，惊恐 (to frighten especially suddenly) 记 联想记忆：s + care(照顾) → 照顾不好，受到惊吓 → 惊吓，受惊
scatter [ˈskætər]	*v.* 散开，驱散 (to separate or cause to separate widely) 同 dispel, disperse, dissipate
schematize [ˈskiːmətaɪz]	*v.* 扼要表示 (to express or depict in an outline)
scintillate [ˈsɪntɪleɪt]	*v.* 闪烁 (to emit sparks; sparkle); (言谈举止中)焕发才智 记 词根记忆：scintill(火花) + ate → 闪烁
scission [ˈsɪʒən]	*n.* 切断，分离，断开 (an action or process of cutting, dividing, or splitting) 记 词根记忆：sciss(切) + ion → 分离，断开
scissor [ˈsɪzər]	*n.* 剪刀 记 词根记忆：sciss(切) + or → 切开时所借助的工具 → 剪刀
scoff [skɔːf]	*v.* 嘲笑 (to sneer; mock); 狼吞虎咽 (to eat greedily) *n.* 嘲笑；笑柄 同 gibe, insult, jeer, taunt, twit
scorch [skɔːrtʃ]	*v.* 烤焦，烧焦 (to dry or shrivel with intense heat) 同 burn, char, sear, singe
scorching [ˈskɔːrtʃɪŋ]	*adj.* 灼热的 同 ardent, baking, boiling, fiery, sultry, torrid
scotch [skɑːtʃ]	*v.* 镇压，扑灭 (to put an end to) 记 和 Scotch(苏格兰)一起记
scowl [skaʊl]	*n.* 怒容 *v.* 生气地皱眉 (to frown angrily); 怒视 (to make a scowl) 同 glower, lower

scar

□ scamp	□ scamper	□ scan	□ scandal	□ scar	□ scare
□ scatter	□ schematize	□ scintillate	□ scission	□ scissor	□ scoff
□ scorch	□ scorching	□ scotch	□ scowl		

scraggly ['skrægli]	*adj.* 凹凸不平的(irregular in form or growth); 散乱的(unkempt)
scrape [skreɪp]	*v.* 刮，擦；擦掉(to remove from a surface by repeated strokes of an edged instrument) 记 联想记忆：scrap(碎屑) + e → 碎屑是被刮下来的 → 刮，擦
scrawl [skrɔːl]	*v.* 潦草地写，乱涂(to write awkwardly or carelessly) 记 联想记忆：s + crawl(爬) → 乱爬 → 乱涂
scribble ['skrɪbl]	*v.* 乱写，乱涂(to write and draw hastily and carelessly) 记 词根记忆：scrib(写) + ble → 乱写，乱涂
scrimp [skrɪmp]	*v.* 节省，精打细算(to economize severely) 同 pinch, scrape, skimp, stint
scripture ['skrɪptʃər]	*n.* 经文，圣典(a body of writing considered sacred or authoritative) 记 词根记忆：script(写) + ure → 写出的东西 → 经文，圣典
scruffy ['skrʌfi]	*adj.* 肮脏的，不洁的(unkempt; slovenly; shaggy) 同 decaying, dingy, scrubby, tatty
scrumptious ['skrʌmpʃəs]	*adj.* 很可口的，美味的(delightful; delicious) 记 可能来自 scrump(*v.* 偷苹果)，偷来的苹果最好吃，所以 scrumptious 有"可口的"的意思
scrutable ['skruːtəbl]	*adj.* 可以了解的，可解读的(capable of being deciphered)
scrutinize ['skruːtənaɪz]	*v.* 详细检查(to examine closely and minutely); 细读 同 inspect, observe, survey, watch
scud [skʌd]	*v.* 疾行，飞奔(to move or run swiftly)
scuff [skʌf]	*v.* 拖着脚走(to scrape the feet while walking; shuffle) 同 scuffle, shamble
scurry ['skɜːri]	*v.* 急跑，疾行(to move in a brisk pace; scamper) 记 词根记忆：s + cur(跑) + ry → 急跑
scurvy ['skɜːrvi]	*adj.* 卑鄙的，下流的(despicable) 记 不要和 scurry(*v.* 急跑，疾行)相混
scutter ['skʌtər]	*v.* 疾走，急跑(to move in or as if in a brisk pace)
seafaring ['siːferɪŋ]	*adj.* 航海的，跟航海有关的(of or relating to the use of the sea for travel or transportation) 记 来自 seafarer(*n.* 水手，海员); sea(海) + fare(过日子) + (e)r(人) → 靠海生活的人 → 水手，海员

38

Word List 39 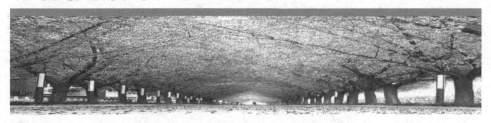 MP3 - 39

seam [siːm]	*n.* 缝，接缝（line along which two edges are joined） 参 seamstress（*n.* 女裁缝）
seamy ['siːmi]	*adj.* 丑恶的，污秽的（unpleasant; degraded; sordid） 记 联想记忆：seam(缝)+y → 裂缝里的 → 污秽的
sear [sɪr]	*v.* 烧焦（to burn or scorch with intense heat）
seasoned ['siːznd]	*adj.* 经验丰富的，老练的（experienced） 搭 seasoned soldier 老兵
secretive ['siːkrətɪv]	*adj.* 守口如瓶的（liking to keep one's thoughts） 搭 be secretive about sth. 对…守口如瓶
secure [sə'kjʊr]	*adj.* 安全的（safe）；稳固的（steady）*v.* 握紧，关牢（to hold or close tightly）；使安全（to make safe） 记 联想记忆：se(看作 see，看)+cure(治愈) → 亲眼看到治愈，确定其是安全的 → 安全的 例 Liberty is not easy, but far better to be an unfettered fox, hungry and threatened on its hill, than a well-fed canary, safe and ***secure*** in its cage.
sedulity [si'djuːliti]	*n.* 勤奋，勤勉（diligence） 记 来自 sedulous（*adj.* 孜孜不倦的）
seep [siːp]	*v.* （液体等）渗漏（to flow or pass slowly; ooze） 同 trickle
self-assertion [ˌselfə'səːrʃən]	*n.* 自作主张（the act of asserting oneself or one's own rights, claims, or opinions） 记 参考 self-consuming（*adj.* 自耗的），self-contained（*adj.* 自制的），self-content（*adj.* 自满的）
senile ['siːnaɪl]	*adj.* 衰老的（of old age） 记 词根记忆：sen(老)+ile → 衰老的
sensible ['sensəbl]	*adj.* 明智的（reasonable）；可感觉到的（noticeable） 记 词根记忆：sens(感觉)+ible → 可感觉到的 例 Human reaction to the realm of thought is often as strong as that to

sensible presences; our higher moral life is based on the fact that material sensations actually present may have a weaker influence on our action than do ideas of remote facts.

sententious [sen'tenʃəs]	*adj.* 说教的(abounding in excessive moralizing); 简要的(terse; pithy) 记 联想记忆: sentence(句子) + tious → 一句话说完 → 简要的
sentient ['sentiənt]	*adj.* 有感觉能力的(conscious of sense impressions); 意识到的(aware) 记 sent(感觉) + ient → 有感觉能力的
sentiment ['sentɪmənt]	*n.* 多愁善感(a tender feeling or emotion); 思想感情 记 词根记忆: sent(感觉) + iment → 感情丰富 → 多愁善感
sentinel ['sentɪnl]	*n.* 哨兵, 岗哨(sentry; lookout) 搭 stand sentinel 站岗, 守卫
sentry ['sentri]	*n.* 哨兵, 步兵(a soldier standing guard) 记 词根记忆: sent(感觉)+ry → 感觉灵敏的人 → 哨兵
sequacious [si'kweiʃəs]	*adj.* 盲从的(intellectually servile) 记 词根记忆: sequ(跟随)+acious(多…) → 跟随大多数的 → 盲从的
sequestrate ['siːkwəstreɪt]	*v.* 扣押, 没收(to place property in custody) 同 seclude, sequester
seraphic [sə'ræfɪk]	*adj.* 如天使般的, 美丽的(like an angel) 记 来自 seraph(*n.* 守卫上帝宝座的六翼天使)
sere [sɪr]	*adj.* 干枯的, 枯萎的(being dried and withered) 记 不要和 sear(*v.* 烧灼)相混
serenade [ˌserə'neɪd]	*n.* 夜曲(a complimentary vocal or instrumental performance) 记 词根记忆: seren(安静) + ade → 夜曲
sermon ['sɜːrmən]	*n.* 布道; 说教, 训诫 记 联想记忆: 布道(sermon)时说阿门(Amen)
serpentine ['sɜːrpəntiːn]	*adj.* 像蛇般蜷曲的, 蜿蜒的(winding or turning one way or another) 记 联想记忆: serpent(蛇) + ine → 像蛇般蜷曲的
serried ['serid]	*adj.* 密集的(crowded or pressed together; compact) 搭 serried ranks of soldiers 密集排列的士兵
settle ['setl]	*v.* 安排(to place); 决定(to decide on); 栖息(to come to rest) 记 联想记忆: set(放置)+tle → 安放, 放置 → 安排
sever ['sevər]	*v.* 断绝, 分离(to divide) 记 和 severe(*adj.* 严重的)一起记
severe [sɪ'vɪr]	*adj.* 严厉的(very serious); 剧烈的(extremely violent) 记 联想记忆: 曾经(ever)艰难(severe)的日子, 一去不复返了 例 There were contradictions in her nature that made her seem an inexplicable enigma: she was *severe* and gentle; she was modest and disdainful; she longed for affection and was cold.

serpentine

39

shabby	*adj.* 破旧的(dilapidated); 卑鄙的(despicable; contemptible)
[ˈʃæbi]	同 scruffy; shoddy
shamble	*v.* 蹒跚而行, 踉跄地走(to walk awkwardly with dragging feet)
[ˈʃæmbl]	同 shuffle
shattered	*adj.* 破碎的
[ˈʃætərd]	记 来自shatter(*v.* 粉碎)
sheaf	*n.* 一捆, 一束(a bundle)
[ʃiːf]	搭 a sheaf of paper 一沓纸
shear	*v.* 剪(羊毛), 剪发(to cut off the hair from)
[ʃɪr]	记 联想记忆: sh(看作she)+ear(耳朵) → 她剪了个齐耳的短发 → 剪发
sheen	*n.* 光辉, 光泽(a bright or shining condition)
[ʃiːn]	
sheer	*adj.* 完全的(complete; utter); 陡峭的(very steep); 极薄的(extremely thin)
[ʃɪr]	记 联想记忆: 绵羊(sheep)在陡峭的(sheer)山坡上吃草
	例 He was indifferent to success, painting not for the sake of fame or monetary reward, but for the *sheer* love of art.
shelter	*n.* 避难所, 遮蔽(place or condition of being protected, kept safe, etc.) *v.* 庇护, 保护(to give shelter to sb./sth.; protect sb./sth.)
[ˈʃeltər]	记 联想记忆: shel(看作shell, 壳)+ter → 像壳一样可以躲避的地方 → 避难所
shield	*n.* 盾 *v.* 掩护, 保护(to protect from harm)
[ʃiːld]	同 defend
shilly-shally	*v.* 犹豫不决(to show hesitation or lack of decisiveness); 虚度时光(to fiddle)
[ˈʃɪliʃæli]	
shipshape	*adj.* 整洁干净的; 井然有序的(trim; tidy)
[ˈʃɪpʃeɪp]	记 联想记忆: ship(船)+shape(形状) → 船的形状 → 整洁干净的
shirk	*v.* 逃避, 回避(to avoid; evade)
[ʃɜːrk]	记 和shirt(*n.* 衬衣)一起记
shoddy	*adj.* 劣质的, 假冒的(cheaply imitative)
[ˈʃɑːdi]	同 second-rate
shove	*v.* 推挤, 猛推(to move sth. by using force)
[ʃʌv]	记 注意不要和shovel(*n.* 铁锹)相混

showy [ˈʃəʊi]	*adj.* 俗艳的(gaudy)；炫耀的(flashy) 同 ostentatious
shrewd [ʃruːd]	*adj.* 机灵的，精明的(marked by clever discerning awareness) 记 注意不要和 shrew(*n.* 泼妇)相混
shriek [ʃriːk]	*v.* 尖叫(to utter a sharp shrill sound)
shudder [ˈʃʌdər]	*v.* 战栗，发抖(to shake uncontrollably for a moment) *n.* 战栗，发抖 记 发音记忆："吓得" → 吓得肩膀(shoulder)直发抖(shudder)
shuttle [ˈʃʌtl]	*v.* (使)穿梭移动，往返运送 (to cause to move or travel back and forth frequently)
sibyl [ˈsɪbl]	*n.* 女预言家，女先知(a female prophet) 同 prophetess
sideline [ˈsaɪdlaɪn]	*n.* 副业，兼职 (a business or activity pursued in addition to one's regular occupation)
sideshow [ˈsaɪdʃəʊ]	*n.* 杂耍，穿插表演(a separate small show at a circus)
sidestep [ˈsaɪdstep]	*v.* 横跨一步躲避(to take a step to the side to avoid)；回避(to avoid) 同 bypass, evade
siege [siːdʒ]	*n.* 包围，围攻(a military blockade of a city or fortified place to compel it to surrender) 记 参见 besiege(*v.* 围攻)
sift [sɪft]	*v.* 筛选，过滤(to separate out by a sieve) 搭 sift sth. out 筛选；剔除
signature [ˈsɪɡnətʃər]	*n.* 签名，署名(person's name written by himself) 记 词根记忆：sign(做记号)+ature → 用名字做记号 → 签名，署名
signify [ˈsɪɡnɪfaɪ]	*v.* 表示(to be a sign of)；有重要性(to have significance) 记 词根记忆：sign(做记号)+ify → 表示
simile [ˈsɪməli]	*n.* 明喻((use of) comparison of one thing with another) 记 词根记忆：simil(相类似的)+e → 把相类似的事物进行比较 → 明喻
simmer [ˈsɪmər]	*v.* 炖，慢煮(to stew gently below or just at the boiling point) *n.* 即将沸腾的状态，即将发作 记 联想记忆：在夏天(summer)，人往往容易充满难以控制的怒火(simmer)
simonize [ˈsaɪmənaɪz]	*v.* 给…打蜡，把…擦亮(to polish with or as if with wax)
simper [ˈsɪmpər]	*v.* 假笑，傻笑(to smile in a silly manner) 同 smirk
simulate [ˈsɪmjuleɪt]	*v.* 假装，模仿(to assume the appearance with the intent to deceive) 记 词根记忆：simul(类似)+ate(使…) → 使某物类似于某物 → 模仿

卖拐
卖拐

simulate

39

simultaneous [ˌsaɪml'teɪnɪəs]	*adj.* 同时发生的(exactly coincident) 记 词根记忆: simul(相同)+taneous(…的) → 同时发生的 搭 simultaneous with 与…同时进行
singe [sɪndʒ]	*v.* (轻微地)烧焦, 烤焦(to burn superficially or lightly; scorch) 记 联想记忆: sing(唱, 唱歌) + e → 烧焦了还唱 → 烧焦
sip [sɪp]	*v.* 啜饮(to drink in small quantities) *n.* 小口喝, 抿; 一小口的量 搭 a sip of wine 一口酒
skim [skɪm]	*v.* 从液体表面撇去(to remove floating fat or solids from the surface of a liquid); 浏览, 略读(to read quickly to get the main ideas)
skirmish ['skɜːrmɪʃ]	*n.* 小规模战斗, 小冲突(a minor dispute or contest) 记 联想记忆: skir(看作 skirt, 裙子)+mish(看作 famish, 饥饿) → 女人会为了裙子而起冲突, 为了穿漂亮的裙子宁可饿肚子 → 小冲突
skirt [skɜːrt]	*v.* 绕过, 回避(to evade) 搭 skirt around / round sth. 避而不提
skit [skɪt]	*n.* 幽默讽刺短剧(a short humorous acted-out scene); 讽刺文章(a short humorous or satirical piece of writing)
skittish ['skɪtɪʃ]	*adj.* 轻浮的, 活泼的(capricious; frivolous; not serious) 搭 skittish financial market 变幻莫测的金融市场
skullduggery [skʌl'dʌgəri]	*n.* 欺骗, 使诈(underhanded or unscrupulous behavior) 记 联想记忆: skull(头颅, 脑袋) + dug(挖) + gery → 挖脑袋 → 想方设法作假 → 欺骗, 使诈
skyrocket ['skaɪrɑːkɪt]	*v.* 突升, 猛涨(to shoot up abruptly) 记 组合词: sky(天空) + rocket(火箭) → 火箭冲向天空, 突然升高 → 突升
slack [slæk]	*adj.* 懈怠的, 不活跃的(sluggish; inactive); (绳)松弛的(loose) *v.* 懈怠, 偷懒
slake [sleɪk]	*v.* 满足; 平息(to satisfy; quench) 记 联想联想: s+lake(湖) → 看到湖水很满足 → 满足
slander ['slændər]	*v.* 诽谤, 诋毁(to defame) *n.* 诽谤, 中伤 记 联想记忆: s+land(地)+er → 把人贬到地上 → 诽谤, 诋毁
slant [slænt]	*v.* 倾斜 *n.* 斜面(a slanting direction); 观点(a peculiar or personal point of view)
slattern ['slætərn]	*adj.* 不整洁的(slatternly) *n.* 邋遢的女人(an untidy slovenly woman) 同 slut
slay [sleɪ]	*v.* 杀戮, 杀死(to kill violently or in great numbers) 记 和 stay(*v.* 停留)一起记
sleight [slaɪt]	*n.* 巧妙手法, 诡计; 灵巧(dexterity; skill) 记 联想记忆: sl(看作 sly, 狡猾) + eight → 八面玲珑 → 灵巧
slew [sluː]	*v.* (使)旋转(to turn, twist) *n.* 大量(a large number) 记 和 slow(*adj.* 慢的)一起记
slice [slaɪs]	*n.* 薄片 *v.* 切成片(to cut into pieces)

slick [slɪk]	*adj.* 熟练的（skillful and effective）；圆滑的（clever）；光滑的（smooth and slippery）
slight [slaɪt]	*adj.* 轻微，微小的（small in degree）*v.* 怠慢，冷落（to treat rudely without respect）*n.* 冒犯他人的行为、言语等 记 联想记忆：s+light（轻的）→ 轻微的 例 In today's world, manufacturers' innovations are easily copied and thus differences between products are usually *slight*.
slink [slɪŋk]	*v.* 溜走，潜逃（to go or move stealthily or furtively） 同 creep
slippage [ˈslɪpɪdʒ]	*n.* 滑动，下降（slipping） 记 来自 slip（*v.* 滑）
slippery [ˈslɪpəri]	*adj.* 滑的；狡猾的（not to be trusted） 记 来自 slip（*v.* 滑）
slit [slɪt]	*v.* 撕裂（to sever）*n.* 裂缝（a long narrow cut or opening） 记 参考 split（*v./n.* 分裂）；slice（*v.* 切开）
sliver [ˈslɪvər]	*n.* 薄长条（a long slender piece）*v.* 裂成细片（to cut into sliver） 记 注意不要和 silver（*n.* 银）相混
slobber [ˈslɑːbər]	*n.* 口水（saliva drooled from the mouth）*v.* 流口水；情不自禁地说 搭 slobber over sb./sth. 对…垂涎欲滴；毫不掩饰表示喜爱
slog [slɑːg]	*v.* 猛击（to hit hard）；苦干（to work hard and steadily） 搭 slog through sth./slog away(at sth.) 埋头苦干；坚持不懈地做
sloppy [ˈslɑːpi]	*adj.* 邋遢的，粗心的（slovenly；careless） 记 联想记忆：slop（溅出，弄脏）+py → 衣服弄脏后显得很邋遢 → 邋遢的
slosh [slɑːʃ]	*v.* 溅，泼（to splash about in liquid）*n.* 泥泞（slush） 搭 a slosh on the ear 一记耳光
slot [slɑːt]	*n.* 狭槽（a long straight narrow opening） 搭 slot machine 投币自动售货机
slouch [slaʊtʃ]	*n.* 没精打采的样子（a tired-looking way）*v.* 没精打采地坐(站、走) 记 发音记忆："似老去" → 没精打采的样子
sloven [ˈslʌvən]	*n.* 不修边幅的人（one habitually negligent of neatness or cleanliness）
slue [sluː]	*v.* (使)旋转（to rotate；slew） 记 slew（*v.* 旋转）的变体
slug [slʌg]	*v.* 猛击，拳击（to strike heavily with or as if with the fist or a bat） 搭 slug it out 决出胜负，一决雌雄
slumber [ˈslʌmbər]	*v.* 睡眠，安睡（to sleep）*n.* 睡眠（a light sleep） 搭 slumber party 睡衣晚会
slump [slʌmp]	*v.* 大幅度下降，暴跌（to fall or sink suddenly） 同 plunge, plummet, tumble

39

□ slick	□ slight	□ slink	□ slippage	□ slippery	□ slit
□ sliver	□ slobber	□ slog	□ sloppy	□ slosh	□ slot
□ slouch	□ sloven	□ slue	□ slug	□ slumber	□ slump

slur [slɜːr]	*v.* 含糊不清地讲(to pronounce words in an indistinct way so that they run into each other) 记 和 blur(*v.* 弄脏, 变模糊)一起记
slurp [slɜːrp]	*v.* 出声地吃或喝(to drink with the sound of noisy sucking) *n.* 啜食, 啜食声
sly [slaɪ]	*adj.* 狡猾的, 狡诈的(clever in deceiving) 搭 on the sly 偷偷地; 背地里
smarmy ['smɑːrmi]	*adj.* 虚情假意的(revealing or marked by a false earnestness) 同 oily, smooth, sleek, unctuous
smattering ['smætərɪŋ]	*n.* 略知(superficial knowledge); 少数(a small scattered number) 同 elements, modicum, smidgen
smear [smɪr]	*v.* 弄脏, 玷污(to overspread sth. adhesive) *n.* 污迹, 污点(a spot) 搭 smeared windows 脏了的窗户
smirch [smɜːrtʃ]	*v.* 弄脏(to make dirty, stained, or discolored) *n.* 污点 同 blemish, soil, sully, tarnish
smirk [smɜːrk]	*v.* 假笑, 得意地笑(to smile in an affected manner) 同 simper
smite [smaɪt]	*v.* 重击, 猛打(to attack or afflict suddenly and injuriously) 搭 be smitten with/by sb./sth. 突然爱上, 完全迷上
smooth [smuːð]	*v.* 使平坦, 使光滑(to make smooth); 消除 *adj.* 光滑的; 平稳的 例 In response to the follies of today's commercial and political worlds, the author does not express inflamed indignation, but rather affects the detachment and *smooth* aphoristic prose of an eighteenth-century wit.
smudge [smʌdʒ]	*n.* 污迹, 污点(a blurry spot or streak) *v.* 弄脏(to smear sth. with dirt, or ink) 记 联想记忆: s + mud(泥) + ge → 污迹, 污点
smuggle ['smʌgl]	*v.* 走私, 私运(to import or export sth. in violation of customs laws) 记 联想记忆: 不断进行反对走私(smuggle)的斗争(struggle)
smut [smʌt]	*n.* 污迹(matter that soils or blackens); 黑穗病 *v.* 弄脏
snappish ['snæpɪʃ]	*adj.* 脾气暴躁的(arising from annoyance or irascibility) 记 联想记忆: snap(劈啪声, 折断) + pish → 脾气暴躁的
snappy ['snæpi]	*adj.* 生气勃勃的(marked by vigor or liveliness); 漂亮的, 时髦的(stylish; smart)
snare [sner]	*n.* 圈套, 陷阱(trap; gin) 记 参考 ensnare(*v.* 使进入圈套)
snarl [snɑːrl]	*v.* 纠缠, 混乱(to intertwine; tangle); 咆哮, 怒骂(to growl) *n.* 纠缠, 混乱; 怒吼声, 咆哮声 同 knot

snatch [snætʃ]	*v.* 强夺，攫取（to take or grasp abruptly or hastily without permission） *n.* 强夺，攫取 记 联想记忆：sna（看作 snap，迅速的）+ tch（看作 catch，抓）→ 迅速地抓 → 强夺，攫取
sneaking ['sniːkɪŋ]	*adj.* 鬼鬼祟祟的，私下的（furtive; underhanded） 搭 sneaking suspicion 私下怀疑
sneer [snɪr]	*v.* 嘲笑，鄙视（to express scorn or contempt） 同 deride, fleer, scoff, taunt
snicker ['snɪkər]	*v./n.* 窃笑，暗笑（suppressed laugh） 同 titter
snide [snaɪd]	*adj.* 挖苦的，讽刺的（slyly disparaging; insinuating） 记 联想记忆：把 n 藏在一边（side）→ 含沙射影的 → 讽刺
snip [snɪp]	*v.* 剪断（to cut with scissors）*n.* 剪；碎片 同 fragment
snipe [snaɪp]	*v.* 狙击（to shoot at exposed individuals from a usually concealed point of vantage）
snitch [snɪtʃ]	*v.* 告密（to tell about the wrongdoings of a friend）；偷（to steal by taking quickly） 记 联想记忆：sni（看作 sin，罪行）+tch → 告密和偷都是罪行 → 告密；偷
snob [snɑːb]	*n.* 势利小人 记 参考 snobbery（*n.* 势利态度，自命不凡）
snobbish ['snɑːbɪʃ]	*adj.* 势利眼的（being, characteristic of, or befitting a snob）；假充绅士的 记 来自 snob（*n.* 势利小人）
snooze [snuːz]	*v.* 打盹儿，打瞌睡（to take a nap） 同 catnap, doze, siesta
snuggle ['snʌɡl]	*v.* 紧靠，依偎（to draw close for comfort or in affection） 记 联想记忆：snug（温暖的）+ gle → 依偎在一起感觉很温暖 → 依偎
soak [soʊk]	*v.* 浸泡，渗透（to lie immersed in liquid; become saturated by, or as if by immersion） 记 联想记忆：soa（看作 soap，肥皂）+k → 在肥皂水中浸泡 → 浸泡
sober ['soʊbər]	*adj.* 清醒的（sedate or thoughtful）；严肃的，认真的（marked by temperance, moderation, or seriousness）
sock [sɑːk]	*v.* 重击，痛打（to strike forcefully） 记 sock 更广为人知的意思是"短袜"
sodden ['sɑːdn]	*adj.* 浸透了的（soaked through; very wet） 搭 a rain-sodden jacket 一件雨水淋透的夹克
soggy ['sɑːgi]	*adj.* 湿透的（saturated or heavy with water or moisture） 同 clammy, dank, sopping, waterlogged
soil [sɔɪl]	*v.* 弄脏，污辱（to become dirty） 记 soil 更广为人知的意思是"土壤"

39

□ snatch	□ sneaking	□ sneer	□ snicker	□ snide	□ snip
□ snipe	□ snitch	□ snob	□ snobbish	□ snooze	□ snuggle
□ soak	□ sober	□ sock	□ sodden	□ soggy	□ soil

solidify [sə'lɪdɪfaɪ]	v. 巩固，(使)凝固，(使)团结(to become solid, hard or firm) 记 词根记忆：solid(固定的)+ify(使…) → 巩固
solitude [ˈsɑːlətuːd]	n. 孤独(the quality or state of being alone or remote from society) 例 Contrary to her customary gregarious behavior, Susan began leaving parties early to seek the *solitude* of her room.
somatic [səʊ'mætɪk]	adj. 肉体的，躯体的(relating to the body) 记 词根记忆：somat(躯体)+ic → 躯体的
somnolent [ˈsɑːmnələnt]	adj. 想睡的(drowsy)；催眠的(likely to induce sleep) 记 词根记忆：somn(睡) + olent → 想睡的
sophism [ˈsɑːfɪzəm]	n. 诡辩；诡辩法(术)(an argument apparently correct in form but actually invalid)
sorcery [ˈsɔːrsəri]	n. 巫术，魔术(the use of evil magical power) 记 词根记忆：sorc(巫术) + ery → 巫术，魔术
soulful [ˈsoʊlfl]	adj. 充满感情的，深情的(full of or expressing feeling or emotion) 摺 a soulful song 一首凄婉的歌
sour [ˈsaʊər]	adj. 酸的(having the acid taste or smell of or as if of fermentation) 记 发音记忆："馊啊" → 酸的
spacious [ˈspeɪʃəs]	adj. 广阔的，宽敞的(vast or ample in extent) 记 词根记忆：spac(=space 地方) + ious(多…的)；注意不要和 specious (adj. 似是而非的)相混
spank [spæŋk]	v. 掌掴，拍打(在屁股上)(to strike on the buttocks with the open hands) 同 smack
spark [spɑːrk]	n. 火花，火星(a small particle of a burning substance) 记 联想记忆：s+park (公园) → 公园是情侣们约会擦出感情火花的地方 → 火花
sparring [ˈspɑːrɪŋ]	n. 拳击，争斗 摺 sparring partner 切磋问题的对手
spasmodic [spæz'mɑːdɪk]	adj. 痉挛的(of a spasm)；间歇性的(intermittent) 摺 spasmodic fighting 零星的战斗
spat [spæt]	n. 口角，小争论(a brief petty quarrel or angry outburst) 记 不要和 spit(v. 吐痰)相混
spate [speɪt]	n. 许多，大量(a large number or amount)；(水流)暴涨，发洪水(flood) 摺 a spate of 一连串，接二连三(通常指不愉快的事物)
spatter [ˈspætər]	v. 洒，溅(to splash with or as if with a liquid) 同 slop, spray, swash
spear [spɪr]	n. 矛；嫩枝(a young shoot, or sprout) v. 用矛刺(to thrust with a spear) 摺 spear fish 叉鱼

specifics [spə'sɪfɪks]	*n.* 细小问题, 细节(details; particulars) 记 来自 specific(*adj.* 详细的)
speck [spek]	*n.* 斑点(a small spot from stain or decay); 少量(a very small amount) 记 参见 peccadillo(*n.* 小过失)
spectacular [spek'tækjələr]	*adj.* 壮观的, 引人入胜的(striking; sensational) 记 来自 spectacle(*n.* 奇观, 壮观); spect(看)+acle(东西) → 看的东西 → 奇观, 壮观
spell [spel]	*n.* 连续的一段时间(a continuous period of time) 记 spell 还有"拼写"、"咒语"等意思 例 The breathing *spell* provided by the moratorium on arms shipments should give all the combatants a chance to reevaluate their positions.
spendthrift ['spendθrift]	*adj./n.* 挥金如土的(人) 记 组合词: spend(花费)+thrift(节约) → 把节约下来的钱全部花掉 → 挥金如土的 同 wasteful
spew [spju:]	*v.* 呕吐(to vomit); 大量喷出(to come forth in a flood or gush)
spiel [spi:l]	*n.* 滔滔不绝的讲话(pitch)
spin [spɪn]	*v.* 旋转(to move round and round); 纺纱(to draw out and twist fiber into yarn or thread) *n.* 旋转(turning or spinning movement)
spindly ['spɪndli]	*adj.* 细长的, 纤弱的(very long and thin) 记 来自 spindle(*n.* 纺锤)
spite [spaɪt]	*n.* 怨恨, 恶意(petty ill will or hatred) 搭 in spite of 尽管, 不管, 不顾
splashy ['splæʃi]	*adj.* 容易溅开的; 炫耀显眼的(exhibiting ostentatious display) 记 来自 splash(*n.* 溅水, 卖弄)
spleen [spli:n]	*n.* 怒气(feelings of anger) 同 rancor, resentment, wrath

39

□ specifics	□ speck	□ spectacular	□ spell	□ spendthrift	□ spew
□ spiel	□ spin	□ spindly	□ spite	□ splashy	□ spleen

431

Word List 40  MP3-40

splice [splaɪs]	*v.* 接合, 拼接 (to unite by interweaving the strands) 记 注意不要和 split (*v.* 破裂) 相混
split [splɪt]	*v.* 破裂, 裂开 (to divide into parts or portions) *n.* 裂开, 裂口 记 发音记忆:"死劈了它" → 破裂, 裂开
spoilsport ['spɔɪlspɔːrt]	*n.* 使人扫兴的人 (one who spoils the sport or pleasure of others) 同 damper, downer, killjoy
spoliation [ˌspəʊli'eɪʃən]	*n.* 抢劫, 掠夺 (the act of plundering) 记 来自 spoliate (*v.* 强夺, 抢劫)
spontaneous [spɑːn'teɪniəs]	*adj.* 自发的 (proceeding from natural feelings);自然的 (natural) 记 词根记忆:spont (自然)+aneous → 自然产生的 → 自发的 例 The Battle of Lexington was not, as most of us have been taught, a *spontaneous* rising of individual farmers, but was instead a tightly organized, well-planned event.
sport [spɔːrt]	*v.* 炫耀, 卖弄 (to display or wear ostentatiously) 搭 sport a beard 故意蓄着大胡子
sportive ['spɔːrtɪv]	*adj.* 嬉戏的, 欢闹的 (playful) 同 frolicsome
spout [spaʊt]	*v.* 喷出 (to eject in a stream);滔滔不绝地讲 (to speak readily) 记 联想记忆:sp (看作 speak, 说)+out (出) → 一直不停地说话 → 滔滔不绝地讲
sprain [spreɪn]	*v.* 扭伤 (to injure by a sudden twist) 记 联想记忆:sp + rain (雨) → 雨天路滑, 扭伤了脚 → 扭伤
spree [spriː]	*n.* 狂欢 (an unrestrained indulgence in or outburst of an activity) 搭 shopping/spending spree 狂购一气;痛痛快快花一通钱
sprint [sprɪnt]	*v.* 短距离全速奔跑 (to run at top speed for a short distance) 记 联想记忆:s + print (印刷) → 像印刷机印钞票一样快地奔跑 → 短距离全速奔跑
spur [spɜːr]	*v.* 刺激, 激励;用马刺刺马 记 联想记忆:美国 NBA 中有马刺队 Spurs

| **spurt** | *n.* (液体等的)喷出，迸发(spout) |
| [spɜːrt] | 同 gush, jet, spew, squirt |

squabble	*n.* 争吵(a noisy quarrel, usually about a trivial
[ˈskwɑːbl]	matter)
	同 bicker, fuss, row, spat, tiff

squabble

squall	*n.* 短暂、突然且猛烈的风暴(a brief, sudden,
[skwɔːl]	violent windstorm); 短暂的骚动(a brief violent
	commotion)

| **squalor** | *n.* 肮脏，污秽(state of being squalid) |
| [ˈskwɑːlər] | 记 发音记忆："四筐烂儿" → 四筐破烂儿 → 污秽 |

square	*v.* 一致，符合(to be or make sth. consistent with sth.; agree with); 结清
[skwer]	(to balance)
	搭 square up 清算账目

| **squat** | *v.* 蹲下(to crouch on the ground) *adj.* 矮胖的(stout) |
| [skwɑːt] | 同 dumpy |

| **squeamish** | *adj.* 易受惊的；易恶心的(easily shocked or sickened) |
| [ˈskwiːmɪʃ] | 记 the squeamish 神经脆弱的人 |

squeeze	*v.* 压，挤(to press firmly together) *n.* 压榨，紧握
[skwiːz]	记 联想记忆：s+quee(看作 queen，女王)+ze → 很想挤进去与女王握手
	→ 挤

| **squelch** | *v.* 压制，镇压(to completely suppress; quell) |
| [skweltʃ] | 搭 squelch a rumour/strike/fire 制止谣言；镇压罢工；控制火势蔓延 |

| **squint** | *v.* 斜视(to look or peer with eyes partly closed) |
| [skwɪnt] | |

| **stab** | *v.* 刺伤，戳(to thrust with a pointed weapon) |
| [stæb] | 搭 stab sb. in the back 在某人背后捅刀子 |

| **stagy** | *adj.* 不自然的，做作的(marked by pretense or artificiality) |
| [ˈsteɪdʒi] | 同 hokey, sensational, theatrical |

staid	*adj.* 稳重的，沉着的(self-restraint; sober)
[steɪd]	记 联想记忆：sta(看作 stay，坚持) + id(看作 ID，身份) → 坚持自己的身
	份 → 稳重的

| **stain** | *v.* 玷污(to taint with guilt or corruption); 染色(to color by processes) |
| [steɪn] | 记 联想记忆：一下雨(rain)，到处都是污点(stain) |

| **stale** | *adj.* 不新鲜的，陈腐的(tasteless or unpalatable from age) |
| [steɪl] | 记 联想记忆：s+tale(传说) → 传说说多了就不新鲜了 → 不新鲜的，陈腐的 |

| **stammer** | *v.* 口吃，结巴地说(to make involuntary stops and repetitions in speaking) |
| [ˈstæmər] | 同 falter, stumble, stutter |

| **stampede** | *v.* 惊跑，逃窜(to cause to run away in headlong panic) |
| [stæmˈpiːd] | 搭 a herd of stampeding elephants 一群狂奔的大象 |

40

stanza	*n.* (诗的)节，段 (a division of a poem consisting of a series of lines)
['stænzə]	记 词根记忆：stan(站住)+za → 诗中停顿的地方 → 节，段
star-crossed	*adj.* 时运不济的 (ill-fated)
['stɑːrkrɔst]	同 cursed, ill-omened, jinxed, luckless
startle	*v.* 使吃惊 (to give an unexpected slight shock)
['stɑːrtl]	同 astound, consternate, terrorize
stationary	*adj.* 静止的，不动的 (fixed in a station; immobile)
['steɪʃəneri]	记 词根记忆：sta(站，立)+tion+ary → 总在一个地方的 → 静止的，不动的
statuary	*n.* 雕像 (a collection of statues)；雕塑艺术 (the art of making statues)
['stætʃueri]	记 来自 statue(*n.* 雕像)
stature	*n.* 身高，身材 (nature height ln an upright position)
['stætʃər]	记 词根记忆：stat(站)+ure(状态) → 站的状态 → 身高，身材
status	*n.* 身份，地位 (social standing; present condition)
['steɪtəs]	记 联想记忆：stat(看作 state, 声明) + us(我们) → 声明我们是谁 → 身份
statutory	*adj.* 法定的；依照法令的 (regulated by statute)
['stætjutɔːri]	搭 statutory offence 法定罪行
staunch	*adj.* 坚定的，忠诚的 (steadfast in loyalty or principle)
[stɔːntʃ]	同 constant, inflexible, stalwart, tried-and-true
stealth	*n.* 秘密行动 (the action of moving or acting secretly)
[stelθ]	记 来自 steal(*v.* 偷)
steep	*adj.* 陡峭的；过高的 (lofty, high) *v.* 浸泡，浸透 (to soak in a liquid)
[stiːp]	记 联想记忆：阶梯(step)中又加一个 e 就更陡峭(steep)
	例 Imposing *steep* fines on employers for on-the-job injuries to workers could be an effective incentive to creating a safer workplace, especially in the case of employers with poor safety records.
steer	*v.* 掌舵，驾驶 (to control the course) *n.* 公牛，食用牛
[stɪr]	记 联想记忆：驾驶着(steer)一艘钢铁(steel)打造的大船
stench	*n.* 臭气，恶臭 (stink)
[stentʃ]	记 注意不要和 stanch(*v.* 止住)相混
stentorian	*adj.* 声音洪亮的 (extremely loud)
[sten'tɔːriən]	记 来自希腊神话特洛伊战争中的传令官 Stentor, 其声音极其洪亮
sterilize	*v.* 使不育；杀菌 (to make sterile)
['sterəlaɪz]	搭 sterilize surgical instruments 给外科手术器械消毒
stickler	*n.* 坚持细节之人 (one who insists on exactness)
['stɪklər]	记 来自 stickle(*v.* 坚持己见)
sticky	*adj.* 湿热的 (humid)；闷热的 (muggy)
['stɪki]	记 来自 stick(*v.* 粘住)

steer

| **stiff** | *adj.* 僵硬的，呆板的，严厉的（not easily bent or changed in shape） |
| [stɪf] | 记 联想记忆：still（静止的）的 ll 变为 ff 就成僵硬的（stiff） |

stiff

| **stifle** | *v.* 感到窒息（to be unable to breathe comfortably）；抑止（to prevent from happening） |
| [ˈstaɪfl] | |

| **stigma** | *n.* 耻辱的标志，污点（a mark of shame or discredit） |
| [ˈstɪgmə] | 同 stain |

| **stigmatize** | *v.* 诬蔑，玷污（to describe opprobrious terms） |
| [ˈstɪgmətaɪz] | 同 brand, label, tag |

| **stimulant** | *n.* 兴奋剂，刺激物（an agent that produces a temporary increase of the functional activity） |
| [ˈstɪmjələnt] | 记 词根记忆：stimul（刺激）+ant → 刺激物 |

| **sting** | *v.* 刺痛；叮螫（to prick or wound） *n.* 螫刺 |
| [stɪŋ] | 记 发音记忆："死叮" → 刺痛；英国有个著名歌手叫斯汀 Sting |

| **stinginess** | *n.* 小气 |
| [ˈstɪndʒinəs] | 记 来自 stingy（*adj.* 吝啬的） |

| **stipple** | *v.* 点画，点描（to apply paint by repeated small touches） |
| [ˈstɪpl] | 记 词根记忆：stip（点）+ple → 用点画 → 点画 |

| **stipulation** | *n.* 规定，约定（a condition, requirement, or item in a legal instrument） |
| [ˌstɪpjuˈleɪʃn] | 记 来自 stipulate（*v.* 规定，明确要求） |

| **stir** | *v.* 刺激（to rouse to activity; to call forth） |
| [stɜːr] | 记 stir 本身是词根，有"刺激"之意 |

| **stitch** | *n.*（缝纫时的）一针 *v.* 缝合（to make, mend, or decorate with or as if with stitches） |
| [stɪtʃ] | |

| **stock** | *v.* 储备 *adj.* 常用的（commonly used; standard） *n.* 存货 |
| [stɑːk] | 例 If you need car parts that the dealers no longer *stock*, try scavenging for odd bits and pieces at the auto wreckers' yards. |

| **stodgy** | *adj.* 枯燥无味的（boring; dull） |
| [ˈstɑːdʒi] | 例 For a young person, Winston seems remarkably *stodgy*; you'd expect someone of his age to show a little more life. |

| **stoke** | *v.* 给…添加燃料（to fill with coal or other fuel） |
| [stoʊk] | 记 联想记忆：给火炉（stove）添加燃料（stoke） |

| **stolid** | *adj.* 无动于衷的（expressing little or no sensibility; unemotional） |
| [ˈstɑːlɪd] | 记 solid（*adj.* 结实的）中间加个 t |

| **stomach** | *v.* 吃得下；容忍（to bear without overt reaction or resentment） |
| [ˈstʌmək] | 同 tolerate |

| **stonewall** | *v.* 拖延议事，设置障碍（to intentionally delay in a discussion or argument） |
| [ˈstoʊnˈwɔːl] | 同 filibuster, stall |

40

□ stiff	□ stifle	□ stigma	□ stigmatize	□ stimulant	□ sting
□ stinginess	□ stipple	□ stipulation	□ stir	□ stitch	□ stock
□ stodgy	□ stoke	□ stolid	□ stomach	□ stonewall	

stooge [stu:dʒ]	*n.* 配角，陪衬(one who plays a subordinate or compliant role to a principal)；傀儡(puppet)
stoop [stu:p]	*v.* 弯腰，俯身(to bend the body)；屈尊(to descend from a superior rank) 记 联想记忆：站(stood)直了别弯腰(stoop)
stouthearted [ˌstaut ˈhɑːrtid]	*adj.* 刚毅的，大胆的(brave or resolute) 记 组合词：stout(勇敢的，坚决的)+heart(心)+ed → 刚毅的，大胆的
straggle [ˈstrægl]	*v.* 迷路(to stray)；落伍(to drop behind)；蔓延(to grow or spread in a messy way) 记 联想记忆：迷路(straggle)了所以在苦苦挣扎(struggle)
straightforward [ˌstreɪt ˈfɔːrwərd]	*adj.* 诚实的，坦率的(honest and frank)；易懂的(not difficult to understand)；直接的(direct) 例 At first endorsements were simply that: *straightforward* firsthand testimonials about the virtues of a product.
straiten [ˈstreɪtən]	*v.* 使为难(to subject to distress, privation, or deficiency)；使变窄(to make strait or narrow)
strand [strænd]	*n.* (绳、线等的)股，缕 *v.* 搁浅(to cause sb. or sth. to be held at a location)
stranded [ˈstrændid]	*adj.* 搁浅的，处于困境的(caught in a difficult situation) 搭 a stranded ship 搁浅的船
strangulation [ˌstræŋgju ˈleɪʃn]	*n.* 扼杀，勒死(the action or process of strangling or strangulating) 记 来自strangle(*v.* 扼杀，抑制)
stray [streɪ]	*v.* 偏离，迷路(to wander away) *adj.* 迷路的(having strayed or escaped from a proper or intended place)；零落的(occurring at random or sporadically) 搭 stray from 偏离
stretch [stretʃ]	*v.* 延伸(to become wider or longer)；伸展(to reach full length or width) 同 elongate, prolongate, protract, unfold
strew [stru:]	*v.* 撒满，散播(to spread randomly; scatter) 同 disseminate
striate [ˈstraieit]	*v.* 加条纹(to mark with striation) 记 联想记忆：stri(看作strip，条、带)+ate → 加条纹
striated [ˈstraieitid]	*adj.* 有条纹的(marked with striations) 记 来自striate(*v.* 加条纹)
stricture [ˈstrɪktʃər]	*n.* 严厉谴责(an adverse criticism)；束缚(restrictions) 记 来自strict(*adj.* 严格的)
strident [ˈstraɪdnt]	*adj.* 尖锐的，刺耳的(characterized by harsh sound) 记 联想记忆：stri(看作stride，大步走)+dent(凹痕) → 大步走进凹坑传来尖声大叫 → 尖锐的
strife [straɪf]	*n.* 纷争，冲突(bitter conflict or dissension) 同 fight, struggle

striking	*adj.* 引人注目的，显著的（attracting attention or notice）
[ˈstraɪkɪŋ]	记 来自 strike（*v.* 打击）
	例 As painted by Constable, the scene is not one of bucolic serenity; rather it shows a *striking* emotional and intellectual tension.
stroke	*v.* 抚摸（to pass the hand over gently）*n.* 击，打（a hit）；一笔，一画（a line
[stroʊk]	made by a single movement of a pen or brush）
stroll	*v.* 漫步，闲逛（to walk in an idle manner; ramble）
[stroʊl]	记 联想记忆：st（看作 street，街道）+roll（转）→ 在大街上转悠 → 闲逛
strut	*v.* 趾高气扬地走（to walk proudly and stiffly）*n.* 支柱（support）
[strʌt]	同 stalk, stride, swagger
stubborn	*adj.* 固执的（determined）；难以改变的（difficult to change）
[ˈstʌbərn]	记 联想记忆：stub（根）+born（生）→ 生根的 → 固执的
	例 In attempting to reconcile estranged spouses, counselors try to foster a spirit of compromise rather than one of *stubborn* implacability.
stubby	*adj.* 短粗的（being short and thickset）
[ˈstʌbi]	同 squat, stocky, stumpy
studied	*adj.* 深思熟虑的（carefully thought about or considered）；认真习得的
[ˈstʌdid]	例 The prospects of discovering new aspects of the life of a painter as thoroughly *studied* as Vermeer are not, on the surface, encouraging.
stuffy	*adj.* 通风不好的，闷热的（oppressive to the breathing）
[ˈstʌfi]	记 联想记忆：stuff（填满）+y → 填满的 → 通风不好的
stultify	*v.* 使显得愚蠢（to make stupid）；使变得无用或无效（to render useless）
[ˈstʌltɪfaɪ]	同 impair, invalidate, negate
stun	*v.* 使震惊，打晕（to make senseless, groggy, or dizzy by or as if by a
[stʌn]	blow）
	记 发音记忆：发音像敲击声"当" → 把人打晕 → 打晕
stunt	*v.* 阻碍（成长）（to hinder the normal growth）*n.* 特技，绝技（an unusual or
[stʌnt]	difficult feat requiring great skill）
stupefy	*v.* 使茫然，使惊讶（to astonish; astound）
[ˈstuːpɪfaɪ]	记 词根记忆：stup（笨，呆）+ efy → 吓呆 → 使惊讶
stupendous	*adj.* 巨大的，惊人的（of amazing size or greatness; tremendous）
[stuːˈpendəs]	记 词根记忆：stup（吃惊）+ endous → 惊人的
stupor	*n.* 昏迷，恍惚（no sensibility）
[ˈstuːpər]	同 swoon, torpor, trance
sturdy	*adj.*（身体）强健的（strong）；结实的（firmly built or constituted）
[ˈstɜːrdi]	记 联想记忆：要想学习（study）好需要身体好（sturdy）
stutter	*v.* 口吃，结巴（to speak with involuntary disruption of speech）*n.* 口吃
[ˈstʌtər]	搭 stutter（out）an apology 结结巴巴地道歉
stygian	*adj.* 阴暗的，阴森森的（gloomy; unpleasantly dark）
[ˈstɪdʒiən]	记 来自 Styx（*n.* 地狱冥河）

40

suavity	*n.* 柔和, 愉快 (gentleness; jolliness)
[ˈswɑːvəti]	记 来自 suave (*adj.* 温和文雅)
subcelestial	*adj.* 世俗的, 尘世的 (worldly)
[ˌsʌbsiˈlestiəl]	记 参考 celestial (*adj.* 天上的, 神圣的)
subjugate	*v.* 征服, 镇压 (to bring under control and governance)
[ˈsʌbdʒugeit]	记 词根记忆: sub (下面) +jug (=yoke 牛轭) +ate → 置于牛轭之下 → 征服
sublimate	*v.* (使)升华, 净化 (to sublime)
[ˈsʌblimeit]	记 来自 sublime (*v.* 使崇高)
sublime	*adj.* 崇高的 (lofty in thought, expression, or manner) *v.* 使崇高
[səˈblaim]	搭 sublime in art 艺术的崇高
submit	*v.* 屈服 (to admit defeat); 提交, 呈递 (to offer for consideration)
[səbˈmit]	记 词根记忆: sub (下面的) +mit (送, 放出) → 从下面递上 → 提交, 呈递
	例 Because the report contained much more information than the reviewers needed to see, the author was asked to ***submit*** a compendium instead.
suborn	*v.* 收买, 贿赂 (to induce secretly to do an unlawful thing)
[səˈbɔːrn]	记 词根记忆: sub (下面) +orn (装饰) → 在下面给人好处 → 贿赂
subpoena	*n.* 【律】传票 (a written order requiring a person to appear in court) *v.* 传讯 (to summon with a writ of subpoena)
[səˈpiːnə]	记 词根记忆: sub (下面) + poena (=penalty 惩罚) → 接下来可能受到惩罚 → 传讯
subreption	*n.* 隐瞒真相, 歪曲事实 (a deliberate misrepresentation)
[səbˈrepʃən]	
subscribe	*v.* 捐助 (to give sth. in accordance with a promise); 订购 (to enter one's name for a publication or service)
[səbˈskraib]	记 词根记忆: sub (下面) + scribe (写) → 写下订单 → 订购
subsequent	*adj.* 随后的, 后来的, 连续的 (later; following)
[ˈsʌbsikwənt]	记 词根记忆: sub (下面) +sequ (跟随) +ent → 跟随在…后面的 → 随后的
	例 Science progresses by building on what has come before; important findings thus form the basis of ***subsequent*** experiments.
subsidiary	*adj.* 辅助的 (furnishing aid or support; auxiliary); 次要的 (of second importance)
[səbˈsidieri]	记 词根记忆: sub (下面) +sid (坐) +iary → 坐在下面的 → 辅助的
subsidy	*n.* 补助金 (a grant or gift of money)
[ˈsʌbsədi]	记 联想记忆: sub (下面) +sid (坐) +y → 坐下来领补助金 → 补助金
subsistence	*n.* 生存, 生计 (the ability to live with little money or food); 存在 (existence)
[səbˈsistəns]	记 来自 subsist (*v.* 生存)
substance	*n.* 主旨, 实质 (most important or essential part of sth.); 物质 (particular type of matter)
[ˈsʌbstəns]	

□ suavity	□ subcelestial	□ subjugate	□ sublimate	□ sublime	□ submit
□ suborn	□ subpoena	□ subreption	□ subscribe	□ subsequent	□ subsidiary
□ subsidy	□ subsistence	□ substance			

例 One of photography's most basic and powerful traits is its ability to give *substance* to history, to present precise visual details of a time gone by.

substantial [səbˈstænʃl]	*adj.* 坚固的，结实的（strongly made）；实质的（concerning the important part or meaning） 例 In contrast to the *substantial* muscular activity required for inhalation, exhalation is usually a passive process.
substratum [ˌsʌbˈstreɪtəm]	*n.* 基础；地基（an underlying support；foundation） 记 词根记忆：sub（下面）+ stratum（层次）→ 下面一层 → 基础
subsume [səbˈsuːm]	*v.* 包含，包括（to include within） 记 词根记忆：sub（下面）+sume（拿）→ 拿在下面 → 包含
subterfuge [ˈsʌbtərfjuːdʒ]	*n.* 诡计，托辞（a deceptive device or stratagem） 记 词根记忆：subter（私下）+ fuge（逃跑）→ 诡计，托辞
subvention [səbˈvenʃn]	*n.* 补助金，津贴（the provision of assistance or financial support） 记 词根记忆：sub（下面）+ vent（来）+ ion → 来到下面作为帮助 → 补助金
suckle [ˈsʌkl]	*v.* 给…哺乳；吮吸 搭 a cow suckling her calves 给小牛吃奶的母牛
sufficient [səˈfɪʃnt]	*adj.* 足够的（enough to meet the needs） 例 Having *sufficient* income of her own constituted for Alice a material independence that made possible a degree of security in her emotional life as well.
suffocate [ˈsʌfəkeɪt]	*v.* （使）窒息，把…闷死（to die from being unable to breathe） 记 词根记忆：suf+foc（喉咙）+ate → 在喉咙下面 → （使）窒息
suggestive [səˈdʒestɪv]	*adj.* 暗示的（giving a suggestion；indicative） 同 evocative, redolent, symbolic
sulky [ˈsʌlki]	*adj.* 生气的（moodily silent） 记 词根记忆：sulk（生气）+ y → 生气的
sullen [ˈsʌlən]	*adj.* 忧郁的（dismal；gloomy） 同 brooding, morose, sulky
summation [sʌˈmeɪʃn]	*n.* 总结，概要（a summary）；总数，合计（a total） 同 summing up
summon [ˈsʌmən]	*v.* 传唤（to order officially to come）；召集（to call together；convene）
sunder [ˈsʌndər]	*v.* 分裂，分离（to separate by violence or by intervening time or space） 记 发音记忆："散的" → 分离
sundry [ˈsʌndri]	*adj.* 各式各样，各种的（miscellaneous；various） 记 组合词：sun（太阳）+ dry（干）→ 太阳晒干各种东西 → 各种的
superannuated [ˌsuːpərˈænjueɪtɪd]	*adj.* 老迈的（incapable or disqualified for active duty by advanced age） 记 词根记忆：super（超过）+ annu（年）+ ated → 超过一定年龄的 → 老迈的

40

□ substantial	□ substratum	□ subsume	□ subterfuge	□ subvention	□ suckle
□ sufficient	□ suffocate	□ suggestive	□ sulky	□ sullen	□ summation
□ summon	□ sunder	□ sundry	□ superannuated		

supererogatory [ˌsjuːprəˈrɔgətɔːri]	*adj.* 职责以外的；多余的 同 superfluous, unnecessary
superfluity [ˌsuːpərˈfluːəti]	*n.* 过剩（a larger amount than what is needed） 记 来自 superfluous（*adj.* 多余的）
superimpose [ˌsuːpərimˈpouz]	*v.* 重叠，叠加（to place or lay over or above sth.） 记 词根记忆：super（在…上面）+ im + pose（放置）→ 放在上面的 → 重叠，叠加
superiority [suˌpiriˈɔːrəti]	*n.* 优越(感)（the quality or state of being superior） 记 来自 superior（*adj.* 优越的）
superlative [suːˈpɜːrlətɪv]	*adj.* 最好的（surpassing all others；supreme） 记 词根记忆：super（在…上面）+lat（放）+ive → 放在别的上面 → 最好的
supervise [ˈsuːpərvaɪz]	*v.* 监督，管理（to keep watch over a job or the people doing it） 记 词根记忆：super（在…上面）+vise（看）→ 在上面看 → 监督
supine [ˈsuːpaɪn]	*adj.* 仰卧的（lying on the back）；懒散的（mentally or morally slack） 同 prone; inactive
supplicate [ˈsʌplikeit]	*v.* 恳求，祈求（to make a humble entreaty） 记 词根记忆：sup（下面）+plic（重叠）+ate → 双膝跪下 → 恳求 supplicate
supreme [suːˈpriːm]	*adj.* 最高的（having the highest position）；极度的（highest in degree） 记 联想记忆：supre（=super 超过）+me → 超越我的 → 最高的
surfeit [ˈsɜːrfɪt]	*n.* 饮食过量，过度（an overabundant supply）*v.* 使过量 记 词根记忆：sur（过分）+feit（做）→ 做过了头 → 过度
surge [sɜːrdʒ]	*v.* 波涛汹涌（to rise and move in waves or billows） 记 本身为词根，意为"升起，立起"
surplus [ˈsɜːrpləs]	*adj.* 过剩的，剩余的（the amount remained）；盈余的（the excess of a corporation's net worth） 记 词根记忆：sur（超过）+plus（加，多余的）→ 剩余的
suspect [səˈspekt]	*v.* 怀疑（to doubt the truth or value of）*n.* 嫌疑犯 *adj.* 可疑的（of uncertain truth, quality, legality, etc.） 记 词根记忆：sus+pect（=spect 看）→ 从上到下地 → 怀疑
suspicion [səˈspɪʃn]	*n.* 怀疑，嫌疑（doubt） 记 来自 suspect（*v.* 怀疑） 例 She worked for recognition and fame, yet she felt a deep *suspicion* and respect for the world in which recognition and fame are granted, the world of money and opinion and power.
sustained [səˈsteɪnd]	*adj.* 持久的，持续的（prolonged） 记 来自 sustain（*v.* 保持） 例 Exposure to *sustained* noise has been claimed to impair blood pressure regulation in human beings and, particularly, to increase hypertension, even though some researchers have obtained inconclusive results that obscure.

svelte [svelt]	*adj.* (女人)体态苗条的(slender; lithe) 同 slim, willowy
swagger ['swægər]	*v.* 大摇大摆地走(to walk with an air of overbearing self-confidence) 记 参考waddle(*v.* (鸭子等)摇摆着走)
swallow ['swɑːloʊ]	*v.* 吞下, 咽下; 忍受(to accept patiently or without question) 搭 swallow a bite (鱼)吞饵上钩
swamp [swɑːmp]	*n.* 沼泽(land which is always full of water) *v.* 使陷入困境(to cause to have a large amount of problems to deal with); 淹没
swank [swæŋk]	*v.* 夸耀, 炫耀(to show; swagger; boast) 记 联想记忆: swan(天鹅)+k → 像天鹅一样骄傲 → 炫耀
swarthy ['swɔːrði]	*adj.* (皮肤等)黝黑的(of a dark color, complexion) 同 brunet, swart, tan
swathe [sweɪð]	*v.* 包, 绑, 裹(to bind, wrap, or swaddle with or as if with a bandage)
sway [sweɪ]	*v.* 摇动, 摇摆(to swing from side to side); 影响(to influence sb. so that they change their opinion) *n.* 摇摆(swaying movement) 记 联想记忆: s+way(路) → 走S型的路 → 摇摆
swear [swer]	*v.* 诅咒(to use profane or obscene language) 同 blaspheme, execrate
swell [swel]	*v.* 肿胀, 增强(to expand gradually beyond a normal or original limit) 记 联想记忆: s+well(泉) → 像泉水一样冒出来 → 肿胀, 增强
sweltering ['sweltərɪŋ]	*adj.* 酷热的(oppressively hot) 记 来自swelter(*v.* 汗流浃背)
swerve [swɜːrv]	*v.* 突然改变方向(to turn aside abruptly from a straight line or course; deviate) 记 联想记忆: serve(发球)中间加w(where) → 发球突然改变方向后都不知道球到哪去了 → 突然改变方向
swig [swɪɡ]	*v.* 痛饮(to drink in long drafts) 同 gulp, guzzle
swill [swɪl]	*v.* 冲洗(to wash; drench); 痛饮(to guzzle) 记 联想记忆: sw(看作swim, 游泳)+ill(有病的) → 游泳之后冲个热水澡才不会生病 → 冲洗
swindle ['swɪndl]	*v.* 诈骗(to obtain money or property by fraud or deceit) 记 联想记忆: s + wind(风) + le → 四处吹风, 搞诈骗 → 诈骗
swine [swaɪn]	*n.* 猪(pig) 记 联想记忆: s + wine(酒) → 喝酒喝多了, 就胖得像只猪一样 → 猪
swing [swɪŋ]	*v.* 摇摆(to move backwards and forwards); 旋转(to move in a smooth curve) *n.* 秋千 记 联想记忆: s+wing(翅膀) → 摇摆翅膀, 在风中转向 → 旋转

40

Word List 41  MP3 - 41

swipe [swaɪp]	*n.* 猛击 (a sweeping blow or stroke) *v.* 猛击 (to hit with a sweeping motion) 记 联想记忆: s+wipe(擦) → 起了磨擦后大打出手 → 猛击
swirl [swɜːrl]	*v.* 旋转 (to move with an eddying motion) *n.* 旋涡 (a whirling motion; eddy) 记 词根记忆: s+wirl(转) → 旋转
swoop [swuːp]	*v.* 猛扑 (to move in a sudden sweep); 攫取 (to seize or snatch in or as if in a sudden sweeping movement)
sybaritic [ˌsɪbəˈrɪtɪk]	*adj.* 骄奢淫逸的, 贪图享乐的 (devoted to or marked by pleasure and luxury) 记 联想记忆: sy(看作 see, 看)+bar(酒吧)+itic → 看着酒吧里放纵的身影 → 骄奢淫逸的
syncretize [ˈsɪŋkrətaɪz]	*v.* (使)结合, (使)融和 (to attempt to unite and harmonize especially without critical examination or logical unity)
syndrome [ˈsɪndroʊm]	*n.* 综合症 (a set of medical symptoms which represent a physical or mental disorder) 记 词根记忆: syn(一起)+drom(跑)+e → 跑到一起 → 综合症 例 The "impostor *syndrome*" often afflicts those who fear that true self-disclosure will lower them in others' esteem; rightly handled, however, candor may actually enhance one's standing.
synopsis [sɪˈnɑːpsɪs]	*n.* 摘要, 概要 (a condensed statement or outline) 记 词根记忆: syn(一起)+op(看)+sis → 让大家一起看 → 摘要
table [ˈteɪbl]	*v.* 搁置, 不予考虑 (to remove from consideration indefinitely) 记 联想记忆: table 原意为"桌子" → 把问题放在桌子上不去看 → 搁置
taboo [təˈbuː]	*adj.* 忌讳的 (banned on grounds of morality) *n.* 禁忌 (a prohibition imposed by social custom)
taciturn [ˈtæsɪtɜːrn]	*adj.* 沉默寡言的 (temperamentally disinclined to talk) 同 mute, reserved, reticent, withdrawn
tackle [ˈtækl]	*v.* 处理 (to take action in order to deal with) *n.* 滑车 (a mechanism for lifting weights)

tactic [ˈtæktɪk]	*n.* 策略，手段(a device for accomplishing an end)；战术(a method of employing forces in combat) 记 词根记忆：tact(使正确)+ic → 策略，手段
taking [ˈteɪkɪŋ]	*adj.* 楚楚动人的，迷人的(gaining the liking of) 同 attractive, charming
tally [ˈtæli]	*v.* (使)一致，符合(to correspond；match) 记 联想记忆：t+ally(联盟) → 目标一致，结成同盟 → (使)一致
tambourine [ˌtæmbəˈriːn]	*n.* 铃鼓，小手鼓(a small drum played by shaking or striking with the hand) 记 来自tambour(*n.* 鼓)
tame [teɪm]	*adj.* 驯服的(submissive；docile)；沉闷的，平淡的(unexciting and uninteresting) 同 domesticated
tamp [tæmp]	*v.* 捣实，夯实(to drive in or down by a succession of blows) 记 发音记忆："踏" → 用力踏 → 夯实
tamper [ˈtæmpər]	*v.* 干预，损害(to interfere in a harmful manner)；篡改(to alter improperly) 记 是temper(*v.* 锻造；调和)的变体
tangy [ˈtæŋi]	*adj.* 气味刺激的，扑鼻的(having a pleasantly sharp flavor)
tantrum [ˈtæntrəm]	*n.* 发脾气，发怒(a fit of bad temper) 记 发音记忆："太蠢" → 大庭广众之下发脾气，真是蠢 → 发脾气，发怒
tarry [ˈtæri]	*v.* 耽搁(to delay in starting or going；dawdle；linger) 同 dally, procrastinate, temporize
tart [tɑːrt]	*adj.* 酸的(acid)；尖酸的(acrimonious；biting) 搭 a tart reply 尖刻的答复
tasty [ˈteɪsti]	*adj.* 美味的(having a pleasant flavor)；有品位的(having or showing good taste)
tatter [ˈtætər]	*n.* 碎片(a part torn and left hanging) *v.* 撕碎(to make ragged) 搭 in tatters 破烂不堪；被毁坏的
tattle [ˈtætl]	*v.* 闲聊(to chatter)；泄露秘密(to tell secrets) 同 leak, snitch, spill, squeal
tatty [ˈtæti]	*adj.* 破旧的，褴褛的，破败的(shabby or dilapidated) 同 decrepit, deteriorated, ragged, shabby
tauten [ˈtɔːtn]	*v.* (使)拉紧，(使)绷紧(to make or become taut) 记 来自taut(*adj.* 绷紧的)
tear [ter]	*v.* 撕裂(to pull into pieces by force) 搭 tear sb./sth. to shreds 彻底毁灭
tease [tiːz]	*v.* 逗乐，戏弄(to make fun of)；强求，强要(to obtain by repeated coaxing) *n.* 逗乐，戏弄(the act of teasing)

41

□ tactic	□ taking	□ tally	□ tambourine	□ tame	□ tamp
□ tamper	□ tangy	□ tantrum	□ tarry	□ tart	□ tasty
□ tatter	□ tattle	□ tatty	□ tauten	□ tear	□ tease

443

teeter [ˈtiːtər]	*v.* 摇摇欲坠；步履蹒跚(to walk or move unsteadily)；踌躇(to hesitate)
	同 totter, wobble
teetotal [ˌtiːˈtoʊtl]	*adj.* 滴酒不沾的(completely abstinent from alcoholic drinks)；完全的，全部的(complete, total)
	记 来自英国戒酒运动拥护者 Turner 在某次戒酒演讲中的一个口误，total 一词因口吃讹音为 teetotal
temerity [təˈmerəti]	*n.* 鲁莽，大胆(audacity; rashness; recklessness)
	记 词根记忆：tem(黑暗的)+er+ity → 摸黑行动 → 鲁莽，大胆
temper [ˈtempər]	*v.* 锻炼(to toughen)；调和，使缓和(to dilute, or soften) *n.* 脾气，性情(disposition)
	记 联想记忆：用锤子(hammer)锤炼(temper)
tempest [ˈtempɪst]	*n.* 暴风雨(a violent storm)；骚动(tumult; uproar)
	记 联想记忆：temp(看作 temper, 脾气)+est → 老天爷发脾气 → 暴风雨
tempestuous [temˈpestʃuəs]	*adj.* 狂暴的(turbulent; stormy)
	搭 a tempestuous relationship 冲突不断的关系
tempo [ˈtempoʊ]	*n.* (音乐的)速度(the rate of speed of a musical piece or passage indicated by one of a series of directions (as largo, presto, or allegro) and often by an exact metronome marking)；(动作、生活的)步调，节奏(rate of motion or activity)
	记 来自词根 tempor(*n.* 时间)
	例 During the opera's most famous aria, the *tempo* chosen by the orchestra's conductor seemed capricious, without necessary relation to what had gone before.
temporize [ˈtempəraɪz]	*v.* 拖延(to draw out discussions or negotiations so as to gain time)；见风使舵(to act to suit the time or occasion)
	记 词根记忆：tempor(时间)+ize → 拖延
tend [tend]	*v.* 照料，照看(to act as an attendant; serve)
	搭 tend the sick 护理病人
tensile [ˈtensl]	*adj.* 张力的(of, or relating to tension)；可伸展的(capable of being stretched)
tenure [ˈtenjər]	*n.* 占有期(the term of holding sth.)；任期；终身职位
	记 词根记忆：ten(拿住)+ure → 始终拿住 → 占有期，任期
terminal [ˈtɜːrmɪnl]	*adj.* 末端的(of, or relating to an end) *n.* 终点，末端(an end or extremity of sth.)
	记 词根记忆：tormin(结束)+al → 终点，末端
terminate [ˈtɜːrmɪneɪt]	*v.* 终止，结束(to bring to an end; close)
	记 词根记忆：termin(结束)+ate → 终止，结束
terminus [ˈtɜːrmɪnəs]	*n.* (火车、汽车的)终点站(terminal)
	记 词根记忆：termin(结束)+us → 结束地 → 终点站

terminate

testify [ˈtestɪfaɪ]	*v.* 见证，证实（to bear witness to） 记 词根记忆：test(看到)+ify → 见证，证实
testimony [ˈtestɪmoʊni]	*n.* 证据，证词（firsthand authentication of a fact；evidence） 记 词根记忆：test(看到)+imony → 所看到的 → 证据 例 The *testimony* of eyewitnesses is notoriously unreliable; emotion and excitement all too often cause our minds to distort what we see.
testy [ˈtesti]	*adj.* 暴躁的，易怒的（easily annoyed；irritable） 记 联想记忆：test(考试)+y → 为考试伤脑筋，很不耐烦 → 易怒的
thaw [θɔː]	*v.* 解冻，融化（to go from a frozen to a liquid state；melt） 记 联想记忆：t+haw（看作 hoe，锄地）→ 冰雪融化便可以锄地了 → 解冻，融化
thermal [ˈθɜːrml]	*adj.* 热的，热量的（pertaining to heat）；温暖的（warm）*n.* 上升的暖气流（a rising current of warm air）
thespian [ˈθespiən]	*adj.* 戏剧的（relating to drama；dramatic） 记 来自古希腊悲剧创始者 Thespis
thrash [θræʃ]	*v.* 鞭打（to beat soundly with a stick or whip） 记 联想记忆：th+rash(鲁莽的) → 一时气急，鞭打别人 → 鞭打
threadbare [ˈθredber]	*adj.* 磨破的（worn off；shabby）；陈腐的（exhausted of interest or freshness） 记 组合词：thread(线)+bare(露出) → 露出线头 → 磨破的
throe [θroʊ]	*n.* 剧痛（anguish；pang）；[*pl.*]挣扎（a hard or painful struggle） 搭 in the throes of sth./doing sth. 正在做，正忙于（尤其指困难或复杂的活动）
throng [θrɑːŋ]	*n.* 一大群（a large number）*v.* 拥挤（to crowd together） 同 concourse, flock, swarm
thrust [θrʌst]	*v.* 猛力推（to push or drive with force）；刺，戳（to stab；pierce） 搭 thrust sth./sb. on/upon sb. 把…强加于；强迫…接受
thump [θʌmp]	*v.* 重击，捶击（to pound） 同 punch, smack, whack
ticklish [ˈtɪklɪʃ]	*adj.* 怕痒的（sensitive to being tickled）；易怒的（touchy） 记 来自 tickle(*v.* 发痒)
tiff [tɪf]	*n.* 口角，小争吵（a petty quarrel） 同 altercation, falling-out, miff
tightfisted [ˈtaɪtfɪstɪd]	*adj.* 吝啬的（stingy） 记 联想记忆：tight(紧的)+fist(拳头)+ed → 抓住不松手 → 吝啬的
tilt [tɪlt]	*v.* (使)倾斜（to slant）*n.* 倾斜（the act of tilting or the condition of being tilted）；斜坡（a sloping surface）
timbre [ˈtæmbər]	*n.* 音色，音质（the quality given to a sound by its overtones） 记 联想记忆：要想乐器音色(timbre)好，必须用好木材(timber)
timely [ˈtaɪmli]	*adj.* 适时的，及时的（appropriate or adapted to the times or the occasion） 记 来自 time(*n.* 时间)

41

| **timeworn** | *adj.* 陈旧的，陈腐的（hackneyed；stale） |
| [ˈtaɪmwɔːrn] | 记 组合词：time（时间）+worn（用旧的）→ 陈旧的 |

timid
[ˈtɪmɪd]

adj. 羞怯的（lacking self-confidence；shy）；胆怯的，怯懦的（fearful and hesitant）
记 词根记忆：tim（害怕）+id → 胆怯的

tinder
[ˈtɪndər]

n. 火绒，火种（sth. that serves to incite or inflame）
记 词根记忆：tind（点燃）+er → 用于点火的东西 → 火绒

tinge
[tɪndʒ]

v. 给…着色（to apply a trace of color to）；使略带…气息（to affect or modify with a slight odor or taste）

tinkle
[ˈtɪŋkl]

v. （使）发出叮当声（to make or emit light metallic sounds）

tirade
[ˈtaɪreɪd]

n. 长篇的攻击性演说（a long and angry speech）
记 词根记忆：tir（拉）+ade → 拉长的话 → 长篇的攻击性演说

to-do
[təˈduː]

n. 喧闹，骚乱（fuss）
同 commotion, stir

toil
[tɔɪl]

v. 苦干，辛苦劳作（to work hard and long）*n.* 辛苦，辛劳（long strenuous fatiguing labor）

toll
[toʊl]

n. 通行费（money paid for the use of a road, bridge, etc.）；代价，损失（loss or damage caused by sth.）*v.* （缓慢而有规律地）敲（to sound with slow measured strokes）
记 发音记忆："痛" → 受伤了，很痛 → 代价，损失
例 In a nation where the economic reversals of the past few years have taken a psychological as well as a financial *toll* on many regions, what most distinguishes the South may be the degree of optimism throughout the region.

tome
[toʊm]

n. 册，卷（a volume forming part of a larger work）；大部头的书（a large or scholarly book）

toothsome
[ˈtuːθsəm]

adj. 可口的，美味的（of palatable flavor and pleasing texture）
同 appetizing, delectable, divine, savory, yummy

topsy-turvy
[ˌtɑːpsi ˈtɜːrvi]

adj. 颠倒的，相反的（with the top or head downward）；乱七八糟的，混乱的（in utter confusion or disorder）

torment
[ˈtɔːrment]

n. 折磨，痛苦（very great pain in mind or body）
记 词根记忆：tor（=tort 扭曲）+ment → 身体和灵魂被扭曲 → 折磨，痛苦

torrent
[ˈtɑːrənt]

n. 洪流，急流（a violently rushing stream）
同 deluge, gush, inundation

torrential
[təˈrenʃl]

adj. 奔流的，洪流的，湍急的（resembling or forming torrents）
搭 torrential rain 大雨如注

torrid
[ˈtɑːrɪd]

adj. 酷热的（intensely hot）
记 词根记忆：torr（使干燥）+id → 酷热的

toss [tɑːs]	*v.* 投，掷（to throw in a careless or aimless way），使摇动，使颠簸（to cause to move from side to side or back and forth）
totter [ˈtɑːtər]	*v.* 摇摇欲坠（to tremble or rock as if about to fall），步履蹒跚（to stagger; wobble）
toy [tɔɪ]	*v.* 不认真地对待，玩弄（to deal with sth. lightly） 搭 toy with sth. 把…当儿戏
track [træk]	*n.* 轨迹，踪迹（a mark or succession of marks left by sth. that has passed），道路，路径（a path, route, or course indicated by such marks），轨道（a path along which sth. moves）*v.* 跟踪，追踪（to follow the tracks or traces of）
tract [trækt]	*n.* 传单（a leaflet of political or religion propaganda），大片土地（a large stretch or area of land）
tractability [ˌtræktəˈbɪləti]	*n.* 温顺 记 来自 tractable（*adj.* 易处理的；易驾驭的）
traduce [trəˈduːs]	*v.* 中伤，诽谤（to slander or defame） 记 词根记忆：tra(=trans 横)+duc(引导)+e → 引到歪里去 → 诽谤
tragedy [ˈtrædʒədi]	*n.* 惨剧，惨事，灾难（a terrible event that causes great sadness） 同 affliction, calamity, catastrophe, woe
traipse [treɪps]	*v.* 漫步，闲荡（to walk or travel about without apparent plan but with or without a purpose）
traitor [ˈtreɪtər]	*n.* 卖国贼，叛徒（one who betrays one's country, a cause, or a trust, especially one who commits treason） 记 参考 traditor（*n.* 叛教者）
tramp [træmp]	*v.* 重步走（to walk, tread, or step heavily） 同 plod, stomp, tromp
tranquility [træŋˈkwɪləti]	*n.* 宁静，安静（the quality or state of being tranquil） 记 来自 tranquil（*adj.* 宁静的，安静的）
transfer [trænsˈfɜːr]	*v.* 转移，传递（to convey or cause to pass from one place, person, or thing to another），转让（to make over the possession or legal title of），调任，调动（to move oneself from one location or job to another） 记 词根记忆：trans(穿过)+fer(带来) → 从一个地方带到另一个地方 → 转移，传递 例 It is a great advantage to be able to **transfer** useful genes with as little extra gene material as possible, because the donor's genome may contain, in addition to desirable genes, many genes with deleterious effects.
transfigure [trænsˈfɪɡjər]	*v.* 美化，改观（to transform outwardly for the better） 记 联想记忆：trans(改变)+figure(形象) → 美化，改观
transgression [trænzˈɡreʃn]	*n.* 违法，犯罪（a violation of a law） 记 来自 transgress（*v.* 越轨；违背）

41

transience [ˈtrænʃəns]	*n.* 短暂，稍纵即逝(the quality or state of being transient)
	搭 the transience of human life 人生的短暂
transpose [trænˈspoʊz]	*v.* 颠倒顺序，调换(to reverse the order or position of)
	记 词根记忆：trans(穿过)+pos(放)+e → 放到另一边 → 颠倒顺序，调换
trapeze [træˈpiːz]	*n.* 高空秋千，吊架(a short bar hung high above the ground from two ropes used by gymnasts and acrobats)
traverse [trəˈvɜːrs]	*v.* 横穿，横跨(to go or travel across or over)
	记 词根记忆：tra(穿过)+vers(转向)+e → 横穿，横跨
travesty [ˈtrævəsti]	*v.* 滑稽地模仿
	记 词根记忆：tra(横)+vest(穿衣)+y → 横过来穿衣 → 滑稽地模仿
treachery [ˈtretʃəri]	*n.* 背叛(violation of allegiance; treason)
	记 词根记忆：treach(=trick 诡计)+ery → 在背后耍诡计 → 背叛
	例 The heretofore peaceful natives, seeking retribution for the *treachory* of their supposed allies, became, justifiably enough according to their perspective, embittered and vindictive.
treaty [ˈtriːti]	*n.* 条约(a formal agreement between two or more states)；协议(a contract or agreement)
	记 来自 treat(*v.* 处理；协商)
trek [trek]	*v.* 艰苦跋涉(to make one's way arduously)
	同 traipse, trudge
tremendous [trəˈmendəs]	*adj.* 恐慌的，可怕的(being such as may excite trembling or arouse dread)；巨大的，惊人的(notable by extreme power, greatness or excellence)
	记 来自 tremble(*v.* 颤抖)
	例 As an outstanding publisher, Alfred Knopf was able to make occasional mistakes, but his bad judgment was tolerated in view of his *tremendous* success.
tremor [ˈtremər]	*n.* 颤动；颤抖，战栗
	记 词根记忆：trem(抖动)+or → 颤动；颤抖
tremulous [ˈtremjələs]	*adj.* 颤动的(characterized by or affected with trembling or tremors; quivering)；胆怯的，怯懦的(affected with timidity)
tribute [ˈtrɪbjuːt]	*n.* 赞词，颂词(eulogy)；贡物(a payment by one ruler or nation to another in acknowledgement of submission)
	记 词根记忆：tribut(给予)+e → 贡物
trifle [ˈtraɪfl]	*n.* 微不足道的事物，琐事(sth. of little value, substance, or importance)
	同 diddly, picayune, triviality
trim [trɪm]	*v.* 修剪(to make neat by cutting or clipping) *adj.* 井井有条的(in good and neat order)

traverse

| **trinket** | *n.* 小装饰品, (尤指)不值钱的珠宝(a small ornament, especially a small, |
| [ˈtrɪŋkɪt] | cheap piece of jewelry); 琐事(a trivial thing; trifle) |

trivia	*n.* 琐事, 小事(trivial facts or details)
[ˈtrɪviə]	记 词根记忆: tri(三)+via(路) → 古罗马时的妇女们常在三岔路口谈论一些
	琐事, 引申为"琐事" → 琐事

| **troll** | *v.* 用曳绳钓(鱼), 拖钓(to fish for by trailing a baited line from behind a |
| [troʊl] | slowly moving boat); 兴高采烈地唱(to sing in a jovial manner) |

| **trounce** | *v.* 痛击, 严惩(to thrash or punish severely) |
| [traʊns] | |

truant	*adj.* 逃避责任的(shirking responsibility) *n.* 逃学者(one who is absent
[ˈtruːənt]	without permission, especially from school); 逃避者, 玩忽职守者(one who
	shirks duty)

| **trudge** | *v.* 跋涉(to walk or march steadily and laboriously) |
| [trʌdʒ] | 同 tramp |

| **trumpery** | *adj.* 中看不中用的(showy but of little value) |
| [ˈtrʌmpəri] | 记 来自trump(*n.* 王牌) |

| **tumble** | *v.* 突然跌倒, 突然下跌(to fall suddenly and helplessly); 倒塌(to fall into |
| [ˈtʌmbl] | ruin) |

| **tumid** | *adj.* 肿起的, 肿胀的(swollen; enlarged) |
| [ˈtjuːmɪd] | 记 词根记忆: tum(肿)+id → 肿起的, 肿胀的 |

tumult	*n.* 喧哗, 吵闹(disorderly agitation or milling about of a crowd usually with
[ˈtuːmʌlt]	uproar and confusion of voices); 骚动, 骚乱(a disorderly commotion or
	disturbance)

| **turgid** | *adj.* 肿胀的(swollen; bloated); 浮夸的(bombastic; pompous) |
| [ˈtɜːrdʒɪd] | 搭 a turgid style of writing 浮夸的文体 |

| **turncoat** | *n.* 背叛者, 变节者(one who switches to an opposing side or party) |
| [ˈtɜːrnkoʊt] | 同 renegade, traitor |

| **tusk** | *n.* (象等的)长牙(an elongated, greatly enlarged tooth) |
| [tʌsk] | 记 联想记忆: 保护好自己的长牙(tusk)是大象们的重要任务(task)之一 |

tutor	*n.* 助教(an assistant lecturer in a college); 导
[ˈtuːtər]	师, 辅导教师(one that gives additional, special,
	or remedial instruction); 监护人(the legal
	guardian of a minor and of the minor's property)
	v. 辅导, 指导(to give instruction to)

小学数学
咋这么难

tutor

tweak	*v.* 扭, 拧, 揪(to pinch and pull with a sudden
[twiːk]	jerk and twist); 调节, 微调(to make usually
	small adjustments in or to)

| **twee** | *adj.* 矫揉造作的, 故作多情的(affectedly or excessively dainty, delicate, |
| [twiː] | cute, or quaint) |

41

twinge	*n.* （生理、心理上的）剧痛（a sharp, sudden physical pain; a moral or
[twɪndʒ]	emotional pang）
	记 联想记忆：twin（双胞胎）+ge → 据说双胞胎有心理感应，能感知对方的
	疼痛 →（生理、心理上的）剧痛

| **typhoon** | *n.* 台风（a tropical hurricane or cyclone） |
| [taɪˈfuːn] | |

| **tyranny** | *n.* 暴政，专制统治（oppressive power exerted by government）；暴行（a |
| [ˈtɪrəni] | cruel or unjust act） |

| **tyro** | *n.* 新手（a beginner in learning; novice） |
| [ˈtaɪrou] | 同 a green hand |

ugly	*adj.* 难看的（unpleasant to look at）；令人不快的（offensive or unpleasant to
[ˈʌgli]	any sense）
	例 The mayor and school superintendent let their dispute over budget
	cuts escalate to *ugly* and destructive proportions.

ulcer	*n.* 溃疡（a break in skin or mucous membrane with loss of surface tissue,
[ˈʌlsər]	disintegration and necrosis of epithelial tissue, and often pus）；腐烂物
	（sth. that festers and corrupts like an open sore）

| **ulcerate** | *v.* 溃烂（to affect with an ulcer） |
| [ˈʌlsəreɪt] | 记 来自 ulcer（*n.* 溃疡） |

| **ultramundane** | *adj.* 世界之外的；超俗的 |
| [ˌʌltrəˈmʌndeɪn] | 记 词根记忆：ultra（超出）+mund（世界）+ane → 超俗的 |

| **umpire** | *n.* 仲裁者（one having authority to decide finally a controversy or question |
| [ˈʌmpaɪər] | between parties）*v.* 对…进行仲裁（to supervise or decide as umpire） |

| **unaffected** | *adj.* 自然的，不矫揉造作的（free from affectation; genuine） |
| [ˌʌnəˈfektɪd] | 记 联想记忆：un（不）+affected（做作的）→ 自然的，不矫揉造作的 |

unanimous	*adj.* 全体一致的（being of one mind）
[juˈnænɪməs]	记 词根记忆：un（=uni 一个）+anim（生命，精神）+ous → 全体一致的
	例 Although some of her fellow scientists decried the unorthodox
	laboratory methodology that others found innovative, *unanimous* praise
	greeted her experimental results: at once pioneering and
	unexceptionable.

unassuming	*adj.* 不摆架子的，不装腔作势的，谦逊的（not arrogant or presuming;
[ˌʌnəˈsuːmɪŋ]	modest）
	记 联想记忆：un（不）+assuming（傲慢的）→ 谦逊的

unbend	*v.* 变直（to become straight）；轻松行事，放松（to behave in a less formal
[ˌʌnˈbend]	and severe manner）
	记 联想记忆：un（不）+bend（弯曲）→ 变直

| **unbidden** | *adj.* 未经邀请的（unasked; uninvited） |
| [ʌnˈbɪdn] | 记 联想记忆：un（不）+bid（邀请）+den → 未经邀请的 |

| **unbosom** | *v.* 倾诉，吐露（to disclose the thoughts or feelings of） |
| [ʌnˈbuzəm] | 同 reveal |

unconscionable	*adj.* 无节制的，过度的，不合理的（excessive; unreasonable）
[ʌnˈkɑːnʃənəbl]	记 联想记忆：un(不)+conscionable(公正的，凭良心的) → 无节制的
uncouth	*adj.* 粗野的，笨拙的（boorish; clumsy in speech or behavior）
[ʌnˈkuːθ]	同 barbaric, coarse, gross, rustic
underbid	*v.* 叫价低于；要价过低（to bid too low）
[ˌʌndərˈbɪd]	记 组合词：under(低于)+bid(出价) → 叫价低于
underdog	*n.* 居于下风者（a loser or predicted loser in a struggle or contest）；受欺负者，受欺压者（a victim of injustice or persecution）
[ˈʌndərdɑːɡ]	记 联想记忆：under(在…下面)+dog(狗) → 受欺负者
	例 The plot of the motion picture *Hoosiers* is trite; we have all seen this story, the tale of an *underdog* team going on to win a championship, in one form or another countless times.
undergird	*v.* 从底层支持，加固…的底部（to strengthen from the bottom）
[ˌʌndərˈɡɜːrd]	记 联想记忆：under(在…下面)+gird(束紧) → 在下面束紧 → 从底层支持
underling	*n.* 部下，下属，手下（subordinate; inferior）
[ˈʌndərlɪŋ]	记 联想记忆：under(在…下面)+ling → 部下，下属
underlying	*adj.* 在下面的；根本的；潜在的
[ˌʌndərˈlaɪɪŋ]	记 联想记忆：under(在…下面)+lying(躺着的) → 在下面躺着的 → 在下面的；根本的；潜在的
	例 Despite the apparently bewildering complexity of this procedure, the *underlying* principle is quite elementary.
understudy	*n.* 预备演员，替角 *v.* 充当…的替角（to act as an understudy to）
[ˈʌndərstʌdi]	
underwrite	*v.* 同意负担…的费用（to support with money and take responsibility for possible failure）；通过保单承担（to take responsibility for fulfilling an insurance agreement）
[ˌʌndərˈraɪt]	记 联想记忆：under(在…下面)+write(写) → 在下面写上自己的名字表示同意 → 同意承担…的费用
undulate	*v.* 波动，起伏（to form or move in waves; fluctuate）
[ˈʌndʒəleɪt]	记 词根记忆：und(波浪)+ul+ate → 波动，起伏
unearthly	*adj.* 奇异的（very strange and unnatural）
[ʌnˈɜːrθli]	记 联想记忆：un(不)+earthly(尘世的) → 不属于这个世间的 → 奇异的
unfasten	*v.* 解开（to undo）
[ʌnˈfæsn]	记 联想记忆：un(不)+fasten(扎牢，扣紧) → 解开
unflappable	*adj.* 不惊慌的，镇定的（marked by assurance and self-control）
[ˌʌnˈflæpəbl]	同 composed, imperturbable, self-possessed, unruffled
unfold	*v.* 展开，打开（to open from a folded position）；逐渐呈现
[ʌnˈfoʊld]	记 联想记忆：un(不)+fold(折叠) → 展开，打开
	例 For those who admire realism, Louis Malle's recent film succeeds because it consciously shuns the stuff of legend and tells an unembellished story as it might actually *unfold* with fallible people in earthly time.

41

ungrudging [ˌʌnˈgrʌdʒɪŋ]	*adj.* 慷慨的；情愿的（being without envy or reluctance） 记 联想记忆：un(不)+grudging(吝啬的；勉强的)→ 慷慨的；情愿的
unification [ˌjuːnɪfɪˈkeɪʃn]	*n.* 统一，一致（the result of unifying） 记 来自 unify(*v.* 统一)
unilateral [ˌjuːnɪˈlætrəl]	*adj.* 单方面的（one sided；affecting only one side） 搭 unilateral nuclear disarmament 单方面裁减核武器
unison [ˈjuːnɪsn]	*n.* 齐奏，齐唱；一致，协调（a harmonious agreement or union；complete accord）
univocal [juːˈnɪvəkl]	*adj.* 单一意思的（having only one meaning） 搭 univocal concept 单一概念
unkempt [ˌʌnˈkempt]	*adj.* 蓬乱的，未梳理的（not combed）；不整洁的，乱糟糟的（messy）
unprepossessing [ˌʌnˌpriːpəˈzesɪŋ]	*adj.* 不吸引人的（unattractive） 记 联想记忆：un(不)+prepossessing(引人注意的) → 不吸引人的
unprovoked [ˌʌnprəˈvoʊkt]	*adj.* 无缘无故的（not caused by previous action）
unravel [ʌnˈrævl]	*v.* 拆开，拆散（to disengage or separate the threads of）；解开（to resolve the complexity of） 记 联想记忆：un(不)+ravel(纠缠) → 拆开，拆散；解开

Genius only means hard-working all one's life.

天才只意味着终身不懈地努力。

——俄国化学家 门捷列夫(Mendeleyev, Russian chemist)

□ ungrudging □ unification □ unilateral □ unison □ univocal □ unkempt
□ unprepossessing □ unprovoked □ unravel

unregenerate [ˌʌnrɪ'dʒenərət]	*adj.* 不悔改的(making no attempt to change one's bad practices) 同 hardened, impenitent, remorseless
unrepentant [ˌʌnrɪ'pentənt]	*adj.* 顽固不化的, 不后悔的(not penitent) 记 词根记忆: un(不)+re(再, 又)+pen(惩罚)+tant → 不再让心灵受惩罚的 → 顽固不化的, 不后悔的
unscrupulousness [ʌn'skruːpjələsnəs]	*n.* 狂妄, 不择手段 记 来自 unscrupulous(*adj.* 肆无忌惮的, 不讲道德的)
unsettle [ˌʌn'setl]	*v.* 使不安宁, 扰乱(to discompose; disorder) 同 agitate, bother, disquiet, distract, disturb
unsettling [ʌn'setlɪŋ]	*adj.* 使人不安的, 扰乱的(having the effect of upsetting, disturbing, or discomposing) 记 来自 unsettle(*v.* 使不安宁, 扰乱)
unthreatening [ʌn'θretənɪŋ]	*adj.* 不危险的 记 联想记忆: un(不)+threatening(危险的) → 不危险的
upbraid [ʌp'breɪd]	*v.* 斥责, 责骂(to criticize severely; scold vehemently) 记 联想记忆: up(向上)+braid(辫子) → 被揪辫子 → 责骂
upfront [ˌʌp'frʌnt]	*adj.* 坦率的(very direct and making no attempt to hide one's meaning) 记 联想记忆: up(向上)+front(举止) → 在行为举止上毫不掩饰 → 坦率的
upheaval [ʌp'hiːvl]	*n.* 动乱, 剧变(extreme agitation or disorder) 记 来自 upheave(*v.* (使)发生混乱)
upright ['ʌpraɪt]	*adj.* 垂直的, 直立的(straight up); 正直的, 诚实的(honest; fair) 同 erect, perpendicular, plumb, upstanding, vertical
uproar ['ʌprɔːr]	*n.* 喧嚣, 吵闹(a heated controversy); 骚动, 骚乱(a condition of noisy excitement and confusion; tumult) 记 联想记忆: up(向上)+roar(吼叫) → 喧嚣; 骚动
uproarious [ʌp'rɔːriəs]	*adj.* 骚动的(marked by uproar); 喧嚣的(loud and full; boisterous); 令人捧腹大笑的(very funny)
upsurge ['ʌpsɜːrdʒ]	*n.* 高涨, 高潮(a rapid or sudden rise) 记 组合词: up(向上)+surge(浪潮) → 浪潮向上 → 高涨, 高潮

□ unregenerate □ unrepentant □ unscrupulousness □ unsettle □ unsettling □ unthreatening □ upbraid □ upfront □ upheaval □ upright □ uproar □ uproarious □ upsurge

453

| **upswing** | *n.* 上升，增长（a marked increase）；进步，改进（a marked improvement） |
| [ˈʌpswɪŋ] | 记 组合词：up（向上）+swing（摆动）→ 向上摆动 → 上升 |

| **utopia** | *n.* 乌托邦（an imagined place or state of things in which everything is perfect） |
| [juːˈtoupiə] | 记 发音记忆：“乌托邦” → 乌托邦 |

| **utter** | *adj.* 完全的（complete）*v.* 发出（声音），说（话）（to make a sound or produce words） |
| [ˈʌtər] | |

| **vacuous** | *adj.* 空虚的，发呆的（marked by lack of ideas or intelligence） |
| [ˈvækjuəs] | 同 bare, blank, empty, inane, vacant |

| **vagary** | *n.* 奇想，异想天开（an erratic, unpredictable, or extravagant manifestation） |
| [ˈveɪgəri] | 记 词根记忆：vag（漫游）+ary → 游移的思想 → 奇想；发音记忆：“无规律” → 奇想 |

| **vagrancy** | *n.* 漂泊，流浪（the state of being a vagrant） |
| [ˈveɪgrənsi] | 记 来自 vagrant（*adj.* 流浪的，漂泊的） |

| **vagrant** | *adj.* 流浪的，漂泊的；*n.* 流浪者，漂泊者（a person who has no home or regular work） |
| [ˈveɪgrənt] | 记 词根记忆：vag（漫游）+rant → 流浪的 |

| **vague** | *adj.* 含糊的，不明确的（not clearly expressed）；模糊的（lacking definite shape, form, or character；indistinct） |
| [veɪg] | 记 词根记忆：vag（漫游）+ue → 思路四处漫游 → 含糊的；模糊的 |

| **vain** | *adj.* 自负的（full of self-admiration）；徒劳的（without result） |
| [veɪn] | 记 联想记忆：他很自负（vain），到头来一无所获（gain） |

| **valediction** | *n.* 告别演说，告别词（an address or statement of farewell） |
| [ˌvælɪˈdɪkʃn] | 记 词根记忆：val（值得的）+e+dict（说）+ion → 告别演说，告别词 |

valedictory	*adj.* 告别的，离别的（used in saying goodbye）
[ˌvælɪˈdɪktəri]	记 词根记忆：val（值得的）+ e + dict（说）+ ory → 告别的
	例 The *valedictory* address, as it has developed in American colleges and universities over the years, has become a very strict form, a literary genre that permits very little deviation.

| **vandalism** | *n.* （对公物等的）恶意破坏（willful or malicious destruction or defacement of public or private property） |
| [ˈvændəlɪzəm] | 例 The acts of *vandalism* that these pranksters had actually perpetrated were insignificant compared with those they had contemplated but had not attempted. |

| **vandalize** | *v.* 肆意破坏（to subject to vandalism；damage） |
| [ˈvændəlaɪz] | 记 来自 Vandal（*n.* 汪达尔人），为日耳曼民族的一支，以故意毁坏文物而闻名 |

| **vanilla** | *n.* 香草，香子兰（any of a genus of tropical American climbing orchids） |
| [vəˈnɪlə] | 搭 vanilla ice-cream 香草冰淇淋 |

| **vanquish** | *v.* 征服，击溃（to defeat in a conflict or contest；subdue） |
| [ˈvæŋkwɪʃ] | 同 conquer, crush, rout, subjugate |

| **vantage** | *n.* 优势，有利地位（superiority in a contest） |
| [ˈvæntɪdʒ] | 搭 vantage point（观察事物的）有利地点 |

| **vapid** | *adj.* 索然无味的，无生气的（lacking liveliness；flat；dull） |
| [ˈvæpɪd] | 记 词根记忆：vap（蒸汽）+id → 蒸汽般的 → 索然无味的 |

vaporize	*v.* (使)蒸发（to convert or be converted into vapor）
[ˈveɪpəraɪz]	记 来自vapor（*n.* 蒸汽）
	例 Despite the mixture's volatile nature, we found that by lowering its temperature in the laboratory we could dramatically reduce its tendency to *vaporize*.

| **vaporous** | *adj.* 空想的（unsubstantial）；多蒸汽的 |
| [ˈveɪpərəs] | 记 来自vapor（*n.* 蒸汽） |

| **variance** | *n.* 分歧，不和（dissension；dispute）；不同，变化（difference；variation） |
| [ˈveriəns] | 例 The notion that cultural and biological influences equally determine cross-cultural diversity is discredited by the fact that, in countless aspects of human existence, it is cultural programming that overwhelmingly accounts for cross-population *variance*. |

| **variegate** | *v.* 使多样化，使色彩斑斓（to exhibit different colors, especially as irregular patches or streaks） |
| [ˈverɪgeɪt] | 记 词根记忆：vari（变化）+ eg（做）+ ate → 做出变化 → 使多样化 |

| **vault** | *n.* 拱顶（an arched structure）；地窖（an underground storage compartment） |
| [vɔːlt] | |

| **vaunting** | *adj.* 吹嘘的，傲慢的 |
| [ˈvɔːltɪŋ] | 记 来自vaunt（*v.* 吹嘘，自夸） |

| **vegetate** | *v.* 像植物那样生长（to grow in the manner of a plant）；无所事事地生活（to lead a passive existence without exertion of body or mind） |
| [ˈvedʒəteɪt] | 记 词根记忆：veg（生活）+et+ate → 无所事事地生活 |

vegetate

不找工作
无所事事

| **velocity** | *n.* 速率，速度（quickness of motion；speed）；迅速，快速（rapidity of movement） |
| [vəˈlɑːsəti] | 记 词根记忆：veloc（快速的）+ity → 速度；迅速 |

| **velvety** | *adj.* 天鹅绒般柔软光滑的（having the character of velvet as in being soft, smooth）；醇口的，可口的（smooth to the taste） |
| [ˈvelvəti] | |

| **vendetta** | *n.* 血仇，世仇（blood feud）；宿怨，深仇（a bitter, destructive feud） |
| [venˈdetə] | 记 词根记忆：vend(=vindic 复仇)+etta → 血仇，世仇 |

| **vengeance** | *n.* 报仇，报复（punishment inflicted in retaliation；retribution） |
| [ˈvendʒəns] | 记 词根记忆：veng（复仇）+eance → 报仇，报复 |

| **vengeful** | *adj.* 渴望复仇的，复仇心重的（showing a fierce desire to punish sb. for the harm they have done to oneself） |
| [ˈvendʒfl] | |

42

□ vantage	□ vapid	□ vaporize	□ vaporous	□ variance	□ variegate
□ vault	□ vaunting	□ vegetate	□ velocity	□ velvety	□ vendetta
□ vengeance	□ vengeful				

venom ['venəm]	*n.* 毒液(normally secreted by some animals (as snakes, scorpions, or bees) and transmitted to prey or an enemy chiefly by biting or stinging); 毒物(poisonous matter); 恶意(ill will; malevolence)
ventilate ['ventɪleɪt]	*v.* 使通风(to cause fresh air to circulate through) 记 来自 vent(*n.* 通风口)
ventriloquist [ven'trɪləkwɪst]	*n.* 口技表演者,腹语表演者(one who uses or is skilled in ventriloquism) 记 词根记忆:ventr(腹部)+i+loqu(说话)+ist(人) → 会说腹语的人 → 口技表演者,腹语表演者
verbal ['vɜːrbl]	*adj.* 口头的(spoken); 言语的 记 词根记忆:verb (字,词)+al → 口头的,言语的 例 Many philosophers agree that the *verbal* aggression of profanity in certain radical newspapers is not trivial or childish, but an assault on decorum essential to the revolutionaries purpose.
verbatim [vɜːr'beɪtɪm]	*adj.* 逐字的,(完全)照字面的(being in or following exact words; word-for-word) 记 词根记忆:verb(字,词)+atim → 逐字的,(完全)照字面的
verbiage ['vɜːrbiɪdʒ]	*n.* 冗词,废话(a profusion of words of little content) 记 词根记忆:verb(字,词)+i+age → 冗词,废话
verboten [vər'boʊtn]	*adj.* 禁止的,严禁的(prohibited by dictate) 同 forbidden, impermissible, taboo
verdict ['vɜːrdɪkt]	*n.* 裁定,裁决(the finding or decision of a jury) 记 词根记忆:ver(真实的)+dict(说) → 说出真话 → 裁定,裁决 例 The widespread public shock at the news of the guilty *verdict* was caused partly by biased news stories that had predicted acquittal.
verdure ['vɜːrdjər]	*n.* 葱郁,青翠(the greenness of growing vegetation); 生机勃勃(a condition of health and vigor)
verge [vɜːrdʒ]	*n.* 边缘(border; edge; rim) 搭 be on the verge of 很接近,濒于
verisimilar [ˌveri'sɪmɪlə]	*adj.* 好像真实的,逼真的(appearing to be true); 可能的(probable) 记 词根记忆:veri(=ver 真实的)+simil(相同的)+ar → 逼真的
veritable ['verɪtəbl]	*adj.* 名副其实的,真正的,确实的(being truly so called; real and genuine) 同 authentic, unquestionable
vernal ['vɜːrnl]	*adj.* 春季的(of, relating to, or occurring in the spring); 春季般的,青春的(fresh or new like the spring)
versant ['vɜːrsənt]	*adj.* 精通的(conversant) *n.* 山坡(the slope of a side of a mountain or mountain range); 斜坡(the general slope of a region)

| **versatile** | *adj.* 多才多艺的（having many different kinds of skills）；多用途的（having many different uses） |
| [ˈvɜːrsətl] | 记 词根记忆：vers(转)+atile → 可向多个方向转的 → 多才多艺的 |

| **vertex** | *n.* (三角形等的)顶角；顶点，最高点（summit; the highest point） |
| [ˈvɜːrteks] | 同 apex, crest, crown, height |

| **vertical** | *adj.* 垂直的，直立的（perpendicular to the plane of the horizon; upright） |
| [ˈvɜːrtɪkl] | 记 来自 vertex(*n.* 顶点) |

| **vertigo** | *n.* 眩晕，晕头转向（a dizzy, confused state of mind） |
| [ˈvɜːrtɪɡoʊ] | 记 词根记忆：vert(转)+igo → 眩晕，晕头转向 |

vertigo

| **verve** | *n.* (艺术作品的)神韵（the spirit and enthusiasm animating artistic composition or performance; vivacity）；(指人)生机，活力（energy; vitality） |
| [vɜːrv] | |

| **vest** | *v.* 授予，赋予（to grant or endow with a particular authority, right, or property） |
| [vest] | |

| **vestment** | *n.* 官服，礼服（an outer garment, especially a robe of ceremony or office）；法衣，祭袍（any of the ritual robes worn by members of the clergy, acolytes, or other assistants at services or rites） |
| [ˈvestmənt] | 记 词根记忆：vest(穿衣服)+ment → 礼服 |

| **veto** | *n.* 否决，禁止（an authoritative prohibition; interdiction）；否决权 |
| [ˈviːtoʊ] | 记 在拉丁文中，veto 的意思是我不准(I forbid)，在英语里则表示"否决"或"否决权" |

| **vibrancy** | *n.* 生机勃勃，活泼（the quality or state of being vibrant） |
| [ˈvaɪbrənsi] | 同 animation, sparkle, vivacity |

| **vibrate** | *v.* 振动，摇摆（to move back and forth or to and fro, especially rhythmically and rapidly）；颤动，震动（to shake or move with or as if with a slight quivering or trembling motion） |
| [ˈvaɪbreɪt] | 记 词根记忆：vibr(振动)+ate → 振动；颤动 |

| **vicar** | *n.* 教区牧师（the priest in charge of an area） |
| [ˈvɪkər] | 记 联想记忆：vi + car(汽车) → 开着汽车在一个区域内四处传道 → 教区牧师 |

| **vicarious** | *adj.* 替代的，代理的（serving in place of sb. or sth. else） |
| [vaɪˈkeriəs] | 记 来自 vicar(*n.* 教区牧师) |

| **vicinity** | *n.* 附近，邻近（proximity; neighborhood） |
| [vəˈsɪnəti] | 记 词根记忆：vicin(邻近的)+ity → 附近，邻近 |

| **vicissitudinous** | *adj.* 有变化的，变迁的（marked by or filled with vicissitudes） |
| [ˌvɪsɪsɪˈtjuːdɪnəs] | 记 来自 vicissitude(*n.* 人生沉浮，兴衰枯荣) |

| **victimize** | *v.* 使受害，欺骗（to cause sb. to suffer unfairly） |
| [ˈvɪktɪmaɪz] | 记 来自 victim(*n.* 受害者) |

| **vie** | *v.* 竞争（to compete） |
| [vaɪ] | 同 contend, contest, emulate, rival |

42

vile	*adj.* 恶劣的，卑鄙的，道德败坏的（morally despicable or abhorrent）	
[vaɪl]	同 abject, contemptible, filthy, loathsome	
vilify	*v.* 辱骂，诽谤（to utter slanderous and abusive statements）	
[ˈvɪlɪfaɪ]	同 defame, malign, revile	
villainous	*adj.* 邪恶的，恶毒的（having the character of a villain）	
[ˈvɪlənəs]	记 来自 villain（*n.* 恶棍）	
vindication	*n.* 证明无罪，辩护（justification against denial or censure；defense）	
[ˌvɪndɪˈkeɪʃn]	同 apology, exculpation	
vintage	*adj.* 经典的（of old, recognized, and enduring interest, importance, or quality）；最好的（of the best）	
[ˈvɪntɪdʒ]		
violet	*adj.* 紫罗兰色的 *n.* 紫罗兰	
[ˈvaɪələt]	记 联想记忆：vio+let（让）→ 让紫罗兰花尽情开放吧 → 紫罗兰	
virile	*adj.* 有男子气的（characteristic of or associated with men；masculine）；刚健的（energetic；vigorous）	
[ˈvɪrəl]	记 词根记忆：vir（力量）+ile → 有力量的 → 刚健的	
virility	*n.* 男子气概；刚强有力	
[vəˈrɪləti]	搭 masculinity virility 男子气	
virtual	*adj.* 实质上的，实际上的（being such in essence or effect though not formally recognized or admitted）	
[ˈvɜːrtʃuəl]		
virtuosity	*n.* 精湛技巧（great technical skill）	
[ˌvɜːrtʃuˈɑːsəti]	例 Winsor McCay, the cartoonist, could draw with incredible *virtuosity*: his comic strip about Little Nemo was characterized by marvelous draftsmanship and sequencing.	
virulent	*adj.* 剧毒的（extremely poisonous or venomous）；恶毒的（full of malice）	
[ˈvɪrələnt]	记 词根记忆：vir（毒）+ul+ent → 剧毒的	
visceral	*adj.* 内心深处的（felt in or as if in the viscera）；内脏的（splanchnic）	
[ˈvɪsərəl]	同 inner, interior, internal, inward	
viscid	*adj.* 黏性的（thick and adhesive）	
[ˈvɪsɪd]	同 glutinous, viscose, viscous	
vista	*n.* 远景（a distant view；prospect）；展望（an extensive mental view）	
[ˈvɪstə]	记 词根记忆：vis（看）+ta → 远景；展望	
vitalize	*v.* 赋予生命，使有生气（to endow with life）	
[ˈvaɪtəlaɪz]	同 energize, exhilarate, invigorate, stimulate	
vituperate	*v.* 谩骂，辱骂（to abuse or censure severely or abusively）	
[vɪˈtjuːpəreɪt]	记 词根记忆：vitu（过失）+per（准备）+ate → 因过失而遭受 → 谩骂，辱骂	
vivacious	*adj.* 活泼的，有生气的，快活的（lively in temper, conduct, or spirit；sprightly）	
[vɪˈveɪʃəs]	记 词根记忆：viv（生命）+aci+ous → 活泼的	

vocation [voʊˈkeɪʃn]	*n.* 天职，神召（a summons or strong inclination to a particular state or course of action）；职业，行业（the work in which a person is regularly employed）；（对特定职业的）禀性，才能（the special function of an individual or group） 记 词根记忆：voc（叫喊）+ation → 受到召唤 → 神召；职业 例 Despite some allowances for occupational mobility, the normal expectation of seventeenth-century English society was that the child's *vocation* would develop along familial lines; divergence from the career of one's parents was therefore limited.
void [vɔɪd]	*adj.* 空的（empty）；缺乏的（completely lacking；devoid）*n.* 空隙，裂缝（empty space）；空虚感（a feeling of want or hollowness）
volition [voʊˈlɪʃn]	*n.* 意志，决断力（will；the power of choosing or determining） 记 词根记忆：vol（意志）+ition → 意志，决断力
volley [ˈvɑːli]	*n.* 齐发，群射（a number of shots fired at the same time）*v.* 齐发，群射（to be fired altogether）；截击 参 volleyball（*n.* 排球）
voracious [vəˈreɪʃəs]	*adj.* 狼吞虎咽的，贪吃的（having a huge appetite）；贪婪的，贪得无厌的（excessively eager；insatiable） 记 词根记忆：vor（吃）+aci+ous（多…的）→ 吃得多的 → 狼吞虎咽的；贪婪的
voracity [vəˈræsəti]	*n.* 贪食；贪婪（the quality or state of being voracious） 同 greed, rapacity
votary [ˈvoʊtəri]	*n.* 崇拜者，热心支持者（a devoted admirer） 记 词根记忆：vot（宣誓）+ary → 发誓追随 → 崇拜者，热心支持者
vouch [vaʊtʃ]	*v.* 担保，保证（to guarantee the reliability of） 例 I can *vouch* for his honesty; I have always found him veracious and carefully observant of the truth.
voucher [ˈvaʊtʃər]	*n.* 证件（a piece of supporting evidence）；收据（a documentary record of a business transaction）；凭证（a form or check indicating a credit against future purchases or expenditures）；代金券（a coupon）
vying [ˈvaɪɪŋ]	*adj.* 竞争的（contending；competing） 记 vie（*v.* 竞争）的现在分词也是 vying
wacky [ˈwæki]	*adj.*（行为等）古怪的，乖僻的（absurdly or amusingly eccentric or irrational）
waddle [ˈwɑːdl]	*v.* 摇摇摆摆地走（to walk with short steps from side to side） 记 发音记忆："歪倒" → 走路走得歪歪斜斜，像要倒下去 → 摇摇摆摆地走
wade [weɪd]	*v.* 涉水（to walk in water）；跋涉（to make one's way arduously） 同 plod, slog, slop, toil, trudge
wage [weɪdʒ]	*v.* 开始，进行（to begin and continue） 搭 wage a war 进行战争

42

---

waggish [ˈwægɪʃ]	*adj.* 诙谐的，滑稽的（humorous） 例 There is perhaps some truth in that *waggish* old definition of a scholar — a siren that calls attention to a fog without doing anything to dispel it.
waive [weɪv]	*v.* 放弃（to relinquish voluntarily）；推迟（to postpone） 搭 waive one's claim 放弃要求
wallop [ˈwɑːləp]	*n.* 重击，猛击（a hard or severe blow）*v.* 重击，猛打（to hit with force） 记 联想记忆：wall(墙)+op → 在生气时用力打墙 → 重击，猛打
wallow [ˈwɑːloʊ]	*v.* 打滚（to roll the body about in or as if in water, snow, or mud）；沉迷（to take unrestrained pleasure）*n.* 打滚（the act or an instance of wallowing） 记 联想记忆：wal(看作 wall，墙)+low(地势低的) → 在墙底下打滚 → 打滚
wan [wɑːn]	*adj.* 虚弱的（feeble）；病态的（sickly pallid） 同 ghastly, haggard, sallow
wanton [ˈwɑːntən]	*adj.* 无节制的，肆无忌惮的（being without check or limitation）；嬉戏的，淘气的（mischievous） 记 发音记忆："顽童" → 淘气的 例 Abandoning the moral principles of his youth, the aging emperor Tiberius led a debauched, *wanton* life.
warehouse [ˈwerhaʊs]	*n.* 仓库，货栈（a large building for storing things） 同 depository, repository, storehouse
warranty [ˈwɔːrənti]	*n.* 保证，担保；根据，理由；授权，批准 搭 under warranty 在保修期内
waspish [ˈwɑːspɪʃ]	*adj.* 易怒的（irascible; petulant; snappish）；尖刻的 记 来自 wasp(n. 黄蜂)
wastrel [ˈweɪstrəl]	*n.* 挥霍无度的人（one who spends resources foolishly and self-indulgently; profligate） 记 来自 waste(n./v. 浪费)
waver [ˈweɪvər]	*v.* 摇摆（to move unsteadily back and forth）；踌躇（to fluctuate in opinion, allegiance, or direction）
wax [wæks]	*n.* 蜡 *v.* 给…上蜡；增大（to grow gradually larger after being small）；（月亮)渐满
waylay [weɪˈleɪ]	*v.* 埋伏，伏击（to lie in wait for and attack from ambush） 同 ambuscade, lurk
wean [wiːn]	*v.* （孩子)断奶；戒掉（to free from an unwholesome habit or interest） 搭 wean sb. off/from 逐渐戒除恶习（或避免依赖）
weary [ˈwɪri]	*adj.* 疲劳的，疲倦的（physically or mentally fatigued）；令人厌烦的，令人厌倦的（having one's interest, forbearance, or indulgence worn out）*v.* （使)厌烦，(使)疲倦（to make or become weary） 例 The Muses are vindictive deities: they avenge themselves without mercy on those who *weary* of their charms.

weird [wɪrd]	*adj.* 古怪的，怪诞的，离奇的（odd; fantastic） 记 联想记忆：we(我们)+ird(看作 bird, 鸟) → 如果我们都变成鸟该多怪异 → 古怪的，怪诞的
weld [weld]	*v.* 焊接，熔接；锻接（to unite or reunite） 搭 weld leg 焊脚
well-groomed [ˌwel ˈgruːmd]	*adj.* 整齐干净的，衣着入时的 记 联想记忆：well(好)+groom(修饰)+ed → 整齐干净的，衣着入时的
welsh [welʃ]	*v.* 欠债不还（to avoid payment）；失信（to break one's word） 记 联想记忆：和威尔士人(Welsh)的拼写一样
wend [wend]	*v.* 行，走，前进（to proceed on） 搭 wend one's way 朝…走去
wheedle [ˈwiːdl]	*v.* 哄骗，诱骗（to influence or entice by soft words or flattery） 同 cajole, coax, seduce
wheeze [wiːz]	*v.* 喘息（to breathe with difficulty, producing a hoarse whistling sound）；发出呼哧呼哧的声音（to make a sound resembling laborious breathing）
whet [wet]	*v.* 磨快（to sharpen）；刺激（to excite; stimulate） 同 acuminate, edge, hone
whiff [wɪf]	*n.* (风、烟等的)一阵（a slight, gentle gust of air） *v.* 轻吹 搭 a whiff of perfume 一股香水味
whim [wɪm]	*n.* 一时的兴致，怪念头（a sudden idea; fancy） 同 caprice, fad, vagary, whimsy
whimper [ˈwɪmpər]	*v.* 啜泣，呜咽（to make a low whining plaintive or broken sound） 同 blubber, pule, sob
whine [waɪn]	*v.* 哀号，号哭（to utter a high pitched plaintive or distressed cry） 同 pule, whimper
whirlpool [ˈwɜːrlpuːl]	*n.* 旋涡（a rapidly rotating current of water; vortex） 记 组合词：whirl(旋转，回旋) + pool(水池) → 旋涡
whisper [ˈwɪspər]	*v.* 耳语，低语（to speak softly） 记 联想记忆：whi(看作 who, 谁)+sper(看作 speaker, 说话者) → 谁在小声说话 → 耳语，低语
whistle [ˈwɪsl]	*n.* 口哨声；汽笛声 *v.* 吹口哨，鸣笛（to make a whistle） 记 发音记忆："猥琐" → 随随便便对女孩子吹口哨很猥琐 → 吹口哨
whit [wɪt]	*n.* 一点儿，少量（the smallest part imaginable; bit） 搭 not a whit 丝毫不；一点也不
wholesome [ˈhoʊlsəm]	*adj.* 有益健康的（good for the body or likely to produce health） 记 联想记忆：whole(完整的)+some → 帮助身体变得完整 → 有益健康的

wheeze

42

whoop [hu:p]	*n.* 高喊，欢呼（a loud yell expressive of eagerness, exuberance, or jubilation）
wicked ['wɪkɪd]	*adj.* 邪恶的（morally very bad）；讨厌的（disgustingly unpleasant）；有害的（causing or likely to cause harm, distress, or trouble）；淘气的（playful in a rather troublesome way） 例 People should not be praised for their virtue if they lack the energy to be *wicked*; in such cases, goodness is merely the effect of indolence.
wield [wi:ld]	*v.* 行使（权力）（to exert one's authority by means of）；支配，控制（to have at one's command or disposal） 参 unwieldy（*adj.* 笨重的；笨拙的）
wiggle ['wɪgl]	*v.* 扭动，摆动（to move to and fro with quick jerky or shaking motions） 记 联想记忆：wig（假发）+gle（看作 giggle，吃吃地笑）→ 戴着假发扭动着身子吃吃地笑 → 扭动
wigwag ['wɪgwæg]	*v.* 摇动，摇摆，摆动（to move back and forth steadily or rhythmically） 同 sway, teeter, totter, waver, weave
wile [waɪl]	*n.* 诡计（a beguiling or playful trick） 同 artifice, craft, gimmick, ploy, ruse
wily ['waɪli]	*adj.* 诡计多端的，狡猾的（full of wiles; crafty） 记 来自 wile（*n.* 诡计）
wince [wɪns]	*v.* 畏缩，退缩（to shrink back involuntarily; flinch） 同 cringe, quail
windfall ['wɪndfɔ:l]	*n.* 被风吹落的果实（fallen fruit）；意外的收获，意料之外（an unexpected gain or advantage）
windy ['wɪndi]	*adj.* 有风的；冗长的；夸夸其谈的（verbose） 搭 a windy speaker 夸夸其谈的人
wink [wɪŋk]	*v.* 使眼色，眨眼示意（to close and open one eye quickly as a signal）*n.* 眨眼，眼色（a winking movement of the eye）
winkle ['wɪŋkl]	*v.* 挑出，剔出，取出（to pry, extract, or force from a place or position）
winnow ['wɪnoʊ]	*v.* 扬，簸（谷物）（to remove chaff by a current of air）；除去 记 注意不要和 minnow（*n.* 小鱼）相混
wiry ['waɪəri]	*adj.* 瘦而结实的（being lean, supple, and vigorous）
wispy ['wɪspi]	*adj.* 纤细的；脆弱的；一缕缕的 搭 wispy hair 一缕缕头发
wither ['wɪðər]	*v.* 干枯，枯萎（to shrivel from loss of bodily moisture） 记 联想记忆：天气（weather）不好植物就会枯萎（wither）
wizened ['wɪznd]	*adj.* 干枯的，干瘪的，干皱的（dry, shrunken, and wrinkled as a result of aging or of failing vitality） 记 来自 wizen（*v.* 起皱，干瘪）；发音记忆："未整的" → 干瘪的

wobble [ˈwɑːbl]	*v.* 摇晃，摇摆（to move with a staggering motion）；犹豫（to hesitate） 同 falter, stumble, teeter, tooter
woe [woʊ]	*n.* 悲痛，悲哀（a condition of deep suffering from misfortune, affliction, or grief）；不幸，灾难（calamity; misfortune）
woo [wuː]	*v.* 求爱，求婚（to sue for the affection of and usually marriage with; court）；恳求，争取（to solicit or entreat especially with importunity）
worship [ˈwɜːrʃɪp]	*n.* 崇拜，敬仰（strong feelings of love, respect, and admiration）*v.* 崇拜，敬仰（to regard with great or extravagant respect, honor, or devotion）
wrath [ræθ]	*n.* 愤怒，愤慨（strong vengeful anger or indignation） 同 exasperation, fury, ire, rage
wreak [riːk]	*v.* 发泄，报复（to inflict vengeance upon）；发泄怒火（to express anger） 同 avenge, redress, requite, vindicate
wrench [rentʃ]	*v.* 猛扭（to move with a violent twist）*n.* 扳钳，扳手 同 jerk, wrest, yank
wrest [rest]	*v.* 扭，拧（to pull, force, or move by violent wringing or twisting movements）；夺取，费力取得（to gain with difficulty by or as if by force, violence, or determined labor）
wretched [ˈretʃɪd]	*adj.* 可怜的，不幸的，悲惨的（(of a person) in a very unhappy or unfortunate state）
wrist [rɪst]	*n.* 腕，腕关节（the joint between the hand and the lower part of the arm） 搭 wrist watch 手表
writ [rɪt]	*n.* 令状（a written order issued by a court, commanding the party to whom it is addressed to perform or cease performing a specified act）；书面命令（an order in writing） 记 联想记忆：write 去掉 e 就变成了 writ
wroth [rɔːθ]	*adj.* 暴怒的，非常愤怒的（intensely angry） 搭 be wroth with 非常生气
wrought [rɔːt]	*adj.* 做成的，形成的（worked into shape by artistry or effort）；精制的（made delicately or elaborately）
wry [raɪ]	*adj.* 扭曲的，歪曲的（twisted or bent to one side）；嘲弄的，讽刺的（cleverly and often ironically or grimly humorous）
yacht [jɑːt]	*n.* 帆船，游艇（any of various recreational watercraft） 搭 a yacht club/race 帆船俱乐部/比赛
yank [jæŋk]	*v.* 猛拉，拽（to pull or extract with a quick vigorous movement） 同 jerk, lurch, snap, twitch, wrench
yen [jen]	*v.* 渴望（to have an intense desire） 同 covet, hanker, long
yielding [ˈjiːldɪŋ]	*adj.* 易弯曲的，柔软的（lacking rigidity or stiffness; flexible）；顺从的，服从的（disposed to submit or comply）

42

□ wobble	□ woe	□ woo	□ worship	□ wrath	□ wreak
□ wrench	□ wrest	□ wretched	□ wrist	□ writ	□ wroth
□ wrought	□ wry	□ yacht	□ yank	□ yen	□ yielding

yowl [jaʊl]	*v.* 嚎叫，恸哭（to utter a loud long cry of grief, pain, or distress） 同 howl, wail
yummy [ˈjʌmi]	*adj.* 美味的，可口的（highly attractive or pleasing to the taste or smell; delicious）
zealotry [ˈzelətri]	*n.* 狂热（fanatical devotion） 搭 religious zealotry 宗教狂热行为
zephyr [ˈzefər]	*n.* 和风（a gentle breeze）；西风（a breeze from the west） 记 来自希腊神话中的西风之神 Zephyros
zest [zest]	*n.* 刺激性（an enjoyable exciting quality）；兴趣，热心（keen enjoyment） 记 联想记忆：对考试（test）有兴趣（zest）
zesty [ˈzesti]	*adj.* 兴致很高的，热望的（having or characterized by keen enjoyment） 记 来自 zest（*n.* 兴趣，热心）
zigzag [ˈzɪɡzæg]	*n.* 之字形 *adj.* 之字形的 *v.* 弯弯曲曲地行进 搭 a zigzag path 弯曲的羊肠小道
zone [zoʊn]	*n.* 地区（a section of an area or a territory established for a specific purpose）*v.* 分成区（to divide into or assign to zones）
zoom [zuːm]	*v.* 急速上升，猛增（to increase sharply） 同 hike, skyrocket, surge

The ideals which have lighted my way, and time after time have given me new courage to face life cheerfully have been kindness, beauty and truth.

有些理想曾为我指引过道路，并不断给我新的勇气以欣然面对人生，那些理想就是———真、善、美。

——美国科学家 爱因斯坦（Albert Einstein, American scientist）

附录：数学词汇

算数-整数

integer *n.* 整数
consecutive integer 连续的整数
positive whole number 正整数
negative whole number 负整数
even/even integer 偶数
odd/odd integer 奇数
real number 实数
divisor *n.* 除数，约数；因子
multiple *n.* 倍数
remainder *n.* 余数
composite number 合数
quotient *n.* 商
prime number 质数，素数
prime factor 质因子，质因数
successive *adj.* 连续的
spread *n.* 范围
score *n.* 二十
consecutive *adj.* 连续的
constant *adj.* 恒定的，不变的

算数-分数

numerator *n.* 分子
denominator *n.* 分母
greatest common divisor/greatest common
    factor 最大公约数
least common multiple 最小公倍数
common multiple 公倍数
common factor 公因子

reciprocal/ inverse *n.* 倒数
mixed number 带分数(带分数就是将一个分数
    写成整数部分+一个真分数)
improper fraction 假分数
proper fraction 真分数
vulgar fraction/common fraction 普通分数
simple fraction 简分数
complex fraction 繁分数
reversible *adj.* 可逆的，可倒转的
nearest whole percent 最接近的百分数

算数-小数

decimal place 小数位
decimal point 小数点
decimal fraction 纯小数
infinite decimal 无穷小数
recurring decimal 循环小数
digit *n.* 位
decimal system 十进制
units digit 个位数
tens digit 十位数
tenths unit 十分位
3-digit number 三位数
quartiles *n.* 四分位数
percentiles *n.* 百分位数
interquartile range 四分位差
negligible *adj.* 可忽略不计的
closest approximation 最相近似的
calculate to three decimal places
    结果保留3位小数

approximately *adv.* 大约，近似
estimation *n.* 估算,近似

算数-实数

absolute value 绝对值
nonzero number 非零数
natural number 自然数
positive number 正数
negative number 负数
nonnegative *adj.* 非负的
rational *n.* 有理数
irrational(number) 无理数

算数-比例

common ratio 公比
direct proportion 正比
percent *n.* 百分比
account for 占(比例)
scatterplot *n.* 点阵图
scale *n.* 比例；刻度

算数-幂和根

cardinal *n.* 基数
ordinal *n.* 序数
exponent *n.* 指数，幂
base/power *n.* 底数/指数，幂
radical sign/root sign 根号
radicals *n.* 根式
square root 平方根
cube root 立方根
product *n.* 乘积
common logarithm 常用对数

算数-集合

subset *n.* 子集
proper subset 真子集
union *n.* 合集，并集
intersection *n.* 交集

empty set 空集
solution set 解集(满足一个方程或方程组的所有解的集合叫做该方程或方程组的解集)
set of data/data set 数据集
sets *n.* 集合
nonempty *adj.* 非空的
mutually exclusive 互斥的
juxtaposition *n.* 并列
disjoint *adj.* 不相交的
elements *n.* 元素
event *n.* 事件
compound events 复合事件
independent events 相互独立事件
sufficient *adj.* 充分的
the sum of A and B/the total of A and B A与B的和
the union of A and B A与B的并集
the intersection of A and B A与B的交集
Venn diagrams 韦恩图

算数-统计

average *n.* 平均数
mean *n.* 平均值；平均数；中数
maximum *n.* 最大值
minimum *n.* 最小值
median *n.* 中数，中点，中线，中值
mode *n.* 众数(在一系列数中出现最多的数)
arithmetic mean 算术平均数
weighted average 加权平均值
weighted mean 加权平均数
　(是不同比重数据的平均数)
geometric mean 几何平均数
　(是指n个观察值连乘积的n次方根)
range *n.* 值域(一系列数中最大值减最小值)
dispersion *n.* 差量，离差
standard deviation 标准方差
to the nearest/round to 四舍五入
round *v.* 保留整数，使成为整数；四舍五入
value *n.* 值，数值
probability *n.* 概率
distribution *n.*(频数或频率)分布

probability distribution 概率分布
frequency distribution 频数分布
normal distribution 正态分布
relative frequency distributions 相关频率分布
standard normal distribution 标准正态分布
factorial notation 阶乘
permutations *n.* 排列；置换
combination *n.* 组合
grid lines 坐标线，网格线
circle graphs 饼图
boxplots *n.* 箱型图
bar graphs/histogram 柱状图；直方图
at random 随机
random variables 随机变量
discrete random variable 离散随机变量
continuous random variable 连续随机变量
equally likely event 等可能事件
roll a fair die 掷骰子
heads up 正面朝上，头朝上
tails up 背面朝上，数字朝上
toss up 掷硬币；(胜败)机会相等

算数-数学运算

add/plus *v.* 加
subtract/minus *v.* 减
multiplication *n.* 乘
multiply/times *v.* 乘
divide *v.* 除
difference *n.* 差
sum *n.* 和
is equal to 等于
total *n.* 总数(用在加法中，相当于+)；
　　总计(用于减法中，相当于−)
divisible *adj.* 可被整除的
division *n.* 除；部分
divided evenly 被整除
dividend *n.* 被除数
the difference of A and B A与B的差
the product of A and B A与B的乘积
prime factorization 质因数分解
less than 小于

greater than 大于
no less than 大于等于
no more than 小于等于
no solution 无解
interval *n.* 区间；间隔
invert *v.* 倒置，颠倒
inverse *n.* 倒数
invert a fraction 求分数的倒数
from subtract 从…减…
in equivalent to 与…相等
increase by 增加了
increase to 增加到
decrease by 减少了
decrease to 减少到
identical *adj.* 相等的
divisibility *n.* 可约性，可除性

代数、方程、不等式

coefficient *n.* 系数
literal coefficient 字母系数
numerical coefficient 数字系数
term *n.* 项
constant term 常数项
quadratic *n.* 二次方程
equivalent equation 同解方程，等价方程
linear equation 线性方程
solution *n.*(方程的)解
inequality *n.* 不等式
expression *n.* 表达式
equation *n.* 方程式，等式
linear *adj.* 一次的，线性的
factorization *n.* 因数分解
function *n.* 函数
inverse function 反函数
trigonometric function 三角函数
complementary function 余函数
variable/variations *n.* 变量
domain *n.* 定义域
sequence *n.* 数列
sequences of numbers 数列
geometric progression 等比数列

arithmetic procession 等差数列
parentheses n. 括号
satify v. 使…成立
equivalent adj. 相等的

几何-直线、垂线

a line segment 线段
midpoint n. 中点
endpoint n. 端点
right angle 直角
perpendicular n. 垂线
perpendicular lines 垂直线
perpendicular bisector 垂直平分线
parallel lines 平行线
bisect v. 平分
partition v. 分割，分开
intercepts n. 截取

几何-相交线和角

acute angle 锐角
obtuse angle 钝角
opposite angles 对角
vertical angle 对顶角
vertex angle 顶角
round angle 周角
straight angle 平角
included angle 夹角
alternate angle 内错角
interior angle 内角
central angle 圆心角
exterior angle 外角
supplementary angles 补角
complementary angles 余角
adjacent angle 邻角
a straight line 直线
angle bisector 角平分线
diagonal n. 对角线
intersect v. 相交
angle measurement in degrees 角度计算

几何-三角形

altitude n. (三角形的)高
arm n. 直角三角形的股
equilateral triangle 等边三角形
hypotenuse n. 斜边，直角三角形的斜边，弦
inscribed triangle 内接三角形
vertex n.(三角形等)顶角，顶点
isosceles triangle 等腰三角形
median of a triangle 三角形的中线
oblique n. 斜三角形
opposite n. 直角三角形中的对边
right triangle 直角三角形
scalene triangle 不等边三角形
similar triangles 相似三角形
leg n. 直角边
included side 夹边
Pythagorean theorem 勾股定理
congruent angles 全等角
congruent line segments 等长线段

几何-四边形和多边形

quadrilateral n. 四边形
pentagon n. 五边形
hexagon n. 六边形
heptagon n. 七边形
octagon n. 八边形
nonagon n. 九边形
decagon n. 十边形
polygon n. 多边形
multilateral adj. 多边的
regular polygon 正多边形
parallelogram n. 平行四边形
square n. 正方形
rectangle n. 长方形，矩形
rhombus n. 菱形
equilateral adj. 等边形的
trapezoid n. 梯形
congruent adj. 全等的
symmetric adj. 对称的

symmetry *n.* 对称，对称性
perimeter *n.* 周长
overlap *v.* 重叠
coordinate geometry 解析几何
corresponding side 对应边
area of a rectangle 长方形的面积
fold *n.* 对折

几何-圆

center of a circle 圆心
circle *n.* 圆形
concentric circles 同心圆
semicircle *n.* 半圆
circumference *n.* 圆周长，周长
chord *n.* 弦
radius *n.* 半径
diameter *n.* 直径
tangent *n.* 正切
inscribe *v.* 内切，内接
circumscribe *v.* 外切，外接
point of tangency 切点
tangent line 切线
circumscribed *adj.* 外接的
radian *n.* 弧度(弧长/半径)
arc *n.* 弧
segment of a circle 弧形
be parallel to 平行
be perpendicular to 垂直
be tangent to 与…相切

几何-立体几何

edge *n.* 边，棱
length *n.* 长
width *n.* 宽
depth *n.* 深度
volume *n.* 体积
surface area 表面积
cube *n.* 立方体
rectangular solid 长方体
regular solid/regular polyhedron 正多面体

cylinder *n.* 圆柱体
cone *n.* 圆锥
pyramid *n.* 角锥
sphere *n.* 球体
faces *n.* 面
cross section 横截面
solid line 实线
dimension *n.* 维数
three-dimensional figures 三维图形
as illustrated 如图所示

几何-几何坐标

coordinate plane 坐标平面
coordinate system 坐标系
rectangular coordinate 直角坐标系
abscissa/x-coordinate *n.* 横坐标
ordinate *n.* 纵坐标
xy-planes *n.* xy平面坐标轴
number line 数轴
origin *n.* 原点
origin O 坐标起点O
axis *n.* 轴
x-axis *n.* X轴
y-axis *n.* y轴
intercept *n.* 截距
x-intercept *n.* x轴截距
quadrant *n.* 象限
four quadrants 四个象限
slope *n.* 斜率
a unique solution 唯一解
parabola *n.* 抛物线
linear functions 线性函数

公式和换算

feet *n.* 英尺
1 billion = 10^9 十亿 = 10^9
1 dozen = 12 1打 = 12个
1 feet = 12 inches 1英尺 = 12英寸
1 gallon = 4 quarts 1加仑 = 4夸脱
1 hour = 3,600 seconds 1小时 = 3600秒

1 mile = 5,280 feet 1英里 = 5280英尺

1 million = 10^6 1百万 = 10^6

1 yard = 3 feet = 36 inches 1码
    = 3英尺 = 36英寸

0! = 1! = 1 0的阶乘为1

多边形内角和 = (n − 2) × 180°

$S_\triangle$ = 1/2底 × 高

$S_梯$ = (上底 + 下底) × h/2

圆周长 = 2 π r(r = radius半径)

$S_圆$ = π r^2

弧长 = (X°/360°) × 圆周长

$S_{立方体}$ = 6 a^2

$S_{圆柱}$ = 2 π r (r + h)

$V_长$ = 长 × 宽 × 高

$V_{圆柱}$ = π r^2 h

$V_{圆锥}$ = $\frac{1}{3}$ π r^2 · h

等差数列 a_n = a_1 + (n − 1) d (d为常数)

等差求和 $S_n = \frac{n(a_1 + a_n)}{2} = na_1 + \frac{n(n-1)}{2}d$

等比数列 a_n = a^1 q^{n-1}

等比求和 $S_n = \frac{a_1(1-q^n)}{(1-q)}$ (q ≠ 1)

利息 − principle(本金) × interest rate(利率)
    × time

句型

be fewer than 小于

be less than 小于

Twice as many A as B A是B的两倍

The ratio of A to B is ⋯ A比B(A/B)

A diminished by B / A minus B /
    from A subtract B A减去B

A multiplied by B A乘以B

A divided by B A/B

A divided into B B/A

A is 20% less than B (B−A)/B = 20%

A is 20% more than B (A−B)/B = 20%

A is a divisor of B A是B的除数(约数)(B/A)

be direct(inverse) proportion at/to 成反比

A is subset of B A是B的子集

be more than twice as many X in A as in B

A里面的X是B里面X的2倍以上

l⊥m line/ l and m are perpendicular
    线l与线m垂直

be proportional to 与⋯成比例的

be drawn to scale 按比例绘制

实际应用

balance n. 余额

cost of production 产品成本

approximate cost 估算成本，约计成本

down payment 预付定金，首付款

installment n. 分期付款

discount rate 折扣率

charter v. 租赁，包租

charge v. 收费

principal n. 本金

simple interest 单利

compound interest 复利

gross profit 毛利

retail price 零售价

sales revenue 销售额

sales taxes 营业税，销售税

property tax 财产税

list price 标价

margin n. 利润；付定金

mark up 涨价

purchases n. 销售数量

rebate n. 退还款，折扣

pointer n. 指针

project v. 预测，估计

corresponding value 对应值

mutual fund 共同基金

expected value 期望值，预期值

intensity n. 强度

intercalary year/leap year 闰年

lifetime n. 寿命

reflection n. 镜射

simplification n. 简化

simplified adj. 简化的

sketch n. 草图，示意图

survey n. 调查

solid color 纯色
concentration *n.* 浓度
weight *v.* 加重量于…，使变重
yields *n.* 产量
central tendency 集中趋势
tie *v.* 打平

其他

blot out 涂掉，删掉
buck *n.* 一美元；一澳元
dime *n.* 一角，十分
clockwise *adj.* 顺时针
constant rate 匀速的
cumulative *adj.* 累积的，附加的
defined *adj.* 已定义的
categories *n.* 种类

in excess of 超过
in terms of 用…的话，用…来表示
in turn 依次，轮流
distinct point 不同点
nearest 0.1 percent 最接近0.1%
inclusive *adj.* 包括在内的
alongside *prep.* 和…一起
preceding *adj.* 在…前的，先前的
simultaneously *adv.* 同时
respectively *adv.* 各自地，分别地
per capita 按照人数分配的，每人
wall *n.* (容器的)壁
truckload *n.* 一卡车的容量
denote *v.* 表示

亲爱的读者，祝贺你完成了本书的学习！GRE考试被戏称为世界上最变态的考试，GRE词汇也被认为是上帝都需要背的词汇。现在，你已经光荣地完成了这项艰巨的任务。在此，让我们以本书作者的经典语录，祝愿你在接下来的学习和工作中再接再厉，梦想成真！

- 绝望是大山，希望是石头，但是只要你能砍下一块希望的石头，你就有了希望。

- 忍受孤独是成功者的必经之路，忍受失败是重新振作的力量源泉，忍受屈辱是成就大业的必然前提。忍受能力，在某种意义上构成了你背后的巨大动力，也是你成功的必然要素。

- 会做事的人，必须具备以下三个做事特点：一是愿意从小事做起，知道做小事是成大事的必经之路；二是心中要有目标，知道把所做的小事积累起来最终的结果是什么；三是要有一种精神，能够为了将来的目标自始至终把小事做好。

- 金字塔如果拆开了，只不过是一堆散乱的石头，日子如果过得没有目标，就只是几段散乱的岁月。但如果把一种力量凝聚到每一日，去实现一个梦想，散乱的日子就集成了生命的永恒。

- 做人最大的乐趣在于通过奋斗去获得我们想要的东西，所以有缺点就意味着我们可以进一步去完善，有缺乏之处意味着我们可以进一步去努力。

- 为什么你不要自傲和自卑？你可以说自己是最好的，但不能说自己是全校最好的、全北京最好的、全国最好的、全世界最好的，所以你不必自傲；同样，你可以说自己是全班最差的，但你能证明自己是全校最差的吗？能证明自己是全国最差的吗？所以不必自卑。

- 每一条河流都有自己不同的生命曲线，但是每一条河流都有自己的梦想——那就是奔向大海。我们的生命，有的时候会是泥沙。你可能慢慢地就会像泥沙一样，沉淀下去了。一旦你沉淀下去了，也许你不用再为了前进而努力了，但是你却永远见不到阳光了。所以我建议大家，不管你现在的生命是怎么样的，一定要有水的精神。像水一样不断地积蓄自己的力量，不断地冲破障碍。当你发现时机不到的时候，把自己的厚度给积累起来，当有一天时机来临的时候，你就能够奔腾入海，成就自己的生命。

- 你说我是猪，不对，其实我连猪都不如。很多人失去了快乐，是因为他太敏感了。别人一句话、一个评论就使自己生气一个月。这是非常无聊的。严重了就成了马家爵，因为别人不请自己吃饭就郁闷地要杀人。

- 人的生活方式有两种。第一种方式是像草一样活着，你尽管活着，每年都在生长，但你毕竟是一棵草，你吸收雨露阳光，但是长不大。人们可以踩过你，但是人们不会因为你的痛苦而产生痛苦，人们不会因为你被踩了，而来怜悯你，因为人们本身就没有看到你。所以我们每一个人，都应该像树一样成长，即使我们现在什么都不是，但是只要你有树的种子，即使你被踩到泥土中间，你依然能够吸收泥土的养分，自己成长起来。当你长成参天大树以后，遥远的地方，人们就能看到你，走近你，你能给人一片绿色。活着是美丽的风景，死了依然是栋梁之才，活着死了都有用，这就是我们每一个同学做人的标准和成长的标准。

读者反馈表

尊敬的读者：

　　您好！非常感谢您对**新东方大愚图书**的信赖与支持，希望您抽出宝贵的时间填写这份反馈表，以便帮助我们改进工作，今后能为您提供更优秀的图书。谢谢！

　　为了答谢您对我们的支持，我们将对反馈的信息进行随机抽奖活动，当月将有 20 位幸运读者可获赠**《新东方英语》**期刊一份。我们将定期在新东方大愚图书网站 www. dogwood. com. cn 公布获奖者名单并及时寄出奖品，敬请关注。

来信请寄：

　　北京市海淀区海淀东三街 2 号欧美汇大厦 19 层
　　北京新东方大愚文化传播有限公司
　　　　　　图书部收

　　邮编：100080　　　　　　　　　　　E-mail：bj62605588@163.com

姓名：_____　　年龄：_____　　职业：_____　　教育背景：_____

邮编：_____　　通讯地址：_____

联系电话：_____　　E-mail：_____

您所购买的书籍的名称是：_____

1. 您是通过何种渠道得知本书的（可多选）：
　　□书店　□新东方网站　□大愚网站　□朋友推荐　□老师推荐
　　□@新东方大愚图书(http://weibo.com/dogwood)　□其他_____

2. 您是从何处购买到此书的？
　　□书店　□新东方大愚淘宝网　□其他网上书店　□其他_____

3. **您购买此书的原因（可多选）：**
   ☐封面设计　☐书评广告　☐正文内容　☐图书价格　☐新东方品牌
   ☐新东方名师　☐其他_____

4. **您对本书的封面设计满意程度：**
   ☐很满意　☐比较满意　☐一般　☐不满意
   改进建议_____

5. **您认为本书的内文在哪些方面还需改进？**
   ☐结构编排　☐难易程度　☐内容丰富性　☐内文版式　☐其他_____

6. **本书最令您满意的地方：** ☐内文　☐封面　☐价格　☐纸张

7. **您对本书的推荐率：** ☐没有　☐1人　☐1—3人　☐3—5人　☐5人以上

8. **您更希望我们为您提供哪些方面的英语类图书？**
   ☐四六级类　☐考研类　☐IELTS类　☐TOEFL类　☐GRE、GMAT类　☐SAT、SSAT类
   ☐留学申请类　☐BEC、TOEIC类　☐英语读物类　☐初高中英语类　☐少儿英语类
   ☐其他_____
   您目前最希望我们为您出版的图书是：_____

9. **您在学习英语过程中最需要哪些方面的帮助？（可多选）**
   ☐词汇　☐听力　☐口语　☐阅读　☐写作　☐翻译　☐语法　☐其他_____

10. **您最喜欢的英语图书品牌：**_____
    理由是（可多选）：☐版式漂亮　☐内容实用　☐难度适宜　☐价格适中
    ☐对考试有帮助　☐其他_____

11. **您对新东方图书品牌的评价：**_____

12. **您对本书（或其他新东方图书）的意见和建议：**_____

    _____

    _____

13. **填表时间：**_____年_____月____日